# The Marshall Plan in Austria

# Contemporary Austrian Studies

Sponsored by the University of New Orleans and Universität Innsbruck



Publication of this volume has been made possible through generous grants from the *ERP*-Fonds of Vienna, the Austrian Culture Institute in New York, and the Bank Gutmann Nfg. AG in Vienna. The University of Innsbruck and Metropolitan College of the University of New Orleans have also provided financial support.

Articles appearing in this volume are abstracted and indexed in HISTORICAL ABSTRACTS and AMERICA, HISTORY and LIFE.

# The Marshall Plan in Austria

*Editors*

Günter Bischof

Anton Pelinka

Dieter Stiefel

Volume 8

Contemporary Austrian Studies

Transaction Publishers

New Brunswick (U.S.A.) and London (U.K.)

This book is printed on acid-free paper that meets the American National Standard for Permanence of Paper for Printed Library Materials.

Library of Congress Catalog Number: 99-087781
ISBN: 0-7658-0679-7
Printed in the United States of America

Library of Congress Cataloging-in-Publication Data

The Marshall Plan in Austria / Günter Bischof, Anton Pelinka, Dieter Stiefel, editors.
p. cm.—(Contemporary Austrian studies ; v. 8)
Includes bibliographical references.
ISBN 0-7658-0679-7 (paper : alk. paper)
1. Marshall Plan. 2. Economic assistance, American—Austria. 3. Reconstruction (1939-1951)—Austria. 4. Austria—Economic conditions—1945- I. Bischof, Günter, 1953- II. Pelinka, Anton, 1941- III. Stiefel, Dieter. IV. Series.

HC265 .M263 2000
338. 91' 730436'09044—dc21 99-087781
CIP

Dedicated to the Memory of

**Joseph Logsdon**

March 12, 1938 — June 2, 1999

# Table of Contents

## III. MACRO- AND MICROECONOMIC IMPACTS



## NON-TOPICAL ESSAYS



## BOOK REVIEWS

**ANNUAL REVIEW**

# Introduction

*Günter Bischof*

The American elite journal *Foreign Affairs* termed the Marshall Plan "perhaps the most important foreign policy success of the postwar period."[1] In both the American and Western European publics, where the memory of the Marshall Plan has been carefully cultivated over the past half a century, such extravagant praise for the European Recovery Program does not appear to be overstated. In Austria the historical memory of the significance of the Marshall Plan for the country's postwar economic reconstruction as a basis for broad prosperity seems largely ignored by the political class and forgotten among the younger generation. Only the contemporaries of the postwar occupation, who lived through the difficult times of postwar want and destitution, seem to remember that the trajectory of Austrian postwar prosperity could hardly have been imaginable without the largesse of the European Recovery Program. It is clear that without Marshall Plan aid Austria would have needed much longer to recover from physical destruction and mental dejection after World War II. This seems strange for a nation that received almost one billion dollars in Marshall aid (1,5 billion if all the American aid programs from 1945 to 1952 are added up). With 132 dollars, Austria was among the top per capita recipients of Marshall Plan aid and arguably profited more than any other country participating in the ERP.[2]

Why this oblivion? Did the wartime generation want to pretend their extraordinary effort in reconstructing had come without any outside aid injection? Did the post-occupation political elite in the grand coalition governments, which led neutral Austria onto its extraordinary trajectory of peace and prosperity, not want to acknowledge how heavily Austria was indebted to this extraordinary American generosity during the occupation decade — a time, it should be noted, when the Soviet Union extracted at least as much in reparations from its Eastern Austrian zone of occupation as the United States poured into the three Western zones with its various postwar aid programs? Does a well-educated, self-centered and often affluent younger generation, with its short historical memory and its neutralist "island-of-the blessed" mentality, no longer care to know about the genesis of their current prosperity and the American contribution to it during extraordinary years of Cold War tensions in Austria's vital geostrategic location? Why have Austrian governments failed to commemorate the recent 50$^{th}$ anniversary of General Marshall's speech at Harvard University[3], which initiated the Marshall Plan, in official ceremonies as did most of the other ERP beneficiaries?[4] Might it be a Cold War legacy in Austria that showing gratitude to the U.S. is an attitude unbecoming to a neutral country? Why is official Austria obsessed with cultivating the memory of the Anschluss in 1938, when the Alpine Republic was a victim of the international system, yet fails to remember the Marshall Plan, when the country happened to be a beneficiary? Why has Austrian contemporary and economic history scholarship been so laggard for so long to produce serious in-depth studies of the Marshall Plan's macro- and microeconomic importance for Austria's postwar reconstruction, when Marshall Plan scholarship in Western Europe and American academia has been a vibrant area of Cold War research? Questions abound crying out to be answered.

Why are so few people aware of the fact that the Marshall Plan is still at work in Austria? How so? In 1962 the U.S. government transferred more than 11 billion Austrian Schillings from its Marshall Plan counterpart accounts to the newly established ERP-Fund *(ERP-Fonds)*. This federal government agency was set up in the Federal Chancellery to continue giving low interest loans to state-owned businesses and small and middle-seized private businesses. Over the past 35 years more than 210 billion Austrian Schillings in low-interest loans have been poured into the capital-starved Austrian economy.[5] It is hardly known that the Marshall Plan has had unique longevity in Austria and is still at work today. Only the West German *Kreditanstalt für Wiederaufbau*, initially also seeded with ERP-counterpart dollars, is a comparable financial investment institution with a similar record of long-term- economic importance in the history of its nation as the *ERP-Fonds* has been having for Austria.[6]

The Center for Austrian Culture and Commerce at the University of New Orleans (CenterAustria) organized a scholarly conference in early May 1998 in New Orleans to answer some of these questions.

This meeting aimed at commemorating the "golden" anniversary of the Marshall Plan in Austria as well as surveying the state of current Austrian Marshall Plan scholarship and identifying important research lacunae in a comparative Western European perspective.[7] The model were previous conferences on Germany and France in a comparative Western European perspective, which explored both the macro- and microeconomic impact of the Marshall Plan.[8] While the political context of the Marshall Plan in Austria and the most important macroeconomic issues had been addressed by previous Austrian Marshall Plan research, sectoral case studies of important branches of the Austrian economy benefitting from the Marshall Plan have been sorely missing. Some sectors like the paper and chemical industry, and individual case studies of well-known Austrian private businesses like the *Fischer* ski company in Upper Austria, or numerous hotels and ski resorts around Western Austria, getting started or taking off with ERP-counterparts, could not be covered in this meeting. In a similar vein, the *Americanization* of Austrian business practices through American management training courses or by entrepreneurs visiting the U.S. on inspection tours, are important lacunae in Marshall Plan research.[9] Similarly, the effects of the American enforced trade embargoes on Austria's traditional East-West trading patterns needs to be studied.[10]

The volume starts out with the **economic legacy** of the Marshall Plan. Ferdinand *Lacina*'s keynote address leaves no doubt about the crucial importance of the Marshall Plan for postwar Austrian economic reconstruction. Lacina has distinguished himself by holding many top-level positions in the Austrian government (at one point overseeing the *ERP-Fonds*) and serving as Austrian finance minister longer than anyone in the postwar Second Republic. Kurt *Löffler* and Hans *Fußenegger* present a detailed history of the contributions of the *ERP-Fonds* in Vienna since the ERP-counterparts were transferred to the Austrian government in 1962. They provide a vital statistical service to Austrian Marshall Plan research by updating the ERP-funds invested into the Austrian economy until 1998.

The two main sections of the volume cover the **political** and the **economic** aspects of the Marshall Plan in Austria. The **political** section starts with two essays that show the difficulties of implementing the ERP in Austria, with the Soviets participating in the quadripartite occupation, and the highly precarious geopolitical location at the iron curtain. Dieter *Stiefel*'s and Ingrid *Fraberger's* contribution subtly analyzes the Austrian perception of the Soviet Union as "enemy" in the context of the postwar Austrian politics of rabid anti-communism. They also summarize the huge Soviet economic exploitation and the reparations taken from postwar Austria. The Austrian shock and surprise about Soviet rapacity is the important counterpart to the great mass appeal of America and U.S. generosity at this time.[11] Andrea Komlosy shows how the Iron Curtain painfully sundered apart old Austrian-Czechoslovak border regions that had interacted and traded for centuries. This is a rare case study of the negative effects of the Marshall Plan on specific East-West border regions. The Marshall Plan completed the division of Europe which the Soviets had started with building their security zone in East Central Europe. Jill *Lewis* and Matthew Paul *Berg* look at the repercussions of the Marshall Plan on Austrian politics and identity. Siegfried *Beer*'s essay begins to answer some of the questions about the secret involvement of the CIA in funding labor unions to protect them from and fortify them against Communist influence. Hans-Jürgen *Schröder*'s analysis of the intensity of Marshall Plan publicity and propaganda demonstrates that the battle for the "hearts and minds (and stomachs)" of the Western Europeans was a vital aspect of the American politics of anti-communism in the early 1950s. The Marshall Plan recipients were constantly reminded that the growing productivity of their economies and increasing prosperity of their citizens were direct results of American Marshall Plan largesse. Schröder also for the first time ventures a brief summary of the Austrian historical memory of the Marshall Plan.[12]

Hans *Seidel* begins the **economic** section with his sweeping survey of the economic impact of the ERP on the postwar political economy and the constant struggle of Austrian economic planners and policy makers to meet the American expectations.[13] Seidel uniquely informed analysis benefits from his insider's expertise — as a young economist he worked in the Austrian Marshall Plan administration himself; he later joined the prestigious *Institut für Österreichische Wirtschaftsforschung*, and in the Kreisky 1970s was involved in setting Austrian economic policy as a State Secretary in the Finance Minstery. Kurt *Tweraser*, Georg *Rigele* and Günter *Bischof* complement Seidel's macroeconomic perspective with sectoral case studies on the over-seized state-owned electrical power and steel sectors, as well as the private tourist industry. Rigele fascinating portrait of the completion of the gigantic Kaprun power plant with ERP-counterparts demonstrates how the Marshall Planners made Kaprun into the TVA of Austria — the symbol of **modernization through electrification** of all branches of the Austrian economy (including agriculture).[14] Tweraser's analysis of postwar bureaucratic jockeying over whether to salvage the huge Nazi-built Linz steel complex with ERP counterpart funds also suggests the intense postwar debates about which direction the Austrian economy should take — focus on state-owned heavy industry, or the traditional private luxury/consumer industries? The complex Austro-American decision-making process about what sectors in the capital-starved Austrian economy should benefit from the bulk of ERP-counterpart funds, would determine the future long-term direction of the Austrian economy. Like the steel sector, the tourist industry's battle for inclusion in the bounty of counterpart investment funds represents another case study of these postwar bureaucratic battles, often tinged by intense partisanship, in the Vienna power centers. In an uphill battle, the conservative People's Party (ÖVP) favored the private sector in its jockeying for Marshall Plan funds, while the Socialist Party (SPÖ) preferred enhancing the state sector, which would become one of its postwar power bases. The intensity of these battles was usually directly proportionate to this partisan political posturing within the all-powerful postwar Austrian coalition government.[15]

At the end of this section, Wilhelm *Kohler*, empirically rich econometric analysis, compares the American aid transfers to Europe in the Marshall Plan era to the projected costs of EU-budgetary transfers to the potential newcomers from East-Central Europe ready to join the European Union in the next round of *enlargement*. Kohler demonstrates that the broad political resistance against such enlargement in Austria and elsewhere due to the expected financial costs is much exaggerated. The *per capita* costs of EU-Eastern enlargement would be much less than what the Americans poured into postwar Western Europe. Such well-informed comparisons of the past with the present can indeed teach valuable lessons.

This volume also features **non-topical essays** by younger scholars who are completing dissertations that will make valuable contributions to the respective historiographical debates. Alexander *Lassner*, a young American with Austrian parentage, revisits the Anschluss era, one of the most contested terrains of Austrian historiography. He adds new documentation to the age-old debate about Austria's military preparedness and strength in March 1938 at the time of the Nazi-invasion. An abbreviated version of Martin *Kofler*'s University of New Orleans M.A. thesis is also published here. Kofler looks at the fall 1960 Austro-Soviet Vienna Summit and shows how Khrushchev tried to utilize Austrian diplomatic mediation in East-West tensions over Berlin. Review essays, book reviews and the annual survey of Austrian politics complete this volume.

It should be noted that most of the original Marshall Plan conference essays in this volume were first published in a German conference volume appearing only half a year after the New Orleans meeting.[16] This English version however is not entirely identical with the original German one. The essays by Berg and Beer—both delivered at the conference—are published for the first time here and were not included in the German volume. Oliver Rathkolb and Anton Pelinka contributed their conference essays to the German volume and are not reprinted in this volume.[17] The Stiefel/Fraberger essay here is considerably expanded with its first section on the traditional Austrian "enemy image" of the Soviet Union, while other essays like Bischof's and Schröder's are only slightly altered and updated.

At the end the pleasant duty remains to thank a number of people and institutions for helping to make the conference an intellectual treat and a memorable success and to shepherd this big volume towards publication. First and foremost the generosity of the *ERP-Fonds* in Vienna must be gratefully acknowledged. Its directors Kurt Löffler and Hans Fußenegger not only recognized the necessity to celebrate the 50th Anniversary of the Marshall Plan with a ceremony in Vienna in 1997—the only official Marshall Plan remembrance in Austria. They also saw the need to assess the importance of the ERP and the *ERP-Fonds* with a scholarly conference. They both graced the meeting in New Orleans with their presence. Hansjörg Gruber was a constant source of help and inspiration at the *ERP-Fonds* and Mr. Penninger was kind enough to help establish the initial contacts there. We are also grateful to the Schumpeter Society in Vienna and the Austrian Cultural Institute in New York for their financial support of the conference. Peter Mikl was our congenial partner at the Cultural Institute. Metro College of the University of New Orleans and the University of Innsbruck kindly supported the meeting out of their annual UNO-Innsbruck symposium budget. Dean Robert Dupont and Gordon "Nick" Mueller, the Director of CenterAustria, as well as Franz Mathis, the coordinator of the UNO friendship treaty in Innsbruck, were instrumental in helping to make the conference a success.

The meeting in New Orleans would not have happened without the tremendous hard work of Martin Kofler and Sabine Schaffer, two Innsbruck graduate students at UNO in 1997/98. Their precision planning and enthusiasm infected all conference participants. Anne O'Herren Jacob of UNO Metro College Conference Services was helpful as always. Gertraud Griessner's savvy management of Center Austria has been invaluable in preparing the conference and completing this volume. She has quickly become indispensable to the well-being of CenterAustria. We are also grateful to David Ellwood (Bologna) for presenting the opening lecture at the New Orleans conference. Franz Mathis (Innsbruck), Herbert Matis (Vienna), David Good (Minneapolis/MN), and Reinhold Wagnleitner (New Orleans/ Salzburg) took time out from their busy academic schedules to attend the conference as expert commentators, adding immeasurably to the scholarly integrity of the meeting. Our distinguished colleagues Radomir Luza and Hermann Freudenberger, both professors emeriti from Tulane University, chaired sessions and added their wisdom in all things Austrian. The conference speakers, whose essays are published here, deserve our most sincere appreciation for their scholarly efforts and discipline in submitting their essays on time.

During the time of the conference Günter Bischof was a guest professor at the University of Salzburg. He would like to thank his students there for the warm welcome. Marianne Dirnhammer not only went out of her way to help track down rare books and provide secretarial support in completing his essay in this volume, she also adopted his entire family. Josef Ehmer, Sylvia Hahn, Fritz Gottas, Christian Dirninger and Robert Hoffmann warmly welcomed him as a colleague.

This volume has severely strained our resources that go into the making of the *CAS* series. Its seize would not have been feasible without the financial contribution of the *ERP-Fonds* in Vienna and the enthusiastic help of *Messieurs* Löffler, Fußenegger and Gruber. Anton Fink has shown again that old friendship can go beyond the call of duty. His help in securing the financial support of the Bank Gutmann Nfg. AG in Vienna is sincerely appreciated. Our experienced production team worked incredibly long and hard to complete this volume. In New Orleans Jennifer's Shimek's high standard in carefully copy-editing more than 20 manuscripts kept us going. The 1998/99 graduate students from Innsbruck Günther Walder (who had already helped with volume 5 of *CAS*) and Daniela Kundmann spent countless hours re-typing and correcting manuscripts, tracking their completion and helping with proof-reading. In Innsbruck Ellen Palli did the lion's share of staying atop of the organizational work, correcting manuscripts, and type-setting the final version of this volume. Her heroic efforts in the end prevailed against all odds.

Authors, sponsors and the production team are all proud to have gone to such length to "build" this scholarly "monument" as a fitting tribute to the memory of the Marshall Plan in Austria and as an Austrian token of gratitude to the people of the United States. Each and every American contributed 80 dollars to the European Recovery Program in those memorable postwar years. Such extraordinary generosity, it should not be forgotten, is extremely rare in the annals of humankind.

Larose, Louisiana, May 1999

While correcting the proofs of this volume, word of the sudden death of my colleague, mentor and friend Joe Logsdon shattered the tranquility of my parents' home in Mellau/Vorarlberg. As chairman of the UNO History Department during part of the 1980s, Joe Logsdon was one of the early protagonists who shaped student and faculty exchanges with the University of Innsbruck. In the spirit of the Marshall Plan he was a visionary of European-American academic exchanges and dialogue. He attended the conference in New Orleans and would have been pleased to see this volume in print, which is dedicated to this memory.

## Notes

1. See the special commemorative session "The Marshall Plan and its Legacy," *Foreign Affairs* 76 (1997): 159-221. For similarly extravangant praise, see the section on the historical memory of the Marshall Plan in the Schröder essay of this volume.

2. Wilfried Mähr, *Der Marshall Plan in Österreich* (Graz: Styria, 1989); Günter Bischof, *Austria in the First Cold War 1945-55: The Leverage of the Weak* (Basingstoke: Macmillan 1999), 78-103.

3. Next to the *ERP-Fonds* (see below), the notable exception was Austrian public radio, which did not forget. The brainy channel *Ö-1* played a four-part documentary on the Marshall Plan in late May 1997, researched by the young Salzburg historian Ewald Hiebl. The Vienna cultural historian Wolfgang Kos, with the expert advice of Georg Rigele, produced a two-hour special in the "*Diagonal*" program on 31 May 1997.

4. See, for example, the publications emanating from such commemorative conferences in the Netherlands and Germany: Hans H.J. Labohm, ed., *The Fiftieth Anniversay of the Marshall Plan in Retrospect and in Prospect: Report of the Seminar organised by The Clingendael Institute in cooperation with the*

*Netherlands' Atlantic Commission, The Hague, 15-16 May 1997*; Haus der Geschichte der Bundesrepublik Deutschland, ed., *50 Jahre Marshall-Plan* (Berlin: Argon 1997). In November 1997 Oslo University in Norway organized a conference on the small nations participating in the Marshall Plan; to date no conference volume has appeared. For the fiftieth anniversary of Marshall's speech at Harvard the prominent *Süddeutsche Zeitung* in Munich published a series of essays on the significance of the Marshall Plan by prominent politicians, entrepreneurs and historians, which are now conveniently published in Hans-Herbert Holzamer and Marc Hoch, eds., *Der Marshall-Plan: Geschichte und Zukunft* (SZ-Aktuell) (Landsberg/Lech: Olzog, 1997).

5. For background, see ERP-Fonds, ed., *25 Jahre ERP-Fonds 1962-1987* (Vienna, 1987). For the 210 billion Schillings in investment loans, see the Löffler/ Fußenegger essay in this volume, which updates the statistics of this commemorative volume.

6. Heinrich Harries, *Wiederaufbau, Welt und Wende: Die KfW—eine Bank mit Öffentlichem Auftrag* (Frankfurt am Main: Fritz Knapp Verlag, 1998)

7. The state of Austrian Marshall Plan scholarship and the specific lacunae are discussed in Günter Bischof, "Der Marshallplan in Österreich," *Zeitgeschichte* 17 (1990), 463-74, and now updated in *idem*, " Zum internationalen Stand der Marshallplan-Forschung: Die Forschungsdesiderata für Österreich," in *Zeitgeschichte im Wandel: 3. Österreichischer Zeitgeschichtetag 1997*, ed. Gertraud Diendorfer, Gerhard Jagschitz and Oliver Rathkolb (Innsbruck: StudienVerlag, 1998), 61-72. For an essay on the comparative Western European persepective see *idem*, "50 Jahre Marshall-Plan in Europa 1947-1952," *Aus Politik und Zeitgeschichte* B22-23 (23 May 1997): 3-17.

8. Charles S. Maier and Günter Bischof, eds., *Deutschland und der Marshallplan* (Baden-Baden: Nomos, 1992); Comité pour l'Histoire Economique et Financière de la France, eds., *Le Plan Marshall et le relèvement économique de l'Europe* (Paris, 1996); see also Hans-Jürgen Schröder, ed., *Marshallplan und Westdeutscher Wiederaufstieg: Positionen - Kontroversen* (Stuttgart: Franz Steiner, 1990), and Gerd Hardach, *Der Marshall Plan: Auslandshilfe und Wiederaufbau in Westdeutschland 1948-1952* (Munich: dtv, 1994). For additional country case studies, see also Richard T. Griffiths, ed., *Explorations in OEEC History* (OECD Historical Series) (Paris: OECD, 1997).

9. Andre Pfoertner is completing a PhD dissertation in this area with Professor Stiefel at the University of Vienna. For the Americanization of West Germany business, see Volker R. Berghahn, *The Americanization of West German Industry, 1945-1973* (Oxford: Berg, 1987); *idem*, "West German Reconstruction and American Industrial Culture, 1945-1960," in: *The American Impact on Postwar Germany*, ed. Reiner Pommerin (rev. ed. Providence, RI: Berghahn Books, 1997), 65-81.

10. For a beginning, see Arno Einwitschläger, *Amerikanische Wirtschaftspolitik in Österreich 1945-1949* (Vienna: Böhlau, 1986).

11. For the irresistible American mass appeal in postwar Austria, see Reinhold Wagnleitner, *Coca-Colonization and the Cold War: The Cultural Mission of the United States in Austria after the Second World War*, transl. Diana Wolf (Chapel Hill: North Carolina University Press, 1994).

12. On the memory of the Marshall Plan in Germany, see also Hans-Jürgen Schröder, "50 Jahre Marshall Plan in Deutschland," *Aus Politik und Zeitgeschichte* B22-23 (23 May 1997): 18-29; on Marshall Plan propaganda in Austria, see also Christiane Rainer, "Der Marshall Plan: Ein Werbefeldzug? Über den Umgang mit Filmquellen in der Zeitgeschichte," M.A. Thesis, Univ. of Vienna, 1999, also available as a "working paper" on the CenterAustria Homepage **Centeraustria.uno.edu**.

13. See also Hans Seidel, "Österreichische Stabilisierungspolitik 1951/53," in: *Von der Theorie zur Wirtschaftspolitik - ein österreichischer Weg: Festschrift zum 65. Geburtstag von Erich W. Streissler*, ed. Franz Baltzarek, Felix Butschek and Gunther Tichy (Stuttgart: Lucius & Lucius 1998), 267-300. Hans Seidel is working on a larger study of postwar Austrian economic reconstruction.

14. See also Georg Rigele, "Kaprun: Das Kraftwerk des österreichischen Wiederaufbaus," in *Inventur 45/55: Österreich im ersten Jahrzehnt der Zweiten Republik*, ed. Wolfgang Kos and Georg Rigele (Vienna: Sonderzahl, 1996).

15. Kurt Tweraser has been a pioneer in applying the bureaucratic approach to Marshall Plan politics in Austria, see his "The Politics of Productivity and Corporatism: The Late Marshall Plan in Austria, 1950-54," *Contemporary Austrian Studies* III (1995): 91-115.

16. With prefaces by Austrian Chancellor Victor Klima and the American Ambassador to Austria Kathryn Walt Hall, see *"80 Dollar": 50 Jahre ERP-Fonds und Marshall-Plan in Österreich 1948-1998*, ed. Günter Bischof and Dieter Stiefel (Vienna: Ueberreuter 1999).

17. Oliver Rathkolb, "Der ERP-Fonds und Optionen zur Transformation der österreichischen Wirtschaft nach 1953," and Anton Pelinka, "Der Marshall Plan und die österreichische politische Kultur," *ibid.*, 103-10, 249-60.

# I. Economic Legacies

# The Marshall Plan—A Contribution to the Austrian Economy in Transition

*Ferdinand Lacina**

One of the aims of the New Orleans Conference on Austria and the Marshall Plan was to gather and disseminate information on the impact the Marshall Plan of on the economic, social and political performance of Austria, a topic hitherto rather neglected by historians. I wonde-red whether I would be able to make a valuable contribution to this discussion, as I am neither an eye-witness to the implementation of the European Recovery Program, nor am I a historian. Rather I am a for-mer politician with some background in economics.

I would like to provide evidence of the long-lasting influence the Marshall Plan exerted in two areas. On the one hand there is the structural development of the Austrian economy, especially its drive for productivity. On the other hand, the Marshall Plan inspired Austrian discussions on development cooperation and the economic and social development in Europe itself.

In its first year (in 1948/49) the Marshall Plan contributed 14 percent to the Austrian national income. According to OECD statistics, the direct aid under this scheme reached an amount of almost $ 100 *per capita* in Austria. Only Iceland and the Netherlands benefitted from higher *per capita* transfers.

The Marshall Plan employed a recovery strategy which was comprised of three stages. Initially in 1948/49 the Marshall Plan offered direct aid; almost half of the deliveries in the first year consisted of food, a quarter was raw materials. The second stage of the

---

* This contribution was the keynote address in the New Orleans Marshall Plan conference.

Plan in 1950/51 was devoted to the reconstruction and adaptation of basic industries, such as steel, chemicals, pulp and paper, non-ferrous metals, and electric energy. In the third stage, 1952/53, manufacturers of finished products and export goods, as well as the tourism industry were the main recipients of aid.

There is almost no sector of the Austrian economy which has not been positively affected by Marshall Plan aid. The rebuilding of railways, bus systems, streets and bridges, agriculture, and housing programs were key ingredients of infrastructure reconstruction.

Doubtless, the economic impact of the Marshall-Plan on postwar Austria was significant, but one should not forget about the political and the social consequences of this program. Austria was a special case in the context of the European Recovery Program (ERP). It was the only recipient country which was partly occupied by Soviet troops. The Soviets controlled a large part of the capital Vienna, and the eastern part of the country. The Soviet zone was confronted with two handicaps: one was the reluctance of private firms to invest in this region; the second was the fact, that the Soviets controlled a large part of manufacturing and oil production in their zone, former "German Property" according to the Potsdam treaty.

This division of Austria into the occupation zones of the Western allies and the Soviet zone was, therefore, not just a threat to the political integrity of Austria. These two economic handicaps could easily have led to a social partition of the country, so it was of utmost importance that the Soviet-controlled part of Austria was not excluded from direct aid. Ironically, U.S. taxpayer's money was thus invested in a region controlled by Soviet troops, and this in the hottest phase of the Cold War.

The fascinating idea of a revolving "counterpart" fund to support economic growth and to improve productivity is, of course, to produce a lasting impact of a once accomplished capital transfer. Up to the present time, the Marshall Plan funds play an important role in Austria's capital formation process. During the last years, between 15 and 20 percent of investment in manufacturing industries were credits financed by funds from the *ERP-Fonds*. Moreover, there exists no skiing resort in Austria which has not been supported by credits either for ski lifts or hotels; there are few farmers who have not received loan at low interest rates.

The concept of the Marshall Plan aid influenced the political debate in Austria in many ways. Bruno Kreisky, Austria's Federal

Chancellor from 1970 to 1983, proposed a Marshall Plan for the developing countries as early as 1958. He spoke before an international seminar for diplomats

> "about the urgent problem which has to be tackled during the next decade, granting aid to developing countries. We have the task of offering aid to the many, many millions of people in Asia and Africa, living below the minimum standards of nutrition. We have to take into account that such an extensive aid program, vividly discussed in many circles of the population, cannot be accomplished without the will and consent of our people. We will need a lot of persuasive power to make the people in the democratic countries understand that they should sacrifice part of their wealth in favor of those people who still are not in the position to buy the goods they are in urgent need of. This is the significance and uniqueness of the Marshall Plan, that the American people in 1948 were determined to make such a gigantic sacrifice."

The idea of the Marshall Plan as an instrument to initiate economic growth and increase productivity in Third World countries was one of the major concepts of Bruno Kreisky pursued throughout his political life. In an attempt to bring about a North-South dialogue on the highest level, he organized—together with President Echeveria from Mexico—the summit of Cancun in 1981, a remarkable gathering of heads of state and governments from the North and the South, among them the newly-elected U.S. President Ronald Reagan. Unfortunately, Chancellor Kreisky could not be present at the meeting himself because of a severe illness. It is useless to speculate what could have been the outcome of such a meeting if he had been able to participate, whether the concept of the Marshall Plan in the North-South context might ever have been realistic scheme. Kreisky himself wrote five years later, "I did not find many friends for this 'Marshall Plan for the Third World,'" but he remained optimistic, still believing the "European Recovery Program had some mechanisms which are quite useful to think about even today. Of course they have to be adapted to the conditions of each country." Despite Kreisky's views, the discussion of development theory and especially development policy looked for new models; the so-called "tigers" of Southeast Asia became more and more the paradigm of successful development. Maybe, now that the Southeast Asia bubble has burst, economists will look for new models again. One of these "new" models celebrated its fiftieth anniversary in 1998.

The Marshall Plan played a certain role in the discussion of the transition from centrally planned to market economies. The former German chancellor Helmut Schmidt firmly advocated a common European and U.S. initiative along the lines of the European Recovery Program. Albeit in this case, too, an unadulterated market doctrine has prevailed over a more gradual approach supplemented by substantial capital transfers, following the pattern of the Marshall Plan.

In the end, the effect of the Marshall Plan on the development of Western Europe needs to be pointed out, which has almost been forgotten in Austria. It was again the former Austrian chancellor Bruno Kreisky who, in a speech before Labor Union functionaries in 1959, pointed to the fact

> that it was the whip of the dollar which we all in Europe needed, the whip which drove us back from the jungle of bilateralism to multilateralism. It was the pressure of the Americans in the OEEC, an organisation created by them, the organisation for the economic cooperation among the Marshall Plan countries, which induced the countries benefitting from Marshall Plan-funds to cooperate systematically in the economic field.

There is no doubt that Western European multilateralism, initiated by the European Payments Union and continued in the OECD, paved the way towards European integration. What we now see in Europe—the formation of a European economic and monetary union—was initiated by some farsighted politicians in the United States and in Europe and was supported by the American taxpayer. Today we look with gratidude at the impressive results of an idea, born in the United States, more than fifty years ago.

# The Activities of the ERP Fund from 1962 to 1998

*Kurt Löffler and Hans Fußenegger*[*]

## The Founding of the ERP Fund

### *General Remarks*

The years 1961 and 1962 marked a decisive turning point in connection with Marshall Plan aid for Austria—due to the conveyance of sole power of disposal over ERP funds from the American to the Austrian government, and as a result of the creation of the ERP Fund. The definitive founding of the ERP Fund occurred in 1962 with the passage of the ERP Fund Act. Before this legislation could be put into law, however, the power of disposal over ERP funds, which had been held by the American government since the initiation of Marshall Plan aid to Austria in 1948, had to be conveyed to the Austrian government. This took place within the framework of the ERP Counterpart Settlement in 1961, signed on March 29, 1961 in Vienna by Austrian Chancellor Julius Raab and US Ambassador Freeman Matthews. This Counterpart Agreement was preceded by an exchange of notes between the US and Austria, which was considered a supplementary understanding of the two governments and took effect simultaneously with the ERP Counterpart Settlement.

This agreement established that the Counterpart funds were to be managed as a legally independent, extra-budgetary fund, and were to continue to be used to support economic development in Austria.

This ERP Counterpart Settlement of 1961 (including the supplementary exchange of notes) thus constituted the precondition for and, at the same time, the basis of the ERP Fund Act (BGBl. Nr.

---

[*] Translated from the original German by Mel Greenwald

207/1962), which was passed by the Austrian government on June 13, 1962 and became law on July 1, 1962.

### The Implementation of the ERP Fund Act in 1962

During the months subsequent to this law having gone into effect, the funds to which the ERP Fund thus became legally entitled were transferred to its accounts at the Austrian National Bank. After this transfer was completed, the assets which the ERP Fund had at its disposal totaled approximately 11.2 billion Austrian Schillings (öS). These funds were divided into two separate endowments: one of about öS 5.66 billion managed by the ERP Fund itself and a second one of about öS 5.55 billion administered by the Austrian National Bank and over which the ERP Fund retained power of disposal.

In July 1962, in accordance with the provisions of the ERP Fund Act, the federal government approved the first ERP annual program, and named the members of both the ERP Credit Commission and the individual expert commissions. Moreover, the fiscal provisions which were to apply to the ERP Fund were established, as specified in the Act, by agreement with the Bureau of Audits and the Ministry of Finance, and the ERP Fund's system of accounting was instituted, whereby the Fund's financial assets and liabilities were set up in accordance with the principles of double-entry bookkeeping. The trustee agreements called for by the Act were also concluded with the authorized credit institutions over the next few months.

### The Most Important Provisions of the ERP Fund Act

The legal provisions in the ERP Fund Act make it quite clear that the most important aspects of the ERP Fund's mission include implementing its credit policy in a way that supports state economic policies, as well as insuring the preservation of its capital through prudent management of the Fund's assets.

The tasks and responsibilities of the ERP Fund are set forth in Paragraph 1 of the Act. According to § 1, Sec. 2, the ERP Fund's mission is "... to further the expansion, increased efficiency, and greater productivity of the Austrian economy, especially by supporting and stimulating production and commerce, and also thereby to promote full employment and increasing GNP, though with full cognizance of the importance of maintaining a stable currency."

In keeping with these provisions, the ERP management has until April of each year to produce an annual program including basic principles underlying its guidelines governing individual ERP programs for the upcoming fiscal year, and to present this to the federal government (also see § 10).

According to § 4, Sec. 1 and 2, the ERP Fund is obliged to "... manage its assets in accordance with sound economic principles" and, aside from certain express exceptions enumerated in the Act, is "... forbidden to expend funds or to engage in activities which would continually diminish the Fund's assets." Furthermore, according to § 4, Sec. 3, the ERP Fund is forbidden to turn over funds to regional or local authorities, and the fund has to be managed separately from the general budget (§ 4, Sec. 4). As a result of these last two provisions, which had already been stipulated in the Counterpart Agreement, ERP funds could no long be dispensed to regional and local authorities or paid out as supplementary cash subsidies, which had been possible previously.

The way in which the ERP Fund was to go about fulfilling these tasks is likewise stipulated in the Act. In concrete terms, the types of loans which the ERP Fund is permitted to make are exhaustively described in § 5. According to § 5, Sec. 1, the ERP Fund may grant "... only medium and long-term, interest-bearing investment credits secured by collateral." These investment credits can be granted in three categories: large (öS 500,000 and up), middle-sized (öS 100,000 - 500,000) and small (öS 10,000 - 100,000). In addition, the ERP Fund may make so-called "miscellaneous outlays" (e.g. economic grants-in-aid to developing countries to facilitate Austrian exports to them), whereby the conditions enumerated in § 4 must be taken into consideration; these are governed by § 5, Sec. 2.

The few small credits that have been granted since the establishment of the ERP Fund were, above all, those made to farming operations in the 1950s. The number of middle-denomination credits has also declined over the years; at present, such loans are made only on rare occasions and exclusively in the non-industrial sector of the economy (agriculture and forestry, tourism, and transport). In the industrial, commercial, trade and energy sectors, ERP middle-sized credits were still relatively significant funding sources during the early years; the number of such credits declined constantly in the 1970s and especially in the 1980s. For this reason, middle-denomination credits were ultimately done away with completely for this sector of the economy in the context of the ERP Fund reform in mid-1985. Since then, only large loans have been made to industrial and commercial enterprises.

The ERP Fund Act also contains special provisions stipulating the organizational structure of the fund (in §§ 6-9), the process of granting credits (in §§ 14-19), as well as the details of pay-out, pay-back and the control procedures (in §§ 20-21).

The personnel of the ERP Fund consists of its administrators who represent the Fund and carry on its business, and the members of the ERP Credit Commission who decide on loan applications submitted to the Fund. It had already been established in § 8, Sec. 2 of the ERP Fund Act that the decision on applications "... in the tourism, agriculture, and forestry sectors as well as in the transport sector ... would be delegated ... to a separate commission of experts." Thus, there are a total of three commissions—an ERP Credit Commission and two expert commissions—legally authorized to decide on the issuance of ERP credits. The federal government appoints the members of these commissions, including 12 members of the ERP Credit Commission and six members of each expert commission (a representative of the ERP Fund as well as a representative of the federal ministry with jurisdiction in the particular sector also sit on each expert commission). The federal government is responsible for overseeing the fund; its affairs and financial condition are subject to examination by the federal Bureau of Audits.

In connection with the process of granting ERP credits, so-called "authorized credit institutions," also known as trustee banks, play a central role. To some extent, the Fund makes use of banking institutions to fulfill its responsibilities and to complete credit transactions. The various parties' rights and obligations are clearly spelled out in the so-called trustee agreements. For the services rendered, the trustee banks receive fees as established by contract.

Basically, any Austrian bank with a certain minimum size and clientele—and, since Austria became an EU member, any such bank headquartered in an EU-member state—can apply for trustee bank status.

According to §§ 14-19 of the ERP Fund Act, all applications for an ERP credit are to be submitted through a trustee bank, with the exception of credit applications from the transport sector which are to be submitted directly to the Ministry of Science and Transport. The trustee bank's job is to review the application and to forward it along with all supporting documentation and its evaluation to the ERP Fund with the request for a determination within the framework of a specific ERP program. In the case of applications that lay within the purview of the ERP Credit Commission (i.e. the industrial/commercial sector), the next step is a comprehensive examination of the submitted investment project by the ERP management staff in conformity with the guidelines in effect for the particular ERP program—in concrete terms, there is an assessment of the project's economic impact, business prospects, and financial feasibility, the latter in a joint investigative committee including representatives of the Austrian National Bank and the Ministry of Finance. In the case of applications that lay within the field of activity of an expert commission (i.e. the tourism, agriculture, and forestry sector, and the transport sector), the assessment of the project's economic impact, business prospects and financial feasibility is the responsibility of the appropriate ministry. The result of this investigation is a proposal to grant an ERP credit (or to deny it), which is then submitted to either the ERP Credit Commission or the appropriate expert commission for a decision. Thus, the law grants the ERP Credit Commission or the particular expert commission authority in reaching a final verdict on an application.

The ERP credit agreement does not directly involve the ERP Fund, but rather is consummated by the trustee bank and the borrower. The basis of this ERP credit agreement is the so-called credit approval declaration which is conveyed by the ERP Fund to the trustee bank which submitted the application. Actually dispensing funds in conjunction with an ERP credit takes place in step-by step-fashion as the credit recipient substantiates having made the approved investment (substantiation of use).

The pay-out of the ERP credit is made through the trustee bank in accordance with general provisions in the trustee agreement as well as specific provisions in the credit approval declaration.

Notwithstanding the oversight duties of the trustee banks, the ERP Fund itself is also entitled to conduct on-the-spot checks of the use of ERP credit funds, as well as of the recipient's compliance with the conditions imposed by the ERP credit agreement.

## Activities of the Fund from its Inception to the ERP Fund Reform in 1985

### *General Remarks*

In all major industrial states over recent decades, the furtherance of private investment activities with the objective of exerting an effect on their level and structure has assumed—alongside public sector infrastructure investments—a central role within the framework of a state's economic policies.

In this connection, Austria possesses a highly developed system to promote investment including both direct and indirect mechanisms. Among the indirect means of furthering investment are various forms of preferential tax treatment; the direct means include providing supplementary outlays, offering loans or credits at below-market interest rates, as well as officially guaranteeing repayment.

Within the context of the direct promotion of investment, a further differentiation can be made with regard to the types of policies used, which essentially can have either an offensive or a defensive structure. An offensive policy structure is understood primarily as the attempt to accelerate the structural transformation of an economy, particularly through support of innovation and diffusion of technology. With the exception of the early 1970s, there have hardly been instances of the use of policies to promote investment as an instrument to moderate business cycle fluctuations.

From a structural policy perspective, promotion of investment thus also serves to compensate for imperfections of the market—as a corrective for inefficient financial markets or as a "reward" for making investments associated with positive external effects.

## The ERP Fund's Policies During this Period

In actual practice, the goal which the ERP Fund set during this period was primarily to pursue an offensive structural policy (though with exceptions mentioned below) and to fortify the economic strength and international competitiveness of Austrian enterprises by supporting modernization, innovation, diffusion of technology, expansion of productive capacity, and the restructuring of various economic sectors. This agenda was meant to enable the Austrian economy to approach the level of the industrially developed states. To reach this goal, guidelines were established for each respective economic sector within the framework of the ERP annual program and its fundamental principles established for individual areas of the economy.

With regard to the worthiness of particular projects to be fostered and promoted, foreign trade considerations—export orientation, import substitution—as well as employment policy aspects—furthering job security or job creation—have played a key role from the very outset. Moreover, promotional guidelines also took into consideration environmental and energy policy aspects, as well as those related to furthering economic competition. Over the years, policies related to fostering individual regions of the country have also been increasingly integrated into the design of ERP programs.

There was only one significant deviation from this offensive structural policy approach. This was in the fiscal year 1972/73, when it was decided to pursue a policy of economic stabilization in order to dampen the business cycle boom prevailing in Austria. Approximately a third of the planned ERP credit budget was not distributed at that time, but rather was "put on ice" for an indeterminate period of time. These ERP funds were ultimately paid out during the fiscal year 1974/75, when the Austrian economy was in a recession and these funds were desperately needed to stimulate the economy (the section on the development of the ERP credit volume discusses this in greater depth).

As previously mentioned, the ERP annual programs are approved each year by the federal government. Thus, a simple mechanism is in place to enable a flexible reaction to current economic policy demands (prevailing conditions). This potential flexibility has been employed above all in connection with the pursuit of special regional policy objectives (discussed in greater detail below). Thus, several of the ERP's special regional programs were instituted as essentially long-term programs (e.g. for the Voitsberg coal mining area), even though they had to receive purely *pro forma* approval from the government over and over again every year. Others, however, were instituted to be able to manage a suddenly-emerging crisis as rapidly as possible (e.g. the short-term ERP special program for the Kirchdorf/Krems district, a situation triggered by the bankruptcy of the Eumig Co. and the skyrocketing unemployment it caused in that area).

Furthermore, since the very beginning of its activities of granting credits and in light of the limited means at its disposal, the ERP Fund has pursued a policy of focusing on those economic sectors which seemed most suited to achieving the objectives established in the ERP

Fund Act (strengthening the Austrian economy in general, with particular concentration on foreign trade and employment considerations). Accordingly, even as early as the 1962/63 fiscal year and throughout the period up to 1985 as well, support was provided to the following sectors of the economy: companies engaged in industrial and commercial production, the energy sector, agriculture and forestry, tourism and shipping/transportation.

The section on the ERP's activities in granting credit to individual sectors of the economy discusses this in greater depth.

## The Importance and Development of Fostering Specific Regions

As mentioned above, ERP Fund activities aimed at fostering specific regions have played an increasingly important role particularly since the early 1970s. The economic situation in a number of regions—especially those communities highly dependent on lignite coal mining—led the ERP to begin making the establishment of regional political goals an ongoing component of the Fund's annual program as early as 1966/67, and to institute special programs for certain disadvantaged regions. (Note: the ERP Fund employs a fiscal year ending June 30.) During the period now under discussion (up to 1985), special regional programs were set up only for the industrial and commercial sector. Indeed, in the other sectors supported by the ERP Fund, there existed no such special programs, but regional policy criteria certainly were taken into consideration in granting credits (especially in the area of tourism). Over the years, these regionally-oriented special programs in the productive sector continually expanded both geographically as well as with respect to the ERP credit volume made available for them. (This is discussed in greater depth below.)

The ERP credits granted in conjunction with these special regional programs included especially favorable conditions in order to strongly stimulate investment in these disadvantaged regions (particularly by attracting firms to relocate there). The terms of such ERP credits generally ran up to 15 years, and provided for no repayments during the first five years in some instances. The interest rate during this no-repayment period was 1 percent per annum in the 1970s and 2 percent p.a. during the first half of the '80s. In the repayment period, the interest rate was, as a rule, 5 percent p.a. (During the years 1980/81 to 1982/83, it was 6 percent p.a.) In comparison, conditions for normal credits in the industrial and commercial sector during this period were as follows: the term was between five and 10 years maximum; the interest rate was generally 5 percent p.a. (6 percent p.a. from 1980/81 to 1982/83); a no-repayment period was generally granted only for a maximum of one year.

The first special regional program was set up for coal mining areas in Styria, Carinthia and Upper Austria and was named the ERP Special Program for Mining Regions. Its declared goal was the creation of new jobs for the surplus workforce in these areas in which coal mining was on the decline because it had ceased to be profitable.

In the 1973/74 fiscal year, the ERP program to foster individual regions was expanded to include an additional structural policy focus. In an effort to do something about the increasing migration away from districts bordering on the Iron Curtain, a series of border areas in Upper and Lower Austria, Burgenland, Styria and Carinthia were declared developmental regions and integrated into the ERP regional support efforts. In addition to the previously existing special program for coal mining areas, a new program—the ERP Special Program to Foster Border Regions—was established to focus on the problems of these areas. In conjunction with this new program, the ERP funds set aside for fostering regional development were increased correspondingly.

During the second half of the '70s and particularly during the first half of the '80s, additional regions—"rust belts," border regions, inadequately developed peripheral zones—were integrated into the ERP program to foster specific regions—for example, in 1977/78 East Tyrol came into the border region program, and was included in the mining region program. In 1980/81, new ERP special programs were established for Upper Styria and Wiener Neustadt-Neunkirchen, regions categorized as older industrial belts currently in decline (the ERP Special Program for the Creation of Industrial-Commercial Jobs in Upper Styria as well as the ERP Special Program for the Creation of Industrial-Commercial Jobs in the Lower Austrian Region of Wiener Neustadt-Neunkirchen).

The funds made available for ERP credits to foster individual regions went hand in hand with the expansion or contraction of the special ERP regional programs which, in turn, depended upon business cycle developments. With the exception of a very few years, the funds made available for ERP credits to foster individual regions rose continuously. Independent of this general trend, though, extraordinarily large sums were used for regional programs in the early 1980s when the Austrian economy was suffering the effects of an international business cycle downswing as a result of the second oil shock. In the ERP fiscal years 1980/81 to 1984/85, the credits granted within the framework of special ERP regional programs made up more than 50 percent of the ERP's entire credit volume in the industrial and commercial sector, and came to between öS 400 million and öS 500 million each year. (An exception was 1981/82, when this amount was öS 340 million.)

In conclusion, it should be mentioned that because of the tremendous structural political significance of the ERP program to foster individual regions, it was not effected by the general contraction of the volume of ERP credits made available in 1972/73 due to overarching economic stability considerations.

**The Development of the Volume of ERP Credits Granted**

On July 1, 1962 the ERP Fund began operations with assets of approximately öS 11.2 billion. Although most of these funds were already tied up as a result of credit commitments from previous years, a total of öS 781 million in credits could be granted in that first year to support the Austria economy.

The next year, the total volume of ERP credits made available increased by more than öS 300 million to approximately öS 1.1 billion. Up to 1970/71, the volume of ERP credits granted amounted to between öS 1.1 billion and öS 1.2 billion annually. Of a total planned credit volume of approximately öS 1.3 billion in the 1972/73 fiscal year, öS 426 million were withdrawn in order to curb the overheating business cycle boom. This reduction impacted primarily the industrial and commercial sector in which ERP credit volume of öS 650 million in 1971/72 was cut back to barely öS 260 million in 1972/73. The agriculture and forestry sector was also hit by this reduction (from öS 200 million in 1971/72 to barely öS 165 million in 1972/73). Thus, it was primarily the industrial credits, as opposed to regional and structural programs, that were impacted during this year.

The funds that had then been "put on ice" were subsequently released during the 1974/75 fiscal year, when the Austrian economy was feeling the powerful effects of the oil crisis and had gone into recession. Thus, the volume of ERP credits made available in that difficult year to support projects in the industrial and commercial sector could be nearly doubled in comparison to the previous year. In concrete terms, ERP credits granted to industrial and commercial firms rose from öS 550 million in 1973/74 to over öS 900 million in 1974/75. (The corresponding figure in 1972/73 had been a "mere" öS 260 million due to the previously mentioned unreleased funds.) The total volume of all ERP credits granted to all sectors to which it provided support could thus be increased to more than öS 1.7 billion. These additional ERP funds which were then released were deployed primarily to support large-scale projects of a regional or structural policy nature.

In the 1975/76 fiscal year, Austria was faced by the worst recession since the end of the Second World War. To provide support for the domestic economy, the ERP Fund made available over öS 1.5 billion in credits. With the exception of the previous fiscal year (and the distribution of previously unreleased funds mentioned above), this sum constituted the largest credit volume in the Fund's history to that date.

In the years thereafter, the volume of ERP credits made available remained about constant. It was not until the early '80s that the volume began to gradually climb, and first reached the öS 2 billion mark in the 1983/84 fiscal year. A table depicting the detailed development of ERP credits granted each year is found in the Appendix.

## ERP Activities in Individual Sectors of the Economy

Since, over the years, the importance of individual economic sectors—especially in connection with cyclical developments within the particular sector—within the framework of the ERP Fund's activities of fostering economic activities changed dramatically in some cases, the following section will describe ERP activities from 1962 to 1985 in each individual sector separately.

### *Industry and Commerce*

From the very beginning, the emphasis in the industrial and commercial sector has been placed on supporting investment by firms engaged in production, export and job creation (although, in certain years, there was an insignificant proportion of firms in the trade and service sectors). In doing so, primary consideration was, in turn, accorded to those investment proposals which served to strengthen the applicant's competitiveness in the domestic and foreign market, especially with respect to European integration, as well as to bring about structural improvements within the particular firm or region. These proposals included investments for the purpose of modernization or automation, measures to enhance product quality, capacity expansion, as well as implementation of state-of-the-art technologies. (Note: prior to the "ERP Fund Era," it was above all Austria's foreign trade relationships with the most important EU member states that were still highly underdeveloped.)

Aside from these general criteria used to assess applications for ERP credits, certain special focal points emerged in particular years. For example, in the late '60s, the textile industry received considerable support. Due to the export orientation of these firms, it was necessary in many cases to construct new production facilities and/or to radically modernize machinery and equipment to achieve the necessary increase in productivity which was a precondition to becoming or remaining competitive in the international market.

An analysis by branch of the ERP credits granted indicates that, in the early years, it was primarily firms in the metal processing, electrical, chemical, iron and steel, sand and gravel, and construction industries that received support. Enterprises in these branches received almost 75 percent of all ERP industrial credits. From the mid-1970s on, mechanical engineering and steel construction assumed increasing importance. Since 1984, the paper industry has also been among the sectors that have been most strongly supported by ERP funds, after the special program providing for low-interest credits for this industry was discontinued by what was then the Ministry for Trade, Commerce and Industry.

In connection with the creation of replacement jobs (primarily by means of business relocations and new start-ups) in problem regions (coal mining areas and "rust belts"), investment plans in the metal processing and electrical industries took on particular significance. The majority of the projects that received ERP support were in these branches. On the other hand, the textile and non-ferrous metals industries dominated in creating jobs in border regions.

In its first fiscal year, the proportion of ERP credits granted to the industrial and commercial sector was approximately 30 percent of all credits extended in all sectors. This figure increased to over 50 percent by the end of the 1960s, and continued to climb in the '70s, when it ranged between 50 percent and 60 percent. In the first half of the '80s, the proportion of credits granted to the productive sector fluctuated between about 64 percent and 68 percent. The actual numbers were öS 250 million in 1962/63 and approximately öS 1.4 billion in 1984/85. Through the expansion of the volume of credits granted to this economic sector, increasing investment in this sector could be supported by ERP funds. The investments supported by ERP credits increased from about öS 700 million in the first fiscal year to approximately öS 5.5 billion in 1984/85. (See the tables in the Appendix on the development of ERP credits granted as well as the investments supported by ERP credits from 1962/63 to 1984/85.)

There were three different programs available for industrial and commercial sector projects during this period: the middle-sized ERP credit (from öS 100,000 to öS 500,000) and the large ERP credit (over öS 500,000) within the framework of the normal program, and the large ERP credit within the framework of the special regional programs. Over the years, the relative importance of these programs has undergone significant and lasting change in accordance with the intentions of the ERP management. Thus, the importance of middle-sized credits declined continuously, until this form of credit was finally discontinued completely in conjunction with the ERP Fund reform in 1985 (discussed in detail below). On the other hand, the large ERP credit was expanded, particularly within the framework of the special regional programs. During the 1970s and especially beginning in the early '80s, a key concern of the ERP Fund in this connection was, on one hand, to provide stronger support to export-oriented enterprises (particularly middle-sized and large firms) and, on the other hand, to create jobs by attracting companies to set up operations in problem regions. Since this agenda concerned itself with large-scale undertakings, the decline of middle-sized credits was a logical consequence.

### *Tourism*

During this entire period, ERP programs to foster the tourism industry were primarily concerned with the modernization of hotels, restaurants and similar facilities. During the 1960s, the chief focus was on betterments to sanitary facilities, overall decor, creation of additional bed capacity, and improvements to staff accommodations. It was not until the early '70s that raising quality standards became the prime criterion for granting ERP funds. At the same time, there was a significant increase in a hotel's required capacity in order for it to qualify for ERP funding: from 15 to at least 30 beds in the case of a going concern, and at least 55 beds for a new project. These stipulations with regard to ERP credit funds granted to the tourism industry accorded recognition both to the rapidly growing trend toward group outings and travel in busses, as well as to the availability of a whole series of other programs designed to support smaller operations.

An additional point stressed by ERP programs to foster tourism particularly in the early '70s was support for swimming pool construction in areas that seemed to require such facilities due to the importance of summer tourism. Even then, particular attention was paid in this process to regions in which tourism was just beginning to emerge as a significant economic factor.

Beginning in the 1965/66 fiscal year, the "spa center" branch of the tourist industry was integrated into the Fund's guidelines. Indeed, the construction or modernization of spas was not one of the ERP's chief concerns; nevertheless, funds to further development in this sector were continually made available in subsequent years. From the early '80s onward, aside from its support for investment in generally increasing quality standards, the ERP Fund increasingly focused its funding activities to foster tourism on expansion of hotels and other forms of guest accommodations and infrastructure in areas in which tourism was just beginning to emerge as a significant economic factor, as well as in measures to prolong the tourism season in "one season" regions.

### *Agriculture and Forestry*

Before the founding of the ERP Fund, a large number of small-scale credits were granted directly to farmers within the framework of ERP programs to foster agriculture. From 1962/63 on, this practice was completely revamped, and ERP funds were henceforth made available, in accordance with a new agenda for this sector, to larger-scale distribution facilities such as co-op organizations and for the purpose of processing and refining agricultural products. Over the entire period but especially in the early years, the chief emphasis was on supporting the construction of silos and multi-purpose structures for the storage, cleaning, drying, ventilation, and cooling of grain and corn, and of storage facilities for grain, fertilizer and mixed feeds. Over the years, however, the emphasis increasingly shifted to the processing and refining of agricultural products, whereby large ERP credits were granted, above all, for the modernization of dairies, slaughterhouses, and meat processing plants (the latter particularly in the '70s and '80s with the goal of enabling these enterprises to export to the European Community). ERP credits were also made available for investment in agricultural infrastructure: in the '70s to build farm roads, and during the entire period—though with diminishing significance—for electrification projects in mountainous areas and border regions.

In the forestry sector, ERP credits were employed primarily for reforestation, building logging roads to open up new stands of trees, and mechanizing the process of bringing in cut timber.

### *Transport*

The ERP Fund's efforts to foster transport made a considerable contribution to the construction of ski lifts (tow, chair, and gondola lifts) in Austria, so that significant new regions could be opened up for tourism, and regions that previously had strictly a summer season could now accommodate tourists in winter as well. Most of the credit volume made available to this sector by the ERP during the '60s and early '70s was employed to foster construction of lift facilities. From the beginning of the '70s on, the primary focus was no longer on the construction of new lifts, but rather on their modernization and the expansion of their capacity, as well as projects in the late '70s related to the consolidation of lift facilities in a single region. During a number of years, much more than half of all investment in lift facilities was financed in part by ERP credits featuring below-market interest rates.

A second main area of focus of the ERP Fund's efforts to foster transport during this period was support of domestic ship transport—particularly passenger ships on the Danube and the lakes of the Salzkammergut region.

In summary, it can maintained that the ERP program to support transport was, in a broader sense, an effort to promote tourism, in that this program helped considerably to finance the necessary infrastructure for this emerging and flourishing economic sector.

### *Energy Sector*

ERP funds were distributed to the energy sector for the purpose of constructing (in early years solely for completing) power plants (steam, hydroelectric, etc.) and district heating systems, as well as for the erection of energy transmission facilities and for the expansion of primary and secondary systems for delivering energy to consumers.

## Miscellaneous Projects of the ERP Fund—Cooperative Development

Among the other accomplishments of the ERP Fund carried out in accordance with § 5, Sec. 2 of the ERP Fund Act since its inception have been its support measures in the framework of cooperative development (developmental aid). In this connection, ERP funds were provided to finance bilateral technical developmental aid projects (e.g. constructing hospitals and water supply facilities) and for productive investments such as electric power plants.

In the case of all projects financed with ERP funds, particular attention was paid to secondary investment effects in Austria of payments made to suppliers of goods and services; on a project basis, the Austrian proportion of these amounts had to be at least 50 percent.

## The ERP Fund Reform of 1985

### *Brief Overview of the Substance of the ERP Fund Reform*

The reform of the Fund's credit-granting process which was initiated in 1985 and essentially put into effect in the 1985/86 fiscal year constituted both a reorganization of the Fund and a reorientation of its policies with regard to fostering development. In this latter respect, there was a thorough reevaluation of the programs then in effect with the aim of reassessing the focal points of the activities pursued up to that point as to their "reasonableness," as well as considering the extent to which new initiatives were necessitated by a changing economic situation.

The most important upshot of these considerations was a shift in the emphasis of the Fund's activities toward increased involvement in fostering development in the industrial and commercial sectors and, simultaneously, a diminishment of efforts in non-industrial sectors. In concrete terms, this meant the complete termination of ERP programs to foster development in the energy sector, as well as a significant reduction of activities on behalf of the tourism industry. There were also cut-backs of ERP programs for agriculture, forestry, and transport. And since there had been a drastic drop in demand for middle-sized credits (i.e. those up to a maximum of öS 500,000) in the industrial and commercial sector, these were also discontinued.

The end of ERP efforts to foster development in the energy sector was primarily the result of investment costs for power plant construction, which had increased to such enormously high levels that an

ERP credit would have covered only a tiny fraction of total outlays. The effects produced thereby would have been only quite marginal; this led to the conclusion that the funds that had been used for this purpose heretofore could be deployed in a much more efficient manner (and with a greater effect upon the activities thus supported) in high-profile areas of the industrial and commercial sector faced with stronger international competitive pressures.

Besides this overhaul of credit-granting activities in general, prime focus was also on considerations with respect to a more selective mode of fostering development within the framework of the Fund's remaining programs. Especially in the industrial and commercial sector, there was a desire to employ the individual special ERP programs as an instrument to bring about an offensive policy of fostering industrial development, whereby the decisive criteria for a project's worthiness to be granted an ERP credit would be the applicant firm's degree of export orientation and the structural improvement effects the credit would bring about within the firm itself.

The more selective granting of development credits also quickly resulted in a marked shift that could be observed within the productive sector toward the technological processing sector and the chemical industry, and away from using ERP credits to support primary producers who had received such credits in the past (an issue discussed in more detail below).

From an organizational perspective, the Fund was reorganized into a service provider organized along the lines of a private firm (removal from the direct administration of the federal government in an organizational sense). In this way, a service-oriented organizational structure could be put into place which no longer had to be oriented upon the organizational structures of the administration of a sovereign state. The ERP Fund could act more efficiently and with a greater orientation toward service as a result of these organizational changes.

## The Period from 1985/86 Until Austria Joined the EEC on January 1, 1994

### *The ERP Fund's Policies of Fostering Development During this Period*

The objective of the ERP Fund's policies of fostering development during this period was to implement the shift of emphasis that had been established within the framework of the ERP Fund reform in

1985/86 and to continue to develop agenda revisions as economic conditions necessitated this. The concrete measures and the most important innovations in this connection are briefly discussed in the following section. During the previous 20 years, growth of the Austrian economy had consistently been a bit stronger than the corresponding rates in the domestic economies of other European OECD states (on average). Nevertheless, Austrian industry's productivity continued to lag behind some other European countries, and it was precisely this improved productivity that was meant to be achieved by the revamped ERP program (see below) for the industrial and commercial sector.

### *Industry and Commerce*

In the '80s, and particularly during the second half of that decade, the intensification of the structural policy approach stood at the centerpoint of the distribution of ERP funds to the industrial and commercial sector, and this was accorded corresponding weight in establishing the guidelines for the individual ERP programs.

Thus, a new emphasis on fostering technology was already introduced in the 1987/88 fiscal year. In the framework of this ERP program, support was provided to projects in the area of production transition, which were consistent with the intentions of federal efforts to foster technology such as the Innovation and Technology Fund (ITF), as well as investments to implement Austrian or foreign research and development (R & D) activities in the field of series production. Furthermore, it ought to be mentioned here that the ERP Fund was commissioned by the federal Ministry for Science and Transport to handle a considerable portion of the ITF's efforts to foster technological development.

The ERP special program for foreign activities was then introduced during the 1988/89 fiscal year. As would subsequently come out, this was a decisive additional point of emphasis within the framework of the ERP program for the industrial and commercial sector. The rationale for this effort was Austrian industry's very low degree of internationalization in comparison to other OECD member states—that is, the level of direct investment of foreign firms in Austria was considerably higher than that of Austrian firms abroad. In order to reduce this deficit, the ERP Fund granted domestic enterprises favorable ERP credits to finance the costs incurred in connection with setting up a foreign subsidiary or joint venture (e.g. start-up or buy-in costs, expenditures associated with opening up new markets, commercial credits to finance the necessary investment). Essential preconditions of this ERP effort was that the credit applicant chiefly did business in Austria and that these activities abroad would improve the firms international market position which would, in turn, have positive repercussions for both the individual enterprise's domestic operations as well as the Austrian economy as a whole. This was not designed to subsidize the export of jobs to cheap-wage countries, but rather to support offensive measures to open up new markets.

The ERP program to further internationalization attained especially great importance during the early '90s when, following the fall of the Iron Curtain, the Austrian economy was confronted by the historic chance to internationalize in newly-reformed Eastern European countries. Due to the close relationships that Austria had maintained with Hungary, the Czech Republic, Slovenia, Slovakia and Poland during the Cold War, Austrian firms enjoyed a favorable starting position during the initial years of restructuring to a free-market economy, which they then had to take advantage of. Between 1990 and 1995, Austria consistently occupied a top position (1st, 2nd or 3rd) among the foreign partners participating in newly-founded joint ventures in these countries (though with the exception of Poland). In order to take these changed circumstances adequately into account, the ERP Eastern Europe program was set up especially for this purpose during the 1990/91 fiscal year. To date, the ERP Fund has supported a total of approximately 350 internationalization projects.

During these years, projects to foster regional development were likewise extremely important and the funds made available through them rose continually. In the period under consideration here, regional programs' credit volume doubled from approximately öS 500 million in 1986/87 to over öS 1.1 billion in 1993/94. The goal was to achieve structural improvement effects and to take pressure off the labor market through intensified investment in problem regions.

Due to its proven record of success and ist know-how based on tremendous experience in the field of fostering regional development, the ERP Fund was also entrusted with the task of implementing various special programs of the federal government in this area. These included the "100,000 Schilling" and "200,000 Schilling" programs instituted in the mid-'80s as combined measures to foster investment and job creation, as well as the "Regional Innovation Premium" and

"Support for Regional Infrastructure" programs sponsored by the Ministry of Science and Transport.

Since the early '90s, consideration has also been given by the ERP to the special situation of small and medium-sized enterprises (SMEs) with respect to obtaining financing on the free market. In comparison to large firms, SMEs often have to pay a far higher risk premium in taking out a loan, and this makes the access to credit much more difficult for these enterprises. Therefore, since the 1990/91 fiscal year, a special SME technology program has been conducted by the ERP to support such enterprises and to foster innovative investment projects. Since, as a rule, the number of projects submitted far outstrips the ERP's budgeted credit funds, and the Fund's policy of fostering development is not based upon the principle of equal shares for all projects worthy of support, but rather to offer extremely generous support to outstanding proposals selected according to clear criteria, an evaluation schema for individual ERP programs was introduced as early as the 1988/89 fiscal year and has been continually refined over the years. (Of course, a precondition is that the project comply with special ERP guidelines.) According to this evaluation catalog, the final assessment of submitted proposals is primarily based on four factors: the economic situation and development of the enterprise, the quality of the project, its impact on the economy (regional significance, environmental implications, etc.) and market development. The individual projects' relevance to structural policy emerges as a result of the evaluation, which is determinative for the amount of support given.

Moreover, an upper credit limit per individual project and per firm as well as a minimum percentage limit for ERP funding were introduced in the 1990s. (These upper limits had previously been öS 100 million; since 1995, this has been increased to a maximum of öS 200 million in connection with the implementation of the EU structure fund credits to foster regional projects.) With regard to the minimum percentage limit, the following rule continues to be valid: projects are excluded from receiving support in cases in which the ERP credit quota—as a result of the upper credit limit—would no longer make up more than 20 percent of total project costs and no other supporting grants from other institutions are available to make up a combined "aid package." Thus, proposals with an investment volume of more than öS 500 million are as a rule excluded from receiving ERP credits. The primary rationale behind this policy was to force large firms to use the capital market to finance major investment projects and, at the same time, to be able to make sufficient ERP funds available to medium-sized enterprises as well as for regionally significant proposals (usually supported by "aid packages") and (usually medium-sized and small) technology projects.

These two measures made it possible to simultaneously achieve the goal of being able to provide very high support to particularly high-quality projects and to significantly increase the ERP credit proportion of total project investment. In the mid-'80s for all ERP-supported projects, the average credit made up approximately 30 percent of the entire project costs; thereafter, this figure rose to almost 60 percent. (See the graph in the Appendix.)

*Tourism*

The ERP program to foster tourism was revived in the 1989/90 fiscal year. Since then, the areas of concentration have been to support:

- automation and modernization of restaurants, hotels and similar facilities in order for them to reach a minimum standard of at least the 3-star category,
- new projects only in border areas and problem regions, and only when the project can make a significant contribution within an overall tourism policy, and
- establishment of tourism operations and facilities to foster active/adventure vacations (whereby swimming pool construction is limited to exceptional cases in developing areas).

Spa hotels and similar luxury-class establishments receive funding only when such projects can be expected to stimulate tourism throughout an entire region.

*Transport*

A new focal point was also established for ERP efforts to foster transport: measures supporting the "road-rail-ship" combined freight transport concept. Due to the rapidly increasing truck traffic on Austria's roads and the simultaneous decline in demand for shipping by railroad and ship, offering incentives to encourage so-called combined freight transport has come to be one of the ERP Fund's most important goals in the area of transport.

A portion of the ERP's funds also continued to be used to support domestic ship transport—particularly passenger ships on the Danube and the Austrian lakes. Over the years, however, the importance of such projects has steadily declined. Support for ski lift projects was discontinued in 1987 to avoid contributing to excess capacity in that sector.

From the early '90s on, practically the entire yearly budget for ERP credits in the transport sector was made available to support special investment to expand capacity within the framework of so-called "combined freight transport."

### *Agriculture*

In the agriculture and forestry area, the goals that had been pursued since the mid-'70s essentially remained in place, although there was a certain shift of focus to projects dealing with processing and refining agricultural products (particularly dairies and meat processing plants).

Two new points of emphasis were introduced into the ERP agricultural program during the second half of the '80s: support for community projects to produce district heating from biomass, and domestic hothouse horticulture. This latter agenda point was an upshot of Austria's balance-of-trade deficit in horticultural products and the reactor catastrophe in Chernobyl.

### *Cooperative Development*

There were no significant changes in the program of developmental aid projects during this period.

## The Development of the Volume of ERP Credits Granted

During the fiscal years from 1985/86 to 1992/93, the ERP was able to increase the annual volume of credits it granted by between öS 200-400 million per year. The figure for 1985/86 came to approximately öS 2 billion; by 1992/93, it had climbed to almost öS 5 billion.

This tremendous increase in ERP credits granted was due primarily to the fact that the maturities of credits were reduced during the '80, and particularly in the case of credits for projects in the industrial and commercial sector. The rationale behind these measures with respect to term to maturity was the rapid pace of technological development—in light of the necessity of increasing productivity in order to maintain the ability to compete in international markets, firms had to upgrade their machinery and equipment much more quickly than in the '60s and '70s.

Due to the weak performance of the Austrian economy in 1993, the Fund made available a special endowment for ERP credits in the amount of öS 1 billion for the 1993/94 fiscal year as a supplement to the regular ERP credit volume in the amount of approximately öS 5 billion. The additional funds primarily benefited firms in the industrial and commercial sector. The ERP Fund's goal was to prevent a potential drop in long-term growth rates due to a decline in private sector R & D activities as a result of the recession. The thinking behind this step was that business cycle declines can lead to substantial losses of economic growth and welfare as a result of decreased R & D activities, and these can no longer be made up long-term, even during an ensuing business cycle upswing.

## ERP Activities With Respect to Individual Sectors of the Economy

Due to the above-mentioned developments with respect to policies to foster investment in the industrial and commercial sector, this period was characterized by intensified support for innovation and technology projects. As for individual sectors, there was a distinct shift in favor or higher "value-added" manufacturers (metal processing, electrical industry, machinery construction, iron and metal goods production, auto components industry), whereas the volume of ERP credits to primary producers declined constantly.

In connection with support for businesses to relocate to problem regions or for the establishment of new firms in such areas, the chief projects were those involving automotive component suppliers, the electrical industry, and the metal processing industry. The proportion of credits granted to the industrial and commercial sector continued to climb in accordance with the shift of emphasis to this economic branch as established in connection with the ERP reform, and constituted approximately 90 percent of all credits granted since the beginning of the '90s.

## The Period Since Austria Joined the EEC in 1994

*General Remarks*

Austrian membership in the EEC—and later in the EC (now the EU)—brought with it a completely new situation with respect to Austria's autonomy in designing policies to foster development. Continuing to pursue a completely independent support policy was no longer possible, since fundamentally new legal circumstances were now binding with regard to the granting of subsidies (Note: in this section, the terms "subsidize," "foster" and "support" are used synonymously.) in Austria, and these applied to all other member states of the EEC and the EU as well. The essential feature was that, once Austria had joined the EEC, the supreme legal authority with respect to laws regulating subsidies was the EFTA Surveillance Authority (ESA) headquartered in Brussels.

The ESA constituted the counterpart of the EU Commission in the field of laws regulating competition. At that time (the beginning of 1994), the ESA was thus responsible for questions related to competition in the six new EEC member states (Finland, Iceland, Liechtenstein, Norway, Austria and Sweden) and the EU Commission in the then-12 EC member states.

In connection with this decisive change with respect to the chief authority regulating subsidies, it should also be mentioned that, within the framework of the EEC, the transport sector as well as agriculture, forestry and fisheries were not included and these sectors were not subject to regulation by the ESA. For these areas of the economy, national autonomy with respect to subsidy matters continued in effect until Austria joined the EU on January 1, 1995.

Thus, for the ERP Fund, this new situation—beginning of January 1, 1994 in some areas and on January 1, 1995 in its entire field of activity—meant a certain degree of restriction of its autonomy in designing support programs. In setting up its annual programs and the basic guidelines for the individual ERP programs until then, the ERP Fund had only to comply with the relevant provisions in the ERP Fund Act and the economic policy goals for the forthcoming year as established by the Austrian government. In 1994 and 1995 respectively, EEC or EU provisions regulating competition constituted the framework conditions for the feasibility of guidelines for the individual ERP programs. Special support policy measures which seemed necessary from the Austrian perspective could be implemented only when they were in accordance with EEC or EU regulations regarding competition.

## EU Regulations Regarding Competition - The Most Important Provisions for the Activities of the ERP Fund

Since, during Austria's one-year membership in the EEC, the same provisions regulating competition applied at that time to competition within the EU (with the exception of the sectors enumerated above), the following discussion will deal exclusively with EU regulations regarding competition.

For simplicity's sake, only a brief description will be provided here of the most important EU provisions regulating competition which are currently valid. Essentially, none of the fundamentals have changed since the beginning of 1995, although there certainly have been some ground-breaking modifications to details (such as the required individual notification of projects in certain branches and sectors, whereby the 1995 EU provisions were far less restrictive than those in effect today).

The essence of the EU provisions regulating competition is that all aid subsidies are forbidden, because it is feared that subsidies distort the competition between EU member states, or would threaten to do so (see Art. 92 of the EC agreement). However, since the EU also pursues certain goals in conjunction with its community policies (e.g. narrowing the economic gap between individual member states, enhancing the EU's competitive position vis-à-vis other economic powers, diminishing dependence upon so-called third-party states, improving environmental conditions in member lands), exceptions to this general ban on aid subsidies have been established. Thus, in order to achieve other highly desirable goals, the EU basically permits subsidies in the following cases:

- R & D
- regional development
- support for SMEs
- environmental protection
- bail-outs and restructuring of firms
- the so-called "de minimis" rule (aid in amounts considered insubstantial)

The special determinations concerning all of these exceptions were enacted in the form of EU announcements and made public in the official EU gazette. These so-called community framework provisions stipulate for what purpose and in what amount aid subsidies may be granted. The following section will describe those which are of significance to ERP programs.

*Community Framework for State R & D Aid*

According to the community framework for R & D, additional amounts can be given out as aid subsidies for basic research as well as for applied research and development (a precise definition of these three R & D categories is contained in the EU rules). The "additionality" of the expenditures plays an important role here—that is to say, an R & D project can be supported only when, collateral to receiving these subsidies, a firm's average R & D expenditures are raised correspondingly. (Ongoing R & D programs as well as outlays purely related to product adaptation can thus not be subsidized.) This condition of so-called additionality is automatically considered satisfied in the case of R & D projects carried on by SMEs; on the other hand, additionality constitutes a make-or-break criterion for R & D projects carried on by large firms.

As the basis for a subsidy, all expenditures incurred in connection with carrying out an R & D project can be taken into account. As a rule, the upper subsidy limit for such projects is 50 percent of gross expenditures for basic research and 25 percent of gross expenditures for applied R & D, whereby additional bonuses amounting to 5 percent to 25 percent of gross expenditures can be granted under certain conditions (e.g. the project is conducted by an SME or in a specially subsidized region, the project is a collaborative effort, etc.). These percentages with regard to the maximum subsidy amount always refer to the "subsidizable" costs; in computing the maximum subsidy amount, all aid subsidy payments for a particular project are to be added together. This general mode of computation applies to all community frameworks in the EU provisions regulating competition; therefore, this need not be gone into further in the subsequent discussions of the individual community frameworks.

*Community Framework for Regional Aid*

With respect to projects to foster development in particular regions (these have been determined by Austria together with the EU Commission on the basis of certain criteria; they include, until the end of 1999, Burgenland, the Mühlviertel district of Upper Austria, the Waldviertel and Weinviertel districts of Lower Austria, Upper, Southern and Eastern Styria, and Eastern Tyrol), so-called tangible "initial investments" (necessary start-up investments in machinery and real property) as well as intangible investments made in connection with carrying out an investment project (such as outside consultants, know-how transfer, costs of patents and licenses) can be supported by subsidies. As a rule, the upper subsidy limit for such projects is 30 percent or 40 percent of net expenditures in the case of Burgenland and 20 percent of net expenditures in the case of the other regions. Here as well, projects conducted by SMEs can be awarded bonuses of up to 10 percent.

*Community Framework for State Aid to SMEs*

Essentially the same provisions apply to the subsidizable costs of projects carries out by SMEs as is the case for regional aid subsidies—both pure investments as well as so-called "soft" expenditures such as those paid for consultants, training, know-how transfer, and feasibility studies qualify for support. A firm is considered an SME (NOTE: the figures below first cite the amount for a small business, followed by that for a medium-sized one) under EU provisions regulating competition if it has no more than 50/250 employees and its yearly gross revenues do not exceed 7/40 million ECUs or its net assets do not exceed 5/27 million ECUs and a large firm owns less than 25 percent of it. The upper subsidy limit for such projects is 15 percent of net expenditures in the case of small business and 7.5 percent of net expenditures in the case of the medium-sized firms, whereby the upper limits according to regional aid provisions come into play in the case of projects in subsidized regions. SME subsidies, however, are not permitted to be granted to firms in the so-called sensitive sectors (discussed below).

*"De Minimis" Rule*

The "de minimis" rule states that subsidies in trivial amounts do not effect competition and are thus permitted. Within the framework of subsidy programs under the "de minimis" rule, a particular firm can receive "de minimis" aid of up to 100,000 ECUs within a three-year period. All "de minimis" subsidies granted to a firm within this three-year period are to be totaled, and the upper limit may not be exceeded. In this cumulative process, those subsidies which were granted within the framework of an EU Commission-approved aid package (e.g. ERP programs) do not have to be included. Furthermore, it ought to be mentioned that "de minimis" subsidies are not subject to notification requirements. "De minimis" subsidies, however, are not permitted to be granted to firms in the so-called sensitive sectors.

In summary, the simple conclusion can be drawn that the greater the extent to which a firm's activities which are to be subsidized are removed from the market, the better the chances of the particular project to receive support (from the perspective of EU provisions regarding competition) and the higher those subsidies might be. Accordingly, the highest subsidy percentages are granted for basic research, whereas costs such as marketing and distribution cannot be subsidized at all. The same applies to the criterion regarding firm size: the smaller the firm, the greater the extent to which a project can be subsidized. Pure investment projects by large firms—with the exception of those in regions in which development is being fostered—do not qualify for subsidies since, respectively, 1994 and 1995. Regional subsidies occupy a special position in this connection. The most important goal of this type of subsidy is to prevent disadvantaged regions and central regions from drifting farther apart, and large firms can make a significant contribution in this respect. Nevertheless, since September 1998, even within the framework of programs fostering regional development, large-scale projects can be supported only under certain specified conditions up to the upper subsidy limit according to the community framework for regional aid subsidies. (The rules which are applicable here are set down in the new multi-sector regional subsidy guidelines for large-scale investment plans.)

Finally, it should also be pointed out in connection with EU regulations regarding competition that special provisions apply to certain sectors in which there is substantial excess capacity throughout the EU as well as to those dominated by a few large firms. These so-called sensitive sectors include the production of iron and steel, motor vehicles, and synthetic fibers, shipbuilding, coal mining, rail and truck transport, inland navigation, agriculture and fisheries.

### The ERP Fund's Policies and Activities During this Period

As previously indicated, the so-called community frameworks based upon the EEC / EU provisions regulating competition constitute the overall rules for the design of specific ERP programs. Moreover, the ESA (for the 1994/95 fiscal year) and the EU Commission (beginning with the 1995/96 fiscal year) have had to be informed in advance of the guidelines of all ERP programs, which had to be approved by these authorities. (The ERP programs for transport, agriculture and forestry for the 1994/95 fiscal year were the sole exceptions to this rule.) It is only after notification of this approval has been received that the individual ERP programs become operational and credit applications can be approved. In order to process these applications in a smooth and timely way despite this long, drawn-out notification process, the ERP Fund proceeds with the task of accepting and investigating applications during this waiting period, so that they can be promptly passed on to the ERP Commission for its decision immediately after receipt of notification regarding individual ERP programs. One of the reasons for this protracted notification process has been the complete lack or severe shortage of personnel in the responsible departments at the ESA and the EU Commission.

However, as a result of the introduction of more selective criteria over the course of recent years—the termination of the ERP normal program and the simultaneous shift of emphasis to innovation, technology, fostering regional development, SMEs and internationalization—the guidelines for individual ERP programs already largely conformed to the criteria contained in the EEC competition provisions in effect at the time Austria joined that organization. Therefore, there was hardly any need to modify or adapt the ERP guidelines in 1994 and/or 1995. Nevertheless, a series of additional and, from the point of view of actual practice, purely formal points had to be adopted into the ERP guidelines, including definitions of SMEs, various research categories, cumulative upper subsidy limits, etc., as such terms are defined in the regulations governing competition.

The only serious cut-backs that had to made in any of the ERP programs were in those focusing on internationalization and Eastern Europe. Despite intensive negotiations and objectively comprehensible grounds (in particular, the fact that Austria continued to lag behind most other OECD states with respect to the degree of internationalization of its economy), it has been impossible to conduct either of these two programs to the extent they were being carried on during the first half of the '90s. The three chief modifications are as follows:

1. subsidizing distribution branches abroad is no longer possible,
2. all projects involving large firms must either be reported to and approved by the EU Commission in advance, or may be granted subsidies only under the "de minimis" rule, and

3. ERP credits can, generally speaking, only be related to material investments; expenditures purely related to opening up new markets can no longer be supported.

The result of these radical restrictions was that ERP financing to foster development in these two areas virtually came to a standstill. In the fiscal years from 1989/90 to 1993/94, from 40 to over 60 such projects were supported each year; in the fiscal years from 1995/96 to 1997/98, the yearly average was five. As previously mentioned, agriculture, forestry and transport were not integrated into the EEC agreement. It was not until Austria joined the EU that these sectors came under the jurisdiction of EU provisions governing competition. Analyses were conducted during the first half of the '90s on the effects of Austria's joining the EU. Since these studies showed that the regulations of a common market would have serious negative short-term consequences for these sectors (e.g. for farmers, the take-over of the communal agricultural policy; for shipping firms, the discontinuation of the practice of independently assessing and collecting duties on behalf of the state), a number of special short-term programs to benefit these sectors were set up in 1994. For example, a special measure was then introduced on behalf of the food and beverage industry in the form of a concerted action bringing together all federal institutions which provide support to this sector. The objective of this special three-year program was to assist these firms as much as possible to implement the required short-term restructuring measures. During the first one and a half years, this special measure continued to be implemented in the context of existing ERP programs (for the industrial and commercial sector and for agriculture) and these projects received extraordinarily generous funding. Beginning in the 1995/96 fiscal year, a separate program, the ERP Eurofit program, was established in addition to the ERP agricultural program that had been in place for many years, since, in the meantime, the TOP Eurofit subsidy program had been discontinued and its objectives were taken over by the ERP Fund. In conjunction with this special program, the ERP Fund supported a total of 120 projects with a total credit volume of öS 3.5 billion during the 1993/94 to 1996/97 fiscal years (within the framework of the ERP programs for the industrial and commercial sector and for agriculture). Thus, the ERP Fund could provide decisive support in financing an investment volume of over öS 7.5 billion in the food and beverage industry.

Aside from these changes to individual ERP programs that were directly connected with Austria's joining the EU, a few other innovations were also introduced. Of particular significance here was the introduction of a new ERP infrastructure program for the industrial and commercial sector during the 1994/95 fiscal year. This effort fostered the establishment or expansion of industrial-commercial infrastructure facilities such as centers for start-up enterprises and technology and research parks in order to stimulate the founding of new businesses in technologically advanced sectors and/or in problem regions, as well as to support the establishment of private-sector industrial research co-operatives.

An additional significant expansion of the ERP's activities to foster development that came about as a result of Austria joining the EU had to do with the implementation of EU structural funds in Austria. In this respect, in deciding for the implementation of the European Fund for Regional Development (EFRD) structural fund subsidies, Austria opted in favor of keeping the existing subsidy system in effect. This has meant that the matching federal funds (co-financing) which are required to supplement the EFRD funds granted must be provided by various different Austrian subsidy instruments. A considerable proportion of the required federal matching funds are provided by the ERP Fund. This co-financing is provided above all by the ERP programs for disadvantaged regions, infrastructure and tourism. Within the framework of these programs, up to 50 percent of the projects subsidized by the ERP Fund receive—in addition to ERP credits with below-market interest rates—supplementary EFRD funds in direct proportion to the credit. Austria's first EU structural fund period extends from the beginning of 1995 until the end of 1999.

To complement its key role as co-financing partner, the ERP Fund was also appointed (following a search process conducted throughout Europe) as the agent to conduct the monitoring throughout Austria for the EFRD on behalf of the federal chancellery.

Moreover, the ERP Fund was commissioned by the Ministry of Agriculture and Forestry to assess cases to be subsidized and to carry out support activities for the so-called sector plans for agriculture and forestry, as well as for a number of other aid projects (biomass, farm road construction, sugar beet processing facilities, etc.). Both sector plans are likewise subsidy programs co-financed by the EU; here, however, the funds are provided by the European Agricultural Guidance and Guarantee Fund, Guidance Section.

The volume of credits granted by the ERP during the 1993/94 and 1994/95 fiscal years was approximately öS 5.7 billion; the corresponding figures during the two subsequent fiscal years were about öS 1 billion higher, and in the 1997/98 fiscal year it increased substantially once again to almost öS 8.2 billion. This continual increase in newly-granted ERP credits has been primarily attributable to premature pay-back of credits, due to the fact that interest rates have dropped considerably since the credits were granted. This last fiscal year also featured a special endowment in the amount of öS 1 billion connected with the creation of an ERP special program for growth and technology offensives discussed in more detail below.

Due to the important role of ERP credits in connection with the deployment of the EU structural funds in Austria following this country having joined the EU, there has been increasing support granted to innovative projects which have created jobs in problem regions. With respect to individual sectors, there has been a further shift in favor of higher "value-added" manufacturers (metal processing, electrical industry, machinery construction, iron and metal good production, auto components industry); at the same time, ERP credits to primary producers have declined steadily.

In connection with support for efforts aimed at attracting new or existing businesses to set up operations in Austria, the focus has remained on the auto components and metal processing industries. The proportion of credits granted to the industrial and commercial sector continued to increase in accordance with the shift of emphasis to this sector established in conjunction with the ERP reform; since the beginning of the '90s, these account for approximately 90 percent of all credits granted by the ERP.

## Current Situation and Future Prospects

The planned changes to the framework conditions of the EU competition guidelines as well as the reform of the EU structural funds (Agenda 2000) are currently at the center of public discussions regarding the design of subsidy programs in connection with direct measures to foster economic development. The way it looks now, regions qualifying for subsidies will be limited over the medium term and the funds made available to support programs in these areas will be decreased. The latitude accorded to individual states in designing programs with special emphases will thus tend to contract. Nevertheless, the following objectives will continue to be of uppermost importance for the ERP Fund as the largest Austrian institution directly fostering economic development:

- securing existing jobs and doing more to stimulate the creation of new ones,
- eliminating obstacles impeding growth—particularly for SMEs, and
- supporting innovation.

To achieve these goals, the ERP Fund will continue to optimize its subsidy programs as circumstances dictate, to strive to make the process of granting credits as clear and comprehensible as possible, and to intensify its efforts to serve the private sector. At the outset of the 1997/98 fiscal year, a series of key innovations related to these objectives were introduced. These include:

*ERP Special Program for a Growth and Technology Offensive—Mobilization of Equity Capital*

Particular attention is being paid to the current state of efforts to eliminate obstacles that impede growth. It is above all innovative small and middle-sized firms that quickly run up against expansion limits as a result of the small domestic market. In many cases, further growth through opening up new markets can be accomplished only by having access to the capital market. Supporting innovative, growth-oriented firms in obtaining financing both through private placements as well as public stock offerings is thus a key objective of the ERP Fund's growth and technology offensive.

Enterprises whose projects conform to the basic principles of the ERP's technology or SME programs and want access to the capital market to obtain financial resources and to finance costs (such as those incurred opening up new markets) which do not qualify for subsidies are offered especially favorable conditions. An ERP credit with a very low rate of interest (0.5 percent p.a.) and a maturity of five years makes available a stable source of working capital which does not participate in profits or growth and thus, in combination with true equity financing, represents part of an attractive mix. Furthermore, as an additional component of a compact aid package, it is also possible to integrate liability assumption through the federal Financial Guarantee Corporation. In addition, negotiations are currently underway to allow for closer cooperation of the ERP Fund with venture capital funds and other such financial institutions in identifying and financing innovative growth projects. With these special programs and accompanying measures, the ERP Fund is making a direct contribution to mobilizing equity capital.

*Expansion of the ERP Infrastructure Program*

Innovation centers, business start-up centers, and facilities enabling technology transfer have long been a part of ERP efforts to foster infrastructure. These impulse generators perform an important function in the national system of innovation as nodes in the innovation network of small and middle-sized firms, and as core elements in the formation of technology clusters and branches. ERP funds from the infrastructure program are also available now for the establishment or expansion of high-level commercial parks equipped with high-tech facilities. This is meant to ease the way for, above all, small firms which, as a result of their rapid expansion or other pressing reasons (such as noise ordinances) must relocate their operations. Moreover, investments for participation in specialized trade shows as technology transfer facilities for SMEs can now receive support from the ERP infrastructure program. ERP funds can thus contribute to greater professionalism and a tighter focus on the part of Austrian trade shows.

*Clear and Comprehensible Criteria for Granting Credits*

Projects that are most worthy of support stimulate high growth and employment, and display a high degree of innovative content. If these factors apply to a low extent, the amount of support granted to a project will be low or it will be deemed unworthy of support.

Establishing the amount of support which a particular project will receive is possible only through close cooperation with other agencies providing similar aid, such as the individual Austrian provinces. The ERP Fund's long years of collaboration with these institutions and the shared perspectives they have come to hold make possible such a mode of working together.

EVALUATION MATRIX

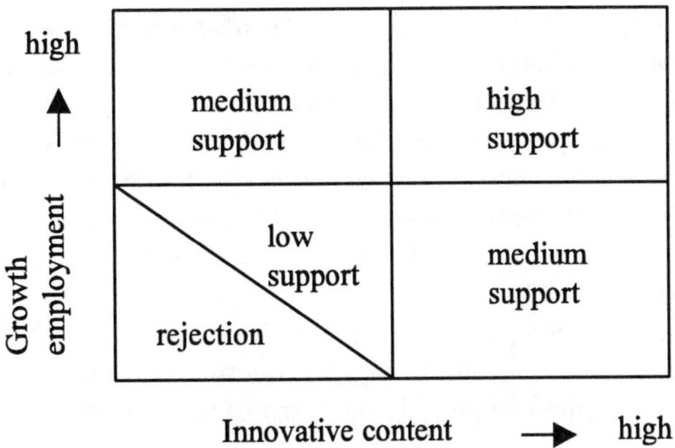


*Stimulus for Higher Employment—Bonus for Jobs and Apprenticeships*

Due to the current labor market situation, creating new jobs is among the most pressing concerns of the ERP Fund. For this reason, firms receive an ERP subsidy bonus if, in connection with carrying out an investment program, they increase employment by at least 10 percent as compared to the size of their workforce prior to the start-up of the project. The compensation comes in the form of an interest rate bonus of 1 percent p.a. over the course of three years as long as the firm proves itself to be successful in this respect. A much more generous financing package is granted to firms with outstanding apprenticeship training programs and to those which have created new apprenticeship positions.

*Improved Services for Firms*

The ERP Fund's particularly intensive efforts on behalf of SMEs have led to the creation of an additional special measure which has only been in effect since July 1998. The introduction of accelerated processing procedures has been designed to assess and decide on applications for ERP credits for amounts under öS 20 million within six weeks of the receipt of all necessary documentation. In doing so, the ERP Fund can also coordinate its support activities with the Financing and Guarantee Corporation and other such agencies fostering development projects. In order to make potential beneficiaries aware of these attractive new possibilities, a special information campaign is being launched during the 1998/99 fiscal year.

Furthermore, the ERP Fund also makes information available in its role as a one-stop shop to provide answers to all question regarding support and subsidies. Fund personnel can advise firms about the ERP Fund aid instruments that are best suited to foster their projects, or can refer applicants to the appropriate agency or institution. If the ERP Fund gets involved in putting together a financial aid package for a particular project, then the Fund can assume responsibility for the overall coordination.

With these measures, the ERP Fund will continue to succeed in making an important contribution to the modernization and growing strength of the Austrian economy in the spirit of the original Marshall Plan.

## Amount of approved ERP-loans from 1962/63 to 1984/85 (in million Schillings)

| | | distribution in economic sectors | | | | | | | |
|---|---|---|---|---|---|---|---|---|---|
| **financial year** | **total** | *industry, commerce and trade* | | | | *energy* | *transport* | *tourism* | *forestry and agriculture* |
| | | large loans | medium-sized loans | loans for regional development | total | | | | |
| **1962/63** | 581 | 200 | 50 | 0 | 50 | 231 | 78 | 72 | 150 |
| **1963/64** | 1,103 | 407 | 38 | 0 | 38 | 270 | 78 | 120 | 190 |
| **1964/65** | 1,107 | 402 | 38 | 0 | 38 | 270 | 82 | 125 | 190 |
| **1965/66** | 1,038 | 336 | 55 | 0 | 55 | 307 | 71 | 106 | 164 |
| **1966/67** | 1,140 | 465 | 59 | 61 | 120 | 200 | 70 | 120 | 165 |
| **1967/68** | 1,064 | 506 | 39 | 18 | 57 | 100 | 70 | 125 | 206 |
| **1968/69** | 1,140 | 564 | 36 | 30 | 67 | 100 | 60 | 150 | 200 |
| **1969/70** | 1,164 | 535 | 49 | 70 | 119 | 100 | 60 | 150 | 200 |
| **1970/71** | 1,282 | 603 | 47 | 122 | 169 | 100 | 60 | 150 | 200 |
| **1971/72** | 1,176 | 621 | 30 | 16 | 46 | 100 | 60 | 150 | 200 |
| **1972/73** | 880 | 236 | 23 | 147 | 170 | 100 | 60 | 150 | 165 |
| **1973/74** | 1,243 | 517 | 33 | 183 | 216 | 100 | 60 | 150 | 200 |
| **1974/75** | 1,705 | 889 | 19 | 252 | 271 | 100 | 60 | 150 | 235 |
| **1975/76** | 1,544 | 637 | 30 | 207 | 237 | 100 | 70 | 300 | 200 |
| **1976/77** | 1,584 | 588 | 26 | 380 | 406 | 150 | 90 | 150 | 200 |
| **1977/78** | 1,372 | 502 | 25 | 275 | 299 | 150 | 70 | 150 | 200 |
| **1978/79** | 1,419 | 583 | 12 | 257 | 269 | 147 | 70 | 150 | 200 |
| **1979/80** | 1,413 | 658 | 6 | 178 | 185 | 150 | 70 | 150 | 200 |
| **1980/81** | 1,637 | 643 | 4 | 420 | 424 | 150 | 70 | 150 | 200 |
| **1981/82** | 1,764 | 779 | 9 | 339 | 348 | 127 | 90 | 200 | 220 |
| **1982/83** | 1,934 | 796 | 4 | 427 | 431 | 127 | 120 | 220 | 240 |
| **1983/84** | 2,076 | 911 | 2 | 463 | 465 | 100 | 120 | 230 | 250 |
| **1984/85** | 2,040 | 894 | 1 | 500 | 501 | 5 | 120 | 250 | 270 |
| **sum** | **31,406** | **13,272** | **635** | **4,345** | **4,981** | **3,284** | **1,759** | **3,668** | **4,645** |

source: annual reports and annual closings of account

## Investments of the ERP-Fund from 1962/63 to 1984/85 (in million Schillings)

| financial year | total | distribution in economic sectors | | | | | | | |
|---|---|---|---|---|---|---|---|---|---|
| | | *industry, commerce and trade* | | | | *energy* | *transport* | *tourism* | *forestry and agriculture* |
| | | large loans | medium-sized loans | loans for regional development | total | | | | |
| **1962/63** | 1,598 | 616 | 90 | 0 | 90 | 360 | 164 | 133 | 234 |
| **1963/64** | 2,998 | 1,177 | 76 | 0 | 76 | 825 | 261 | 3,365 | 294 |
| **1964/65** | 2,852 | 1,166 | 65 | 0 | 65 | 842 | 194 | 265 | 320 |
| **1965/66** | 3,121 | 1,172 | 97 | 0 | 97 | 1,196 | 180 | 203 | 269 |
| **1966/67** | 5,890 | 1,430 | 108 | 110 | 217 | 3,554 | 162 | 247 | 279 |
| **1967/68** | 4,289 | 1,512 | 76 | 26 | 103 | 1,851 | 178 | 292 | 354 |
| **1968/69** | 3,753 | 1,741 | 76 | 78 | 153 | 1,074 | 120 | 308 | 357 |
| **1969/70** | 3,666 | 1,765 | 97 | 172 | 269 | 854 | 122 | 331 | 698 |
| **1970/71** | 5,777 | 3,333 | 94 | 206 | 300 | 1,376 | 132 | 321 | 315 |
| **1971/72** | 9,606 | 4,496 | 83 | 23 | 106 | 4,135 | 136 | 402 | 331 |
| **1972/73** | 5,759 | 1,496 | 54 | 272 | 326 | 3,039 | 147 | 478 | 273 |
| **1973/74** | 9,119 | 2,969 | 68 | 468 | 535 | 4,630 | 140 | 514 | 331 |
| **1974/75** | 7,523 | 5,076 | 56 | 728 | 784 | 638 | 170 | 402 | 454 |
| **1975/76** | 11,105 | 4,259 | 65 | 530 | 595 | 4,921 | 154 | 734 | 442 |
| **1976/77** | 14,088 | 3,318 | 65 | 970 | 1,034 | 8,764 | 343 | 312 | 316 |
| **1977/78** | 6,176 | 3,148 | 64 | 756 | 820 | 1,178 | 275 | 377 | 378 |
| **1978/79** | 7,846 | 4,890 | 31 | 566 | 598 | 1,222 | 206 | 499 | 431 |
| **1979/80** | 8,126 | 3,693 | 16 | 502 | 518 | 2,850 | 172 | 424 | 470 |
| **1980/81** | 8,587 | 5,262 | 8 | 1,473 | 1,481 | 924 | 151 | 347 | 422 |
| **1981/82** | 7,906 | 4,641 | 26 | 1,277 | 1,303 | 761 | 224 | 498 | 479 |
| **1982/83** | 8,445 | 4,976 | 8 | 1,295 | 1,303 | 599 | 369 | 797 | 581 |
| **1983/84** | 7,504 | 4,411 | 7 | 1,093 | 1,099 | 425 | 370 | 626 | 572 |
| **1984/85** | 7,275 | 4,278 | 3 | 1,243 | 1,246 | 36 | 452 | 694 | 569 |
| **sum** | **153,009** | **70,825** | **1,333** | **11,788** | **13,121** | **46,054** | **4,822** | **12,569** | **9,169** |

source: annual reports and annual closings of account

## Amount of approved ERP-loans from 1985/86 to 1997/98 (in million Schillings)

| financial year | sum of ERP-loans | distribution in economic sectors | | | | | | | | | | |
|---|---|---|---|---|---|---|---|---|---|---|---|---|
| | | *industry and commerce* | | | | | | | | *transport* | *tourism* | *forestry and agriculture* |
| | | large & medium sized loans | promotion of regional development | promotion of technology | promotion of SMEs | promotion of investments in foreign countries | promotion of infrastructure | Eurofit | total | | | |
| **1985/86** | 1,995 | 1,292 | 403 | 0 | 0 | 0 | 0 | 0 | 1,695 | 100 | 0 | 200 |
| **1986/87** | 2,802 | 2,027 | 495 | 0 | 0 | 0 | 0 | 0 | 2,522 | 80 | 0 | 200 |
| **1987/88** | 2,968 | 2,082 | 500 | 146 | 0 | 0 | 0 | 0 | 2,728 | 40 | 0 | 200 |
| **1988/89** | 3,140 | 1,812 | 491 | 297 | 0 | 200 | 0 | 0 | 2,800 | 40 | 100 | 200 |
| **1989/90** | 3,480 | 1,730 | 500 | 312 | 0 | 488 | 0 | 0 | 3,030 | 50 | 180 | 220 |
| **1990/91** | 4,480 | 1,358 | 764 | 618 | 160 | 1,075 | 0 | 0 | 3,975 | 60 | 200 | 245 |
| **1991/92** | 4,520 | 300 | 1,107 | 837 | 363 | 1,369 | 0 | 0 | 3,975 | 60 | 240 | 245 |
| **1992/93** | 4,986 | 0 | 1,125 | 1,092 | 433 | 1,766 | 0 | 0 | 4,416 | 70 | 250 | 250 |
| **1993/94** | 5,748 | 0 | 1,128 | 1,944 | 739 | 1,291 | 56 | 0 | 5,158 | 70 | 270 | 250 |
| **1994/95** | 5,694 | 0 | 1,683 | 1,452 | 815 | 1,109 | 20 | 0 | 5,079 | 0 | 365 | 250 |
| **1995/96** | 6,569 | 0 | 4,329 | 973 | 380 | 0 | 155 | 112 | 5,949 | 27 | 308 | 285 |
| **1996/97** | 6,576 | 0 | 3,504 | 1,296 | 445 | 120 | 137 | 335 | 5,836 | 0 | 500 | 240 |
| **1997/98** | 8,207 | 0 | 5,326 | 1,598 | 387 | 40 | 202 | 0 | 7,553 | 0 | 433 | 222 |
| **sum** | 61,165 | 10,601 | 21,355 | 10,565 | 3,722 | 7,458 | 570 | 447 | 54,716 | 597 | 2,846 | 3,007 |

**Investments of the ERP-Fund from 1985/86 to 1997/98 (in million Schillings)**

| financial year | sum of ERP loans | distribution in economic sectors | | | | | | | | | | |
|---|---|---|---|---|---|---|---|---|---|---|---|---|
| | | *industry and commerce* | | | | | | | | *transport* | *tourism* | *forestry and agriculture* |
| | | large & medium sized loans | promotion of regional development | promotion of technology | promotion of SMEs | promotion of investments in foreign countries | promotion of infrastructure | Eurofit | total | | | |
| **1985/86** | 7,401 | 5,132 | 1,438 | 0 | 0 | 0 | 0 | 0 | 6,571 | 284 | 0 | 546 |
| **1986/87** | 9,697 | 7,406 | 1,378 | 0 | 0 | 0 | 0 | 0 | 8,784 | 308 | 0 | 605 |
| **1987/88** | 9,587 | 7,345 | 1,062 | 351 | 0 | 0 | 0 | 0 | 8,758 | 227 | 0 | 602 |
| **1988/89** | 9,540 | 6,425 | 1,045 | 764 | 0 | 509 | 0 | 0 | 8,742 | 84 | 206 | 508 |
| **1989/90** | 14,769 | 9,082 | 1,604 | 1,231 | 0 | 1,715 | 0 | 0 | 13,632 | 83 | 458 | 595 |
| **1990/91** | 17,574 | 6,353 | 2,817 | 2,654 | 551 | 4,014 | 0 | 0 | 16,389 | 143 | 404 | 638 |
| **1991/92** | 15,934 | 917 | 4,171 | 2,975 | 1,212 | 4,513 | 0 | 0 | 13,788 | 353 | 1,145 | 648 |
| **1992/93** | 14,459 | 0 | 3,230 | 3,404 | 1,123 | 5,210 | 0 | 0 | 12,967 | 112 | 614 | 765 |
| **1993/94** | 15,505 | 0 | 2,666 | 5,474 | 1,605 | 4,038 | 116 | 0 | 13,900 | 98 | 851 | 656 |
| **1994/95** | 12,423 | 0 | 3,425 | 3,354 | 1,646 | 2,567 | 32 | 0 | 11,024 | 0 | 1,012 | 388 |
| **1995/96** | 14,691 | 0 | 9,856 | 2,070 | 771 | 0 | 264 | 243 | 13,204 | 37 | 799 | 652 |
| **1996/97** | 12,513 | 0 | 6,437 | 2,259 | .842 | 263 | 406 | 767 | 10,974 | 0 | 1,105 | 433 |
| **1997/98** | 14,986 | 0 | 9,463 | 2,883 | 724 | 98 | 563 | 0 | 13,732 | 0 | 876 | 379 |
| **sum** | 169,079 | 42,660 | 48,592 | 27,419 | 8,474 | 22,927 | 1,381 | 1,010 | 152,465 | 1,729 | 7,470 | 7,415 |

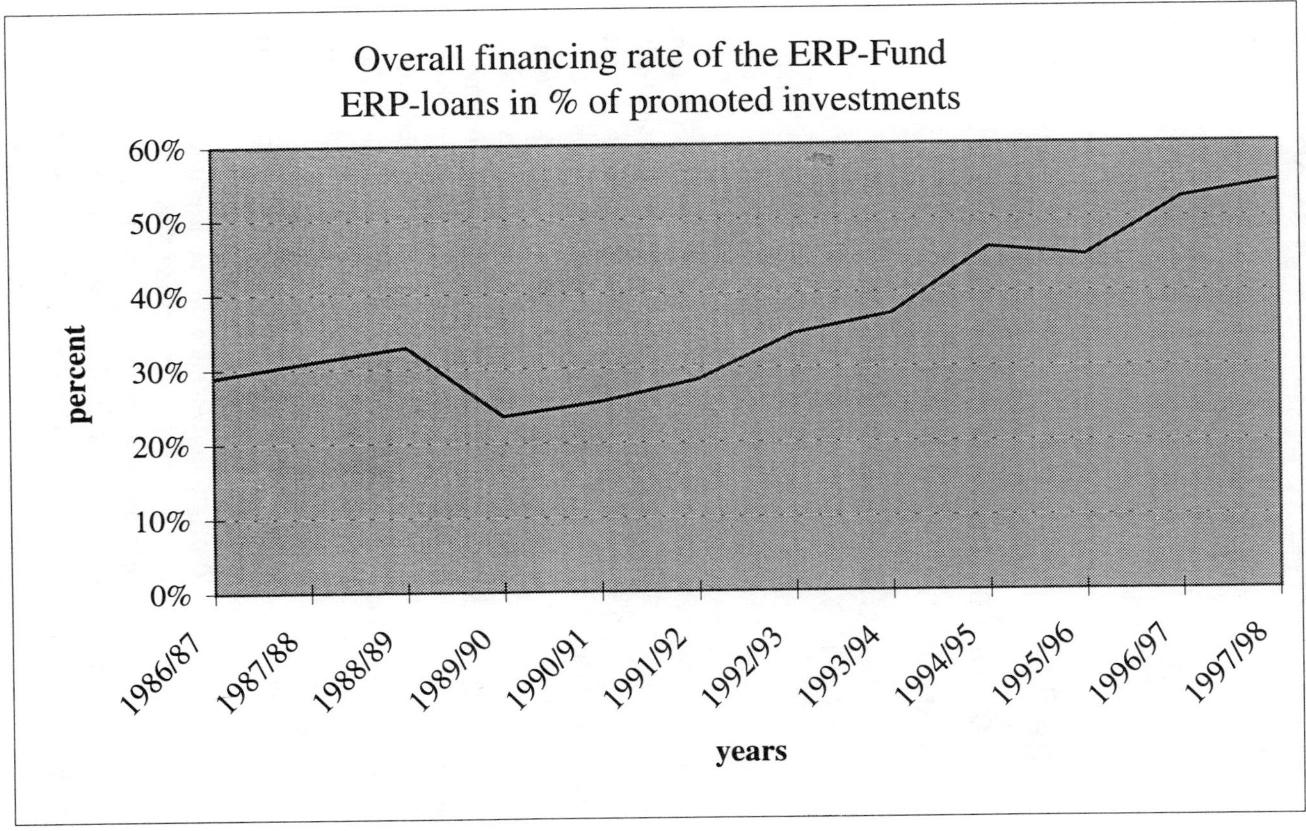

Overall financing rate of the ERP-Fund
ERP-loans in % of promoted investments
percent
60%
50%
40%
30%
20%
10%
0%
1986/87
1987/88
1988/89
1989/90
1990/91
1991/92
1992/93
1993/94
1994/95
1995/96
1996/97
1997/98
years

# II. Politics, Identity, Propaganda

# "Enemy Images": The Meaning of "Anti-Communism" and its Importance for the Political and Economic Reconstruction in Austria after 1945

*Ingrid Fraberger and Dieter Stiefel**

In recent years, scholars in Germany have begun to take a detailed and comprehensive look at the alien and hostile image associated with Russia.[1] Austrian research in this field still clearly lags behind. Aside from individual publications dealing with the nineteenth century,[2] and a few works—only some of which can be characterized as scholarly—on the history of the immediate postwar years,[3] research on the Austrian image of Russia has barely gotten beyond the preliminary stages.[4] From its very approach, the analysis of enemy images is interdisciplinary and has recourse to a wide variety of scholarly fields including psychology, sociology, and sociobiology.[5] Biological or anthropological hypotheses, however, are of only limited value to the process of historical inquiry, since they tend to expound on potential for aggression rather than demonstrate the concrete historical or social form in which it manifests itself. There has also been much detailed work done in the field of group dynamics on the friend/foe and in-group/out-group schemas. "Concepts of the enemy thus evoke feelings and reactions such as fear, aversion, aggression, and hate."[6] The group dynamics approach, though, is conceived as being applicable to groups containing a limited number of persons and not to larger social entities

---

* Translated from German by Mel Greenwald, Salzburg.

or even nations. Thus, it is rather the culturally generated form of enemy images that is significant for historical research, which Ulrich Beck emphasizes with respect to the postwar period.

"Enemy images" in this sense are prejudices and heterostereotypes that permit the transvaluation of values. They provide a source of legitimation for modern nation-states. Beck makes particular reference to the integrative—in this sense, positive—characteristics of enemy images. "Without enemies there is no funding, no legitimacy, perhaps even no nation-state integration and legitimation, no unity within, for example, the conservative parties, which were actually glued together by their shared anti-Communism." He poses the question: "Is the creation and activation of enemy images perhaps one tool—or even the primary tool—used by states to reintegrate a society where solidarity is on the wane?"[7] According to this view, postwar Western society was held together not only by a shared tradition and democratic values, but rather above all by a common enemy: Communism. "Communism, both in and of itself and measured against its own standards, may not have proved very positive. As an actual living enemy, however, it met the most stringent requirements—in terms of size, virulence and stability ... Its reliably hostile stance has been a fountain of health for the West."[8]

What significance did the enemy image "Communism" have for the political and economic reconstruction of Austria, a land situated right on the front lines of the Cold War? To a certain extent, Austrians' image of Russia had already been equated with the enemy image of Communism since the interwar period. Only the Austrian labor movement had been, at times, fascinated by the Soviet Union. In the 1920s, delegations of Austrian workers and young people visited the Soviet Union; their journeys were planned every step of the way and participants were under constant supervision. The Soviets left nothing to chance. The delegations were continuously accompanied by "official persons" such as interpreters and escorts; "choruses of cheers" greeted them at every stop on their itinerary. The Austrians were thus conveyed the impression of happy and satisfied Soviet men and women. Most of these Austrians were so taken by the image of life in the Soviet Union as presented to them that only a very few called it into question.[9] Nevertheless, a variety of opinions prevailed within the labor movement. Whereas the position of the party leadership could vacillate according to political and tactical considerations, the rank and file generally held fast to their positive attitude toward the Soviet

Union—indeed, more for emotional reasons than as a result of actual knowledge about conditions prevailing there.[10]

Conservative elements in Austria, the bourgeoisie and the rural peasantry, opposed the Soviet Union with emotional intensity from the very start. The leftist-revolutionary events which occurred immediately after World War I in Austria and neighboring countries were perceived as an existential threat. With the corporatist state dictatorship in Austria beginning in 1934—as the Austrian brand of fascism—this politically aggressive hostility was enforced by means of violence. Opposition to the leftist labor movement was a key element of the corporatist state, which thus also opposed the Soviet Union as the motherland of Communism.[11]

In 1938, with the Anschluß on the Third Reich, Austria came under the direct influence of Nazi propaganda. Its enemy image stopped short of no extreme. The Soviet Union's population was made up of eastern peoples, Bolsheviks, beasts.[12] The essential features of the National Socialists' image of Russia were anti-Communism, racism, and a touch of anti-Semitism. For the Nazis, the Russians were the Mongolian peril which, under the banner of Communism and the leadership of the Jews, threatened European culture.[13] This image was a concise summary of everything to which one was opposed.

Nevertheless, during the years of Nazi rule, even in Germany there had not been a truly uniform image of Russia; rather, what was purveyed was "tantamount to a pliable, mutable image whose appearance could be revised in accordance with a concrete situation and political necessities."[14] The National Socialist image of Russia was highly contradictory. On one hand, the Russians were said to be a people too weak "to shed the yoke of the Jews through their own efforts," one that lacked "the capabilities to conduct the affairs of state," which was why "the end of the Jewish domination of Russia (would be) the end of Russia as a state as well."[15] The Soviet Union was apostrophized as "a colossus standing upon feet of clay." At the same time, though, the danger from the east was played up. In this context, even the services of Napoleon were called upon: "Scratch a Russian and you find a Tatar." Leibbrandt, head of the Eastern Section in the Nazi Party's Foreign Policy Office, spoke in this connection of a bastardization of the formerly Nordic—and thus, in the eyes of the National Socialists, positive—character of the Russians due to interbreeding with "Mongolian-Asiatic" instincts.[16] This image of "Asiatic" Russia has had a long tradition in the Germans' confrontation with that land, having originated in the early sixteenth century at the time of the Polish-Russian wars.[17]

In the 1930s, the political-ideological campaign against Communism stood at the forefront of both foreign and domestic policy initiatives in Germany. The racial-ideological approach was of secondary importance during these years.[18] The aim of this propaganda campaign was to take the wind out of the German Communists' sails. In accordance with the friend/foe schema, it was held that "every opponent of the Third Reich is an ally of Bolshevism."[19] The signing of the German-Soviet Nonaggression Pact in 1939 was thus also a major surprise for Nazi propagandists. During the subsequent two years up to the military campaign launched against Russia in 1941, Nazi propaganda exercised total restraint on the subject of the Soviet Union. For war-related tactical reasons, Joseph Goebbels forbade any negative depiction of Russia even immediately prior to the beginning of the campaign.[20]

Attacking the Soviet Union changed everything. The German troops' rapid advance initially seemed to confirm the image of a "colossus of clay." By August 1941, Goebbels' Propaganda Ministry had already launched an extensive media campaign against the Soviet Union. This was what established that image of Russia which people would keep in mind long after the end of the Third Reich. Goebbels' propagandists were assigned the task of contriving an image of a gigantic system of fraud and exploitation in which people were degraded to behaving like animals eking out an indescribably miserable existence under conditions unfit for human beings. The Russians were forced to live in filthy villages with streets in complete disrepair, in wretched houses and apartments infested with lice. Through the manipulative selection of graphics, a repulsive enemy image was designed. Bolsheviks reduced to the level of animals were contrasted to the open and honest countenances of German workers, filthy Soviet barracks to the tidy housing developments of working-class Germans, roads of bottomless mud to German highways.[21] Symbolic imagery and catch phrases were used, like disheveled, dirty, absence of a sense of order, lack of drive and ambition, crude and negligent. Russian men were depicted as lazy, whereas the women had to do hard labor. There was talk of an enormous arms build-up, whereas it was simultaneously maintained that economic mismanagement had assumed unheard of proportions so that, despite its wealth of natural resources, the land was actually poor. The manner and appearance of the Soviet *Nomen-*

*klatura* was made out to be vulgar; it was barely conceded that they were capable of eating with a knife and fork. In the Soviet Union, there was "no middle class, nothing distinguished or elegant, and no family culture." In short, "when Russia became Soviet, it turned its back on Europe" and the Germans' job was thus to "bring (Russia) back home to Europe."[22] However, as the military situation in the Soviet Union became increasingly unfavorable for the Third Reich, the more the National Socialist propaganda machinery turned the Russians into murderous monsters. In contrast to the military campaign on the western front, the war in the east increasingly resembled one of total destruction conducted with immeasurable brutality.[23]

The National Socialists' enemy image of the Soviet Union displayed extraordinarily persistent tendencies in Austria even after the war. In order to provide an explanation for this, we must call to mind the situation in 1945. Without a doubt, postwar Austria found itself in a political identity crisis. Just what sort of republic would now emerge or reemerge? During the entire interwar period, the tiny new state had never been able to find itself and to succeed in developing a positive national identification. "*Autriche c'est qui reste*" as Clemenceau had formulated it during the peace treaty process in 1919, and one of the major political discussions of the day focused on the "economic non-inviability" of the Republic of Austria which had been dislodged from its position imbedded within the Austro-Hungarian Monarchy.[24] Behind this economic argumentation of "non-inviability" stood the political objective of an annexation to Germany. These efforts to bring about an Anschluß were carried on by a number of different political groups and were kept up with varying levels of intensity during the entire interwar period.[25] So it was no wonder that many Austrians welcomed the actual Anschluß in 1938, even if its initial manifestations were poli-tically problematic. It was not until the military situation took a turn for the worse and with the increasing terror of the Nazi regime that a process of rethinking took place. Nevertheless, the events of 1945 were perceived as a defeat by the majority of Austrians just as they were by most Germans. The land was destroyed, occupied by foreign troops, and about 500,000 Austrian men were prisoners of war. The dream of an Anschluß had been played out—but what was this Austria now? Top political leaders reacted quickly. According to the Moscow Declaration of 1943, Austria was "the first victim of National Socialism." The state had never ceased to exist; it had only been unable to act on its own behalf. At the same time, the "mentality of the camps" was played up, since several Christian Socials and Socialists from Austria had done time together in concentration camps where, in the resistance struggle against the Nazis, they had put aside their class struggle mentality.

The "victim hypothesis" was a thoroughly useful tool from the point of view of international law, but neither it nor the "mentality of the camps" corresponded to the experiences of the majority of the population and was thus hardly appropriate as elements to endow the Second Republic with a sense of identity. "Living a lie" may certainly make sense from a political perspective, but it cannot create meaning itself. Rather, this function was assumed to a great extent by the enemy image "Communism." Up to now, only passing reference has been made to the significance of this enemy image. Heidemarie Uhl, for example, has written:

> "The line of argument that depicts Austria as a victim represents only one side of efforts to interpret the past, namely the one unsaid in official presentations, schoolbooks and official publications. In domestic politics opposing views could be heard soon after the war. This was partly due to the escalation of the Cold War, as even former Nazis were able to identify with anti-Communism and the concept of the Soviet enemy".[26]

Manfried Rauchensteiner also stresses that the minimal ideological consensus of the grand coalition early in the occupation period had been anti-Communism. In Austria, this was older than its American counterpart, and was a clear sign of Austrian independence. "In Austria, the formation of a new identity went hand in hand with the sovietization of Hungary and Czechoslovakia. The occupation thesis, which once again established a clear demarcation vis-á-vis Germany, was well suited to this, as was the role of bulwark fortifying the east which was promoted by the Western Allies and was thoroughly fitting to Austrians' conception of themselves."[27] And Günter Bischof has established that the chief explanation for the Austrian population's increasing orientation toward the West was not so much its attachment to the treasures of the advanced culture of Western civilization, but rather its deep-seated anti-Communism. He quoted an American observer in September 1945: "The hatred against the Russians is almost universal," whereby "Russians" and "Communism" were perceived by the population as more or less identical. The deep-seated aversion held by most Austrians for the Russians was widespread above all in Vienna and in the East Zone where there was contact with them on a daily basis. A U.S. poll expressed it in this way: "The Russians are violently disliked in Vienna." The population's anti-Communist orientation went hand in hand with its increasingly pro-Western disposition. In February 1950, Geoffrey Keynes, U.S. high commissioner in Austria, expressed the probably somewhat exaggerated opinion that 90 percent of Austrians were "Western minded" and would be ready to fight against Communism. U.S. Secretary of State John Foster Dulles could assure the National Security Council in October 1953 that Austria had the weakest Communist movement in the world: "There was no country in the world with less indigenous Communist strength." This anti-Communism of the people was like the mortar that cemented together the two leading parties—the People's Party (ÖVP) and the Social Democrats (SPÖ)—in the governing coalition, and accompanied that coalition on the way to its pro-Western policies.[28]

Images of domestic enemies—such as class conflicts, for instance—further polarization; images of foreign enemies, however, have a harmonizing effect internally.[29] The enemy image of Communism took on such an integrative function in Austria. There are at least three reasons why this fell onto such fertile soil. First, Austria was one of the first "theaters" of the Cold War, and the conflict between East and West took place between the occupation powers on Austria's own territory. It was not until the establishment of neutrality in connection with the State Treaty (*Staatsvertrag*) in 1955 that Austria was able to move out of the direct "line of fire" in the Cold War.

Second, the shared enemy image of Communism facilitated the process of integrating ex-Nazis into Austrian political life and society. It was not by mere chance that the amnesty of former National Socialists coincided with the Marshall Plan and the beginning of the Cold War. National Socialism had been anti-Communist from the very outset, and the East-West conflict could thus also be interpreted as a belated confirmation of Nazi anti-Soviet propaganda. Had there not been many National Socialists who, after the defeat of the Third Reich, had wanted to join together with the Western Allies and resume the fight against the Soviet Union? In this way, the German war of annihilation in the East seemed to be again transformed into a matter of honorable soldiering, the remembrance of which was carried on in the veterans' organizations being formed at this time. The problem of social reintegration of National Socialists was a burden for more than the 536,000 individuals directly affected. Since they comprised almost 15 percent of the adult population, every Austrian was connected to them in some way—as relatives, friends and acquaintances, or as coworkers.[30] Joining forces under the common banner of anti-Communism already made a "harmonization" of Austrian society possible only a few years after the war. Anti-Communism thus covered up the Nazi past without society having to deal critically with this issue any longer. To go about this, it had not even been necessary to transform the enemy image of the Soviet Union, as was the case in the United States. This nation had been an ally of the Soviet Union during the war, and political agitation directed at the motherland of Communism had been correspondingly mild. It was not until the increase in political tensions after the war that Communism became public enemy number one in the United States. Fascism and Communism were subsumed under the common term totalitarianism as an anti-capitalist, anti-Christian, and anti-democratic system. Communism was turned into "red fascism," whereby, emotionally, the struggle became a continuation of the fight against the Nazis.[31] For the Austrians, however, anti-Communism by no means meant a rejection of National Socialism and, thus, of their own past; on the contrary, it was a continuation of a pre-1945 enemy image. With the coming of the Cold War, Austria went from loser to "clandestine ally" of the West, a function with which former Nazis could also identify. With this, Austria got over the total defeat of 1945 and landed in the camp of the Western victors.

Finally, anti-Communism in Austria could fall back on even older enemy images going back to the nationality conflicts in the Monarchy prior to 1918.[32] Socialism as adopted in actual practice and the planned economy were above all phenomena to be found in Slavic lands. Slavic culture and Communism were equated, which also corresponded to a considerable extent to the political self-conception of the peoples of these lands. Anti-Communism provided a new label for the old national conflicts from the time of the Monarchy. After all, had not practically all the peoples of the Monarchy—with the exception of the "German-Austrians"—disappeared behind the Iron Curtain?[33]

Enemy images exclude the possibility of neutrality. "When the relationship between enemies worsens, third parties, the neutrals who live and think on both sides, are destroyed ... The principle of mutual exclusion—either friend or foe—eliminates differentiation and permits the noncommitted to become externalized."[34] In the parliamentary elections held in November 1945, the Communists received a mere 5 percent of the vote, and were thus confronted with a surprisingly clear rejection by the people. Whoever came out in favor of Communism was against Austria, and collaboration with the Soviet occupation force was perceived as tantamount to high treason. One had to show one's true colors; there was no way to evade the matter or to hold a complex, differentiated position. When composer Gottfried von Einem attempted to secure Bertold Brecht's participation in the Salzburg Festival and, to make this possible, was able to obtain an Austrian passport for Brecht, who was a stateless person at the time, there began a hate campaign directed at Einem which ultimately cost him all of his official functions and discredited him for many years. He had thus violated a fundamental enemy image and was isolated accordingly. At the parliamentary elections held in 1949, the ÖVP used campaign posters that clearly recalled National Socialist propaganda. They attempted to shift the SPÖ into Communism's corner and thus to discredit it.

Enemy images are culturally produced, sometimes even against the will of the so-called "enemy." Since information is negatively filtered, the enemy hardly has a chance to escape from this role. "The following characteristics belong here: negative anticipation, putting blame on the enemy, identification with the evil, zero-sum thinking: what is good for the enemy is bad for us and vice versa, stereotyping, deindividualisation and refusal to show empathy."[35] Indeed, the Soviet Union was an extremely practical enemy image, and the Soviet occupation authorities often gave the impression of doing everything they could to live up to their negative image. Events that took place during the occupation of Austria seemed merely to reconfirm many of the prejudices which were already firmly in place. Even the initial impressions which concentrated on the "appearance" of the Russians were for the most part negative, as contemporary eyewitnesses substantiate to this day.

"After the Russians, there came a lot of Mongolians, supposedly partisans. They were dirty, and some of them had on coveralls like those worn by mechanics." (1)[36]

"The first troops were the totally wild ones, the Asians." (2)

"The stomping of hundreds of boots worn by Russian soldiers and their military gun molls in their sloppy, yellow-brown uniforms resounded up from the street. The members of the Russian Army were preceded by their reputation for terrible misdeeds like rapes, abductions, arbitrary shootings and a good deal more." (3)

> "Among the first Russian soldiers were some guys who looked really rough and tough. Slant-eyed, coarse and wild. From Mongolia." (4)
>
> It was also reported over and over again that the Russians indiscriminately drank anything they could lay their hands on. "Russian" and "vodka" are considered synonyms to this day.
>
> "In other schools, the Russians opened up the jars containing biological specimens (snakes, lizards, insects, etc.) and drank the alcohol." (5)

The eating habits of the Russian soldiers also provoked shudders of disgust on the part of some Austrians—one example is the casserole of partially—plucked chickens, potatoes, spices, vodka and plum jelly (6), or their peculiar custom of eating raw onions as if they were apples (7). Another notorious "Russian delicacy" which many Austrians still recall today is the shipment of peas donated in 1945. Although it was not the Red Army's fault that the peas were already spoiled—they were old Wehrmacht provisions—the Soviets alone were held responsible for them nevertheless. It did not take long for the first jokes to begin circulating: "Stalin is our old Pea King, he pledges much and does nothing".

Another of the Russians' "peculiar ways" which was a source of considerable trouble for the Austrian population was the notorious command "*Uhra, Uhra*" [translator's note: Uhr is watch in German].

> "At the mouth of the valley, we encountered two Russian soldiers. The ordered us to halt, fleetingly eyeing our baggage. 'Uhra?' one of them asked. 'We don't have any watches,' we said, shaking our heads ... Further along, we again met up with two young Russians. 'Uhra?' 'No Uhra.' They stood there almost timidly with disappointment on their faces." (8)
>
> "Suddenly, a Russian mounted on horseback rode out of the forest, blocked my path, and shouted at me: 'Where watch? Where ring? Where chain? Where gold?' He was already wearing at least 10 watches on each wrist, all of them taken by him from frightened Austrians. I said: 'No watch, no chain—all gone! All I've still got is this' and showed him my rosary. He spat, cursed in Russian and galloped off as if the devil were hot on his tail." (9)

> "My first encounter with the Russians was as follows: a Russian with a drawn revolver approached me and said: 'Uhra, Uhra!' I told him I didn't have one. But he frisked me and found the alarm clock in my pants pocket. Grinning, he took it and said: 'Tick, tock!'" (10)

The story is told of a Russian soldier who forced his way into a house looking for watches. A whole collection of them already hung from his belt, including a few alarm clocks. Suddenly, one of them started to ring. He ripped off his belt, threw it to the floor, and began firing at the clocks and watches with his machine gun. All of them were destroyed, of course. Another anecdote that made the rounds dealt with the Russians' perplexity when faced with Western-style toilets. Not only were they said to drink from them; one Russian soldier is supposed to have washed apples or cherries in one such toilet bowl. When he depressed the handle and they were flushed away, he flew into a rage and shot the fixture to pieces with his machine gun. Of course it is a contradiction that a purportedly dirty Russian washes his fruit; the story is, above all, testimony to cultural arrogance.

It is not of primary significance whether or not either of these two stories is true. Solely as a result of their dissemination and retelling, they attain a value of their own and become part of a country's culture. They are rather more along the lines of legends and myths, orientational aids that endow events with meaning. Their degree of truth is of secondary importance; regardless of it, they give expression to culturally conformist thinking and behavior.[37]

A difficult psychological problem in the relations to the Russians was, above all, the state of insecurity. People were simply rounded up on the streets and put to work as clean-up crews. No one knew for sure whether they would not one day simply be whisked off the street by the Russians and abducted to the Soviet Union.[38]

> "The Russians were not overly scrupulous to be sure. The prisoner transports that passed through almost every day were often missing a few men who had made a daring escape. Since the company of guards was responsible for the exact number of prisoners that had been turned over to them, they replenished their contingents—particularly here on the border—with men they just arrested at random." (11)

> "Even when the war was over, our lives were far from carefree. The Russians repeatedly came into our homes, or

were out on the streets. You never knew for sure if you would be simply sent off somewhere to work." (12)

"Horrified, we looked over toward the army base and saw several Russians gesticulating wildly, forcing passers-by inside. The rifle, ready to fire, was aimed at those who failed to do what they were told. ... Do you have any idea what it meant to follow their orders? It meant scrubbing the floor that the Russians spat on; cleaning out the stopped-up bathtubs which they filled when they themselves were not constipated, because they took them to be communal facilities for use when several had to go at the same time. It also meant peeling potatoes and washing mountains of dirty dishes covered with dried-on food." (13)

The most horrible memories of the Austrian civilian population, however, are connected with the many rapes at the end of the war. In all recollections of the year 1945, such accounts assume a prominent place. There is talk of an "enormous number of rapes," "99 percent of which went unreported," and that "there were villages in which all women were raped."

"Women were also said to have been raped on the steps leading up to the altar." (14)

"Several women were raped; several were infected and had to be hospitalized for treatment. On Wienerstraße, there was a clinic for those with venereal disease. Once, the wife of an engineer asked for directions to walk to Vienna. She was gang raped more than 20 times and had to go to the hospital." (15)

"Hundreds of women came from near and far to be treated at the clinics. Wherever the Russian troops had marched through, they had left their traces behind. Many women were injured or mutilated." (16)

"The cries for help of the women being raped could be heard all the way down to the cellar." (17)

"The coast was clear again for only a short time, until the next soldiers showed up. Many women and girls were raped. A seven-year-old girl and her grandmother with whom I was acquainted were abused and raped. The girl suffered from the consequences for years afterwards." (18)

> "One night, as we lay on our plank beds, we heard that the Russians had arrived. Not far from the medical society headquarters, there was a monastery; from there, we heard the cries for help and shouts for the guards to come. The nuns were raped by the Russians." (19)

In Vienna alone, from April to June 1945, between 70,000 and 100,000 women in all age groups were said to have been raped; in Styria, the figure was about 5,000.[39] For the year 1945 in the Melk district, the proportion of rape victims was established as having been at least 5.8 percent. In the Soviet Occupation Zone in Germany as well, the number of rape victims was set at 6 percent-7 percent of all women; the number of unreported cases was surely much higher.[40] Rapes were a problem above all in the Soviet-occupied areas, although the military occasionally handed out very harsh punishments in such cases. Indeed, the other occupation forces also committed such assaults, but the Western Allies were responsible for this to a far lesser extent. Why did such incidents occur so frequently on the Soviet side? For the Soviet Zone in Germany, Norman M. Naimark has summarized several of the explanatory approaches.[41] Such behavior cannot simply be dismissed as a disciplinary problem of troops in the elation of victory, since these incidents did not last for just a few days, but for weeks and months. Nor can the fact that the soldiers had been separated from their women for a long time due to the war—that is, a purely physical sexual problem—provide a satisfactory answer; after all, that applied equally to virtually all men in this situation, regardless of which uniform they wore. The effect of excessive alcohol consumption in lowering inhibitions surely played some role; nevertheless, it is important to get a more detailed and comprehensive picture. The behavior of Soviet soldiers differed according to their region of origin and level of education. During their advance, Red Army troops did not behave in the same way everywhere they went. Slavic women in Poland, Czechoslovakia, Bulgaria, and Serbia suffered far less from such assaults than did German, Austrian, and Hungarian women.[42] This suggests that the rapes were committed as a form of revenge, and that, psychologically, they were a continuation of the war with other means. The extremely high degree of violence—not stopping short of murder and manslaughter—points to this interpretation, as does the many rapes committed in public, acts of violence which not only strangers but also husbands, children, and other family members had to stand by and witness. The Soviet society was still a patriarchic one to a much greater extent than those of the Western Allies. Gerda Lerner has shown that in such traditional societies, rape is directed against the men just as much as it is against the women. "The impact on the conquered of the rape of conquered woman was two-fold: it dishonored the woman and by implication served as a symbolic castration of their men. Men in patriarchal societies who cannot protect the purity of their wives, sisters and children are truly impotent and dishonored."[43]

Figures are highly problematic here, since many cases went unreported. Why was this so? Filing a complaint with the Russians was dangerous, and the Austrian authorities were powerless. In addition, pressing charges increased the number of those who knew of the rape, which could lead to further humiliation of these women on the part of the local populace. In the present context, what is important is not so much the number of such incidents—as horrible as these rapes were for the female victims—but rather that these rapes by Russian soldiers have become deeply embedded in the collective consciousness of the Austrian people. They were a confirmation of the National Socialist image of Russia, provided a feeling of moral superiority, and were, at the same time, an excuse for "unmanly" behavior since it had been possible only with great difficulty to protect women.[44] They have become a part of Austrian culture as a collective memory, in the sense that they are a stereotype that continues to be associated with the Russian occupation to this day. No matter which contemporary eyewitnesses one interviews, rape is one of the initial responses to the very mention of the "Russian occupation" regardless of whether they themselves had witnessed such an incident or not. The historian Hugo Hantsch summarized this lasting impression: "These people will never forget what the Red Army did to our woman. The present feeling of the simple people that the Russians are Untermenschen will last as long as this generation lives."[45]

This attitude of the Austrians toward the Soviet Union, which was already strained by the burdens of the past, was considerably intensified by economic factors. The "Russians" were also evaluated according to the economic treatment of and development in their East Zone, compared with the western occupation zones. In this respect, the situation was poor from the beginning. To be sure, in taking Vienna, they had conquered "the second German capital." Nevertheless, the eastern parts of the country had been disadvantaged long before the beginning of the occupation era.[46] This is even reflected in demographic developments. Between 1934 and 1951, the population of the eastern Austrian provinces declined by 389,000—in Vienna by 16.5 percent, in Lower Austria by 3.2 percent and in Burgenland by 7.8 percent, whereas the number of inhabitants of the western provinces, due to immigration and an excess of births over deaths, grew by a total of 563,000, representing an increase of 18.5 percent.[47]

For Austria, the entire period from 1938 to 1955 was a phase of relative economic decline. The initial basis for this developmental process had already been set in place during the time of National Socialism.[48] After the Anschluß, most investments in production vital to the war effort flowed into the western provinces, so that by 1947, a clear shift in industrial employment had already taken place.

**Table 1:** Distribution of Industrial Employment (in Percent)[49]

| | 1937 | 1947 | 1954 |
|---|---|---|---|
| Eastern Austria (V, LA, Bgld.) | 60 | 49 | 46 |
| Western Austria | 40 | 51 | 54 |

**Table 2:** Industrial Employment Index 1937 = 100[50]

| | 1947 | 1951 |
|---|---|---|
| Austria | 121 | 174 |
| Lower Austria | 88 | 134 |

From 1936 to 1958, industrial employment in Upper Austria, Salzburg and Tyrol more than tripled, and in Styria, Vorarlberg and Carinthia, it doubled. In the eastern provinces, however, it rose by only about 50 percent.

The damage caused by bombardment, combat, destruction by retreating German troops (Nero order), plundering, and arson was also considerably higher in the east than in the west. Damage caused directly by the war to industrial facilities were estimated (in 1945 Schilling values) for Vienna, Lower Austria, and Burgenland at öS 1.3 billion and for western Austria at öS 100 million. The East Zone—excluding parts of Upper Austria—thus suffered 93 percent of this destruction.[51] As a result of war-related destruction and dismantling, Vienna and Lower Austria lost 60 percent of their capacity in the iron and steel industry and 70 percent in machinery manufacturing, in contrast to approximately 30 percent in the western provinces. In the east, almost 60 percent of all rail lines were impassable; in the west it was a mere 30 percent. Therefore, from the very beginning, the Eastern Zone clearly lagged behind in the reconstruction process. At the beginning of 1947, industrial capacity utilization in the west was estimated at 50 percent whereas in the east, it was a mere 20 percent to 25 percent—attributable, above all, to difficulties related to transport and raw materials.[52]

To this damage can be added the absolutely ridiculous partition of a country with six million inhabitants into four occupation zones—plus one international zone in the center of Vienna—in accordance with the treatment of Germany, which was about ten times as large. The zonal borders, such as the one along the river Enns separating the U.S. and Soviet occupation zones, were regarded from the beginning as an extreme hindrance to the process of economic normalization. Indeed, it was not so much the new internal borders which hindered reconstruction. This complaint reflected "the psychological state of the nation to a greater extent" than the actual course of events. "It was a reflection of a situation characterized by insecurity, in which potential barriers could easily be mistaken for real obstacles."[53] Then, with the signing of the 2nd Control Agreement of 26 June 1946, the four Allied Occupation Powers reconveyed governmental jurisdiction over the entire country to Austria, whereby the partition into zones was eliminated for the most part. Thus, in contrast to Germany, Austria had already achieved "reunification" in 1946, though the difficult circumstances of an Allied occupation continued until 1955.

It is thoroughly remarkable that the lagging economic development of the Eastern Zone hardly seems to have manifested itself in overall economic growth rates in Austria.

**Table 3:** Austria's Gross National Product[54]
(real prices up to those of 1954)

| | 1937 = 100 | Growth versus Previous Year in Percent |
|---|---|---|
| 1946 | 58 | |
| 1947 | 64 | 10.3 |
| 1948 | 81 | 26.9 |
| 1949 | 97 | 18.9 |
| 1950 | 109 | 12.4 |
| 1951 | 116 | 6.8 |
| 1952 | 116 | 0.0 |
| 1953 | 121 | 4.4 |
| 1954 | 134 | 10.2 |
| 1955 | 149 | 11.5 |

Four years after the war, the prewar GNP level had already been reached; by 1955, it was 50 percent higher. There had been no such economic success stories during the entire interwar period. Indeed, West Germany displayed a growth rate that was about 2 percent higher, which might well suggest the retarding effects attributable to the lagging Eastern Zone in Austria. On the whole, though, the process of reconstruction, once it had gotten underway, had not simply made satisfactory progress, but rather had moved forward with unanticipated speed.

The disadvantaged state of eastern Austria must therefore be considered in a way that covers many different aspects. The greater dynamism of the western provinces—which was even further amplified through the preferred treatment accorded by the Marshall Plan—would have emerged to some extent even without political influences. The "old" industries were represented to a higher degree in eastern Austria, which for the most part had undergone industrialization earlier, whereas the new economic sectors tended to be located in the west. This is totally consistent with the way in which an industrial society tends to develop, whereby, at a higher level of maturity, industrialization spreads out across the entire country—achieving blanket coverage, as it were, and encompassing regions that previously had been excluded. The relative economic decline of the east, however, was intensified by:

1. the burden of the Soviet-administered business concerns;
2. the precisely targeted, politically motivated use of ERP funds; and
3. the Western orientation of the Austrian economy as a result of the Iron Curtain.

On the basis of the Potsdam Agreement concluded by the Allies in August 1945, German property located abroad was claimed as war reparations. Thus, in accordance with Article VII, all German assets in Austria became the property of the occupation power on whose territory it was situated. Of the $3.6 billion (in 1938/9 purchasing power) of German assets located abroad, $1.5 billion (42 percent of the total and 62 percent of such assets in Europe) were located in Austria.[55] The large German share of the Austrian economy was connected with the Anschluß, German investment in arms production, property transfers made voluntarily and as a result of applied pressure, and with the large-scale "Aryanization" of Jewish assets. Since Austria did not want to allow such a considerable segment of its economy to be subject to foreign influence, these enterprises were taken over by the state in 1946/47. The Western Allies ultimately accepted this procedure with certain restrictions; the Soviet Union, however, merged all German property in its occupation zone into a Soviet-administered conglomerate and in this way snubbed the Austrians.

The Soviet Union thus claimed the right to utilize the extensive German property in Austria actually as war reparations. The United States could easily assume a more generous stance, since the losses it had suffered in World War II had not even approached those of the Soviet Union, whose sacrifice of human life had been the greatest of all participants in the war. Within its own borders, the United States had hardly been affected by the war, whereas the Soviet territory occupied by the Germans had been among the most highly developed economic regions of the Soviet Union prior to World War II.[56] Real *per capita* GNP in the United States rose, correspondingly, from 1938 to 1945 by 63 percent;[57] whereas the USSR had lost 25 percent of its capital stock as a result of the war, losses which even significantly exceeded those suffered by Germany (the future FRG) by 13 percent.[58] While the U.S. economy boomed due to the war, the Soviet Union had been no better off than the losers—the land was decimated, its industry and infrastructure mostly destroyed, and 1946 and 1947 were years of pronounced hunger.[59] Thus, in 1945, the Soviet Union was a poor country whose standard of living was certainly even lower than that prevailing in the portions of eastern Austria it occupied.

For these reasons, it was impossible for the Soviet Union to provide economic aid like the United States. Quite the contrary—assets extracted from the Austrian economy in the form of the spoils-of-war program, dismantled plants, and the ongoing production of goods assumed absolute priority, regardless of the legal title under which this would take place.[60] To a certain extent, this may well have been completely understandable and perhaps even acceptable to the Austrians. Far worse than the material war reparations, however, was the arbitrary and unpredictable way in which the Soviet Union pursued its aims. Austria's own political policies were partially to blame for this. The new state was "living a lie." On the basis of its claim to be considered the first victim of National Socialism which thus, on principle, exempted it from reparations, it was impossible to demand a lump sum from Austria and then to leave the country to its own devices to manage how to raise this amount. The Soviet Union therefore had to come up with other procedures in order to secure for itself the war reparations that were absolutely essential. What then took place were apparently indiscriminate expropriations, the introduction of an incomprehensible administrative system, and countless actions and operations which contravened Austrian legal principles and persisted throughout the entire occupation period. This **unpredictability** of the Soviet occupation forces produced insecurity, fear, and disapproval.

The economic actions and operations of the Soviet occupation forces in Austria—to the extent that they can be assessed on the basis of Austrian source material—were divided into two phases. The initial one was a military phase from April 1945 to early summer of 1946, the "spoils of war and trophy campaigns" characterized by seizing booty, dismantling plants[61] and the necessity of provisioning occupation troops. The legal principle on which this was based was martial law.[62] Due to the Cold War, there were wide-ranging estimates of the amounts extracted during this period; nevertheless, the resulting loss to the Austrian economy certainly exceeded $ 200 million or öS 4 billion (in 1951 values).[63]

The second phase got away from thinking oriented on the spoils of war and shifted to the exploitation of ongoing production. It was characterized by the creation of a Soviet economic organization in Austria. From the early summer of 1946 on, Soviet assets in Austria were appraised, confiscated, and organized by the "Department for the

Investigation of German Property." The legal principle on which this was based was the Potsdam Agreement—which, indeed, had never been officially recognized by Austria—and Order Nr. 17 issued on 27 June 1946 by the supreme commander of the Soviet occupation force in Austria, General V. V. Kurasov. This led to the founding of the USIVA (*Upravlenie sovetskim imushchestvom v vostochnoi Avstrii*, that is, Administrative Authority for German Property in Eastern Austria) which was later renamed USIA *(Upravlenie sovetskim imushchestvom v Avstrii*, that is, Administrative Authority for Soviet Property in Austria). The initial core of the USIA was the afore-mentioned "Department for the Investigation of German Property," which was incorporated into the USIA and worked together with the Austrian Communist Party (KPÖ). The Soviet conglomerate also encompassed the Soviet Petroleum Authority (SMV), the Danube Steamship Company (DDSG, a line with a long-established tradition in Austria), *Wien-Film*, and the Soviet Military Bank. The Soviet retail chain (USIA Shops), the Soviet state trucking company, Juschwnesch-trans, as well as INTRAC and the KPÖ enterprises assumed particular importance within the USIA.[64]

The administration of the USIA was divided up into nine departments corresponding to the ministries of the Soviet administrative system. The number of these enterprises changed constantly; figures cited in different sources vary widely. In 1955, Austrian Vice Chancellor Schärf mentioned 419 as the number of USIA businesses, of which over 300 were in the industrial sector. Together with the operations of the SMV and the DDSG, the number of Soviet-managed businesses in Austria could be put at 454.[65] However, 160 are cited in an "Austrian Final Report on the Soviet Economic Administration" which provides a detailed breakdown and complete listing by name of all USIA enterprises (not including SMV, DDSG, trading and shipping operations, as well as agricultural and forestry properties) for 1954.[66] The number of employees they were said to have had fluctuated accordingly. It was 22,000 at the time of the Soviet takeover in 1946, but rose to 45,000 in February 1948, and was estimated at 50,000 to 60,000 in 1951.[67] The Final Report, however, indicates 36,191 employees in 1954.[68]

The USIA businesses' percent share of individual industries varied to a great extent. They played a minor role in the food and beverage sector, whereas they exerted a strong influence in other areas. Their share of total Austrian industrial capital in specified industries was as follows: glass, 60 percent; leather, 43 percent; iron and steel, 40 percent; non-ferrous metals, 32 percent; machinery construction, 22 percent; car and truck manufacturing, 17 percent.[69] Although the USIA's share of total Austrian industrial production was a mere 5 percent, in Vienna and Lower Austria this figure amounted to a substantial 30 percent. One negative consequence resulted from the dearth of desperately needed export revenues. Thus, an average of approximately 63 percent of the crude oil extracted in Austria was shipped to the Soviet Union. Austria had to be satisfied with a 27 percent share and, as a result, even had to use foreign exchange to import crude oil from the West.[70] According to "calculations based on quite reliable evidence" in the Final Report, exports by USIA industries and the petroleum sector to the Eastern Bloc nations came to between öS 14.06 billion and öS 17.48 billion.[71]

In the process of selecting the businesses to be confiscated, the Soviet Union proceeded according to an extremely liberal interpretation of the term "German property." Only eighteen of the USIA businesses were specified as German property in the 1946 Austrian law establishing state control over such enterprises. Some of these firms were expropriated solely because they had received German loans. One of the reasons used to justify the confiscation of Prince Esterhazy's extensive land holdings was that in 1806 one of his ancestors had been made a knight of the Holy Roman Empire, which thus qualified his possessions as German property.[72] Most problematic was the takeover of forty-one previously Aryanized businesses. Since Aryanization had been connected with financial compensation—whereby the former Jewish owner had received only a fraction of it and often nothing at all—the Soviets proceeded under the assumption of a formal property transfer, and such firms thus fell under the Soviet definition of German property.[73]

The foreword to the 1958 Austrian "Final Report on the Soviet Occupation Economy in Austria" displays the deep and lasting impression made by the occupation period and the Cold War. The otherwise so cautious, detailed, and dryly formulated study refers emotionally to an "economy of exploitation in colonial style amid a highly developed European economy, the extent and the economic success of which are actually astounding." It had subsequently come out "how extraordinarily systematically this economic enclave of the occupation economy in Austria was used to fortify the economic potential of its bloc, to pursue its political objectives and, finally, to function as an economic bridge positioned directly opposite western Austria and the Western world as a whole."[74] Thus, the point had been "to exploit Austria's natural and human resources as profitably and systematically as possible."[75] The goal was to align to the highest possible degree Austrian economic potential to the requirements of Soviet production plans. The expropriated portion of the Austrian economy was designed to provide the Soviet Union with products subject to manufacturing bottlenecks and goods in short supply. Simultaneously, through perforations in the Iron Curtain, the USIA was used to obtain scarce items from the West and peddle surplus goods to obtain foreign exchange from the West. These surplus items were sold in Austria by the USIA retail chain, and the Schillings were exchanged, either on the black market or officially in Zurich, for Western currency.[76]

However, according to the view taken by the Austrian report, the Soviets had not achieved their actual goal. "Namely, the amalgamation of the Austrian Eastern Zone, which had been totally permeated by their occupation management system, with the overall economy of the Eastern Bloc, and thus, ultimately, the political absorption of this Eastern Zone—or perhaps even the whole of Austria—into this bloc."[77] After all, the Soviet occupation economy would have had to increasingly adapt to conditions prevailing in the Austrian economy in order to continue to survive. There were a number of reasons for this: the overestimation of the possibilities of a planned economy, the Austrian economy increasingly developing "a life of its own" in the Eastern Zone of occupation as well, and the growing economic dynamism of Austria and the West.[78]

This had been a consequence of successful reconstruction and the Marshall Plan. Favorable business cycle developments in western Austria and the enterprises in eastern Austria which were not under Soviet influence had also had an impact on the USIA—which ultimately had been economically interconnected with them—and they had exerted a pull away from the Soviet economic bloc. Therefore, the Soviets had not achieved their final objective "due to the mental and physical resistance put up by Austria and the entire Western world."[79]

The Soviets were never able to bring themselves to conceive of their property within the territory of the Republic of Austria in the Western sense. After all, other foreign corporations also had property in Austria, but these abided by the legal statutes of the land. The Soviet Union would have preferred to acquire legal legitimation of its holdings beyond the basis of martial law and the Potsdam Agreement, but Austria did not recognize the Soviet confiscations and, accordingly, refused to record ownership in land registers and the official registry of firms. In retaliation, the USIA continually violated the Austrian state's sovereign right to collect taxes. Thus, sales tax, trade tax, and wealth tax were basically not paid. The authority to collect customs duties was constantly violated, and regulations regarding raw materials, business practices, and shipping were likewise not observed. Moreover, the Soviets recognized the legal jurisdiction of the Austrian state only when it was convenient for them. Verdicts enforceable against Soviet-managed firms were often set aside by order of Soviet military authorities. Business dealings between the Austrian private sector and USIA enterprises were therefore problematic, since valid legal title could not always be enforced. "As a result of these and many other factors, the presence of Soviet property in Austria had totally different consequences than those which normally accompany the existence of assets belonging to foreign nationals in another state."[80]

Organizations analogous to the USIA also operated in Czechoslovakia, Hungary, East Germany, Finland, Bulgaria, and Rumania. The fact that the "Soviet Union constructed the same economic model in both its German and Austrian occupation zones"[81] certainly did not contribute to building trust in Austria. Even the names they gave to them were very similar to those of the USIA enterprises. Similar to the HO shops that were founded in the German Eastern Zone, a chain of retail stores began to be set up in the Eastern Zone of Austria in 1948. Another similarity to these countries was the attempt to establish joint ventures to which practically all the Soviets would contribute was the assets they had confiscated, and Austria would have to supply the capital.[82] Although this solution got a positive reception in some quarters on the Austrian side—particularly in the petroleum industry—it was ultimately not implemented due to objections from the United States, which feared a prolongation of Soviet influence beyond the period of occupation. By the end of 1953, the Soviet Union had conveyed its equity in SAG companies back to the GDR; in the same year, they also began to return former German assets in Finland. This development was carried on in other eastern European states as well. Thus, the transfer of Soviet shares of joint ventures in Bulgaria, Rumania, and Hungary—with the exception of strategically vital operations like uranium production—took place in 1954. But by far the most long-lived Soviet claim was the one based on the Potsdam

Accords to former German property in the Soviet occupation zone of Austria.[83]

The foreignness of the Soviet economic body in Austria is evident from its organizational structure alone. No fewer than eleven Moscow ministries and agencies—as far as we know—had a say in the management process, which naturally led to complications and tensions. Thus, there was no centralized administration in Moscow with sole responsibility for and authority over Soviet assets abroad. In addition, there was the Office of the Soviet High Commissar as well as military authorities who maintained contact with Austrian government agencies. A striking feature of the Soviet economic organization's structure was thus the fragmentation of authority, though this may well have been the rule for the Soviet system of planning and typical of totalitarian systems. "The dual-track policy of duplicate jurisdictions facilitated supervision and control. It made those in positions of authority somewhat insecure and also limited their possibilities of carrying out assignments in an autocratic style."[84] Dealings on the part of official administrators or other managers of confiscated enterprises with Austrian authorities for the purpose of exchanging information and giving instructions were forbidden and punished as economic espionage against the USSR.[85] Not only the Soviet management staff but also the Austrian employees were obliged to maintain the strictest secrecy; "every actual or apparent effort to disregard this stipulation or the attempt to provide information about the organization was punished as espionage according to Russian military law."[86]

A special role was played by the Soviet Military Bank, which, for a time, tried to obtain an Austrian bank charter. This was denied, however, to prevent this institution from establishing itself as a long-term presence in the Austrian economy. It had evolved from a field bank for soldiers and was a subsidiary of the Gosbank (*Gosudarstvennyi bank SSSR*, that is, State Bank of the USSR) in Moscow. It was the sole financial institution for the entire Soviet conglomerate in Austria, and determined financial policies as far as loans for operating funds and circulating capital were concerned. The various Moscow agencies were responsible for approving investments. Along with the NKVD and the KPÖ—which was very widely represented among the personnel throughout the entire organization—the Soviet Military Bank, as the clearing house and central treasury, was an instrument for restandardization of the discordant division of authority within the economic enterprise.[87]

The organization of the USIA—as far as we have ascertained up to now—consisted of a chairman, who was characterized as the "chief executive," and his three assistants, one each for political, personnel, and commercial matters.[88] The very fact that a political officer occupied a top-level position in the organization must have been a cause for uneasiness. Moreover, the USIA had a "secret service" that worked closely with the NKVD; military guards were always posted at the entrance to this department, which was normally off-limits to Austrians. Up to 1949, USIA enterprises were mostly headed by officers of the Soviet occupation forces; thereafter, they were replaced by trained Russian "managers." For example, the job of running the Austrian construction firm Porr AG was assigned to a Russian officer who was neither able to speak German nor trained in business administration. He was said to have been a dance instructor in Moscow before the war.[89] The rapid succession of individuals holding top posts in the Soviet economic administration also inspired little confidence, and this surely served to prevent close contacts with Austrians from developing. Thus, in the nine years of its existence, the USIA had no fewer than five "chief executives," as did the DDSG. In this brief period, the SMV had four different chairmen and five head book-keepers, all of whom came from the Soviet Union.[90] The final report indicates that the careers of many of these USIA executives even ended in arrest and imprisonment.[91] Thus, in the USIA's nine years of operation, top executives were replaced about every two years. In politics as in business, however, continuity of personnel plays a key role in establishing one's reliability and building trust with ones partners.

Up to 1951, the Soviet economic undertakings expanded along with the overall business cycle upswing and generated healthy profits. The deployment of the economic organization to achieve political goals occurred during this time. "This phase is also characterized by the initial attempt to totally align the Soviet economic enclave toward linkage with the economic sphere of the Soviet Union and its satellites."[92] The Soviets at first held the naive view that the Austrian businesses in their possession would be fully integrated into the Soviet planned economy. The set-up of the USIA reveals the Soviet intention "to employ appropriate economic measures—that is, with the help of the USIA—to prevent the Western economic system of capitalism from becoming operative in the Soviet occupation zone, or at least to restrict its influence there."[93] It very soon became apparent, though, that it was poor economics to completely isolate these firms from the Austrian economy and to insist that every single screw be ordered from the Soviet Bloc. Shortly after the founding of the USIA, it therefore became necessary to permit exchange to some extent with the rest of the Austrian economy, so that exports to the East by USIA firms ultimately made up 38 percent of the total, and the majority of their output thus remained in Austria. The "Russian businesses"[94] were thus forced to partially integrate themselves into the Austrian economy, if for no other reason than because the Austrian government made the supplying of raw materials and energy dependent upon it.[95]

The Soviet-administered firms thus actually constituted an enclave of planned economies, which fostered scant trust and, with the outbreak of the Cold War, were perceived as a threat as a result of their resemblance to organizations in Soviet satellite states. It is no wonder, therefore, that the Austrians and the Western Allies resorted to countermeasures which necessarily has disadvantageous economic consequences for the Eastern Zone. This orientation of Austria toward the Western powers led to a policy of containment of Communism by integration with the West.[96] By 1947, in response to the alleged report of a "Soviet Economic Program for Austria" which foresaw a stronger economic integration of the Austrian East Zone, the United States had already developed a "neutralization plan" designed to economically starve the Russian zone. The "neutralization plan" was meant to make Austria independent of the USIA enterprises. The financial credits which were to be provided by the United States would have been tied to conditions such as a reduction of energy and raw materials deliveries to Soviet firms and a restriction of their means of transportation, and they foresaw a deliberate policy of Western financing of substitute investments. This scheme was made superfluous by the introduction of the Marshall Plan.[97]

Instead, a "Strategic Control Plan" was drawn up as a means to supervise and direct Austria's economic contacts with the East. It called for implementing all measures necessary to prevent U.S. imports within the framework of the ERP program from falling into the hands of USIA enterprises unless these were supplying the Austrian market with vital necessities. A second element had to do with surveillance of Austrian economic contacts with the East to ensure that the country not become dependent upon this region.[98] With the help of ERP funds, replacement factories were built in the west with the main objective of preventing the development of one-sided dependencies in industries in which the USIA dominated the market, such as glass, chemicals, and metals, to name a few. This intensified the already-operative trend to relocate production facilities out of the Soviet zone and into the west. In Upper Austria, for example, there had been 500 to 600 industrial firms in 1937, and another 100 were added during the war; in the first two postwar years, though, 400 new enterprises were founded.[99] The reciprocal competitive pressure exerted by the USIA and the Western replacement firms led to a deterioration of the economic position of the USIA firms, which were no match in the competitive struggle due to their lower investment budget and their organizational structure not attuned to a market economy. The west-east gradient thus became even steeper.[100] Klambauer even proceeds under the assumption that the inferior development of the Eastern Zone was chiefly the result of the USIA firms' disadvantaged position with respect to investment financing, whereby these firms were cut off from Western credits not only from the ERP but from Austrian banks as well. ERP financed imports were also brought in to break the monopoly.

Marshall Plan funds were thus intentionally deployed *against* the Eastern Zone. The *per capita* rate of loans granted per industrial employee in Styria was two and a half times as high as in Lower Austria; the multiple in Carinthia was five, in Salzburg twelve.[101] The regional distribution of ERP funds even more solidly established the preferential treatment accorded to the western provinces. A summary of the "Special Mission to Austria for Economic Cooperation" contained in an "End-Use Report" for the period ending 31 December 1952, stated that the western occupation zones had received 75 percent of the $538.6 million worth of financed commodities which had been delivered up to that point, and got a full 92 percent of the $504.6 million worth of Counterpart Funds released to the Austrian Government. Thus, the region including Vienna, Lower Austria, and Burgenland—with an approximately equal population—had to be satisfied with 25 percent of US-financed commodities and 8 percent of ERP aid.[102] The Marshall Plan had thus intensified the westward shift of the regional center of gravity. It may be an exaggeration to say that this had turned the Soviet zone of occupation into an industrially and agriculturally depressed area,[103] but it was, in any case, partially excluded from the investment that poured into the land during the time of reconstruction.[104] Without ERP aid, the USIA firms' industrial plant and equipment was very much substandard for Austria, since an investment program proposal to receive Marshall Plan funds could not be submitted by an enterprise in the Russian sector of Austria.[105] In general, ERP funds could be granted in the Eastern Zone only when it could be proved that the goods were not being produced for the Eastern Bloc.[106] Even if the amount of ERP funds distributed in the Eastern Zone of Austria was small, their political significance is certainly undeniable. This was the only case in which any Marshall Plan funds were handed out in Soviet-occupied territory, and the Austrian government placed tremendous value on the participation of the East Zone to maintain the country's economic and political unity.[107]

These policies oriented toward the West were buttressed by the U.S. foreign trade embargo of the Soviet Union.[108] Delivery of strategic goods to Communist countries was forbidden. Since the term "strategic goods" was defined very broadly, there was very little in the way of technology that did not fall under the ban. Although Austria did not officially participate in this embargo policy, it upheld its provisions for the most part after the Korean War. Furthermore, the U.S. ECA Mission in Vienna kept up careful surveillance of the embargo.[109] Compliance with U.S. trade policies was made a condition of Marshall Plan aid.[110] After all, the Soviet Union, with its USIA businesses, the eastern border of Austria under its control, and the open zone border to western Austria, enjoyed what amounted to a hole in the Iron Curtain, which it could use to evade the US embargo during the period of the intensified embargo policy between 1949 and 1953.

This anti-Soviet orientation was also supported on the Austrian side through a policy of public institutions boycotting USIA firms to the greatest extent possible. In response to a query, Vienna City Councilman Bauer stated: "The City of Vienna Purchasing Department basically does no business with USIA firms."[111] Exceptions had to be justified. For this purpose, there existed lists of Soviet-influenced enterprises, and for some businesses it became a matter of survival to be removed from them. Other firms, like the previously mentioned construction company Porr AG finally got fed up with having the Soviets' will imposed upon them. They withdrew their personnel and equipment from the Soviet zone of Vienna to Salzburg, where they founded a new corporation. What they left behind for the USIA was not much more than an empty shell which then lived off Soviet contracts. When this USIA operation reverted back to the owners in 1955, the managers who had continued to work together with the

Soviets were immediately fired, since their actions were viewed as a breach of loyalty to the firm.[112]

Between 1951 and 1955, the signs of crisis in the Soviet economic organization became increasingly clear. In the early 1950s, there was a general slowdown of economic growth in Austria. In the USIA, this manifested itself in lower gross revenues and profits, and resulted in the liquidation and consolidation of firms. During the occupation period, about 100 USIA enterprises were shut down or merged.[113] Finally in 1955, the Soviet economic complex was liquidated and turned over to Austria for a lump-sum payment agreed to in the *Staatsvertrag*. The Final Report mentions one last yeoman service of the Soviet economic administration: with the withdrawal of the occupation troops, practically all written documentation concerning the USIA enterprises disappeared as well.[114]

After the signing of the *Staatsvertrag*, the Austrians attempted to perform a final accounting of the economic burden attributable to the Soviet occupational presence. Along with the more or less quantifiable losses, it also summed up those more difficult to put into numbers:

- the numerous plants dismantled immediately after the war, which had been a shock for the Austrian economy;
- the expropriation of foodstuffs and consumer goods, which led to ongoing shortages in the immediate postwar period;
- the alignment of production according to Soviet needs, whereby some machinery which finally reverted back to Austria had to be completely written off;
- neglecting to provide training for skilled laborers and specialists, which made for tremendous problems after 1955;
- the meager sums invested: in virtually every business the Soviets had managed, several hundred million schillings were required to catch up on long-overdue investment; and
- the losses attributable to the activities of the USIA retail chains which paid no taxes and customs duties, and the highly dubious dealings of the Soviet trucking firm. Since Austria's eastern border was controlled by Soviet occupation forces, this freight carrier had amounted to nothing less than a smuggling operation.

The value of the output produced by Soviet firms in Austria from 1946 to 1955 has been estimated (on the basis of 1955 values) at between 27 and 36 billion Schillings. To this can be added öS 9.15 billion from crude oil production and refining, so that total production can be set at between öS 36.15 billion and öS 45.15 billion. Their profit, which had to be paid over at that time to the USIA under the heading of "taxes" in all sectors including the petroleum industry, has been calculated at öS 12.83 billion. Adding to this the final deliveries to the USSR as agreed to in the *Staatsvertrag*, which amounted to öS 8.6 billion, the numerically ascertainable profit the Soviets made in Austria came to öS 21.43 billion ($1.072 billion).[115] Günter Bischof has put together an estimate of the Austrian "reparations" paid to the Soviet Union between 1945 and 1964 which takes into account the dismantled plants, USIA profits, losses attributable to unpaid taxes and customs duties, and the final payments in accordance with the *Staatsvertrag*. Since these losses resulting from dismantled plants and uncollected taxes and duties are difficult to quantify and thus—depending upon ones political assumptions—are open to considerable evaluative latitude, he put the amount of Austrian "reparations" paid to the Soviet Union at between $1.325 billion and $2.425 billion. However, the Austrian Final Report on the activities of the USIA set their profits at $722 million as compared to the $500 million figure cited by Bischof. The total amount of "reparations" would thus have to be raised by $222 million, yielding a range between $1.547 billion and $2.647 billion.[116] It was thus approximately twice as much as the $909 million in aid received from the Marshall Plan.[117] Austria thus led all countries in *per capita* "reparations" paid to the Soviet Union. And this lead is even further strengthened if one takes into account disinvestment due to lack of new investments on the part of USIA firms, which had to be made up for once they were returned to Austrian hands.

Due to the Austrian people's largely negative experience with the Soviet occupation powers, the country's political, cultural, and economic reorientation towards the West was further intensified and accelerated. Another factor contributing to this was the Soviet domination of the central and eastern European countries with which Austria had traditionally been closely interlinked economically; these turned into an "Eastern Bloc" and disappeared behind the Iron Curtain. This economic reorientation—in contrast to the cultural and political one—can be documented quite well with figures.

**Table 4:** Proportion of Total Austrian Foreign Trade (in Percent)

| Year | Export | | Import | |
|---|---|---|---|---|
| | Future EU (12) | Eastern States | Future EU (12) | Eastern States |
| 1922 | 24 | 28 | 23 | 29 |
| 1937 | 44 | 28 | 34 | 32 |
| 1946 | 28 | 22 | 38 | 23 |
| 1955 | 58 | 10 | 59 | 9 |

**Source:** Felix Butschek, *Statistische Reihen zur Österreichischen Wirtschaftsgeschichte*, Österreichisches Institut für Wirtschaftsforschung, Vienna 1996. The eastern states include Bulgaria, Czechoslovakia, East Germany, Poland, Hungary, Rumania, and the USSR.

The importance of western Europe (in the form of the future EU nations) had already grown considerably during the interwar period, although the eastern European states' share of Austrian foreign trade could be maintained at about 30 percent. In 1946, both regions' proportions decreased, with the exception of imports from the future EU nations. This certainly reflected, among other factors, the significance of aid shipments from Switzerland, Scandinavia and North America. Taking the extraordinary circumstances of 1946 into account, though, both regions maintained relations comparable to those prevailing before the war. Developments from 1946 to 1955, however, clearly show the effects of the Cold War and the Austrian economy's shift toward western Europe. The share of Austrian exports to the future EU nations doubled, while that of the eastern European states was cut in half.[118]

This change of trend is revealed even more clearly if we examine the two most prominent cases: Germany and Czechoslovakia. Prior to the war, these two nations were Austria's most important foreign trading partners. Czechoslovakia and Austria were the chief industrial heirs of the Monarchy and were correspondingly closely linked with one another. This interrelationship was still evident during the interwar period and did not diminish significantly until 1937.[119]

Here as well, it becomes clear that the trade situation with these two countries did not change dramatically during the interwar period, except for imports from Czechoslovakia which declined by about a third. This was, to a lesser extent, attributable to the world economic crisis, and rather more the result of Austria's intentional policy of reducing its chronic balance-of-trade deficit with this country. On the other hand, the share of exports to Germany increased by about a half,

**Table 5:** Proportion of Total Austrian Foreign Trade (in Percent)

| Year | Export | | Import | |
|---|---|---|---|---|
| | Cz | FRG | Cz | FRG |
| 1922 | 7.1 | 10.8 | 16.4 | 15.5 |
| 1937 | 7.2 | 14.8 | 11.0 | 16.1 |
| 1946 | 19.1 | 2.1 | 16.9 | 23.8 |
| 1955 | 1.5 | 25.1 | 1.7 | 35.4 |

**Source:** Felix Butschek, *Statistische Reihen zur Österreichischen Wirtschaftsgeschichte*, Österreichisches Institut für Wirtschaftsforschung, Vienna 1996

which can be traced back to, among other factors, the business cycle upswing driven by rearmament in the Third Reich. The 1946 figures display a few abnormalities: on one hand, with respect to exports and the intentional effort by the Allies to separate Austria from Germany in all possible respects;[120] on the other hand, the share of imports ran contrary to this plan, in that Czechoslovakia maintained its interwar position, and imports form Germany had already increased in significance. The development from 1946 to 1955, however, makes the reorientation of the Austrian export economy patently clear.[121] Czechoslovakia's share became insignificant, falling below 2 percent, whereas the FRG's shares rose, accounting for a quarter of exports and a third of imports. The economic Anschlu§ was a matter of fact at this point. Among other factors, developments in the area of foreign trade can be introduced into evidence as an economic basis for the different levels of esteem for the United States and the USSR.

Whereas the United States' share of Austrian imports climbed far above 20 percent in conjunction with the Marshall Plan from 1949 to 1951, that of the Soviet Union generally remained so minute as to be statistically insignificant. Indeed, these numbers fail to take into account the role of "illegal" imports by the Russian occupation authorities, mostly through the USIA; nevertheless, these certainly did not contribute to the USSR's esteem in the eyes of the Austrians. Moreover, a significant proportion of U.S. imports through the Marshall Plan were "grants," reconstruction aid that was free of charge; whereas imports from the Soviet Union had to be paid for.

**Table 6:** Proportion of Total Austrian Foreign Trade (in Percent)

| | USA | USSR |
|---|---|---|
| 1937 | 6.0 | 0.5 |
| 1946 | 3.5 | 0.2 |
| 1947 | 3.4 | 0.0 |
| 1948 | 7.9 | 0.0 |
| 1949 | 28.9 | 0.0 |
| 1950 | 23.2 | 0.0 |
| 1951 | 22.2 | 0.0 |
| 1952 | 18.3 | 0.0 |
| 1953 | 12.5 | 0.0 |
| 1954 | 8.8 | 0.2 |
| 1955 | 10.5 | 0.5 |

**Source:** Felix Butschek, *Statistische Reihen zur Österreichischen Wirtschaftsgeschichte*, Österreichisches Institut für Wirtschaftsforschung, Vienna 1996

**Table 7:** Foreign Aid Proportion of Austrian Imports (in Percent)

| | |
|---|---|
| 1945/6 | 88 |
| 1947 | 68 |
| 1948 | 57 |
| 1949 | 50 |
| 1950 | 43 |
| 1951 | 31 |
| 1952 | 16 |

Up to 1947, this aid was contributed by a number of different countries—with the United States always providing a considerable share—as well as proceeding under the auspices of the UN. From 1948 on, though, this support came almost exclusively from the U.S's occupation authorities. From the Soviet side came absolutely nothing. This Western orientation of Austria's foreign trade also had considerable political-cultural significance.[122] The Soviet Union remained as alien to Austrians as it had ever been, whereas consumer products, durable goods, and equipment from the U.S. brought not only U.S. technology but also organizational know-how, the English language and a better understanding of American culture to Austria. Thus, as early as 1946, a Soviet diplomat criticized the political propaganda which depicted "the United States as a ready-to-help angel" and the Soviet Union as a "devil stripping the land."[123]

## Notes

1. Most notable among these is the Wuppertal project led by Mechthild Keller investigating the history of German-Russian enemy images, "West-östliche Spiegelungen: Russen und Rußland aus deutscher Sicht und Deutsche und Deutschland aus russischer Sicht von den Anfängen bis zum 20. Jhdt." The period from the 9th century until 1925 ("Russen und Rußland aus deutscher Sicht") has been completed up to now. There are also several books and articles dealing with specific aspects of Russia's image, such as Ekkehard Klug's, "Das 'asiatische' Rußland. Über die Entstehung eines europäischen Vorurteils," *Historische Zeitschrift* 245 (1987): 265-289; Hans-Erich Volkmann, ed.; *Das Rußlandbild im Dritten Reich*, (Cologne: Böhlau, 1994); *Deutsche, Deutschbalten und Russen. Studien zu ihren gegenseitigen Bildern und Beziehungen*, ed. Klaus Meyer, (Lüneburg: Nordostdt. Kulturwerk, 1996).

2. Harald Heppner, *Das Rußlandbild in der öffentlichen Meinung* Österreichs 1848-1856 (Graz: Zur Kunde Südosteuropas, 1945), 2,4). Gertraud Marinelli-König, *Rußland in den Wiener Zeitschriften und Almanachen des Vormärz* (1805-1848): *Ein Beitrag zur Geschichte der österreichisch-russischen Kultur- und Literaturbeziehungen* (Vienna: Österr. Akademie der Wissenschaften, 1990, Veröffentlichungen der Kommission für Literaturwisschenschaft der Österreichischen Akademie der Wissenschaften, Sitzungsberichte der Philosophisch-Historischen Klasse 10, 552).

3. Among the multitude of works dealing with the history of individual Austrian regions and districts during the Soviet occupation—many of which are reminiscences by contemporary eyewitnesses—a few scholarly works can be singled out for mention here. Margarete Hannl, *Mit den Russen leben: Ein Beitrag zur Geschichte der Besatzungszeit im Mühlviertel 1945-1955* (M. A. thesis., University of Salzburg, 1988). This master's thesis also appeared as a journal article entitled "Mit den 'Russen' leben. Besatzungszeit im Mühlviertel, 1945-1955," *Zeitgeschichte* 16 (1989) 5: 147-166; Marianne Baumgartner, "*Jo, des waren halt schlechte Zeiten...*" *Das Kriegsende und die unmittelbare Nachkriegszeit in den lebensgeschichtlichen Erzählungen von Frauen aus dem Mostviertel* (M. A. thesis., University of Vienna, 1994). Franz Severin Berger and Christiane Holler, *Trümmerfrauen. Alltag zwischen Hamstern und Hoffen* (Vienna: Ueberreuter, 1994).

4. In 1988, the ORF broadcast a series of discussions on the subject of Austrian images of aliens and enemies. The ORF also published these discussions as a book entitled *Feindbilder: Wie Völker miteinander umgehen. Die Dokumentation zur Fernsehserie* (Vienna: Kremayr und Scheriau, 1988). An entire session within this series of broadcasts was dedicated to the image of alienness and hostility associated with "Russia." Also see the corresponding chapter "Sowjetunion: Jeder Schuß ein Ruß?," in Ibid., 106-116. Another work dealing with this issue is the master's thesis by Heike Vigl, *Stereotypen: Feind- und Fremdbilder. Rußland aus der Sicht eines Südtiroler Kriegsgefangenen* (Dipl.-Arb., University of Innsbruck, 1997).

5. Ragnhild Fiebig-von Hase, "Introduction," in *Enemy Images in American History*, eds. Ragnhild Fiebig-von Hase and Ursula Lehmkuhl (Providence: Berghan, 1997), 4ff.

6. Kurt R. Spillmann and Kati Spillmann, "Some Sociobiological and Psychological Aspects of Images of the Enemy," in *Enemy Images*, eds. Fiebig-von Hase/ Lehmkuhl, 50-51.

7. Ulrich Beck, "The Sociological Anatomy of Enemy Images," in *Enemy Images*, eds. Fiebig-von Hase/Lehmkuhl, 69-71.

8. Ibid., 79.

9. Hans Schafranek, "Die Avantgarde der Einäugigen - Österreichische Arbeiterdelegationen in der UdSSR," in Barry McLoughlin, Hans Schafranek and Walter Szevera, eds., *Aufbruch - Hoffnung - Endstation: Österreicherinnen und Österreicher in der Sowjetunion, 1925-1945* (Vienna: Verlag für Gesellschaftskritik, 1996, Österreichische Texte zur Gesellschaftskritik 64), 13-48. Hans Hautmann, "Über einige Aspekte des Verhältnisses der österreichischen Arbeiterbewegung zur Sowjetunion in den Zwanzigerjahren," in *Österreich und Sowjetunion 1918-1955, Beiträge zur Geschichte der österreichisch-sowjetischen Beziehungen*, ed. Historikersektion der Österreichisch-Sowjetischen Gesellschaft (Vienna: Österreichisch-Sowjetische Gesellschaft 1984), 63-65.

10. Hautmann, "Verhältnis der österreichischen Arbeiterbewegung zur Sowjetunion," 70-71.

11. Dieter Stiefel, "Utopie und Realität: Die Wirtschaftspolitik des Ständestaates," in, *Tirol und der Anschluß. Voraussetzungen, Entwicklungen und Rahmenbedingungen,* eds. Thomas Albrich, Klaus Eisterer and Rolf Steininger (Innsbruck: Haymon, 1988).

12. Manfred Weißbecker, "'Wenn hier Deutsche wohnten...' Beharrung und Veränderung im Rußlandbild Hitlers und der NSDAP," in *Das Rußlandbild im Dritten Reich*, ed. Hans-Erich Volkmann (Cologne: Böhlau 1994), 41.

13. Hitler himself regarded Bolshevism as the attempt by the Jewish people to achieve world domination. Adolf Hitler, *Mein Kampf* (Munich: Volksausgabe, 1937), 751.

14. Weißbecker, "Rußlandbild Hitlers und der NSDAP," 53.

15. Hitler, "*Kampf*," 742-743.

16. Weißbecker, "Rußlandbild Hitlers und der NSDAP," 27.

17. Although Russia—as a result of its Christianization by Byzantium in the late tenth century—can be regarded from a cultural-historical perspective as belonging to Europe, it was nevertheless characterized as lying outside the "*orbis christianus*" in a number of different sixteenth century German works on Russia. This hypothesis originated during the early sixteenth century in Poland and Lithuania, which were then at odds with Moscow. Ekkehard Klug, "Das 'asiatische' Rußland. Über die Entstehung eines europäischen Vorurteils," *Historische Zeitschrift* 245 (1987) 265-289.

18. Wolfram Wette, "Das Rußlandbild in der NS-Propaganda. Ein Problemaufriß," in *Das Rußlandbild im Dritten Reich*, ed. Hans-Erich Volkmann (Cologne: Böhlau 1994), 63.

19. Cited in Weißbecker, "Rußlandbild Hitlers und der NSDAP," 26.

20. Wette, "NS-Propaganda," 63.

21. Ibid., 64-66.

22. Herbert Kraus, *Rußland 1941: Volk, Kultur und Wirtschaft* (Vienna: Süd-Ost-Echo Verlag, 1942), 24-25, 61, 86, 150-151.

23. Wette, "NS-Propaganda," 56ff.

24. Karl Bachinger, *Umbruch und Desintegration nach dem Ersten Weltkrieg*, (Manuskript, Vienna 1981), Ch. IV.

25. Gerhard Botz, "Das Anschlußproblem (1918-1945) aus österreichischer Sicht," in *Deutschland und Österreich*, eds. Robert A. Kann and Friedrich Prinz (Vienna: Jugend und Volk, 1980, Bilaterale Geschichtsschreibung 2), 184.

26. Heidemarie Uhl, "The Politics of Memory: Austria's Perception of the Second World War and the National Socialist Period," in *Contemporary Austrian Studies, vol. 5, Austrian Historical Memory & National Identity*, eds. Günter Bischof and Anton Pelinka (New Brunswick: Transaction, 1997), 73-74.

27. Manfried Rauchensteiner, "Das Jahrzehnt der Besatzung als Epoche in der österreichischen Geschichte," in *Österreich unter alliierter Besatzung 1945-1955*, eds. Alfred Ableitinger, Siegfried Beer and Eduard G. Staudinger (Vienna: Böhlau, 1998), 30-31.

28. Günter Bischof, "Österreich - ein 'geheimer Verbündeter' des Westens?," in *Österreich und die europäische Integration 1945-1993*, eds. Michael Gehler and Rudolf Steininger (Vienna: Böhlau, 1993), 427-428.

29. Ulrich Beck, "Sociological Anatomy," 79.

30. Dieter Stiefel, *Entnazifizierung in Österreich* (Vienna: Europa Verlag, 1980), 211.

31. Les K. Adler and Thomas G. Paterson, "Red Fascism: The Merger of Nazi Germany and Soviet Russia in the American Image of Totalitarism, 1930's - 1950's," *The American Historical Review 75* (1969-70): 4, 1046 ff.

32. Also see Adam Wandruszka and Peter Urbanitsch, eds., *Die Habsburgermonarchie 1848-1918, vol. III: Die Völker des Reiches* (Vienna: Verlag der Österreichischen Akademie der Wissenschaften, 1980), particularly the articles by Robert A. Kann, "Zur Problematik der Nationalitätenfrage in der Habsburgermonarchie 1848-1918," 1304ff., and Peter Urbanitsch, "Die Deutschen," 240ff.

33. Hungary and those areas of the Monarchy which were taken over by Italy were, of course, exceptions not considered here.

34. Beck, "Sociological Anatomy," in *Enemy Images*, eds. Fiebig-von Hase/Lehmkuhl, 77.

35. Spillmann and Spillmann, "Aspects of Images," in *Enemy Images*, eds. Fiebig-von Hase/Lehmkuhl, 50-51.

36. Statements (1) - (19) cited here are excerpts from unpublished biographical reminiscences of Austrian contemporary eyewitnesses. These have been collected by and archived at the Institut für Wirtschafts- und Sozialgeschichte in the framework of the "Dokumentation lebensgeschichtlicher Aufzeichnungen" project under the leadership of Univ.-Prof. Mitterauer. For reasons of confidentiality, the names of these individuals cannot be made public. Mag. Günter Müller was kind enough to make some of these reminiscences available to us for this work.

37. Herbert Matis and Dieter Stiefel, *Unternehmenskultur in Österreich: Ideal und Wirklichkeit* (Vienna: Service-Fachverlag an der Wirtschaftsuniversität, 1987), 88.

38. Stefan Karner, "Zur Politik der sowjetischen Besatzungs- und Gewahrsamsmacht," in *Alliierte Besatzung 1945-1955*, ed., Ableitinger/Beer/Staudinger, 409-414.

39. Klaus Eisterer, "Österreich unter allierter Besatzung 1945-1955," in *Österreich im 20. Jahrhundert*, vol. 2, eds. Rolf Steininger and Michael Gehler (Vienna: Böhlau, 1997), 150; Günter Bischof, *Between Responsibility and Rehabilitation: Austria in International Politics, 1940-1950*, vol. 2, (Ph.D. diss., Harvard University 1989), 246.

40. Marianne Baumgartner, *Das Kriegsende und die unmittelbare Nachkriegszeit in lebensgeschichtlichen Erzählungen von Frauen aus dem Mostviertel* (M. A. thesis., University of Vienna, 1992), 83.

41. Norman M. Naimark, *The Russians in Germany: A History of the Soviet Zone of Occupation 1945-1949*, (Cambridge, MA: Harvard University Press, 1995), 107-114.

42. Among the Soviet soldiers' rape victims were also quite a few Russian and Ukrainian women, the *Ostarbeiterinnen* brought in to work in the Third Reich. Also see Pavel N. Knyschewskij, *Moskaus Beute: Wie Vermögen, Kulturgüter und Intelligenz nach 1945 aus Deutschland geraubt wurden* (Munich: Olzog Verlag, 1995), 28-31. As far as we know, Moscow was informed about the numerous physical assaults and rapes on the part of Soviet soldiers, but did not react to them for reasons still unknown.

43. Gerda Lerner, *The Creation of Patriarchy* (New York: Oxford University Press, 1986), 450.

44. Erich Kuby, *Die Russen in Berlin 1945* (Munich: Scherz, 1965), 313.

45. Leonard Hankin (OSS), "Subject: the Russian Occupation of Ravelsbach, Lower Austria: A Personal Report," in *Gesellschaft und Politik am Beginn der Zweiten Republik. Vertrauliche Berichte der US-Administration aus Österreich 1945*, ed. Oliver Rathkolb (Vienna: Böhlau, 1985), 300.

46. Dieter Stiefel, "Fünf Thesen zu den sozio-ökonomischen Folgen der Ostmark" in *Politik in Österreich, Die Zweite Republik: Bestand und Wandel*, ed. Wolfgang Mantl (Vienna: Böhlau, 1992, Studien zu Politik und Verwaltung 10), 43.

47. According to Felix Butschek, *Statistische Reihen zur österreichischen Wirtschaftsgeschichte. Die österreichische Wirtschaft seit der industriellen Revolution*, 2.3. Bevölkerungsbilanz nach Bundesländern (Vienna: WIFO, 1996).

48. Fritz Weber, Wiederaufbau zwischen Ost und West, in Österreich 1945-1995, Ges*ellschaft-Politik-Kultur*, ed. Reinhard Sieder, Heinz Steinert and Emmerich Tálos (Vienna: Verlag für Gesellschaftskritik, 1996), 74.

49. Fritz Weber, "Die wirtschaftliche Entwicklung," in *Handbuch des politischen Systems Österreichs*, ed. Herbert Dachs, P. Gerlich et. al. (Vienna: Manz, 1991), 31.

50. F. Kranzelmayer, *Die Wirtschaftsstruktur Niederösterreichs*, (Ph.D. Diss., University of Vienna, 1959), 228.

51. *Vier Jahre Wiederaufbau* (Vienna: 1949), 46.

52. Herbert Matis, "Das Jahr 1945 - Die wirtschaftliche Ausgangssituation," *Österreich in Geschichte und Literatur* ( 1979): 289ff.

53. Fritz Weber, "Wiederaufbau," 74.

54. According to Felix Butschek, *Statistische Reihen*: 1955 real prices up to those of 1976.

55. Christian Kimmel, *Die wirtschaftlichen Folgen der Reparationszahlungen Deutschlands* (Freiburg, 1973), 134.

56. These areas produced a third of the Soviet Union's industrial output (measured in 1926/27 prices). Most severely affected were heavy industry (here, above all, armaments manufacturing), metals production, and mining. Moreover, these were among the most important Soviet agricultural regions: they accounted for 40 percent of the entire grain harvest, 60 percent of the country's entire swine population, and almost all sugar production. In 1941/42, the Soviet government indeed attempted to evacuate as many industrial plants as possible; nevertheless, this succeeded only partially and at the cost of productivity in other industrial sectors. It has been estimated that about 3/8 of this region's industrial capacity was involved in the evacuation process (that is 1/8 of the Soviet Union's total assets at that time). Mark Harrison, "The Second World War," in *The Economic Transformation of the Soviet Union 1913 - 1945*, ed. R. W. Davies, Mark Harrison and S. G. Wheatcroft (Cambridge: Cambridge University Press, 1994), 253-254.

57. Alan S. Milward, *Der zweite Weltkrieg, Krieg, Wirtschaft und Gesellschaft 1939 - 1945* (Munich: Deutscher Taschenbuch-Verlag, 1977), 420.

58. Angus Maddison, *Economic Policy and Performance in Europe* (London: 1973).

59. The mortality rate of the urban population rose in 1947 by 48 percent versus 1946; the corresponding figure for the rural population was 37 percent, but these figures only reflect officially registered cases. The number of unrecorded cases is said to have been higher. V. F. Zima, *Golod v SSSR 1946-1947 godov: proiskhozhdenie i posledstviia* (Moscow: Institut Rossiiskoi istorii RAN, 1996), 161.

60. Otto Klambauer, *Die USIA-Betriebe* (Ph.D. Diss., University of Vienna, 1978), 79.

61. According to the latest Russian research based upon Soviet Ministry of Defense archive material made public to date, 206 plants are said to have been dismantled in Austria between 2 March 1945 and 2 March 1946. By way of comparison, the corresponding figures in other nations were as follows: Germany, 2,885; Poland, including Silesia, 1,137; Hungary, 11; Czechoslovakia, 54; and Manchuria, 96. To transport this plant and equipment back to the Soviet Union, 142 railroad cars were loaded with 25,412 tons of freight. Knyschewskij, *Moskaus Beute*, 44-47.

62. Wilfried Aichinger, "Die Sowjetunion und Österreich 1945-1949," in *Die bevormundete Nation. Österreich und die Allierten 1945-1949*, ed. Günter Bischof and Josef Leidenfrost (Innsbruck: Haymon, 1988), 277.

63. Günter Bischof, *Austria in the First Cold War 1945-55: The Leverage of the Weak*, (Basingstoke: Macmillan, 1999), Table 1 in Chapter 4.

64. *Die sowjetische Besatzungswirtschaft in Österreich. Endbericht über die Ergebnisse des Forschungsauftrages* (Vienna, May 1958), 1, Nachlaß Figl, Niederösterreichisches Landesarchiv Kt. 204, 7. The names of the authors of this study are unknown.

65. Klambauer, *USIA-Betriebe*, 256.

66. *Sowjetische Besatzungswirtschaft*, 139.

67. Klambauer, *USIA-Betriebe*, 257.

68. *Sowjetische Besatzungswirtschaft*, 139.

69. W. Brunner, *Das deutsche Eigentum und das Ringen um den österreichischen Staatsvertrag 1945-1955*, (Ph.D. Diss., University of Vienna, 1976), 144.

70. *10 Jahre ERP 1948-1958*, 86.

71. *Sowjetische Besatzungswirtschaft*, 26

72. Klambauer, *USIA-Betriebe*, 266.

73. Felix Romanik, *Der Leidensweg der österreichischen Wirtschaft* (Vienna: Österreichischer Bundesverlag 1957), 38; William B. Bader, *Austria between East and West 1945 - 1955* (Stanford: 1966), 123.

74. *Sowjetische Besatzungswirtschaft*, 1.

75. Ibid., 22.

76. Ibid., 22f.

77. Ibid., 1.

78. Ibid., 2.

79. Ibid., 3.

80. Ibid., 12.

81. Klambauer, *USIA-Betriebe*, 241.

82. William Stearman, *Die Sowjetunion und Österreich 1945 - 1955* (Bonn: Siegler, 1962), 31; Klambauer, *USIA-Betriebe*, 132ff.

83. Klambauer, *USIA-Betriebe*, 247.

84. *Sowjetische Besatzungswirtschaft*, 10.

85. Klambauer, *USIA-Betriebe*, 335.

86. "Die USIA-Betriebe - Bewertung - Forderungen - Schulden," in *Wirtschaft 1955* 22: 3.

87. *Sowjetische Besatzungswirtschaft*, 18f., 234f.

88. Ibid., 14.

89. Herbert Matis and Dieter Stiefel, *Mit der vereinigten Kraft des Capitals, des Credits und der Technik. Die Geschichte des österreichischen Bauwesens am Beispiel der Allgemeinen Baugesellschaft A. Porr Aktiengesellschaft*, vol. 2 (Vienna: Böhlau, 1994), 31.

90. *Sowjetische Besatzungswirtschaft*, 65. Since the financial statements had to be prepared in accordance with Soviet accounting principles, Soviet bookkeepers were brought in. This position was much more important than the equivalent in the market economy. He was practically the second most important man after the chief executive officer, whom he had to monitor and whose decisions he had to countersign in many instances.

91. Ibid., 15.

92. Ibid., 8.

93. Klambauer, *USIA-Betriebe*, 271.

94. Hermann Mitteräcker, "Russenbetriebe," in *Weg und Ziel*·5 (Vienna 1947).

95. H. Feigl and A. Kusternig, eds., *Die USIA-Betriebe in Niederösterreich. Geschichte, Organisation, Dokumentation* (Vienna: 1983), 79.

96. Günter Bischof, "Die Planung und Politik der Allierten 1940-1954," in *Österreich im 20. Jahrhundert, Band 2: Vom Zweiten Weltkrieg bis zur Gegenwart*, ed.: Rolf Steininger and Michael Gehler (Vienna: Böhlau, 1997), 119.

97. Wilfried Mähr, *Der Marshallplan in Österreich*, (Graz: Styria, 1989), 96ff.

98. Ibid., 96.

99. Roman Sandgruber, *Ökonomie und Politik. Österreichs Wirtschaftsgeschichte vom Mittelalter bis zur Gegenwart* (Vienna: Ueberreuter, 1995), 455.

100. Klambauer, *USIA-Betriebe*, 365-366.

101. *Jahrbuch der Handelskammer Niederösterreich 1952.*

102. Memorandum, Thibodeaux to Ambassador L. Thompson, Vienna 10 March 1953, National Archives RG 59, 863.00/3-1053. The Soviet zone of occupation in Vienna was about 22 percent of the total area, but was assumed to be exactly one quarter.

103. Franz Heissenberger, *Der Wiederaufbau in Österreich: Die finanzielle Kulisse 1945 - 1960* (Frankfurt: F. Knapp, 1961), 41.

104. Alexander Vodopivec, *Die Balkanisierung Österreichs*, (Vienna: Molden, 1966), 25.

105. Klambauer, *USIA-Betriebe*, 374.

106. Hannes Hofbauer, *Westwärts. Österreichs Wirtschaft im Wiederaufbau* (Österreichische Texte zur Gesellschaftskritik, Vienna: Verlag für Gesellschaftskritik, 1992), 157.

107. Günter Bischof, "Österreich - ein 'geheimer Verbündeter' des Westens? Wirtschafts- und sicherheitspolitische Fragen der Integration aus der Sicht der USA," in *Österreich und die europäische Integration 1945-1993*, ed. Michael Gehler and Rolf Steininger (Vienna: Böhlau, 1993), 432-433.

108. Mähr, *Marshall Plan*, 117.

109. Arno Einwitschläger, *Amerikanische Wirtschaftspolitik in Österreich 1945-1949* (Vienna: Böhlau, 1986), 76-94; Mähr, *Marshall-Plan,* 211-216.

110. Florian Weiß, "'Gesamtverhalten: Nicht sich in den Vordergrund stellen.' Die österreichische Bundesregierung und die westeuropäische Integration 1947-1957," in *Österreich und die europäische Integration 1945-1993*, ed. Gehler/Steininger (Vienna: Böhlau, 1993), 37.

111. Klambauer, *USIA-Betriebe*, 329.

112. Matis/Stiefel, *A. Porr Aktiengesellschaft*, Volume 2, 37ff.

113. A breakdown of the individual firms is to be found in Gerhard Geissl, *Die Probleme des industriellen Wiederaufbaus in der sowjetischen Besatzungszone (1945-1951) mit einer Darstellung der Situation im Raum Wiener Neustadt* (M.A. thesis, University of Vienna, 1997), 45ff.

114. The Final Report itself is based upon official Austrian sources, and was produced in co-operation with Austrian former employees of the USIA.

115. *Sowjetische Besatzungswirtschaft*, 24.

116. These "reparations" consisted of trophy campaigns and dismantled plant and equipment, the proceeds taken in by the Soviet business conglomerate, Austrian final payments in conjunction with the *Staatsvertrag* in 1955, as well as the costs of the occupation.

117. Günter Bischof, *Austria in the First Cold War 1945-55*, Table 1 in Chapter 4.

118. Also see Fritz Breuss, "Österreichs Wirtschaft und die europäische Integration 1945-1990," in *Österreich und die europäische Integration 1945-1993*, ed. Gehler/Steininger (Vienna: Böhlau, 1993), 451.

119. Dieter Stiefel, *Die große Krise in einem kleinen Land. Österreichische Finanz- und Wirtschaftspolitik 1929-1938* (Studien zu Politik und Verwaltung 26, Vienna: Böhlau, 1988), 313 ff.

120. Klaus Eisterer, "Österreich unter Allierter Besatzung 1945-1955," in *Österreich im 20. Jahrhundert*, Vol. 2, eds. Steininger/Gehler, 165.

121. Also see Jürgen Nautz, "Wirtschaft und Politik. Die Bundesrepublik Deutschland, Österreich und die Westintegration 1945-1961," in *Österreich und die europäische Integration 1945-1993*, ed. Gehler/Steininger (Vienna: Böhlau, 1993), 149.

122. Reinhold Wagnleitner, *Coca-Colonization and the Cold War: The Cultural Mission of the United States in Austria after World War II* (Chapel Hill: University of North Carolina Press, 1994).

123. *Foreign Relations of the United States 1946*, Vol. V. 377, cited in Klambauer, *USIA-Betriebe*, 1.

# The Marshall Plan and the Making of the "Iron Curtain" in Austria

*Andrea Komlosy*

What do we actually mean when we speak of the Iron Curtain, one of the main ideological slogans of the post-World War II period? Today one almost automatically thinks of the technical barricades at the closed frontier between Western and Eastern Europe, set up by the Soviet Union and its satellites between 1949 and 1989. But what did the contemporary people, East or West, bear in mind, when they heard the term "Iron Curtain," and how did they describe the division line of Europe? What different kinds of concepts were linked with the notion of the Iron Curtain? What was its function for either side? How did it affect the bordering regions?

Usually the first use of the terms "Iron Curtain" is ascribed to Winston Churchill who, at his Fulton lecture in March 1946, used it to warn of the influence the Soviet Union was exercising over the Central and Southeastern European countries which had been liberated by the Red Army. In fact, the term was not invented by Churchill, but was initially used by Joseph Goebbels in February 1945 in order to legitimize the battle against the "*iron russian steam-roller*", which he expected to be expanding into Germany: "*If the German people stopped fighting, the Soviets would, despite the treaties between Roosevelt, Churchill and Stalin, occupy eastern and south-eastern Europe including large parts of the Reich. An iron curtain would go down before this huge territory.*"[1] This is something of which Churchill supposedly was aware on the occasion of a speech by Schwerin-Krosigk, foreign minister of the post-Hitler cabinet Dönitz, which was reported in "The Times" of 3 May 1945. Churchill personally used the term in a letter to Truman on 12 May.[2] It is most likely that the term Iron Curtain was created by a German speaker and not by Churchill.

In German it denominates the safety curtain separating a theatre stage form the spectators' hall, whereas the English language offers other terms (for example, fire-proof curtain).[3]

Churchill used the term to question the influence the Soviet Union was exercising over the territories and governments within its sphere of interest. He wanted to challenge the expansion of communism and asked for its containment. As at that time there was no actual danger of Soviet troops expanding beyond the demarcation lines Stalin had agreed upon with him and Roosevelt in Yalta, any request for containment was a call for the isolation of the Soviet Union and its partners (satellites). For Truman, who attended Churchill's lecture, it represented a formidable trial balloon qualified for testing the reaction of the American public on a policy of severity against the former war-ally.[4]

Every curtain separates a whole in two pieces. We therefore have to examine the so-called Iron Curtain from the West and from the East as well as from the perspective of the regions situated at its border. Investigating the case of Austria, these regions are located at the borders with Czechoslovakia, Hungary, and Yugoslavia.[5] They will be analyzed on a local level, because their social and economic life has traditionally been based on cross-border contacts. Because of their occupation by Soviet military forces, the eastern and north-eastern parts of Austria represent a special area within Austria. They were not only surrounded by borders with foreign countries, but also by the border-line separating the Soviet from the occupation zones of the Western allies. To deal with the "Iron Curtain" on a local and regional level requires the investigation of its origins and the underlying intentions as well as the specific way of functioning as a multiplex border-line.

Starting the investigation from the eastern or the western side already affords a supposition of what has to be included in the considerations when speaking of the Iron Curtain. We do not want to revive the antagonism between the so-called "traditionalists" and their "revisionist" critics, ambitiously arguing about who was responsible for the onset of the Cold War.[6] The contrast is rather between those concentrating on the military threat and the conflict between the systems on the one side and the argument regarding the economic and political interests of the United States and the Soviet Union to have caused the shift from inter-allied wartime cooperation to an atmosphere of Cold War on the other. Do we have to consider the Marshall Plan to be first of all an instrument of the Cold War, as Geir Lunestadt suggests[7], or should we rather follow John Gimbel who stresses the reconstruction of Western Europe and especially of Western Germany to be the main objectives of the Marshall Plan?[8] In this article, the main impetus behind the politics of the Great Powers is considered to be the restoration of Western Europe as a competitive partner in the case of the United States[9] and the continuation of the inter-allied wartime coalition to profit from the U.S. financial capacities to pay for recovery and reconstruction in Eastern Europe in the case of the Soviet Union.[10] These primarily economic motivations are intertwined with the strategic as well as the systemic antagonism between the two Great Powers. As a result, the necessity to stay in a friendly relationship with the war-ally differed. The Soviet Union, suffering heavy losses from the war, considered it to be vital. For the United States, it was not very important; it finally turned out to contradict the need to build close relations with Western Germany. Another big difference is to be seen in the importance of Eastern Europe. For the Soviet Union, it was a *"cordon sanitaire"* against a new German attack on a military level and a source for lacking industrial products economically; for the United States, the Eastern part of Europe was peripheral, not profitable enough to invest in its recovery nor important enough to oppose Soviet domination.[11] We suggest considering the different levels of socio-economic development, the degree of war damages, and the position of the respective States and regions—United States and Soviet Union, Western and Eastern Europe—in the world economy. Thus, we can discuss questions of integration and disintegration of Europe in connection with the necessities of capital accumulation on a worldwide scale, the strive of every region for hegemony and competitivness and the struggle of peripheral regions to catch up.

## The Approach of the West

Although participation in the European Recovery Program (ERP) had also been formally offered to the Soviet Union and the east and south-eastern European states, the ERP was dedicated to help reconstruct the industrialized western parts of Europe. The ERP expenditures were aimed at the economic integration of the western part of Europe and, at the same time at the disintegration of the European East. Marshall Plan aid for the West was inseparably linked with the embargo policy the United States exercised against the East.

By connecting aid with trade embargo, the Marshall Plan was the instrument to make the receipient states follow the United States' directions. The result was the establishment of a sharp economic division line throughout Europe.

The first laws and directives to prevent exports to Western European partners from reaching the East were enacted by the United States in 1947. The Commerce Department was implementing a general control system for all exports to Europe. From January 1948 exports to Eastern Europe were only possible with special export licences. The Economic Cooperation Act (ECA) of 3 April 1948 finally contained regulations concerning trade with Eastern Europe. Chapter 117d explicitly prohibited the ECA administrators from approving the export of goods into a participating country, "which [would] go into the production of any commodity for delivery to any non-participating European country, which commodity would be refused export licences to those countries by the United States in the interest of national security."[12] A very clear definition of the embargo regulations was expressed by the Mutual Defense Assistance Control Act of 1951. The Act did more than list the eventual export restrictions for military as well as civilian goods. Paragraph 203 contained the sanctions, which were imposed against any country receiving military, economic or financial assistance, "when the president determines that the receipient country (1) is not effectively cooperating with the United States pursuant to this title, (2) is failing to furnish to the United States information sufficient for the President to determine that the receipient country is effectively cooperating."[13] The embargo laws and regulations were followed by lists of goods the export of which was subjected to strict embargo, to control, or to supervision. The first list contained goods, which were not allowed to be exported to the East. The second one listed those items which required special licences. List number three gave a summary of those items that were not subject to embargo regulations at the moment, but which were registered, in order to be put on another list in the future. In the early 1950s, 1700 items were registered on the embargo lists and forbidden to be sold to Eastern Europe. A Joint Comittee on Foreign Economic Cooperation (alias the Watchdog Committee) was installed, and Secretaries of Economic Defense at the United States' European embassies had to exercise control over the trade from West to East.

Although the embargo was negotiated in the Organization of European Economic Cooperation (OEEC) as well as in the UN Economic Commission for Europe (ECE), there was no official document or body responsible for the policy of embargo on the European level. According to Gunnar Myrdal, at that time executive secretary of the ECE, there was too much dissent among the American and the European members about how far the boycott should go in order not to direct itself against national economic interests. At the beginning, the embargo was planned by a secret committee under U.S. leadership including British, French, Italian, Belgian, Swedish, Dutch, Norwegian, and Swiss members.[14] Only on 22 November 1949, they agreed to institutionalize their Consultative Group (CG) by forming an informal organization, called the Coordinating Comittee (COCOM). The COCOM headquarters were located in Paris; founding members were England, France, Italy, the Netherlands, Belgium, Luxemburg and the United States. These were joined in 1950 by Norway, Denmark, Canada, and Western Germany, and later by Portugal, Japan, Greece, and Turkey. While at the level of the Consultative Group ministers were planning the general lines of the embargo, the Coordinating Committee was an executive body consisting of diplomats and technical experts who decided what was to be put on the embargo lists and how the embargo was to be controlled.[15] All other countries were committed to follow the embargo because it was linked with U.S. aid and credits. In addition to the general regulations of the Economic Cooperation Act, the Battle Act, and other control laws, the United States signed bilateral agreements with each participating country in order to form their domestic economic reconstruction as well as their relations with foreign countries.[16]

There has been much discussion about the reasons for this rigid policy of economic boycott, which was often contested by European partners and in many cases was impossible to effectively control. At the time, some arguments stressed the military threat from a Soviet Union eager to support the spread of communism towards Western Europe. In contrast, some arguments assert that the embargo was considered to be primarily a means of containment against the Soviet Union. We rather want to stress the question of creating a dangerous enemy in order to raise public support for foreign economic aid. The construction of the Soviet danger was much more important than its effective threatening potential. The recovery of world trade was the main aim of supporting the economic reconstruction of Europe. The United States had improved its world economic position during the war; Great Britain, the former rival, had suffered big damage and its economy was down. The crisis of the 1930s as well as the war itself had not only destroyed the production capacities of the industrialized Western countries, but had also deeply interrupted traditions of international cooperation and division of labor. The United States were only able to realize their economic hegemony if world trade were restored. It was necessary to find markets and partners for the expansion in order to avoid a possible post-war depression. It therefore made sense to reconstruct Western Europe. Truman expressed it, in his Message to the Congress on 20 December 1947, when he said that in the past the exchange of raw materials and industrial products between Western Europe, Latin America, Canada, and the United States had united these parts of the world into one system of commerce; exports from the Far East to the United States contributed to pay for the European goods sold to the Far East. Thus, Europe was considered to be an important part of world trade. If this huge system of commerce could not be revitalized, Truman expected a deterioration of the economic situation of the whole world, from which the United States would suffer as would other countries.[17]

Eastern Europe in its vast majority was not considered a part of this Europe. For various reasons, including its geographical position and historical structures, its occupation by competing foreign powers and the inability of its countries and regions to play a dynamic role in the world's economic division of labor, it was a predominantly agrarian region. The programs of land reform and industrialization the new governments had started after having achieved political independence in 1918 were interrupted by the Great Depression and ended in subordination to Nazi Germany or occupation by the *Wehrmacht*. To support Eastern Europe at the end of World War II did not make much sense to the United States. Not only was the Red Army standing in that part of Europe, there were no economic and social structures appropriate to fit into the United States' needs for expanding markets and competitive partnership. Financial support for the East could become virtually unlimited. Given the fact that the potential of U.S. aid was restricted and that it was not easy to mobilize public support in order to finance foreign aid, funds had to be concentrated on those parts of the European economy whose recovery would strengthen the U.S. economy. This would not have been the case in Eastern Europe; therefore, there was not much interest in building up relations with that part of Europe by supporting it financially. This reluctant attitude becomes visible if we compare the amount of financial support given to the different parts of Europe prior to the Marshall Plan. While those countries that later participated in the ERP received loans and credits between July 1945 and June 1947 amounting of $ 7.4 billion, Eastern Europe received only $ 546 million. During the same period, the humanitarian aid was $ 3 billion for the West and $ 1 billion for the East.[18]

Of course, there might also have been considerations how to undermine the Soviet Union's and Eastern Europe's ability to recover from the war's destruction, which were much higher in Eastearn Europe than in the West, for political and ideological reasons. An embargo, and a refusal to give loans and to integrate the East into a common European reconstruction seemed to be appropriate measures to prevent a possible Soviet and communist expansion. However, there is no evidence of the extent to which the Soviet Union and her partners were affected by the embargo. First, the embargo did not always work properly and was weakened by illegal transactions. Second, it is possible that the embargo was indirectly contributing to national programs of industrialization and import-substitution in the single countries as well as in the international co-operation within COMECON, founded in 1949 as a direct response to the exclusion of the East from trans-European reconstruction. Gunnar Myrdal therefore considered the embargo to be an important element in the consolidation of the communist block. At any rate, it was an easy pretext for the sovietization of the East European states, which followed the isolation of the East from the West.[19] Stalin would have had to invent the embargo, had it not been offered to him by the United States, Myrdal argued.

Western European countries were traditionally much more involved in trade relations with East and Southeastern Europe than the United States. If they wanted to participate in the ERP, these western European countries had to give up these relationships and re-orient their exports and imports to Western partners. The embargo conditions of the Economic Cooperation Act of April 1948 and some other U.S. laws regulating the conditions for exports did not leave them any other choice. Each participating country signed a treaty accepting direct influence of U.S. advisers and ECA administrators on various kinds of domestic economic decisions. Austria's Marshall Plan treaty with the United States was signed on 2 July 1948.

## Austria and the Embargo

Being a successor state of the Austrian-Hungarian Monarchy, Austria had a special history of co-operation with the countries of East and Southeastern Europe. Despite the rupture caused by the break-up of the monarchy and the foundation of sovereign states, each trying to build up an independent national economy, Austria was pursuing close trade relations with the other Habsburg successor states. In 1930, 41 percent of Austria's exports and 31 percent of the imports were exchanged with Czechoslovakia, Hungary, Yugoslavia, and Poland.[20] Austria's main trading partners in the inter-war period were Germany and Czechoslovakia, followed by Hungary and Italy. It kept a balance in its foreign economic co-operation, looking eastward as well as westward, thus using Vienna's former contacts to build a bridge between the developed industrialized Europe and the states of the agrarian periphery, which put much effort in copying the Western model. As a consequence of the decline in prices and Western European demand for Eastern cash crops and raw materials after the big crisis of 1930, Hungary and the Southeastern European states relied more and more on Germany in their foreign trade relations; Hitler-Germany was accepting raw materials in exchange for German manufactured goods, thus binding the peripheralized economies into the German *Großraumwirtschaft* on a subordinate level[21]. In Czechoslovakia, the economic crisis led to a sharp decline in foreign trade[22]. Austria's trade with the above mentioned four successor states had declined to 32.5 percent of exports and 26 percent of imports in 1937,[23] before the country was subjected to a sharp re-orientation of its trade patterns toward the West by the *Anschluß*, its integration into the German Reich.

At the end of World War II, Austria's economic structure had completely changed. During the Nazi period, there had been an enormous investment in heavy industry and the military sectors, which had led to a shift from the production of consumer goods to basic and strategic industries linked with the replacement of the traditional medium sized firms by big (German owned) companies. By concentrating industrial activities in the west of the *Ostmark*, especially in Upper Austria (Oberdonau), southern Lower Austria, till now in close co-operation with Upper Styria, the leading centre of mining and metal industries, Austria had lost its hegemony as a leading industrial region. In 1945, large parts of Austria's industrial landscape were destroyed.

Enterprises suffered from lack of machines, workers, raw materials, and markets.

The breakdown of industrial production at the end of the war caused a lot of poverty. However it also offered the possibility for a new orientation. Should reconstruction go on with the structures the Germans had created by integrating Austria into the Reich in line with the needs of the German war machine? Should efforts be concentrated on the big companies in basic and heavy industries despite the fact that there was no more need for these products on the domestic market? Or should Austria take on the diversified industrial landscape of the inter-war period and build up the consumer goods industries which had been neglected by the Nazis? Both options had implications for foreign economic relations. The basic and heavy industry model was directed towards the West; there, after a period of political uncertainty including the option of a united Germany, the Reich was replaced by Western Germany in terms of demand for Austrian energy, steel, and semi-finished products. The consumer goods industry model would have been based on domestic demand; exports as well as joint business ventures would have had to find their partners in the successor states of the Habsburg Monarchy.

While intellectuals were discussing the pros and cons of the different models of reconstruction,[24] politicians and businessmen were pursuing the path of what was possible. On one hand, they were trying to have close relationships with the Western allies in order to participate in relief and aid programs. On the other hand they were building economic relationships with their Eastearn European neighbors, especially with Czechoslovakia, whose economy was in a much better shape than that of Austria. Between August 1945 and May 1946, a total of 42 percent of Austrian exports and 39 percent of imports were exchanged only with Czechoslovakia.[25] In 1946, 25 percent of Austrian foreign exchange activities were taking place with Czechoslovakia, Hungary, Poland, and Yugoslavia; 19 percent concentrating on Czechoslovakia alone.[26] So the restrictions of the post-war situation offered a real option to rebuild the close relationship among the Central European nations prior to 1938, which had been perverted by their integration and subordination under Nazi *Großraumpolitik*. The following view, expressed in an Austrian newspaper in April 1948, illustrates the Austrians' pragmatic will to combine a general political orientation towards the West with good trade relations with the East:

> Most Austrians welcome the integration of Western and Central European countries against the bolshevist bloc of Eastern European states eager to expand. But nobody wants our state borders to be surrounded by an Iron Curtain. We want to live in peace with all our neighbors. Everybody is to be happy in his own way, but the opportunity must be created to trade with Eastern Europe (...). The ill-famed Iron Curtain is not as close as it was supposed to be. In 1947 goods were imported for öS 300 million, only half of that amount was exported. We have to be grateful to the Western powers, but as soon as a state treaty will be signed and we will again be able to dispose of our industry, as soon as financial aid will be over, relations with Northeastern and Southeastern Europe have to be established.[27]

The article finally concluded: "Decisive for the course of the world are economic facts, not political slogans."[28]

The United States was aware of these close economic ties, and a document issued as early as 1 January 1945 shows that they did not necessarily object to them: "Austria must also seek a partial solution for its foreign trade problems by entering into special regional arrangements with neighboring contries (especially Czechoslovakia and Yugoslavia) aimed at developing their mutual trade. The U.S. should not oppose such arrangements unless they threatened seriously the evolution of broader multilateral trade patterns."[29] At the end of the year, the U.S. position was no longer so liberal. On the one hand the United States agreed to the delivery of Austrian iron ore to the Czech steel plant of Trinec "to prove at the proper time that it was the U.S. forces in Austria which permitted the operation of a very important iron and steel plant in Czechoslovakia (...) and not the Russians who were most anxious to prove to the Czechs that the orientation of Czech economy towards the East was not only advantageous but possible."[30] On the other hand, these exchanges were "to be held on a purely orientative level, since specific and detailed U.S. policy on the disposal of the Hermann Goering Iron and Steel Works apparently was not decided on, and since the Goering Works are U.S. war booty."[31] When the Austrian government wanted to sell unused VOEST blast furnaces in exchange for Czech coal in December 1946, U.S. High Commissioner General Clark objected to the deal.[32] Although the U.S. occupation forces had turned over the former *Hermann Goering Werke* under the administration of the Austrian government, which had decided to nationalize the former German property and build up a complex of state industries with the consent of the Western allies, the United States still owned it. The same objections were made in the spring of 1948 to sell spare VOEST equipment to Czechoslovakia or Yugoslavia. At that time, the U.S. "no" was already directly justified with the "embargo of heavy machinery to Czechoslovakia" because the export "of certain capital equipment. (...) would contribute to Soviet war potential.[33]

In order to avoid economic deals contradicting U.S. strategic concepts, the United States could rely on their ownership of German property which was assessed to the occupation forces at the Potsdam Conference of July/August 1945. With the beginning of the Marshall Plan, they were entitled to control further aspects of the Austrian economy. Receiving Marshall Plan aid required countries to follow the embargo, and U.S. administrators were entitled to oversee economic transactions on the level of government, ministries, and companies. Not only did ECA administrators control the sectors and companies in which Marshall Plan financed imports as well as credits financed from the counterpart funds were allowed to flow, they also cared about the destination of the commodities produced with the help of the Marshall Plan. Many items being excluded from export to the Soviet Union and its allies, Austria's exports to Eastern European countries (CS, Hu, Po, Yu) had gone down from 25 percent in 1946 to 17 percent in 1948, the first year of the Marshall Plan. In the following years it fell under the 10 percent-limit.[34] The Marshall Plan and its counterpart, the embargo against Eastern Europe, were in this way contributing to the rise of an Iron Curtain before the Soviet Bloc was enclosing itself with a metal fence.

## The Approach of the East

The Soviet Union and the Eastern and Southeastern European countries, which were under the military influence of the Red Army at the end of the war, had suffered heavy war damages. All of them were interested in western aid, credits, and an all-European program of recovery. From the beginning, it was evident, however, that the flow of western aid and credits to this part of Europe was dilatory.

The Soviet Union was interested in continuing their cooperation with the Western allies which had made possible the defeat of the *Wehrmacht*. Now their main concern was to find a common solution for the German question in such a way that Soviet aspirations for reparations could be satisfied. A precondition for the Soviet Union to get access to the industrial assets concentrated in the western part of Germany, especially in the Rhine and Ruhr regions, was a united Germany. Therefore, the Soviet Union very much strove for the unification of Germany, which, like Austria, was split in four occupation zones, while at the same time promoting German neutralization in order to appease its western flank. Even when there seemed to be no more hope to achieve this goal after the foundation of the Federal Republic of Germany (FRG) and, as a response, the German Democratic Republic (GDR) in 1949, Stalin made a last effort for reunification in 1952, conceding free elections, a peace treaty, and the withdrawal of foreign occupation forces.[35]

In order to carry on the wartime coalition, the Soviet Union was participating in the international conferences leading to the foundation of the World Bank and the International Monetary Fund in 1944. Although the proclamation of the Truman doctrine on 21 March 1947 could be interpreted as the end of the cooperation, Stalin was still ready for further negotiations.[36] Molotov, the Soviet minister of foreign affairs, met his British and French colleagues in Paris in June 1947. They debated a Soviet participation in the ERP.[37] The conditions of the Marshall Plan did not offer hope that an all-European settlement could be worked out. To receive help was only possible if the receiving country agreed to accept U.S. control over various aspects of economic life. From its first anouncement by George C. Marshall in his Harvard speech on 5 June 1947, the ERP had a clear anti-eastern as well as anti-communist tendency by linking aid with embargo; for those being faced or menaced by the embargo it was difficult to act at the same time as if they were benefiting from the program. A main reason for the Soviet Union identifying the Marshall Plan as an instrument not for cooperation but one directed against its vital interests was rooted in the the handling of the German question. The recognition of the German West as a pillar of Western Europe's recovery, which became obvious after the failure of the Four Power negotiations in March and April 1947, was an indicator of the end of the inter-allied trans-systemic cooperation. After the U.S. integration of Western Germany into a Western recovery program, the Soviet Union lost the main industrial capacities necessary to pay for reparations.[38] At this stage, participation in the ERP did not represent an option for the Soviet Union any more. They definitely refused to take part and left the June 1947 foreign ministers' meeting in Paris ahead of time. As a result, this put pressure on the Eastern European allies who were invited, in spite of the break with the Soviet Union, to participate in an all-European conference preparing the Marshall Plan, which was going to take place in mid-July.[39] Poland, Bulgaria, Romania, and Hungary did not accept the invitation, nor did Finland. Czechoslovakia, which had already agreed to take part in the preparatory meeting, revised its decision. Especially for Czechoslovakia, this was a bitter experience. The government did not expect the Soviet Union to oppose its participation. But at a meeting with Stalin, a Czech delegation was informed about the Soviet "*Niet*". Gottwald and Masaryk immediately sent home a telegram obliging the government to revise its decision : "According to Stalin, we should withdraw our acceptance to participate. (...) We regard it as an imperative that you agree to the withdrawal of our acceptance to the joint conference at Paris (...)."[40]

U.S. politicians as well as State Department diplomats responsible for the Marshall Plan, including George F. Kennan and William L. Clayton, unmistakably stated that the possibility of the Soviet Union taking part in the ERP had never been considered a realistic option by the United States.[41] The same applied to Ernest Bevin and Georges Bidault, the British and French foreign ministers, who were appointed to coordinate the European participants. At the Paris meeting, they did not show much interest in achieving a compromise with the Soviet delegation over the main issues in dispute, the participation of former European war enemies, especially Germany. Still negotiating, Bevin already admitted to have "anticipated and wished" for the "breakdown of the conference": "This conference will break up tomorrow. I am glad that the cards have been laid on the table and that the responsibility will be laid at Moscow's door."[42] It was a tactical approach obliging the Soviet Union to reject the plan; while at the same time, it put a wedge between the Soviet Union and her partners over the question of participation. It was obvious that the countries of East Central and Southeastern Europe, the more they were situated in the West and had developed industries, the more they were interested in having close economic relationships with the industrialized European West, hoping to benefit from reconstruction programs. For the United States, the advantages resulting from such support were not so obvious; on the contrary, they were considered to be few. Therefore, in the period prior to the Marshall Plan, aid was given only in quantities which were neglegible compared with what the western part of the continent received. The U.S. State Department did not want to explicitly exclude Eastern Europe from participation, however. But in case of conceiving a foreign aid program "as a proposal for general European (not just western European) cooperation (...) it would be essential that this be done in such a form that the Russian satellite countries would either exclude themselves by unwillingness to accept the proposed conditions or agree to abandon the exclusive orientation of their economies," Chief of the Policy Planning Staff, George Kennan, argued.[43] Nobody actually believed that Eastern European states would participate after the Soviet rejection of the Marshall Plan.

A special case was that of Czechoslovakia. Apart from the German Democratic Republic, it was the only country within the military and political influence of the Soviet Union which had a developed industrial landscape traditionally interconnected with Western Europe. It was worth being integrated into what was to become the European West. Czechoslovakia was overwhelmingly liberated by the Red Army, which controlled the country up to the line connecting Karlovy Vary with České Budějovice. The regions in the far West, however, were liberated and held by U.S. troops at the end of the war. At the end of 1945, Soviet and U.S. troops had withdrawn from Czechoslovakia, leaving it as the only Eastern European country without any foreign troops. Nevertheless, the government and the people, 38 percent of whom had voted for the Communist Party in the elections of 26 May 1946, held close ties with the Soviet Union. They resulted mainly from the British and French agreement to the German occupation of the Czech border regions in Munich in September 1938 and the proclamation of a German protectorat over the Czech lands in April 1939. The United States was interested in loosening these ties by offering cooperation. However, the United States was disappointed by the Czechoslovak approach to economic planning as well as by their friendship with the Soviet Union. As a result of the 1946 elections, the U.S. enthusiasm for turning Czechoslovakia into a proper member of Western Europe had already cooled, leading to the refusal of credits. By the end of 1946, even credits already agreed upon were ineligible for further payment.[44] Nevertheless, Czechoslovakia was invited to take part in the negotiations regarding Marshall Plan participation and was even considered to join a committee of five countries which would work out European proposals for U.S. assistence.[45] The Czechoslovak Republic (ČSR) had tried to develop its own national agenda of economic development and social reform, pursuing good relations with both East and West. This was no longer viable when the break-up of the wartime coalition gave way to a Cold War between the Great Powers. The country had to opt for one side, and this decision was made as a result of the prevailing circumstances rather than as a result of their own free will.

It cannot be taken for granted, however, that Czechoslovak participation at the Paris meeting would have led to an agreement on the ERP. The United States had expressed clear political and economic conditions under which it would accept Czechoslovak participation, and disapproved of the ČSR's decision to be open to East and West.[46] In President Beneš' own words: "Culturally we are Europeans. We will not range ourselves solely with the East nor solely with the West, but with East and West simultaneously."[47]

So European postwar reconstruction was realized in two different forms. The industrialized West of the continent, including the mediterranean countries (except Spain), was within the U.S. sphere of influence which was exercised by the conditions linked to accepting Marshall Plan aid. One of the conditions consisted in obeying the embargo. The industrially less developed European East was under control of the Soviet Union. The more the split between East and West became inevitable, the more the Soviet Union was imposing its model of socialism upon the small Eastern and Southeastern European countries. To maintain relations with both sides, as Czechoslovakia sought to do, was no longer possible. So the split became perfect and exclusive. Its consequence was the sovietization of the Eastern and Southeastern European countries, which consisted in establishing the Communist Party as the leading political factor of society, and re-structuring of the economy along the Soviet model of planning and the separation from capitalist interference. This established a strict control of trade, traffic, and the movement of people at the borders of the socialist block. Within the socialist block, which was institutionalized by the foundation of the COMECON in 1949, the participating countries were concentrating on the development of their own national economies and therefore often objected to stronger international integration aspired to by the Soviet Union. With the exception of Czechoslovakia, parts of which had been among the main industrial regions of the Habsburg Monarchy, the national Communist Parties considered the socialist model of reconstruction to be an instrument of industrialization which their countries had not been able to realize after independence (achieved in the nineteenth century and later with the break-up of the Habsburg and the Zarist Empire in 1917/18).

### The Iron Curtain as a Specific Type of Border Line

One main element of the sovietization of the Eastern European countries was the establishment of a technical barrier along the border of the countries, which was most effective at the exterior borders of the socialist block with the West. Its function was a political, a military, and an economic one, enabling the public authorities to control every movement and transaction crossing the demarcation line between East and West. The border fortifications of the Iron Curtain went beyond the responsibility of the individual governments of those states bordering the West. They were serving the interests of the whole block under Soviet hegemony. Nevertheless, the technical logistics as well as the organization of border control were up to the individual governments, and they differed from country to country.

In common, they had a metal fence behind the borders at a distance of one or two kilometers inside the country. The fence consisted of two parts enclosing some meters of bare land showing the foot-prints of everybody stepping on it. People were not permitted to enter the border area outside the fence except for military and border police. Inside the fence, there was a broader border zone of up to 15 kilometers, which was under military control. In Hungary, the villages located within the zone were inhabited, thus separated from the outside by two border-lines; in Czechoslovakia, most of the villages within the zone were depopulated and the houses blown up. Along the fence there were watchtowers and barracks allowing control of the territory and eventual prosecution of persons trying to overcome it illegally. The technical means of control, deterrence and prosecution, were developing from very crude forms right after the erection of the barriers in the early 1950s up to more sophisticated methods in the 1970s and 1980s. In the case of Hungary following its erection in 1949 and its rebuilding after the suppression of the Hungarian uprising in 1957, the fence was supported by mines; they were only taken away in the middle of the 1960s, when the fence was equipped with an alarm system signalling every crossing to the military in the border barracks.[48] Within minutes policy they were able to catch the refugee, who in the majority of cases turned out to be a rabbit, however.[49] In Czechoslovakia, the system was similar, with the exception that there were usually no mines, but there was a much more rigid destruction of settlements within the confines of the border zone, mainly due to the fact that most of these villages before were inhabited by Germans expelled from the country after 1945.[50] The most rigid surveyance could be observed along the border between FRG and GDR.[51]

The existence of technical barriers at the border was first mentioned in Austria in October 1948 at the border between the southeastern part of Austria, called Burgenland, and Hungary. A local newspaper described the difficulties of farming at the border in an article entitled "Wires and mines."[52] On 9 March 1949, a newspaper mentioned a "wire as tall as a man" near Mattersburg, Burgenland.[53] In the following months, several articles described the character of the new barriers at the border between Austria and Hungary and warned of the mines which were a danger to the population.[54] In Czechoslovakia, the building-up of border barriers started later than in Hungary. The rise of an "Iron Curtain" was first mentioned right after the communist take-over in March 1948,[55] however, it had not yet risen in the form of literal fences. It was used in a more general sense to describe the interruption of international contacts between Czechoslovakia and the West. Prior to the creation of a border fence and a security zone was the reorganization of the security forces responsible for border control.[56] In May 1945, three units were charged with border security: a quickly recruited army was responsible for the recovery of the state border of 1937; border control was split among special police forces (SNB, Corps of National Security) as well as by pre-war type customs officers. After February 1948, a militarization of border control could be observed: while the customs bodies of the Ministry of Finance were dissolved, the police units split into a special unit for border control, equipped with heavy arms, under the command of the newly created Ministry of State Security (SNB-PS, Corps of National Security - Border Police) and regular police forces (SNB). A system of technical barriers only came up in the second half of the 1950s, when a new "Defence Law" was giving way to the establishment of unarmed working units charged with building-up border fortifications.[57] In July 1951 a new "Law on the Protection of the State Borders" was defining the proceeding and the responsibilities of border control.[58] From now on the Iron Curtain type border with wire fence and border zones, started to take on shape. According to a Czech forest officer, a continuous metal fence at the Austrian-Czech border only existed as of 1952.[59] In this very year, the Ministry of National

Security was abolished, and the responsibility for the armed units of border control again became the agenda of the Ministry of Interior Affairs. In the case of Czechoslovakia, further steps of modernization of the border system were usually first introduced at the border with Western Germany, then only with a brief delay reaching the Austrian border, and—with further delays and modifications—the borders with the German Democratic Republic, Poland, and Hungary. In 1962, the initial border fence at the Austrian-Czechoslovak border was renewed and equipped with an electrical alarm system.

If we regard the character of the Iron Curtain, we can observe an almost singular type of border regime due to the overlapping of various borders. Remarkably, it closely followed the dividing line separating Europe into a more developed West and a less developed East established at least since the sixteenth century, but dating back into Charlemagne's time. "It is as if Stalin, Churchill and Roosevelt had studied carefully the status quo of the age of Charlemagne on the 1130th anniversary of his death."[60] When the bordering regions of this European dividing line became independent states in 1918, state formation was linked with the establishment of political borders. As soon as the individual states became parts of two different economic and social orders, the dividing line took on a systemic character.

As soon as the border was equiped with wire, mines, and electric alarm systems, the term "Iron Curtain" changed its meaning. Originally conceived in a much more general way to describe the demarcation line between East and West, it became an expression to denominate the border barriers surrounding the socialist states. The use of the term was restricted to the West, however, while being heavily contested in the East. The East used terms such as border fence, border barrier, or metal fence. In Eastern Europe, the border fortifications were officially justified as a necessary means of defense against Western interference. As such, the fences were the subject of high level state propaganda. Being directed against the free movement of the citizens, the fences were at the same time kept top-secret and virtually out of bounds. The technical barriers at the border were considered to be a consequence of the division of Europe which was attributed to the West. Paradoxically, the East was ready to pay for the costs of isolation, relieving the western neighboring states of the pressure of uncontrolled immigration.

The Iron Curtain exercised a form of total border control. Theoretically, it can be seen as an extreme of a broad spectrum of borders ranging from total closure to total permeability. In reality, borders usually represent a combination of closure and openness resulting in a state of semi-permeability.[61] Who and what is entitled to cross the border depends on the relationship between the bordering states, not necessarily taking into consideration the needs of the immediate border regions. If the relationship between the neighbouring states is a balanced one, the border will not interfere very much in the cross-border contacts and will not represent a strong dividing line. If the relationship is characterized by different levels of economic development, the border will play the role of a link between center and periphery. The more advanced economy will open its borders for what they want to import or export to the periphery, including labor, in some cases practicing free trade, in others trade restrictions and limitations. The peripheries' capacities to shape the border according to their domestic needs is restricted by economic dependency and a weaker bargaining power. As sovereign states they can decide to restrict or not to restrict trade, migration, and the flow of capital. With every measurement for the protection of their domestic market, however, they risk the deterioration of the relationship with the more developed neighbor on whom they rely because of export markets, access to capital, and technology.

The groups of states being separated by the Iron Curtain did not only belong to two different social and economic systems. With some exceptions, the West stands for the industrialized, rich center, the East for the poor agrarian periphery, for centuries tied together by an unequal division of labor. The lack of interest by the United States to support the post-World War II recovery of the European East can be explained by the region's lack of a modern economic structure comparable to that of Western Europe. So the United States hesitated to support and invest in Eastern European reconstruction. A second reason to neglect and finally boycott the East involved the lack of control the West was able to exercise over states under Red Army occupation with strong Communist Parties, one of them even democratically voting for a communist government. Under these circumstances, the United States decided to isolate the small Eastern and Southeastern European countries, just as they had isolated the Soviet Union. At the same time, they were using any opportunity to break-up the solidarity among them and the Soviet Union, thus weakening the possible success of the communist model of development. Disposing of the embargo as a means of isolation, which every Western European country receiving Marshall Plan aid had to respect in its own interest, the West did not depend upon a primitive fence at the demarcation line. Whatever was not to cross the line could be hindered by this means.[62]

After the end of World War II, the free flow of goods and people across the border which would later become the Iron Curtain did not have much opportunity to flourish. The immediate postwar period was characterized by soldiers and prisoners coming home from the war, as well as by the movements of prisoners released from the concentration camps, displaced workers of all countries subjugated by the Nazis who had been forced to work and now were looking for their families, refugees who tried to escape political persecution, and the huge masses of German minorities who were expelled and evacuated from countries previously dominated by the Third Reich. Then there were the occupation forces of the allied powers establishing military and political control over the territories liberated from the *Wehrmacht*. They also were exercising border control between their zones of occupation, which did not necessarily coincide with state borders. When all the postwar troubles were calming down in 1947, the Cold War was already developing, severing many relationships which had just been established. A further result of the recovery program to Western Europe, which isolated the countries in the East was that the Soviet Union was giving up the initial attempts to carry on the Anti-Hitler Coalition. A conference of European Communist Parties in September 1947 in Poland could be taken as a decisive date marking the shift from cooperation to the beginning of the Cold War. At that meeting the Secretary of the Central Comittee of the Communist Party of the Sovient Union, Andrei Shdanow, formulated the picture of the two antagonistic camps: "the imperialist anti-democratic one on one hand and the anti-imperialist democratic one on the other," thus taking on the Western characterization of the Iron Curtain.[63]

In order to meet the boycott by the West, Stalin decided to sever the reconstruction of the Soviet Union and the small states within its sphere of interest from the West. This offered the possiblity to undertake enormous efforts to enforce the industrialization by the means of socialist transformation. One of the preconditions for improving industrialization was to cut the relationship with the developed capitalist countries. So the weapon directed against the successful recovery of the Soviet Union and its allies was turned into an instrument of development. Severing connections with the West allowed the Soviet Union to build up the productive forces of the socialist countries without accepting Western standards of productivity as the scale for development. This severing also kept the West from being able to undermine the setting up of self-reliant socialist industrialization in the individual Eastern European countries. A strict regime of border control made it possible to regulate the flow of goods, capital, and people, and to prevent the market from deciding which industries could exist. At the same time, the border regime intended to prevent political ideas and conceptions of development not corresponding with the Soviet model from entering the socialist bloc. The border fortifications referred to as Iron Curtain were one main element of a complex set of measurements of active severing which was imposed on all countries belonging to the Soviet bloc—whether they liked it or not.

As soon as Stalin turned passive exclusion into an active strategy of development, he was gaining power. He was gaining power vis-à-vis the West and vis-à-vis the East and Southeastern European partners, who—under the protection of the embargo—were driven into sovietization, which finally led to the seizure of power by the Communist Party in those countries which were governed by democratic governments until 1947/48. So the embargo and the Soviet industrialization, conceived to be antagonistic measurements, actually turned out to be a form of dialogue the Great Powers were leading by means of the Cold War.

One argument in this dialogue was the shape of the border. By imposing an embargo against the Soviet Union and Eastern Europe, the United States put economic pressure on the Soviet Union and the countries under its protection, so enforcing the old economic gap between Eastern and Western Europe. By closing the borders and erecting total border control, the Soviet Union was regaining political control over the economic function of the border between regions with different levels of economic development, which now were also regions belonging to different systems of social and economic order.[64]

## Looking at the Border Regions

### *Eastern Austria: the Soviet Occupation Zone*

The regions south and west of Vienna traditionally belonged to the industrial cores of the Habsburg Monarchy. During the Nazi occupation, new industries had been established in and around Linz, converting Upper Austria into a second economic centre of the *Ostmark*. Following the Potsdam Agreement of July/August 1945, the Allied Powers were entitled to assess the German properties in their occupation zones as reparations. At the end of the war more than 60 to 70 percent of Austria's industries belonged to German owners (in 1937, the share of German ownership was only 10 percent) and 62 percent of the German property abroad was located in Austria.[65] Immediately after the war, all occupation forces were confiscating and dismantling industrial objects under the title of captured enemy material also known as war booty.[66] While the United States, Great Britain, and France very soon made clear that they would not claim the German assets in their occupation zones, the Soviet Union, which had suffered the highest war damages, depended on reparations. A joint Soviet-Austrian administration of former German properties, which was suggested by the Soviet Union in the summer of 1945, was vetoed by the Western allies and rejected by the Austrian government.[67] In June 1946, the Soviet Union declared possession of all firms previously owned by Germans and created an administrative body, the Administration of the Soviet Property in Eastern Austria (USIA) which was under the direct control of Soviet ministries as well as planning institutions. In Lower Austria, the number of people employed in USIA firms amounted to 27 percent of those employed in industry.[68] Paradoxically, the nationalization program of the Austrian government, passed on 26 July 1946, was inspired by an attempt to prevent the Soviet assessment of German property.[69] It was supported by all Austrian parlamentarians including the deputies of the Communist Party. Whereas the Western allies did not object to its realization, the Soviet Forces prevented the nationalization of the German property from being implemented in their zone. So a considerable part of the economy was outside of Austrian influence.

Because of the Soviet occupation and because the Soviet Union controlled an important part of the economy, Eastern Austria was neglected when Western humanitarian aid was distributed right after the war.[70] Also, only a very modest share of the funds contributed by the Marshall Plan reached the eastern part of the country. The amount of ERP aid invested per capita was öS 14.600.- in Styria, öS 21.800.- in Upper Austria, öS 28.000.- in Carinthia and öS 66.000.- in Salzburg. In Vienna it was below öS 5.000.- and in Lower Austria öS 5.500.-. Only öS 407 million, that is 6.2 percent of ERP funds given

## Document 1

This identity card, issued by *Polizeidirektion Wien*, 13 June 1946, was necessary to cross the border between the Soviet and the Western occupation zones. When crossing from the Soviet to the U.S. zone, the bearer was subjected to desinfection by DDT.

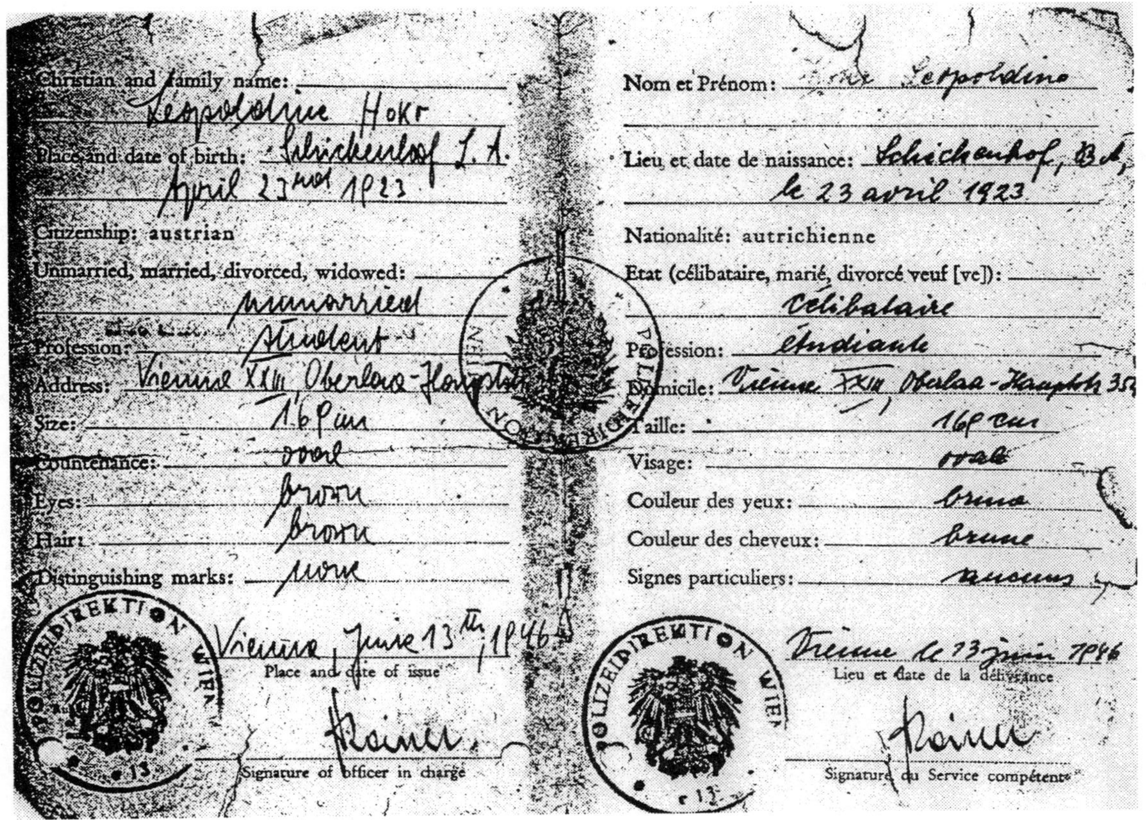

Christian and family name: Leopoldine Hokr

Place and date of birth: Schlickenhof

April 23rd 1923

Citizenship: austrian

Unmarried, married, divorced, widowed:

unmarried

Profession: student

Address: Vienna XIII Oberlaa-Hauptstr.

Size: 1.68 m

Countenance: oval

Eyes: brown

Hair: brown

Distinguishing marks: none

Vienna, June 13th, 1946

Place and date of issue

Signature of officer in charge

Nom et Prénom: Leopoldine

Lieu et date de naissance: Schlickenhof,

le 23 avril 1923

Nationalité: autrichienne

Etat (célibataire, marié, divorcé veuf [ve]):

célibataire

Profession: étudiante

Domicile: Vienne XIII Oberlaa-Hauptstr. 35

Taille: 168 cm

Visage: ovale

Couleur des yeux: brune

Couleur des cheveux: brune

Signes particuliers: aucuns

Vienne le 13 juin 1946

Lieu et date de la délivrance

Signature du Service compétent

**Source**: private.

## Document 2

This Austrian passport, issued by *Polizeidirektion Wien*, 20 May 1953, contains visas to Czechoslovakia, Eastern Germany, and Denmark (June 1953).

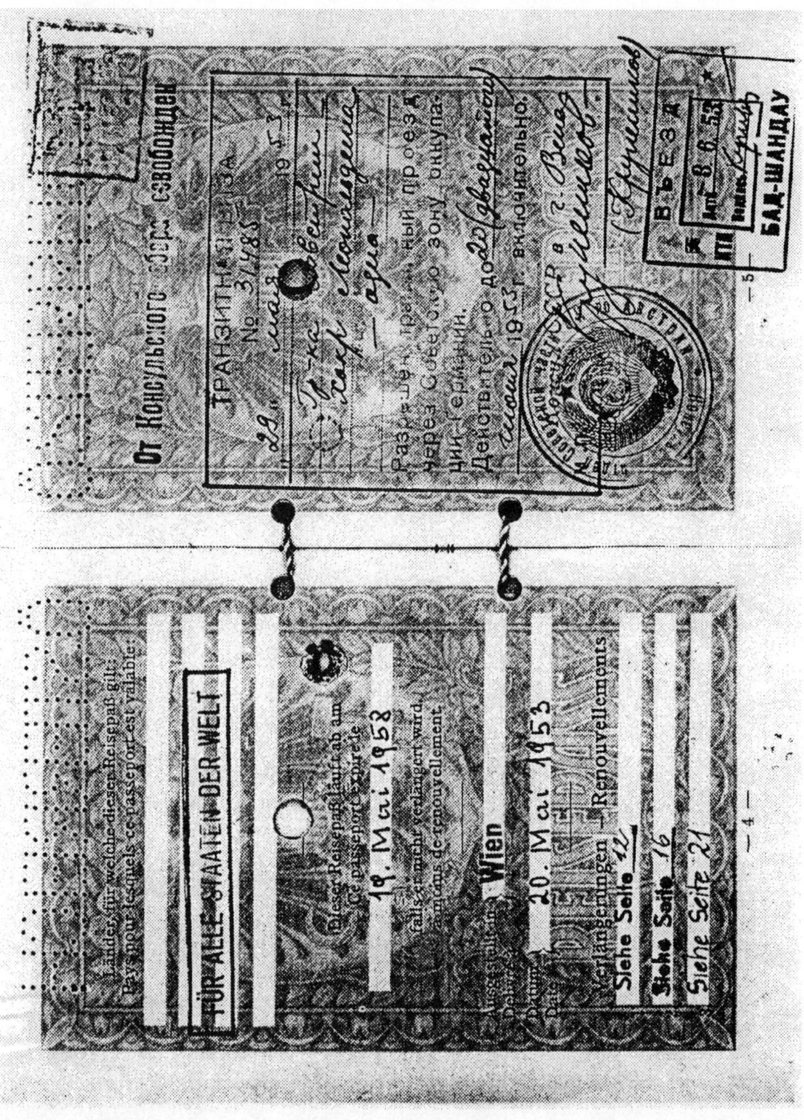

Länder, für welche dieser Reisepaß gilt:
Pays pour lesquels ce passeport est valable:

FÜR ALLE STAATEN DER WELT

Dieser Reisepaß läuft ab am
Ce passeport expire le

19. Mai 1958

falls er nicht verlängert wird.
à moins de renouvellement.

Ausgestellt in
Delivré à
Wien

Datum
Date
20. Mai 1953

Verlängerungen — Renouvellements

Siehe Seite 12

Siehe Seite 16

Siehe Seite 21

— 4 —

От Консульского сбора освобожден

ТРАНЗИТНАЯ ВИЗА

№ 31485

29 мая 1953 г.

Разрешен транзитный проезд через Советскую зону оккупации Германии.

Действительно до 20 (двадцатого) июня 1953 г. включительно.

ССР в г. Вена

ВЪЕЗД

КПП

8.6.53

БАД-ШАНДАУ

— 5 —

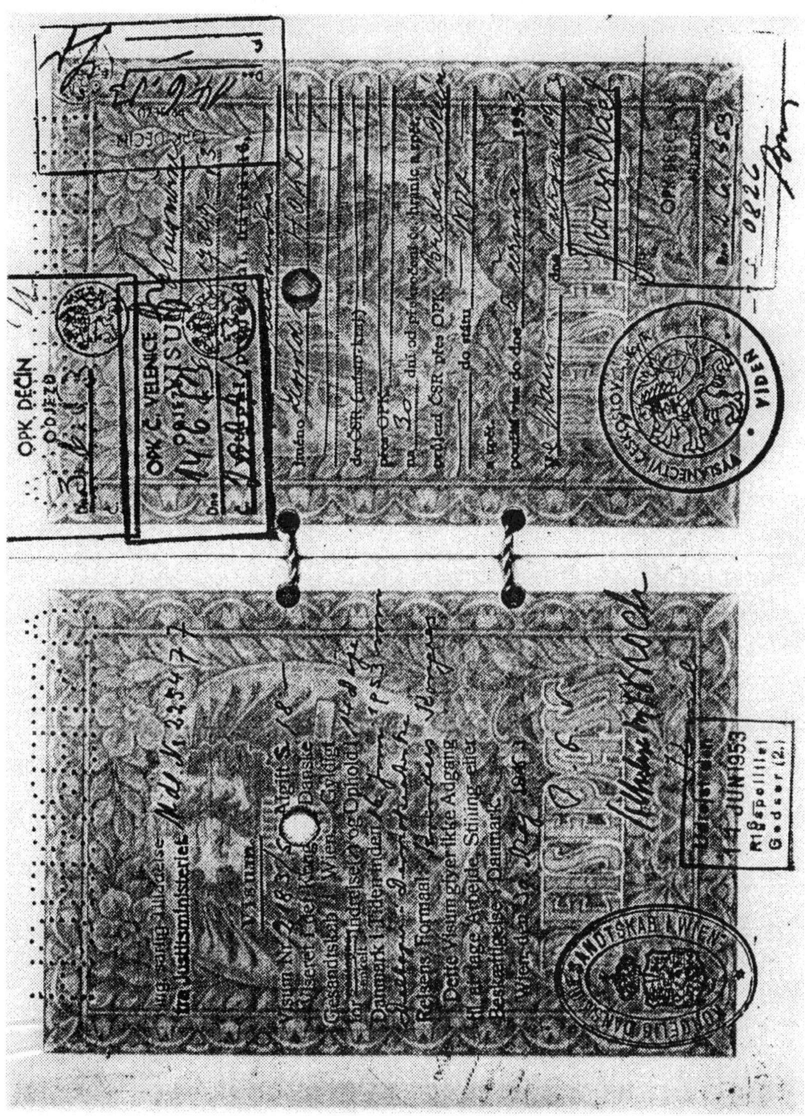


**Source**: private.

to Austria between 1948 and 1952, reached the Soviet Zone.[71] With minor exceptions, they did not reach the USIA complex at all.[72]

Factory-owners in eastern Austria were in an economically disadvantaged position. More or less excluded from Marshall Plan aid and faced with the political insecurity resulting from Soviet occupation, they were reluctant to invest and modernize. In many cases, they founded subsidiary companies in the Western zones in order to avoid political and economic risks.[73] Austrian capital was moving westwards, leaving the eastern part of the country in an often desperate economic situation. As a consequence of this neglect, the dynamics of economic development were more significant in the western parts of Austria than in the eastern ones.

The eastern region of Austria was situated between two borders. A state border separated Austria from its Czechoslovakian, Hungarian, and Yugoslav neighbors. The second border surrounding eastern Austria was the border between the Soviet and the U.S. occupation zone. At the end of the war, it was as difficult to cross it as it was to cross the state borders. Border control as well as the issue of passports and identity cards was controlled by the occupation forces. Not only did these borders restrict travelling and trade, they were also preventing Marshall Plan aid from reaching the Soviet zone.

Despite of the uneven distribution of funds, the ERP was considered to be an all-Austrian program meant to be applied in the Soviet zone as well. Any firm in the eastern zone of Austria applying for Marshall Plan funds was properly checked. It was considered to be a brigde-head in a hostile surrounding. Although the Austrian east was profiting much less from the benefits of the ERP, the enterprises located in this zone nevertheless had to accept the conditions prescribed by the Marshall Plan. They had to stick to the embargo and reorient their trade relations from their eastern neighbors to the European West. Traditionally being much more oriented towards the successor states of the Monarchy than the western regions, the imposed exchange of trade partners was causing economic disintegration and a loss of the ability to be competitive, for both individual enterprises as well as the eastern region as a whole.

The USIA companies located in the Soviet zone were regarded as being under Soviet influence and were therefore subjected to a kind of embargo similar to that of the Eastern European countries. Indeed, they represented a separate administrative body under direct Soviet control. The production of goods was first of all dedicated to supply the Soviet troops in Austria and to export scarce commodities to the Soviet Union and Eastern Europe. Trade with the West should have permitted access to hard currency. The existence of Soviet companies in a Western country could also serve as a means to undermine the embargo against the East.[74] According to an investigation on the customers of USIA products during the period from 1946 to 1955, 20 percent of the turnover was sold to other USIA enterprises, 38 percent to Eastern Europe, and 42 percent to other Austrian firms. Only 1 percent was exported to the West.[75] Especially when a USIA firm was the only supplier of a certain product, sales to Austrian firms did take place.[76] But this trade had to correspond with the general embargo regulations against the East. Raw material, for example, was only sold to a USIA firm if it guaranteed that the manufactured product would stay in Austria and not be traded with Eastern Europe.[77] In case of a USIA monopoly, however, the Austrian government was encouraged to build substitute companies with the help of the ERP in the West.[78] So USIA firms increasingly suffered from the lack of raw materials and had growing difficulties in finding Western markets. Serving as a means to realize reparations for the Soviet Union, they also were generally suffering from a lack of investment and modernization.[79] One exception to this was the oil industry, which was strongly expanding under Soviet ownership.

The border toward Eastern Europe was practically non-existent for the USIA sector. Goods were able to pass the border without being subjected to Austrian customs and international embargo regulations. This gave way to the idea of the existence of a breach in the Iron Curtain.[80] Staying beyond the control of Austrian authorities, trade with eastern countries was carried on in spite of the intensification of the strict border regime along their western borders. The more USIA firms were boycotted by Austrian and western companies, the more they were intensifying their orientation towards the East. Many of these exchanges with the East were taking place on the level of direct exchange relations out of reach of the Austrian tax authorities and border controls. The USIA complex seemed to have had a more or less extra-territorial status within the geographical limits of the Austrian state.[81]

What the Soviets had in mind for the USIA companies and what the principles were that guided their administration will hopefully be investigated by a research project under the direction of Dieter Stiefel.[82] It will for the first time open access to sources the Soviets had taken with them after the occupation ended, making possible the analysis of this sector of the Austrian economy from a Soviet point of view. In summary, the USIA complex was weakly integrated with the Austrian economy and priority was given by the Soviet administrators to the needs of the Soviet Union and its eastern partners over that of Austria. The existence of that sector was contributing towards weakening the position of Eastern Austria at a time when the Austrian West was able to rely on Marshall Plan support for its reconstruction. Thus the Eastern zone of Austria was surrounded by a double fence. Both frontiers had features resembling the characteristics of the Iron Curtain, while in other respects they were open for trade and political relations.

*Regions Along the Borders with the East*

At the end of the Habsburg Monarchy, the Austrian, Bohemian, and Moravian border regions were interconnected by close cooperation on a regional and local level. *Mühlviertel*, *Waldviertel*, and *Weinviertel* on the one side as well as the South of Bohemia and Moravia on the other, being economic peripheries, were dependent on their respective cores, above all on the capital of the Empire, Vienna. So while the economic, political, and cultural orientation of the border regions towards Vienna, Prague, Brno, and Linz was gaining importance, the local cross-border contacts were losing significance. The same applies to the Austrian regions bordering Hungary and the countries which later became Yugoslavia—with the big difference, however, that these borders were changing their course after World War I. Western Hungary became Austrian territory, forming the Burgenland, and Southern Styria was becoming part of Yugoslavia, so that the new state borders were separating regions which had formed a political unit before.

In spite of the establishment of new states after the break-up of the Habsburg Empire, the regions along the borders, whether old or newly drawn, held close relations amongst each other. Regional centers were attracting people from both sides of the borders, and children were spending a year with another family in order to learn the language of the neighbors, a phenomenon which was not restricted to state borders. On an economic level, enterprises were buying and selling across the borders as well as holding capital shares. In many cases, farmers possessed land abroad, which they could cultivate with no problem.

The peaceful cross-border contacts were terminated by the expansion of the Third Reich and the Second World War. Austria was made a province of the Reich. Hungary kept its sovereignty, becoming a satellite-like ally of Germany. In this case, the effects on the border regions stayed relatively small. The Yugoslav border region formerly being part of Styria was annexed and re-united with Styria. The Slovenian population was expelled and driven southward, completely disrupting the inter-ethnic relationships on the regional level. Following the Agreement of Munich between Germany, Great Britain, France, and Czechoslovakia, the Czech border regions, containing a majority of German-speaking people, were occupied by the *Wehrmacht* in October 1938. The Czech minority—as well as Jews and German social democrats and communists—were under pressure to leave the country, partly being replaced by new German settlers.[83] The abolition of the Austrian-Czech border was a subject of strong propaganda, celebrating the break-down of borders on a highly symbolic level.[84] At the same time, a new border line was drawn between the Reich and the Czechoslovak Republic, the Bohemian and Moravian part of which was put under German protectorate on 16 April 1939. The new political border was now more or less overlapping the ethnic situation.

After the defeat of the *Wehrmacht*, the borders prior to World War II were restored. The Potsdam Agreement foresaw the expulsion of the German-speaking population inhabiting the Czech, Slovak, Hungarian, and Yugoslav border regions, which already started at the end of the war by individual as well as organized actions of the local population and paramilitary groups. These actions often were characterized by hatred and violence against the Germans who were accused of collective responsibility for the Nazi aggression, destruction, and extermination.[85] The country the most affected by the transfer of the Germans was Czechoslovakia, where the German population reached more than three million in the interwar-period. The following considerations are therefore drawn from the Czechoslovak example.

Big tensions existed between Germans and Czechs during the First Czechoslovak Republic, and the inter-ethnic relationship had deteriorated in the 1930s. An overwhelming majority of the Czechoslovak Germans supported the *Sudetendeutsche Partei* of Konrad Henlein and welcomed Adolf Hitler annexing the border regions and breaking up the Czechoslovak State.[86] After 1938, the good relationship between Germans and Czechs, which in the border regions had resisted the nationalist hostilities for a long time, came to an end.[87] As long as Germans and Czechs cohabitated in the protectorate as well as in the border regions, contacts between the nationalites went on, however. With the expulsion of the Germans after the war, these contacts were completely severed. The contradictions along the state border, which now equally represented an ethnic and linguistic one, anticipated in many respects the separation later on enforced by the Iron Curtain.

This attitude must not be generalized, however. Between 1945 and 1948, the Austrian-Czech border region was not only characterized by spontaneous expulsions, the resettlement of the German population, and soldiers, prisoners and refugees crossing the border regions from one part of Europe to the other, but also by much economic cooperation. On the local level, the cross-border movements consisted of short-range traffic including personal visits, trade exchange, smuggling and activities linked with cross-border cultivation of land.[88] To liquidate former joint business ventures also required a lot of border crossings. The crossing of a state border at that time required a passport, the consent of the occupation forces, and a visum. Private travelling, in general, was not permitted; official and business visits were allowed only in urgent cases. Local border crossings were facilitated by special "*rasses*" legitimations issued by Soviet occupations authorities and the so-called *"Kommandaturen,"* or Austrian district authorities.

The general alienation between Czechs and Germans did not hinder economic cooperation. Immediatly after the war, Czechoslovakia turned out to be Austria's main trading partner, acounting for 40 percent of Austria's foreign trade.[89] The economic contacts suffered a great deal, since embargo regulations prior to as well as accompanying the Marshall Plan were disintegrating the exchange between Austria and Czechoslovakia on an inter-state as well as on an interregional level. The corresponding step from the Czechoslovak side, resulting in the termination of the cross-border relations, was the takeover of power by the Communist Party in February 1948. Subsequently, both sides were erecting barriers minimizing diplomatic relations, which were overshadowed by various conflicts,[90] and Austrian foreign trade with Czechoslovakia fell much below the previous share of nearly 20 percent in 1946, reaching a share of 5 percent in 1950.[91]

New trading partners in Western European countries were able to compensate for some of these losses on a supra-regional level, but not

## Document 3

This "pass" for brief border crossings was issued by Soviet authorities the district authority, in Gmünd, Lower Austria, on 2 January 1947.

**Bezirkshauptmannschaft Gmünd, N.-Oe.**

Nr. 302

# Bescheinigung

für den kleinen Grenzverkehr.

# Osvědčení

pro malý pohraniční styk.

Inhaber (Vor- und Zuname) / Majitel (Jméno a příjmění): Hauer Hilda

Geboren am / Narozen dne: 29.7.1927

in / v: Erdweis

Beruf / Povolání: Hilfsarbeiterin

Wohnort / Bydliště: Zuggers 66

Staatsangehörigkeit / Státní příslušnost: Österreich

Gültig zum Grenzübertritt / Platí k přestupu hranice

von / z: Zuggers

nach / do: Breitensee

zwecks / za účelem: Arbeit

Gültigkeitsdauer / Doba platnosti: [crossed-out handwritten entries, illegible]

Gültig nur in Verbindung mit diesem Personalausweis: 34220

Platní jen ve spojení s tímto osob. prukazem: 34220

Lichtbild

Personenbeschreibung / Popis osoby:

Gestalt / Postava: 163 cm

Gesicht / Obličej: oval

Nase / Nos: normal

Mund / Ústa: normal

Haare / Vlasy: braun

Augen / Oči: braun

Besondere Kennzeichen / Zvláštní znamení: keine

Hauer Hilde

Eigenhändige Unterschrift des Inhabers / Vlastnoruční podpis majitele osvědčení

Gmünd, am 2.1.1947

Viděl: / Gesehen:

Der Bezirkshauptmann: I.A.

Source: Dokumentationsarchiv für das Obere Waldviertel, Gmünd.

within the border regions. Finally, the contacts were terminated by the build-up of the border fortifications commonly referred to as the Iron Curtain and by the total closure of the border for private visitors by the Czechoslovak authorities following the communist take-over. During the first half of the 1950s, Czechoslovak citizens were hardly allowed to travel abroad or to welcome visitors. Later, travelling to the West was rather expensive and required many bureaucratic efforts. To cross a Western border not only required a passport and a visum, but also a permission to change hard currency or an invitation by relatives as well as an exit permit issued by the ministry of interior or exterior affairs. In the early 1950s, after the economic crisis of 1961, and after the suppression of the Prague Spring in 1968, travelling was very difficult.[92] Austrians only required a visum issued at the Czechoslovak Embassy in Vienna. A short-range border traffic did not come up again from either side. After a while, the inhabitants of the border regions almost forgot that there were people living on the other side.

Even in the case of the Iron Curtain, separation must be considered to be a process rather than a sudden split. Due to the close interactions and overlapping ownerships, farmers continued to cultivating their lands after the Cold War had broken out. People continued to visit their friends and relatives on the other side, when crossing was forbidden and the fortifications were already built. Lovers used the dark in order to meet a girl on the other side.[93] Sometimes very small incidents reported in local newspapers indicated that people were not ready to accept a political decision which destroyed their traditional freedom of action from one day to the other. In some cases, only fees, punishments, and trials could keep them from that to which they had been accustomed.

Trans-border contacts often were carried on using railway lines crossing the territory of the neighboring state. Some of these lines had been given up between 1945 and 1948. In other cases, the supra-regional traffic was dependent on their maintainance, for instance, the line connecting Gmünd, with Litschau in the Upper *Waldviertel*, the rails crossing Czech territory for some kilometers.[94] On the border between Burgenland and Hungary, the railway line connecting Mattersburg with Deutschkreuz, led through a Hungarian corridor. Although it was forbidden to leave the train in both cases, the corridor-situation offered opportunities for contacts. In the case of Gmünd the Czechoslovak authorities obliged Austria to build a new line on Austrian territory in 1950. The last train crossing Czechoslovak territory left on 17 December 1950.[95] Before this day, an Austrian signal-man had come to work every day from the Austrian border town Gmünd to the Czech town České Velenice to regulate the traffic at the railway crossings. When he once used the opportunity to smuggle sacharin, which in Austria was a scarce commodity at that time, he was arrested and fined as were the people who had bought from him.[96] His story illustrates that there were still ways to slip through the Iron Curtain. In the case of the Burgenland, the corridor train through Hungary was operating during the whole period of the Cold War. When Austrians and Hungarian emigrants wanted to get in contact with their relatives, they took a trip on the train to look at each other, wave hands, and drop letters and packets. On one day in 1957, a man could not resist jumping from the corridor train when crossing his former home region, risk arrest by Hungarian border police.[97]

Finally, the Iron Curtain was accepted as a reality which could no longer be challenged. Personal and cultural contacts were cut and regional economies lost their partners and hinterlands. There was practically no Marshall Plan aid supporting local entrepreneurs who wanted to build up their companies, which, in the majority of cases, were much too small and insignificant to attract ERP funding. Austrian authorities concentrated on economic projects in the central industrial regions, neglecting the regions on the border. So the peripheral regions along the Iron Curtain, suffering from economic peripheralization since the eighteenth century[98], were developing into veritable crises zones. Unable to make a living, people were forced to migrate or commute to the towns and industrial regions, leaving behind the villages at the border. So the Austrian border regions were undergoing a process of depopulation, thus contributing to one of the features characterizing the Iron Curtain: no man's land.

## Notes

1. Joseph Goebbels, "Das Jahr 2000," *Das Reich*, 25 February 1945, cited in: Franz Kernic, 'Der Eiserne Vorhang:' "Zur Geschichte des Stacheldrahtzaunes zwischen Ost- und Westeuropa," Der *Truppendienst* 6 (Vienna 1991): 514.

2. Ibid., 514.

3. Ibid., 515.

4. Truman in *Time*, 18 March 1946, quoted in Helmut W. Kahn, *Der Kalte Krieg, vol. 1: Spaltung und Wahn der Stärke 1945 bis 1955* (Köln: Pahl Rugenstein, 1986), 75.

5. The special case of Yugoslavia will not be dealt with in this article.

6. For an overwiew on the positions of various authors and tendencies see Günter Bischof, "Zum internationalen Stand der Marshall-Plan-Forschung: Die Forschungsdesiderata für Österreich," in *Dritte Österreichische Zeitgeschichtetage 1997*, ed. Oliver Rathkolb, et. al. (Innsbruck: Studienverlag, 1999).

7. Geir Lundestad, "Der Marshall-Plan und Osteuropa," in *Der Marshallplan und die europäische Linke*, ed. Othmar Haberl and Lutz Niethammer (Frankfurt: EVA, 1986), 69.

8. For the discussion between Gimbel and Lundestad compare Lundestad, "Der Marshall-Plan," 69; John Gimbel, *The Origins of the Marshall Plan* (Stanford: Stanford, 1976) as well as Gimbel, "Die Entstehung des Marshall-Plans" in *Der Marshallplan und die europäische Linke*, ed. Othmar Haberl and Lutz Niethammer (Frankfurt: EVA, 1986), 25-35. Gimbel's article was reprinted *in Marshall-Plan und westdeutscher Wiederaufstieg*, ed. Hans-Jürgen Schröder (Stuttgart: Franz Steiner Verlag, 1990), 11-21, with a critical answer by Manfred Knapp, "Das Deutschlandproblem und die Ursprünge des europäischen Wiederaufbauprogramms. Eine Auseinandersetzung mit John Gimbels Marshall-Plan-Thesen," 22-32, stressing the necessity to embed the Marshall Plan into the framework of the conflict between East and West.

9. Rainer Brähler, *Der Marshallplan. Zur Strategie weltmarktorientierter Krisenvermeidung in der amerikanischen Westeuropapolitik 1933 - 1952* (Köln: Pahl Rugenstein, 1983).

10. Othmar N. Haberl, "Die sowjetische Außenpolitik im Umbruchsjahr 1947," in *Der Marhall-Plan und die europäische Linke*, ed. Othmar N. Haberl and Lutz Niethammer (Frankfurt: EVA, 1986), 75-98.

11. Lundestad, "Der Marshall-Plan," 70f.

12. This quote is found in Gunnar Adler-Karlsson, *Western Economic Warfare 1947-1967. A Case Study in Foreign Economic Policy* (Stockholm: Almquist and Wiksell, 1968), 23; compare Arno Einwitschläger, *Amerikanische Wirtschaftspolitik in Österreich 1945 - 1949* (Vienna: Böhlau, 1986), 76-80; Hannes Hofbauer, *Westwärts. Österreichs Wirtschaft im Wiederaufbau* (Vienna: Verlag für Gesellschaftskritik, 1992), 84f.

13. Mutual Defense Assistance Control Act, quoted in Adler-Karlsson, *Western Economic Warfare*, 29.

14. Adler-Karlsson, *Western Economic Warfare*, 43.

15. Ibid., 51.

16. Hofbauer, *Westwärts*, 86.

17. Truman in *New York Times*, 20 December 1947, quoted in *Europa-Archiv* 3 (1948): 1267.

18. Haberl, "Die sowjetische Außenpolitik," 67.

19. Gunnar Myrdal, "Foreword, " in Adler-Karlsson, *Western Economic Warfare*, XII.

20. *Beiträge zur österreichischen Statistik* 1 (1946).

21. Alice Teichova, *Kleinstaaten im Spannungsfeld der Großmächte. Wirtschaft und Politik in Mittel- und Südosteuropa in der Zwischenkriegszeit* (Vienna: Verlag für Geschichte und Politik, 1988), 175.

22. Andrea Resch/Zdeněk Sládek, "Integrations- und Desintegrationstendenzen. Die Handelsbeziehungen 1921 - 1937," in *Österreich und die Tschechoslowakei 1918 - 1938: Die wirtschaftliche Neuordnung in Zentraleuropa in der Zwischenkriegszeit*, ed. Alice Teichova and Herbert Matis (Vienna: Böhlau, 1996), 285-304.

23. Ibid.

24. See for instance, Ernst Kübler and Anton Tautscher, *Die Lebensfähigkeit Österreichs. Untersuchungen und Ausblick* (Vienna: Stocker, 1946); Kurt Rothschild, *The Austrian Economy Since 1945* (London: Royal Institute of International Affairs, 1950).

25. *Monatsberichte des Instituts für Wirtschaftsforschung* 7 (1946): 98.

26. *Statistische Nachrichten* 2 (1947).

27. *Oberösterreichische Nachrichten*, 24 April 1948; the newspaper was founded by the U.S. forces in Upper Austria.

28. Ibid.

29. Headquarters United States Forces in Austria, USACA Section, APO 777, *U.S. Army,* Record Group (RG) 260: Memorandum "Economic Treatment of Austria," 2.1.1945, quoted in Einwitschläger, *Amerikanische Wirtschaftspolitik*, 30.

30. RG 260: "Information received form Czech sources concerning the Czech position fo Iron Ores and coal," 4.12.1945, quoted in Einwitschläger, *Amerikanische Wirtschaftspolitik*, 34.

31. RG 260: "Exchance of Iron Ore for Czech Coke," 14.12.1945, quoted in Einwitschläger, *Amerikanische Wirtschaftspolitik*, 34.

32. Ibid., 45.

33. RG 165: 4.3.1948, quoted in Einwitschläger, *Amerikanische Wirtschaftspolitik*, 46.

34. *Beiträge zur österreichischen Statistik* 1946; *Statistische Nachrichten* 1948; *Statistisches Handbuch* 1950.

35. Wolfgang Harich, *Keine Schwierigkeiten mit der Wahrheit. Zur nationalkommunistischen Opposition 1956 in der DDR* (Berlin: Dietz, 1993), 18.

36. Haberl, "Die sowjetische Außenpolitik," 82.

37. Ibid., 85.

38. Ibid., 89.

39. Lundestad, "Der Marshall-Plan," 67; Alice Teichova, "For and against the Marshall Plan in Czechoslovakia," in *Le Plan Marshall et le relèvement économique de l'Europe. Colloque tenu à Bercy les 21, 22 et 23 mars 1991 sous la direction de René Girault et Maurice Lévy-Leboyer* (Paris: Ministère des Finances, Comité pour l'histoire économique et financière de la France, 1993), 107-118.

40. Reported by the U.S.-Ambassador in Czechoslovakia, Steinhardt, to Marshall, on 10 July 1947, *Foreign Relations of the United States (FRUS)* 1947, vol. III (Washington, D.C.: Government Printing Office, 1972), 319f; Karel Kaplan, *Der kurze Marsch. Kommunistische Machtübernahme in der Tschechoslowakei 1945-1948* (Munich: Oldenbourg, 1981), 107f.

41. Lundestad, "Der Marshall-Plan," 61-67; Haberl, "Die sowjetische Außenpolitik," 84f.

42. Reported by the U.S.-Ambassador in France, Caffery, to Marshall, on 1 July 1947, *FRUS*, 1947, III, 301-303.

43. Kennan to Secretary of State Dean G. Acheson, 23.5.1947, *FRUS* 1947, III, 228.

44. Teichova, "For and Against the Marshall Plan," 112.

45. *FRUS*, 1947, III, 292, quoted in Teichova, "For and against the Marshall Plan," 116.

46. Teichova, "For and Against the Marshall Plan," 115.

47. President Beneš, speech of 6 May 1947 is quoted in Teichova, "For and Aainst the Marshall Plan," 115.

48. Eva Varga, Technische und mentalitätsgeschichtliche Aspekte des "Eisernen Vorhangs" in den Jahren 1949 - 1957; Andreas Schmidt, Motive im Vorfeld des Abbaus des Eisernen Vorhangs 1987 - 1989, both lectures held at the *conference "Die Grenze im Kopf - Annäherungen an das Phänomen "Grenze,"* Budapest, 14 - 15 April 1997.

49. Ibid.

50. Jiří Petraš and František Svátek, "Transport über die Grenze. Geschichte und Vorgeschichte der Aussiedlung der deutschen Bevölkerung aus Südböhmen 1945-1947," in *Kulturen an der Grenze. Waldviertel - Weinviertel - Südböhmen - Südmähren*, ed. Andrea Komlosy, et al. (Vienna: Promedia, 1995), 323-336; Hanns Haas, "Das Ende der deutsch-tschechischen Symbiose in Südmähren. Muster und Verlauf ethnischer Homogenisierung unter Zwang 1938-1948," in *Kulturen an der Grenze. Waldviertel - Weinviertel - Südböhmen - Südmähren*, ed. Andrea Komlosy, et al. (Vienna: Promedia, 1995), 311-322.

51. Kernic, "Eiserner Vorhang," 518.

52. *Kremser Zeitung*, Nr. 39, September 1948.

53. *Arbeiter-Zeitung*, 9 March 1949.

54. *Arbeiter-Zeitung*, 10 June 1949, 24 July 1949.

55. *Oberösterreichische Nachrichten*, 25 March 1948.

56. The following information about the Czechoslovak border system were submitted to the author by František Svátek, Prague. They are based on Czechoslovak sources and literature on the questions of security and control of the state borders.

57. *Branný zákon* (Defence Law) (Praha 1950).

58. *Tisk Národního shromáždění, přijetí zákona o ochraně státních hranic, 11.7.1951* (Negotiations of the National Assembly about the Law on the Protection of the State Borders) (Praha 1951).

59. Information by Jiří Pólak, České Velenice, April 1998. As a forest officer, Mr. Polák was responsible for cartography and forest patrol in the border zone.

60. Jenö Szücs, "The Three Historical Regions of Europe," *Acta Historica Academiae Scientiarum Hungaricae* 29, 2-4 (1983), 133.

61. See the typologies of different kinds of borders and trans-border relations in Andrea Komlosy, "Wo die österreichischen an die böhmischen Länder grenzen: Kleinraum - Zwischenraum - Peripherie," in *Kontakte und Konflikte Böhmen, Mähren und Österreich: Aspekte eines Jahrtausends gemeinsamer Geschichte*, ed. Thomas Winkelbauer (Horn: Waldviertler Heimatbund, 1993), 494-498; Martin Seger and Pal Beluszky, *Bruchlinie Eiserner Vorhang. Regionalentwicklung im österreichisch-ungarischen Grenzraum (Südburgenland/Oststeiermark - Westungarn)* (Vienna: Böhlau, 1993), 13-18.

62. Of course there were ways to overcome the embargo finally leading to its diminishing significance. At its peak between 1947 and 1953, the embargo nevertheless contributed to reduce the Western European countries' trade with Eastern Europe to a neglegible dimension. See Adler-Karlsson, *Western Economic Warfare*, 22-36, 83-89.

63. Haberl, "Die sowjetische Außenpolitik," 91; Kaplan, *Der kurze Marsch*, 102f.

64. Komlosy, "Wo die österreichischen an die böhmischen Länder grenzen," 516.

65. Otto Klambauer, *Die USIA-Betriebe* (PhD. diss., Vienna, 1978), 44-46.

66. Einwitschläger, *Amerikanische Wirtschaftspolitik*, 52; *Die USIA-Betriebe in Niederösterreich. Geschichte, Organisation, Dokumentation*, ed. Helmut Feigl, Andreas Kusternig (Vienna: Institut für Landeskunde, 1983), 5.

67. Einwitschläger, *Amerikanische Wirtschaftspolitik*, 164; *Die USIA-Betriebe*, 10f.

68. Klambauer, *Die USIA-Betriebe*, 257f; also see the Fraberger/Stiefel essay in this volume.

69. Einwitschläger, *Amerikanische Wirtschaftspolitik*, 167; Hofbauer, *Westwärts*, 31.

70. Einwitschläger, *Amerikanische Wirtschaftspolitik*, 54, 181.

71. *Jahrbuch der Handelskammer von Niederösterreich für das Jahr 1952* (Vienna: 1953), 167; also see the appendices to the Bischof essay in this volume.

72. Einwitschläger, *Amerikanische Wirtschaftspolitik*, 125.

73. *USIA-Betriebe,* 71; Andrea Komlosy, *An den Rand gedrängt. Wirtschafts- und Sozialgeschichte des Oberen Waldviertels* (Vienna: Verlag für Gesellschaftskritik, 1988), 220.

74. *Die Sowjetische Besatzungswirtschaft in Österreich. Endbericht über die Ergebnisse eines Forschungsauftrages (Wien Mai 1958)*, Niederösterreichisches Landesarchiv, Nachlaß Figl (K. 204), 21-23; USIA-Betriebe, X.

75. Sowjetische Besatzungswirtschaft, 141f.

76. *USIA-Betriebe*, 58-60.

77. Einwitschläger, *Amerikanische Wirtschaftspolitik*, 126; *USIA-Betriebe*, 78.

78. *USIA-Betriebe*, 69.

79. Sowjetische Besatzungswirtschaft, 135.

80. The picture of a gap in the Iron Curtain has often been used by contemporaries as well as analysts; see Klambauer, "USIA-Betriebe," 378.

81. *USIA-Betriebe*, 69.

82. Dieter Stiefel with Ingrid Fraberger, *Die wirtschaftlichen Interessen der Sowjetunion in Österreich 1945-1955* (Vienna: Forschungsprojekt, 1997).

83. Hanns Haas, "Die Zerstörung der Lebenseinheit 'Grenze' im 20. Jahrhundert" in *Kontakte und Konflikte Böhmen, Mähren und Österreich: Aspekte eines Jahrtausends gemeinsamer Geschichte*, ed. Thomas Winkelbauer (Horn: Waldviertler Heimatbund, 1993), 374-377.

84. See photographs showing the pulling-down of boundary posts, in *Kulturen an der Grenze. Waldviertel - Weinviertel - Südböhmen - Südmähren*, ed. Andrea Komlosy, et al. (Vienna: Promedia 1995), 76f.

85. Petraš and Svátek, "Transport über die Grenze," 323-336; Haas, "Das Ende der deutsch-tschechischen Symbiose," 311-322.

86. Jindřich Pecka, "Zwischen Okkupation und Befreiung. Bewegungen im südböhmischen Grenzland in der Zeit der nationalsozialistischen Herrschaft", in *Kulturen an der Grenze. Waldviertel - Weinviertel - Südböhmen - Südmähren*, ed. Andrea Komlosy, et al. (Vienna: Promedia, 1995), 305-310.

87. A research project under the direction of Hanns Haas, *"Verfeindete Brüder an der Grenze. Böhmen, Mähren und Niederösterreich: Die Zerstörung der Lebenseinheit Grenze 1938-1948,"* has been studying how modern nationalism ended in breaking up the local co-existence of the German and the Czech ethnicity in South Bohemian and Moravian villages.

88. Cross-border co-operation between Mühlviertel and South Bohemia are documented in Michael John, "Vom Sprachenstreit zum 'Eisernen Vorhang'. Oberösterreich und Südböhmen: Grenzen in Politik, Wirtschaft und Alltag im 20. Jahrhundert," in *Kulturen an der Grenze. Waldviertel - Weinviertel - Südböhmen - Südmähren*, ed. Andrea Komlosy, et al. (Vienna: Promedia, 1995), 104-107. For the communication across the Hungarian border with the Burgenland, see Traude Horvath and Eva Müllner eds., *Hart an der Grenze. Burgenland und Westungarn* (Vienna: Verlag für Gesellschaftskritik, 1992), 153-174.

89. *Monatsberichte des Österreichischen Instituts für Wirtschaftsforschung* 7 (1946): 98.

90. Oliver Rathkolb, "Sensible Beziehungen. Österreich und die Tschechoslowakei 1945-1989", in *Kulturen an der Grenze. Waldviertel - Weinviertel - Südböhmen - Südmähren*, ed. Andrea Komlosy, et al. (Vienna: Promedia, 1995), 79-81.

91. *Statistisches Handbuch 1950.*

92. I am grateful for information on travelling conditions provided by Jiří Dvořák (České Budějovice), Ivan Jakubec (Prague), Jiří Polák (České Velenice), Mikulaš Teich and Alice Teichova (Cambridge - Wien) and Eva Zajíčková (Studená).

93. John, "Sprachenstreit," 107.

94. Franz Drach, "Eisenbahnen im Lainsitztal," in *Die Lainsitz. Natur- und Kulturgeschichte einer Region*, ed. Andrea Komlosy and Herbert Knittler (St. Pölten: Institut für Landeskunde von Niederösterreich, 1997), 166.

95. *Waldviertler und Wachauer Nachrichten. Sozialistisches Wochenblatt für das Viertel ober dem Manhartsberg*, Nr. 51/52, 23 December 1950.

96. Information by Alfred Drach, Gmünd, April 1998.

97. Interview with a Hungarian German expelled from Hungary in 1946, winter 1996.

98. Komlosy, "An den Rand gedrängt."

# Dancing on a Tight-rope: The Beginning of the Marshall Plan and the Cold War in Austria

*Jill Lewis*[*]

In June 1950, during discussions on yet another currency crisis, Viktor Kienböck described the Austrian government's position as "dancing on a tight-rope" (*auf einem Seile tanzen*).[1] The term is apt for the whole period of Allied occupation, but most particularly for the earlier years, from 1945 to 1950. The subject of this article, the complex economic and political conditions in which the initial negotiations for Marshall Aid took place, is one example of this. This article argues that assessment of the Marshall Plan should not be limited to the economic factors stressed by the European Recovery Program, such as productivity and industrial output, nor should the political implications be confined to international politics. The Marshall Plan must also be considered in the domestic political context. This article concentrates on the food, wages, and prices crises of 1947 and 1948 and argues that during this period, when the details of Marshall Aid were being negotiated, the domestic situation in Austria was extremely dangerous. The popularity of the Marshall Plan was not as obvious as has been suggested, most notably in this initial phase. In the longer term, Marshall Aid did bring considerable benefit to the Austrian economy, but the transition from Anschluß to western

---

[*] This paper is part of a larger project on Austrian labour relations between 1945 and 1950. I would like to thank the British Academy/Leverhulme Trust for providing a Research Fellowship in 1996-97, the Austrian State Archives and the Verein der Geschichte der Arbeiterbewegung for access to documents, as well as Eleonore Breuning, Gerhard Jagschitz, Franziska Meyer, and Noel Thompson.

affluence was neither simple, nor pre-planned.[2] In particular, the concept of "tutelage," the term often used in preference to "reeducation" to describe the relationship between the Allies and Austrian politicians, is an over-simplified analysis of a complex situation, which often assumes, incorrectly, a passive role on the part of Austrian politicians.[3] On the contrary, the Austrian government after 1946 had extended, though still limited, powers. It began to display the ability to react to adverse circumstances, at times turning these to its own advantage. During the period of occupation (1945-1955), the seeds were sown for the Austrian "model" of political and economic life based on formal consensus and shared elite decision-making. This was done in the face of Soviet opposition to the westernization of the country and American suspicion of post-war European "national capitalism," which advocated economic recovery based on state intervention and full employment rather than full economic liberalization.[4] Moreover, the Austrian government was faced by critical and conflicting demands in its bid to create an independent, economically viable, and politically stable state. To achieve independence, it had to negotiate with not one but four occupying powers representing two opposing camps in the intensifying Cold War. Economic recovery required foreign/American aid, the first stage of which was provided by the United Nations Relief and Rehabilitation Administration (UNRRA) and the second under the more stringent terms of Marshall Aid. But there were also domestic considerations, primarily the need to maintain political consensus and allay serious domestic pressures for increased living standards, which ran counter to Marshall Aid criteria. The backdrop to all of this was the precarious position of Austria and the ever-present threat of Soviet expansionism, a threat which was often exaggerated by Austrian politicians, either consciously or subconsciously, both internally and in their relations with the Western Allies.

In the winter of 1944 and spring of 1945, Central Europe was "liberated" from Nazi occupation by the advancing Soviet Army. The release was a mixed blessing. By 1950, Europe had been effectively "partitioned" into East and West, with the dividing line falling across Central Europe; all that had been liberated by the Soviet army remained under Soviet dominance or influence until 1989. All to the west was heavily influenced by the United States. One exception to this rough division was the small area of the former Austrian Republic, which had been absorbed into Nazi Germany in 1938 and liberated from the east by the Soviets on 29 March 1945. Yet, unlike its neighbors who also experienced Soviet occupation, Austria did not become a Soviet satellite. In fact political power was returned to Austrian politicians with surprising speed: within weeks, the Soviet authorities asked a former Chancellor, Karl Renner,[5] to form a provisional coalition government consisting of representatives of the People's Party (ÖVP), the Socialist Party (SPÖ), and the Communist Party (KPÖ), thus confronting the other Allies with a *fait accompli* when they arrived in Vienna in the summer of 1945 from the south and west. The country was divided into four zones of occupation, each of which was administered separately for the first year: the Soviet zone consisted of Burgenland, Lower Austria and Upper Austria north of the Danube, the British of Carinthia and Styria, the American of Salzburg and Upper Austria south of the Danube, and the French of Tyrol and Vorarlberg. Vienna was also divided, but with an international zone in the center.[6] National elections were held in November 1945, after which the Communist Party's influence was reduced: it won only 5.4 percent of the vote. Six months later under the second Control Agreement, the new government was given extensive, though not absolute, jurisdiction over domestic politics and law and order. But liberation did not mean independence.

The "ambiguous" status of Austria in the war, deemed by the 1943 Moscow Declaration to be both the "first victim of Nazi aggression" and at the same time bearing "co-responsibility" for the part Austrians played in subsequent Nazi aggression, was to continue:[7] she was both "victim" and "perpetrator," "liberated" but remaining occupied under what has been termed Allied "tutelage;" her politicians were forced to prove their democratic credentials before being granted autonomy.[8] Real power lay in the Joint Allied Council which initially vetoed all Austrian legislation and, after the passing of the second Control Agreement on 28 June 1946, retained a right of veto. As a result, the authority of the Austrian State was limited for ten years by the presence of the four occupying forces, as protracted negotiations took place over an Austrian State Treaty. These negotiations were affected not only by internal developments, but also by the increasingly antagonistic relations between the Allies in the initial phase of the Cold War. Between 1949, when Germany was divided, and 1955, when the Austrian State Treaty was finalized, Austria was the only state under joint four-power occupation.[9] Her geographical position exaggerated her strategic importance: this was the European territory where East and West continued to confront each other eye-to-eye during the early years of the Cold War, the crossroads between East and West, which provided the setting of intrigue and espionage for Graham Green's *The Third Man*. The United States granted liberal Marshall Aid and sent in Mickey Mouse and Coca Cola.[10] The Soviet Union seized "German" property and unsuccessfully sought to encourage workers and unions to reject the westernization of the new state. Under occupation, Austrian politicians were engaged in an intricate and delicate political chess game designed to restore the domestic economy and political life and to regain political autonomy. In October 1955, the Allies finally and unexpectedly agreed to the Austrian State Treaty guaranteeing Austrian independence and leading to Austria's declaration of permanent neutrality, after which the Allies withdrew their troops. Austria, a country which had been dismissed as economically non-viable in 1919, destroyed by political conflict and civil war and then absorbed into Nazi Germany for seven years, later went on to become one of the most economically successful states in Europe. Such a transition appeared impossible immediately after World War II.

Major political and economic problems faced the Austrian government in 1945, all of which were compounded by the presence of four separate occupation zones; the occupation costs themselves accounted for almost 30 percent of the national budget in 1946.[11] The country had also emerged from the Second World War with a disintegrated, chaotic, and weak economy, which lacked resources, infrastructure, raw materials, markets, power and a skilled labor force. Food supplies had to be imported and paid for, and so did coal, raw materials, and power. But the currency was unstable, industrial production was dangerously low, capital investment was urgently needed, and real wages were amongst the lowest in Europe.[12] There was also a constant threat of galloping inflation. Austria depended on foreign aid, first through the United Nations and later through Marshall Aid and the European Recovery Program, aid which was intended for industrial investment to increase productivity and foreign earnings, not to pay for imported food.

Although its industrial plant had suffered less war damage than that of neighboring countries, output in the first few years remained critically low; in 1947, when a new production index was published, it showed that combined production of investment and consumer goods was 61 percent of the 1937 level, and 1937 itself had been a poor year.

Moreover, the figures showed a marked discrepancy between output of investment goods and that of consumer goods: the former had reached 84 percent of the 1937 level whilst the latter was only 42 percent of the 1937 level.[13] This could have been good news, because of Austria's dependence on foreign trade and her need to export. But in the immediate postwar years, when her balance of payments was in chronic deficit, the goods she was exporting, raw materials and semi-manufactured goods, had low added value. In the case of goods produced in Soviet-controlled plants, there was no direct benefit to the Austrian economy. Many of these goods, including oil and semi-manufactured goods, were also required by Austria's own engineering industries, where they could have earned higher added value for the export market.

Austria was exporting low value-added goods in return for power and raw materials. The chronic weakness of her consumer market meant that economic revival was dependent on the export market—the domestic market was too weak. But which markets? Austria's traditional trading area to the east was becoming increasingly closed off, and her goods were uncompetitive in western markets, many of which were facing similar problems. She also had to import consumer goods to provide essentials for the domestic market—chiefly food. The country required a stable currency, new markets, and large-scale investment to compete on the world market. By 1947, Austria had attained none of these.

The most pressing domestic problem since 1945 had been food: the population could not be fed without large-scale foreign aid. Domestic agricultural production, which had accounted for no more than 75 percent of food requirements before the war, fell yet further. In 1945, the urban population was on the point of starvation. Basic daily rations fell from 2000 calories in 1944 to between 350 and 800 calories in the spring and summer of 1945.[14] There was talk of a "hunger catastrophe".[15] During these early weeks the Viennese population was saved from actual starvation by an unrelenting diet of worm-ridden dried peas provided first by the Russians and then by UNRRA.[16] The Black Market and looting also played important roles, but the situation remained critical. A report by the United States Forces in Austria, Economics Division, written in December 1946, commented that "for over 18 months Austrian peoples [sic] have been subsisting on a near-starvation diet. Malnutrition has resulted in a serious reduction of workers' productive capacity. This too has caused a substantial delay in the previously anticipated industrial recovery."[17] Rations remained under the 2000 calorie level, considered at the time to be the minimum for a healthy diet, until the autumn of 1947.

The food problem had political as well as economic dimensions and illustrated the crucial dilemmas confronting the Austrian government in relations with its own people and with the Occupying Powers. It was faced with two specters from the First Republic—the threat of civil violence stemming from a politically divided populace and the fear of a non-viable economy. The long-term political solution to the first problem was to foster a sense of Austrian national identity, emphasizing consensus and a common struggle for reconstruction.[18] The more immediate problem was to contain the popular discontent which might result from the low standard of living and food shortages. Immediate danger was averted by UNRRA aid, which provided 64 percent of Austrian basic ration requirements between March 1946 and June 1947. However, this aid was also intended to stimulate industrial growth by increasing capital investment. It failed to do so, partly because of the severity of the food crisis: no new machinery was imported into Austria before 1948.[19] Food was heavily subsidised, leaving domestic agricultural prices far below world market prices, and adding to the supply problem: farmers complained that their incomes were low despite subsidies. In 1946, a drought caused serious disruption to domestic food production and power, which relied heavily on hydro-electric plants. This was followed by one of the severest winters on record and the 1947 harvest, the most disastrous, brought in only 44 percent of the 1937 total for wheat and rye, 30.3 percent for potatoes, and 33 percent for coarse grains such as maize, barley, and oats.[20]

Food supplies were again an acutely critical issue, and hunger demonstrations broke out in towns in all zones. Rising prices in 1946 had also led to a series of protests over wages. The reaction of the centralized Austrian Trade Union Federation (ÖGB) was to oppose *ad hoc* protests and to press the government for greater price controls. By the end of that year, as wages began to rise, there were strong indications of increasing inflation. Labor productivity, which had remained low after the war, began to fall still further, and there were demands for a stabilization of the schilling.

In 1947, the economy appeared to be spiralling into disaster, and street protests were increasing. The timing of this was unfortunate for the government; it was not the moment for civil unrest. In June 1947, as the last shipments of UNRRA aid were delivered and it became clear that the State Treaty negotiations had not achieved a speedy end to the occupation, the United States announced its plans for a new European Recovery Program (ERP)—the Marshall Plan. Based on the principle of "self-help" rather than direct aid, the plan required recipient states to submit detailed proposals for economic reconstruction based on the principles of free trade within an integrated European market. Central to these plans was the need for stable convertible currencies, reduced tariff barriers, and a commitment to invest funds in capital goods to increase industrial productivity and stimulate growth. Such sustained reconstruction, it was argued, would require short-term controls on consumption, but would, in the long term, lead to prosperity. It also required acceptance of the laws of economics as interpreted by the United States as well as acceptance of the right of U.S. agencies to oversee European economic policy. In June 1947, Austrian delegates attended the first meeting of recipient states in Paris, thereby confirming the western orientation of their economy and activity.[21] Over the next six years, Austria received 962 million dollars in Marshall Aid, one of the highest allocations in terms of aid per head of population.

The impact of Marshall Aid on the economic development of Austria and the political constraints it placed on Austrian policy-making are still a matter of debate.[22] In the context of this article, the actual implementation of the policy is not at issue; detailed plans for Austrian requirements were not drawn up until late 1947, and the first consignments of aid only appeared in March 1948. In the summer of 1947, the crucial questions were whether the Soviet Union would allow Austrian participation, having blocked moves by Poland and Czechoslovakia to join, and what effect the more stringent terms of Marshall Aid, which specifically sought to preclude spending on food in favor of investment in machinery and raw materials, would have on food supplies and rations.

The Soviet authorities did not succeed in barring Austria from joining the ERP. Protests were made in the Allied Council about the June interim aid agreement on the grounds that it violated the Moscow Declaration and undermined Austrian independence by subjugating the economy to American control.[23] This was an accusation which was also directed at the Marshall Plan and dominated Soviet and Austrian Communist Party propaganda for the following years. But the Soviet sector also benefited from American aid: plants in the Soviet sector could not be excluded from the reconstruction program, although restrictions were imposed by the ERP in order to restrict aid to projects which were essential to the Austrian economy and to prevent plants, machinery, and goods from being shipped to the east.[24]

For the government, the nub of the second problem, the effect of the terms of Marshall Aid, was how to finance reconstruction. Would the working population accept continued low wages and a low standard of living in order to allow greater capital investment, as demanded by the ERP? Official government figures attempted to show that wages had in fact kept up with rising prices, but the figures were themselves disputed, not least by local union members.[25]

There were signs that, in the deteriorating international situation, the United States was modifying its position on the seriousness of the food crisis in Austria. In June 1947, it issued interim aid of $300 million, although the urgency of the matter was not understood in Congress: the decision on an Austrian proposal to increase official rations from 1550 calories to 1800 calories in July was delayed until November while Congress prevaricated over agreeing to issue the necessary funds.

The government feared that the delay would boost support for the Communist Party in the forthcoming shop-steward elections.[26] When confronted with the 1946/47 food crisis, it was haunted by a deep-seated fear of Soviet intentions and suspicion that domestic unrest, in the shape of strikes and demonstrations, was being exploited both by the Soviet authorities and the Austrian Communist Party in order to undermine the state. Relations with the Soviet occupying forces had deteriorated steadily since 1945. Wide-spread theft, looting, and rape by Soviet troops in the early months of liberation, followed by reported waves of kidnappings, had fuelled popular animosity, which was placated neither by summary shootings of offenders nor by the dismissal of the Soviet Commandant in Austria.[27] For many Austrians, these outrages were paralleled by official Soviet policy, particularly delays in the return of Austrian prisoners of war from the Soviet Union and Soviet claims to plant and machinery. In the first three months of occupation, Soviet forces had begun to remove plant and machinery from Austrian territory as "war-booty," targeting primarily heavy industry and engineering. The issue was raised at the Potsdam Conference (17 July to 2 August 1945), when the official justification for the requisitioning switched to the question of reparations: the Allies agreed that the Soviet Union could requisition "German Property" in its

Austrian zone, although the definition of such property remained vague.[28] The legal case for this decision and its ramifications is complex and beyond the scope of this article. But the consequences for Austrian political and economic recovery were severe: Soviet exactions included not only large sections of Austrian heavy industry, engineering, chemicals, and textiles, but also the oil industry and the Danube Shipping Company. The negative effect which the seizure of "German Property" had on Austria's own economic recovery was compounded by Soviet refusal to pay taxes or to abide by Austrian trade laws. French attempts to find a solution to this problem at the first session of the Austrian State Treaty negotiations in April 1947 failed, and the issue of "German Property" remained a point of bitter contention.

In addition to the economic consequences of the Soviet occupation, there was also the question of the influence it had on Austrian workers employed in Soviet plants. In 1946, a central authority, *Upravleniye Sovietskovo Imushchestva v Avstrii* (Administration of Soviet Property in Austria—USIA) was set up to administer approximately two hundred and eighty Soviet-controlled firms, with Soviet managers overseeing fifty thousand Austrian workers. The chief objective of the USIA managers appears to have been to maximize economic gains for the Soviet Union, exporting oil, scrap iron, and steel, among other resources, to aid economic reconstruction in the East. An American report on the USIA plants written in 1948 commented that the Soviets "display a surprising partiality for short-term economic benefit as against long-term political advantage."[29] This was not a view shared openly by the Austrian government, which repeatedly argued that the USIA plants were training centers for Communist saboteurs, spearheaded by the *Werkschutz,* a factory guard of Austrian Communists variously estimated to number between 1,600 and 12,000 members, whose job was to "protect" Soviet property. The fact that these guards were armed raised another major issue—complaints by the Austrians that their own police and gendarmerie were so under-armed that they would not be able to put down a violent demonstration without Allied intervention. After one demonstration on 5 May 1947, the Austrian government made a public approach to the Joint Allied Council to demand the increased arming of the police.[30] A British military report concluded that the Viennese police failed to stop demonstrators from marching into the city because they lacked crowd control weapons. Describing a meeting between the Interior Minister,

Oscar Helmer, and the British Deputy High Commissioner in Austria, General Winterton, it went on:

> General Winterton said that in his opinion the most important question was to equip the Vienna police with some means of competing with a crowd and that for this purpose a truncheon was really more suitable than a lethal weapon. Dr Helmer agreed, but said that the rubber truncheon had a bad reputation in Vienna from Nazi days. General Winterton pointed out that the London police found a wooden truncheon satisfactory and that such a truncheon should be equally suitable for Vienna. Dr Helmer professed to disbelieve this but was nevertheless impressed by the argument and asked General Winterton to obtain sample truncheons from England.[31]

The report also stated that the British authorities had rejected a call for military intervention in the international First District, fearing that this would trigger conflict between Allied troops.

In 1947, there were also wider suspicions of Soviet intentions in Austria as relations between the Soviet Union and the United States deteriorated. The fusion of the U.S. and British zones in Germany and the announcement of the Truman Doctrine led to rumors that Soviet troops would consolidate their hold on Austria and force a partition of the country. The Communist take-over in Hungary and violent strikes in France and Italy in which Communists were involved led to fears that widespread discontent about the food situation in Austria was being exploited by the Communist Party to kindle revolt.

In 1946 and the first half of 1947, thousands of women signed petitions and joined in demonstrations demanding better rationing and greater controls on hoarding and black marketeering. The protests were led by Communist women, but found resonance in areas as far flung as Innsbruck and Klagenfurt, where Communist influence was minimal.[32] On 5 May 1947, following a month in which full food rations were not distributed, the potato ration again failed to materialize. Demonstrators from Simmering, in the Soviet zone of the city, marched into the center of Vienna and were joined by others. The demonstration turned violent. Next day in Cabinet, ministers blamed the Soviet authorities for preventing potato supplies from coming into the city and said the demonstrators were led by Communists, Greeks, and Albanians who were intent on wrecking the State Treaty negotiations and undermining the Austrian State itself. Chancellor Figl reported that the demonstration had had characteristics previously not seen in the Second Republic: a delegation of strike leaders he had met had not voiced economic grievances, but had criticized the westernization of Austrian policy. The demonstration, he argued, had been politically, not economically, motivated.[33]

The 1947 hunger demonstration was the first of several events which Austrian politicians described as Communist "putsch" attempts.[34] Fears of an imminent Soviet take-over in 1947 were not unwarranted, considering the wider political climate, but the reality of the threat of a "putsch" may have been exaggerated. As Martin Herz wrote a year later in the wake of the Czech "putsch," the organization and goals of the Austrian Communist Party were no different from those of other Communist parties in Europe—to seize power. However, the KPÖ lacked support amongst the Austrian electorate and, more important, from the Soviet Occupying Power.[35] Herz cited several examples, including agreement to the 1947 currency reforms and arbitrary increases in the price of Austrian oil, where Soviet policy directly contradicted explicit Austrian Communist Party policy, adding that "at times they [the Soviets] showed such disregard for the propaganda position of the Communists that they harmed and embarrassed them." Without Soviet support, a KPÖ putsch could not succeed. Outlining several possible scenarios in which the Soviets decided to increase pressure on Austria, Herz concluded that such action could only be deterred by a western commitment to use force, "by making its price seem high, by making bloodshed and a major incident appear the price."[36] It was a point which was frequently echoed by Austrian politicians.

The food problem, concern at the terms under which Marshall Aid would be issued, and fears of Soviet economic and political intervention and the influence this might have on grass-roots politics came to a head in August 1947 when the Austrian government took decisive action in the shape of the announcement of what was to prove the first of a series of Wages and Prices Agreements. The first agreement was designed as an *ad hoc* measure to last for three months to cool the inflationary wage tendencies and to set price increases for public utilities, which were underpriced, and for agricultural products, which had seen steep rises in May and June and showed signs of escalating still further. The rates set for public utilities went up by between 50 percent and 100 percent and those for agricultural prices were raised by an average of 58 percent. Wages were increased on a sliding scale to cover most, though not all, of the ensuing rise in the cost-of-living, with the provision that the trade unions could demand further wage increases if the actual rise in the cost-of-living index went above 10 percent. In the event it did, showing an increase of 14.5 percent by December, but the Trade Union leadership agreed to abide by the terms of the Agreement for a further twelve months.[37]

The importance of the first Wages and Prices agreement should not be exaggerated. In economic terms, it managed to hold down wage increases, but was less successful in controlling prices. Nor did it solve the immediate food crisis, despite arguments that the increase in agricultural prices would discourage farmers from selling on the Black Market and so release more domestic food onto the legitimate market. (The ability to raise rations was dependent on United States aid, as was shown earlier.) Finally, the Wages and Prices Agreement did not stop wage or food protests. In November 1947, a series of strikes broke out in the British zone in Styria when local shortages of milk and fat supplies led to cuts in the rations. The strikes occurred in Fohnsdorf, Donawitz, Zeltweg, and Eisenerz, all in plants with Communist shop-stewards and, according to the British, were orchestrated to boost support for the Austrian Communist Party in the forthcoming shop-steward elections.[38] But the Communists were not the only people to object to wage restraints, as the 1948 shoemakers' strike and protests at successive Wages and Prices Agreements were to show.

The real significance of the first Wages and Prices Agreement lay in the way in which it was drawn up. The terms of the Agreement had been negotiated by representatives of the three Chambers of Labor, Trade, and Agriculture, and leaders of the Austrian Trade Union Federation. Their recommendations were sent to the government's Economic Committee and submitted to the Cabinet for ratification on 29 July 1947. Despite earlier disagreements over the conflicting importance of living standards and increased prices, all sides agreed to a compromise. This is an early example of elite consensus, then new to Austria, which became the basis of its postwar political stability and economic recovery. Two specific aspects of this are of particular importance. The first is the role which non-elected bodies were given in shared decision making at an important macro-economic level. The second is the role of the leaders of the Trade Union Federation, who continued to support the need for wage restraint as a necessary step on the road to economic recovery. Their most vociferous critic was the Communist Party, which linked the Wages and Prices Agreement with the demands laid down by the United States regarding aid and the westernization of the economy. From 1947 onwards, labor conflicts in Austria were increasingly identified by both the government and the Trade Union Federation as attacks on the state itself. Equally significantly, the Austrian government had used the authority invested in it by the second Control Agreement to legislate on prices and wages and to produce an economic framework which began as a short-term solution to a specific crisis.

The existence of this framework did not prevent political and economic interests from competing. In both 1949 and 1950, there is evidence that disagreement between the political parties over the Third and Fourth Wages and Prices Agreements seriously threatened the stability of the coalition government.[39] In the case of the Fourth Wages and Prices Agreement, the minutes of the government economic committee show that as late as July 1950, just six weeks before the Agreement was announced, there was considerable reluctance to resort to yet another round of wage controls.[40] Since the 1949 agreement, there had been many reports of large-scale popular discontent over wages and rising prices. So why take the risk? The answer lies in the proposed reductions in Marshall Aid and delays in the release of Counterpart funds in 1950, which necessitated the removal of subsidies and the regulation of the exchange rates through which the subsidies had been maintained. In August and September 1950, as the details of the Fourth Wages and Prices Agreement were being worked out, there were frequent meetings with John Giblin, the acting head of the ECA mission in Vienna, to ascertain the U.S. attitude toward specific Austrian proposals for raising grain and fodder prices and for currency reform.[41] The Austrian government did not set the economic agenda, and its economic policy required U.S. approval. But the mechanism for drawing up policy by close consultation with the Chambers and trade unions deflected open public criticism and debate at moments of economic crisis, and presented a united front to the electorate and so reduced potential political conflict. It was crucial for the development of labor politics in the Second Republic.[42] Moreover, the threat posed by the presence of the Soviet occupation forces and the weakness of the Austrian Communist Party created a situation in which a Communist putsch was unlikely, but could not be ruled out. This was useful in Austrian negotiations with the Americans over the speed and degree of economic "liberalization" and the use of Counterpart funds.[43] One example of this occurred in December 1950, when the United

States government released ÖS 50 million of Counterpart funds to alleviate unemployment in the light of the "high unemployment in Austria which is increasing in a politically dangerous manner."[44]

The success of the Marshall Plan in Austria was not a foregone conclusion in 1948. The domestic situation was unstable, and the presence of mutually hostile occupying forces exacerbated this. In addition, the initial terms of Marshall Aid sought to shift investment away from food to capital investment—itself highly dangerous. It was in this situation that one of the early roots of the Social Partnership developed, but the question remains, what influence did this have on the decision-making process in Austria and on the political culture and language of the Second Republic?

## Notes

1. Kienböck had been Minister of Finance and president of the Austrian National Bank in the First Republic. The comment was made during a meeting of the Wirtschaftliches Ministerkomitee, on which he sat as an adviser. Archiv der Republik (AdR), Bundeskanzleramt (BKA), Wirtschaftliches Ministerkomitee Protokolle (WiMiPro), Sitzung 76, 20 June 1950.

2. Alan Milward cites Austria as one of the two states where Marshall Aid made a substantial contribution to economic recovery. Alan S. Milward, *The Reconstruction of Western Europe, 1945-1951* (London: Routledge, 1992), 92.

3. This point was made by Robert Knight, "Besiegt oder befreit? Eine völkerrechtliche Frage historisch betrachtet," in *Die bevormundete Nation: Österreich und die Alliierten 1945-49*, ed. Günter Bischof and Josef Leidenfrost (Innsbruck: Haymon, 1988), 75-92.

4. The reference is to Fred Block, quoted in Robert Wood, "From the Marshall Plan to the Third World," in *Origins of the Cold War: An International History*, ed. Melvyn P. Leffler and David S. Painter ( London and New York, 1994), 206-7.

5. Karl Renner had been the Socialist president of the last elected parliament, which was prorogued by Chancellor Dollfuss in March 1933. The Soviet decision to ask Renner to form the first provisional government was unexpected: Renner had been on the right wing of the *Sozialdemokratische Arbeiter Partei* (SDAP) and had publicly and controversially supported Anschluß in 1938. See Anton Pelinka, *Karl Renner zur Einführung (*Hamburg: Junius, 1989) and Manfried Rauchensteiner, *Der Sonderfall: die Besatzungszeit in Österreich 1945-1955* (Graz: Styria, 1995), 66-75.

6. For details of war-time Allied plans for a post-war Austria, see Rauchensteiner, *Der Sonderfall*, 15-45.

7. Günter Bischof, "Die Instrumentalisierung der Moskauer Erklärung nach dem 2. Weltkrieg," *Zeitgeschichte,* 11/12 (November/December 1993): 345-366.

8. For a fuller criticism of the use of the term "tutelage," see Robert Knight, "Narratives in Post-war Austrian Historiography," in *Austria 1945-1955: Studies in Political and Cultural Re-emergence,* ed. Anthony Bushell ( Cardiff: University of Wales Press, 1996), 11-36. The term "tutelage" (*Bevormundung*) has been adopted by many Austrian historians in preference to the German term re-education (*Umerziehung*).

9. For details of the treaty negotiations, see Gerald Sturzh, *Geschichte des Staatsvertrages 1945-55: Österreichs Weg zur Neutralität,* 3rd. ed. (Graz: Styria, 1985). For an example of differences about who was responsible for the delays in reaching a settlement, see the articles by Günter Bischof and Oliver Rathkolb in *Austria in the Nineteen-fifties,* vol. 3, *Contemporary Austrian Studies* (New Brunswick: Transaction, 1995).

10. Reinhold Wagnleitner, *Coca-Colonisation und Kalter Krieg: Die Kulturmission der USA in Österreich nach dem Zweiten Weltkrieg* (Vienna: Verlag für Gesellschaftskritik, 1991).

11. Ernst Hanisch, *Der lange Schatten des Staates. Österreichische Gesellschaftsgeschichte im 20. Jahrhundert. Österreichische Geschichte 1890-1990* (Vienna: Ueberreuter, 1994), 407.

12. K.W. Rothschild, *The Austrian Economy Since 1945* (Aberdeen: University Press, 1950).

13. Ibid.

14. Roman Sandgruber, "Vom Hunger zum Massenkonsum," in *Die "wilden" fünfziger Jahre,* ed. Gerhard Jagschitz and Klaus Dieter Mulley (Vienna: Verlag Niederösterreichisches Pressehaus, 1985), 112.

15. The provisional government set up a Food Office on 27 April 1945. A report on the food situation to the SPÖ conference in 1949 argued that the breakdown in domestic food supplies had been the result of the relaxation of draconian Nazi controls on agriculture and unresolved currency problems. Bericht an den Parteitag, Volksernährung 1945-1949 (18.11.1949). Schärf Papers, Box 44 4/294, Verein der Geschichte der Arbeiterbewegung, Vienna.

16. Irene Bandhauer-Schöffmann and Ela Hornung, "Geschlechtsspezifische Auswirkungen von Hungerkrise und 'Freßwelle'," in Thomas Albrich et al., eds., *Österreich in den Fünfzigern* (Innsbruck: Österreichischer Studien-Verlag, 1995), 15-19. This fascinating article stresses the role women played in the reconstruction and also subsequent selective memory: the peas were invariably wormridden and were always associated with the Russians in popular memory. The Russians later demanded repayment for this emergency relief. Rauchensteiner, *Der Sonderfall*, 64.

17. "Austria's Import Requirements and Balance of Trade for the year 1947 (To be referred to as "Project R")," prepared by Economics Division USACA Section, Headquarters, United States Forces Austria. AdR, BKA/AA, WPol.Wi.Europe, 1947. Box 87, Marshallplan.

18. See Robert Knight, "Narratives."

19. OEEC report, Paris 19 July 1949. AdR, Bundesministerium für soziale Verwaltung (BMfsV), Section III, Sa. 11, Box 216, 12932/III.

20. Rothschild, *The Austrian Economy Since 1945*, 29.

21. Wilfried Mähr, *Der Marshallplan in Österreich* (Graz: Styria, 1989), 74-80.

22. See Mähr, *Der Marshallplan*, and Hannes Zimmermann, "Wirtschaftsentwicklung in Österreich 1945-51 am Beispiel der Lohn-Preis-Abkommen und des Marshallplans" (Ph.D. diss., Vienna University, 1983).

23. Reinhold Wagnleitner, ed., *Understanding Austria: The Political Reports and Analysis of Martin F. Herz* (Salzburg: Wolfgang Neugebauer Verlag, 1984), 260-61.

24. Ibid.

25. Zimmermann, "Wirtschaftsentwicklung," 148-154.

26. Unsigned letter to the Austrian special envoy in Washington, 19 September 1947, BKA/AA, W.Pol. Wi. Eur. Box 87.

27. Marshal Tolbukhin, Soviet Commander in Austria from April 1945, was reported to have been relieved of his command in the summer of 1945 because of the behavior of his troops at this time. NA, RG 59, 740.00119 Cont. (Aust)/ 11-2345. Quoted in Oliver Rathkolb, ed., *Gesellschaft und Politik am Beginn der zweiten Republik* (Vienna: Böhlau, 1985), 342.

28. Wilfried Aichinger, "Die Sowjetunion und Österreich 1945-49" in Bischof and Leidenfrost (eds.), *Die bevormundete Nation*, 274-292.

29. The report was written by Martin F. Herz, then Second Secretary of the American Legation in Vienna. His edited papers have been published in Wagnleitner, ed. *Understanding Austria*: p. 606.

30. AdR, BKA Ministerrats-Protokolle (Minratpro), Sitzung 67, 6 May 1947. Anton Staudinger, "Zur Geschichte der B-Gendarmerie," *Öst. Milit. Zeitschrift* 5 (1972): 343-348. Rauchensteiner says that the *Werkschutz* was first set up in April or May 1946. Rauschensteiner, *Der Sonderfall*, 228.

31. ACABRIT to Foreign Office (German Section), 15 May 1947. Foreign Office (FO)/1020/245, Public Record Office (PRO), London.

32. Siegfried Mattl, "Frauen in Österreich nach 1945" in Rudolf G. Ardelt et al., eds., *Unterdrückung und Emanzipation*: *Festschrift für Erika Weinzierl* (Vienna: Geyer-Edition, 1985), 101-126.

33. Minratpro, Sitzung 67, 6 May 1947. It was after this demonstration that the Austrian government asked for the increased arming of their police.

34. Adolf Schärf in Günter Bischof, " 'Prag liegt westlich von Wien': Internationale Krisen im Jahre 1948 und ihr Einfluß auf Österreich," quoted in Bischof and Leidenfrost, eds., *Die bevormundete Nation*, 315-347.

35. According to the minutes of a meeting between Andrej Zhdanov and Austrian Communist leaders on 13 February 1948, Zhdanov rejected an Austrian Communist request for Soviet forces to remain on Austrian territory, saying that "the independence of the country cannot be based on the presence of foreign forces" and that without a defense of "national sovereignty" the Austrian Communist Party would have no future. S. Pons, "The Twilight of the Comin-

form," in *The Cominform. Minutes of the Three Conferences 1947/1948/ 1949*, ed. G. Procacci (Milan: Feltrinelli, 1994), 489-90.

36. Wagnleitner, *Understanding Austria*, 606.

37. This was despite criticisms of the way in which the cost of living index was calculated. See Zimmermann, "Wirtschaftsentwicklung," 148-154.

38. PRO, FO/1020/113. Short Brief on Industrial Unrest in Styria, 16 October 1947.

39. In a personal memo Adolf Schärf commented on ÖVP astonishment at the SPÖ agreement to the Third Wages and Prices Agreement: "It is being asserted in ÖVP circles that what has been achieved as a result of the new wages and prices agreeement, in addition to the economic gains which it has proved possible to obtain through this agreement for industry, trade and agriculture in the shape of price roll-overs etc., is above all that the SPÖ has been definitively put at a political disadvantage. The ÖVP are therefore describing the Wages and Prices Agreement not only as an economic success for those represented by the ÖVP, but above all as a political triumph, which will mean attaining a majority in the elections, and a substantial and irretrievable loss of votes by the SPÖ." [*"Man erklärt in ÖVP Kreisen, daß es nunmehr durch das neue Lohn- und Preisabkommen endgültig gelungen sei, neben den wirtschaftlichen Vorteilen, die man durch dieses Abkommen, durch die Preisüberwälzungen usw. für die Industrie, Gewerbe und bäuerlichen Kreise herausholen konnte, vor allem die SPÖ dadurch endgültig politisch in die Hinterhand zu bringen.... Man bezeichnet daher das Lohn- Preisabkommen von seiten der ÖVP nicht nur als einen wirtschaftlichen Erfolg für die von der ÖVP vertretenen Kreise, sondern vor allem als einen politischen Triumpf der die Erringung der Mehrheit bei den Wahlen und einen nicht aufzuholenden erheblichen Stimmenverlust der SPÖ bedeutet."*] Schärf Papers, Box 43 4/283. No date (c. June 1949).

40. BKA. WiMiPro, Sitzung 77, 4 July 1950.

41. Minutes of inter-party discussions show that the Americans were being consulted about the price of grain on 31 August 1950. Schärf Papers, Box 20 4/134, Parteibesprechungen. Lohn- und Preisfrage. Giblin met Austrian finance ministers on 1, 5 and 26 September, Schärf Papers, Box 20 4/135.

42. On 24 August 1950 Otto Probst wrote a letter to the editor of the Tyrolean newspaper, *Volkszeitung*, conveying Johann Böhm's displeasure at the publication of an article on wages: "He [Böhm] thinks that it would be dangerous for our Party press to start making trouble over the wages question." ["*Er* [Böhm] *meint, daß es gefährlich sei, wenn unsere Parteipresse in der Lohnfrage zu zündeln beginnt.*"] The editor replied that "what is said in this article expresses in a subdued way what shop stewards have been saying at all the conferences." ["... *die Feststellungen dieses Aufsatzes sprechen in einer gedämpften Form aus, was die Vertrauensmänner in allen Konferenzen ... ausgesprochen haben.*"] Probst Correspondence, SPÖ Documents, Verein der Geschichte der Arbeiterbewegung, Vienna.

43. In December 1950, the Austrian envoy, Kleinwächter, reported that he had received confidential information from the U.S. State Department. The American government is prepared to assist Austria in a productive campaign against unemployment and has released fifty million Austrian Schillings for building projects. The State Department has asked whether an early further release of 100

million Schillings is desired." ["... *habe vom amerikanischen State Department die vertrauliche Mitteilung erhalten.... Die amerikanische Regierung wäre bereit Österreich bei der produktiven Bekämpfung der Arbeitslosigkeit zu unterstützen und hat aus den Counterparts 50 Millionen öS für Bauten freigegeben. Das State Department fragt an, ob eine baldige weitere Freigabe von 100 Millionen öS erwünscht wäre.*"] BKA/AA. W.Pol/50, Wi Europa, Gz 142429, "Freigaben aus Counterpartsfonds," 16 December 1950.

44. "[der] *starken und politisch bedrohlich zunehmenden Arbeitslosigkeit in Österreich* ..." Ibid.

# "Caught Between *Iwan* and the *Weihnachtsmann*": Occupation, the Marshall Plan, and Austrian Identity

*Matthew Paul Berg*

> A Russian soldier was fishing from one bank and an American from the other along the Enns River. The Russian soldier took the fish he caught and killed them by dashing their heads against a rock. The American took his off the hook and stroked them. The Russian asked if that wasn't the wrong way to go about it, to which the American replied: "They die this way, too."[1]

For many effective jokes, the element of truth is what often lends a story its humor. In this case, the truth conveyed is the prevailing sense among Austrians that, during the occupation years, the very existence of the Austrian state and society were contingent upon either the whim or the cold calculations of Soviet policy on the one hand, and the sugar-coated, largely U.S.-led power politics of the Western Allies on the other. Moreover, it is consistent with the Austrian notion of victimization—first as a result of the Anschluß, then at the hands of those who had "liberated" them but deferred the restoration of Austrian sovereignty as promised in the Moscow Declaration of autumn 1943.

Outstanding scholarly work has been done on Austrian circumstances within the context of great power politics, most prominently in the areas of diplomacy,[2] denazification,[3] and economic issues (reparations, nationalized industry, and USIA).[4] Rather less has been undertaken in the way of inquiry into the experiences of occupation—partly because the results seem somehow more impressionistic and less tangible, partly because the techniques of oral history have become more refined and thus only recently more widely-accepted. This essay explores ways in which the experiences of Soviet and U.S. occupation may have contributed to a sense of "Austrianness" between 1945 and 1955. Taking as my point of departure the tension between the nurturing and violation of the individual's democratic rights and protections as they are stated or implied in the *Bundesverfassungsgesetze*, rather than a concern with issues related to the violation of state sovereignty, I explore the circumstances under which contact with Soviet and U.S. authorities contributed to cultural and political perceptions, and address the Marshall Plan as a significant contribution to Austrian identity formation in the early postwar years.

On the one hand, violations of fundamental rights such as freedom of expression, the right to private property, and the safeguarding of the person against arbitrary search and seizure, arrest, or violence perpetrated by the Soviet occupation forces helped shape prevailing opinion towards the USSR and reflected badly on the weak and widely-scorned Austrian communists. On the other hand, the initial postwar food relief provided primarily from U.S. storehouses and, later, the finances and materiel advanced by U.S. authorities won a high degree of support from the Austrian public. Such aid did not come without what some critics characterized as the sting of American arrogance or the shallowness of U.S. consumer democracy. Nonetheless, U.S. aid and the generally positive Austrian response to the behavior of Western troops, as compared to that of Soviet troops, reinforced for Austrians the long-standing conviction that Austria was a bulwark of Western culture and values set against the twentieth century threat from the east, Soviet-style socialism.

## Rape, Robbery, and Other Crimes

"To the victors go the spoils" may be a centuries-old maxim, but the unprecedented destruction of human lives and property between 1941 and 1945 brought to it a meaning hitherto unknown. For the Soviets, in particular, both defense of the homeland against a merciless invader and Manichaean ideological considerations contributed to the bitterness of the war, and the Soviet government demanded thorough compensation for the extensive damages suffered. The behavior of Soviet soldiers, and to a lesser extent that of western Allied troops, makes plain that many individual soldiers were determined to seize their own personal share of the spoils through acts of bullying and thievery, or continued to take the war to the German and Austrian populations—very frequently under the influence of alcohol—once hostilities ceased. As a result, rape, intimidation, robbery, and kidnapping became an enduring source of menace or awful realities for the inhabitants of German-speaking Europe between 1945 and 1955. In practice, the Moscow Declaration's statement of Austria-as-victim of aggressive Nazi Germany's foreign policy resulted in rather little difference between the way many Soviet soldiers, and the Soviet occupation regime on the whole, dealt with individual Austrians or eastern Germans.

Unquestionably, this occupier/occupied dynamic is more complex than the characterization of Russians as beastly and the Austrians as continually put-upon. Margarete Hannl has made a strong case for rethinking the coexistence between Soviet troops and Austrian civilians in her careful revisionist study of everyday life in the *Mühlviertel*, while Klaus-Dieter Mulley's examination of everyday life in Lower Austria between 1945-1948 concludes that in every fundamental respect (the workings of the military government and its interaction with the *Landesregierung*, quartering troops; requisition of goods and robbery; rape; the Soviet role in denazification), Soviet forces were regarded as occupiers rather than liberators.[5] While acknowledging that exceptions clearly existed to the prevailing *Feinbild* of the Soviet occupation forces, I suggest that, for most Austrians, violent behavior served both to confirm Nazi-era perceptions of Russians and other Soviet peoples for some and reinforced anti-communist sentiments in the new Second Republic that had been deeply-rooted since 1918. As Anton Pelinka has argued, the fact that the majority of the Austrian population thoroughly identified the Austrian Communist Party (*Kommunistische Partei Österreichs*, KPÖ) with the Soviet occupation regime served frequently to embarrass the KPÖ. While they could hardly have approved of the misbehavior of Soviet soldiers, the Austrian Communists knew that without the Soviet Military Administration they were politically insignificant. Thus, they were compelled to stand largely uncritically—and at times uncomfortably—on the side of the Soviet Union, supporting its policies and ignoring its excesses.[6]

Recent scholarship has shed new light on the long-taboo subject of rape in both eastern Germany and eastern Austria.[7] The extent of the phenomenon was frighteningly widespread. Atina Grossmann estimates that between 100,000 and almost one million women were raped in Berlin alone; the higher figure taking into account women who were attacked repeatedly. All told, Grossman surmises that perhaps 1.9 million women were rape survivors in Soviet-occupied Germany; furthermore, Norman Naimark suggests that smaller towns tended to suffer most severely from such attacks by Soviet troops (and even junior officers), even though this behavior sometimes met with swift and occasionally deadly punishment meted out by Russian commanders.[8] Rape was, indeed, perpetrated by western soldiers too, albeit far less frequently. While none of the Western Allies' armies were above reproach, those cited more frequently in rape incidents were generally French colonial troops or U.S. servicemen, yet their numbers pale in comparison to those on the Soviet side.[9]

In Eastern Austria, the circumstances were no different. Mass rape was attributed solely to Soviet soldiers among those Marianne Baumgartner interviewed for her study of conditions in Vienna and Lower Austria during 1945. The same fear of, and disgust with, "Asiatic" Soviet soldiers was expressed by German women, to no small degree the product of traditional notions fears harbored by self-proclaimed "civilized people" towards alleged "Asiatic barbarians" (Huns, Turks, etc.)[10] and reworked via National Socialist propaganda, and was expressed vividly in the recollections of Austrian women who lived through the worst of the rampant period of rape during the several months following the conclusion of hostilities.[11] This experience must have had the effect of confirming elements of racist thinking among many people who experienced Red Army excesses, and left men and women alike without any particular fondness for the Soviet occupation forces or for communism, although their antipathy towards the latter had deeper roots. The research of Atina Grossman and Maria Mesner suggests interesting continuities between pre- and post-1945 attitudes in another, closely-related respect. Abortion procedures were made readily available by German and Austrian authorities in cases where women had become impregnated as a result of rape by Soviet soldiers, and were based on National Socialist legal guidelines for dealing with *Rassenschande*.[12] While pregnancies that resulted from either rapes committed by western soldiers or voluntary union with them were often considered only marginally less disgraceful under prevailing Austrian opinion, Mesner points out that the termination of such pregnancies was rarely permitted.[13]

Closely linked to the issue of *Rassenschande* was what Marianne Baumgartner isolates as the patriarchal element central to "rape syndrome": the marked tendency for men throughout Lower Austria (certainly in Vienna as well) to harbor deep-seated resentment towards the Red Army for having emasculated them by "devaluing" their women. This widespread male perception of Austrian women who had survived rape as "damaged goods" was undoubtedly reinforced by the staggering increase in cases of sexually-transmitted disease among women who had come into contact with Soviet troops.[14] Soviet soldiers, themselves, could only rarely have understood their actions as a form of ethnic cleansing, yet the phenomenon of mass rape seems to have been interpreted in terms not entirely dissimilar to these by Austrian men. Moreover, taking German-speaking women may have been seen as part and parcel of the victors' spoils, through which revenge would be wrought upon Germans (and to a lesser, but still large extent on Hungarians as well). By contrast, Soviets soldiers tended to regard Slavic societies as having been liberated rather than defeated, and it has been suggested that this may help account for only rather limited incidence of rape in Poland, Bulgaria, parts of Yugoslavia, and in Czechoslovakia.[15]

There were exceptions to characterizations of Soviet soldiers as brutal and barbaric, of course. Atina Grossman notes that many German women remembered cases of "the cultivated officer who spoke German, had memorized Dostoyevsky and Tolstoy, deplored the excesses of his comrades, and could be relied upon for protection even as he sought to educate his captives about German war crimes." On the other hand, "'cultivated' status was rarely achieved by the American occupiers, who were persistently categorized as primitive and vulgar, even if not so dangerous, since they could supposedly achieve their conquests with nylons and chocolate rather than by rape." Indeed, one of Grossmann's sources recalled that, within her circle of friends, prevailing wisdom on the difference between eastern and western occupiers was "the Americans and the British ask the girls to dinner and then go to bed with them, while the Russians do it the other way round."[16] Ingrid Bauer's investigation of relations between women in the province of Salzburg and the American occupiers points to concerns that would, in part, corroborate these perceptions. Women who took up with American soldiers, whether to secure a higher standard of living, out of loneliness, or because of love, were castigated by returning demobilized *Wehrmacht* soldiers as "Ami whores" whose favors *often were*, in fact, purchased with nylons and chocolate.[17]

The worst of the Soviet mass rape epidemic seems to have abated by the end of 1945, the result of a somewhat greater enforcement of discipline. In a rather rare instance in Freistadt, within the Soviet-occupied portion of Upper Austria, the mayor and city council entered into negotiations with the Russian commandant to create a brothel for Soviet troops, effectively reducing the rape of Austrian women to isolated incidents.[18] This seems to have been an anomalous solution, however. Although rapes did occur in the three western zones into the later 1940s and early 1950s, widespread sexual assault remained a concern endemic to the Soviet occupation zone.

The literature on Soviet troops in eastern Germany and in eastern Austria invariably associates the occurrence of rape with heavy binge drinking in most instances. For example, Naimark notes that while soldiers in each of the occupation armies drank to excess,

> [i]t was not the amount that Soviet soldiers drank that proved so disastrous for women—in comparison, for example, to how much American soldiers drank—but rather the way they drank. As scholars of Russian drinking habits have repeatedly noted, Russians drink in binges, reaching a stage of intense intoxication over a period of several days, and then they are quite sober before the next binge. The availability and high quality of alcohol available in Germany did not help the situation.[19]

Hannl dismisses this as a stereotype in her examination of Soviet occupation of the *Mühlviertel*, although Soviets troops were characterized as wild drinkers and extraordinarily dangerous even in Russian accounts of 1945 and the occupation years, for example in the work of Lev Kopelev, not merely in those accounts provided by Austrian or German writers. This linkage of Soviet criminality with excessive alcohol consumption is significant in that it was central to the perception of the occupied populations who experienced excesses of rape, other forms of physical violence, destruction of property, or theft. According to U.S. Office of Strategic Services' report from Vienna during the summer of 1945, the arbitrariness of such violence, through which "[t]he womenfolk and the property of men back from concentration camps, of many Jews, of pro-Soviet adherents, and of Communists were violated equally with those of Nazis and of 'bourgeoisia' [sic]," was said to stimulate the strongest of emotional reactions among the Viennese and colored their perceptions of Soviet control significantly.[20] Alcohol was a factor in the behavior of Soviet soldiers in a large number of such cases throughout the occupation years according to Austrian police and newspaper reports.

Careful analysis of the extensive catalogue of criminal reports involving all four occupation powers compiled by the *General Direktion für öffentliche Sicherheit* during the course of 1946 reveals a staggering number of cases involving "men in Russian uniform"—well over ninety percent of the year's entire caseload, and quite frequently linked to alcohol consumption. Among these reports were undoubtedly the occasional instances of Austrian criminals masquerading as Soviet troops. Americans were responsible for most of the 5 to 7 percent of crimes not committed by "men in Russian uniform" during 1946, followed by French and then British soldiers, and the incidents reported tended to involve brawls between the soldiers of rival nationalities or with Soviet troops. Reports concerning members of the Western occupation armies bullying or intimidating Austrian civilians usually involved verbal harassment in the street or in a bar, the occasional fist fight, and incidents of property damage in bars, restaurants, or cafés; the soldiers involved were most often inebriated. The Soviet-sponsored *Österreichische Zeitung* went to great lengths to portray American servicemen as "drunkards, thieves, gangsters, rapists, pimps, and hold-up men"[21] in response to criticism leveled against the behavior of Soviet troops. The U.S. State Department political official Martin Herz acknowledged that the extravagantly detailed descriptions of interracial altercations between American servicemen, night club brawls, and sexually-transmitted disease "undoubtedly made interesting reading for people who already hated America or who were disposed in that direction. Public opinion research showed that particularly the reports of racial trouble—such as about white soldiers evicting Negro soldiers from night clubs—gained considerable circulation in Vienna."[22] The gravity of such incidents notwithstanding, the absence of abundant references to misdeeds committed by Western troops in the Interior Ministry archival record, in the non-communist press, and in oral histories are telling. Western—particularly U.S. troops—were guilty of boorish and insensitive behavior that did cross into the criminal, but the occurrence of forceful dispossession of Austrians by Western troops was quite rare compared with Soviet behavior. Undoubtedly this had a great deal to do with the fact that the British and U.S. forces had far more to eat and had more money to spend than either their Soviet counterparts or the Austrians themselves; thus, there was less incentive to steal livestock or other valuables. The prestige and, undoubtedly, the occasionally swaggering expression of power that issued from American purchasing power, which at times was capable of eliciting feelings of resentment from Austrians, was probably far more attractive for most troops than what could be gained from looting.

On the other hand, the average Soviet soldier encountered unfamiliar and dazzling wealth in Germany and Austria, even after the effect of years of war-induced privation and the destruction on Central Europe, and the widespread requisitioning or looting done by Soviet troops might be thought of as a form of "personal reparations." Indeed, it is not uncommon to encounter police reports that note the intervention of western soldiers on behalf of Austrians who were threatened with physical violence or loss of property at the hands of Soviet troops.[23] These incidents were not confined to police file cabinets, however; they also were frequently printed in mass circulation newspapers, which must have lent the impression that indiscriminate disregard for life, limb, and property was an inchoate form of Soviet behavior, *particularly* if drink was involved. Content analyses of such papers—for example, the *Arbeiter-Zeitung* and *Das Kleine Volksblatt*—show that during the entirety of the occupation period, the Austrian Socialist Party (*Sozialistische Partei Österreichs*, SPÖ) and the Austrian People's Party (*Österreichische Volkspartei*, ÖVP) downplayed crimes committed by Western soldiers and emphasized criminal acts perpetrated by their Soviet counterparts. The *Arbeiter-Zeitung* was particularly militant in its criticism of the Soviet occupation authority's policies and demonstrated an extraordinary vigilance in reporting the transgressions of its personnel—indeed, at the expense of noting any such misdeeds by Western soldiers. Only rarely did the *Arbeiter-Zeitung* report on incidents demonstrating humane or conscientious behavior on the part of Soviet troops—for example, the case of a Soviet soldier who drove an elderly pedestrian to the hospital in the Hollabrunn district, saving his life, after he had been struck by another Soviet serviceman in a hit-and-run incident.[24] The overwhelmingly negative press coverage of Soviet behavior confirmed for a great many Austrians that their fate lay in reinforcing the cultural identity they shared with western peoples. Such sentiments had deeper roots than the experiences of occupation: for example, long-standing fears of Easterners as marauding barbarians harbored in nurtured collective memory of the Turkish invasions, and more recently direct experiences of post-Russian Revolution anti-Bolshevik sentiment and racist Nazi anti-Communism.

## Infringements Upon Basic Democratic Rights

In response to concerns expressed by beleaguered inhabitants, the following remarks by a Berlin-based Soviet Military Administration representative in November 1948 could just as easily have been uttered in Eastern Austria:

> Can one equate the great, historical, human, and noble deeds of the Soviet Army with a watch taken or a bicycle stolen? A watch taken away is nothing in comparison with the freedom that was brought. Today, one can easily say: Tell me how you relate to the Russians and I will tell you who you are. There can be no honest democrats and freedom-loving people who are against the Soviet Union and go around telling anti-Soviet jokes or stories.[25]

This succinct expression of Soviet attitudes towards the inhabitants of German-speaking occupied regions called upon genuine anti-fascists not to allow a few negative experiences to taint Austrians' perceptions of the heroic efforts of the Red Army. As noted earlier, the indiscriminate, almost anarchic character of looting during 1945, followed by the all too frequent drunken rampages in subsequent years, made it extraordinarily difficult for most Germans and Austrians to warm up to the Soviets. Moreover, if democracy were the alleged alternative to fascism, interference in matters involving acceptable (that is, non-fascist) political free speech belied any genuine Soviet support for the democratic principle emphasized in the first article of the *Bundesverfassungsgesetze*. While it is now widely accepted among historians that Austrians were reluctant democrats in 1945—both because they had not previously experienced a functioning democracy, and because they were most concerned with achieving sustained material security in the wake of severe privation—Anglo-American wealth and stability likely confronted most Austrians with a seductive instrumentalist logic that they had more to gain from the establishment of a successful of western-style democracy than from democratic centralism. Given that the parameters under which a new Austrian authority would take shape were expressly anti-fascist and democratic, it stands to reason that post-Nazi *Politikverdrossenheit* and cynicism towards Allied motives notwithstanding, the eventual restoration of sovereignty could only have been understood as contingent upon the success of Austrian democracy.[26]

Soviet intrusion into the realm of freedom of speech and dissemination of information, then, represented an additional and significant factor shaping Austrian perceptions of the Soviet occupation authorities. U.S. interference in the exercise of freedom of speech was not unheard of, however. U.S. military authorities were not above interfering with demonstrations, particularly when they were unauthorized, or in those instances where the purpose or nature of the protest was controversial. A case in point was the Bad Ischl demonstration of 20 August 1947, where a protest against changes in food rationing was transformed into heated action against the alleged black market activities of local displaced persons (DPs) housed in a hotel-turned hostel. Protesters played on the fact that most of these DPs were of Jewish background and shouted anti-Semitic epithets and hurled rocks through windows of the hotel. U.S. military police arrested several protesters, who were convicted and sentenced to heavy sentences—later reduced—for violating the proscription against using free speech as an incitement to race hatred and interfering with activities assisting DPs. Martin Herz suggested that the KPÖ was responsible for the demonstration, and had shamelessly "attempted to picture the defendants as ordinary citizens or meritorious anti-Nazis who were being persecuted for having asked for milk for their children."[27] The U.S.-sponsored *Wiener Kurier* explained the American military government's only restricted free speech where it was misused to incite race hatred, to interfere with activities jeopardizing the work of the U.S. Armed Forces in peacekeeping or DP assistance—an admittedly elastic range of possibly restrictive scenarios—or where the threat of violence existed as the result of the exercise of free speech.[28] A wide range of cases might be cited to underscore Soviet interference with the democratic process inside Austria, and these incidents were frequently, but not exclusively, linked to election campaigns. In the autumn of 1945, for example, Lower Austrian social democratic officials reported to the SPÖ leadership in Vienna that the KPÖ newspaper, the *Österreichische Volksstimme*, in the districts of Krems and Neunkirchen was consistently delivered with cars driven by Soviet soldiers. When the SPÖ office in Krems requested that the daily social democratic newspaper be delivered in a similar manner, the local military commander replied bluntly that this would not be in the interests of the Red Army.[29] In Klosterneuburg the following year, the local SPÖ leader found himself in the frustrating position of having to submit all *Wandzeitungen*, announcements, and party posters for an unprecedented additional round of scrutiny by Soviet censors before receiving permission to post them, which he suggested was an abuse of the terms of the Allied Control Agreement.[30] The SPÖ in Freistadt found itself consistently at odds with the local Soviet commandant over freedom of speech; in March 1947 officials from the local district office complained that the Soviet commandant had ordered removal of all copies of a poster with the words *"Der Faschismus verspricht—Der Sozialismus verwirklicht!"*, having based his directive on the clumsy translation provided by his political officer that "socialism is the realization of fascism".[31] Several years later, Freistadt again made the news when the Soviet commandant ordered confiscation of an SPÖ broadsheet entitled "*Urteilen sie selbst!*". The poster compared the average annual consumption of dietary staples in Austria, Hungary, and the USSR, and pointed out that under the categories of meat, fat, sugar, and flour, the rations on which Soviet citizens subsisted lagged miserably behind those of Austrians and Hungarians.[32]

The *Volkspartei* and its members were subjected to similar treatment. In February 1949, the *Wiener Zeitung* reported that campaign materials printed for the election later that year and the truck carrying them had been confiscated *en route* from Vienna to Upper Austria by Soviet authorities. The reason for the seizure of the 250,000 leaflets was that they featured a stylized representation of a communist attack on Austria and neighboring states with the text: *"Wir wollen keine Volksdemokratie!"*[33] The *Wiener Zeitung* article proclaimed in angry bold print that "[c]anvassing for a party, the collection of campaign funds, and political slogans directed against communism are inalienable elements of democratic freedom, the protection of which is the avowed task of the occupation powers."[34] After the two drivers were subjected to separate three-hour interrogation sessions, they were released and permitted to climb into their truck—the sides of which had been smeared with manure to conceal the ÖVP symbol—and return to Vienna. Just prior to the 1949 elections, another instance of Soviet censorship was made known to the Austrian public. Two anti-communist *Volkspartei* electoral posters were banned—one depicting a giant octopus with tentacles stretching westward towards Austria with the text "*Erkenne die Gefahr*," the other an illustration of a worker burdened down with an oversized hammer and sickle on his back and the accompanying admonishment "*Damit dies nicht dein Schicksal sei—wähl Österreichische Volkspartei.*"[35] The frustrations of many an Austrian were given voice in a *Wiener Kurier* editorial in November 1949 that denounced censorship of free speech in all forms, from political party canvassing to personal letters:

> … inhabitants of the western [zones] utilize their God-given right [sic] to curse politicians and taxes, the weather and whatever else so abundantly that already overworked censors would collapse under the additional burden—but they don't carry such a burden, for the western powers neither exercise censorship nor white-out portions of letters … The extravagance and the virulence of Soviet lies … only proves that someone has stepped powerfully on Ivan's toes as he did a little illegal sniffing around.[36]

Repeated complaints lodged by the Austrian government concerning Soviet censorship and interference in the exercise of democratic rights prompted the Western Allies to raise the issue in the Allied Control Council. The Soviet representative refused to accept the wording of a proposed Four Power declaration that censorship of posters did not fall under the jurisdiction of the Council.[37] Subsequently, Austrian newspaper reports of Soviet encroachment on free speech became bolder, particularly during the so-called *Plakataffäre* of 1954. This controversy stemmed from another round of confiscation of ÖVP electoral posters throughout the Soviet occupation zone, posters that criticized the USSR for failing to cooperate with the Western Allies at the recently concluded Berlin Conference of foreign ministers. The poster expressed frustration with the ongoing occupation, and depicted a map of Austria with photos of marching Russian soldiers superimposed over it and a scrawling "*Njet!*" across the length of its surface. A second poster linked the fortunes of Berlin and Vienna with the caption "Two cities—one destiny!"[38], a motif which the Soviet authorities alleged was evidence of sentiment in favor of a new *Anschluß*, and a clear indication of the importance of continued occupation. Austrian authorities remained firm but careful when confronted with Soviet threats and intimidation, but small groups of frustrated Austrian civilians translated widespread annoyance with Russian intransigence on state treaty negotiations into action by distributing anti-Soviet leaflets, with consequences as severe as ten years' hard labor if apprehended by Soviet patrols.[39]

Even reluctant democrats came to understand that the restoration of Austrian sovereignty rested in significant measure upon the success of democratic institutions. Soviet abuses of fundamental democratic principles such as freedom of speech not only violated rights which the Allies agreed to restore to Austria, they also represented a negation of Austrians' status as victims, as touted in the Moscow Declaration. Soviet intransigence over a state treaty seemed a contradiction—why would a "victimized" society require occupation? The Western presence, while certainly not uniform in character across the three zones, never carried with it the onerous associations that the Soviet presence did, and this had a great deal to do with the volume of material aid and public relations triumph that was the European Recovery Program versus Soviet misbehavior, meddling, and extensive reparations demands.

## The Marshall Plan and Perceptions of the Occupation

My intention to this point has been to explore how Soviet behavior, press coverage of it, and individual Austrians' experiences with it combined to shape admittedly generalized, but nonetheless pervasive, perceptions of the Soviet occupation forces. Rape, looting, seemingly arbitrary arrest, and interference in free speech—not to mention the threat of political kidnapping or Soviet-assisted KPÖ mischief, such as the short-lived autumn 1950 uprising[40]—contributed to a complex and perhaps not entirely consistent sense of Austrianness. This sentiment may have emerged on the *Lagerstrasse* for a relative few, for more it may have come from a dissatisfaction with the course of the war. Above all, though, I would suggest that the discrepancy between Austrian "victimization" as expressed in the Moscow Declaration of 1943 on the one hand,[41] and the limits imposed upon state and individual sovereignty by the occupation on the other, helped to foster an Austrianness built on the foundation of anti-Communism which was based on interwar experience and reinforced during the Nazi era. This attitude was reinforced after the war by skepticism, if not outright hostility, towards the Soviet system. At the other pole from Sovietization was an assimilation of elements of Americanism; the earnest search for a *dritter Weg* notwithstanding, social democrats and Catholic conservatives alike emphasized that Austria was decidedly part of the West, even as they sought to give meaning to a rhetoric of an "Austrian mission to the East" within the context of a divided Europe. This entailed *de facto* integration into the West, although Austrian authorities and cultural critics warned against permitting U.S.-style capitalism and its accompanying crass consumerism to destroy traditional Austrian values or to threaten the institutions of social partnership and the nationalized industrial sector. Still, when juxtaposed with rough-edged Soviet behavior, the seeming altruism of American aid and the effectiveness of the U.S. model for modernization appeared all the more attractive, and can be regarded, I suggest, as a central factor contributing to the formation of a sense of Austrian identity.

It is a truism that Marshall Plan aid contributed vitally to the nourishment of Austrian citizens and provided a basis for the reconstruction of an Austrian economy that experienced greater setbacks through the loss of trade with Eastern European lands than did any other European Recovery Plan (ERP) recipient.[42] Alan Milward, despite his skepticism *vis-à-vis* the far-reaching exigency for the Marshall Plan,[43] provides convincing evidence for the impact of aid on Austria's economy, in particular. Milward estimates that between 1 July 1948 and 30 June 1949, Austria led all ERP recipients with 14 percent of its national income represented by ERP aid; the Netherlands followed with 10.8 percent, and Ireland was third with 7.8 percent—whereas ERP assistance to western Germany represented only 2.9 percent of its national income![44] The significance implied in these figures for the initial stimulus to Austria's economy is implied for present purposes, rather than developed; it is not my intention to explore Marshall Plan-related diplomacy and the ERP's influence on the Austrian domestic politics or political economy. For consideration of these issues, one is best served by referring to the authoritative work of the late Wilfried Mähr and the keen insights of Kurt Tweraser.[45] Instead, I turn below to a case study in U.S. propaganda for the Marshall Plan and Soviet reactions to it, and offer an example of Austrian reactions to this manifestation of a broader postwar U.S. agenda.

"In the most profound sense," the historian Michael Hogan has written, the postwar U.S. agenda "involved the transfer of attitudes, habits, and values as well, indeed, of a whole way of life that Marshall-planners associated with progress in the marketplace and social relationships as much as they did with greater output in industry and agriculture."[46] And as John Gimbel reminds us:

> Within the State Department there was a strong inclination to regard the end of the war as the beginning of an opportunity … It was an opportunity to root out Nazis, Fascists, and others who had led their people to war, to reduce political and economic nationalism, to further the principles of free trade, to strengthen the forces of liberalism—in short, to do missionary work.[47]

The impetus for the U.S. interest in western integration must, of course, be considered in the context of a cluster of other postwar developments as well for example, the Berlin Blockade, the Truman Doctrine, and a concern on the part of the U.S.-led western Allies to preempt widespread appeal for communism through rapid reconstruction and the creation of democratic societies. These societies would be shaped by what then-West German Economics Minister Ludwig Erhard characterized as

> the freedom of all citizens to shape their lives in a form adequate to the personal wishes and conceptions of the individual, within the framework of the financial means at their disposal. This basic right of consumer freedom must find its logical counterpart in the freedom of the entrepreneur to produce or distribute whatever he thinks necessary and potentially successful in a given market context.[48]

Erhard's linkage of democracy and economic freedom, which he juxtaposed to the dyad of dictatorship and a state-controlled economy, represent the quintessence of the German Christian Democratic and Liberal emphasis upon the *market* element in Erhard's concept of the social market economy. While the *social* element in Austria's *Sozialpartnerschaft* system carried somewhat stronger currency than in the German context, Erhard's notion of consumer democracy is applicable to Austrian circumstances as well—even though we must keep in mind, as Wilfried Mähr duly noted, that while the SPÖ rank-and-file supported the Marshall Plan overwhelmingly, they were reminded by critical voices in the party that the acceptance of U.S. aid would not necessarily preserve the freedom of movement necessary for the establishment of democratic socialism.[49]

The announcement of the European Recovery Program, and the Austrian government's eagerness to participate in it, prompted immediate and trenchant criticism from Austrian communists. KPÖ chairman Johann Koplenig declared that "[f]ar from being a humanitarian aid plan, the Marshall Plan is quite something else: It is a plan to divide Europe into two hostile camps, to create a bulwark against the East, with Western Germany as its center and America as its outpost. This is what the Marshall Plan means for Austria."[50] Consistent with the communists' stance as champions of Austria's national interest, he added

> [t]he chaining of Austria to American policy for Europe means a reduction of our living standard to the level of colonial slaves. The American zone of Germany today is an example of how a Europe dominated by the US would look: No land reform, no nationalization, and labor or social policies according to the American pattern ... The inhabitants of the American zone are treated practically like natives in a colonial empire. That is the kind of democracy which America wants to give us on the basis of its aid under the Marshall Plan.[51]

U.S. reports on the Austrian population's perceptions of the Allies and reactions to the Marshall Plan told a somewhat different story. Eighty percent of Austrians polled in November 1947 expressed confidence that the United States would support Austrian interests at the upcoming London Conference of Foreign Ministers, as against 2.4 percent who felt the USSR would represent Austrian concerns adequately.[52] A second poll, conducted specifically in Vienna, revealed that 90 percent of Austrians questioned were ill-informed with respect to the features of the European Recovery Program; however, once the American investigators provided them with an explanation of how the plan was to affect the Austrian economy, just over 86 percent voiced their approval, as opposed to under 2 percent who opposed it. The rest were undecided.[53] Ultimately, massive campaigns by the United States, the ÖVP-SPÖ government, and by each of these political camps for the benefit of their respective constituencies provided the public with rather more extensive information on the workings of the Marshall Plan.[54] The social democratic-dominated Austrian Trade Union Federation was particularly instrumental in persuading its rank-and-file that standards of living, the chance for an intelligently-planned economy, and the possibility of an enhanced role for the unions during and after reconstruction warranted support for the plan. This pro-ERP groundwork proved instrumental in rallying a vital segment of the Austrian population behind participation in the program.[55]

The material impact of the Marshall Plan notwithstanding, the great significance of U.S. aid during the years 1945-1948 and throughout the course of the ERP was that it confirmed for most Austrians their perceptions of the rival superpowers. This, in turn, reaffirmed Austria's western value-orientation, despite the emerging discussion of a Second Republic which would remain free from identification with either Cold War power bloc. Selling the Marshall Plan to the Austrian public was a relatively easy task; for example, whereas in West Germany authorities were careful in their approach to advertising the Marshall Plan and deliberately avoided developing symbols or creating posters that might in any way have led people to draw unsavory comparisons to Nazi-era propaganda techniques,[56] it is not apparent that the authorities were preoccupied with the same concern when it came to promoting the plan in Austria. Information about this extensive aid program was made available to the Austrian public via radio broadcasts, newspaper reports, and articles in the journals of the political parties, trade unions, and interest groups. Dissemination of information through these channels found its complement in a series of extensive U.S. cultural policy initiatives explored so thoroughly in the work of Reinhold Wagnleitner.[57] The U.S. cultural mission during the later 1940s and early 1950s did not limit itself to an adult audience, however. In order to safeguard the stability of a future, post-reconstruction Austria and to reproduce an "Austrianized" version of U.S.-style consumer democracy, children were targeted closely as well. Apart from Wagnleitner's research, this important theme has been essentially ignored in studies of U.S. cultural politics in Austria. I offer, then, the following case study as an additional exploration into the ways the U.S. and Soviet occupation authorities attempted to influence children's perceptions of their respective systems. Through children, the Cold War adversaries sought to influence and eventually reproduce a still embryonic Austrian identity.

The U.S. Economic Cooperation Mission had set the precedent for introducing political materials into Austrian classrooms as early as September 1950 with the delivery of a series of twenty-four large posters detailing economic aspects of ERP-sponsored European integration to Austrian secondary schools.[58] Austrian schoolchildren had been encouraged to give thanks in the form of prose, verse, or drawings for U.S. food aid provided by the CARE program a few years earlier,[59] but an enhanced emphasis on propaganda in the classroom enabled the United States to present its global agenda in a positive light at the beginning of a new school year that coincided with the emerging Korean conflict. Delivery of these pamphlets was supplemented well into 1951 by continued large-scale shipments of materials from the CARE Mission, among them packages of English-language books for Austrian schools.[60] Included in these shipments were some 200,000 copies of an ERP pamphlet, entitled "*Von guten Dingen und wie sie zu Euch kamen*." This pamphlet announced an international contest in which children up to sixteen years of age in eighteen different nations were encouraged to create drawings or paintings depicting the significance of the Marshall Plan for their respective countries.[61] The text of the brochure read as follows:

> During the war and shortly thereafter people here were only able to get very few things which they needed. As soon as it was possible, the United States of North America began to help Austria and the other lands in Europe with things they needed. This system through which other lands were helped was named the Marshall Plan. First it brought food and clothing to Austrians. But then it also brought coal, machines and trucks so that Austria could produce more foodstuffs for itself and could manufacture more things. It was known that it would be better for Austria to be able to help itself insofar as it was possible.
>
> In Austria everything has, indeed, become better. The Marshall Plan still brings many goods to Austria, for its activity is still not complete. The Americans give to the Austrians all that they want so that Austria will become a land in which it is possible to live a good life. But they are not doing this merely out of friendliness. The Americans know that the whole world must work together, they know that everyone in the whole world must be happy if the people in any of the various countries are to be happy.[62]

Prizes ranged from öS 2,500 for first place to öS 50 for those finishing between twenty-sixth and 250th place. Another 250 children could win ERP hats or pins and a personalized diploma of recognition, as well as the chance for larger money awards or travel prizes in the international competition, including an all-expenses-paid trip to Washington, D.C. as the grand prize. The response among schoolchildren was enthusiastic.[63] Marshall Plan public relations activity directed towards children and the gradual increase of nutritional and material well-being for the overall population allowed the United States to cast itself in the best possible light as it set about to integrate Western Europe as both a region in which U.S. firms might do business and which would be more resistant to communist solicitations. Geopolitical and broad economic interests may have been tempered somewhat by humanitarian concerns, but the former considerations were the driving force behind the carefully-marketed product that Austrian consumers were all too eager to enjoy. Of course, the favorable perception of U.S. policy and the generally positive perception of American soldiers made it easier for most Austrians to accept the ERP; if the USSR had advanced it own comprehensive aid package, it is difficult to imagine that the population would have been as enthusiastic, given the track record of the occupation regime and the profoundly negative feelings towards the behavior of Soviet troops. During the course of the 1950s and beyond, however, the *cachet* so widely associated with things American led to what many Austrian cultural critics decried as the formation of a generation nurtured on "*Schmaltz and Coca-Cola*," to employ Wagnleitner's term.[64] This perceived inundation of base U.S. popular culture—particularly rock 'n' roll and Hollywood films—at the expense of traditional Austrian values represented the undesirable byproducts of Austrians' ready embrace of U.S. assistance. In this sense perhaps there was an element of truth in Koplenig's criticism of the Marshall Plan,[65] insofar as Austria gradually became another market for Americana and, eventually, a consumer democracy in its own right—even if Austria did not exactly become the sort of colonial outpost of the United States that Koplenig envisioned it would be.

As Austrians began to benefit tangibly from Marshall Plan aid by the early 1950s, the Soviet authorities in Eastern Austria were determined not to allow the Americans unchallenged access to the classroom—much to the dismay of SPÖ and ÖVP officials alike. One particularly well-documented incident involved an inquiry sent to the Federal Minister of Education in April 1951 by social democratic delegates in the *Bundesrat* regarding the charge that

> [t]he district commander of Floridsdorf has given the responsible school authorities twenty copies of a poster from the Soviet Information Service with firm instructions to send them to ... [list of schools in Vienna XXI followed].

> The above-mentioned headquarters demanded, further, a list of these schools with the remark that the Executive Commission of the [Soviet] occupying power was certain that the order would be carried out. A copy of the poster is included in this inquiry. It does not require any extensive explanation that the introduction of political propaganda into schools implies a severe impairment of educational work. As a rule in democratic states, these kinds of methods attain exactly the opposite effect of that desired from the propaganda. Moreover, according to the opinion of the elected members of the *Bundesrat*, this mission signifies a breach of the Control Agreement.
> ... Is the Herr Minister of Education, in the name of the Austrian Federal Government, prepared to register a protest to the Soviet occupation force against this procedure, and to appeal [for] the recalling of the command to bring propaganda posters into Austrian schools?[66]

The posters, printed by the Soviet Information Service in Vienna, were illustrated with reproduced photographs of anti-U.S. protests in Seoul, London, Berlin, and Düsseldorf, as well as of peace demonstrations in Stockholm, Sofia, and Warsaw. The text included a call to convene a conference of representatives of the five permanent members of the UN Security Council to discuss the peaceful resolution of existing differences, a demand that Germany and Japan not be rearmed, categorical rejection of interference in the internal affairs of other states, an insistence that all states reduce their armaments to 50 percent of current levels, and the demand of independence for all colonial peoples.[67]

An investigation undertaken by the Education Ministry uncovered that a Floridsdorf district school inspector had been ordered to distribute the posters at a film showing of Russian fairy tales to local schoolchildren. The inspector reported that the Soviet authorities had demanded a list of the schools to which the posters were distributed in order that they might verify his compliance. Before proceeding with this command, however, he had brought the matter to the attention of the president of the Vienna City School Council, the mayor, and the federal vice-chancellor.[68] According to the Education Ministry report, after this incident was revealed to the press, the inspector was summoned to the chief Soviet cultural officer. This official denied outright the accusation that the Soviet district commander had given the order to distribute the posters to the schools, yet demanded to know why this school inspector did not want the posters affixed in the schools. When he heard that the stated policy of the Viennese City School Council forbade political propaganda on school premises,

> the cultural officer produced the brochure on the ERP drawing competition for Austrian children and said "But these have been distributed. These pamphlets were placed in the hands of every child. We only want to have the posters brought into the schools." He handed the district school inspector an additional package of posters with the words "It is not an order or a commission, only a suggestion, but if you don't give these to the schools then you must tell me why the piece on the Marshall Plan [was accepted] and not our poster."[69] [This particular poster showed the good conditions under which a Russian family lives, and included a laudatory text.]

The *Arbeiter-Zeitung* denounced this consistent pressure to introduce propaganda brochures and pamphlets into the classroom, complaining that school officials throughout the Soviet zone were being summoned before the occupation authorities and pressured to cooperate with Soviet designs. Comparing this sort of heavy-handedness to the "voluntary coercion" ("*freiwilliger Zwang*") of the Nazi era, the *Arbeiter-Zeitung* reminded its readers that forcing school officials to introduce materials into the classroom that had not been sanctioned by the provincial school board was a violation of the Control Agreement.[70] Other newspapers subsequently gave voice to this same complaint. According to *Das Kleine Volksblatt*:

> [F]irst and foremost, we want our children entrusted with a knowledge of the language, culture, and history of their own homeland. Still, an understanding of the form and substance of foreign cultures was always cultivated in our schools; that was so and will continue to remain so. To that end, however, we don't need support from local Soviet commandants.[71]

Austrian authorities instrumentalized the issue of censorship, decrying Soviet interfence in the free dissemination of information and overlooking the practice of occasional censorship within the Austrian government and within the political parties, as well as within the

Western Allied occupation governments. When Austrian officials or newspapers made pronouncements such as those noted above, they were guilty of a certain hypocrisy. This, in combination with the willingness to allow Marshall Plan propaganda into the classroom, plainly substantiated the Soviet assertion that Austrian education officials, from the provincial school councils up to Federal Ministry of Education, were willing to selectively introduce political material into schools to the benefit of the United States. As legitimate as their grievance was regarding the presence of ERP propaganda in the classroom, evidence does not indicate that either thinly-veiled Soviet threats or the distribution of Russian propaganda pamphlets and brochures at showings of fairy-tale cartoons swayed Austrian children significantly enough to create future grassroots KPÖ supporters—or even prompted parents to deem such propaganda distressing enough to lodge complaints with district school councils.[72] By the early 1950s, it had become clear that the Soviet occupation authority had not won, and was not likely to win, "the hearts and minds" of the Austrian population.

## Conclusion

As Austrian society slowly began to feel the initial effects of reconstruction during the 1950s, the State Treaty brought the occupation to a conclusion, and the principle of Austrian neutrality was established, a composite Second Republic identity first began to develop as a rallying point for most Austrian citizens. This newly-emerging sense of Austrianness was based as much on the repression of civil war enmities and the Nazi past as the promotion of a sometimes uneasy commitment to pluralism and solidarity. Created from selective elements of imperial, Catholic, and social democratic traditions, and a new sense of internationalism built upon neutrality. This new, composite identity allowed Austria to remain open to both blocs, yet assert its cultural roots in the western tradition, and to pursue domestic and international political interests while grounded in the *Bundesverfassungsgesetze* and a new political culture derived from—and reinforced by—coalition, *Proporz*, and *Sozialpartnerschaft*.

Interwar tensions, the Nazi years, postwar occupation and the Cold War division of Europe, and the Marshall Plan each contributed significantly to this still-evolving, and often contested Austrian identity and its link to a functioning democratic system. For the founders of the Second Republic, among whom there were some reluctant democrats, this identity meant a hybrid of constitutional patriotism, pride in pre-republican and only partially successful First Republic achievements, and a particularly dogged aversion to critical self-scrutiny concerning Austrians' participation in the crimes of the Third Reich. This is not to suggest that the creation of a constitutional patriotism has been either an unmitigated success or a frictionless process. If one reflects upon Jürgen Habermas' criticism of the lack of a German constitutional patriotism, the Austrian case has been a *relatively* successful one, the emergence of a strong political right notwithstanding.[73] Nonetheless, it is important to recognize that Austrians were compelled by a combination of circumstance and conviction to embrace democracy as the best means to regain and retain their sovereignty, and during the occupation, only two models were available from which to choose: "democratic centralism" or western liberal-capitalist democracy.

Austrian politicians and private citizens alike found themselves in the position to weigh the rhetoric of U.S. and Soviet propaganda against the realities of U.S. and Soviet action, at the level of individual soldiers' behavior towards individual Austrians and of occupation policies towards the broader Austrian community. Even the convivial behavior of some Soviet officials and soldiers was heavily outweighed by the damaging behavior of many members of the Red Army occupation forces, and those incidents of criminality and infringements against the fragile, newly-found democratic consensus served to confirm a visceral antipathy towards communism and suggested a certain residual racism *vis-à-vis* perspectives of the Russian and Soviet Asian peoples. In the end, those children who associated the U.S. presence with the generosity of the *Weihnachtsmann*, and who went on to become ardent consumers of U.S. pop culture in the 1950s and 1960s, provided the State Department and corporate America with convincing evidence that the ERP had been successful, even if many of these young people became critical of U.S. policies in the 1960s. In general, for the older generations, U.S. occupation and western-style democracy came to appear all the more attractive when they considered what the United States and its Western Allies *spared* the Austrian population as well as what they *offered* it in the form of CARE and Marshall Plan assistance.

## Notes

1. Bruno Kreisky, *Im Strom der Politik: Der Memoiren zweiter Teil* (Vienna: Kremayr & Scheriau, 1988), 79.

2. See, for example, Gerald Stourzh, *Geschichte des Staatsvertrags 1945-1955: Österreichs Weg zur Neutralität* (3rd ed., Graz: Verlag Styria, 1980); Manfried Rauchensteiner, *Der Sonderfall: Die Besatzungszeit in Österreich, 1945-1955* (Graz-Vienna: Verlag Styria, 1979); Audrey Kurth Cronin, *Great Power Politics and the Struggle over Austria, 1945-1955* (Ithaca, NY: Cornell, 1986); Günter Bischof, "Österreich—ein 'geheimer Verbündeter' des Westens? Wirtschafts- und sicherheitspolitische Fragen der Integration aus der Sicht der USA," in *Österreich und die europäische Integration, 1945-1993: Aspekte einer wechselvollen Entwicklung*, ed. Michael Gehler and Rolf Steininger (Vienna: Böhlau Verlag, 1993), 425-450; Oliver Rathkolb, "Von der Besatzung zur Neutralität: Österreichs Neutralität in den außenpolitischen Strategien des Nationalen Sicherheitsrates unter Truman und Eisenhower," in *Die bevormundete Nation: Österreich und die Allierten, 1945-1949*, ed. Günter Bischof and Josef Leidenfrost (Innsbruck: Haymon-Verlag, 1988), 371-406.

3. The classic monographic study of Austrian denazification remains Dieter Stiefel, *Entnazifizierung in Österreich* (Vienna: Europaverlag, 1981); see also Sebastien Meissl, Klaus-Dieter Mully, and Oliver Rathkolb, eds., *Verdrängte Schuld, verfehlte Sühne: Entnazifizierung in Österreich, 1945-1955* (Munich: R. Oldenbourg, 1986).

4. Alois Brusatti, "Entwicklung der Wirtschaft und der Wirtschaftspolitik," in *Österreich: Die Zweite Republik*, vol. II, ed. Erika Weinzierl and Kurt Skalnik (Graz: Verlag Styria, 1972), esp. 424-29; Fritz Weber, "Österreichs Wirtschaft in der Rekonstruktionsperiode nach 1945," in *Zeitgeschichte* 15 (1987): 267-98; Felix Butschek, *Die österreichische Wirtschaft im 20. Jahrhundert* (Vienna: Österreichisches Institut für Wirtschaftsforschung, 1985).

5. Margarete Hannl, "Mit den 'Russen' leben: Besatzungszeit im Mühlviertel, 1945-1955," *Zeitgeschichte* 16 (1987): 147-66; Klaus-Dieter Mulley, "Befreiung und Besatzung: Aspekte sowjetischer Besatzung in Niederösterreich 1945-1948" in *Österreich unter alliierter Besatzung 1945-1955*, ed. Alfred Ableitinger, Siegfried Beer, and Eduard G. Staudinger (Vienna: Böhlau Verlag, 1998), 361-400.

6. See Anton Pelinka, "Auseinandersetzung mit dem Kommunismus" in *Österreich: Die Zweite Republik*, II: 169-201, esp. 183.; on the Austrians' anti-communist *Feindbild* also see the Fraberger/Stiefel essay in this volume.

7. See, for example, Norman M. Naimark, *The Russians in Germany: A History of the Soviet Zone of Occupation, 1945-1949* (Cambridge, MA: Belknap/Harvard, 1995), 69-140; Atina Grossmann, "A Question of Silence: The Rape of German Women by Occupation Soldiers," in *West Germany under Construction: Politics, Society and Culture in the Adenauer Era*, ed. Robert G. Moeller (Ann Arbor: Michigan, 1997), 33-52; Marianne Baumgartner, "Vergewaltigung zwischen Mythos und Realität: Wien und Niederösterreich im Jahr 1945," in *Frauenleben 1945—Kriegsende in Wien. 205. Sonderausstellung des Historischen Museums der Stadt Wien* (Vienna, 1995), 59-71; Maria Mesner, *Frauensache? Zur Auseinandersetzung um den Schwangerschaftsabbruch in Österreich* (Vienna: Jugend & Volk, 1994), 36-46; Klaus-Dieter Mulley, "Befreiung und Besetzung," 387-90.

8. Grossmann, "A Question of Silence," 35; Naimark, *The Russians in Germany*, 84.

9. Naimark, *The Russians in Germany*, 106, 138.

10. Hannl, "Mit den 'Russen' leben," 149.

11. Baumgartner, "Vergewaltigung zwischen Mythos und Realität," 61.

12. Grossman, "A Question of Silence," 44-48; Mesner, *Frauensache?*, 36-39. Consider also the following comment by a resident of Ravelsbach, Lower Austria: "If the Russians would start suddenly being kind and considerate, if they could discipline their troops well enough so that the panic and insecurity could fade from the hearts of people, undoubtedly much of the intensity would disappear quickly. But never all. These people will never forget what the Red Army did to our women. The present feeling of the simple people that the Russians are *Untermenschen* will last as long as this generation lives." Leonard Hankin (OSS) on "The Russian Occupation of Ravelsbach, Lower Austria: A Personal Report, 1 September 1945," cited in *Gesellschaft und Politik am Beginn der Zweiten Republik: Vertrauliche Berichte der US-Militäradministration aus Österreich 1945 in englischer Originalfassung*, ed. Oliver Rathkolb (Vienna: Böhlau Verlag, 1985), 300.

13. Mesner, *Frauensache?*, 37.

14. Baumgartner, "Vergewaltigung zwischen Mythos und Realität," 62.

15. Susan Brownmiller, *Against our Will: Men, Women, and Rape* (New York: Simon & Schuster, 1975), 64.

16. Grossmann, "A Question of Silence," 48.

17. Ingrid Bauer, "'Ami-Bräute'—und die österreichische Nachkriegsseele," in *Frauenleben 1945*, 74. Bauer refers ironically to the *Heimkehrer* as "'twice' defeated heroes."

18. Hannl, "Mit den 'Russen" leben," 152.

19. Naimark, *The Russians in Germany*, 113.

20. Leonard J. Hankin (OSS) Report on Soviet Zone of Occupation in Austria, RG 43, International Conferences EAC, Austria 100 (3 July 1945) in Rathkolb, *Gesellschaft und Politk*, 277.

21. Reinhold Wagnleitner, ed., *Understanding Austria: The Political Reports and Analyses of Martin F. Herz, Political Officer of the U.S. Legation in Vienna 1945-1948* (Salzburg: Wolfgang Neugebauer Verlag, 1984), "Bi-monthly Report on Political Developments in Austria for August and September, 1947," 263.

22. Ibid.

23. See for example, AdR/BMfI, Abteilung 2 (GDföS), Tagesbericht of 21 March 1946, Box Nr. 2, in which two U.S. soldiers prevented two Russian troopers from stealing a poor peasant woman's horse and wagon. Numerous other examples abound in which Soviet soldiers, were prevented from stealing livestock, bicycles, or committing rapes, usually by western soldiers but occasionally by Russian officers.

24. SOWIDOK-AK Wien, Mappe "Sowjetische Besatzungselement": *Arbeiter-Zeitung* 5 August 1951, "Ein Russe hilft einem Schwerverletzten."

25. Cited in Naimark, *The Russians in Germany*, 139.

26. Along these lines, Herz noted in 1947 that three-quarters of Austrians surveyed in an opinion poll associated democracy with freedom and communism with dictatorship. See Wagnleitner, *Understanding Austria*, "Report on Austrian Publig Opinion, 18 March 1947," 133.

27. Ibid, "The Bad Ischl Trial, 16 October 1947." 258.

28. Ibid, 258-59.

29. Verein für die Geschichte der Arbeiterbewegung/Politisches Archiv der SPÖ (hereafter VGA/PAdSPÖ)—Zentralsekretariatskorrespondenzen mit der niederösterreichischen Landesorganisation, 27 October 1945.

30. VGA/PAdSPÖ—Zentralsekretariatskorrespondenzen mit der niederösterreichischen Bezirksorganisationen, 22 October 1946.

31. VGA/PAdSPÖ—Zentralsekretariatskorrespondenzen mit den oberösterreichischen Bezirksorganisationen, Sektion Freistadt, 1 March 1947.

32. SOWIDOK—AK Wien, Mappe "Sowjetische Besatzungselement": *Arbeiter-Zeitung* 9 August 1951, "Die Russen beschlagnahmen eine Wandzeitung der Sozialistischen Partei!"

33. SOWIDOK—AK Wien, Mappe "Sowjetische Besatzungselement": *Wiener Zeitung*, 19 February 1949, "Freie Wahlen oder Terror?"

34. Ibid.

35. SOWIDOK—AK Wien, Mappe "Sowjetische Besatzungselement": *Die Presse*, 28 September 1949, "Die Sowjets verbietein zwei Plakate der Volkspartei."

36. SOWIDOK—AK Wien, Mappe"Sowjetische Besatzungselement": *Wiener Kurier*, 3 November 1949, "Wer ist der Zensor?"

37. SOWIDOK—AK Wien, Mappe "Sowjetische Besatzungselement": *Arbeiter-Zeitung*, 1 November 1952, "Die russische Plakatenzensur: Ergebnislose Debatte im Allierten Rat."

38. VGA/Oskar Helmer Nachlaß—H/4, Mappe 15/I (Innenressort, sowjet. Besatzungsmacht.) "Sicherheitsdirektion Niederösterreich, Zl. Präs 132/3 S.D. an das Bundesministerium für Inneres, Gen. Dion f.d. öff. Sicherheit—Abteilung 2, 16.3.1954."

39. SOWIDOK—AK Wien, Mappe "Sowjetische Besatzungselement": *Weltpresse*, 28 May 1954, "Wieder ein russisches Terrorurteil gegen einen Österreicher: 10 Jahre für Flugzettelverteiler"; *Weltpresse*, 10 June 1954, "Russen verurteilen eine Oesterreicherin zu 10 Jahren Zwangsarbeit."

40. Günter Bischof, "'Austria looks to the West': Kommunistische Putschgefahr, geheime Wiederbewaffnunf und Westorientierung am Anfang der fünfziger Jahre," in *Österreich in den Fünfzigern*, ed. Thomas Albrich et al. (Innsbruck: Österreichischer StudienVerlag, 1995), 183-209.

41. See idem, "Die Instrumentalisierung der Moskauer Erklärung nach dem zweiten Weltkrieg," *Zeitgeschichte* 20 (1993): 345-66.

42. Idem, "Der Marshall Plan und Österreich," *Zeitgeschichte* 17 (1990): 466.

43. Alan Milward, "Was the Marshall Plan Necessary?" in *Diplomatic History* 13 (1989): 231-253.

44. Idem, *The Reconstruction of Western Europe* (Berkeley: California, 1984), 96, Table 15. See also Wilfried Mähr, *Der Marshall-Plan in Österreich* (Graz: Verlag Styria, 1989).

45. See Mähr, *Der Marshall-Plan in Österreich*; Kurt K. Tweraser, "Marshall Plan, Sozialpartnerschaft und Produktivität in Österreich," in *Österreich in den Fünfzigern*, 211-36.

46. Michael Hogan, *The Marshall Plan: America, Britain and the Reconstruction of Western Europe, 1947-1952* (Cambridge: Cambridge, 1987), 415.

47. John Gimbel, *The Origins of the Marshall Plan* (Stanford, CA: Stanford, 1976), 30.

48. Ludwig Erhard, *Wohlstand für alle* (Düsseldorf: Econ-Verlag, 1960), 14. For an extended discussion of consumer democracy in the German context, see Erica Carter, "Alice in the Consumer Wonderland: West German Case Studies in Gender and Consumer Culture," in *West Germany under Construction*, 347-71.

49. Mähr, *Der Marshallplan in Österreich*, 165-66.

50. Speech before Central Committee of the KPÖ, 26 September 1947, as reported in the *Österreichische Volksstimme* of 27 September 1947. See Wagnleitner, *Understanding Austria*, 254.

51. Ibid, 255. For a more comprehensive look at the KPÖ and Soviet responses to the introduction of the Marshall Plan into Austria, see Mähr, *Der Marshallplan in Österreich*, 106-117.

52. Wagnleitner, *Understanding Austria*, "Third Report on Austrian Public Opinion, 26 February 1948," 334.

53. Ibid.

54. By April 1948, the Information Services Branch of the United States Forces in Austria had compiled statistics suggesting that the Austrian population was better informed about the Marshall Plan than several months earlier. In Vienna 80.3 percent of those polled had heard something about ERP aid; among them, 89.5 percent were generally in favor of it, and 89 percent of these people felt that it would improve their quality of life. In Linz the poll results showed 73.4 percent of those questioned had heard of the ERP, with 88 percent of them generally in favor of it and 85 percent inclined to think it would improve their circumstances; in Salzburg the figures were 71.2 percent, 88.5 percent, and 86 percent, respectively. These poll results indicated that those questioned were under no illusions as to US motives. Seventy-seven percent of Viennese asked if the American government was using the Marshall Plan to hinder communist expansion in Europe responded in the affirmative, vs. 81 percent in Linz and 74 percent in Salzburg. Among Viennese, only 45 percent felt that the U.S. was honestly concerned with helping Europe get back on its feet as the primary

reason for ERP aid, as opposed to 64 percent in Linz and only 45.5 percent in Salzburg. The author would like to thank Oliver Rathkolb for sharing this data from his private collection.

55. Mähr, *Der Marshallplan in Österreich*, 166-72.

56. Klaus Schönberger, "'Hier half der Marshallplan': Werbung für das europäische Wiederaufbauprogramm zwischen Propaganda und Public Relations," in *Propaganda in Deutschland: Zur Geschichte der politischen Massenbeeinflussung im 20. Jahrhundert*, ed. Gerald Diesener and Rainer Gries (Darmstadt: Primus Verlag, 1996), 196.; also see the Schröder essay in this volume.

57. Reinhold Wagnleitner, *Coca-Colonization and the Cold War: The Cultural Mission of the Unites States in Austria after the Second World War* (Chapel Hill: North Carolina, 1994).

58. See ÖStA/AdR, BKA 518.170-ERP/1/1950, ÖStA/AdR, BMU 7.952-IV/15/1951.

59. See schoolchildren's drawings from 1947 depicting the generosity of U.S. occupation forces in Wagnleitner, *Coca-Colonization*, 176ff.

60. ÖStA/AdR, BMU 9.328-IV/18/1951.

61. ÖStA/AdR, BKA 524.457-ERP/1/1950, as cited in ÖStA/AdR, BMU 10.318-IV/15/1951.

62. Ibid.

63. Ibid.

64. Wagnleitner, *Coca-Colonization*, 275-96.

65. Ibid, 166-274. For a comparison with the East and West German cases, see Uta G. Poiger, "Rock 'n' Roll, Female Sexuality, and the Cold War Battle over German Identities," *Journal of Modern History* 68 (1996): 577-616.

66. *Anfrage an den Bundesminister für Unterricht betreffend der Anbringung kommunistischer Plakate in den Schulen*, 11 April 1951, Präs. Nr. 46/J-BR/1951, in ÖStA/AdR, BMU 19.543-IV/18/1951.

67. ÖStA/AdR-BMU 30.518-IV/18/1951.

68. ÖStA/AdR, BMU 19.543-IV/18/1951.

69. Ibid. Education Minister Hurdes followed up District School Inspector Kotrba's letter to Vice-Chancellor Schärf regarding the Soviet posters with one of his own and asked that the matter not be publicized any further, given the great difficulties in ignoring the Soviet "suggestion" until the matter could be brought formally to the Soviet authorities; see Hurdes to Schärf, 30 July 1951, ÖStA/AdR, BMU 30.518-IV/18/1951. Within the Executive Committee of the Allied Council for Austria, the western Allies accused the Soviet zone occupation authorities of unilateral censorship of posters in Austrian schools by attempting to control the distribution of posters. EXCO/P(52)112, Minute # 2703, 24 October 1952, reel 12; ALCO/M(52)181, Minute # 1639, 31 October 1952, reel 7; and ALCO/P(52)67, Minute # 1469, 14 November 1952, reel 7. The western Allies urged that Chancellor Figl received word from the Executive Committee

to the effect that Austrian school officials were not required to submit posters for approval prior to publication. The Soviet member stood firm in his insistence that control of posters was consistent with the Press Decree of 1 October 1945 which forbade publication of any material which slandered the occupation forces or praised National Socialism. No agreement proved possible, and school officials in each zone remained subject to different standards.

70. SOWIDOK—AK Wien, Mappe "Sowjetische Besatzungslelement": *Arbeiter-Zeitung*, 25 October 1951, "Weg mit der russischen Propaganda aus den Schulen!"

71. SOWIDOK—AK Wien, Mappe "Sowjetische Besatzungsmacht": *Das Kleine Volksblatt*, 18 January 1952, "Schule und Besatzungsmacht."

72. ÖStA/AdR, BMU 28.476-IV/1954. This document, a report from the Landesschulrat für Oberösterreich in Linz to the BMU dated 9 January, 1954, details an Austro-Soviet Society film outing undertaken by a *Volksschulklasse* in Gallspach and the distribution of propaganda materials such as "Legal Protection of Mother and Child in the USSR." The social legislation focus of these brochures was probably well over the head of the seven to ten-year-old *Volksschüler*, and were most likely designed for their parents. Residents of the Soviet-occupied Traunviertel in Upper Austria, in which Gallspach lies, consistently rejected the KPÖ in parliamentary elections. The Communists averaged only 4.66 percent in electoral contests between 1945 and 1953. See Peter Gerlich et al., eds., *Wahlen und Parteien in Österreich*, vol. III, (Vienna: Österreichischer Bundesverlag, 1967).

73. Jürgen Habermas, "Der DM-Nationalismus," *Die Zeit*, 30 March 1990.

# The CIA in Austria in the Marshall Plan Era, 1947-1953

*Siegfried Beer*

### Background: Sources and Contexts

Even though the genre of intelligence studies has started to claim its rightful place in the fields of military, diplomatic, and even political history in the last two decades, this has not meant that authoritative studies on the role and impact of intelligence activities on the national level, that is, concerning specific states over an extended period of time, have so far been attempted in great numbers.[1] Austria is no exception here. Great Britain, the United States, and Canada certainly are. In order to understand the role which the Central Intelligence Agency (CIA) might have played in Austria during the crucial era of the Marshall Plan, it will be imperative to understand the general intelligence environment into which the representatives of the CIA were placed in Austria at the end of 1947 and in which they continued to function up to 1953 and beyond.[2]

At this point, one of the great myths or at least misunderstandings about U.S. intelligence, of which even experts of U.S. foreign policy or of international relations have frequently become victims, needs to be corrected. The CIA, in the late 1940s and early 1950s, and especially now, has been and is only *one* among several providers of intelligence to U.S. civilian and military decision makers. It clearly has to be seen in the context of all the others. During the period under review, the CIA, which was enacted in July 1947, was essentially in the process of development; however, by 1953 it had reached a stage of first maturity and had become a major tool of U.S. foreign policy.[3]

It is estimated that today some 80,000 Americans work for the entire U.S. intelligence establishment, at a yearly budget of approximately \$30 billion.[4] Only 10 percent of that amount is allotted to the

CIA; close to 85 percent goes to the Department of Defense which runs, among other agencies, the super-secret National Reconnaissance Office (NRO) and the National Security Agency (NSA) which, by the way, came into existence in 1952 and is probably the largest center of computer, satellite, and surveillance technology in the world. It employs the great majority of specialists in U.S. intelligence.[5]

One can assume that the CIA today probably has a staff of approximately 15,000 people, of which no more than 2,000 are stationed abroad and more often than not, are working out of embassies or consulates and trade, industrial, or press organizations.

Today at least five ministries (State, Defense, Justice, Finance, and Energy) are involved in foreign intelligence activities, so that when we speak of the CIA we are, strictly speaking, referring only to a relatively small part of the U.S. intelligence community. However, and most importantly, the Director of Central Intelligence (DCI) since 1947 has also been the director of the CIA. It is he who reports directly to the President of the United States and to the National Security Council (NSC). It is this connection which makes the equalization of the CIA and the entire U.S. intelligence community quite understandable.

A crucial issue must now be addressed openly and honestly: what are the sources of historical knowledge about this topic, and how can at least a basic modicum of reliable information about the early CIA, or more precisely, about U.S. intelligence efforts in Austria by the U.S. government as one of the major players in the battle for intelligence or espionage supremacy in the era of the First Cold War, roughly the period in question, 1945/47 to 1953, be obtained? What is the state of information and knowledge, primary and secondary, about postwar U.S. intelligence generally and about the activities of the various U.S. intelligence organizations in Austria specifically? Generally speaking, the quantity and quality of available sources are not very satisfactory in the area of operational intelligence, but they are fairly good about organizational matters. There is a steadily growing and scientifically researched body of interpretation about the roots, birth, and bureaucratic development of the CIA which goes well beyond the first decade of its existence;[6] however, the documentation of the information gathering, analysis, and distribution processes as they pertain to geographical regions or specific countries is still very rudimentary. This is even more true about covert action and counter-intelligence. The records of the CIA have been exempt from the standards and regulations of the Freedom of Information Act (FOIA), and even though in the early 1990s, several CIA directors have announced and publicly committed to a policy of opening the records for serious research and scholarship, the subsequent release of documents has, at best, been selective and piecemeal.[7] Nevertheless, the last five years have seen a remarkable output of serious and reliable, often autobiographical and/or co-authored body of works on selected topics of the intelligence struggle during the Cold War, particularly on questions like Cuba, Guatemala, Vietnam, Kim Philby, or most recently, Berlin.[8]

As to the specific question of U.S. intelligence documentation on the Marshall Plan years in Austria, such intelligence information is fragmentary and almost non-existent about the CIA. Broad archival documentation about U.S. intelligence efforts exists only for the period of the Office of Strategic Services (OSS) and the Strategic Services Unit (SSU) in Austria, that is, up to the fall of 1946; for much of the work of army intelligence, G-2 and Military Intelligence Service (MIS) documentation exists up to about 1950; and for the activities of the Counter Intelligence Corps (CIC), documentation exists for the entire period of U.S. occupation in Austria.[9] All of the operational and even organizational records of the CIG and CIA in Austria have remained tightly closed.[10] The CIA has finally provided access to the first seven country studies or national estimates about Austria, reaching from February 1947 to May 1955, undertaken by the Office of Research and Evaluation (ORE) through 1949 and by the Office of National Estimates (ONE) since 1950.[11]

The first and only volume of FRUS, the quasi official Foreign Relations of the United States series, dealing entirely with organizational intelligence matters, was published only in 1996 and contains just a few documents referring to organizational questions concerning the period of the Central Intelligence Group (CIG) and the CIA in Austria.[12] A few documents touching upon Austria can also be found in one of the more recent editions of declassified records published by the Center for the Study of Intelligence, the History Staff of the present CIA.[13] This is about all that exists for documentation. There are also several books and maybe an occasional article, written by former CIA, CIC, or G-2 employees, which include vital information on U.S. intelligence operations in Austria. Oral history interviews are another source of information.

Four books on this topic deserve specific mention. First and foremost, William Hood's *Mole,*[14] a non-fictional account of the first major defection from the Soviet military intelligence organization

GRU, deals primarily with the case of Pyotr Popov, which began in Vienna in 1952 and provided major insights into the hitherto hidden world of Soviet military intelligence, not the least in Central Europe.[15] Secondly, several chapters of the book *The Secret World* (1959), provide an autobiographical account of an equally important defector in Austria, the KGB officer Pyotr Deryabin, who one day in early 1954 walked into the Viennese *Stiftskaserne* and became one of the longest serving informants and experts on Soviet intelligence for the Americans, writing and publishing well into the 1980s.[16] A third book is James Milano's slightly self-defensive account of a major CIC operation in or from Austria in a volume entitled *Soldiers, Spies and the Rat Line: America's Undeclared War against the Soviets* (1995).[17] Finally, there is the autobiographical story of the fourth CIA chief-of-station in Vienna, Peer de Silva, whose book *Sub Rosa*: *The CIA and the Uses of Intelligence* (1978)[18] promises more than it delivers, but covers the last year of the allied occupation of Austria and, even more importantly, describes the role of CIA Austria in the handling of the Hungarian crisis of 1956.

I have interviewed as many U.S. intelligence veterans with connections to Austria as I could discover and reach. So far, the number interviewed comes close to two dozen. Five of these veterans had also served in the CIA in the period under review, one of them being the first CIA station-chief in Vienna.[19] The testimony of these intelligence officers is obviously crucial, but it can never replace the existing, but unfortunately still practically inaccessible, archival documentation.

## U.S. Intelligence: The CIA and Beyond

I am convinced that one cannot possibly understand the position and role of the CIA in Austria from 1947 to 1953, roughly the years of the Marshall Plan in Austria, or even up to 1955, the end of the allied occupation in Austria, without taking into account the work and impact of all the other U.S. intelligence units or organizations operating before and during that same period. This is particularly true of the OSS and of its successor or caretaker units, the SSU and CIG, bridging, as they did, the crucial period from fall 1945 to fall 1947.

I believe it can legitimately be claimed that the experiences and traditions of the wartime Office of Strategic Services, the first U.S. central, and despite the war, largely civilian intelligence organization of pre-Pearl Harbor origin, have greatly influenced and shaped the philosophy behind the CIA as an instrument of the national security state. Four of the strongest DCIs, and thus CIA directors, were veterans of the OSS: Allen Dulles, John Foster's brother, in the 1950s; Richard Helms in the late 1960s and early 1970s; William Colby in the mid-1970s, and William Casey in the 1980s. Three of these had been heavily involved in Central European affairs during World War II; Helms was also involved in the period under review here. A significant quantitative indicator of continuity between the OSS and the CIA is provided by the fact that, in 1948, fully a third of the personnel of the CIA had formerly served in the OSS.

By 1944, the OSS had been active on almost all continents and in practically all areas of intelligence then known and practiced.[20] The OSS in Central Europe was active in the areas of intelligence gathering and analyzing, in gray and black propaganda, and since 1944, in attempts to penetrate the Third Reich,[21] as well as in postwar planning for Germany and Austria.[22]

In May of 1945, OSS officers were among the first U.S. military personnel to enter Austria and, as I would claim, may well have been the best-informed allied unit on Austrian territory between the liberation of Austria and the first free Austrian elections after the war in late November 1945. In August 1945, close to 200 full-time members of the OSS were stationed in Austria, most of them by then in Vienna and Salzburg. President Truman dissolved the OSS as of 1 October 1945, but several of its major branches continued to serve in Washington and in just a few countries abroad, among them Austria. These branches were the Research and Analysis Branch (R&A), incorporated into the State Department, and the SSU, consisting of SI (Secret Intelligence) and X-2 (Counter-Intelligence), placed under the War Department.[23]

While the OSS in Austria concentrated its efforts on what was going on in Austria at the time, politically, militarily, economically, and socially, the SSU soon shifted its focus from mainly Austrian matters to monitoring events and developments in the neighboring countries to the southeast. By the beginning of 1946, SSU Austria, under the leadership of former Lt. Cdr. Alfred C. Ulmer, later to become the first CIA station-chief in Vienna, was reduced to a staff of about sixty, most of them operating out of Vienna and mainly targeting the Soviet zone in Austria, Hungary, and, increasingly, Yugoslavia. By the end of April 1946, just as the political and economic situation seriously deteriorated in all of Central Europe, the SSU was further reduced to a personnel ceiling of thirty-seven. In May 1946, the Austrian SSU Mission was decentralized and put under new cover arrangements. Only a small administrative unit remained under G-2 at Headquarters United States Forces in Austria (USFA); the Trieste Unit remained under cover of the U.S. military government, while the Salzburg station which also housed the headquarters of counter-intelligence (X-2 Austria), only partly operated under cover of the U.S. military government in Salzburg and partly under cover of USDIC, the U.S. Detailed Interrogation Center there. In August 1946, Ulmer asked for the adoption of a new cover designation for the SSU: Field Operations Branch in the Executive Division of the Allied Commission for Austria, but it was by then rapidly turning into a mostly civilian organization. The new target priorities of SSU Austria are convincingly reflected in its report tabulation for September 1946: forty-three reports on Yugoslavia, seventeen reports on Hungary, thirteen reports on the Soviet zone in Austria, and only four reports on the U.S. zone of occupation. The same survey lists twenty-one different sources or chains of informants.[24] Clearly the emphasis in intelligence gathering by the SSU during 1946 had shifted from Austria to the Soviet Union and its emerging satellite countries of southeastern Europe.[25]

In October 1946, SSU Austria was liquidated in name, but its tasks were simultaneously taken over by the CIG, the immediate precursor of the CIA. It was renamed Office of Special Operations (OSO) and as such became the nucleus around which CIA Austria was organized about a year later.[26] OSS Austria under the Joint Chiefs of Staff (JCS) and under USFA, SSU Austria under the War Department and USFA and OSO-Austria under the CIG and USFA were only one major type of U.S. intelligence provider in quadripartitely-occupied Austria. Compared to Army Intelligence, these, at first partly, and by spring 1946 mainly, civilian intelligence units, were limited in size. However, Air Intelligence (A-2) and particularly the Office of Naval Intelligence (ONI) in Austria were even smaller.[27]

Army Intelligence was organized as tactical intelligence, referred to as S-2 at the regimental level, and G-2 at the general staff level, from division through field army. The purpose of the S-2/G-2 staffs was to collect information from the combat units on the position of the enemy during the war and early postwar phase and, as part of the occupation force, to collect positive intelligence gained by technical intelligence army personnel consisting of interrogators, document analysts, order of battle specialists, and counter-intelligence agents. For the occupation, these units were combined into a Military Intelligence Service (MIS) which provided the backbone for intelligence operations supporting the U.S. military government. The 7769th MIS in Austria collected military, political, economic and cultural intelligence.[28] The latter, for example, was also carried out in conjunction with the army's Information Services Branch (ISB), which at first controlled and later monitored all Austrian media in the U.S. zone and, of course, also analyzed the Soviet military and Soviet-controlled press in Austria.[29] The combined resources of the army provided an overwhelming amount of information which had to be coordinated, harmonized, and made available to the U.S. Military Commander, not the least in his other role as U.S. High Commissioner in Austria. This coordinating task fell to Col. Edwin M.J. Kretzmann, who headed the Intelligence Coordination Branch (ICB) which provided daily, weekly, and, later, bi-weekly USFA intelligence summaries for the Commander-in-Chief and the other decision-makers in the U.S. element of the Allied Commission for Austria (USACA).[30]

Until the summer or even the fall of 1946, these USFA intelligence summaries included virtually no information on the Soviet forces or on subversive communist activity. This changed only towards the end of 1946 when the 7769th MIS in Austria was reorganized into internal and external security sections. It was not until 1947 that army intelligence information had coalesced into a clear depiction of the Soviet Union as a definite danger to the security of the United States. Only by February 1948 did military intelligence reports uniformly characterize the Soviet Union and the Austrian Communist Party as subversive influences in Austria.[31]

However, some elements of U.S. army intelligence in Austria, that is certain sections within the Army's Counter-Intelligence Corps under Major James Milano, had been collecting and submitting critical reports on the Soviets and Austrian Communists practically from the onset of the occupation. Such intelligence had come from deserters, escapees, monitored telephone lines, or recruited secret agents. At first, this adverse information was not included in the G-2's periodic intelligence reports and was not mentioned in the official reports of the High Commissioner to the Joint Chiefs of Staff. Only by the end of 1946 did the MIS in Austria provide positive intelligence on military and industrial targets inside the Soviet Union. While initially the U.S. had envisaged no long-term security interests in Austria, by mid-1947 the new USFA Commander, General Keyes, in May received the following assessment by the Joint Chiefs of Staff:

> This government continues to regard Austria as of the greatest political and strategic interest. We cannot afford to let this key area fall under exclusive influence of the Soviet Union, for if this should happen it would only consolidate Soviet domination of Danubian and Balkan areas but would also weaken our position in Italy, Germany and Czechoslovakia. This government will therefore continue to support in every feasible way, any government in Austria that preserves an independent or neutral orientation.[32]

Almost immediately, General Keyes embarked on a personal mission to uphold the U.S. position in Austria.[33] By mid-1948, this shared perception led directly to a secret military assistance program, code-named Operation KISMET, the purpose of which was to help establish a nascent Austrian military force that could resist potential communist expansion.[34] By that time, of course, the First Cold War in Austria was in full swing. Three years later, Hans J. Morgenthau, in a study for the State Department Policy Planning Staff defined U.S. interest in Austria in no uncertain, almost cruelly honest, terms of self-interest:

> ...we are interested in the political social, and economic stability of Austria, not because we are interested in Austria per se, for humanitarian or other reasons, nor because we like democratic stability per se but because the military and political interests of the United States demand stability in Austria.[35]

Before turning to the central question about the CIA in Austria in the era of the Marshall Plan, a word on the role of the 430th CIC in Austria also appears necessary. The original and primary mission of the CIC in postwar Austria was to carry out the denazification program.[36] In 1946, that mission began to change markedly. The CIC started to concentrate its efforts on combatting the Soviet threat to U.S. forces and to Austrian independence. For this purpose, it did not even shy away from employing former German or Austrian Nazi intelligence functionaries. The following names of former *Abwehr*, SS and SD officers, mostly Austrian by birth, exemplify this approach in

Austria: Jan Robert Verbelen, Wilhelm Höttl, Hermann Milleder, Stefan Schachermayer, Karl Kowarik, and Erich Kernmayr.[37]

By 1946, the CIC and other army intelligence units began to turn their attention to the phenomenon of desertion from the Red Army or other Soviet organizations in Austria, which allegedly averaged twenty to twenty-five per month over these early years. While at the beginning of the occupation period a significant number of Soviet deserters in Red Army uniforms were returned, by early 1947 this practice had ceased, and U.S. security organizations began to collect and use the information provided by escapees and started analyzing the motifs and reasons for Soviet desertion. By early 1948, G-2 became convinced that a majority of Soviet deserters believed that the world was on the verge of a hot war between the capitalist and communist powers. As one Soviet deserter put it: "Stalin tells us that war is inevitable."[38] By mid-1947, the stream of deserters and low-level defectors to the West over the Austrian borders and from Soviet organizations in Austria had become steady, just as reliable information on the Red Army, Soviet activities in Eastern Europe, and Soviet objectives generally turned into a much sought-after commodity in Vienna, but more importantly in Washington.[39] Austria was, by then, fully recognized as an almost ideal listening post into the Soviet empire in Eastern Europe. It was at that point that the 430th CIC in Austria developed the infamous Rat Line, that is, an escape route from Austria via Italy to South America for all important Soviet defectors and often for their families as well. It was a simple idea: recognize an important, that is, knowledgable deserter/defector, debrief him, establish a new identity and a visa for him and then send him off to a new life somewhere in South America. However, running those rat lines was a tricky, sensitive, and, above all, costly operation. It needed good connections to the Vatican where a former fascist Croatian priest provided the genuine visa papers and good relations to the Genova harbor police as well as to the Italian border police. The Rat Line was clearly created for Soviet deserters defectors, but eventually was also used for or by fascist war criminals. Jim Milano's book provides a chilling account of this type of activity by U.S. Army counter-intelligence units stationed in Austria.[40]

Towards the end of 1949 or at the beginning of 1950, the CIA in Austria took over the Rat Line, and even though the then CIA chief in Austria, John Richardson, professed not to be interested in it, it was definitely re-opened in early 1951. It was reopened for a long-time

CIC agent in Germany who, it turned out, had been the head of the *Gestapo* in Lyon during the German occupation and had figured large on every important war criminal search list. His name was Klaus Barbie. It was his case which, after his capture in Bolivia in the early 1980s, threw open the hitherto hidden history of the Rat Line from Austria.[41]

The CIC considered itself as the U.S. agency most actively committed to the struggle against communism in peace time. In 1955, it was responsible for fifty-three targets in Austria. These targets were categorized in six priorities:[42]

Priority I:
Indications of impending hostility
Overthrow of the Austrian government
Activities of Soviet satellite intelligence agencies
Priority II:
Complaint investigations
Security surveys and inspections
Priority III:
KPÖ activities
Priority IV:
Labor screening
Marriage investigations
Priority V:
Activities of KPÖ Front Groups
Priority VI:
Extreme right wing

Part of the routine tasks of the CIC was also the gathering of general positive intelligence, among which was, for example, the surveillance of major Austrian politicians.[43] CIC Austria had an average staff size of around 500 people over the entire decade of the occupation.

## Agendas and Activities

Sallie Pisani, in her book *The CIA and the Marshall Plan*, published in 1991, convincingly demonstrates that overt Marshall Plan aid and a new covert organization, founded in June 1948 and entrusted with new types of non-military operations in peace time, were part of one over-arching strategy to counter communism in Western Europe.[44]

It was called the Office of Special Projects, but was soon and quite understandably, albeit less appropriately, renamed Office of Policy Coordination (OPC). Through NSC directive 10/2 of 18 June 1948, the OPC was empowered to conduct covert operations defined as "activities against hostile foreign states or in support of friendly foreign states which are so planned and executed that, if uncovered the U.S. government, can plausibly disclaim any responsibility for them."[45] In October 1948, its chief, Frank G. Wisner, Assistent Director of Policy Co-ordination, spelled out the specific functions of the OPC on the following lines of clandestine activity:[46]

- Functional Group I - Psychological Warfare
  - Program A - Press (periodical and non-periodical)
  - Program B - Radio
  - Program C - Miscellaneous (direct mail, poison pen, rumors, etc.)
- Functional Group II - Political Warfare
  - Program A - Support of Resistance (Underground)
  - Program B - Support of DPs and Refugees
  - Program C - Support of anti-Communists in Free Countries
  - Program D - Encouragement of Defection
- Functional Group III - Economic Warfare
  - Program A - Commodity operations (clandestine preclusive buying, market manipulation, and black market operation)
  - Program B - Fiscal operations (currency speculation, counterfeiting, etc. )
- Functional Group IV - Preventive Direct Action
  - Program A - Support of Guerillas
  - Program B - Sabotage, Countersabotage and Demolition
  - Program D - Stay-behind
- Functional Group V - Miscellaneous
  - Program A - Front Organization
  - Program B - War Plans
  - Program C - Administration
  - Program D - Miscellaneous

The OPC grew in leaps and bounds. While in 1949 it had a combined staff of 302 and a budget of approximately $5 million, by the end of 1952 it had expanded to a staff of 2,812 at home and to 3,142 operators working in forty-seven stations around the world with a budget of close to $200 million.[47] During Truman's presidency, eighty-one covert actions were authorized.[48]

Besides the hardly coincidental beginning of both the European Recovery Program (ERP) and of the OPC in mid-1948, the main revelation in Pisani's book pertained to the claim that 5 percent of the ERP Counterpart Funds, collected in European currencies but set aside for dollar aid, were allegedly made available to the OPC to finance its covert efforts in political, economic, and psychological warfare against communism.[49] Allegedly, very few Marshall Plan officials even at the top level were aware that such a sizeable percentage of the counterpart sources set aside were used directly for funding the OPC, not even Paul G. Hoffman, the chief of the Economic Cooperation Administration (ECA). Pisani argues that the OPC's first major assignment, in effect, was covert political assistance to the Marshall Plan in the various ERP countries. CIA-in-house critics of Pisani's theory, which she derived mainly through oral history interviews, have argued that the CIA/OPC played only a relatively small part in the entire context of the Marshall Plan policy.[50] Nevertheless, there are significant links between central intelligence and the ERP. For example, one notices a strong staff continuity between OSS/SSU and the ERP at the upper and middle echelon, as well as at the lower level of the ECA.[51] Also, there were other links.

By 1947/48 a variety of western, mainly U.S. inspired organizations drew up programs of covert operations disguised to subvert communist influence in Europe. Together with the OPC, they formed a kind of covert network of operations intended to destabilize the Soviet Union and its satellites.[52] One such U.S. covert operation was the funding of the European Movement through the American Committee on United Europe (ACUE) which was directed by senior figures from the U.S. intelligence communities, among them William J. Donovan and Allen W. Dulles and several members of the European resistance community during World War II. ACUE was seen by them as "the unofficial counterpart" to the Marshall Plan.[53] The OPC was thus only the vanguard of a broad set of clandestine operations and organizations active in postwar Europe in five major areas: first, the covert support of the political parties of the non-communist left and center, as evidenced most dramatically in the Italian parliamentary elections of 1948;[54] second, the struggle for the control of international labor organizations and, even more importantly, against the Soviet-controlled World Federation of Trade Unions (WFTU);[55] third, the attempt to influence the cultural and intellectual elites of Europe through the funding of various groups, conferences, and publications; (The best documented example for this type of strategy is the founding and funding of the Congress for Cultural Freedom in 1950.[56] From the spring of 1951, these cultural and other clandestine activities were conducted by a new department of the CIA, the International Organizations Division (IO) which promoted the utilization of private organizations as so-called "fronts", particularly of U.S. foundations[57]); fourth, subversive operations meant to provoke dissonance within the USSR, but directed also against the Soviet satellite states (These efforts were carried out primarily through the National Committee for a Free Europe, later known as Free Europe Committee, which ran Radio Free Europe and Radio Liberty out of Munich.); and fifth, the OPC itself, which in 1952 was fully integrated into the CIA; by then it was already in the midst of a determined effort to forge stay-behind networks in resistance against an expected Soviet incursion into western Europe and to penetrate *emigré* agents into Eastern Europe.[58]

Early in 1949, the OPC entered into a formal relationship with the Free Trade Union Committee (FTUC) of the AFL through which it then started funnelling funds to non-communist trade unions in western Europe in the amount of $170,000 in 1950, for example.[59] The OPC also invested considerable amounts of couterpart funds for labor projects in various strategically important European countries. Even though we do not have exact figures for Austria, we now know that a good number of the regional and national ECA officers cooperated or had close contact with the OPC/CIA, either through Washington or through local connections and that most of the labor *attachés* in the ECA were recipients of CIA subsidies. These were to be used to secure the full-hearted support of the non-communist trade union elites. Even though this policy was at first mainly directed towards Italy, France, and the western zones in Germany, it can be assumed that after the communist coup in Prague and the first Berlin crisis, Austria was given disproportionate attention. The names Jay Lovestone, Irving Brown, Henry Rutz, and Wesley Cook as representatives of the AFL and the CIO stand prominently for this type of strategy.[60] Despite the lack of incontrovertible documentary proof, the overlapping goals of the ERP and the OPC make it very plausible that a good deal of strategic coordination did occur; it certainly made good Cold War common sense.[61]

Moreover, the ECA, also in Austria, was used heavily as a new and convenient cover organization for CIA operators. One of these operators almost certainly must have been Irving Ross who, as ECA trade negotiator with the Soviets, was murdered in the Russian zone in Vienna on the night of 30/31 October1948. He may have been lured there by a female Soviet double agent named Dana Superina with whom he had a romantic liaison and who had pretended to be a Croatian anti-communist agent.[62] Needless to say, all intelligence records pertaining to this case have remained tightly closed ever since. Irving Ross was only one of several American victims of the bitter intelligence battle which was fought in Austria, foremost in Vienna, and which had greatly escalated in 1948. As the Cold War battle over the Marshall Plan for Austria intensified, abductions, kidnappings, and beatings became almost daily occurrences, particularly during the later weeks of 1948. Some of the more spectacular kidnappings involved upper echelon Austrian civil servants, among them highly placed security officers like Anton Marek of the *Staatspolizei* or Franz Kiridus of the Austrian *gendarmerie*. No doubt, Austrian police and *gendarmerie* officers were among the most important collaborators or informants for the CIA as well as for the NKVD/MVD. Espionage for the United States was the charge most often leveled against the kidnapped. More often than not it may have been a legitimate accusation.[63]

It appears that U.S. intelligence managed to develop very close relations not only with members of the Austrian Cabinet (foremost among them Leopold Figl, Karl Gruber, Adolf Schärf, and Oskar Helmer) but also with leading civil servants in charge of ministerial sections and particularly of security, among them section chief Maximilian Pammer of the Interior Ministry and the head of the *Staatspolizei*, later to be director of Public Safety, Oswald Peterlunger; and most likely also Josef Holaubek, the Viennese police chief. Further known or probable informants, some of them possibly paid agents, were to be found in Austrian media press circles (press and radio) and among the financial and industrial elites.[64]

I suspect Austria must have been considered a special case and place for the CIA because, in Vienna, it certainly did not have to start from scratch. The first chief of CIA Austria, Alfred C. Ulmer,[65] had been stationed in Vienna since the end of the war, after having been involved in OSS planning for the agent penetration into Austrian territory from the Bari/Caserta base of Allied Forces Headquarters

(AFHQ) in Italy since the summer of 1944. By mid-1946, he had forged a small but experienced team in Vienna and Salzburg, which had developed intelligence chains into Hungary, Yugoslavia, Trieste, and even into Poland.[66] Even though CIA Austria was heavily outnumbered by the various military intelligence agencies operating in Austria, probably by a factor of between eight to twelve, I believe it would be wrong to underestimate the contribution and competence of CIA Austria even in the first couple of years of its existence. Certainly by 1949, when the process of civilianization of the U.S. occupation authorities greatly intensified, the CIA took on more and more of the tasks hitherto handled by G-2 and CIC. We have reason to assume that by 1949, the OPC, which was operating under the auspices of the CIA, but at first was primarily directed by the State Department, was well-established in Austria and had already started planning for covert action operations into southeastern Europe. As William Hood confirmed, just one of the OPC missions in Austria was to "shake the Hungarian Government to its knees."[67] Frank Lindsay, also a veteran of the OSS and the Marshall Plan Administration, who was in charge of planning and executing infiltration missions into Eastern Europe, spoke of the unrealistically high expectations and pressures in and from Washington for subversive paramilitary action, both within the CIA and within the U.S. government.[68] Most of the refugee agent parachute missions into communist Europe and into the Soviet Union itself, undertaken from the early 1950s, were to end as tragic failures.[69]

The CIA in Austria had extensive offices in Vienna in the *Stiftskaserne* and in the *Allianz Versicherungsgebäude* in the *Währingerstraße*. The chief-of-station, his secretary, and the communication specialists were housed in the American Legation or, later, Embassy. It is impossible to prove, but based on available evidence, I would hazard the guess that by 1950 CIA Austria had a staff of about fifty to sixty full-time employees. When the OSO and the OPC were merged in 1952, and a steady build-up took place, the CIA in Austria probably reached a size of about eighty to one hundred staff and officers by 1955. Both William Hood and Peer de Silva estimate that Soviet intelligence outnumbered the Americans by a factor of four to five. In April 1948, the CIA estimated Soviet security strength in Austria at 2,500 (MVD and GRU), probably about four times the size of the combined U.S. security apparatus.[70] Pyotr Deryabin, the KGB defector who changed sides in Vienna, claimed that between 60 to 70 percent of the Soviet intelligence staff worked under diplomatic cover.[71] The U.S. percentage for that was much smaller, probably around 25 percent.

Who, then, were the main partners of the CIA in Austria? It can be said with much confidence that the Austrians proved generally to be very susceptible to U.S. goods, ideas, and even values.[72] Small wonder then that they also proved to be very cooperative, even eager, to serve the Americans, not least as informants and even agents. This was actually the case with all U.S. intelligence agencies. Cooperation and collaboration reached into public and private institutions alike; it was valued by the Americans particularly when it addressed present and future elites and opinion makers; this is why the CIA during those years secured the cooperation of student organizations in Austria, newspaper journalists, magazines, authors, and broadcasters. What little propaganda was really needed to keep the Austrians in tow was organized and sponsored through newspapers like the *Wiener Kurier*, the *Salzburger Nachrichten* and *Oberösterreichische Nachrichten*, all three of which had, of course, been controlled for years by the U.S. Information Services Branch (ISB) and had then probably been funded by the CIA.[73] The CIA had certainly also subsidized Fritz Molden's *Die Presse*, Radio Rot-Weiss-Rot, and the Austrian Congress of Cultural Freedom journal *Forum*, edited since January 1954 by Friedrich Torberg.[74] Other important allies were found and financed within the Austrian trade union movement. Franz Olah, the head of the transportation workers union and, after the strike movement of October 1950, in charge of the so-called *Sonderprojekt*, is the best-known case in point.[75] One must not forget Radio Free Europe, a CIA operation, which ran an Austrian Program from Munich, or the OPC/CIA financed visits to the U.S. by academics, managers, and trade unionists.[76] The CIA bought shares in publishing houses, engaged in the production and distribution of films, and placed agents in major news agencies. It also cooperated with major foundations and think tanks like the Council of Foreign Relations or the Rockefeller and Ford Foundations and its sub-organizations around the world. One such CIA front may, at least in the beginning, well have been the Ford Institute in Vienna.

Among the more spectacular CIA projects run during this period in Austria was Operation SILVER (Operation LORD for the British), a tunnel project begun by the British intelligence organization SIS/MI6 in 1951 and run jointly by the British and Americans from 1952 to 1954. It was a telephone wiretap operation monitoring Soviet telephone lines from a seventy foot tunnel underneath a building in Schwechat, a town just outside of Vienna. These successful interceptions may have provided London and Washington with some assurances that the Soviets had no plans to take military actions in Europe during the period of the Korean War.[77] Operation SILVER became the model for the CIA planned undertaking called Operation GOLD, a similar, but technically much more complicated, project in Berlin a few years later.[78]

NSC Document 10/ 4 of January 1951 authorized the CIA to organize "assistance to underground resistance movements, guerillas and refugee liberation groups."[79] Operation EASEFUL was run under this title; it eventually resulted in the preparation of around eighty weapons caches sites in western Austria which, as will be remembered, baffled the Austrians for a while in 1996. They represent the gist of the thinking of the "determined interventionists" of the OPC during these years in Austria.[80]

However, it needs to be stressed and remembered that the CIA of the Marshall Plan era was still primarily conceived and organized as an agency of intelligence collection, counter-intelligence and intelligence analysis. ORE's and NIE's country studies, though prepared in Washington, were to a large extent based on the OSO's observations in the field. No doubt they improved over the years, but they were succinct and usually highly accurate assessments of the current situation in Austria already during these early years of the CIA in Austria. Again a few examples must suffice. A CIG study of February 1947 claimed: "The USSR desires an Austrian regime subservient to Soviet policy. The Soviets want a treaty which imposes maximum restrictions on the sovereignty of the Austrian Government and legalizes future Soviet interference in Austrian affairs."[81] In April 1948, an ORE report argued: "Austria from a U.S. point of view is of considerable importance but almost entirely in a negative sense. The USSR could absorb Austria only by military force."[82] A study on "Possible Developments in Soviet Policy Towards Austria" of February 1949 addressed the question of a Berlin-type crisis: "A blockade of Vienna, similar to that of Berlin, is a Soviet capability and may not be entirely discounted. It is, however, considered unlikely. The Kremlin would be reluctant at this time to take the risk of war entailed in a blockade of Vienna."[83] In a more elaborate study of August 1949, perhaps reflecting a greater insight into structural problems of Austria gained by ECA administrators in close touch with the CIA, the following was said about Austrian internal security:

> Internal security within Austria rests not only upon the police and gendarmerie (some 200,000 men) but also upon the presence of the occupation forces who have, to date, exerted a restraining influence upon any disturbing elements. The Communists enjoy an artificial importance by virtue of the Soviet-occupation forces but the USSR has given no evidence of desiring an overt attempt to disrupt internal security, possibly because active Soviet support of the communists would threaten partition of the country and because the Western Powers could effectively control any such attempt in the Western Zones.[84]

This certainly proved to be an accurate estimate in view of what happened only a year later. Many more examples could be given. In any case, these estimates reached the highest offices in Washington, from the Office of the President or the Office of the Secretary of Defense to the Joint Chiefs of Staff. Perhaps they should not be discounted lightly. I, for one, do not believe that the CIA in Austria until 1955 played only a highly marginal role (" eine höchst marginale Rolle"), as was recently argued by an Austrian historian.[85]

Reporting and analyzing was the bread and butter task of the CIA, but Washington wanted more. It was hungry for inside information on the main enemy: "Your job is to recruit Russians. Until we've done that we've failed," wrote William Hood, one of the main CIA operators in Vienna, of the real challenge to CIA Austria.[86] Counter-intelligence was the higher task, and Vienna proved to be a fertile ground in those years. Popov of the GRU and Deryabin of the KGB were prize defectors for the early CIA, and they were both handled extremely skillfully.[87] Also competently handled was the case of Otto Verber and Kurt Ponger, two Austrian emigrants and intelligence agents who, after working for the Americans during the war and early postwar period and returning to Austria, changed their allegiance to the Soviets, were caught and in 1952 were taken to the U.S. for a trial which was in the end averted through confession. Ponger was given five to fifteen years, Verber three to ten. They were later paroled and allowed to return to Vienna.[88]

By mid-1953, with Allen W. Dulles just appointed DCI, Stalin's death, the ceasefire in Korea, and the figures for the Austrian economy and trade starting to improve noticeably, due in large measure to the impact of the ERP, a new optimism must have set in also among the personnel of CIA Austria. After eight years of battling the Soviet intelligence apparatus and their satellite intelligence organizations in Central Europe and elsewhere, the American intelligencers had reason to believe that they were finally starting to hold their ground.

In any case, the first dozen or so years of the CIA were a period of practically uncontrolled activities and limitless development of the organization as a whole; during these years even the most critical U.S. print media refrained from excessive interest in this most secret weapon of the Cold War arsenal.[89] This could only have enhanced the sense of self-importance and self-confidence among the men on the very frontlines of the ideologically-based struggle of the intelligence avant gardes. In some respects, these were, even more so in retrospect, the golden years of the agency. Nevertheless, in places like Berlin and Vienna, they were, potentially at least, also dangerous to one's health and life.

## Conclusion

By the time the Marshall Plan was implemented in Austria, U.S. intelligence organizations had been active in this small country for over three years. This at least in part explains why the Office of Policy Coordination, as a new covert action unit operating under the auspices of the CIA, was capable of establishing its presence in Austria within a relatively short period of time. In the escalating tension of the early years of the First Cold War, Austria, not necessarily a country of great traditional interest for the United States, became of undisputed strategic importance for both military and diplomatic decision makers in Washington and in Austria. The OPC/CIA presence at this central European junction of the escalating super-power conflict favored the continued active and substantial involvement of intelligence resources in Austria. The men of OPC/CIA recognized the potential for a major contribution in the containment of the Soviets in the Danubian heartland of Europe by complementing, wherever possible, the massive U.S. foreign aid program in Austria. This at least partially explains why Austria and its capital were to remain a significant arena in the battle for intelligence supremacy in Central Europe for years to come.[90]

## Notes

1. Significantly, the Netherlands and Germany, both countries where quite recently national associations for the study of intelligence have been established (The Netherlands Intelligence Studies Association, NISA, in Holland and the Arbeitskreis Geschichte der Nachrichtendienste in Germany) are notable European exceptions. Cf. Bob de Graaff and Cees Wiebes, *Villa Maarheeze: The Netherlands Foreign Intelligence Service* (The Hague: Sdu Uitgevers, 1998); and Wolfgang Krieger and Jürgen Weber, eds., *Spionage für den Frieden? Nachrichtendienste in Deutschland während des Kalten Krieges* (Munich: Olzog, 1997).

2. Reliable information on the roots and early years of the CIA can be drawn from Tom Braden, "The Birth of the CIA," *American Heritage: The Magazine of History* 28 (February 1977): 4-13; and John Ranelagh, *The Agency* (London: Weidenfeld & Nicolson, 1986). An overview of U.S. intelligence endeavors concerning Austria before the creation of the CIA is provided in Siegfried Beer, *Target Central Europe: American Intelligence Efforts Regarding Nazi and Early Postwar Austria, 1941-1947* (Working Papers in Austrian Studies 97/1, Minneapolis, MN 1997).

3. This viewpoint is shared by several historians of the CIA, e.g. Harry Howe Ransom, "Secret Intelligence in the United States, 1947-1982: The CIA's Search for Legitimacy," in Christopher Andrew and David Dilks, eds., *The Missing Dimension. Governments and Intelligence Communities in the Twentieth Century* (London: MacMillan, 1984), 203; or William M. Leary, ed., *The Central Intelligence Agency. History and Documents* (The University of Alabama Press, 1984), 52. Oliver Rathkolb is on record as doubting the relevance and/or effectiveness of the early CIA in Austria; however, he has so far failed to substantiate his negative assessment. Cf. Oliver Rathkolb, ed., *Gesellschaft und Politik am Beginn der Zweiten Republik. Vertrauliche Berichte der US-Militäradministration aus Österreich in englischer Originalfassung* (Vienna: Böhlau, 1985), 18 and idem, *Washington ruft Wien. US-Großmachtpolitik und Österreich 1953-1963* (Vienna: Böhlau, 1997), 188.

4. The present Director of Central Intelligence (DCI), George Tenet, only recently broke the habitually held silence on the annual U.S. budget for national intelligence purposes when he released the figures for 1998: $ 26.7 billion covering thirteen agencies altogether. This accounts for about a tenth of the total U.S. defense budget. Cf. *International Herald Tribune*, December 5-6, 1998. The CIA's annual budget for 1998, approximately $30 billion, constitutes a nominal increase of financial resources over the budget of the predecessor agency OSS in 1945, approximately $30 million, by a quotient of 100.

5. Cf. James Bamford, *The Puzzle Palace: A Report on America's Most Secret Agency* (Boston: Houghton Mifflin, 1982).

6. Cf. Thomas F. Troy, *Donovan and the CIA: A History of the Establishment of the Central Intelligence Agency* (Fredericks, MD: University Press of America, 1981); Rhodri Jeffreys-Jones, *The CIA and American Democracy* (New Haven, CT: Yale University Press., 1989) and Loch K. Johnson, *America's Secret Power. The CIA in Democratic Society* (New York: Oxford University Press, 1989).

7. The CIA's practice of releasing selected documents on self-chosen topics ("targeted openings") has drawn greatly deserved criticism from the scientific community. Cf. Zachary Karabell and Timothy Naftali, "History Declassified: The Perils and Promise of CIA Documents," in *Diplomatic History* 18 (1994): 4, 615-626 and Warren F. Kimball, "Classified!," in *Perspectives. AHA Newsletter* 35 (1997): 2, 9f. and 22-24.

8. Just two representative examples must suffice here: Aleksandr Fursenko and Timothy Naftali, *"One Hell of a Gamble": Kruschev, Castro, and Kennedy, 1958-1964* (New York: W.W. Norton, 1997) and David E. Murphy, Sergei A. Kondrashev, and George Bailey, *Battleground Berlin: CIA vs. KGB in the Cold War* (New Haven, CT: Yale University Press, 1997).

9. They are mainly to be found in the following Record Groups (RG) of the National Archives (NA): RG 226 (COI, OSS, SSU, some CIG); RG 260 (G-2); RG 263 (CIA); RG 319 (CIC); RG 338 (CIC, G-2); RG 341 (A-2) and RG 407 (S-2, G-2, CIC).

10. I have continually and consistently worked on U.S. intelligence efforts undertaken during the years 1941 to 1946 in or concerning Austria, having made yearly pilgrimages since 1984 to the National Archives of the United States on Pennsylvania Avenue in Washington, D.C. and now for the last several years at College Park, MD. I have personally researched about 600 boxes of records of the COI/OSS/SSU/CIC and MIS/G-2 and gathered about 10,000 pages of photocopied documents in the process.

11. Cf. Siegfried Beer, "Early CIA Reports on Austria," *Contemporary Austrian Studies (CAS)* 5 (1996): 247-288.

12. Cf. e.g. *FRUS, 1945-1950: Emergence of the Intelligence Establishment* (Washington, DC: U.S. Government Printing Office, 1996) 240.

13. It is entitled *The CIA under Harry Truman*, ed. Geoffrey Warner (Washington, DC: Center for the Study of Intelligence, 1994).

14. William Hood, *Mole* (New York: Ballantine Books, 1982) and re-issued by Brassey's (Washington, D.C., 1993).

15. Popov was given the code name ATTIC. He was able to provide the CIA with an extensive history of GRU operations in Austria, providing the names and functions of every GRU officer in Vienna and the cryptonyms of hundreds of illegal agents working in the West. Cf. Wendell L. Minnick, *A World Wide Encyclopedia of Persons Conducting Espionage and Covert Actions, 1946-1991* (Jefferson, NC: McFarland, 1992), 184.

16. Peter Deriabin and Frank Gibney, *The Secret World: KGB* (New York: Time Inc., 1959).

17. James V. Milano and Patrick Brogan, *Soldiers, Spies, and the Rat Line: America's Undeclared War Against the Soviets* (Washington, D.C.: Brassey's, 1995).

18. Peer de Silva, *Sub Rosa: The CIA and the Uses of Intelligence* (New York: Times Books, 1978).

19. Alfred C. Ulmer, Jr., interviewed by the author at Washington, D.C. in August of 1991. Several of these interviews have been conducted in connection with the "OSS Oral History Project" directed by Christof Mauch and funded by the Center for the Study of Intelligence, Washington, D.C.

20. The exception was signals intelligence which was conducted by the army's Signal Intelligence Service, later called the Special Branch, and the navy's Communication Security Unit, also known as OP-20-G.

21. For a general overview of the structure and value of OSS, cf. Bradley F. Smith, *The Shadow Warriors: OSS and the Origins of the CIA* (New York: Basic Books, 1983); and George C. Chalou, ed., *The Secrets War: The Office of Strategic Services in World War II* (Washington, D.C.: National Archives and Records Administration, 1992).

22. Cf. Oliver Rathkolb, "Professorenpläne für Österreichs Zukunft. Nachkriegsfragen im Diskurs der Forschungsabteilung Research and Analysis," in *Geheimdienstkrieg gegen Deutschland,* ed. Jürgen Heideking and Christof Mauch (Göttingen: A. Francke, 1993), 166-181; and Siegfried Beer, "Research and Analysis about Austria, 1941-1949. American Intelligence Studies on the Reconstruction of Central Europe," *Wiener Beiträge zur Geschichte der Neuzeit* 24 (1999, forthcoming).

23. For a more detailed description of the activities of the SSU in Austria see Beer, *Target Central Europe.*

24. SSU Report "The Austrian Mission", 23 September 1946, NA, RG 226, E(ntry) 108B, B(ox) 75, F(older) 619.

25. Among the projects run by SSU Austria in the fall of 1946 were the PENTATHOL and ANACIN Projects into Poland, the MIDAL Project into Romania, and the UNQUENTINE and KILKENNY Projects into the USSR. SSU-Survey "Recapitulation of Expenses", 19 October 1946, NA, RG 226, E 199, B 2, F 25.

26. It can be assumed that SSU/OSO Austria was among the vanguard of U.S. intelligence efforts vis-a-vis the Soviet Union in 1946/47, at a time "when Washington knew virtually nothing about the U.S.S.R.", as one of the most experienced CIA functionaries of the whole Cold War period characterized it thirty years later. Cf. Harry Rositzke, "America's Secret Operations: A Perspective," *Foreign Affairs* 53 (January 1975): 335.

27. So far very little concrete information exists about the activities of these two small intelligence units in Austria, the sole exception being a short piece on the potential scenario of a Berlin-style blockade of Vienna by Erwin A. Schmidl, "'Rosinenbomber' über Wien? Alliierte Pläne zur Luftversorgung Wiens im Falle einer sowjetischen Blockade 1948-1953," *Geschichte und Gegenwart* 17 (1998): 195-210.

28. Until quite recently, very little research attention had been paid to the wide range of activities carried out by the several U.S. army intelligence units, particularly in the postwar period, during which they were of particular importance in the various U.S. occupational zones. Three American scholars have begun to fill the void: Ralph W. Brown III, Elisabeth B. White, and James Carafano. Their contributions will be cited below.

29. On the strategic importance of the cultural mission of the Americans in Austria, particularly during the early years of the Allied occupation of Austria, the several scholarly contributions of Oliver Rathkolb and Reinhold Wagnleitner should be consulted.

30. In retirement, Col. Kretzmann wrote a 105 page personal memoir of his experiences in postwar Austria entitled "'Four Powers in Three-Quarter Time'. Tales of the Austrian Occupation. Vienna 1945-1948." A copy of these unpublished remembrances is in my possession. Further elucidation on the early work of G-2 in Austria was provided me by one of Kretzmann's assistants during the first year of occupation, Lt. Henry Delfiner, who granted the author a two-hour taped interview in Cambridge, MA in May 1997.

31. Cf. James J. Carafano, "'Waltzing into the Cold War.' U.S. Army Intelligence Operations for Postwar Austria, 1944-1948," *CAS* 7 (1999): 165-189.

32. JCS to Keyes, 24 May 1947, printed in *FRUS*, 1947, Vol. II, 1177.

33. Cf. James J. Carafano, "'Battling State.' General Keyes' Campaign for Securing Austria, 1947-1950." Unpublished paper kindly provided me by Col. Carafano.

34. Cf. Christian Stifter, *Die Wiederaufrüstung Österreichs. Die geheime Remilitarisierung der westlichen Besatzungszonen 1945-1955* (Vienna: Studienverlag, 1997).

35. Quoted by Rathkolb, *Washington ruft Wien*, 283.

36. During the first three months in Austria, the 430th Detachment made approximately 4,000 arrests.

37. Cf. Oliver Rathkolb, "'Dritte Männer'. Ex-Nazis als US-Agenten," *Das jüdische Echo* 39 (1990): 85-89; Siegfried Beer, "Von Alfred Redl zum 'Dritten Mann': Österreich und ÖsterreicherInnen im internationalen Geheimdienstgeschehen 1918-1947," *Geschichte und Gegenwart* 16 (1997): 24; and Elizabeth B. White, "'Babes in the Woods'. The U.S. Army Counter Intelligence Corps in Postwar Austria." Paper delivered at the 63rd SMH-Meeting in Washington, D.C. on 21 April 1996. An official history of the 430th CIC Detachment was published by the U.S. Army Intelligence Center: *Occupation of Austria and Italy* (History of the Counter Intelligence Corps XXV, Baltimore, MD, 1959).

38. Ralph W. Brown III, "'Stalin Tells us that War is Inevitable': What American Military Intelligence in Austria Learned from Soviet Deserters, 1946-1948." Paper delivered at the 63rd SMH Meeting in Washington, D.C. on 21 April 1996.

39. Some of the defectors changing sides in Austria wrote noteworthy autobiographical accounts, for example, Peter Pirogov, *Why I Escaped* (London: Harvill Press, 1950); and A. I. Romanov (Boris I. Baklanov), *Nights Are Longest There: Smersh from the Inside* (London: Hutchinson, 1972).

40. Milano desperately claims that as long as the rat lines were run by CIC Austria they were not used for the escape of Nazi war criminals. Cf. Milano, *Rat Line*, xi.

41. Cf. Tom Bower, *Klaus Barbie: Butcher of Lyons* (London: Joseph, 1984).

42. General Briefing, 430$^{th}$ CIC Detachment, May 1955, NA, RG 319, B 61.

43. Cf. Siegfried Beer, "Monitoring Helmer: Zur Tätigkeit des amerikanischen Armeegeheimdienstes CIC in Österreich 1945-1950. Eine exemplarische Dokumentation," in *Geschichte zwischen Freiheit und Ordnung: Gerald Stourzh zum 60. Geburtstag,* ed. Emil Brix, Thomas Fröschl and Josef Leidenfrost (Graz: Styria, 1991), 229-259.

44. Sallie Pisani, *The CIA and the Marshall Plan* (Lawrence, KS: University Press of Kansas, 1991).

45. NSC 10/2, 18 June 1948. Printed in *FRUS, 1945-1950: Emergence*, Doc. Nr. 292.

46. Memo Wisner to DCI Hillenkoetter, 29 October 1948, Ibid., Doc. Nr. 306.

47. Cf. Beatrice Heuser, "Subversive Operationen im Dienste der 'Roll-Back'-Politik 1948-1953," *Vierteljahrshefte für Zeitgeschichte* 37 (1989): 291.

48. Cf. Gregory F. Treverton, *Covert Action: The Limits of Intervention in the Postwar World* (New York: Basic, 1987), 14.

49. 5 percent of ERP counterpart was worth approximately $200 million per annum. A good portion of this was made available as a "slush fund" for use on secret projects. Cf. Evan Thomas, *The Very Best Men. Four Who Dared: The Early Years of the CIA* (New York: Simon & Schuster, 1995), 40.

50. See, for example, the review of Pisani's book by John R. Mapother, a CIA-officer in the mid-1950s in *Foreign Intelligence Literary Scene* (FILS) 11 (1992): 8. John A. Bross, an OSS/CIA veteran interviewed by Pisani, felt that the OPC Marshall Plan connection was not planned but had evolved naturally. Pisani, *CIA-Marshall Plan,* 143.

51. Among these ECA officers in Europe were a number of senior intelligence officers of the OSS, for example David Bruce and Milton Katz, as well as several former OSS field operators in Central Europe, like Franklin A. Lindsay, Albert A. Jolis, and Jacob J. Kaplan. Cf. Albert Jolis, *A Clutch of Reds and Diamonds: A Twentieth Century Odyssey* (Boulder, CO: Columbia University Press, 1996), 211-217.

52. Cf. Eric Thomas Chester, *Covert Network. Progressives, the International Rescue Committee, and the CIA* (New York: M.E. Sharpe, 1995).

53. Cf. Richard J. Aldrich, "OSS, CIA, and European Unity: The American Committee on United Europe, 1948-60," *Diplomacy and Statecraft* 8 (March 1997): 184-227, here 195. The origins of ACUE can actually be traced back to a plea for assistance from the Austrian exile Richard Coudenhove-Kalergi who already in 1947 lobbied for U.S. congressional support for the idea of European unity.

54. See James E. Miller, "Taking off the Gloves: the United States and the Italian Election 1948," *Diplomatic History* 7 (1983): 35-46.

55. Cf. George Morris, *CIA and American Labor:The Subversion of the AFL-CIO's Foreign Policy* (New York: International Publishers, 1967); Ronald Radosh, *American Labor and United States Foreign Policy* (New York: Random House, 1969); and Frederico Romero, *The United States and the European Trade Union Movement, 1941-51* (Chapel Hill: University of North Carolina Press, 1993).

56. Cf. Peter Coleman, *The Liberal Conspiracy: The Congress for Cultural Freedom and the Struggle for the Mind of Postwar Europe* (New York: Free Press, 1990).

57. See Pisani, *CIA Marshall Plan*, 47-52.

58. See Aldrich, *European Unity*, 188f.

59. Recent access to archival collections of the AFL-CIO International Affairs Department at the George Meany Memorial Archives in Silver Spring, MD has made it possible to establish the scope of the utilization of U.S. labor by the OPC/CIA. From 1949 to 1958, the FTUC was the recipient of almost a half million dollars which the OPC/CIA transmitted mainly to Jay Lovestone, the executive secretary of the FTUC and to Irving Brown, its European representative. See Anthony Carew, "The American Labor Movement in Fizzland: The Free Trade Union Committee and the CIA," *Labor History* 39 (1998): 25-28.

60. Needless to say, the records of the Offices of the Labor Advisor and of the Labor Information Division in NA, RG 469: Records of U.S. Foreign Assistence Agencies 1948-61 provide no clue as to this kind of clandestine cooperation.

61. Richard Bissell, by many considered the main force behind the Marshall Plan Administration in Washington, saw in the ECA "an aggressive, innovative organization that should perhaps have served as a prototype of how to achieve foreign policy objectives in the postwar era." Richard M. Bissel, Jr., *Reflections of a Cold Warrior: From Yalta to the Bay of Pigs* (New Haven: Yale University Press, 1996), 69. Evan Thomas believes that Bissell and others saw in the ECA "the model for the CIA as a small, elite group, privately manipulating the world with American funds and power" (Thomas, *Very Best Men*, 97).

62. See cable Keyes to Department of the Army, 5 December 1948, NA, RG 263, B 188.

63. Despite claims to the contrary, this author believes that even Margarethe Ottillinger, who was officially pardoned after the collapse of the Soviet Union, was a case in point. For a dissenting view cf. Stefan Karner, "Zur Politik der sowjetischen Besatzungs- und Gewahrsamsmacht. Das Fallbeispiel Margarethe Ottillinger," in *Österreich unter alliierter Besatzung 1945-1955,* ed. Alfred Ableitinger, Siegfried Beer and Eduard G. Staudinger (Vienna: Böhlau, 1998), 401-430.

64. I have refrained from mentioning further specific names of likely former CIA contacts and informants as a substantial number of these men are still politically or professionally active in Austrian public affairs. See also Arnold Kopeczek, "*Fallbeispiele des Kalten Krieges in Österreich, 1945-1965,*" Ph.D. diss., University of Vienna, 1992, 57-66.

65. Through interviews and various printed sources I have been able to establish the names of the CIA station chiefs in Vienna over the period of the first decade of CIA Austria. These were Alfred C. Ulmer, Jr. (1947/48); John H. Richardson (1948-1952); Bronson Tweedy (1952-1955); and Peer de Silva (1955-1957).

66. By then, Ulmer ran five desks: an Austrian Desk headed by Charles B. Friediger; a Hungarian Desk headed by Martin Himler; a Polish Desk headed by Maj. Burton B. Lifshultz; a Yugoslav Desk headed by John Richardson; and a Romanian Desk headed by Maj. Homer Hall.

67. Cf. Hood, *Mole*, 95 and my interview with William Hood at Scarborough, ME on 12 August 1997.

68. Personal interview with Franklin A. Lindsay by the author at Cambridge, MA on 14 January 1997. Lindsay ran the OPC paramilitary projects from Germany and Austria under the cover of the U.S. Army's External Survey Detachments. Cf. Christopher Simpson, *"Gladio - Type Guerilla Operations in Austria."* Unpublished Report, 1990, 8.

69. Cf. for example, in Albania see Nicholas Bethell, *The Great* Betrayal (London: Hodder & Stoughton, 1984); and John Prados, *Presidents' Secret Wars: CIA and Pentagon Covert Operations from World War II through Iranscam* (New York: Quill/ William Morris, 1988), 45-52.

70. ORE 13-48, 28 April 1948, printed in *CAS* 6 (1996) 272.

71. Peter Deriabin, "The Difficult Intelligence Business," *Show* (March 1964): 40.

72. Cf. Reinhold Wagnleitner, "The Irony of American Culture Abroad: Austria and the Cold War," in *Recasting America: Culture and Politics in the Age of the Cold War*, ed. Lary May (Chicago: University of Chicago Press, 1989), 285-301.

73. See Oliver Rathkolb, "U.S.-Medienpolitik in Österreich 1945-1950: Von antifaschistischer 'Reorientierung' zur ideologischen Westintegration," *Medien-Journal. Informationen aus Medienarbeit und -forschung* 8 (1984): 2-9.

74. Cf. Oliver Rathkolb, "Die Entwicklung der US-Besatzungspolitik zum Instrument des Kalten Krieges," in *Kontinuität und Bruch 1938 - 1945 - 1955. Beiträge zur österreichischen Kultur- und Wissenschaftsgeschichte,* ed. Friedrich Stadler, (Vienna: Jugend und Volk, 1988), 42; and Frank Tichy, *Friedrich Torberg: Ein Leben in Widersprüchen* (Salzburg: Otto Müller Verlag, 1995), 188 and 216-222.

75. On the involvement of Franz Olah with the OPC and later with the CIA, see Wilhelm Svoboda, *Franz Olah. Eine Spurensicherung* (Vienna: Promedia, 1990), 34-43; as well as Helmut Konrad and Manfred Lechner, *"Millionenverwechslung:" Franz Olah, Die Kronenzeitung, Geheimdienste* (Vienna: Böhlau, 1992), 63-87.

76. Cf. Pisani, *CIA Marshall Plan*, 99; and Gene R. Sensenig, *Österreichisch-amerikanische Gewerkschaftsbeziehungen 1945 bis 1950* (Köln: Pahl-Rugenstein, 1987), 118.

77. Cf. David C. Martin, *Wilderness of Mirrors* (New York: Ballantine Books, 1981), 74-76.

78. See Murphy/ Kondrashev/ Bailey, *Battleground Berlin*, 205-209.

79. NSC 10/4, 16 January 1951, NA, RG 273. See also: *Es muß nicht immer Gladio sein* (ZOOM 4-5/1996).

80. A fitting term used by Sallie Pisani, though objected to by some of the men so characterized. Pisani, *CIA Marshall Plan*, 3.

81. "The Situation in Austria," ORE 13/1, 20 February 1947, NA, RG 263, ORE Reports, B 1, printed in *CAS* 5 (1996) 260.

82. "The Current Situation in Austria," ORE 13-48, 28 April 1948, NA, RG 263, ORE Reports, B 2, printed in *CAS* 5 (1996): 266.

83. ORE 28-49, 10 February 1949, NA, RG 263, ORE Reports, B 3, printed in CAS 5 (1996) 273.

84. "The Current Situation in Austria," ORE 56-49, 31 August 1949, NA, RG 263, ORE Reports, B 3, printed in *CAS* 5 (1996) 287.

85. Rathkolb, *Washington ruft Wien*, 188.

86. Hood, *Mole*, 9.

87. Popov is widely acknowledged as the "main agent source on Soviet matters during the fifties for the U.S. Government." Cf. Rositzke, *America's Secret Operations*, 336. He was able to report on Soviet conventional weapons as well as on tactical missile systems and nuclear submarines, saving the Pentagon "at least a half-billion dollars in its research and development program." Idem, *The CIA's Secret Operations. Espionage, Counterespionage, and Covert Action* (Boulder, CO: Westview, 1977) 69. On Deriabin cf. Gordon Brook-Shepherd, *The Storm Bird: Soviet Postwar Defectors* (New York: Weidenfeld & Nicolson, 1989), 85-109.

88. Cf. Hans Moses, "The Case of Major X," in *Inside CIA's Private World. Declassified Articles from the Agency's Internal Journal, 1955-1992,* ed. H. Bradford Esterfield (New Haven, CT: Yale University Press, 1997), 450-477; and Wilhelm Höttl, *Einsatz für das Reich: Im Auslandsgeheimdienst des Dritten Reiches* (Koblenz: Verlag S. Bublies, 1997), 394.

89. Cf. Bradley F. Smith, "An Idiosyncratic View of Where We Stand on the History of American Intelligence in the Early post-1945 Era," *Intelligence and National Security* 3 (1988): 113f.

90. Cf. Harald Irnberger, *Nelkenstrauß ruft Praterstern: Am Beispiel Österreich: Funktion und Arbeitsweise geheimer Nachrichtendienste in einem neutralen Staat* (Vienna: Promedia, 1983); and Kid Möchel, *Der geheime Krieg der Agenten: Spionagedrehscheibe Wien* (Hamburg: Rasch and Röhring, 1997).

# Marshall Plan Propaganda in Austria and Western Germany

*Hans-Jürgen Schröder*

When Secretary of State George C. Marshall delivered his Harvard speech on June 5, 1947, to announce a European Recovery Program, nobody would have been able to predict that this was the beginning of the most successful foreign aid program ever. Within a few years, essential steps towards Western Europe's economic recovery had been achieved, and the economic stabilization was a vital prerequisite for social stability and democracy. Due to its impressive achievements, the Marshall Plan has repeatedly been recommended as a model for solving economic problems in all parts of the world.
American statesmen in particular have repeatedly emphasized George Marshall's contribution to European recovery. Again and again, the Marshall Plan has been referred to as the most important element of United States foreign policy since World War II. In June 1950, while the European Recovery Program was still in progress, President Truman already gave an overall positive evaluation:

> "In the first 2 years of the European recovery program, with our essential aid, the peoples of Europe have made great strides in rebuilding their economies. This has enabled them to preserve and strengthen their free institutions, and to deal successfully with the threat of communism on their own soil. They are drawing closer together in common purpose and in common defense."[1]

Similarly, on the occasion of the tenth anniversary of the Harvard speech, President Eisenhower commemorated the event in a personal letter to George Marshall:

"Only ten years ago, the nations of free Europe stood on the brink of economic collapse and political chaos. Millions of men and women who had fought and suffered in World War II to regain peace and freedom were confronted by a new danger infinitely more complex but no less terrifying than war itself. The fate of all Western Civilization hung in the balance, and there were many to whom disaster seemed inevitable. That this tragedy was averted is due in large measure to the bold and imaginative undertaking which you proposed and which rightfully bears your name. Today, on the tenth anniversary of the pronouncement that launched this undertaking, free Europe has recovered a remarkable degree of economic health, accompanied by an upsurge in political stability, military power, and spiritual vitality."[2]

These statements by both Truman and Eisenhower are just two examples of a long list of positive comments on the Marshall Plan by American politicians and diplomats. In 1997, the fiftieth anniversary of the Harvard speech again offered many opportunities to remember the European Recovery Program and to remind the public of what had been achieved by the Marshall Plan and that its "spirit" is still alive.

The significance of the Marshall Plan has always attracted historians who have intensified their research since more and more archival material became open after the 1970s. A broad set of questions has been asked and most of them have been answered: the economic and political goals and achievements of the European Recovery Program (ERP), the interdependence of economic and political developments, and the militarization of the Marshall Plan are just a few major examples. These topics have been supplemented by studies with special emphasis on Britain, France, Germany, and Italy. More recently, attention has been paid to Austria's special role in the context of the European Recovery Program. With the growing illusion of unlimited access to Russian archives, Soviet policy towards the Marshall Plan has become a topic of empirical research.[3] Given the huge number of publications on the Marshall Plan, it is surprising, however, that until recently one important element had been neglected: propaganda.

## Launching the Publicity Campaign

The Truman Administration undertook extensive propaganda initiatives to enlist support for the Recovery Program, both at home and abroad. First, it was essential to win support from the American people and from Congress, the political body which would allocate the funds required by the executive branch. The White House used various means, both official contacts and informal channels, to achieve this goal. The most prominent non-governmental organization was the New York Council on Foreign Relations with its Committee for the Marshall Plan.[4] Once the aid program had become law, the Truman Administration launched a propaganda campaign overseas. The Economic Cooperation Administration (ECA), which was created to handle the aid program, thought it to be of vital importance to win active support of the Europeans if the Marshall Plan were to be a success. The ECA office in Washington, the Office of the Special Representative in Europe (OSR), and the missions in all recipient countries were committed to selling the Marshall Plan. The files of these offices, which are accessible in the National Archives, are a rich source for any historian interested in ECA propaganda efforts.[5] Of special interest are the records of the Division of Information and the Division of Labor Information.

The ERP overseas information program had basically four general functions, as they were summarized by the ECA's Office of Information.[6]

1. To make available to both the U.S. and the international press material that could be used in reporting about the various activities of the Marshall Plan.
2. To "promote an understanding among the European People of the motives of the United States in extending recovery aid, to explain the objectives and methods of the program, to tell the amount of help which America is extending, and to create an awareness in Europe about the ERP, its progress and operations."
3. To explain the close relationship of the ERP to U.S. foreign policy in Europe and to "counteract" Communist propaganda against the Marshall Plan.
4. To inform the recipient countries about the steps which were necessary if economic stability was to be attained by the end of the Marshall Plan in 1952.

To achieve these goals, the ECA missions launched intensive field work using all available media: newspapers, pamphlets, postcards, postal stamps, cancellation stamps, posters, stickers, radio and motion pictures. In addition, the public was mobilized by exhibits and various Marshall Plan competitions such as poster contests. The perhaps most important feature of the propaganda campaign was the Marshall Plan emblem. The American shield and the American flag were graphically combined. It carried two important messages, the main goal of the Marshall Plan and the key importance of the United States: "For European Recovery—Supplied by the United States of America." This slogan, which was used until 1950, could easily be translated into the languages of the recipient countries. "*Für den Wiederaufbau Europas —Geliefert von den Vereinigten Staaten von Amerika.*"

In the context of Marshall Plan propaganda, Austria and Germany were major targets for a number of reasons. These two countries were of special importance for U.S. interests in Europe and therefore played a key role for both the formulation and application of the Marshall Plan. When, in the spring of 1947, former President Herbert Hoover summed up the results of his fact-finding mission to Austria and Germany, he left no doubt about the countries' serious economic conditions. The disastrous food shortages, he argued, required American support: "It may come as a great shock to American taxpayers that, having won the war over Germany, we are now faced for some years with large expenditures for relief for these people. Indeed, it is something new in human history for the conquerer to undertake."[7] Austria was in a similar situation.

> "The problem of how soon Austria can become self-supporting by exports with which to buy her own food is of the first interest to the American taxpayer. No report on Austria that does not face this situation is worth preparation. So long as such a balanced economy cannot be created (unless we wish to see terrible starvation) a large part of the deficit will fall upon the taxpayers in the United States and other nations."[8]

It was not only the economic and financial situation, however, which required immediate attention by U.S. diplomacy. Economic problems were closely interrelated with various political and strategic considerations. The main factors that shaped United States policy towards Austria and Germany can be summarized as follows:

1. Austria and Germany were both occupied by the armed forces of the Big Four.
2. Both countries had frontiers with the emerging Soviet bloc in East Central Europe.
3. Austria and Germany were important "battlefields" in the Cold War
4. The containment of Soviet ideological, political, and economic expansion in the respective Western zones was regarded as impossible unless economic chaos could be avoided.
5. The economic stabilization of the Western zones was of vital U.S. financial interest, since the American taxpayer would not indefinitely tolerate subsidizing the Western zones.
6. In both countries, the food situation was aggravated by "displaced persons" and a growing number of refugees.
7. Before the war, a large share of Austrian and German foreign trade had been oriented towards the East; losses in this trade had to be compensated in the West.
8. Finally, the emerging Cold War economic progress in the respective Western zones was of vital importance to demonstrate superiority of the Western economic system which was challenged by Soviet anti-capitalist propaganda.

In their information campaigns, the ECA missions made use of modern marketing methods, which were applied in close cooperation with the governments to which they were assigned to. The great importance of Marshall Plan propaganda is reflected in the various bilateral agreements that were concluded between the U.S. government and the recipient countries. Marshall plan publicity was an integral element of these treaties. In the Austrian-U.S. treaty of 2 July 1948, it was recognized by both governments "that it is in their mutual interest that full publicity be given to the objectives and the progress of the joint program for European recovery and of the actions taken in furtherance of that program." It was further recognized that "wide dissemination of information on the progress of the program is desirable in order to develop the sense of common effort and mutual aid which are essential to the accomplishment of the objectives of the program." Both governments wanted to "encourage the dissemination of such information and will make it available to the media for public information." The Austrian government agreed to "take all practical steps to ensure that appropriate facilities are provided" to the media for public information.[9] In the Economic Cooperation Agreement between the United States and the Federal Republic of Germany, both governments recognized "that it is in their mutual interest that full publicity be given to the objectives and progress of the joint program for European recovery and of the actions taken in furtherance of that program." The "wide dissemination of information on the progress of the program" was regarded as "desirable in order to develop the sense of common effort and mutual aid which are essential to the accomplishment of the objectives of the program." The West German government agreed to "encourage the dissemination of such information both directly and in cooperation with the Organization for European Economic Cooperation" and to "make such information available to the media of public information."[10] Marshall Plan propaganda was projected as a joint effort by ECA and the recipient country's government.

**Exhibits**

Marshall Plan exhibits were a widely used instrument to inform the public on the major elements of the ERP. Touring exhibitions carried the Marshall Plan message not only to the big cities but also to areas beyond the main centers. Auto caravans, ships, and special trains were sent to many European countries. The "Train of Goodwill and Peace," which was organized by the German National Railways was officially dedicated in Bonn on 14 September 1950 by the President of the Federal Republic, Theodor Heuss, the Vice Chancellor and Minister for the Marshall Plan, Franz Blücher, and the American Deputy High Commissioner, General George Hays. It consisted of 15 cars of displays which explained the importance of ERP for Germany and Europe. More than 350 companies from West Germany and West Berlin displayed their products in the ERP context. The Train made two trips through West Germany in 1950 and 1951. The train stopped at fifty cities and towns and it was visited by more than 1,300,000 people.

More important from an international perspective was another ERP train, "The Train of Europe." After a preview in Paris, it proceeded to Munich for the opening show on 21 April 1951. The train consisted of seven cars. The interiors of four cars formed the principal exhibition area. In a fifth car, about seventy people could be seated to watch films and puppet shows. Alternatively, this car could be stripped of seats and devoted to exhibits relating the main theme of cooperation of the sponsoring nation's economy. The other two cars provided crew quarters and storage space. The visitors were greeted by a dedication panel, explaining the train's mission: "The Train of Europe is dedicated to cooperation among the free people of Europe for their economic strength and freedom." "Europe Working Together" was the leitmotif of the various displays, which visualized key ERP elements: "Economically divided, Europe is weak—cooperating, Europe is strong. Together for strength, together for progress, together for security, together for peace and freedom." The "Train of Europe" visited eight countries in a two year period. It stopped in West Germany, West Berlin, Norway, Denmark, the Netherlands, Belgium, France, Italy, and Austria. The train ended in Vienna in mid-1953, about half a year after the official end of the Marshall Plan.[11]

The "Europe Train" with its Marshall Plan exhibits arrives in Austria in 1952. Wilhelm Taucher, the director of the ERP in Austria welcomes it to Vienna.

Source: National Library, Vienna, # US 22266-B/C

Vienna and Berlin were of particular importance for ECA exhibits. As "outposts" of the Free World, both cities were ideal places to counteract Soviet propaganda. The ECA mission was already presented at the Vienna spring fair of 1949. The following year, a Marshall Plan exhibit was shown, which summarized the first two years of ERP activities. At the 1950 Berlin industrial fair, an ERP Pavilion was opened. In West Berlin and in Vienna, visitors from the Eastern zones could be directly informed about the Marshall Plan.

## Photos, Graphs, and Posters

Marshall Plan publicity also relied heavily on still pictures to visualize ERP activities and achievements of Marshall Plan projects. Virtually any ERP conference, any exhibit, and any ERP supported economic activity was documented by ECA photographs. Huge construction projects seemed to be as important as daily life. The most important hydro-electric project in Austria, the Limburg Dam Project at Kaprun was extensively covered, of course. In addition, examples showed how Marshall Plan aid helped relieve living conditions in Austria. Life had become "easier for women, since victuals and articles for every day life are available in Austria again, thanks to Marshall Plan aid," and the Austrian housewife "no longer needs to worry of a breakdown in the supply of electricity, the power supply having been secured with the help of Marshall Plan aid. 180 million counterpart schillings have helped to construct twenty power plants. Special occasions were also documented by ECA photographers. When the four millionth ton of goods supplied to Austria by the Marshall Plan arrived in Austria in May 1950, this event was marked by ceremonies at Trieste, the frontier town of Arnoldstein and in Vienna as part of the ECA publicity campaign.

Numerous photos were widely distributed to the press and could be printed free of charge. This was an important method to achieve cumulative information effects. These photos, which primarily focused on making economic progress visible to the public at large, obviously represented "reality" and could be more convincing than any propaganda slogan. A huge collection of these ECA photos is preserved in the National Archives at College Park, Maryland. They are a rich source for the historian of the Marshall Plan and other U.S. foreign aid programs. The collections on Austria and Germany are particularly voluminous and include many impressive documents of economic reconstruction in both countries.

A good example of how photos helped visualize the Marshall Plan by publicizing what had already been achieved, is found in the book *The Marshall Plan in Pictures*, which was published in late 1950.[12] More than ninety photos, which were combined with various diagrams, visualized the broad scope of the European Recovery Program. The ERP's mid-point offered an excellent opportunity to demonstrate what had already been achieved. The book's first pages give a general introduction about the goals of the ERP and its structure. The main part consists of pictures and diagrams about ERP support of nearly any segment of the Austrian economy: coal production, power plants, production of iron ore, steel production, the electrical industry, various other industrial sectors, tourism, and agriculture, among others. The central message of all the pictures was "ERP-schillings help"

Another important instrument of Marshall Plan propaganda included all kinds of contests, such as essay or painting competitions. These offered an opportunity to mobilize the population through active participation and to integrate participants into the propaganda process. One of the most impressive and widely publicized competitions was the ECA Poster Contest of early 1950 on the subject of "Intra-European Cooperation for a Better Standard of Living."[13] Designers from thirteen Marshall Plan countries submitted more than 12,000 posters. An international jury of art experts, each from a different ERP country[14], awarded twenty-five prizes. The poster winning the first prize had been designed by the Dutch artist Reijn Dirksen: his "All Colours to the Mast" symbolized European cooperation. The fully rigged ship "Europe" is shown sailing safely through a rough sea. The ship's colorful sails show the flags of the OEEC countries.

The "classical" poster "All Colours to the Mast" was just one of the many other designs visualizing European cooperation in many different ways. According to the poster contest's theme, most entries emphasized improved living standards as immediate results of European cooperation: "cooperation means prosperity,"[15] "prosperity, the fruit of cooperation;"[16] "Whatever the weather—We only reach welfare together;"[17] or "a united Europe carries prosperity"[18] were typical texts which were in most cases added to the designs. While Europe was the central focus point of most Marshall Plan posters, U.S. contributions and even Washington's leading role were sometimes also visualized in a very subtle way, for example, by showing the American flag in a superior position. Some artists reflected on the political implications of the ERP and its effects on peace: "Peace through intra-

European cooperation."[19] It was symbolized by doves of peace in some designs. Some posters effectively combined the messages of prosperity and peace by referring to a new Europe as distinct from the war-torn continent of the past: "Towards a better future—European Recovery Program,"[20] "We build a new Europe." [21]

While most ERP posters championed the idea of European cooperation, many others addressed specific needs of individual recipient countries. There was no doubt that European cooperation did not mean neglect of the problems these countries were confronted with. On the contrary, "Marshall Plan Europe" and the United States' leading role were the keys for national recovery and the improvement of living conditions for the people. The poster "America helps Germany with textiles" might be cited as an example.[22] In addition, economic interdependence obviously had political implications. In a very subtle way, Austrians and West Germans were informed not only about the economic benefits of ERP participation, but also about its political implications. In a European context, Marshall Plan aid appeared to be much more than a hopelessly one-sided institution. This interdependence was stressed by various Austrian posters: "Austria needs 18 countries—8 countries need Austria."[23] A West German poster showing the flags of all OEEC countries was even more explicit: "West Germany shares in decisions!"[24] These were important political messages: Austria and Germany, both occupied by armed forces, could contribute to the revival of Europe. These contributions manifested themselves in their membership in OEEC, for example. And this was seen as a possibility to partly offset the loss of national sovereignty, to overcome postwar isolation and to return to the international arena through economic cooperation.[25]

### Marshall Plan Films

Another important element of Washington's ERP propaganda was the medium film, which had already played an important role during World War II to support the war effort. During the late 1940s and the early 1950s, more than 200 films were produced. These Marshall Plan films are excellent examples of how the United States Government effectively visualized the goals and achievements of the ERP.[26] About half of the film produced by the Economic Cooperation Administration are accessible in the National Archives at College Park. These films cover an extremely broad spectrum of topics. They attempt to combine

The idea of European cooperation leading towards European integration was expressed in slogans like: "Austria needs 18 countries - 18 countries need Austria: The U.S. contribution to European Reconstruction"

Source: Archives of the *ERP-Fund*, Vienna

national specialties with intra-European necessities. Of special importance were numerous film series such as *E.R.P. in Action: A Monthly Film Digest of the Facts and Figures of European Recovery*, *One - Two - Three*, and *The Marshall Plan at Work*. These series were supplemented by those films which dealt with specific projects in the recipient countries. The main task of the ECA film program was to inform the public both in the United States and in Europe about the origins and goals of the European Recovery Program and to visualize what had already been achieved in the respective Marshall Plan countries. For the countries under discussion, two excellent examples are the films *The Marshall Plan at Work in Western Germany*[27] and *The Marshall Plan at Work in Austria.*[28]

*The Marshall Plan at Work in Austria*[29] starts with a brief description of Austria's situation after the war, the foreign policy orientation, and support through the ERP. The situation after World War II is compared with the pre-World War I period. This comparison helps explain why Vienna is characterized as an "imperial city without an empire":

> "Now Vienna rules only a small damaged country of six million people, the Austria of today. That is what makes Austria's recovery from the Second World War slow and difficult: territories which once fed a people and provided the most raw materials have become independent states or satellites of Russia. While repairing their shorn and shattered land, Austrians must look elsewhere. Yes, the friendship of this little nation now governed by a democratic parliament freely elected is vital to the Western world. Symbolic of the importance of strategic geography as thrust on Austria is the fact that Vienna is policed by each of the four occupying powers. Today, Austria is receiving from the West the friendly help she needs; for her own efforts to build a new economy are being helped by Marshall aid."

This general introduction is followed by a description of the main tasks of reconstruction: improvement of agricultural output through productivity, stimulation of industrial production, and expansion of tourism. Increasing agricultural production was designed to improve the provisioning of the population, reduce dependency on agricultural imports and free up labor for industry. Increasing industrial production, so the argument went, would lead to more exports, which in turn would net the foreign currency needed to finance vital imports. Austria's lack of foreign currency could be further improved by expanding the tourist sector (see the Bischof essay in this volume). All these policies had already been initiated, were interdependent and would spark Austrian recovery. The new Austria would be "a land, where wider horizons are opened again and where the joy of living is astir once more. With confidence today, Austria shows herself to the world. With the help of friends across the sea there is rising at her hills and lakes the strength of modern nationhood. Helping people to help themselves: the Marshall Plan." This optimism is symbolized by the construction of Austria's hydroelectric industry. Twenty such projects are mentioned, and Kaprun's significance is especially pointed out.

The Kaprun project is extensively covered in the film *The Invisible Link.* The significance of water power for Austria's future development is repeatedly stressed and interpreted as a major step towards Austria's independence: "A little country like this, we have to make the most of what we got. And with American help we can do it." The film ends with the statement: *The Invisible Link.*[30]

These two films on Austria are structured in a way that suggests visual parallels with the United States during the 1930s. The New Deal is not mentioned explicitly, but the Roosevelt presence is obvious. Progress of the Marshall Plan would help to build the "new Austria." As in the United States during the New Deal era, dam projects and electricity were portrayed as modernizing agriculture and industrial production and contributing to another economic take-off for the whole economy. During the war, water power was advertised as the first step towards air power and victory; now, after the war, water power could inject strength into the economy. Electrification of the railway system seemed to combine power, movement, and progress. The New Deal analogy and Austria's support by the United States were presented as seals of approval.

The film *The Marshall Plan at Work in Western Germany* differs from the film on Austria, because its focus is on industrial problems and Germany's economic significance for European reconstruction: "Today, industrial Germany is still the factory of Europe." The film's makers leave no doubt that the nations of Europe "need her goods as they never did before." The wheels of Europe are still closely geared to the wheels of German industry. "The recovery of Europe must surely lag and falter until these German factories are in full production once again." Given the extent of war destruction the problems are manifold. But due to ERP assistance and the introduction of American production methods, progress is already visible: "Help people to help each other: the Marshall Plan."

In the film, the economic reconstruction of West Germany is defined as a major goal, and important steps towards progress are visualized. But unlike Austria's reconstruction, the West German economic recovery is not seen as an end by itself. West Germany's reconstruction is presented as a necessary step towards European reconstruction. West German economic structure and the close interdependence of Germany's economy with that of other European nations seem to leave no alternative. This seemed to be the only way to justify economic support for a country that was responsible for war and economic chaos. The concentration on strictly economic problems obviously seemed to be a strategy used to avoid political criticism.

With its focus on the close interdependence of German reconstruction and European recovery, the film also reflects the thinking within the State Department. In a memorandum, George F. Kennan's Policy Planning Staff expressed the view that the "importance of Germany to general European recovery is well known and requires no statistical illustration. No impartial student of Europe's pre-war economy can fail to appreciate the vital significance which German productivity and German markets have had for the well-being of the continent." This fact had not been altered by the war: "This is not a political judgement but a bitter economic reality."[31] And Secretary of Commerce Harriman summarized his impressions of a trip to Germany in a similar way: "We cannot revive a self-supporting Western European economy without a healthy Germany playing its part as a producing and consuming unit."[32] By 1948, this analysis had become official U.S. policy towards Western Germany as it was summarized in a Policy Statement of August 1948:

> "Our interest in Germany´s relation to ERP arises from the importance of Germany´s economic position in Europe. Germany is potentially one of the most important European suppliers of such acutely needed commodities as coal, mining machinery, and industrial equipment. At the same time she is potentially an important market for European goods. German economic recovery is therefore vital to general European economic recovery. On the other hand, German economic recovery is largely dependent on the economic recovery of other European countries since they are the chief markets of

> their goods. It is U.S. policy that the fullest possible recognition be given this interdependence in order to achieve the greatest over-all benefits for the European Recovery Program."[33]

George Kennan stressed West Germany's key role for Washington's Marshall Plan strategy when he wrote that the United States should "accept no arrangements which would inhibit the Germans from participating in ERP. To do so would place Germany economically at the mercy of Russia and would defeat the purpose of the program."[34]

The samples of American Marshall Plan advertisement in Germany and Austria discussed here are only a small portion of a very extensive ECA film program. Apart form the Marshall Plan propaganda in general, ECA aimed at providing detailed factual knowledge through film in particular. For the industrial sector numerous films demonstrated to both entrepreneurs and workers advanced production techniques and efficiency methods. Farmers were instructed in American agricultural planting and rationalizing. In some instances, films intended to provide technical assistance also managed to address special needs of Marshall Plan participant countries. This was true for the film "Productive Potato Planting—The Method of Longer Germination" directed by Georg Tressler from Vienna, which was produced in cooperation with the Institute of Plant Physiology and Plant Protection of the Agricultural University of Vienna.[35] New ways of planting potatoes were explained to Austrian mountain farmers. To increase the acceptance among these farmers, Tressler refrained from using high German. He remembers that he presented the film "in the very broad dialect that these mountain folks talked." Thus the viewer was very shrewdly informed of the contribution of the Marshall Plan, when the camera panned over a logo with the letters ERP, "very discreetly, but very pointedly," in the words of Tressler. A peasant informed the viewers: "... supported by Marshall Plan funds."[36]

Films designed to advance the technical knowledge of viewers were spreading the key message - the increase in productivity, which was the wherewithal for improving prosperity in all segments of society, workers included. The pay-off for their hard work now would be a higher standard of living in the future. The best example of this intense productivity campaign is the movie "Productivity—Key to Progress."[37]

While most film productions had a medium- or long-range character, some films were produced to visualize specific events. On the occasion of the Marshall Plan's second anniversary, the Vienna ECA mission and the Federal Chancellery's Central Bureau for ERP Affairs produced a short film *Way out of Chaos* (*Der Weg aus dem Chaos*). During the first month, the film had already been shown in 182 motion picture theaters. The Federal Chancellery called it "one of the biggest propaganda successes of the last two years." In light of this success, it was suggested "to repeat such propaganda programs from time to time."[38]

## Your Eighty Dollars

ERP mid-point celebrations were not only a highlight of Marshall Plan propaganda, they also mark the ERP's new emphasis. Since the outbreak of hostilities in Korea, military preparedness had become a major goal of ERP. The ECA agencies were absorbed by the Mutual Security Administration (MSA), which was created in 1951. Political and strategic considerations had always been inherent in the Marshall Plan, but during the first two years of ERP economic recovery, they had been the main theme of Marshall Plan publicity. After 1950, it had become necessary to stress the close interdependence of European reconstruction and Western defense. However, American diplomats hesitated to introduce a purely military aid program, since this might have been be regarded by European public opinion "as a cynical attempt by the Americans to hire foreign mercenaries and to prepare a safely distant battleground for a possible conflict with Soviet Russia." Therefore, the defense effort was "designed as much to restore Western Europe's political stability and economic vitality as to revive its military potential." Western defense "should be developed in the context of European political and economic unification as well as of continued progress throughout the free world toward improved living standards and greater security for the individual." This would be of help in "reconstructing the social fabric of Western Europe, for it will strengthen European self-confidence and faith in a secure future."[39]

"Strength for the Free World" was the motto that marked ERP's shift towards militarization of the Marshall Plan. By 1951, it had become a central element of Marshall Plan propaganda both in Europe and the United States. This new emphasis, the shift from economic aid to strategic cooperation, was clearly expressed in a new Marshall Plan emblem. The design remained unchanged, but the original text "For European Recovery—Supplied by the United States of America" was substituted by "Strength for the Free World—from the United States of America." In late 1953, a new emblem symbolizing all United States foreign aid activities of the FOA was adopted as a "world wide symbol of Mutual Security": two clasped hands on a red, white, and blue American stars-and-stripes shield carrying the words "United States of America." It was "believed to become one of the best known and most widely issued labels in the world."[40]

The growing importance of military aspects in the implementation of the Marshall Plan was also reflected in the film program. *Strength for the Free World* was the title of a new motion picture series. The series' subtitle clearly expressed its main goals: *A weekly program presenting documentary evidence of the progress the free world is making for its strength through mutual security*. The film program was designed to inform the public both in Western Europe and the United States how the people of the free world worked together to establish a permanent peace. All films of the series stressed the close interdependence of economic progress and military defense: "On this foundation of greater economic and social strength the rearmament of the allied nations is being built. All around the world the free peoples are uniting with American aid to resist want and to withstand aggression."

An impressive example of how this message was visualized is the film *Your Eighty Dollars*.[41] It was produced in 1952 and primarily addressed an audience in the United States. The film starts with impressions of well-known European monuments, such as the Coliseum, the Acropolis, Tower Bridge, and Notre Dame to remind people of the cultural ties between the United States and Europe: "This is Western Europe, the old world. From the shadows of landmarks such as these most Americans can trace their heritage and the roots of our nation. And we are proud to do so [...] From this continent first came knowledge and the science, the skills and the culture on which the United States was built."

The relations between Western Europe and the United States were not seen as a dead end road. The film's makers loose no time in drawing attention to America's commitment to the reconstruction of war-torn Europe: "But we can also be proud that over the past few years every man, woman, and child in America has made an investment to keep this mother civilization alive and free. The twelve billion dollar investment of Marshall aid, equivalent of eighty dollars from every American, a generous investment that began four years ago." It is a business-like approach. The European Recovery Program is not identified as foreign aid, but as an investment. The American audience was to be convinced that it has been a sound investment that paid off for the United States. This point is supported by a look backwards at the European situation after World War II, the origins of the Marshall Plan, and the Soviet threat in Europe. Through the economic reconstruction of Europe, it is argued, the Europeans had been put into a position to make an economic contribution to Western defense. This European contribution to U.S. security is interpreted as the investment's dividend. At the same time, there is no alternative to America's commitment in Europe. Free Europe is referred to as the "heartland of the continent." In case of war, Europe would play a key role: "Europe is still the decision area in any world conflict of any kind. Her wealth can make its controller ruler of most if not all of the earth." These arguments leave not doubt that the Marshall Plan, while being a European Recovery Program, had worldwide implications. The Marshall Plan had become an instrument within the framework of a global battle between the two super powers.

### Communist anti-Marshall Plan agitation

The Soviet Union and the communist parties throughout Europe tried to discredit the Marshall Plan as an instrument of U.S. capitalism. Walter Ulbricht, deputy leader of the East German communists, thought it quite "obvious" that "the Marshall Plan would bring about a triple enslavement of the German people."[42] East German politicians tried to convince the public that there was no need for any kind of Marshall aid and that the Germans would stimulate the economy themselves ("*Wir brauchen keinen Marshallplan, wir kurbeln selbst die Wirtschaft an*").[43] Communist production planning was advertised as being superior to the Western capitalist system. This was the argument to enlist support for East Germany's half-year, two year and five year plans.[44] Propaganda posters offered direct comparison between the so-called Germany Plan and the Marshall Plan.[45] While the former was presented as a guarantee for employment, the Marshall Plan was identified with unemployment. Another "big difference" was presented by the Communists.[46] The European Recovery Program would not only bring about unemployment, but would finally result in an overall eco-

"Get out of here! We do not need a Marshall-Plan, we crank up the economy ourselves!"

Source: Haus der Geschichte, Bonn

nomic crisis and produce huge profits for a few capitalists only. State planning, on the other hand, meant "growing wealth" for the people.[47] Therefore, the Communist argument stated, the East German plans would be "victorious."[48] The five year plan would prove that peace, reconstruction, and prosperity could be achieved by the German people.[49] The anti-Marshall Plan agitation was part of a "Yankee, go home" propaganda which was illustrated in East German posters and cartoons.[50]

A similar anti-ERP campaign was launched in Austria. However, the Soviets found themselves in a more difficult position. In Eastern Germany, the Soviets exercised unlimited control and could rely on a German puppet regime which fulfilled Soviet expectations. In Austria, the Soviets found themselves in a less advantageous position. This might explain why Soviet origins of anti-ERP actions could be better identified. Soviet newsreels reported anti-Marshall Plan demonstrations by Austrian workers.[51] Radio broadcasts from Moscow tried to instill in an Austrian audience an anti-ERP mood. These broadcasts implied that the Marshall Plan meant "enslavement" of the European working class. And Austria's "Marshallization" would result in a loss of sovereignty.[52]

Within Austria, the Communist Party was the only domestic instrument of Soviet propaganda. Similar to East Germany's half-year, two year, and five year plans, the Austrian Communists formulated a three year plan. In June 1948, the one hundred page pamphlet was presented to the public as an alternative to the Marshall Plan: "The Road to Prosperity. An Austria Economic Plan"[53] attacked U.S. policy in Austria and the whole Marshall Plan strategy on the grounds that they allegedly prevented any autonomous Austrian development. The pamphlet stated: "America has not only shaped the Marshall Plan in whatever way she wished, but she also exercises an actually dictatorial power to execute the 'plan'." The authors of the three year plan wanted to fight the disastrous theory of Austria's "inability to live its own life" and to prove that Austria had possibilities for economic recovery other than "selling itself out to the United States by way of ERP which is nothing but a limited relief program that is largely based on strategic considerations of the United States." The three year plan had been drawn up "to show to the Austrian people that it is not true that there is only one alternative; no, there are also other decisions than those presented to us every day by a propaganda directed by special interests." The KPÖ claimed that its three year plan wanted to strengthen Austrian independence. The Austrian economy had to be rebuilt in a way that would make foreign aid and "gifts" from abroad unnecessary as soon as possible. However, the Austrian Communists did not hesitate to call for a close cooperation with the neighboring countries in the East and the Soviet Union.

The ECA mission in Vienna supplied a detailed analysis of the KPÖ's three year plan. The Communist three year plan was believed "to be fairly sound in scope but definitely incomplete in the proposed extent." The plan was "too vague" to be "anything other than an introduction to more specific plans to come." Since it appeared "quite impossible that the communist party anticipates being called upon to introduce such a plan in Austria, it is believed that the three year plan was conceived solely for its negative propaganda effect." This raised the question of the propaganda target. Since considerable efforts were exerted in the Communist plan to "prove that the recommended economic measures are sound," the Vienna ECA mission believed that the three year plan was "directed at an audience which ordinarily would not be receptive to run-of-the-mill communist propaganda." However, there was no doubt that the three year plan had "a certain negative value because it might provide the necessary 'source data' to those who reject ERP aid for reasons of their own."[54]

Soviet propaganda was regarded as a serious threat to U.S. policy in Austria. It was therefore extensively analyzed by American diplomats, who also supplied recommendations for counteractions. This was reflected in the Vienna ECA mission's "ERP Information Summaries," "Weekly News Briefs in Austria," and the "Weekly Press Comments of Communist Press." In hindsight, it seems obvious that, in the long run, Communist anti-ERP agitation in Austria, West Germany, and West Berlin lacked any kind of credibility, since the Marshall Plan turned out to be a success. However, this extremely positive development could not have been foreseen by contemporaries. In addition, recovery of the national economy did not necessarily invalidate Soviet anti-American and anti-capitalist critiques. Again and again, Austrian Communists and Soviet newspapers described the Marshall Plan as a device to enslave or colonize the participating countries. The argument claimed that, by rendering the nations dependent on U.S. aid, the United States could put itself in a position to dictate their economic lives, to exploit the working class, and to dictate political developments as well. The European Recovery Program was even attacked as a plan for war against Russia.

Since Communist propaganda was primarily geared to winning over the "working class," the ECA missions in Europe undertook specific efforts to enlist labor's support for the ERP. Here, Austria played a key role for the Labor Information Division's activities. It established contacts with leaders of non-communist unions and disseminated information about labor unions in Europe and the United States, international labor union conferences and, above all, about the Marshall Plan. The Vienna mission issued a special "Labor Information Service."[55] The first page carried the ERP emblem and the Austrian flag designed as an American shield to demonstrate Austrian-U.S. solidarity.

In the propaganda battle with the Soviet Union, Washington diplomacy was able to enlist support from the Austrian Trade Union Federation (ÖGB). "Austrian workers have long ago recognized the importance of ERP for the Austrian Economy," its president Johann Böhm wrote in 1950: "It is an undeniable fact that ERP has put Austria on her feet again. Therefore, the overwhelming majority of Austrian workers who are again working to-day with a chance for a better future, welcome the European Recovery program."[56] This positive attitude towards the ERP was seen as a result of the Marshall Plan's success, which could already be recognized by 1950. One of the most marked elements of economic progress, a member of the OSR office in Paris argued, "has been the maintenance of a high, stable level of employment." This full employment had boosted industrial production.[57]

Any ERP progress report was even more impressive when Marshall Plan activities were compared with Moscow's dismantling policy in the Soviet Zone: "For the Alpine towns of Deuchendorf and Weiz the Marshall Plan has meant the difference between life and death. In both places the Russians stripped factories of machines and equipment and at the same time inhabitants of their means of livelihood. But neither was fated to become a ghost town. Today they are more flourishing than ever. New modern Marshall Plan equipment have returned the factories to full operation and steady jobs and income to the town's workers."[58]

## Propaganda or Information?

American officials observed and conducted detailed public opinion surveys on these advertisement campaigns, particulary in West Berlin and West Germany. In a report written in October 1950 success stories were registered in these information campaigns but continuing these efforts was deemed mandatory as well.[59] The German public needed to be informed with even more persuasive intensity about the ERP and the United States taking the lead in it. The local Marshall Plan partners were reminded again and again that they were contractually obligated to keep their respective publics informed. American diplomats reminded the *Kreditanstalt für Wiederaufbau* that ERP-funded projects had to be clearly marked with the ERP logo. The *Kreditanstalt für Wiederaufbau*, headquartered in Frankfurt am Main, sent a flood of letters to the recipients of ERP credits, admonishing them: "In the United States the idea of 'publicity' is strongly developed and public opinion is considered crucially important. We are fully supportive of these goals. We must not forget that ultimately the American tax-payers have provided these Marshall Plan funds. The Senate, the House of Representatives, the Executive Branch and the Washington bureaucracy are only representatives of the American people. The American public will be more inclined to continue sending reconstruction aid if they are convinced that the aid recipients value such help."[60]

This publicity campaign was continued even after the Marshall Plan had come to an end. After 1952, the public was informed about those projects which were supported by counterpart funds. This was a reminder of the "help by the American people."[61]

The Marshall Plan publicity campaign undoubtedly was one of the biggest propaganda blitzes ever launched in peace time. It should be noted, however, that the elite Marshall Planners felt most uneasy with the term "propaganda". Ever since "propaganda" had become associated with totalitarian states, Western democracies deemed it disreputable. Therefore, political actors abandoned the term "propaganda" to distance themselves even in linguistic usage from Soviet propaganda campaigns. Instead, they preferred terms such as "information", "advertisement", "publicity", or even "psychological offensive", at least in public debates. They never succeeded in gaining acceptance for any one of these terms, which can also be derived from the frequent usage of the term "propaganda" in their internal correspondence.

This debate over semantics sometimes surfaced in public. In one of the periodic reports of the West German Government we can read: "The Federal Minister for the Marshall Plan [Blücher] never considered publicity for the Marshall Plan a propaganda tool. He rather intended to win the confidence and support of the German public by reporting the facts faithfully—in the sense of true democracy and what Americans call "public relations".[62]

Looking back, the film official Toby E. Rhodes also stressed the idea of keeping the public well informed: "We wanted to inform and enlighten, we did not want to launch a propaganda campaign." Every once in while critics attacked the U.S. about unleashing a vast Marshall Plan propaganda campaign. In such instances ERP officials always replied that one could never know enough about the Marshall Plan "... if you want to call it propaganda, o.k., go ahead and call it propaganda."[63] Defining propaganda in the moderate sense of the *Oxford English Dictionary* as "systematic propagation of information or ideas by an interested party," in a way takes care of this war about words.[64]

Apart from the problem of semantics one has to note that Marshall Plan publicity was driven by the most modern marketing methods used in U.S. business practises. This is clearly expressed in a memo by the Office of the Special Representative (OSR) in which the parallels in ECA-information policy with private sector marketing were deemed obvious: "Research on consumer attitudes and copy themes is essential in planning or appraising an advertising campaign ('information program'). New products (a customs union, an international grid) need extensive consumer research before being put on the market. Voters (and their leaders) are just as difficult to persuade as buyers, and ECA's whole success depends on voters (and their leaders)—abroad as well as at home."[65]

The Marshall Plan propagandists did not always succeed in pitching their publicity campaign appropriately and subtly as internal debates over intensifying and improving their information campaign suggest. Yet in spite of occasional misdirection, Marshall Plan propaganda featured a tremendous asset which defined its overall success—**credibility**. Most goals outlined by the ERP were reached. The Marshall Plan was the big success story of Western European postwar economic reconstruction. It has been stressed that such success lent credence to the claim that "propaganda was good public relations." Usually no further political arguments needed to be made whenever the ERP logo proclaimed the support of the Marshall Plan for towns and products. The excellence of the Marshall Plan as a **brand name** worked wonders as an implicit propaganda tool. The broad availability of Marshall Plan goods to millions of consumers was much more persuasive than explicit sloganeering. This demonstrated “that in advertising the ERP the mass appeal of public relations was less dependent on heavy-handed ideological indoctrination than on certain social conditions and economic prosperity.”[66] The very visible success story of the ERP and the effectiveness of the ad campaign were highly interdependent. The publicity blitz convinced both the people of the United States and the recipient countries that the ERP was absolutely necessary. This conviction in turn reinforced the positive outcome of the Marshall Plan.

The visible results of ERP had also opened new perspectives for Washington’s overall foreign policy. Marshall Plan publicity became an important weapon of the Soviet-American global propaganda battle. This is clearly documented in a memorandum of June 1950 “Psychological Pressures—Our Global Objectives,” which was compiled by the Office of the Special Representative’s Information Division. Three “psychological activities” were regarded as particularly significant in the propaganda battle with the Soviet Union: 1. developing a healthy international community; 2. deterring the Soviets from further encroachments; and 3. rolling back Soviet power.[67]

This study confirmed that the Truman Administration’s ERP propaganda was an integral part of U.S. foreign policy. The Marshall Plan propaganda concentrated on a broad spectrum, which can be summed up as follows:

1. ERP in the context of United States foreign policy,
2. Economic progress through the ERP,
3. Increased productivity in both industry and agriculture,
4. Technical assistance, namely the transfer of know-how from the United States to Europe,
5. European Integration (more precisely: West European integration),
6. Liberalization of foreign trade,
7. The idea of Western defense,
8. The peaceful character of Marshall aid,
9. A reminder that Marshall aid came from the United States, and
10. The unspoken assumption of U.S. leadership.

## Public Memory

Marshall Plan propaganda certainly contributed to ERP’s success in many ways. It helped to counterbalance Communist anti-Marshall

Plan campaigns, it enlisted the support of the non-Communist left in Europe, and supported the idea of European integration. In addition, the various propaganda campaigns established an overall positive image. This is particularly true for Western Germany. In the Western zones of occupation, the Marshall Plan, the currency reform, and the founding of the Federal Republic are closely interrelated. These events paved the way for West Germany's economic recovery which culminated in what has been called the "*Wirtschaftswunder*" of the 1950s. But the Marshall Plan did not only offer economic aid, it also provided for Germany's reemergence as a political actor in international affairs. National sovereignty could be regained through economic prosperity and cooperation, first of all with the United States of America. Economic recovery and close cooperation with the United States became the rationale of the new West German state. Therefore, it is no surprise that all (West) German governments have done the utmost to keep public memory of the Marshall Plan alive. On numerous occasions, all Federal Chancellors have commemorated the Marshall Plan and U.S. contributions to the recovery of Germany and Europe. In his last government statement, Konrad Adenauer thanked the people of the United States for their generous support.[68] On the occasion of the twentieth anniversary of the Harvard speech, Chancellor Kiesinger applauded the Marshall Plan as "one of the greatest political achievements of our century."[69] On the fiftieth anniversary of General Marshall's Harvard speech, Willy Brandt praised the genius of the Marshall Plan.[70] On 3 June 1977, Helmut Schmidt thanked the American people and their government for the "generous achievements." The Marshall Plan had been the "economic take-off for the reconstruction of a destroyed country that had destroyed other countries."[71] Chancellor Helmut Kohl was one of the most ardent supporters of the Marshall Plan idea and always expressed his belief that U.S. support of Germany and Europe had to be remembered and that this memory should be an integral part of German attitudes towards the United States.

West German commemoration of the Marshall Plan was not limited to official statements by leading politicians. Since the early days of the ERP, many endeavors have been undertaken to remind a broader public of the Marshall Plan and its meaning for Germany. Postal stamps were issued, for example, in 1950, 1960, and 1997. In the city of Frankfurt, a Marshall fountain was built to honor George Marshall and his initiatives. It was dedicated on 27 October 1963, in the presence of Mrs. Marshall, Chancellor Ludwig Erhard, and Secretary of State Dean Rusk. In Germany, memory of the Marshall Plan was further intensified on the occasion of the fiftieth anniversary of the Harvard speech, when the Kohl government initiated various events. The *Haus der Geschichte* of the Federal Republic of Germany presented an exhibition, which compared the free market economy with the realities of a state planned economy.[72] Central components of the Marshall Plan were exhibited for the general public. In addition, the *Haus der Geschichte* sponsored an international conference on the European Recovery Program.[73] The (West) German interest to preserve and intensify the public memory on the Marshall Plan is probably best evidenced in the founding of the German Marshall Fund of the United States in 1972, twenty-five years after the Harvard speech. The fund was established as "A Memorial to the Marshall Plan" to commemorate "the generous assistance provided for the recovery of Germany and Europe by the Marshall Plan." In a speech at Harvard, Willy Brandt expressed his wish "to arouse in the younger generation that mutual trust which in those days exhorted the Europeans to make peace among themselves. They must not forget that the interdependence of states on both sides of the Atlantic proclaimed by John F. Kennedy must remain a moral, cultural, an economic and a political reality."[74]

Unlike the (West) German regimes, most Austrian governments have refrained from actively shaping public memory of the Marshall Plan. This is due primarily to fundamentally different political and strategic situations. Before the Austrian State Treaty was concluded, the presence of Soviet occupation forces necessitated a cautious policy. After 1955, it was neutrality that required Austria to refrain from pro-United States manifestations. These attitudes were reflected in various postal stamp issues.[75] In February 1948, Austria gave publicity to its reconstruction efforts through a ten stamp set, but no mention was made of the Marshall Plan. Neither was the European Recovery Program referred to in an eight stamp set issued in March 1951, nor in other commemorative stamps issued in 1962 and 1971. The latter showed important projects that had been financed by Marshall Plan counterpart funds: the VOEST steelworks at Linz, which had been completely destroyed during the war, the Kaprun reservoir and power station, and the Brenner highway. Huge projects such as Kaprun are visible monuments of the Marshall Plan's achievements.

Although Austrian governments have given less attention to the memory of the Marshall Plan than politicians in Western Germany, three important publications that commemorate the Marshall Plan and its achievements have to be mentioned. In 1958, the Austrian government published a volume *Ten Years of ERP in Austria*, which is an impressive documentation of what had been achieved by 1958.[76] The publication was dedicated to the "unknown American taxpayer to whom the Austrian economy owed millions for its reconstruction."[77] The publication was introduced with contributions of prominent Austrian politicians; Chancellor Raab described the Marshall Plan as an event of "global significance" that should be remembered by future generations. "Unfortunately," it was not "customary" to build a monument for economic initiatives. Therefore, the book documented and reminded Austrians of the fact that the Marshall Plan was an ideal form of aid, since it enabled the recipients "to stand on their own feet again." Austria was saved from economic destruction, and "America's man in the street deserves Austria's gratitude."[78] The Minister of Commerce and Reconstruction added that "Austria's economic miracle" had emerged from "two very concrete factors," Austria's own economic efforts and the Marshall Plan.[79] What already had been achieved by 1958 is documented on 250 pages describing and also illustrating numerous specific industrial and agricultural projects supported by ERP funds. The power plants are referred to as "a monument of ERP."[80]

In 1987, on the fortieth anniversary of Marshall's Harvard speech, the Austrian *ERP-Fonds*, which had been created in 1962 to administer the ERP counterpart funds, summarized the first twenty-five years of its work in a 200 page book.[81] In his introductory remarks, Chancellor Franz Vranitzky described the European Recovery Program as "one of the most important and most successful economic programs in modern history," and he used the opportunity to thank the American people for their generous economic aid. He reminded Austrians "what this economic aid had meant for us" and stressed the ongoing activities of the *ERP-Fonds*. Vranitzky also drew attention to the Marshall Plan's psychological effects. ERP assistance had brought about a "flourishing economy," and this had created in Austria "a climate full of optimism that helped to finally definitely overcome the psychological depression of the 1930s and the 1940s." This had changed the course of Austrian history in a positive direction.[82]

The U.S. ambassador Ronald S. Lauder shared this view that the Marshall Plan "was meant to do more than simply revive the economic health" of Europe. "It was designed to help create an environment in which Europe and America could build a community of common democratic values which would support a lasting peace." Due to the foresight of President Truman, George Marshall and their contemporaries, "we can look back on the advances of the last four decades with justifiable pride." The ambassador left no doubt that the "finest tribute which Europeans and Americans can pay to their memory is to emulate the vision which they showed, and rededicate ourselves to support those values they believed in and in which we continue to believe: freedom, justice and the dignity of the individual."[83] Remarks by acting politicians and diplomats were supplemented by short memoirs of prominent people who had been present at the creation, among them former Minister of Foreign Affairs Karl Gruber and former Chancellor Bruno Kreisky. Looking back, Gruber left no doubt that the Marshall Plan had been a "vital matter for our country." Without Marshall Plan aid, Austria's reconstruction would have been delayed by decades.[84] Kreisky stressed the long-range effects of Marshall Plan. The European Recovery Program had not only been instrumental for Austria's development towards a modern industrial state, but ERP counterpart funds had also been a "decisive factor" in overcoming the economic crisis of the early 1970s. In addition, the Marshall Plan's political dimensions could not be overestimated. The Americans had been "Austria's big friends," and nobody knows whether Austria's unity could have been preserved without their help. "Americans had unselfishly transferred much money to Austria." To a large extent, Austria's "economic miracle" or "Austria's way" was due to the take-off initiated by the Marshall Plan.

To commemorate the fiftieth anniversary of the inauguration of the Marshall Plan, the Austrian ERP-Fonds sponsored an international symposium "The Marshall Plan in Austria. An Economic and Social History," that was organized by the Center for Austrian Culture and Commerce of the University of New Orleans in cooperation with the University of Innsbruck and the Schumpeter Society of Vienna. A collection of numerous conference contributions in German was edited by Günter Bischof and Dieter Stiefel in late 1998.[85] In his preface to the publication, Chancellor Viktor Klima thanked the American people for their "generous economic aid" which had been instrumental for Austrian economic reconstruction after the war. Moreover, the

Marshall Plan had created a political and social environment which had been a prerequisite for the development of democratic institutions in Austria. The Marshall Plan's political dimensions were also stressed by former Finance Minister Ferdinand Lacina. The Marshall Plan had preserved Austria's territorial and political integrity as it had prevented a social division of Austria, since the Soviet occupied zone had not been excluded from Marshall aid. In addition, the United States had insisted on a minimum of intra-European cooperation, and this had been an important towards European integration. It includes a compact survey of the *ERP-Fonds'* main activities since it was established in 1962. This article is a reminder that the Marshall Plan is an ongoing story (see the Lacina essay in this volume). In the years to come, the *ERP-Fonds'* capital, which originates from former counterpart credits, "will achieve an important contribution to the modernization and the strengthening of the Austrian economy in the spirit of the Marshall Plan."[86]

## Notes

1. Statement by the President Upon Signing the Foreign Economic Assistance Act, 5 June 1950, in: *Public Papers of the Presidents of the United States, Harry S. Truman*, vol. 1950 (Washington: Government Printing Office, 1965), 454.

2. Eisenhower to Marshall, 3 June 1957, in Eisenhower Library, Abilene, KS, President's Personal File.

3. Mikhail M. Narinsky, The Soviet Union and the Marshall Plan, Washington 1994 (Cold War History Project Working Paper, Nr. 9); Vojtech Mastny, *The Cold War and Soviet Insecurity: The Stalin Years* (New York: Oxford University Press, 1996).

4. Michael Wala, "Selling the Marshall Plan at Home: The Committee for the Marshall Plan to Aid European Recovery", *Diplomatic History 10* (1985): 91-105; idem, *Winning the Peace: Amerikanische Außenpolitik und der Council on Foreign Relations, 1945-1950*, (Stuttgart: Franz Steiner, 1990), 204ff.; idem, "Selling War and Selling Peace: The Non-Partisan Committee to Defend America and the Committee for the Marshall Plan", *Amerikastudien/American Studies* 30 (1985): 95-105.

5. An excellent description is given by Kenneth Heger, "Publicizing the Marshall Plan: Records of the U.S. Representative in Europe, 1948-50", *The Record, News from the National Archives and Records Administration*, 5.1, (September 1998): 24-26.

6. NA, RG, 469, Office of Information, Office of the Director, Subject Files 1949-53, Box 6.

7. Herbert Hoover, The President's Economic Mission to Germany and Austria. Report No. 1: German Agriculture and Food Requirements, 1947, 20.

8. Herbert Hoover, The President's Economic Mission to Germany and Austria. Report No. 2: Austrian Agriculture and Food Requirements—Economic Reorganization, 1947, 8.

9. "Economic Cooperation Agreement Between the United States of America and Austria," in *United Statutes at Large*, vol. 62 (1948), part 2, pp. 2137-2171, quotation 2143f.

10. Abkommen über Wirtschaftliche Zusammenarbeit zwischen der Bundesrepublik Deutschland und den Vereinigten Staaten von Amerika/Economic Cooperation Agreement between the United States of America and the Federal Republic of Germany, 15 December, 1949, English and German texts in: Bundesgesetzblatt (Bonn), 31 January, 1950, 10-21, quotation 17.

11. ECA memorandum "The Train of Europe," 31 January, 1951, NA, RG 469, OSRI, LD, Box 19. A photo collection on the train is held by the Haus der Geschichte, Bonn.

12. Der Marshallplan in Bildern. Der Wiederaufbau der österreichischen Wirtschaft. Reproduktionen aus der ERP-Wanderausstellung, Wien 1950; about the size of the first edition, see Memo Wilson, 16 November 1950, NA, RG 469, Mission to Austria, Administrative Division Subject Files, 1948-55, Box 77.

13. Important details on the results of the contest are contained in the inventory 286-MP-Poster Contest and General File, NA, Still Picture Branch, RG 286. Unfortunately, the posters are not in the National Archives. Numerous posters are in possession of the following institutions: Library of Congress, Washington D.C.; Deutsches Historisches Museum, Berlin; Haus der Geschichte der Bundesrepublik Deutschland; German Marshall Fund of the United States, Berlin.

14. The Austrian member was Professor Viktor Slama of the Acadamy of Fine Arts, ibid., entry no. 7.

15. The German Marshall Fund of the United States, Berlin.

16. Marshall Fund of the United States, Berlin.

17. Haus der Geschichte, Bonn.

18. German poster text: "Einiges Europa trägt Wohlstand," The German Marshall Fund of the United States, Berlin.

19. German poster text: "Frieden durch innereurop. Zusammenarbeit," Haus der Geschichte, Bonn.

20. The German Marshall Fund of the United States, Berlin.

21. The German Marshall Fund of the United States, Berlin.

22. German poster text: "Amerika hilft Deutschland mit Textilien," reprinted in *Danke Amerika, Journal für Deutschland. Ein Magazin des Presse- und Informationsamtes der Bundesregierung* (August/September 1997), 21.

23. German poster text: "Österreich braucht 18 Länder - 18 Länder brauchen Österreich," Österreichisches Gesellschafts- und Wirtschaftsmuseum/ERP-Fonds, Wien.

24. German poster text: "Deutschland spricht mit!", Stadtarchiv Giessen.

25. Werner Bührer, Westdeutschland in der OEEC. Eingliederung, Krise, Bewährung 1947-1961 (Munich: Oldenbourg, 1997).

26. Albert Hemsing, "The Marshall Plan's European Film Unit, 1948-1955: A Memoir and Filmography", *Historical Journal of Film, Radio and Television* 14 (1994): 269-297; Catalogue of Information Films Produced in Europe for the Marshall Plan 1948-1953 by the Film Section, Information Division, Special Representative in Europe, Economic Cooperation Administration, Mutual Security Agency, July 1954, George C. Marshall Foundation, Lexington, Virginia.

27. NA, Motion Picture, Sound, and Video Branch, RG 306.00107.

28. NA, Motion Picture, Sound, and Video Branch, RG 306.04004.

29. On Marshall Plan films on Austria, see: Christiane Rainer, Der Marshallplan: Ein Werbefeldzug? Über den Umgang mit Filmquellen in der Zeitgeschichte. M.A. thesis, University of Vienna, 1999.

30. NA, Motion Picture, Sound, and Video Branch, RG 306.81.

31. Working Paper of the Policy Planning Staff "Certain Aspects of the European Recovery Problem from the United States Standpoint, 23 July 1947," NA, RG 59, Records of Charles E. Bohlen.

32. Harriman to Truman, 12 August 1947, Harry S. Truman Library, Independence, Missouri, President's Secretary File, Germany.

33. Department of State Policy Statement, Germany, 16 August 1948, *FRUS, 1948*, II, 1310.

34. Policy Planning Staff Paper, 12 November 1948, *FRUS, 1948*, II, 1330.

35. Hans Beller, *Marshall Plan in Action.* Filme für Europa, Videoproduktion Munich 1997.

36. Interview with Tressler. ibid.

37. NA, Motion Picture, Sound, and Video Branch, RG 306/6059.

38. Taucher to King, 14 June 1950, NA, RG 469, Mission to Austria, Administrative Division Subject Files, 1948-55, Box 78.

39. See the lengthy memorandum "The Potential Military Contribution of the ERP Countries to the Common Defense of the West," 22 May 1950, NA, RG 469, Agency for International Development, ECA, Deputy Administrator, General Subject Files of the Mutual Security Program 1950-51.

40. Memo of the Foreign Operations Administration, undated (September 1953), mimeographed copy, BA, B146/379.

41. NA, Motion Picture, Sound, and Video Branch, RG 306.8997.

42. Walter Ulbricht, *Brennende Fragen des Neuaufbaus Deutschlands* (Berlin: Dietz, 1947), 9.

43. Poster Nordrhein-Westfälisches Staatsarchiv Detmold, file D81, no.1586; see also the pamphlet: "Wir brauchen keinen Marshallplan, wir kurbeln die Wirtschaft selber an. Das ist die Parole von Grotewohl," Pieck, Ulbricht in der Sowjetzone, Cologne n.d. [1951].

44. Numerous Posters in BA, No. 100ff.

45. Poster "Deutschland-Plan," BA, No.100/32/12.

46. Poster "Der große Unterschied," BA, No. 100/32/15.

47. Ibid.

48. Poster "Mit uns siegt der Plan!", BA, No. 100/29/21.

49. Poster "Unser Friedensplan" with a quotation from an Ulbricht speech of 10 August, 1950, BA, No. 100/29/44; see also the Poster "Fünfjahrplan heißt Aufbau und Frieden," BA, No. 100/29/42.

50. In interesting photo of a Communist youth parade of 1950, which "trumpets the Soviet line," is printed in *Newsweek*, May 1997, 20.

51. Novosti Dnia vom April und Juli 1949, NA, Motion Picture, Sound, and Video Branch, RG MID242.5260 und .5264.

52. Quoted in ERP Information Summary, 21 December 1948, NA, RG 469, Mission to Austria, box 5.

53. Der Weg zum Wohlstand. Ein österreichischer Wirtschaftsplan. Ausgearbeitet von der Wirtschaftspolitischen Kommission beim Zentralkomitee der Kommunistischen Partei Österreichs, Vienna 1948.

54. Memorandum Duerr, 12 August 1948, NA, RG 469, Records of the U.S. Foreign Assistance Agencies 1948-1961, Mission to Austria, Administrative Division Files, 1948-55, box 3.

55. Gewerkschaftlicher Nachrichtendienst der ECA. Labor Information Service of the ECA-Marshall Plan.

56. Quoted by Charles Levinson in his Report on Labor's Benefits from ERP and Trade Union Attitudes Toward ERP, September 1950, NA, RG 469, OSR, LID, Planning and Policy Section, Box 23.

57. Ibid.

58. Ibid.

59. Office of the U.S. High Commissioner for Germany, Report No. 39, 12 October 1950: The Effectiveness of the ERP Information Program in Western Germany, NA, RG 306.

60. Undated sample letter, Historical Archives, Kreditanstalt für Wiederaufbau, Frankfurt/M., file HA/BS 19.

61. USIS Bonn (Hodges) to Bundesminister für den Marshallplan, 21 May 1954, Bundesarchiv Koblenz, B146/379.

62. Bundesminister für den Marshallplan, Fünfter und Sechster Bericht der Deutschen Bundesregierung über die Durchführung des Marshallplans (Bonn 1951), 179.

63. *The Oxford English Dictionary* (2[nd] ed., Oxford: Oxford University Press, 1989), 632.

64. Memorandum Hayes to Hoffman, 16 July 1948, NA, RG 469, Records of the U.S. Foreign Assistance Agencies 1948-1961, Office of the Deputy Administrator Subject Files, 1948-49, Box 6.

65. Klaus Schönberger, "Hier half der Marshallplan. Werbung für das europäische Wiederaufbauprogramm zwischen Propaganda und Public Relations," *Propaganda in Deutschland. Zur Geschichte der politischen Massenbeeinflussung im 20. Jahrhundert*, ed. Gerald Diesener and Rainer Gries (Darmstadt, 1996), 208.

66. Carroll Memorandum: Psychological Pressures—Our Global Objectives, 12 June 1950, NA, RG 469, Records of the U.S. Foreign Assistance Agencies 1948-1961, Mission to Austria, Administrative Division Subject Files, 1948-55, Box 77.

67. Verhandlungen des Deutschen Bundestages. Stenographische Berichte, vol 1 (1949): 487.

68. Speech of 2 June, 1977, Bulletin der Bundsregierung, no. 59, 6 June, 1967, 504.

69. Bulletin der Bundesregierung, no. 83, 7 June, 1972, 1139.

70. Bulletin der Bundesregierung, no. 60, 7 June, 1977, 559.

71. Haus der Geschichte der Bundesrepublik Deutschland, ed., *Markt oder Plan: Wirtschaftsordnungen in Deutschland 1945-1961* (Frankfurt, 1997).

72. Haus der Geschichte der Bundesrepublik Deutschland, ed., *50 Jahre Marshall-Plan* (Berlin: Argon, 1997).

73. Willy Brandt, "Thanking America." A speech marking the 25[th] Anniversary of the Marshall Plan, mimeographed copy supplied by the German Marshall Fund of the United States.

74. William C. Norby, *American Aid and the Marshall Plan in the Reconstruction of Europe*, (Bensenville, IL, 1988) (American Philatelic Society, Europa News, Bulletin of the European Study Unit, Monograph Series, No. 5, private print, copy in: George C. Marshall Foundation, Lexington, VA.).

75. *Zehn Jahre ERP in Österreich 1948/58. Wirtschaftshilfe im Dienste der Völkerverständigung*, ed. by the Austrian Printing Office with the cooperation of the Federal Chancellery, Economic Coordination Section (Vienna: Government Printing Office, 1958).

76. *"Gewidmet den unbekannten amerikanischen Steuerzahlern, deren Steuerleistung die österreichische Wirtschaft die Millionen des guten Willens zum Wiederaufbau verdankt."* Ibid. 3.

77. Ibid., 5f.

78. Ibid., 13.

79. Ibid., 63.

80. *25 Jahre ERP-Fonds 1962-1987* (Vienna: ERP-Fonds, 1987).

81. Ibid., 7.

82. Ibid., 11.

83. Ibid., 44.

84. Ibid., 60 ff.

85. Günter Bischof and Dieter Stiefel, eds., *"80 Dollar": 50 Jahre ERP-Fonds und der Marshall-Plan in Österreich 1948-1998* (Vienna: Ueberreuter, 1999).

86. Kurt Löffler and Hans Fußenegger. "Die Tätigkeit des österreichischen ERP-Fonds von 1962 bis 1998," ibid., 21-56, quotation 56 (a translation of this essay is included in this volume).

# III. Macro- and Microeconomic Impacts

# Austria's Economic Policy and the Marshall Plan

*Hans Seidel**

## Introduction[1]

> "How long should we subsidize this outfit and get them to fight the Russkis when they are, in the long run, licked?" (Kindleberger, August 1946)[2]

The scientific community has repeatedly analyzed the Marshall Plan in general and its importance for individual countries. Their findings differed in many respects. Eichengreen and Uzan (1992) offered the following classification: The authors of the first generation[3] predominantly welcomed the Marshall Plan; the next generation thought it was not very effective or was even redundant;[4] the third generation found that the Marshall Plan had a lasting effect although for different reasons than the first generation.[5] Generally speaking, the authors of the third generation underrated the transfer of real resources initiated by the Marshall Plan.[6] They emphasized the creation of new institutions and the shift in economic policy that the Marshall Plan brought about.

The international literature has uncovered many facts and relationships that help to understand the role of the Marshall Plan for

---

* The author started his career after World War II as a junior economist in the Austrian Institute of Economic Research (WIFO). In this capacity he was involved in various Marshall Plan activities. He drafted reports for the government, participated in governmental meetings, and represented Austria at sessions of the OEEC (Organization for European Economic Cooperation).

Austria. However, one must not forget: Austria was in a especially bad, some would even say desperate, situation both politically and economically. Kindleberger, during his visit to Vienna in the summer of 1946, regarded the Austrian case as almost hopeless. Milward (1984, p. 82) mentioned that his critique of the European countries did not include Austria.

The United States acknowledged the "special case" by providing Austria with more aid (per capita or per unit of output) than most other countries. The objection of some scholars that the Marshall Plan was not large enough to have sizeable macroeconomic effects does not apply to Austria. Foreign aid was important compared with macroeconomic magnitudes such as GDP, imports or investment. Therefore, it seems to be justified to diverge from the contemporary research and to focus this paper on the transfer of real resources.

The transfer of resources from a donor to a receiving country can be seen in two ways: First, foreign aid provides the receiving country with foreign exchange. Hence, this country can spend more dollars than it earns. Second, if the goods are sold in the domestic market foreign aid provides the receiving country with investible funds in local currency. Consequently, it can invest more than it saves. In the case of Austria—it will be demonstrated—both the "dollar side" (dollar gap) and the "schilling side" (savings gap) of the Marshall Plan mattered.

## The Dollar Gap

> "...no amount of domestic effort will immediately produce the needed imports of food and certain crucial commodities." (Allan W. Dulles,1948).[7]

### *Pre-ERP Aid*

The Marshall Plan did not start before the middle of 1948. In the first three years after the war, Austria had to rely on foreign aid from other sources. The Marshall Plan differed from the aid received before in various aspects. It emphasized rehabilitation rather than relief. It offered a medium-term perspective and it was still available when production surpassed the prewar level. Nevertheless, for many purposes it is useful to stress the continuity of aid.[8] Since aid was flowing continuously there was no "market-shock"[9], neither when the Marshall Plan was announced nor when deliveries started.

The ad hoc programs in the first three years and the subsequent Marshall Plan provided Austria over a period of seven years with $ 1.6 billion dollars in foreign aid, mostly from the United States. At purchasing power parities that was almost six times as much as the international loan Austria got after World War I in order to stop hyperinflation (Nemschak, 1955, p. 22). Moreover, the postwar foreign aid was given almost exclusively as grants. Austria had not to repay the principal and was not obliged to pay interest. Serving a debt of $ 1.6 billion at 11 percent interest (the rate of the international loan of 1922) would have required yearly interest payments of $ 176 million or öS 4.58 billion (3.2 percent of GDP). Austria would have been an early candidate for a debt crisis if it would have had to carry such a burden in addition to the obligations of the State Treaty after 1955.

Although this paper is primarily concerned with the Marshall Plan a few remarks on pre-ERP aid appears to be useful. The younger generation often asks with an ironic undertone: Would the Austrians have died of famine without the Marshall Plan? Probably not. At that time, a larger set of opportunities was already available. However, in the immediate postwar years, there was a real danger that malnutrition would lead to chaos. In the industrial districts in Lower Austria, food rations for some time did not exceed 900 calories per day. Domestic supplies covered only 40 percent of the meager food rations of the non-farm population. The survival of the Austrian population depended crucially on help from outside.

Immediately after the war, the occupying forces provided some food out of military stocks in their zones in order to prevent "disease and unrest." Beginning in April 1946, the United Nations Relief and Rehabilitation Administration (UNRRA) delivered food and some other goods essential for survival, like pharmaceuticals. In the fall of 1946, a critical situation developed. The UNRRA support ended in the first half of 1947, the domestic harvest was very poor, and little food could be expected from commercial trade with neighboring countries (some of them also received UNRRA aid).

The tensions between the Austrian government and the Allied Military Council grew.[10] The Council criticized Austria, saying that it was not doing enough to organize production and distribution of food. It asked for a four year plan with short notice. The Austrians complained that they could not use their resources fully, that the country was divided in four-zones, and that military personnel were engaged in black market transactions.[11]

In this critical situation, the United States (and the Britain) decided to provide substantial financial assistance to Austria. As early as August 1946, Kindleberger, in his letters from Vienna, mentioned the intention of the U.S. administration to help (Kindleberger, 1989, p. 82). Various estimates tried to sort out how much help Austria needed (Bischof 1989, pp. 484-495). Strategically important was the so-called **Dort-Plan** or **R-Plan**, drafted by a group of U.S. and British economists. Starting from the import requirements and the export prospects they estimated a trade deficit of $200 million for 1947, only a small part of which could be covered by the remaining UNRRA deliveries.[12] The R-plan became a reference model for the subsequent Austrian estimates of the trade deficit before the Marshall Plan. The *Notprogramm* (emergency import plan) for 1948 explicitly was called a modified version of the R-plan.[13]

In 1947, the United Kingdom, although burdened with grave economic problems, gave Austria a credit of £10 million mainly in order to buy raw materials. A large part of it was later declared grant. The U.S. War and State Department provided Austria with the most needed food and some free dollars, mainly to buy coal in Europe. In the first month of 1948, an "interim aid" helped Austria to bridge the gap until the beginning of the Marshall Plan. Including military surplus goods, Austria received more $600 million foreign aid before the Marshall Plan.[14] In other words, pre-ERP aid was flowing at a rate of $200 million per year.

The decision of the United States and Britain in the fall of 1946 to help Austria as a whole (and not just their occupation zones) provided not only the most needed food and coal. What was at least as important: it made the Austrians confident that the West is ready to help. But the donor countries will do so directly (and not via UN organizations) with all the implications connected with this commitment. The occupation zones of Austria might have drifted apart, if the United States and Britain would have just cared for their zones.[15]

### *Two Stages of Reconstruction*

The Austrians argued that the pre-ERP aid just sufficed to prevent the population from starving and to operate the economy at a subsistence level. In order to initiate a reconstruction process, substantially more foreign aid was needed. The setback of the Austrian economy in the extreme cold winter 1946/47 seemed to confirm this pessimistic view. However, after the spring of 1947 industrial production expanded very strongly. Hence, rehabilitation was well under way before the Marshall Plan started. The "folk image" (De Long and Eichengreen, 1993, p. 194) that the European economy was on the edge of collapsing before the Marshall Plan was not even true in the case of one of its weakest parts.[16]

Obviously, the distinction between relief and rehabilitation was not sharp. The Austrians began reconstruction immediately after the cease-fire. The first steps to be take were straightforward. Almost everybody helped to remove the rubble from the bombing and fighting. The public utilities restored systems of transportation and communication, at least on a minimum scale. Workers and entrepreneurs patched damaged buildings and factories in order to prevent further decay. For this pick and shovel work not much additional foreign equipment was necessary, except for spare parts from Germany. This held especially true since the industrial capacity of Austria reached its prewar level, notwithstanding the damages by bombing and the dismantling of machinery and equipment by the Soviet Union.

In line with the repair of physical capital, human capital was built up. As in other countries suffering from war, the Austrian government hesitated to force labor into jobs where additional workers were most needed, notably in agriculture, forestry, and mining. Incentives in the form of additional food rations were only partly successful. Those who happened to survive the atrocities of the war were determined to build up their own careers irrespective of the short-term pressing needs of the economy.[17] These investments in human resources contributed to future economic growth, but delayed recovery in the short run.[18]

The crucial point is the following: Austria was only able to invest in human and physical capital because the United States provided food and coal. The import of these goods, contrary to a widespread belief, was highly productive.[19] Of course, the question arises: How did the Austrian policy makers know that foreign assistance would be forthcoming? The answer was, they did not. Nevertheless, they embarked on a reconstruction path that could only be maintained with foreign aid. In the language of some of the conservative critics of the Marshall Plan, Austria was "overspending" and manoeuvered the United States in a position where they could not refuse to provide help.

Was there an alternative? A "survival" program with no or only limited foreign aid would have been much tougher to design and implement—perhaps too tough for a democratic government. It is not very difficult to sketch the outline of such a survival program.

Compulsory labor recruitment,[20] concentration of industrial production in few units running at full capacity,[21] and continued overcutting of woods would be some of the necessary measures to be taken, not to mention the sale of art treasures.

To understand the attitude of the Austrian government, one has to consider that it felt only partly responsible for the gloomy economic situation of the country. Without the burden of the occupying forces and with reasonable "reparations" to cover their "partial responsibility" for the war, Austria would have had enough economic potential to survive without much foreign help. As was demonstrated by Bischof (1999, p. 138) the costs of occupation and the transfers to the Soviet Union were almost as high as the foreign aid Austria received.

Around 1948, reconstruction entered a second phase. The most urgent repair work having been done, a sustainable progress depended on new investments. Incidentally, when the ERP started, the Ministry in charge of economic planning had just finished development plans (called *Konstitutionspläne*) for some industries: for the iron and steel industry, for non-ferrous metals, for coal mining, and for electrical power plants. Plans for industries producing finished goods for various reasons proved to be more intricate and did not succeed as quickly as desired. (At the end of 1949 the Austrian government decided to dissolve the Ministry of Planning, leaving many *Konstitutionspläne* unfinished.) These ambitious plans did not merely seek to restore something that had already existed in the past. They had the much more ambitious aim of creating a new economic structure conducive to economic growth. For these purposes, new machines and equipment had to be imported.

The adequacy of investment goods delivered under the Marshall Plan was discussed intensively, though in an unsystematic way. In the early phases of the Marshall Plan, the lack of foreign investment goods could have restricted investments more than the supply of savings.[22] That was especially true if one wanted to revamp manufacturing industry at an accelerated pace. However, according to the Austrian "long-term program" prepared at the end of 1948,[23] only 12 percent of the planned supply of investment goods had to be imported. (Incidentially, this was exactly the share of investment goods in Marshall Plan direct aid.) Expressed in real terms, one of the main functions of the ERP remained to supply food for the workers in the domestic investment goods industries, especially in the building industry. This industry had been expanded disproportionaly both with respect to domestic savings and to historical benchmarks. In 1951, the value added of the building industry was three times as high as 1937 while agricultural production was still lower than before the war. (Those who criticized the Marshall Plan as an "emergency program"[24] did obviously not mean that U.S. building firms should have built the dams for electric power plants in the Alps with American workers.)

*Import Plans and Dollar Allocations*

For the reasons mentioned above, Austria expected from the Marshall Plan substantial more foreign aid that it actually got. In the fall of 1947, it presented to the coordinating committee of the participating countries (CEEC) a balance of payments forecast containing a deficit of approximately $650 million both in the fiscal year 1948/49 and 1949/50. The cumulative deficit over the four year period totaled more than $2 billion[25] calculated at 1947 prices.

That proved to be wishful thinking. The requirements of the participating countries added up to something like $30 billion, much more than the United States was willing to pay. The figures presented by the member countries had to be cut drastically.

Austria seemed to be in an especially awkward position. The U.S. administration[26] suggested aid for Austria in the first Marshall Plan year ranging from $151 million (annex to the Marshall Plan bill) to $197 million (Brownbook of the State Department). These estimates assumed that the Marshall Plan will only cover the deficits in the western hemisphere and not those vis-à-vis European member countries. The Austrian government maintained that Austria needed more imports than it could pay for by exports. It further stressed that the U.S. experts overestimated the feasible food imports from Eastern Europe. Consequently, it intervened heavily in order to get a larger share. The Austrian position was explained in a "note ii".[27] A delegation was sent to Washington in order to convince the U.S. authorities that Austria needed more help than was suggested in the U.S. documents.[28] These interventions were partly successful.[29] Austria got an advanced payment of $70 million for the second quarter of 1948.

Actually, the U.S. Congress fixed only the global amount for the first year and left it to the OEEC in Paris to determine the shares of individual countries. For that purpose, the OEEC asked from each member country two estimates of its balance of payments: a "budget" estimate based on the deficit mentioned in the Brownbook, and a "requirement" estimate based on the perceived needs of a country.

Austria originally refused to provide the requirement version of the estimate, claiming a "special case" status.[30] After deducting the prepayment of $70 million for the second quarter of 1948, only $126.8 million were left for the remaining three quarters of the first Marshall Plan year. For food and coal alone $230 million were regarded as necessary, not to mention other requirements.

Finally, the outcome of the horse trading in Paris was not too bad. Austria received for the first Marshall Plan year direct aid of $217 million covering the deficit in the dollar area and an indirect aid (so-called drawing rights) of 63,5 million $ covering the deficit in intra-European trade. The aid granted for 1948/49 ($280.5 million) was less than half the amount that was originally expected, but more than the aid received in 1947 ($225 million according to the balance of payments compiled by the National Bank). Compared with the estimates presented to the CEEC at the end of 1947, the requirements for nearly all groups of commodities had to be curtailed. Food imports were cut drastically. The plans to provide the non-farm population with more and better food had to be postponed.

In the following years, the gap between requested and received aid was relatively small. The market for aid, so to speak, became more transparent. It was generally understood that foreign aid would be reduced gradually (by approximately 30 percent per year). Furthermore, the ECA announced for planning purposes (before the approval of the Congress) tentative figures for the next fiscal year. Finally, in the fall 1949, the participating countries agreed on a formula for the distribution of aid. According to the so-called Snoy-Marjolin formula,[31] Austria's share was fixed at 4.252 percent of the direct foreign aid as decided by the US Congress. For 1949/50, Austria received $259 million and for 1950/51 $180 million direct and indirect aid.

Despite these negotiation routines, decisions concerning the Marshall Plan aid for a specific year could not be reached quickly. The member countries agreed on the Snoy-Marjolin formula only after a lengthy and heated debate. More often than not, the Austrian ERP Bureau had to revise its balance of payments forecast several times and to adjust the import plans accordingly. But the rules of the game were well known. This well-behaved system was shocked by the outbreak of the Korean War. The boom in raw materials reduced the real value of the aid granted for 1950/51. In the fiscal year 1951/52, the United States decided to concentrate on military aid and to reduce economic aid drastically. This point will be elaborated in the last section of this paper.

*How much help did Austria really need?*

The big difference between the aid Austria originally requested from the Marshall Plan and the aid it finally received raises the question: How much help did Austria really need? Was there a rock-bottom figure? If Austria could do with $280 million in the first Marshall Plan year instead of $650 million as requested, would have $140 million provoked a disaster? These are difficult questions for which no easy answers exist. However, some insights can be gained by analyzing the relevant factors.

A convenient starting point is the trade gap. In 1947, before the Marshall Plan, Austria's imports (of goods and services) were three times as high as its exports. In the first two Marshall Plan years the gap was still approximately 100 percent. Even in 1951, the year before the Marshall Plan was scheduled to end, exports fell short of imports by one-third.

**Table 1:** The Trade Gap

| Year | Imports* $ million | Exports* $ million | Imports in % of Exports |
|---|---|---|---|
| 1947 | 335.0 | 110.5 | 303.17 |
| 1948 | 495.8 | 228.58 | 216.90 |
| 1949 | 624.7 | 329.31 | 189.70 |
| 1950 | 510.13 | 378.06 | 134.93 |
| 1951 | 700.25 | 523.98 | 133.64 |
| 1952 | 704.74 | 600.19 | 117.42 |

* Goods and services according to the balance of payments statistic of the Austrian National Bank.

Austria could only afford to import more than it exported because foreign aid was available. There is no doubt about the direction of causality. Contrary to the period after World War I, Austria had practically no foreign assets that could eventually be used to finance net imports. Private capital failed to perceive the growth potential of Europe let alone those of occupied Austria. At the beginning of the

1950s, the value of U.S. direct investment in Austria did not exceed the level of 1937.[32] Long term credits were granted by some government sponsored foreign credit institutions on a modest scale.[33] Until 1952, even the World Bank refused to finance projects in Austria. (The first project presented to the World Bank was an energy power plant in Huben-Dorfertal.[34] When the project was taken up decades later, it was not realized because of environmental concerns). The first purely commercial credit was a Swiss loan, in 1953. In order to get this loan Austria had to earmark part of its gold reserves.

Given these constraints, until 1950 the deficit on current account was practically equal to foreign aid. Later on, short-term capital transactions, notably shifts in the terms of payment, played a certain role, and the National Bank could accumulate modest foreign exchange reserves.[35] Nevertheless, up to 1952 the cumulative deficit on current account surpassed foreign aid only by small margin. It was not before the stabilization policy of 1952/53 that (induced and autonomous) capital transactions became relevant. The close relationship between foreign aid and the deficit in the foreign account is confirmed by a simple regression analysis.

A univariate regression of the current account deficit (CAD) on foreign aid (FA), both magnitudes expressed in percent of GDP, for the period 1947/55 gives the following results:

$$CAD= \quad 1.57 \quad — \quad 1.09\ FA$$
$$(1.96) \quad — \quad (8.69)$$

$R^2$=0.92 DW=2.21

The coefficients are robust. They remain fairly constant, if other variables, lags or 2SLS estimation techniques are introduced.

The gap between exports and imports is not the only indicator and probably not the decisive one for estimating the need for foreign help. If domestic goods can be exported easily or are a close substitute for imported goods, then even big gaps in the foreign account can be closed with no adjustment costs. In this case there is no foreign exchange constraint (although there might be a savings constraint). The notion that the foreign balance can be adjusted smoothly to foreign shocks (as in macroeconomic models with one composite good) played a certain role in the international discussion of the Marshall Plan and the dollar gap.[36] It certainly did not fit the postwar conditions of Austria. For this purpose a simple structural model such as was used by the contemporary economic policy makers seems to be more realistic.

The structural argument runs as follows. The Austrian economy needs inputs from abroad in order to employ its factors of production. These necessary inputs include a minimum of food (which in this respect can be regarded as an input to provide labor services). If for any reason whatsoever the complementary inputs from abroad are not available, then the factors of production cannot be used fully or efficiently. Actual production falls short of potential production. In other words, within a certain range, the GDP is an increasing function of imports and with given exports, also of foreign aid. The drastic fall of industrial production in the cold winter 1946/47 and its steep rise during the year 1947 were typical examples of this dependence.

One of the big disadvantages of this country in the postwar era was the lack of coal and of food. Both products were scarce and expensive. They could only bought against payments in dollars or in exchange for goods of comparable scarcity. On the other hand, goods and services which Austria could offer at a comparative advantage, like traditional consumer goods and tourism, were discriminated as "non-essentials." In this respect Austria was in a worse situation than most other European countries.

The commodity composition of Austria's foreign trade was reflected by adverse terms of trade and a huge dollar deficit. In the first Marshall Plan year, 1948/49, only 11 percent of the programmed expenditure of $234 million in the Western Hemisphere could be covered by receipts denominated in dollar.[37] Even this meager 11 percent resulted mainly from the refunds of occupation costs by the United States and payments for refugees. If there ever was a country suffering from a dollar shortage, it was Austria.

Certainly, not all of the imports from the United States were necessary in the sense that these goods could not be bought elsewhere without dollar payments. To a certain degree, by providing dollars, the United States promoted the sale of U.S. goods. Due to the postwar boom, however, the pressure to sell U.S. goods was relatively small and cannot be compared with the export promoting character of many aid programs for developing countries later on. (Perhaps the most important exception was the rule that ERP goods had to be shipped on U.S. cargo boats.)

"Unnecessary" spending of dollars mainly occurred because some goods were cheaper or (and) easier to get in the United States than elsewhere.[38] That was especially true when the effective exchange rate for Austrian exports was around 14 schillings per dollar compared with an official rate of 10 schillings per dollar. Therefore, the devaluation in the fall of 1949 and the subsequent abolishment of multiple exchange rates somewhat reduced the dollar shortage. Nevertheless, it seemed to be very unlikely that feasible changes in relative prices could have eliminated the dollar deficit altogether.

This was especially true, since Austria had not only a dollar gap vis-à-vis the Western Hemisphere but also vis-à-vis Europe. Trade in Europe, on principle, was steered by bilateral trade agreements, distinguishing between "essential" and "non-essential" goods. The current account had to be balanced not only between countries, but also between types of commodities. If enough essential goods could not be offered, payment in dollars was required. The indirect aid (drawing rights) of the Marshall Plan provided the receiving countries with dollars to buy essential goods in Western Europe. Austria used its drawing rights mainly for purchases of coal from the Ruhr and of raw materials from the sterling zone.

The following example illustrates the trade and payments practices before the establishment of the EPU.[39] In preparing a trade and payments agreement between Austria and the tri-zone of Germany for 1949/50, a list of "dollar-worth" commodities was set up. According to this list, Austria offered $22 million exports (including $6 million electric current) and wanted $66 million imports of "dollar-worth" goods. The import surplus of $44 million was equal to the required coal deliveries. It should be covered by drawing rights.

That leaves trade with Eastern Europe. In the postwar era, East-West trade was not just an economic issue, but had an eminent political character, even before embargo lists reduced the scope for profitable business.[40] Unfortunately, the discussion was biased by ideology, and not enough empirical work has been done. From the Austrian files it appears that Eastern Europe would not have been able (or willing) to provide Austria with the goods it needed most urgently, namely grain and coal, in sufficient quantities and in exchange for Austrian finished goods.

As far as coal is concerned, Poland was prepared to deliver hard coal, but until the beginning of the 1950s, between 40 and 60 percent of the coal bill had to be paid in dollars. (Already part of the "free" dollars provided by Congressional aid in 1947 had been spent for Polish coal.) Contrary to the prewar supply conditions, the Ruhr became the most important source for coal imports, partly because coal from West Germany was cheaper than alternative supplies.[41] In 1937, 80 percent of the coal imports came from Eastern Europe, in 1948 only 40 percent.

Bread grain was not available from Eastern European sources in the first postwar years. According to an international survey[42] based on country reports for 1947/48, only the Western Hemisphere expected crops exceeding their domestic requirements (half of the exportable surplus came from the United States). The supply in the Eastern European countries, the former granary of Western Europe, was barely sufficient to cover the most urgent domestic needs. In the trade agreements with Austria, the Eastern European countries were not prepared to include an option for Austria in case crops will be higher than expected.[43] In the course of the reconstruction period, the food supplies from Eastern Europe gradually became more elastic. Coarse grain, meat, vegetables, and other foodstuffs were imported from these countries in exchange for Austrian industrial products. However, according to the Austrian Economic Report, as late as 1950/51, at most one-fifth of import requirements of bread grain (560,000 t) could be covered by Eastern Europe.[44]

The structural deficiencies of Austria's foreign trade were adequately described in a Report of the US National Security Council as late as 1951:

> The nature of the Austrian economy is such that it cannot earn enough dollars to support its essential imports from the dollar area in the absence of United States aid. Until a greater measure of convertibility of currencies is achieved, it cannot measurably increase its direct earnings of dollars.[45]

The concept of a structural balance of payment deficit created by the lack of coal and food fitted the facts pretty well during the first half of the Marshall Plan. It lost explanatory power approximately from 1950 on because it neglected two important factors:

- The structure of production and demand is rigid only in the short run. One is entitled to ask: Did economic policy in Austria make reasonable efforts to overcome the bottlenecks that had plagued the economy since the end of the war?
- The dollar shortage eased at the beginning of the 1950s. When intra-European trade was liberalized and the European Payments Union established that the distinction between "essential" and

"non-essential" goods was meaningless, dollars could be earned by exports to Western European countries.

As to the first objection, one might argue that Austria had not done enough to alleviate the food and energy situation. It took eight years (until 1953) for agricultural production to regain the prewar level, although more machines and fertilizers were used. At the same time, industrial production was already 70 percent higher than in 1937. After World War I, agricultural production attained the prewar level of 1924 without much more additional inputs. Agriculture suffered from a lack of labor. Farm hands looked for jobs in industry at a time when food rations for the non-farm population were insufficient. The booming building activity and extra rations for workers engaged in certain giant projects supported the shift in employment from agriculture to industry. Efforts to keep labor at the farms failed as did attempts at increasing the area under cultivation.

When it comes to coal, great efforts were taken to increase the domestic production of brown coal (lignite). Hard coal had to be imported. In 1948, when the Marshall Plan started, Austria consumed 1/3 more coal than it had in 1937. The energy coefficient (the consumption of energy per unit of output) was almost 40 percent higher. One might question if such a high energy coefficient was really unavoidable. The vast energy requirements resulted from the shift of production towards energy intensive basic industries and from ambitious recovery programs. Both factors could be influenced by appropriate policy measures. In the reconstruction period, economic policy kept prices for energy as low as possible and relied on administrative controls to contain demand. Economic agents did not have sufficient incentives to save energy. As far as investment programs are concerned, more energy was needed "today" in order to save energy "tomorrow." Not much attention was given to the rate of substitution between present and future energy requirements.[46]

Austria undoubtedly could have improved its dollar balance, if the pace of reconstruction would have been slower and if energy and capital intensive projects would have been postponed. In that case, it could have offered its European trading partners more "essentials" like timber, steel, and electricity. The exports of these products were licensed, giving reconstruction and full employment a high priority.

The second objection refers to the fact that the market conditions changed considerably within a few years. De Long and Eichengreen

(1995, p. 212) assumed that in the Marshall Plan years, bottlenecks played only a minor role, except, perhaps, at the initial stages of the plan. In this paper, it is argued that they were important for Austria at least until the middle of the Marshall Plan period. Nevertheless, things did change. The recovery of production in Europe, the devaluation of most of the European currencies in fall 1949, the upswing of the U.S. business cycle after the recession 1948, the rearmament boom financed by the United States after the outbreak of the Korean War—these and other factors reduced the dollar shortage. Since the establishment of the EPU and the liberalization of intra-European trade, dollars could be earned by accumulating a surplus in the trade with Western Europe. Such a surplus did not merely depend on the supply of a few scarce goods. It could be achieved by improving competitiveness over a broad range of goods and services. The renewed introduction of controls for important commodities during the Korean war did interrupt the tendency towards a market economy, but only temporarily.

This line of reasoning leads to the following conclusion. The gloomy picture of a country on the edge of starvation may have been true for Austria in the immediate postwar period. In the Marshall Plan era, Austria could have done with less or even without help given an appropriate economic policy. However, adjustment costs might have been high, especially if foreign aid would have been reduced at an early date and if this cut would have caught Austria's economic policy unprepared. In this case, either technological unemployment (caused by a shortage of inputs) or structural unemployment (caused by a low level of aggregate demand) would have been liable to occur.

Austria's economic policy stance, encouraged by the Gray report[47], was based on the assumption that aid will be available even after the scheduled end of the Marshall Plan. It placed high priority on reconstruction and undertook only moderate efforts to settle the foreign balance. The radical reduction of foreign aid at the end of 1951, therefore, brought about substantial adjustment difficulties. The possible outcome of an earlier stabilization policy can be estimated by a comparison with Western Germany. This country introduced, in 1948, a currency reform and established a high degree of internal and external stability. The "social market economy," however, provoked a relatively large structural unemployment and was only gradually accepted by the public. A persistent "breakthrough" occurred not before 1950, partly as a result of the Korean boom (Wolf 1993, p. 43). It is very unlikely that the Austrian coalition government could have agreed on such a strategy approximately at the same time as Western Germany.

### *The Savings Gap*

> *"An der Person Porsche bin ich nicht interessiert. Sein Versuch, einen Volkswagen zu konstruieren, hat keine Aussicht auf Erfolg."* (Krauland, *Minister für Vermögensicherung und Wirtschaftsplanung*[48])

Immediately after the war, economic policy primarily looked at the "dollar side" of foreign aid. Although the goods delivered were sold in the domestic market and therefore local currency funds (counterpart funds) accumulated, no consistent ideas existed how these funds should be used. Concerning the UNRRA funds a special interministerial commission drafted a preliminary program[49] which, however, was not carried out. According to this program, the receipts should be distributed among different ministries mainly to meet additional public expenditures over a few years. Actually, until the end of 1947, most of the pre-ERP funds remained unspent (25 percent were cancelled by the monetary reform at the end of 1947).

In the first month of 1948, policy makers "discovered" that large sums were piling up. The Ministry of Finance estimated that until mid—1948 öS 2 billion counterpart funds would be available. With the beginning of the Marshall Plan, a continuous stream of receipts was to be expected over some years. Spending plans mushroomed. The government provided some funds for aged persons. Within a few months, it granted öS 600 million subsidies to farmers (for milk and later on for grain). Also öS 200 million were requested as start-up capital for a newly created housing fund. Not least, the nationalized industries needed large sums for their ambitious investment projects (they had already received a bridging loan of öS 300 million).

In order to coordinate the mounting claims, in August 1948 the government set up a comprehensive plan of counterpart releases for 1948.[50] An amount approximately equal to the accruals in 1948 was to be spent, while the balance already existing at the beginning of the year was to be sterilized. Since the ECA was not willing to subsidize farm prices, counterpart funds of a comparable size were requested to finance investment programs contained in the federal budget.

The ECA accepted the first application for releases largely unchanged and at short notice. Only the proposed spending for general housing was rejected. Subsequently, the release procedures proved to be rather cumbersome. The ECA delayed decisions in order to clarify controversial issues or simply refused to release funds until certain conditions were met. The yearly programs were split up into parts, leaving the Austrian government in the dark as to whether or not the yearly programs will be financed. Bridging operations became the rule.

### *Counterpart Funds and Economic Policy*

The struggle over the use of counterpart funds can be easily explained. The ECA regarded the releases as a major instrument to achieve the goals set by the Marshall Plan. Roughly speaking, the dollar allocations were supposed to cover the present needs of the participating countries, while the counterpart allocations were supposed to strengthen the economy and thereby reduce the future needs for foreign aid. In particular, the local currency funds were supposed to be used to enhance financial stability and to promote productivity, especially in the exposed sector of the economy. These two goals were not easy to reconcile and caused some inconsistencies.[51]

In order to comply with the mentioned twin goals, the yearly release programs presented by the Austrian government contained two steps. First, it had to be determined how much spending of counterpart funds was compatible with financial stability. Second, the admissible global amount had to be allocated to specific investment projects.

In order to determine the appropriate releases for the coming year, the following procedure was adopted. It was estimated how much money would be generated in the coming year and how much monetary expansion will be compatible with a prudent fiscal and monetary regime. The difference should be made up from the counterpart funds. This early exercise in "monetarism" was not very well designed, because at that time, the demand for money was not a stable function (of income, wealth, or other variables). Its main aim was to draw attention to the factors shaping excess demand and inflation. The Austrian authorities did not take this exercise very seriously. They usually found that spending the receipts of a certain year did not violate financial stability. The planning authorities felt that it was more important to carry out their investment projects than to achieve a bit more financial stability. The monetary authorities by and large pursued an accommodating policy stance. They were prepared to finance the cost-push type price-wage-settlements of the social partners and felt only responsible for price increases stemming from the demand side.

On two occasions, in 1949 and 1952, the ECA urged the Austrian government to adopt a more cautious (less inflationary) fiscal and monetary policy. In order to support their demands, they held back releases of counterpart funds.

In 1949, the federal budget was about to get out of control. The budget estimate for this year showed a deficit of öS 1,4 billion. Actually, a much larger deficit was to be expected, since the costs of the occupying forces and of displaced persons were not contained in the budget. Furthermore, tax revenues (especially from the tobacco tax) were overestimated and current expenditures underestimated. Under these circumstances, the ECA[52] argued, it would be imprudent to release counterpart funds.[53] Confronted with the lack of funds for projects, most of which had already been started, in May 1949 the Austrian government launched a consolidation program with tax increases of about 2 percent of GDP. It remains an open question what budgetary policy would have been followed without the intervention of the ECA. On the one hand, the government had only limited access to the National Bank. Therefore, some consolidating steps had to be taken anyhow. On the other hand, elections were due in the fall of 1949. Probably the government would have undertaken some bridging operations and postponed painful consolidating measures until the election was over.

The 1952 intervention was a byproduct of the Korea War. The United States concentrated its foreign aid on military assistance and wanted to finish its economic aid to Austria as soon as possible. They therefore asked the Austrian government to put on the monetary and fiscal brakes. Internal and external financial stability was to be achieved regardless of short term negative effects on employment and production. The stabilization recession will be described in some detail in the last section of this article. It had to be stressed, however, that up to 1952, the ECA had not urged the Austrian government to attain price stability at any cost. They more or less accepted the inflationary bias of the price and wage agreements organized by the social partners.[54]

In the second step the allocation of funds to individual projects or, as far as small business was concerned, groups of projects had to be decided. This was a delicate task since the ministries and interest groups concerned defended their projects stubbornly. After the internal coordination, the release program had to pass the review of the ECA. The hope that the Americans would more or less accept the outcome of the internal decision making process proved to be premature. The ECA (and the National Advisory Council) scrutinized carefully all big projects and rejected those they considered less important.[55]

In accordance with the general goals of the Marshall Plan, the ECA established a few principles for the use of counterpart funds:

- The funds should finance investments rather than private or public consumption.
- Investments in immediate productive sectors should be preferred to infrastructure investments.
- Priority should be given to investment projects with a direct impact on the balance of payments.

Yet, as in the case of financial stability, the ECA did not enforce these principles rigorously. According to the bilateral agreement between Austria and the United States, the goods delivered under the Marshall Plan had be sold at world market prices calculated at the official exchange rate. Nevertheless, the ECA temporarily accepted the sale of agricultural products at domestic prices which most of the time were lower than those prevailing at the world markets. Although the ECA put a constant pressure on the Austrian government to abolish the "price gap," it did not achieve this goal before the middle of 1951. According to rough calculations, approximately one fifth of the receipts of the ERP were used for food subsidies and presumably supported private consumption. (To justify subsidies, one could argue that low food prices helped to moderate wage pressure and allowed comfortable profit margins in manufacturing.)

By the same token, the ECA reduced only gradually releases for infrastructure investments in the federal budget—mainly for railways and postal services. It did, however, from the very beginning refuse to provide counterpart funds for general housing, although the Austrian government repeatedly asked for it. It was not before 1952 when the flow of counterpart receipts began to dwindle that the ECA strictly rejected any financing of government investments with the argument:

> I do not consider it economically sound to retain workers on relative unproductive public works by means of counterpart expenditures, when the same worker could be much more

usefully employed by using this counterpart to finance essential industrial projects".[56]

**Table 2:** Investment financing from counterpart funds*

| Year | Federal Budget | Industry | Other Sectors | Total Financing out of Counterpart Funds |
|---|---|---|---|---|
| | | öS million | | |
| 1948 | 588.0 | 600.0 | 50.0 | 1238.0 |
| 1949 | 852.7 | 544.3 | 178.0 | 1575.0 |
| 1950 | 365.0 | 1231.0 | 565.1 | 2161.1 |
| 1951 | 387.1 | 2093.2 | 826.6 | 3306.9 |
| 1952 | 31.1 | 1084.7 | 298.0 | 1413.8 |
| Total | 2223.9 | 5553.2 | 1917.7 | 9694.8 |
| Share % | 22.9 | 57.3 | 19.8 | 100.0 |

* Releases from (ECA and non-ECA) counterpart funds. Without debt redemption.
**Source**: WIFO-Monatsberichte

As far as counterpart releases for industry (including electricity) was concerned, the Austrian proposals were by and large accepted. That was remarkable, since Austria embarked on a bold industrial policy. During the war, the Germans had established some large-scale enterprises that did not seem to fit in the traditional landscape of the Austrian industry. One group of experts (industrialists and engineers mainly in the Ministry of Planning) argued that a new industrial structure should be created with emphasis on basic industries. Another group, among them prominent political economists, pleaded for strengthening the processing industries.[57]

The supporters of strong basic industries gained acceptance mainly for the following reasons:

- In the postwar era, basic products were scarce and offered high earning prospects even if domestic prices were controlled.
- The basic industries and most of the energy projects were mainly located in the Western zones of Austria. The United States would hardly have agreed to finance big projects of military importance[58] in the Russian zone. Only 15 percent of the counterpart funds went to the Eastern part of Austria.

- The Austrian planning authorities correctly assessed the chances of the basic industries, but failed to appreciate those of the investment goods industries in a world of explosive economic growth (see the quotation at the beginning of the chapter). The investments of the postwar period had a lasting effect on the industrial structure of the country.
- The basic industries (including electric power plants) were nationalized. Nationalized firms, at least at the beginning of the ERP, developed more ambitious investment plans than private firms or firms owned by the banks. Later on, when high growth rates became a widely accepted fact, more private projects were coming forward. The structure of counterpart financed investment was shifted somewhat in favor of the processing industries. Nevertheless, the basic industries still got the lion's share.

The Marshall Plan administration took up the discussion about an adequate industrial policy at the end of 1949. It questioned the concentration of investments in energy and steel. Investing more in the processing industries could improve the balance of payments quicker than the existing investment program. In order to clarify this issue, the ECA urged a detailed long term investment program. In the meantime, it reduced counterpart releases to a minimum.[59] Understandably, the Austrian government was annoyed. It had just tightened the fiscal belt as requested and expected to be rewarded by ample counterpart releases. The discussion ended abruptly when the Korean conflict triggered an armament boom. Basic products became scarce again and had to be rationed. The United States even asked Austria to put into operation an additional blast-furnace.

Comparing the intentions of the Austrian government with the outcome of the negotiations with the ECA, one comes to the conclusion that if the Austrian government would have been free to dispose of the funds, it would have spent more for subsidies and infrastructure investments (including housing). Therefore, less would have been available for the immediate productive sectors of the economy, inflationary financing excluded.

It is worth noting that the ECA was against subsidies for consumption but did not mind subsidizing enterprises via low nominal interest rates. In the years of high inflation, borrowing by industrial firms at 4.25 percent produced an enormous leverage effect. Standard calculations show that 1 million ERP credits taken in 1948 up to 1952 generated an additional net value of approximately the same size. Thus, counterpart transactions boosted profits, unless prices were kept low by government regulations. These links have to be taken into account when microeconomic data of cash flows and investment are analyzed. It is unlikely that the nationalized industries (including power stations) could have played such an important role in the postwar era without the counterpart programs accepted by the United States despite their dislike of nationalization.

### *Investment and Growth*

Thanks to foreign aid, Austria could (and did) consume and invest more that it produced. Domestic absorption surpassed domestic production by a wide margin. By selling the ERP goods in the domestic market, purchasing power was siphoned off, that could be used for investment. This is true regardless of whether the counterpart funds were spent for specific purposes or mobilized indirectly by other financial transactions. (The technique of financing determined, however, the distribution of investment.)

According to the capital account of the national income statistics—which, admittedly, was not very reliable at that time—in 1948 and 1949 foreign aid was almost as high as the flow of domestic savings (net). It covered nearly one half of gross investment in durable assets. Thereafter, the domestic savings took the lead. Nevertheless, in the next two years, the share of foreign aid ("foreign savings") remained relatively high, partly because the devaluation of the Austrian schilling in November 1949 boosted the local currency receipts. Even in 1951, foreign aid covered one third of gross investment in fixed assets.[60]

**Table 3:** Financing of gross asset formation

| | Gross Asset Formation | | | | Financing | | |
|---|---|---|---|---|---|---|---|
| | Invest-ment in Fixed Assets* | Stock Buil-ding** | Credits to Foreign Residents *** | Total | Depre-ciation | Domestic Savings Net | Foreign Aid |
| | in % GDP | | | | in % GDP | | |
| 1948 | 12.35 | 7.31 | 0.39 | 20.04 | 9.01 | 5.10 | 5.93 |
| 1949 | 14.77 | 9.68 | 0.11 | 24.57 | 9.50 | 7.80 | 7.26 |
| 1950 | 16.89 | 8.69 | 3.02 | 28.60 | 9.78 | 11.61 | 7.21 |
| 1951 | 18.79 | 9.76 | -0.19 | 28.37 | 9.31 | 12.76 | 6.29 |
| 1952 | 18.62 | 3.00 | 3.09 | 24.71 | 9.96 | 12.03 | 2.73 |

**Source**: National Income Statistics (VGR), WIFO 1963 and 1965.
* gross, ** including errors and omissions, *** net; the increases of 1950 and 1952 reflect mainly the accumulation of foreign exchange reserves and shifts in the terms of payment.

Without foreign aid Austria could not have invested so much. After the end of the Marshall Plan, it took until 1960 to re-establish the high rate of investment achieved in 1951. In the postwar years, it was difficult to generate domestic savings sufficient to finance the ambitious investment plans. Given the low real wages and the flat distribution of income, saving out of wages was negligible. Not much additional funds were to be expected if financial assets had offered high returns (which was not the case). Additionally, there was not much room to compress the share of wages in national income, thereby allowing firms to self-finance investments (business savings). Nor would it have been feasible to raise taxes sufficiently to generate a budget surplus[61] on current account (public savings). The proposal of J.R. Hicks (1947, p. 155) to use the wartime technique of "forced" savings to finance reconstruction was hardly applicable in Austria (mainly because economic policy could not efficiently control a "repressed inflation").[62] Therefore, one might conclude that even if the foreign exchange constraint was not binding (for example because Eastern European countries were able to provide Austria with food and coal), the Marshall Plan was important as a major source of financing a high rate of investment.

If net investment (NI) in fixed assets is regressed on foreign aid (FA), both variables expressed as percentage of GDP in the period 1948/55, one gets a "suitable" regression coefficient of approximately 1, if a linear time trend is added. The coefficient, however, is sensitive to changes in specification.

$$NI = -5{,}03 + 0{,}94\ FA + 2{,}02\ Trend$$
$$(-1{,}40) \quad (2{,}46) \quad (4{,}20)$$
$$R2 = 0{,}85 \quad DW = 2{,}08$$

Taking as a fact that Austria could not have invested so much without foreign aid raises the question: how important was it to achieve a high rate of investment? The answer is more complicated than it looks at the first sight. The conventional wisdom has it that a speedy reconstruction required high investments. In old movies investments were glorified. One could observe how a hard working labor force repaired the damages caused by the war and the dismantling of plants. New plants emerged from scratch and huge dams were built under extremely difficult conditions in order to gain electric current.

Yet the super-growth of the Austrian economy (and by the same token, the German economy) in the first postwar years cannot—or at most only partly be explained by high investments. That can be shown by simple calculation. In order to achieve a high rate of growth merely by using more capital, unrealistically high rates of investment would be necessary. Assume, for example, the national product grows at a rate of 15 percent per annum and the capital coefficient (the relation between the capital stock and output) is 4. Then the share of investment in national product (both magnitudes measured net, without depreciation) ought to reach 60 percent, if the capital stock has to grow at the same rate as production (in case of a declining capital productivity, more than the national income had to be invested). Very high rates of growth, therefore, almost invariably are accompanied by a declining capital coefficient. According to rough estimates[63] the capital coefficient of the Austrian economy fell from 4.6 at the beginning of 1948 to 3.74 at the beginning of 1952 and 3.27 at the end of the period investigated (beginning of 1956).

The extremely high rates of growth and the accompanying decline in the overall capital output ratio can be explained in the following way. The productive capital stock had suffered from war damages and dismantling less than was originally expected. Since investments in Austria had been high during the war, at the beginning of the reconstruction period, the capital stock was only marginally lower than in 1938. In industry as well as in agriculture, it was even higher. Yet this capital stock could not be used fully and efficiently. Raw material and energy were lacking, inadequate food rations impaired the productivity of workers, the infrastructure was partly destroyed, and there were gaps in the structure of the productive capital stock. Furthermore, the traditional ties with the economies of Eastern Europe, but also with the German economy, were interrupted. In the language of the institutionalists, information was scarce and transaction costs high. As a result of these and other factors, after the war production fell more than the capital stock. The (conventionally measured) capital coefficient was high.

To the extent that these and other bottlenecks were overcome, the existing capacities could be utilized and production picked up strongly. According to statistics of the Chamber of Commerce, capacity utilization in manufacturing increased steadily in the reconstruction period. At the end of 1947, 64.1 percent of all firms used less than 50 percent of their capacities. Until 1951 this percentage dropped to 28.2 percent. From this point of view, investments were just one element, although an indispensable one and hardly a separable element of the set of factors responsible for the boost of production in the postwar era.

Important supply constraints were gradually overcome during the first half of the Marshall Plan period. The food situation improved in the course of 1949. Fixed rations could be scheduled, and the rationing of bread was abolished at the end of the year. Many of the bureaucratic controls of non-farm business were relaxed. Most firms got the raw material and the energy they needed (only in winter did energy have to be rationed). The overall improvement of business conditions let the industrial production soar. From the beginning of 1947 until the end of 1949, it rose at the exceptional rate of 43 percent on an annual basis.

Similar interpretations of the postwar recovery are offered in the international literature. Both in Italy and in Western Germany,[64] the industrial capacity was found to be higher after the war than before. Eichengreen (1995) observed that between 1947 and 1952 those countries which had suffered most from the war experienced the largest increase in production. For the following "golden age" (1952-1970), this correlation vanished. In this period, the gap *vis-á-vis* the United States became an important source of economic growth. It is therefore appropriate to distinguish between "recovery" (from the damages caused by World War II) and "catch-up" (closing the gap vis-á-vis the United States). Wolf (1995, p. 325) in an analysis of the German economy coined the expressions "soft growth" and "hard growth."

At the beginning of the 1950s the capacity utilization effects were more or less exhausted. Economic growth depended largely on new investments that were started in the last years with the help of counterpart financing. Understandable, the rate of growth declined but nevertheless remained impressive. One possible explanation is that new investments were more productive than the neo-classical growth theory predicts (see Kohler, 1998, p. 5-6). But this is a debatable question, and more research is needed.

As far as the quality of investment is concerned, two conflicting tendencies could be observed. On the one hand, many investment projects were long-lived, and it took some years to finish them. In the short run they had a large income and a low capacity effect. Low interest rates furthered long-lived projects.[65] The ECA was only partly successful in urging the member countries to focus on investments that promised high short run returns.[66] On the other hand, vintage effects and both static and dynamic economies of scale enhanced the productivity of investments. The new machines incorporated a much more advanced technology than the old ones they had replaced. When after the end of the war the network of industrial input-output relations broke down, many Austrian firms tried to fill the gaps with a diversified production program at high costs. With market size increasing, large economies of scale could be exploited by concentrating on a few products and applying specialized equipment. Finally, in many branches learning processes played an important role. For example, it took a few years for the Austrian iron and steel industry to produce high quality steel for the automotive industry. Farmers had to learn to use tractors efficiently, and local mechanics had to learn to service the growing stock of agricultural machinery.

## Political aspects

> This expansion [the westward expansion of the Soviet Union] was not stopped at the gates of Austria by the force of arms ...It has been stopped by resistance from the Austrian themselves. But this resistance would never have been offered if there had not been a conviction, among the Austrians, that

we would not let them fall into a state of starvation and despair ...[67]

The Marshall Plan had an economic and a political component. The economic aim was to help the war-devastated European countries to rebuild their economy. The political aim was to contain Communist expansion. The economic and the political goals were not necessarily incompatible. Well-paid workers have more to "lose than their chains." In reality some conflicts were liable to arise. Historians complain that some aid was "wasted" for "populist" actions in order to keep week governments in office.[68] Moreover, military considerations influenced trade and investment policies.

*Austria: A Special Case*

The Austrian authorities repeatedly claimed that Austria was a "special case". Therefore, it deserved a relatively large allocation of Marshall Plan aid and could not adopt certain policy measures suggested by the ECA or the OEEC (for instance import liberalization). The "special case" argument had an economic (objective) and an political component.

The objective component resulted from the limited economic resources, the occupation by four powers, and the Cold War:

- Austria, as was discussed in detail, had to import food and coal. Both products were especially scarce in the postwar era and had to be paid for (at least partially) in dollars. The Cold War and the growing divergence in their respective economic systems restricted Austria's trade with its traditional trading partners in Eastern Europe. At least as important, although largely neglected by the relevant research, was the interruption of the inter-industrial network with German firms.
- Austria was the only country that participated in the Marshall Plan and at the same time was partly occupied by the Soviet Union. That created many administrative problems. Specific techniques of control had to be developed for the Marshall Plan goods distributed in the Russian zone. Austria had to postpone the OEEC-wide liberalization of goods on the list of the "battle bill" in order to prevent its export to Eastern Europe.[69] Economic policy was hampered by the fact that Austria could not fully control its resources and no clearly defined property rights existed. Measures

with short-term adverse effects had to be taken with care because they might increase the risk of Soviet interventions.

The political (anticommunist) aspects of the Marshall Plan has been given ample attention in the relevant literature. The quotation at the beginning of this article is contained in a little known source, a memorandum of the USFA (United States Forces Austria) titled "The Economic Rehabilitation of Austria" of 1947. The political aspects were mentioned in many official documents of the United States, for example, in the country chapter of the Marshall Plan bill at the end of 1947,[70] or in a document dealing with Austrian East-West-trade in 1952.[71] The good relations between the Austrian Socialist Party and the United States can be partly explained by the anticommunist attitude of the Austrian labor force.

The political argument could be put forward even when economic arguments failed to convince. During the stabilization process in 1952, one Austrian ambassador pleaded for a less restrictive macroeconomic policy stance by arguing that Austria from an economic point of view may be a burden for the West, but politically it is an asset.[72]

For quite some time, it was clearly beneficial to underline the Austrian position be referring to the special conditions prevailing in this country. Nevertheless, one gets the impression that the Austrians used the special case argument too often and for too long. Consequently, the argument lost credibility, especially when the Marshall Plan was phased out. The bureaucrats abused the argument as an excuse for doing nothing, and the politicians abused it to stall unpleasant adjustments. Economic problems were shifted from the technical to the diplomatic level before its implications were fully understood.

Some of the tensions between the ECA and the Austrian government derived from communication problems. The Austrian bureaucrats, badly paid and undernourished, did a remarkable job of preserving law and order under the most difficult conditions of the postwar era. However, only a few of them were qualified for handling the problems raised by foreign aid. To negotiate efficiently, one needed specific qualifications: a basic knowledge of economics, a good command of the English language, and some experience of horse trading in international forums. In addition managerial abilities were welcome in addition to legal competence.

These qualifications were not easily met. Already, Charles P. Kindleberger in his Vienna letters of August 1946 complained the lack of competence on behalf of the Austrian bureaucracy.[73] The author heard the same complaints some years later from ECA staff members in Vienna with whom he had fairly close contacts. As late as 1953, the Americans[74] criticized the Austrians for not having been able to collect economically relevant data for the USIA - complex (such as turnover, value added, or capital equipment at repurchase costs).

Economists are not experts capable resolving all socioeconomic problems all the time. But in order to communicate one has to speak a common language and share a common view of how the economy works.[75] That was especially important because, at that time, international economic policy was quick in introducing new analytical tools. The following example illustrates this point. In November 1948, Mr. Marjolin, the general secretary of the OEEC, requested the member countries to base their reports on national income statistics and analysis. The amount of aid would depend on a statistically and analytically adequate presentation of a countries needs and efforts.[76] At that time, an internationally comparable system of national accounts was just about to be developed. The first data that Austria presented in Paris were widely off the mark. (The author knows what he is talking about because he produced these deficient data.)

The discussions in the early phases of the ERP had one useful consequence: the reorganization of the Austrian ERP Bureau at the end of 1949. When the Marshall Plan started, the government set up the ERP bureau as part of the Ministry of Foreign Affairs with restricted responsibilities.[77] Other ministries did the relevant work, notably the Ministry of Planning and the Ministry of Finance, while interministerial committees performed coordinating functions. The bureau was designed to present the government's decisions with diplomatic skill to all foreign organizations dealing with the Marshall Plan. That did not work properly, because the experts of the Marshall Plan organizations wanted to talk to those who made the plans and not just to those who tried to sell them. The new ERP bureau took over part of the staff of the Ministry of Planning that was dissolved at the end of 1949. It was headed by Wilhelm Taucher, a former minister and university teacher with plenty of experience in negotiating with international bodies. The WIFO supported the bureau with technical expertise and drafts for economic reports.

*U.S. Interference in Austria's Economic Policy*

The U.S. authorities recommended, more or less forcefully, many policy measures. Mähr (1989, p. 201ff) and Bischof (1990, p. 469) dealt with these interventions under the heading "Dancing to a Foreign tune?". They concluded that the Austrians in many cases did not act as requested and developed special techniques to avoid or postpone unpleasant measures.

That is certainly true, but it is not the whole story. In order to obtain a balanced view, one has to consider certain realities. Donor countryies or institutions usually demand some sort of conditionality and surveillance if they grant foreign aid on highly concessional terms. The conditions for loans of the International Monetary Fund are well known and very often heavily criticized. Perhaps less well known are the harsh conditions of the international loans arranged by the League of Nations after World War I. Austria received such a loan in 1922 in order to stop hyperinflation. Although it paid almost 11 percent interest, it had to accept a foreign State Commission with far reaching power to control its economic policy. This Commission, by the way, ordered a reform of the Austrian railways, a measure that the Austrian government flatly refused to take when the ECA suggested it.

Generally speaking, the U.S. interventions in Europe were only partly successful as Milward (1984) and Esposito (1995) have shown in their detailed studies. The European countries followed their country-specific policy mix, notwithstanding attempts on behalf of the United States to "standardize" economic policy. Nevertheless, in important cases, the United States pushed successfully through their intentions. This is especially true as far as European economic integration is concerned. The EPU was established against objections of the British, and German rehabilitation was launched against objections of the French.

There are some signs that in the initial stages the Austrian government was not aware (or did not want to admit) that the Marshall Plan aid came with "strings attached." The decision to participate in the Marshall Plan and to sign the bilateral agreement between Austria and the United States were taken by the cabinet without formal consent of the parliament.[78] It therefore came as a surprise when in the first year of the Marshall Plan the chiefs of the ECA mission in Vienna became active in a businesslike matter. They proposed to the Austrian government a series of detailed policy measures. Since some of the suggestions or demands were presented in an undiplomatic way, the chancellor felt offended personally. The diplomats had to come to the rescue. (These episodes were described in detail by Mähr, 1989). Afterwards, the dialogue between the ECA and the Austrian authorities followed the usual diplomatic and bureaucratic rules and habits.

The relationship between the United States and Austria can best be described as a continuous dialogue on current economic issues. In the course of this permanent dialog the U.S. authorities raised many points and suggested policy measures of different kinds with different emphasis. In some cases, policy measures were presented for consideration. In others, such measures were strongly recommended with a tendency to compromise after lengthy negotiations. A typical example was the devaluation of the Austrian schilling in November 1949. The Americans suggested a premium rate for invisibles of 29 schillings per dollar, while the Austrians wanted a rate of 22.[79] As a compromise, the premium rate was set at 26 schillings per dollar.

In three important issues of economic policy, as was mentioned before, the ERP insisted on specific measures and took sanctions when the Austrian authorities hesitated to act accordingly. In all three cases of blocking counterpart funds, the U.S. interventions could be defended as measures to foster external and internal stability. A prudent minister of finance and a responsible manager in charge of industrial policy may have taken the same steps. However, counterpart releases were still used as a "negotiating device" even after the end of the Marshall Plan (Rathkolb, 1997).

An important topic in the relevant research of the scientific community has been how much the Marshall Plan contributed to the establishment of a market-orientated economic order. De Long and Eichengreen ( p. 218) argued that the Marshall Plan tipped the balance of the mixed economies of Europe towards a market economy. But one has to add that, by and large, the United States favored a gradual transition from the wartime controls towards free markets. The ECA regarded the Italian and German decisions to abolish controls and enforce macroeconomic stability by a restrictive monetary and fiscal policy as premature.

The Austrian experience confirms the "gradual" approach of U.S. policy. Especially in the immediate postwar years, efficient government controls of important markets were called for. The Congressional aid (P.L.84) in mid 1947 was provided under the provision that a ration and price control system should be maintained. All classes of the population, irrespective of purchasing power, should receive a fair share. The country chapter on Austria contained in the draft of the Marshall Plan criticized Austria for having no long-term economic plan and for not efficiently controlling the use of coal. The bilateral agreement of the Marshall Plan did not mention rationing and price control. The U.S. administration, however, hesitated to accept proposals to relax rationing of food. (Until October 1949, the Austrian government was obliged to make monthly plans for the supply and distribution of rationed food that had to be accepted by the Allied Council). The ECA did not take sides in the heated internal debate about abolishing price controls and rationing in the years 1948 to 1950.

Probably the most important deviation from the rules of a free market economy was the central planning of investments. The ECA asked Austria to design multi-year investment plans,[80] containing all investments and not just those financed out of counterpart funds. Accordingly, the Austrian Investment Plan 1950/52 states:

> The investment program is not limited to the allocation of public funds...in particular Counterpart funds, but is also an attempt at controlling and coordinating all public and private investment. (The Austrian Investment Program 1950/52).[81]

Considering that all projects financed with counterpart funds had to be accepted by the *Kreditlenkungskommission*, a coordinating body in which all important economic policy institutions were represented, it is a small wonder that a leading socialist economist (H. Kienzl) claimed that Austria had learned planning in the Marshall Plan period.

It was not before the middle of the Marshall Plan when market orientated policies were given more weight (although during the Korean War many controls were again introduced). The most important step came from trade policy. The liberalization of imports from the OEEC area and the multilateral payment system gradually increased competition, although with a considerably delay. The plea for an active competition policy was not successful (as in other countries such as Germany or Italy). In 1953, the United States suggested in vain the introduction of the U.S. banking system.[82] Mr. Johnstone (1951), a staff member of the Special Mission in Vienna, wrote a much debated report on the restraint of competition. The report recommended not only more competition, which is understandable given the many restrictions that existed in Austria at that time, it also suggested the abolition of institutions and organization upon which the Austrian system of social partnership was based.

The Austrian steeple-chase race towards a free market economy, as seen in the highly critical 160-page "Johnstone Report" of 1951, which suggested the nostrums for structural reform of the Austrian corporatist economy

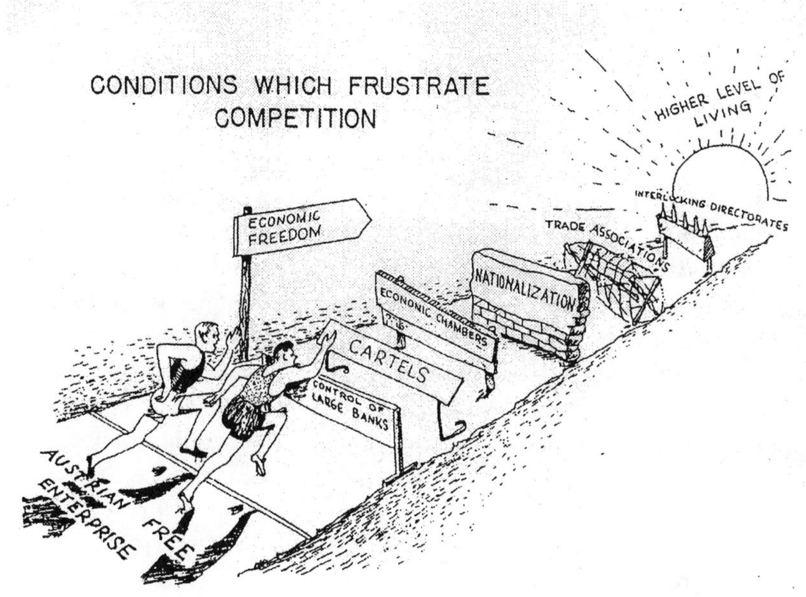


Source: The Johnstone Report, 1 Dec. 1951, in: 863.00/12-151, RG 59, NA

## Stabilization Policy and the End of the Marshall Plan

This section[83] deals with the end of the Marshall Plan and the Austrian stabilization policy from 1951 to 1953. This policy was both popularized and criticized under the label *Raab-Kamitz-Kurs*. With the information available, it is difficult to disentangle the interplay of foreign and domestic threads of that strategy. The following remarks focus on the role of the Marshall Plan organizations. From the files the author studied, one conclusion emerged clearly: The "classical" stabilization policy[84] could not have been carried out in Austria without the leadership of or at least strong support from the United States.

In the fiscal year 1951/52, the United States concentrated their foreign aid on military assistance. They reduced economic aid for Austria to $120 million, in real terms approximately one half of the aid received in 1950/51. Further cuts were announced for the following years. Therefore, in late 1951, the Marshall Plan organizations decided that Austria should take appropriate measures to live within its own means. Such measures seemed to be warranted since in this year, GDP surpassed the prewar level by almost 30 percent (industrial production by 60 percent), while exports were lagging. Obviously, domestic absorption was too high.

At a hearing[85] of the European Payment Union (EPU) in November 1951 the Managing Board criticized Austria for not doing enough to achieve internal and external financial stability. The Board concluded that both instabilities have a common root: the excessive domestic demand fueled by credit expansion and price-wage agreements. The Board furthermore noted that Austria should take corrective actions while there was still some foreign help available. Later on, higher adjustment costs would have to be expected.

The Austrian government reacted to the critique of the EPU by introducing a first anti-inflationary package in December 1951. The National Bank raised the bank rate from 3.5 percent to 5 percent, the credit control agreements were sharpened, and stronger controls of foreign exchange transactions and holdings were introduced. The Minister of Finance, when explaining these measures to the Ministerial Council, explicitly referred to the recommendations of the EPU.[86]

The Mutual Security Agency (MSA), the successor of the ECA, did not consider these measures as sufficient. On 7 January 1952, Mr. Meyer, Chief of the Special Mission in Vienna (MEC), after consultations with Washington, wrote a letter to the Austrian government asking, for among others, three additional stabilization measures:[87]

- the Federal budget should be balanced without releases from counterpart funds,
- the expansion of credits should be stopped,
- qualitative credit controls should ensure that speculators sell their inventories.

Since the Austrian government did not react immediately, the MSA stopped releases of counterpart funds and blocked $ 11 million of direct aid.

At end of May 1952, the Austrian government[88] answered the Meyer letter, describing what measures it has adopted in the meantime. It could emphasize that it did take painful steps in order to balance the budget. Subsequently, the MSA lifted the sanctions. However, it still held back öS 500 million counterparts, because it still feared inflationary tendencies. In order to comply with U.S. demands, in June 1952 the Austrians launched a second anti-inflationary package: the discount rate was raised to 6 percent and strict ceilings for commercial credits were introduced. The Socialists were strictly against raising the bank rate. According to the records, the *Generalrat* of the National Bank accepted this step only under the pressure of foreign demands.

The U.S. authorities did not change their position in the second half of 1952, although a formidable stabilization recession was unfolding. Of course, they did not openly admit that a strict antiinflationary policy would cause at least temporarily unemployment. No politician could be so outspoken. But in their letters[89] of 13 June they made clear that stabilization had priority. What they were looking at was the highest level of employment compatible with internal and external stability and not the other way round (the highest level of stability compatible with full employment). The U.S. position is described very clearly in a briefing prepared for a meeting of Mr. Kenney, the assistant director of the MSA, with Austrian top politicians on 9 August, 1952:

> Emphasize that we are anxious to have the necessary stabilization measures carried through as quickly as possible so that expansion of the economy can be resumed, on a healthy basis, as soon as possible.[90]

The meeting showed that the Austrians at that stage did not want to push the anti-inflationary pressure further. The minister of finance, Kamitz, who held the chair, pleaded for an additional release of öS 300 million counterparts for the federal budget and warned that selective credit controls should not be pushed too far in order to avoid unemployment. If "overshooting" occurred, it was not primarily the fault of the Austrian government.

The stabilization policy achieved internal and external financial stability. Prices that had risen during the year 1951 by 40 percent, fell somewhat in 1952 and 1953. The trade unions left out one wage round. Still more impressive, the balance of payments deficit disappeared. In 1953 and 1954, the current account showed a surplus of $71 and $69 million respectively. Since Austria still received some foreign aid (in 1953, $38 million) and large receipts poured in from unknown sources (mostly short-term capital), the monetary reserves of the National Bank ballooned.

The other side of stabilization policy was a deep stabilization recession with relatively high unemployment. Nevertheless, the stabilization was a success: the internal and external stability attained proved to be permanent, while the rise in unemployment was of a temporary nature. Austria, no more a special case, became a respected member of the group of industrialized countries even before the State Treaty.

## References

Werner Abelshauser, *Wirtschaft in Westdeutschland, Rekonstruktion und Wachstumsbedingungen in der amerikanischen und britischen Zone* (Stuttgart: Deutsche Verlagsanstalt, 1975).

Sydney S. Alexander, "Europe's need and prospects," in *Foreign Economic Policy for the United States,* ed. Seymour E. Harris (Cambridge, Mass.: Harvard University Press, 1948), 351-73.

Günter Bischof, *Austria in the First Cold War, 1945-55* (London: MacMillan, 1999).

"Between Responsibility and Rehabilitation: Austria in International Politics, 1940-1950," Ph.D. Diss., 2 vols, Harvard University 1989.

"Der Marshallplan und Österreich," *Zeitgeschichte 17* (August/September 1990): 463-73.

Oliver Blanchard, "Panel discussion," in *Postwar Economic Reconstruction and Lessons for the East Today*, ed. Rudiger Dornbusch, Wilhelm Nölling and Richard Layard (Cambridge, Mass.: MIT Press 1993), 231-34.

J. Bradford De Long and Barry Eichengreen, "The Marshall Plan: History's Most Successful Structural Adjustment Program," in *Postwar Economic Reconstruction,* ed., Dornbusch, 189-230.

Nicholas Crafts and Gianni Toniolo, eds., *Economic Growth in Europe Since 1945* (London: Center for Economic Policy Research, 1996).

Isabelle Cassiers, "From 'Belgian miracle' to Slow Growth: The Impact of Marshall Plan and the European Payments Union," in *Europe`s Post-war Recovery*, ed. Barry Eichengreen (Cambridge University Press, 1995): 271-91.

Marcello De Cecco, Francesco Giavazzi, "Inflation and Stabilization in Italy: 1946-1951", in *Postwar Economic Reconstruction,* ed., Dorn-busch, 57-81.

Rudiger Dornbusch, Wilhelm Nölling, Richard. Layard, eds., *Postwar Economic Reconstruction and Lessons for the East Today* (Cambridge Mass.: The MIT Press 1993).

Allen, W. Dulles, *The Marshall Plan*, ed. by Michael Wala (Oxford: Berg, 1993).

Barry Eichengreen, ed., *Europe`s Post-war Recovery* (London: Cambridge University Press, 1995).

Barry Eichengreen and Marc Uzan, "The Marshall Plan: Economic Effects and Implications for Eastern Europe and the Former USSR," *Economic Policy 14* (1992):13-75.

Arno Einwitschläger, *Amerikanische Wirtschaftspolitik in Österreich 1945-1949* (Vienna: Böhlau, 1986).

Chiarella Esposito, "Influencing aid receipients: Marshall Plan Lessons for Contempory Aid Donors," in *Europe's Post-war Recovery*, ed. Eichengreen, 68-90.

Gottfried Haberler, "Dollar Shortage?" in *Foreign Economic Policy*, ed. Harris, 426-45.

Gottfried Haberler. "Some Economic Problems of the European Recovery Program," *American Economic Review 38* (September 1948): 496-525.

Seymour E. Harris, ed., *Foreign Economic Policy for the United States* (Cambridge MA: Harvard University Press, 1948).

J.R. Hicks, "World Recovery after War – A Theoretical Analysis," *The Economic Journal* 57 (June 1947): 151-64.

Michael J. Hogan, *The Marshall Plan* (Cambridge Mass.: Cambridge University Press, 1987).

Calvin B.Hoover, "What Can Europe Do for Itself?" in *Foreign Economic Policy*, ed. Harris, 298-316.

Hans Igler, "50 Jahre Marshall-Plan in Österreich – eine Erfolgsstory," mimeographed, Vienna, 1997.

Charles P. Kindleberger, *The Marshall-Plan Days* (Boston: Allen & Unwin, 1987).

Charles P. Kindleberger, *The German Economy 1945-1947* (Westport, CN: Meckler, 1989).

Wilhelm Kohler, "El-Expansion into Eastern Europe: A New Marshall-Plan for the East? New Orleans Conference, 1998.

Wilfried Mähr, *Der Marshall-Plan in Österreich* (Graz: Styria, 1989).

C. S. Maier, Günter Bischof, eds., *Deutschland und der Marshall-Plan* (Baden-Baden: Nomos, 1992).

Alan S. Milward, *The Reconstruction of Western Europe 1945-51* (Berkeley-Los Angeles: Univ. of California Press, 1984).

Franz Nemschak, *Zehn Jahre österreichische Wirtschaft*, 1945-55 (WIFO: Vienna, 1955; OEEC, Annual Reports, Paris).

Oliver Rathkolb, ed., *Gesellschaft und Politik am Beginn der Zweiten Republik* (Vienna: Böhlau, 1985).

Oliver Rathkolb, *Washington ruft Wien* (Vienna: 1997).

Georg Rigele, *The Marshall-Plan and Austria's Hydroelectric Industry*; New Orleans Conference, 1998.

Hans Seidel, "Die österreichische Stabilisierungspolitik 1951/53," in: *Von der Theorie zur Wirtschaftspolitik - ein österreichischer Weg.* Festschrift zum 65. Geburtstag von Erich W. Streissler (Stuttgart, 1998).

Kurt Tweraser, *The Marshall-Plan and the Austrian Steel Industry*, New Orleans Conference 1998.

Holger Wolf, "Post-war Germany in the European context: domestic and external determinants of grwoth", in: Barry Eichengreen, ed., *Europe's Post-War Recovery* (Cambridge: Cambridge Univ. Press, 1995) 323-352.

*WIFO-Monatsberichte.*

WIFO, Österreichs Volkseinkommen 1950 bis 1960. Sonderheft Nr. 13, 1963.

WIFO: Österreichs Volkseinkommen 1913 bis 1963 (Kausel-Nemeth Seidel), Sonderheft Nr. 14, 1965.

## Notes

1. This paper draws heavily on documents from the *Archiv der Republik Österreich* (hereafter cited AR). In addition, G. Bischof and O. Rathkolb provided the author with some files from U.S. archives.

2. Kindleberger (1989, p. 78).

3. For example, Alexander (1948) and Hoover (1948). The support of the Marshall Plan was, however, far from unanimous at the initial stages. The critics at the political level called the Marshall Plan "operation rathole" The economist Hazlitt wrote an influencial booklet "Will Dollars Save the World ?" (Dulles, 1993).

4. See especially, Abelshauser (1975) and Milward (1984).

5. Most authors are in Dornbusch et al. (1993) and Eichengreen (1995).

6. Eichengreen and Uzan (1992), in an econometric analysis challenged the conventional wisdom that the Marshall Plan stimulated economic growth by financing the dollar gap (closing bottlenecks) and enhancing the rate of investment. More quantitative research on this crucial issue, however, would be welcome. Eichengreen in subsequent papers (1993,1995) weakens somewhat his econometric findings by emphasizing that the Marshall Plan made deflationary policies unnecessary and that part of the technical progress is embodied in physical assets.

7. Published by Wala (1993).

8. In Western Germany, for example, Marshall Plan aid gradually replaced the aid of the U.S. forces (GARIOA). In other countries, the Marshall Plan allowed governments to run a dollar deficit, after they had depleted their foreign exchange reserves and their credit facilities.

9. Eichengreen and Uzan (1992, p. 15) assumed that the additional supplies provided by the Marshall Plan led to lower prices and to stabilizing reactions of consumers and investors. The Austrian data do not confirm this assumption. The black market prices showed a declining trend over the whole postwar period until the end of rationing. The only shock discernible in the series was caused by the currency reform at the end of 1947.

10. Allied Council resolutions and memorandums from June until December 1946, 1706-U/46, 2628-U/46, 2262-U/46, Bundeskanzleramt, Archiv der Republik, Vienna (hereafter cited BKA, AR).

11. See among others Schärf (1955, pp. 127-130).

12. Dort-Plan (R-Plan), 15 February 1947, 515-U/47, BKA, AR.

13. Memorandum (Notprogramm), 2 October 1947, 1365_U/47.

14. Eleanor Dulles estimated the pre-ERP aid at $ 677 million (Bischof, 1989, p. 521).

15. This view was emphasized by Bischof (1989, p. 514).

16. Industrial production in West Germany recovered in 1947 at a comparable pace. That led Abelshauser (1975) to conclude that Germany did not need the Marshall Plan. The conclusion drawn here is much weaker. It simply states that the rate of foreign aid in 1947 was sufficient to support a strong recovery process. Whether the recovery was sustainable without foreign aid is another question.

17. The individualist attitude of the population was noticed by many observers. Kindleberger (1987, p. 17) complained that entrepreneurs and workers did not act in the interest of the community.

18. To illustrate this point: The author continued his university study in 1946, although he had some experience with farm work. (In this case, though, it might be questioned if the social returns calculated at a reasonable interest rate justified this decision.)

19. Alexander (1949, p. 354) noted with respect to Western Europe: "Foreign aid, principally American, was available to help keep people alive, and they themselves reorganized their shattered economics and raised their production well above the low levels to which it has been reduced by the war."

20. At the request of the Allied Council a Compulsory Labor Law was enacted in April 1946, but was only applied in a few cases. At the end of 1946, only 255 workers were forced to work in agriculture. At the same time, the Minister of Agriculture complained that agriculture was short 50,000 farm hands.

21. Capacity utilization was low because coal and raw materials were lacking. The distribution of insufficient quantities of coal among many firms mitigated energy efficiency (as was already noted in the Austrian chapter of the Marshall Plan bill).

22. Eichengreen and Uzan (1992, Appendix A) demonstrated in a formal model under what circumstances the foreign exchange constraint is binding rather than the savings constraint.

23. The Austrian Long Term Program, 15 October 1948, 5120-U/48, BKA, AR.

24. For example, Einwitschläger (1986, p. 117).

25. File from 30 December 1947, 163722-Wpol/47, Amt für Auswärtige Angelegenheiten, Archiv der Republik, Vienna (hereafter cited AfAA, AR).

26. Files of 16 Februrary 1948 (7363-15/48) and 12 May 1948 (35331-15/48), Bundesministerium für Finanzen, Archiv der Republik, Vienna (hereafter cited BMF, AR).

27. 7. Interministerielle Planungskommission, 6 July 1948, 48050-15/48, BMF, AR

28. Report Leopold and Igler on negotiations in Washington, April to June, 17 August 1948, 60020-15/48, BMF, AR.

29. Igler (1997, S. 5).

30. Memorandum Austria (48), 12 July 1948, 54070-15/48, BMF, AR.

31. File of 22 September 1950, 208426-Wpol/50, AfAA, AR.

32. U.S. Department of Commerce Study, 6 November 1953, 416846-Wpol/53, AfAA, AR.

33. At the end of 1951, the outstanding foreign debt of the Republic of Austria (including guarantees, but without prewar debt) was as low as $ 18,2 million. Ministerrat Figl 2 , No.279, 5 February 1952, AR.

34. Ministerrat Figl 2 , No. 290, 29 April 1952. AR.

35. At the end of 1951, the foreign exchange reserves (including gold) of the Austrian National Bank covered the imports of two months. The lack of adequate foreign exchange reserves let Austria hesitate to liberalize its imports according to the liberalization code of the OEEC until 1954.

36. For an early survey of the dollar problem, see Seidel (1951).

37. Revised program 1948/49, 9. Sitzung Interministerielle Planungskommission, 3 September 1948, 64369-15/48, BMF, AR.

38. A typical example was tobacco. The Austrian tobacco monopoly asked for dollar allocations mainly because tobacco was much cheaper in the United States than in the Near East.

39. Ministerrat Figl 1, No158, 17 May 1949, 126848-Wpol/49, AfAA, AR.

40. Different opinions about East-West trade are described in Bischof (1989, p. 486); also see the Komlosy essay in this volume.

41. In the second half of 1947, Ruhr coal was priced at $ 11t, Polish coal at $ 17/t (coal from the United States was much more expensive because of high transport costs). The price disparities shrank somewhat in the following years. However the "law of one price" was never established.

42. Report of the International Food Emergency Conference in July 1947, Ministerrat Figl 1 , No.76, 15 July 1947, AR.

43. Ministerrat Figl 1,.No. 117, 22 June 1948, AR.

44. Wirtschaftliches Ministerkomitee, 28 November 1950, 227701-Wpol/50, AfAA, AR.

45. National Security Council, NSC Determination No.2: Report on "Trade Between Austria and the Soviet Block...", 15 July 1951, 197578-Wpol/51. AfAA, AR.

46. One of the most intriguing features of the postwar area was the lack of conscious intertemporal decisions. Too many projects were started at the same time.

47. Ministerrat Figl 2 , No.218, 19 September 1950, AR.

48. Statement at the Cabinet Meeting. The minister said that he is not interested in the person "Porsche". His attempt to develop a "Volkswagen" has no chance to be realized. Ministerrat Figl 1, No.148, 8 March 1949, AR.

49. Establishment of UNRRA Fund, 14 May 1947, 2178-U/47, BKA, AR.

50. On the distribution of ERP counterpart funds, 6 January 1949, 26-15/49, BMF, AR.

51. The annual releases fell short of the receipts, except in 1951 when inflation reached a postwar peak.

52. Mähr (1989) and Einwitschläger (1986) discussed in detail the controversies between the chiefs of the ECA mission in Vienna and the Austrian government during the first Marshall Plan year, but did not mention the blockage of counterparts and the measures to contain the budget deficit in spring 1949.

53. Ministerrat Figl 2 , No.153, 12 April 1949, AR.

54. The ECA, in general, preferred a "gradual stabilization process" (Reichlin, 1995, p. 47).

55. The discussion about energy projects is described by Rigele's contribution to this volume; with regard to tourism, see the Bischof essay.

56. Letter from Meyer to Figl, 7 January 1952, 700435-ERP/3/52, BKA, AR.

57. See the Tweraser essay in this volume.

58. Einwitschläger (1986) described to what extent military considerations influenced investment decisions.

59. Reports of 15.April 50 (165564-Wpol/50) and 31 July 1950 (195125-Wpol/50), BKA, AR.

60. In West Germany foreign aid covered 31 percent of gross domestic asset formation in 1948. Until 1951 the share dropped to 7 percent (Reichlin, 1995, p. 44).

61. It should be noted, though, that some Scandinavian countries managed to obtain big a budget surplus on current account.

62. The Vienna Chamber of Labor suggested this method of financing in its yearbook for 1948. That indicates that some labor economists were familiar with the British literature.

63. Based on an extrapolation of the net capital stock calculated by WIFO.

64. In Italy, by 1947 industrial capacity was 37 percent higher than before the war. (De Cesso and Giavazzi, 1993, p. 61). In West Germany the capital stock exceeded the level of 1938 by 16 percent. (Wolf, 1995, p. 326).

65. According to the managers of electric power plants, building huge dams required low interest rates. If market rates were high, then subsidies were required.

66. See the discussion about Kaprun in Rigele's paper included in this volume.

67. USFA, The Economic Rehabilitation of Austria, 23 September 1947, 164289-Wpol/47, AfAA, AR.

68. According to Esposito (1995), this was especially the case in France and in Italy where the Communist party held a relative high share of votes.

69. File of 2 December 1953, 420316-Wpol/53, AfAA, AR.

70. Chapter Austria in the Marshall Plan bill (German translation), 16 February 1948, 7363-15/48, BMF, AR.

71. National Security Council, 14 July 1951, 195578-Wpol/51, AfAA, AR.

72. Department of State, Conversation with Löwenthal, 14 July 1952, NA, RG59 (copy from Bischof).

73. Kindleberger (1989), p. 78.

74. Vienna Embassy, Austria's Economic Position after the State Treaty, 29 September 1953, NA, RG59 (copy from Bischof).

75. Fortunately, at that time the tribe of economists differed less than usual on major issues. Some version of Keynesianism served as mainstream economics. According to Kindleberger (1987, p. 159) by 1948 most economists in the U.S. government were Keynesians.

76. Letter from Marjolin, 9 November 1948, 86312-15/48, BMF, AR.

77. Ministerrat Figl 1, No. 13, 25 May 1948,155670-Wpol.1948, AfAA, AR.

78. Ministerrat Figl 1, No. 118, 29 June 1948.

79. Ministerrat Figl 2, No. 181, 14 November 1949.

80. In the ERP period, two multi-year plans had to be developed: the Long-Term Program in fall 1948 and the Investment Program 1950/52 in spring 1950.

81. Wirtschaftliches Ministerkomitee, No.75, 31 May 1950, AR.

82. This had nothing to do with the so-called "dollar-diversion," the misuse of ERP dollars by an Austrian bank. A similar proposal was made in Germany and turned down by the Germans, see Oliver Rathkolb, "Der ERP-Fonds und Optionen zur Transformation der österreichischen Wirtschaft nach 1953," in *"80 Dollar"*, ed. Günter Bischof and Dieter Stiefel (Vienna: Ueberreuter, 1999), 103-110.

83. This is a summary of a larger, still unpublished study. A shorter version of this study was published in Seidel (1998).

84. The stabilization policy did not only rely on orthodox fiscal and monetary measures, but also applied "heterodox" measures of cost stabilization which, however, were not controversial.

85. EPU Hearing Austria, 5 November 1951, 234753-Wpol/51, AfAA, AR.

86. Ministerrat Figl 2 , No. 62, 4 December 1951, AR.

87. See footnote 68.

88. Reply of the Austrian government to the letter of Meyer from January 7, 29 May 1952, 711066-ERP/3/52, BKA, AR.

89. Letter from Meyer to Figl, 13 June 1952, 711668-ERP/3/52, letter from Kenney to Figl, 13 June 1952, 711882-ERP/3/52, BKA, AR.

90. Department of State, Record of Meeting, 9 August 1952, NA, RG59 (copy from Rathkolb).

# The Marshall Plan and the Reconstruction of the Austrian Steel Industry 1945-1953:

## The Bureaucratic Politics of Trusteeship, Nationalization, and Planning as Reflected in the Rise of the United Iron and Steel Works in Linz

*Kurt Tweraser*

### Introduction

After a promising start, the task of penetrating the complexity of the Marshall Plan in Austria and of analyzing the details of its implementation got stuck in its infancy.[1] On the basis of the scanty serious literature, the following generalizations seem warranted: Nobody has doubted that the Marshall Plan in Austria was essential in overcoming critical bottlenecks in investment and production in the years 1948 to 1953.[2] Without it, the industrial boom of the 1950s and 1960s could only have been achieved through a politically dangerous further lowering of an already low general standard of living. Yet, the initial emphasis of the Marshall Plan on investments in the capital goods industries at the expense of the finished products industries aroused the vigorous opposition of Austrian politicians and economists who apparently favored a return to pre-Anschluss conditions and practices. Undoubtedly, the Marshall Plan in Austria re-enforced the orientation towards a build-up of the capital goods industries and the trend towards larger enterprises already initiated during the National Socialist (NS) regime. Thereby the weight of the Western Austrian provinces, especially Upper Austria, increased to the detriment of the Viennese and Lower Austrian but also Styrian interests.[3]

For a deeper understanding of the Marshall Plan it is not enough to analyze its effects at a high national level. Generally speaking, while great efforts have gone into researching the origins of the Plan and its diplomacy, little is known of its effective application country-by-country. One must examine sectors of the economy, if not single enterprises to determine this. The United Iron and Steel Works in Linz excellently lend themselves to a microanalysis of the Marshall Plan. After all, the enterprise was one of the largest single recipients of Marshall Plan aid; as so-called "German Property" it became an essential part of the complex of nationalized industries and was a bone of contention for Austrian as well as U.S. interests. The basic question for the enterprise, reconstruction and conversion to an integrated steel complex or razing it to the ground, engaged the passions of Austrian national and regional elites and workers as well as those of the Marshall Plan administrators and the representatives of other U.S. Departments in Vienna, Paris and Washington.[4] Rather than analyze the Marshall Plan as an instrument of a rational actor on the international stage (rational actor model), U.S. as well as Austrian decision-making will be explained as the result of often contrary, but also frequent, parallel institutional interest (bureaucratic politics model). Decision makers follow scripts largely written by the organizations whom they speak in order to preserve their agency's influence against domestic rivals. Policy recommendations are thus tailored to prevail in that continuing struggle.[5] This article emphasizes the interactions of donors and recipients, open or hidden cooperation, the resigned acceptance of constraints and the gradual regaining of a scope for action. To characterize the bargaining process between donors and recipients as tutelage or economic coaching or a dance to a foreign tune does not quite capture the reality of interactions.[6]

The officials of the Marshall Plan organization, whether in Vienna, Paris, or Washington, could not realize their conceptions of what Europeans should do to become more like Americans. There is bound to exist a considerable gap between what planners and managers of modernization hope to achieve in the way of cultural, social, political, and economic changes in a country they are occupying for a brief spell, historically speaking, and what actually transpires in the course of the occupation. The image of an all-powerful occupation compelling a subject people to change their errant ways and institutions is rarely helpful in explaining outcomes which are much more the result of decisive intervening processes growing out of the deeply ingrained historical past of the occupied country. Whatever illusions the Marshall planners and managers might have had, after two years of actually administering the aid, disillusionment, but also realism, triumphed. The disillusionment expressed itself in a lamentation over an Austrian political culture which stood in the way of a free market economy which was based on the U.S. model:

> As in most European countries, elements of socialization are omnipresent stretching from huge nationalized enterprises to government-provided housing, fixed prices, and governmental funeral services. Meanwhile, elements of corporatism are prevalent, with industrial, agricultural, labor and trade groups accorded formal representation in many of the processes of government. The vigorous champions of "private enterprise", none too numerous, must provide support and comfort to the bigger partner in the coalition to provide strength against the homogeneous Socialist Party which carries the vote of organized industrial labor. Again, as in most European countries, it is to be noted that free enterprise to its Austrian champions is a far different concept than the American version lauded by its Austrian supporters . . .
>
> The huge bureaucracy inherited from the Hapsburg empire adds little to efficiency and contributes greatly toward socialism. In general, it is the case that private initiative is seriously hampered by the effects of socialism, "corporativism," and statism.[7]

Quite clearly, the U.S. administrators found obstacles to competition wherever they looked, especially in the strong tendency towards a "chamber state," in the obligatory membership in the various chambers, in the quasi-cartels of the nationalized industries and banks, in the numerous cartel agreements which turned Austria into a veritable paradise for cartels, and in the hidebound traditionalism of small and backward businessmen. Above all, they were disappointed in the all-pervasive politicization of the economy in Austria against which they set the supposedly "apolitical" aim of enhancing productive efficiency through scientific management, business planning, and industrial cooperation. Yet, "Europe was not a blank slate, and the economic policies that the United States tried to thrust upon it, could not avoid partisan implications even when they were deemed apolitical."[8] No matter what U.S. cultural-economic ideals were, the

U.S. practice in Austria had to adjust to an admittedly unpleasant reality. The fight against economic misery and political extremism forced the acknowledgment, even the sanctioning, of political and economic institutions and practices which were considered unthinkable for the United States. At any rate, the establishment of a free market economy in the U.S. image was no condition for U.S. aid. The overriding goal was the achievement of political and economic stability for which the cooperation of conservative and socialdemocratic indigenous forces was essential, but which limited the achievement of U.S. political-economic desiderata. The fallback to realism was already apparent in the U.S. acquiescence to nationalization in Austria.

### The Nationalization of German External Assets

According to the Potsdam Agreement, the German properties in Austria would go to the occupation powers on a zonal basis.[9] Whereas the Western Allies construed the Potsdam Agreement narrowly, the Soviet authorities stuck to a broad interpretation, which meant that a sizable part of Austrian industrial production would permanently remain under Soviet control. In order to escape these politically and economically unacceptable terms, the Austrian government decided to secure its legal claims to these properties through nationalization.[10] Some seventy industrial corporations and financial institutions were covered by the 1. Nationalization Law, unanimously passed by the Austrian Parliament on 26 July 1946.[11] Among them were the two largest iron and steel producers in Upper Austria and Styria. With the support of the Western Allies, Austrian authorities were able to implement the provisions of the Nationalization Law in the western-occupied zones. Indeed, already on 16 July 1946, ten days before the Austrian Nationalization Law, the U.S. High Commissioner, Gen. Mark Clark, designated the Austrian Government to become custodian of German assets in the U.S. zone. In contrast, Soviet opposition to the Austrian definition of "German Property" led to the creation of a Soviet administration for the industrial and trading companies formerly under German ownership, a situation that lasted until 1955. Among the nationalized enterprises were the Iron and Steel Works at Linz, a product of the reorganization and expansion of the Ostmark's iron and steel industry after the Anschluss. After the German defeat, the Linz steel mill was registered as *Vereinigte österreichische Eisen- und Stahlwerke A.G.* (VÖEST). There was no doubt that the works were a

German External Asset and as such subject to Allied reparations claims according to the Potsdam Agreement.[12] At the same time, the State Department espoused the principle that German property in Austria should primarily remain there as part of the Austrian economy. Transfers should only take place if they did not prejudice the economic growth of an independent Austria.

Prior to the transfer of German assets to the trusteeship of the Austrian Government, a struggle had taken place between the State Department and the U.S. occupation authorities in Austria. Thus, not only were there differences among the Austrian elites, the U.S. authorities, too, were divided on the question of nationalization. The U.S. military in Austria were principally hostile to it and expended considerable efforts to find solutions for the German External Assets that would result in privatization rather than nationalization. The *Steyr-Daimler-Puch A.G.*, a huge industrial property under the control of the U.S. military government, but not nationalized, was chosen for the development of a basic plan of reorganization which could be applied to other assets such as the VÖEST. The principal purpose was to assure that Austrian enterprises should be operated to the greatest extent by Austrian private ownership. The urgency of continuing the operation of industries in the U.S. zone which were deemed essential for the reconstruction of the Austrian economy, but which might be subject to reparations claims, induced the High Commissioner Mark Clark to suggest a privatization plan to his superiors in Washington. It consisted of the following major parts: he would ask the Austrian government to maintain the Steyr plants in operation, giving U.S. assurances that those parts of the Steyr factories in the U.S. zone deemed essential to the Austrian economy will not be removed as reparations. He also might secretly assure the Austrian government that the U.S. intended to waive its claims to German External Assets and to use its good offices to induce the other Western powers to do likewise. However, since it was clear that a very large segment of industry would revert to the Austrian state if reparations claims were waived and would in effect bring pressure on Austria to nationalize former German assets, Clark's plan also included some provisions for the investment of the Austrian people in company stock to provide working capital, satisfy simultaneously reparations claimants through the issuance of preferred stock and maintain complete control of the corporation through a Board of Directors on which American representatives would call the shots.[13] Given the lack of a capital market in Austria, the Clark plan quite unrealistically maintained that the necessary capital stock in the corporation should be underwritten by a syndicate of banks and then offered to the public under an agreement prohibiting the retention of any substantial amount in the bank syndicate's hands.[14]

In contrast to West Germany where the U.S. Army proved more skilled in the bureaucratic fighting over nationalization, in Austria it was the State Department that triumphed.[15] The State Department considered the final disposition of German assets, as suggested by Clark, premature, since it still hoped for an overall settlement of the German assets question on a quadripartite basis. As to the question of nationalization, the State Department forcefully reminded Clark that it was U.S. policy to leave the question for local determination on a democratic basis, as long as proper compensation for private owners was provided.[16] As for the presence of U.S. citizens on a supervisory board, the State Department reminded Clark that the operation of the Potsdam Reparations Agreement with respect to German assets in Austria should not be such as to substitute Allied for German penetration. As a solution, Washington ordered the designatation of the Austrian government as the trustee of German assets in the U.S. zone, with the power to appoint and dismiss directors and managers, operate the companies, arrange for the financing, and render accounting to U.S. authorities only at quarterly intervals, though the Austrian government was not permitted to dispose of company assets that were subject to restitution.[17] In execution of State Department policy General Clark informed the Austrian government on 10 July 1946 that the U.S. would hand over all German assets in the U.S. zone with the Austrians acting as trustees. In a solemn public ceremony the former "Hermann Göring" works in Linz were turned over to the Austrians. The High Commissioner assured the Austrians that the German assets may immediately be used for purposes of reconstruction without fear of removal of the plants and equipment.[18]

The policy decision of the U.S. State Department could not hide the fact that the U.S. military occupation bureaucracy only grudgingly gave up its obsession with the lurking dangers presented by socialistic tendencies, an obsession that was widespread in the military, in the business world, and in the U.S. Congress. Even John Erhardt, Clark's usually sober and reasonable foreign policy adviser, was carried away by the privatization fantasies. In the end, pragmatism triumphed over ideological preferences. After all, private capital necessary for starting the key industries was simply not available outside the government; on the other hand, nationalization held out the hope—in vain, as it turned out—to counter Soviet claims and privatization at some future date. The business wing of the Austrian People's Party (ÖVP) acquiesced to nationalization for similar reasons. Furthermore, nationalization was not just an Austrian affair, but part of an overall European tendency.[19] It appeared to be the better part of political wisdom to acquiesce in it as long as nationalization was executed by national governments who were based on free elections and proper compensation for expropriation was provided.[20] Once more, the decisive importance of the Austrian election of November 1945 and of a functioning national government was demonstrated. Lastly, there was the expectation that nationalization was only a transitory emergency solution to be rectified in the future through some form of "people's capitalism." Although the priority of the U.S. military was to administer their zone in such a way as to avoid Congressional and public criticism for the "pro-socialistic" solution, in the end, they could not deny the Austrians the right to reach a decision reflecting the existing internal political balance of forces. Obviously, trusteeship was not transfer of property. By insisting on preserving Allied rights according to Potsdam, the United States secured important possibilities for intervention. It was now the task of the Austrians to create political and economic realities which could not be repealed by the U.S. "proprietors" without creating a most undesirable political crisis in Austria. In moments of great frustration with what they considered Austrian mismanagement of the nationalized industry, some of the U.S. authorities were sorely tempted to reinstate direct control until cooler heads reminded them of the adverse political consequences of such action.[21] Nothing came of such implausible schemes.

## The VÖEST in Linz; the Problem Child of the Americans

During the National Socialist regime, the Iron and Steel Works at Linz were, together with the Alpine Montan Company in Styria, part of the *Reichswerke A.G. Alpine Montan Betriebe* "Hermann Göring." With the German defeat in 1945, the Reichswerke were dissolved, and the Linz works made into an independent enterprise. At the end of the war, the Linz complex possessed a huge pig iron capacity and large coking facilities, but only a small steel mill and inadequate rolling facilities.[22] In May 1945, U.S. troops occupied Linz, and they established property control over the Linz plants of the *Reichswerke.* The plants had been hit by over 6000 bombs and presented themselves to the superficial viewer as a miserable "industrial cemetery," although more sober assessments came to the conclusion that only about 8.5 percent of capital assets had been destroyed.[23]

During the period from 1945 to 1950, within the fate of the VÖEST gave rise to vigorous, even acrimonious, discussions and between Allied authorities as well as between various regional and national Austrian agencies and experts. In these debates the U.S. and Austrian advocates of reconstruction and of making the Linz complex part of a reorganized iron and steel sector triumphed, but there was plenty of opposition. Highly qualified economists in the Austrian Institute for Economic Research in Vienna voiced great skepticism about developing the Linz complex from the very beginning:

> The integration of overdimensioned plants created during the National Socialist Regime will pose extraordinary difficulties. The danger exists that huge investment funds will be required to keep them operating whereas at some future date it will be realized that the plants cannot be maintained at all or only under the greatest of sacrifices. These plants are out of proportion for small Austria and made sense only in a Grossraumwirtschaft.[24]

The salient question was whether the steel market could bear the addition of another iron and steel center besides the old established Styrian complex, a question whose answer invariably aroused regional animosities and bureaucratic politics. The tradition-rich Styrian iron and steel industry, concentrated in Donawitz, viewed the VÖEST as a competitor which ought to be dismantled. However, important Upper Austrian politicians such as the conservative Provincial Governor Heinrich Gleissner and the Socialist mayor of Linz, Ernst Koref, regarded the continued existence of the iron and steel complex in Linz a matter of highest priority and seized the initiative by lobbying the regional U.S. authorities and the Renner Government in Vienna.[25] Competent expertise was provided by Hans Malzacher, a brilliant iron and steel man, whose National Socialist past was conveniently discounted by the politicians.[26] Support was also furnished by the U.S. regional industry officer Lt. Col. Engeseth whose identification with "his" iron and steel works was astonishing.[27] From the very beginning of the occupation, finding top managers for the Linz complex who were both competent and had a clean political past proved to be an almost impossible task for the U.S. and the Austrian authorities.[28]

As for the ultimate future of the VÖEST, the U.S. authorities in Linz and Vienna left the door open. In the meantime, whether for purposes of reparations or reconstruction, the economic assets represented by the plants required immediate attention in order to avoid their dissipation or waste. A skeleton crew was, therefore, kept at the works; they started almost immediately on a program of repairing the plants, but also became active in repairing rolling stock, locomotives, bridges, and agricultural machinery. Obviously, the issue could not be decided by the regional military government; it seemed reasonably clear that any solution for Linz had to fit into the wider framework of the Austrian iron and steel sector.[29] In overcoming Styrian and Viennese resistance to the VÖEST, the Upper Austrian politicians faced a difficult task. When the Western Allies recognized the Renner Goverment in October 1945, Provincial Governor Heinrich Gleissner saw a chance to plead the VÖEST case. He argued that because of its modern equipment and the relatively small damages suffered in the war, the VÖEST constituted an important sector for the reconstruction of the Austrian economy. He further suggested the formation of a Commission, composed of representatives from the national government, the provincial governments of Upper Austria and Styria, and recognized iron and steel experts.[30] It took, however, several strong interventions by Gleissner and by the national government before the discussions with the Styrian interests could begin in earnest in April 1946.

It seems that the Styrian delaying tactics found the approval of the British occupation power. In the fall of 1945, the British had come to the conclusion that the Linz complex was a "white elephant" which in its present form was not economically viable since it lacked adequate steelworks and rolling mills. The acquisition and installation of the missing elements would cost huge sums and take several years to complete. Since Linz was remote from both iron ore and coal, it would probably continue to be unproductive even if the steel works and rolling mills were be built. Thus, in the eyes of the British and their Styrian clients, the problem of the VÖEST resolved itself by making use of Linz's existing equipment in Donawitz and dismantling the rest.[31]

The opinion that Linz was unnecessary and could not be fitted into the framework of Austria's future economy because it would be too costly to complete, extremely costly to operate, and unlikely to find markets, initially was shared by some of the U.S. authorities in Vienna. Thus, the Chief of the Industry Branch of the Economics Division, U.S. Allied Commission, Austria, recommended in March 1946 to keep only three of eight cokery batteries at Linz to produce coking gas for the operation of the nearby nitrogen works; the remaining five batteries should be relocated, sold, bartered, dismantled, or destroyed.[32] Additionally, USACA recommended that four of the six modern blast furnaces in Linz should be disposed of; one should be used to supply spare parts for an incomplete furnace at Donawitz; one should be used for the operation of the nitrogen fertilizer plant. A Siemens-Martin furnace at Linz should be eliminated from Austria's steel production. What installations remained in Linz should be placed under the management of the Alpine Montan in Styria.[33] At the quadripartite level, no agreement could be reached in the Industrial Functional Committee of the Allied Control Council in determining the position of the Linz works in the Austrian iron and steel industry. In the Soviet view, the plants in Linz were designed for purely military purposes and were entirely unnecessary for the Austrian economy. Only one or two batteries of coke ovens should be operated, retaining the chemical fertilizer plant. Of the four occupying powers, the United States was the most sympathetic towards Upper Austrian interests and supported the maintenance of one blast furnace; whereas the other three powers saw the principal use of the Linz installations solely as a support for the nitrogen plant.[34]

Meanwhile the Austrian Ministry of Property Control and Economic Planning (the Krauland Ministry) had been engaged for several months in a tough bargaining process to hammer out an understanding between the regional interests of Upper Austria and Styria.[35] Under U.S. prodding, a small planning unit in the Krauland Ministry developed a concept for the production of steel which included thoughts about a possible role for the Linz complex. The planning unit arrived at the following conclusions: the main problem in Linz was the enormous disparity between the blast furnace capacity and the steel making and rolling capacity; the proper remedy would be the sale of three of the six blast furnaces, the acquisition of a hot strip mill, and the introduction of a new steel Metallurgy process. The plan submitted by the Krauland Ministry corresponded measurably to the ideas advanced by U.S. authorities who felt responsible for the reconstruction of the Austrian economy rather than the safeguarding of reparations assets.[36] The Ministry also emphasized that the modern plant in Linz was of the utmost importance for Austrian economic survival, because the coke and coke gas needed for industry and the production of nitrogen for agriculture could only be accomplished with a blast furnace plant. The Ministry felt that one blast furnace should be kept operating, and two others kept in reserve for future expansion. Furthermore, the ore dressing plant, the slag plant, the heavy plate mill, the finishing plants (foundry, forge, engineering works and steel construction), and the caloric power plant should be kept in operation. Obviously, something more than the mere production of fertilizer was intended.[37]

The U.S. occupation bureaucracy saw the solution of the Linz problems primarily in terms of their respective bureaucratic missions. Thus, a committee charged with looking into the fiscal affairs of the Linz plants considered it a fallacy to regard this large installation as a going concern or business enterprise. Before loans could be extended, the VÖEST must have been assured a place in a properly worked out industry plan. As a business institution, the report concluded, VÖEST was in a very unsound condition under its present management and should be closed down and liquidated or reorganized, unless its continued operation could be justified on the grounds of military necessity or short term economic necessity.[38] The matter was dropped into the lap of the Economic Division of USACA to work out a definite commitment as to the place the VÖEST was to occupy in the industry plan for Austria. The German External Assets (GEA) Branch, a subunit of the Property Control Division, was primarily focused on the preservation of the company assets for satisfying reparations claims. Furious about the constant crises of management which threatened the mission of the GEA Branch, it advocated as late as the summer of 1948 to fire the "local opportunists" administering the plant in Linz and to hand over control of management to the Alpine Montan, which alone had the necessary expertise and integrity.[39] The Economics Division saw as its mission, however, the promotion of the longterm reconstruction of the Austrian economy and had increasingly become convinced that the VÖEST was destined to play a large role in it. Thus, according to this division, far from treating the VÖEST as merely an object of reparations claims or of dismantling the Linz complex as a "monstrous war baby," it would be the better part of political and economic wisdom to bring about a balance between the overdimensioned blast furnace capacity and the underdimensioned steel producing and rolling capacity.[40]

When by mid 1946 it was obvious that no agreement about German assets at a quadripartite level could be achieved, the U.S. authorities indicated their readiness to act unilaterally in their zone. The "friends" of the VÖEST in the Economics Division gained ascendancy over the "enemies" of the VÖEST in the internal bureaucratic wrangling. While close working relations developed between U.S. and Austrian officials, differences remained. In both U.S. and Austrian offices, bureaucratic politics thrived. A telling example of the continued difficulties with the VÖEST is the politics surrounding the sale of the three surplus blast furnaces. They were considered much in excess of domestic requirements and of the potential export markets. Originally, the VÖEST management hoped to deliver three of the six furnaces to Czechoslovakia in exchange for urgently needed coal. The negotiations began in September 1946 and stretched into February 1948.[41] In the meantime, one of the furnaces was actually sold to Sweden for $ 1.27 million. Since the blast furnace was a company asset, U.S. agreement for the use of the sales proceeds was required according to the Trusteeship Agreement. Indeed, the dollars were used as partial payment for a hot strip mill of U.S. origin. The sale of the two remaining blast furnaces ran into one delay after another, partly because of U.S. objections, partly because of parallel objections voiced by Austrian steel experts in the Krauland Ministry.[42] The Communist take-over in Prague in February 1948 put an end to the negotiations with the Czechs. The two blast furnaces became an integral part of the VÖEST expansion of its pig iron production. Of greater importance than the Czech sale for the fate of the VÖEST was the so called *"Schwedengeschäft"*, a triangular transaction. Sweden paid dollars to Poland for the delivery of coal to the VÖEST; the Linz enterprise, in turn, would deliver pig iron and rolled products to Sweden. The delivery of the coal enabled the VÖEST to blow on the first blast furnace on 14 June 1947.[43]

The following summary of the three postwar years of the Austrian iron and steel industry seems warranted. After the cessation of hostilities, the industry was nationalized. It had been re-equipped by the Germans, bombed by the Americans and dismantled by the Soviets. The period was used by the plant management to repair the bomb damages, to make small improvements in the operation of the works, and to install machinery that had been previously discarded and left on the scrap heap. The industry was able to operate in a somewhat makeshift manner, largely on the strength of a huge unfilled consumer demand at home and abroad.

## The Iron and Steel Plan: To Be Ready Means Everything

From 1946 on, the task for the Austrian authorities was to plan for production capacities which, on the one hand, would be acceptable to the Western Allies, who insisted on a capacity of not more than one million tons crude steel, but, on the other hand, would allow for production increases should circumstances change. Intense planning sessions stretched over one and one-half years and involved tough bargaining between the relevant iron and steel interests. A small planning unit in the Krauland Ministry under the leadership of Margarete Ottillinger succeeded in finishing an Iron and Steel Plan just at the time when the Austrian government was expected to submit planning and program figures for its participation in the Marshall Plan. The Iron and Steel Plan had three main goals: 1. the maximum utilization of existing plant capacities; 2. the widening of production through the provision of new capital; and 3. the coordination of production programs among the steel producing companies.[44] The members of the planning unit were a productive mixture of experienced iron and steel experts, including Franz Leitner, former technical director-general at Böhler, and young, eager management types not yet affected by bureaucratic circumspection, such as Hans Igler and Hans Blumauer-Montenave. Igler's motto seems to have been "Let us plan as if we had the money."[45] In retrospect, one can only marvel at the coolheadedness, some would say vision, others chutzpah, with which the Austrian planners formulated the future of the iron and steel industry. The basic message with respect to Linz was that the value of the works, despite the bomb damages they suffered, was far higher than the investments necessary to round out the capacities to achieve economic production results.[46] Therefore, it would be foolish to forego the utilization of the Linz works. This, then, was the situation at the beginning of the Marshall Plan: Austrian planners, confronted with the alternatives of either investing in the steel industry or facing eventual reduction of operations and a possible shutdown of a considerable portion of its plant, opted for major investments. Had they followed a course of reduction, it would have meant a possible annual expenditure of $30 million for importing iron and steel products of commercial quality for Austrian secondary industries. Since it was doubtful that any investment made in the finished goods industries would have balanced such a drain on the national economy, it was decided to follow the expansion course and keep the steel industry alive.

New Morgan steel-rolling equipment installed with the help of ERP funds in at the Alpine-Montan Company in Leoben, Styria, in 1950

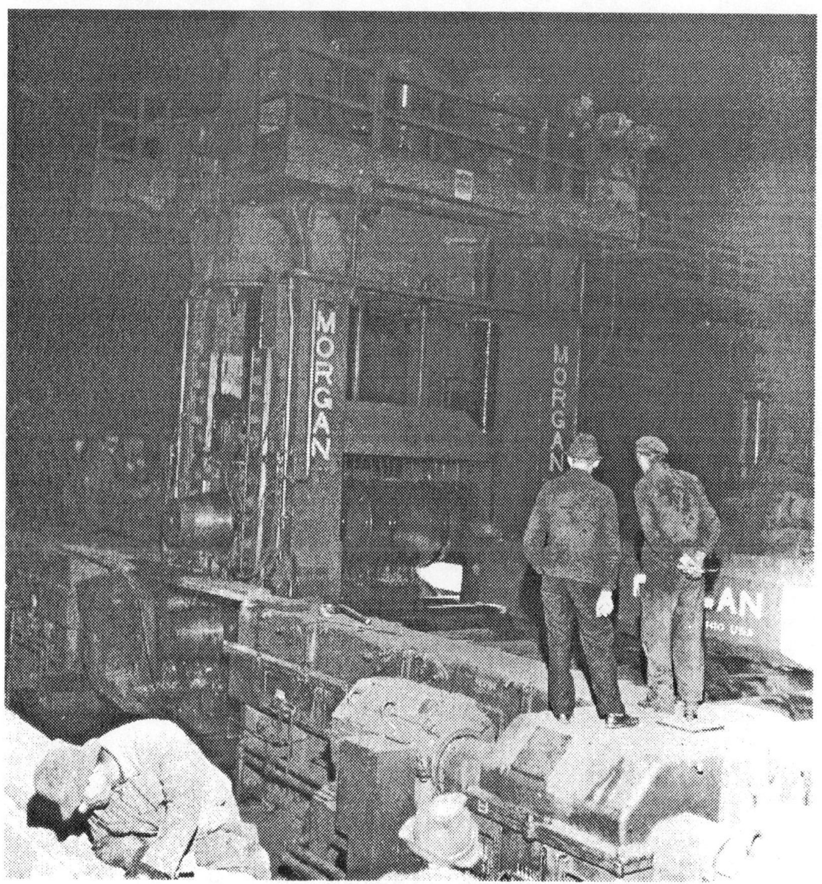


Source: National Library, Vienna, # US 21162

New Morgan steel-rolling equipment installed with the help of ERP funds in at the Alpine-Montan Company in Leoben, Styria, in 1950

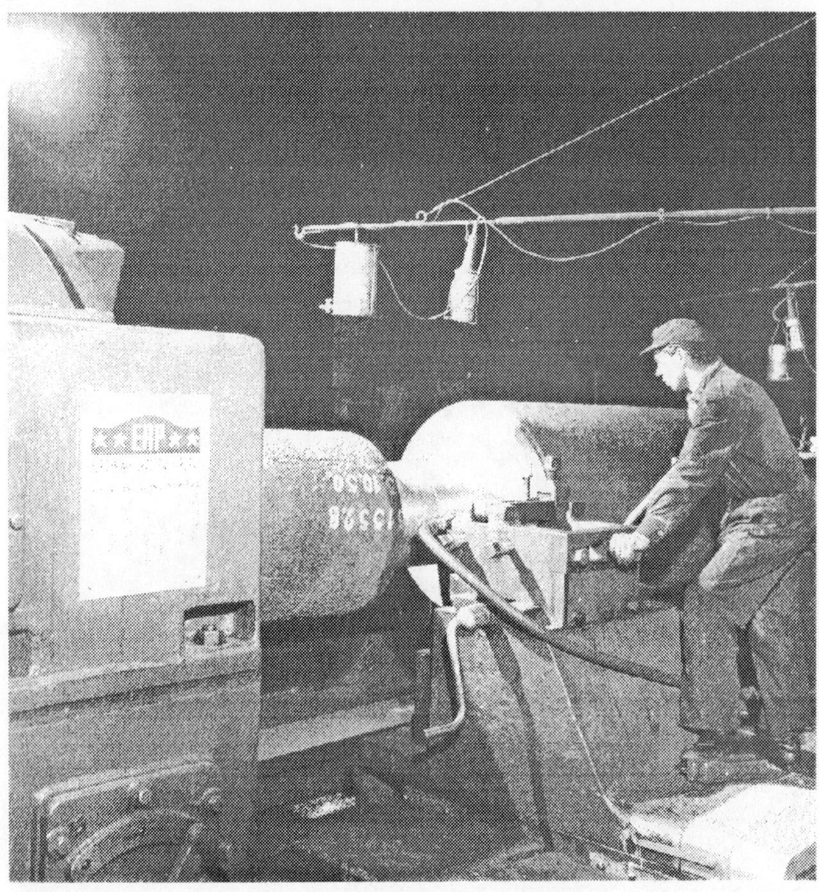


Source: National Library, Vienna, # US 21165

The Iron and Steel Plan provided for a far-reaching reallocation of production programs. Mass production steel manufacturing was to be distributed between Linz and Donawitz. Whereas in Donawitz production would concentrate on profiles, Linz would become the sheet capital of the iron and steel industry. The following projects, almost equally benefiting Alpine Montan and VÖEST, were contemplated, amounting to about $30 million ($13 million for Alpine, $17 million for VÖEST). Projects for Alpine Montan included:

rehabilitation of the iron ore mine at Erzberg, so that the blast furnaces could be provided with a greater portion of domestic ore ($1.9 million); import of a new blooming mill to replace the one in operation since 1897 ($3.9 million); of a billet mill ($3.1 million); and a structural mill to replace older equipment ($4.1 million). Projects for VÖEST included: import of a slabbing mill ($ 3.9 million); import of a hot strip mill, which would permit the plant to produce plate and sheet at competitive costs for Austria and for export ($8 million); and in order to complete the rolling installations, the purchase of a cold strip mill ($4.5 million) was also planned.[47]

The Iron and Steel Plan also contemplated further improvement in metallurgical practice in order to decrease scrap and solid fuel retirements, anticipating, one must say rather optimistically, the novel LD process, that was to revolutionize the production of steel all over the world. The plans for the re-equipment and re-organization of the steel industry demanded the importation of expensive capital goods, which could only come from the United States. The aim was to provide the steel industry with the most basic modern equipment for producing commercial grades of steel at competitive costs and in quantities that were adequate to meet anticipated Austrian demand at home, while also providing a surplus for export. In Linz, the chief goal was to secure the maximum advantage for Austria from the basic plant left at the end of German rule.

In the summer of 1948, Marshall Plan deliveries began. They consisted mainly of foodstuffs and ran counter to the intentions of the Marshall planners who wanted to get away from relief measures and concentrate on rehabilitation. Tough negotiations between Marshall Plan officials and their Austrian counterparts about the relative extent of foodstuff deliveries versus investment goods were their constant companions during the first two years of Marshall aid. As for investments in industry, the Economic Cooperation Administration (ECA) Mission was guided by the principle of enabling recipient countries to economically develop indigenous basic resources in order to provide the finished goods industries with cheap raw material and half-finished goods. This meant that the basic industries would initially get preferential treatment in the allocation of Marshall funds. Under these guidelines, it was obvious that the iron and steel industry would become one of the main beneficiaries of U.S. largesse.

The Iron and Steel Plan was officially adopted in July 1948 by the Federal government. It served as a major basis for the industrial aspects of the Austrian Long-Term Program 1948/49 - 1951/52 (also called Four Year Plan) submitted to the ECA authorities. The first version of the Austrian Long-Term Program, submitted in the latter part of 1948, was rejected by the United States since "it appeared to be hastily prepared, inadequately coordinated and largely incomplete." Only a few portions of the Program were found promising, among them the steel industry "where scheduled investments . . . are believed to be closer to reality than the original Austrian Steel Plan which was over-ambitious."[48] The Industry Branch of the ECA Mission in Vienna, in close cooperation with representatives of the Krauland Ministry, worked out a second Long Tem Program which was submitted to the Chief of the ECA Mission on 15 January 1949. It was considered to provide a sound working basis for all future industrial planning.[49] Or so it seemed.

After the first Austrian Long-Term Program had become public knowledge, it received severe criticism not only from ECA authorities, but also from an Austrian coalition of interests which voiced vigorous objections to what it called imbalances in the Austrian plan. The loose coalition consisted of top representatives of the Chamber of Commerce (Julius Raab and Reinhard Kamitz), the Chamber of Labor (Stefan Wirlandner) and academia (Wilhelm Taucher and Franz Nemschak).[50] Spokesman for the strange coalition was Franz Nemschak, the Director of the Institute for Economic Research in Vienna. In a private talk with a member of the ECA Mission, he denounced the Four Year Program as "so much incompetent nonsense cooked up by an amateurish Krauland staff, having a strong iron and steel bias." Among the architects of the Long-Tem Program, he singled out those who were young, inexperienced or biased: Peter Feldl, age twenty-five, an ex-journalist; Hans Igler, age twenty-eight, from the iron and steel industry, with ambitions to return; and Margarete Ottillinger, age thirty, previously with the iron and steel industry.[51] The criticism of the mostly conservative politicians and economists was also directed against Minister Krauland, ironically one of their own (ÖVP).

Nemschak was not satisfied with a verbal denunciation. He produced a forty-seven page paper in which he expanded upon the question of the optimal constitution of the Austrian economy, the financing of investments, the organization of foreign trade and, more specifically, on the plans for individual economic sectors.[52] Nemschak's list of grievances were the following:

1. The Long-Term Program was based on the autarchic tendencies characteristic of a technocratic mentality. The authors of the Long-Term Program were inspired by the idea of a self-balanced economy within a large territory (*Grossraumwirtschaft*) and tried to adapt the concept of an extensive self-contained economic macrocosm to the microcosm of the Austrian national economy.
2. In the era of a highly developed international division of labor and specialization, the Austrian economy could not achieve its optimum level through an equalized development of all stages of production, but fundamentally only through development of those production sectors in which Austria had favorable competitive costs, and met relatively advantageous conditions. For good reasons, such as lack of capital, slow capital formation, a relative scarcity of raw material resources, small internal markets, large reserves of overly qualified people and relatively low wage standards, Austria did not appear to be a suitable capitalistic producer of raw materials and semi-finished goods. Rather, it was a country of quality production requiring a great amount of skilled labor.
3. The Long-Term Program called for a forced stepping-up of basic production (iron, steel, metal, and coal), which, from a standpoint of production costs, was less profitable in Austria than in other countries. At the same time, the finished goods industries which were closely geared to export, were neglected. The result of both policies would be an inability to export.
4. Iron and steel planning was erroneously calculated with over-estimated future requirements rather than actual demand. The planning was unrealistic, since it was based upon the unreal demand of technical dream projects. The basic flaw was the relegation of price and production costs to a secondary place, subordinating them to technical considerations linked with the desire to reach the greatest possible independence from foreign countries. Economically irresponsible projections of industry requirements would not only waste portions of valuable ERP aid, but would also considerably encumber the federal budget and taxpayer and endanger currency stability.
5. Economic planning must not be left to the exclusive judgment of technocrats. On the contrary, it was economic planning which must initially prescribe the financial limits to be observed. Economic planning should also closely concur with representatives

> of business and labor. Economic planning should be undertaken by a relatively small staff of capable persons in a non-bureaucratic manner and must not be shackled by a cumbersome bureaucratic machine.[53]

Basically, then, Nemschak argued that the first version of the Long-Term Program, which projected an extensive expansion and modernization of Austria's iron, steel, coal, and power industries, was an entirely fallacious and unnatural approach to the nation's economic development. Austria, he maintained, was a high cost, low quality producer in these areas and could never compete with these commodities in the world market. On the other hand, the nation's traditional export articles, finished high quality goods, were completely neglected in the Long-Term Program. Nemschak concluded that the government plan's emphasis on heavy industry at the expense of quality goods production would most certainly, in the long term, precipitate serious economic dislocation and reduce the nation's living standards. In short, Nemschak believed that, if based on the Long-Term Program, the Economic Recovery Program (ERP) in Austria would fall far short of intended objectives.

The ECA mission had already invested considerable effort and prestige in the Long-Term Program and since the publicity surrounding the Nemschak paper was a threat to the execution of the ECA program. After all, critics in Paris (Organization for European Economic Cooperation—OEEC, Office of the Special Representative—OSR) and Washington would not miss such an opportunity to challenge the Austrian Government and ECA Vienna. Therefore, the Industry Branch of the Mission prepared a detailed analysis, and rebuttal where appropriate, of the industrial aspects of Nemschak's comments.[54] The most important finding of the Mission was that the Nemschak paper was based on the first version of the Long-Term program which, for the same reasons as advanced by Nemschak, had been rejected by the Mission. The Mission agreed with Nemschak's critique of the unbalanced nature of the planning projects in the basic materials producing and finished goods industries. In fact, the Mission had insisted on an increase of the planning figures for the finishing industries. In the first version of the Long-Term Program, $55 million or 56.4 percent out of a total of $97.5 million were earmarked for the basic industries; the second version scheduled only $48.85 million or 38.5 percent for the basic industries out of a total of $126.7 million, while the remainder of $77.856 million was earmarked for the finishing industries.[55] However, instead of shifting the planning figures from the heavy goods industries to the finished good industries, the Mission preferred to increase the total industrial investments at the expense of non-industrial items.

The Mission tried to induce the Austrian planners to increase the figures for the finishing industries even further and to make the necessary additional funds available from other sectors of the Austrian economy, particularly the food sector, to no avail. The Austrian negotiators successfully insisted that larger amounts for industrial goods imports could not be scheduled during the first two years of ERP because of Austria's dire food situation. On the planned investments for the iron and steel industry the Mission did not budge. The reduction from $45 million to $44.75 million was minimal. The Mission drew attention to the fact that Nemschak's idea of drastically reducing the role of the iron and steel industry in the planning scheme was an unpalatable alternative, the consequences of which he neither faced or discussed. It would mean at least a partial suspension of operations and throw a considerable portion of the 44,000 highly skilled workers employed in the steel industry out of work. It would also mean at least a partial loss of equipment which could not be dismantled and sold. Obviously, realizing Nemschak's ideas, however sound they may have been from the point of view of an economic theorist, would have required political measures whose grave economic and social consequences neither the Austrian government nor the ECA Mission were prepared to underwrite. The Nemschak paper supplied welcome ammunition for those forces in Paris and Washington who were worried about the general expansion of the European iron and steel sector and were advocating a cutback so as to avoid overproduction. Thus, the OEEC Executive Committee tried to cut $10.6 million earmarked for steel projects from the Austrian program, which, if successful, would have resulted in the suspension of orders already placed for steel mill equipment and would have been tantamount to the abolishment of ECA aid for the re-equipment of the Austrian steel industry. Taking the cue from OEEC, the Chief of the Austrian desk at OSR in Paris also began to harbor grave doubts about the Austrian steel program.[56]

The Austrian government immediately issued instructions to its representatives in Paris and Washington to dispel any doubts the Nemschak paper might have created at OEEC, OSR, and ECA Washington.

The démarche was based on arguments supplied by an experienced official in the U.S. legation in Vienna.[57] In order to strengthen the Austrian position the ECA mission and the High Commissioner Gen. Geoffrey Keyes in June 1949 engaged William E. Brewster, a recognized iron and steel industry expert, to undertake a thorough examination of the Austrian iron and steel sector with special emphasis on the appropriateness of the VÖEST projects. After almost five months of research, Brewster delivered a positive judgment. He was particularly impressed with the modern production capacity and the physical outlay conducive to conducting steel operations efficiently. He approved the expansion in plate and sheet production which would remove the bottleneck in steel flow and output. He also observed good teamwork and cooperation between employers and workers and testified to the thorough competence on the part of the entire management personnel. In Richter-Brohm, the Director-General, a German, Brewster found an energetic and ambitious executive, thoroughly imbued with the restoration of private enterprise, but still afflicted with many of the prejudices carried over from his National Socialist past.[58]

Even the pugnacious Nemschak appeared to retreat considerably from his original stand which had received so much publicity in Paris and Washington, especially after a project of the Alpine Montan encountered trouble. In an apologetic letter to the Mission, Nemschak stressed that his criticism of Austrian planning for heavy industry did not, of course, refer to the projected structural mill for Donawitz.[59] His skeptical attitude about the VÖEST projects did not change. He still viewed the Iron and Steel Plan as "colossal stupidity" and pleaded for a stop to the importation of heavy machinery for the VÖEST. The risk of losing the already undertaken investments must be accepted.[60] Nemschak was supported in his intransigence by the *Vereinigung Österreichischer Industrieller*, whose main spokesman demanded that a still larger part of Marshall investments should go into the finished goods industries.[61] Within the iron and steel sector, the differences between VÖEST and Alpine continued to smoulder. Oberegger, the Director-General of the Alpine Montan, made it known that he could never agree to a policy which apportioned such a large slice of the ECA cake to Linz.[62]

The ECA Mission could not ignore the more or less public exchanges which had reached the ministerial level. After all, queries about the squabbles in the Austrian steel industry would inevitably be forthcoming from Paris and Washington.[63] In the opinion of the

Mission, it was, much too late for a drastic revision of the iron and steel program. The Mission found it useful, however, to discuss the Austrian industrial modernization program with the opposition. These endeavors did not mean that the Mission was prepared to drastically change its attitude towards the iron and steel program. The whole situation was helped when in December 1949, under U.S. prodding, the Austrian ERP Administration was reorganized. A new ERP Central Office, located directly in the Chancellor's Office and headed by the highly respected Wilhelm Taucher, took over the ERP business. The new institution undertook a renewed examination of the iron and steel program, but Taucher, loyal to the Americans, thwarted all of Nemschak's attempts to bring about substantial changes, although Taucher himself was skeptical about the program.[64] A new opportunity for an attack by Nemschak arose January 1950 when the hot strip mill earmarked for Linz became the focus of a great debate. The proponents of the strip mill in the ERP Central Office, in which Hans Igler played an ever-increasing role, had the better arguments.[65]

In the meantime, a change had taken place in the estimates about the future sheet metal demands in the European market. In June 1949, the ECA Administrator Paul Hoffman had made dire predictions about steel overproduction, reflecting the pessimistic forecasts in the United Nations, OEEC, and ECA. In October 1949, a much more optimistic estimate of future demand in the European sheet metal market allayed the fears of overproduction.[66] The renewed optimism gave momentum to finalizing the VÖEST orders for a slabbing mill and the hot strip mill in November 1949. But new dangers arose to the VÖEST projects in the early months of 1950. A fundamental attack on the thrust of the ECA's steel investment policy was carried out, in front of the U.S. Senate, by a Staff Report of the Joint Committee on Foreign Economic Cooperation. The report criticized the piecemeal approach which had led the ECA to approve most of the plans presented by individual countries, without any prior attempt to establish selective criteria for the whole of Western Europe. Because of the need for economies of scale, especially for the strip mills, it would have been more appropriate to locate the plants only in the areas with the best productivity record. Moreover, it seemed inappropriate to help rebuild steel industries, such as the Italian and Austrian ones, whose costs were thought to be high and whose origins were regarded as being of a "political" nature. In fact, according to this body of congressional opinion, what the ERP should have been doing was aiding those countries in eliminating their steelmaking facilities.[67]

While the Congressional "Nemschakian" attack had no serious repercussion on the VÖEST and it appeared that all hurdles in the way of modernizing the VÖEST had been cleared, bureaucratic politics within the United States caused a significant delay in the delivery of the heavy machinery ordered from U.S. firms. While the delivery of the slabbing mill for the VÖEST was on time, difficulties arose with respect to the delivery of the hot strip mill.[68] Although the OEEC, ECA in Vienna, Paris, and Washington, and even the Vienna Screening Committee for Strategic Goods had approved the delivery and there was a valid contract between the VÖEST and the Mesta Machine Company in Pittsburg, Pennsylvania, the Defense Department refused to issue an export license. Even the presidential go-ahead with the delivery in August 1950 did not change the attitude of the Defense Department. The military stubbornly argued that the equipment to be delivered had a potential capacity considerably greater than the utilization planned in the ECA project. The military further argued that this potential capacity would tend to increase the export of militarily important steel products to the Soviet bloc, since the controls of Austrian exports of strategic items to the East were ineffective under quadripartite occupation. Furthermore, since the plant was located across the river from the Soviet zone, the installations would, in all probability fall to the Soviets in case of war.[69]

ECA Washington and the State Department tried to calm the strategic worries of the military with political arguments. Denial now, they argued, when the equipment is ready for shipment and after top level approval for ECA financing, would be a damaging blow to Austrian morale. Moreover, denial would be followed by a Soviet propaganda campaign to the effect that the Western countries were ready to abandon Austria. The political effects would be interpreted in Europe as a sign of U.S. retreat. However, it was only in January 1952, when the State Department decided to again call the Linz project to the attention of the presidential level, thereby threatening to reveal the non-execution of a presidential order by the Defense Department, that the military gave up their resistance without changing their strategic concerns. As a high Defense Department official put it: I do not want to stand any longer in the way of what appears to be the consensus of judgment on the part of other agencies. I do not agree with that judgment, but under the circumstances I do not propose to press further the Defense Department's appeal to the National Security Council.[70]

No further delays for the delivery of the equipment arose. Both the hot strip mill and the cold strip mill began functioning in 1953. Investments in plate and sheet metal production demanded the rapid modernization of crude steel production, a feat that was achieved with a breakthrough in metallurgy, the LD process. At the end of 1953, the first stage of the VÖEST modernization towards an integrated steel complex was achieved. Roughly half of it was financed through ECA. The delay in the delivery of the heavy machinery for the VÖEST, caused by the Cold War hysteria of the U.S. military, should not obscure the fact that already during the spring of 1950 the bargaining about the final shape of the Austrian investment program resulted in compromises which satisfied both the Austrian government and the ECA Administration. The program, negotiated by Taucher and his staff with the ECA in Vienna and Washington, approved by the Austrian government on 31 May 1950 and by ECA Washington in June 1950,[71] raised the expectations that Austria, too, would participate in the grand Marshall design: to bring down the cost of production, thereby working towards the elimination of protective barriers and State subsidies; to expand industrial capacity, thereby contributing to the balance of payments and narrowing the dollar gap; and to make the Austrian steel industry competitive with the other European steel producers.

That Austria could live up to those great ECA expectations was in no small measure due to the introduction of a new steel producing method, the LD oxygenblast method. The decisive breakthrough occurred in the summer of 1949 in Linz.[72] The method reduced furnace time from ten to twelve hours in a 200 to 250 ton Siemens-Martin furnace to approximately thirty-five minutes in the LD furnace. The LD method, named for Linz and Donawitz, gave Austria a technological lead that assured it sizable advantages in steel production. Capital costs in the construction of new facilities were about 25 to 30 percent below those of older technologies. The adoption of the new technology greatly reduced production costs for Austrian steel producers during the 1950s.[73] Unfortunately, the mishandling of licensing agreements and patent rights by the management of the VÖEST and the Alpine led to the adoption of the revolutionary technology by numerous foreign competitors, among them the Japanese. The technological lead of the Austrian steel industry had disappeared by the end of the 1950s.[74] Besides making it competitive in the international markets, the steel industry's cost effectiveness also allowed low domestic steel prices that strengthened Austria's manufacturing industries internationally. As an OECD study concluded: "By charging low domestic prices for these raw materials and semi-finished goods, in accordance with the government's price policy, these industries made an important contribution to the stabilization of the general economic situation and to the favorable development of the, mostly privately owned, finished goods industries."[75]

## Conclusion

The investments in the heavy industry sectors, partially financed by the ECA, created a strong nationalized part of the Austrian economy which strengthened the power of the organizations of labor (Socialist Party, Österreichischer Gewerkschaftsbund, Chamber of Labor) for decades to come. The U.S. decision to transfer German external assets as trusts to the Austrian government and then to equip these nationalized enterprises with state-of-the-art machinery aimed, of course, at the containment of Soviet expansionism and not at the promotion of socialism. The results, namely the adoption of planning and programming concepts and the modernization of the capital goods industries, were also based on sympathetic personnel in the ECA Mission, the Krauland Ministry, and the ERP Central Office. More specifically, the Marshall Plan made a significant contribution to finish in Linz what the Germans had begun. It allowed the VÖEST to become the leading Austrian firm in the market for thin flat products.

While the positive short and middle term consequences of the emphasis on the capital goods industries can be demonstrated, such as dynamic growth and real subsidies for the secondary economic sectors through low steel prices, it is difficult to reach final conclusions with respect to negative long-term consequences such as latent structural problems and the fitting of huge enterprises into an economic structure dominated by small and medium sized firms. A judgment could, perhaps, be reached with the help of counterfactual history: what would have happened, had the Marshall Plan in Austria put the initial emphasis on investments in the finished goods industries?[76] Yet, judgments based on a history that has not taken place are neither verifiable nor falsifiable. All one can maintain with some degree of certainty is that the long-term structural thinking, "Austria, the classic land of labor-intensive production of quality finished goods," could not overcome the lures of heavy demand for iron and steel creating a seller's market.[77] The motto "Go Heavy Metal, Austria" had a convincing ring during the first two decades after World War II.[78] It was also in tune with what appears, in retrospect, to have been one of the basic premises implicit in the Marshall Plan, namely the idea that big was beautiful. As Charles Maier put it: "Mass production and integrated markets promised prosperity. The economic enterprise that most typified the postwar reconstruction schemes was the integrated steel mill . . . The Marshall Plan in effect diffused a particular stage of industrial technology. It built naturally on a vision of production that dominated from the 1930s to the 1960s and then began to fade."[79]

## Notes

1. Wilfried Mähr, *Der Marshallplan in Österreich* (Graz: Styria, 1989); Günter Bischof, "Der Marshallplan und Österreich," *Zeitgeschichte* 17 (1990): 463 - 474; and "Der Marshallplan in Europa 1947 - 1952," *Aus Politik und Zeitgeschichte* B 22-23/79): 3 - 16.

2. Even the skeptics who deny the essentiality of the Marshall Plan for the reconstruction of Western Europe usually exempt Austria from their doubts. Alan S. Milward, *The Reconstruction of Western Europe 1945 - 51* (Berkeley: University of California Press, 1984), 90 - 125.

3. Stefan Koren, "Die Industrialisierung Österreichs - vom Protektionismus zur Integration," in *Österreichs Wirtschaftsstruktur gestern - heute - morgen*, ed. Wilhelm Weber (Berlin: Duncker and Humblot, 1961), 322-334;Felix Butschek, *Die österreichische Wirtschaft im 20. Jahrhundert* (Stuttgart: Fischer, 1985), 65-78; and *Die österreichische Wirtschaft 1938 bis 1945* (Stuttgart: Fischer, 1978), 100-114; Herman Freudenberger and Radomir Luza, "National Socialist Germany and the Austrian Industry, 1938 - 1945" in *Austria Since 1945*, ed. William E. Wright (Minneapolis: Center for Austrian Studies, University of Minnesota, 1982), 74-100; Fritz Weber, "Wirtschaft und Wirtschaftspolitik in der Ersten und Zweiten Republik," in *Österreichs Erste und Zweite Republik: Kontinuität und Wandel ihrer Strukturen und Probleme*, ed. Erich Zöllner (Vienna: Österreichischer Bundesverlag, 1985), 129-133; and "Die wirtschaftliche Entwicklung," in *Handbuch des politischen Systems Österreichs*, ed. Herbert Dachs et al. (Vienna: Manz'sche Verlags- und Universitätsbuchhandlung, 1992), 30-31; and "Spuren der NS-Zeit in der österreichischen Wirtschaftsentwicklung," *Österreichische Zeitschrift für Geschichtswissenschaften* 2 (1992): 135 - 165; Dieter Stiefel, "Fünf Thesen zu den sozialökonomischen Folgen der Ostmark," in *Politik in Österreich*, ed. Wolfgang Mantl (Vienna: Böhlau, 1992), 49-61.

4. This article is part of a comprehensive research project about the U.S. economic influence in Upper Austria from 1945 to 1955. It is based on material in the National Archives II, College Park, Md., especially Record Group 260 United States Forces Austria (USFA), U.S. Allied Commission, Austria (USACA)

including the German External Assets Branch, the Property Control Division and the Economic Division, and Record Group 469, Records of U.S. Foreign Assistance Agencies 1948 - 61, including the Industry Division, the Productivity and Technical Assistance Division, and the Office of the Labor Adviser. In addition, documents from the *Archiv der Republik*, Vienna, the Upper Austrian Provincial Archives, the City Archives and the VÖEST Archives in Linz were consulted.

5. The fact that the Economic Cooperation Administration (ECA) was established as an agency independent from the State Department, but with a mandate to disband after four years, points to bureaucratic politics which also included an assertive role of the legislature in the foreign aid policy regime. The ECA Missions in participating countries administered the business of the ECA; they were the local arm of the ECA bureaucracy, reporting to the Special Representative of the ECA in Europe (OSR), headquartered in Paris, who in turn reported to the head of the ECA in Washington. A separate agency, other than the State Department, was thus put in place in order to deal with what remained basically a foreign policy matter, reflecting the congressional distrust of State Department's proverbial "softness" on Communism. For an application of the bureaucratic politics model, see Irwin M. Wall, "The American Marshall Plan Mission in France," in *Le Plan Marshall et le relèvement économique de l'Europe*, ed. Comité pour l'histoire économique et financière, Ministère des Finances (Paris: 1993), 133 - 143. See also Günter Bischof, "Between Responsibility and Rehabilitation: Austria in International Politics, 1940 - 1950," Ph. D. diss., Harvard University, 1989.

6. Wilfried Mähr, "Der Marshallplan in Österreich: Tanz nach einer ausländischen Pfeife?" in *Die bevormundete Nation: Österreich und die Alliierten 1945-1949*, ed. Günter Bischof and Josef Leidenfrost (Innsbruck: Haymon, 1988), 245-272; Kurt Tweraser, "The Politics of Productivity and Corporatism: The Late Marshall Plan in Austria, 1950 - 54" in *Austria in the Nineteen Fifties*, Vol. 3, *Contemporary Austrian Studies*, ed. Günter Bischof, Anton Pelinka, and Rolf Steininger (New Brunswick, NY: Transaction Publishers, 1995), 91 - 118.

7. Mission Analysis and Recommendations on the Austrian Government's Proposed 1951 Counterpart Program, 20 July, 1951, Box 8, Productivity and Technical Division, Record Group (RG) 469, National Archives II, College Park, Md. (NA II)

8. Charles S. Maier, "The Politics of Productivity: Foundations of American International Economic Policy after World War II," in *The Cold War in Europe: Era of a Divided Continent*, ed. Charles S. Maier (New York: Markus Wiener Publishing, 1991), 169 - 201, here 181.

9. William B. Bader, *Austria Between East and West 1945-1955* (Stanford: Stanford University Press, 1966), 26 - 40; Reinhard Bollmus, "Ein kalkuliertes Risiko? Grossbritannien, die USA und das "Deutsche Eigentum" auf der Konferenz von Potsdam," in Bischof and Leidenfrost, eds., *Bevormundete Nation*, 107 - 126.

10. Renate Deutsch, "Chronologie eines Kampfes. Geschichte der Verstaatlichung in Österreich," in *In Sachen* 4 (1978), 23-25.

11. Edmond Langer, *Die Verstaatlichungen in Österreich* (Vienna: Verlag der Wiener Volksbuchhandlung, 1966),34-62: Rupert Zimmermann, *Verstaatlichung in Österreich* (Vienna: Verlag der Wiener Volksbuchhandlung, 1964), 37 - 51;

Wilhelm Weber, ed., *Die Verstaatlichung in Österreich* (Berlin: Duncker and Humblot, 1964); Eduard März and Fritz Weber, "Verstaatlichung und Sozialisierung nach dem Ersten und Zweiten Weltkrieg - eine vergleichende Studie," *Wirtschaft und Gesellschaft* 4 (1978): 115 - 141; Franz Mathis, "Zwischen Lenkung und freiem Markt: Die verstaatlichte Industrie," in *Österreich in den Fünfzigern*, ed. Thomas Albrich, et al. (Innsbruck: Studienverlag, 1995), 169 -180; Erich Andrlik, "The Organized Society: A Study of 'Neo-Corporatist' Relations in Austria's Steel and Metal Processing Industry," Ph.D. diss., Massachusetts Institute of Technology, 1983.

12. Secretary of State to Ambassador in the United Kingdom (Winant), 29 November 1945, *Foreign Relations of the United States*, Vol. III, 1945: *European Advisory Commission: Austria, Germany* (Washington: Government Printing Office, 1968), 668-673.

13. Cable, Clark to JCS Pass to Secretary of State, 6 May 1946, Box 174, German External Assets Branch (GEA), RG 260, NA II.

14. Grove to MacIntosh, Proposed Method of Future Operation for the Steyr Daimler-Puch AG, 3/18/46, Box 174, GEA, RG 260, NA II.

15. Werner Link, "Der Marshall-Plan und Deutschland," in *Marshallplan und Westdeutscher Wiederaufstieg: Positionen - Kontroversen*, ed. Hans-Jürgen Schröder (Stuttgart: Steiner, 1990), 87 - 90; Dörte Winkler, "Die amerikanische Sozialisierungspolitik in Deutschland 1945 - 1948," in *Politische Weichenstellungen im Nachkriegsdeutschland, 1945 - 1953*, ed. Heinrich August Winkler (Göttingen: Vandenhoeck and Ruprecht, 1979), 88 - 110.

16. Cable P-8882 War Signed WDSCA to USFA, 14 June 1946, Box 174, GEA, RG 260, NA II.

17. Ex.Div. Disentanglement Com. to ADC, Plan for financing Steyr Plant, 18 June 1946, Box 174, GEA, RG 260, NA II.

18. Mark Clark to Chancellor Figl, Agreement, 11 July 1946, Exhibit No. 14, Box 2, GEA, RG 260, NA II.

19. Barbara Ward, "Europe Debates Nationalization," *Foreign Affairs* XXV (1946): 44 - 58.

20. With respect to compensation of private owners, the Austrian government promised to pass a law in 1946; actual passage of a compensation law did not take place before 1954. Siegfried Hollerer, "Verstaatlichung und Wirtschaftsplanung in Österreich (1946 - 1949)," Diss. Hochschule für Welthandel, 1974, 27 - 28.

21. As late as 1948 U.S. authorities charged with the supervision of the management of the Linz Steel Mill advanced schemes of privatization and of employing American steel and management experts to run the works. Memo to General Keyes, Review of Activities of Stanley N. Brown, 9 December 1948, Box 4, Economics Division, RG 260, NA II. Stanley Brown, a steel expert, suggested a reorganization plan for the VÖEST, pleasing to U.S. officials in the German External Assets Branch. Arno Einwitschläger, *Amerikanische Wirtschaftspolitik*" in *Österreich 1945 - 1949* (Vienna: Böhlau, 1986), 47. Einwitschläger neglects to mention that Stanley Brown's influence on U.S. policy in Austria was negligible.

22. Helmut Fiereder, "Reichswerke 'Hermann Göring'" *in Österreich 1938 - 1945* (Vienna: Geyer, 1983).

23. Helmut Fiereder, "Die Hütte Linz und ihre Nebenbetriebe von 1938 bis 1945," in *Historisches Jahrbuch der Stadt Linz 1981* (Linz: Stadtarchiv, 1982), 179 - 219; similar estimates in Report, The United Iron and Steel Works of Austria, August 1945, Box 29, GEA, RG 260, NA II.

24. Fünftes Sonderheft, Österreichisches Institut für Wirtschaftsforschung, (April 1948), 31.

25. Schuber 187 and 344, VÖEST, Koref Akten, Stadtarchiv Linz; Z 5314, Präsidialakten 1945 - 46, Oberösterreichiches Landesarchiv.

26. Kurt Tweraser, *US Militärregierung Oberösterreich.Bd. 1: Sicherheitspolitische Aspekte der amerikanischen Besatzung in Oberösterreich-Süd 1945 - 1950* (Linz: Oberösterreichisches Landesarchiv, 1995), 195 - 197.

27. An interesting survey of the situation in the Linz Steel Mill is provided by a number of OSS Reports in *Gesellschaft und Politik am Beginn der Zweiten Republik: Vertrauliche Berichte der US-Militäradministration aus Österreich 1945 in englischer Originalfassung*, ed. Oliver Rathkolb (Vienna: Böhlau 1985), 70 - 93, 237 - 240.

28. The management crisis in the VÖEST could finally be solved with the appointment of Walter Hitzinger, a forceful manager, although with some brown patches on his vest. Hitzinger epitomized the young manager who started out as a Socialist, but made a career during the National Socialist period in important technical positions. After 1945, he returned to the Socialist Party to become part of a growing stratum of "socialist managers." "The smoothness with which many of these new managers adapted themselves to the traditional ways in the exercise of their official functions, as well as their private life style, reflects the lack of depth of their socialist convictions." Kurt L. Shell, *The Transformation of Austrian Socialism* (New York: State University of New York, 1962), 205 - 206.

29. *Oberösterreichiche Nachrichten*, 4. 7. and 21. 7. 1945.

30. Gleissner to Renner, Österreichische Eisen- und Stahlindustrie, 24. Oktober 1945, Schuber 187, Koref Akten, Stadtarchiv Linz.

31. Memorandum Wiggs, Alpine Montan, Donawitz and Hermann Göring Linz, 14 November 1945, FO 1020/1324/XC 8713, Public Records Office. The author thanks Eduard Staudinger, Institut für Geschichte, Abteilung Neuzeit, Universität Graz for the documents.

32. The Linz nitrogen works had been constructed during the National Socialist Regime in the vicinity of the Iron and Steel Works. Although the nitrogen works were an enterprise separate from the VÖEST, the two were functionally so interrelated that they were practically one enterprise.

33. Major Koraniyi, Chief, Industry Branch to Chief, Economics Division, USACA, Report on the Integration of the Hermann Göring Works, Linz into the Iron and Steel Industry of Austria, 13 March 1946, Box 3, GEA, RG 260, NA II.

34. Quarterly Historical Report, USACA Section, USFA 1946, 272 - 274, Box 32, Historical File, RG 260, NA II.

35. *Oberösterreichische Nachrichten* 23.3., 30.3. and 28.6.1946.

36. John G. Erhardt to Secretary of State, Austrian Government Plan for the Iron and Steel Industries, 5 August 1946, Box 178, GEA, RG 260, NA II; Minutes of Planning Board Held in Leoben from llth to 22nd June 1946, Box 3, GEA, RG 260, NA II; Handelskammer Graz, Fachgruppe Eisenerzeugende Industrie an Bundesministerium für Vermögenssicherung und Wirtschaftsplanung, Fachgruppengutachten, 19.April 1946, Protokolle der Sitzungen des Planungsausschusses Linz - Donawitz von April bis Juni 1946, Ordner Rauscher, Archiv des Geschichteclubs VÖEST.

37. Krauland to Economic Directorate, Austrian Goverment Plan for the Iron and Steel Industries, 5 August 1946, Box 3, GEA, RG 260, NA II.

38. Report of Subcommittee, Determination of Fiscal Policy, United Iron and Steel Works, Linz, 5 February , 1946, Box 3, Property Control/Trusteeship, RG 260, NA II.

39. Garrison, Chief, RD & R Divison, IRS Iron and Steel Works Linz, 19 October 1948, Box 178, GEA, RG 260, NA II. The report warned that "every precaution should be taken by this Headquarters to assure that Alpine Montan is free from political pressure which is certain to be exerted by the Krauland Ministry and the Linz politicians in event the above plan is carried out. The Krauland Ministry will certainly object to any action on the part of this Headquarters which would place Linz under Alpine Montan Management. The Ministry will wish to protect the VÖEST opportunists at all costs. Alpine Montan is not popular with the Krauland Ministry because it has resisted all efforts on the part of that Ministry to staff the company with political favorites."

40. Staff Study of the United Austrian Iron and Steel Works, 6 July 1948, Box 178, GEA, RG 260, NA II.

41. Aktenkonvolut in Ordner Verkauf Hochöfen, Archiv des Geschichteclubs VÖEST; Helmut Fiereder, "Der Weg zu LD und Breitband. Die Hütte Linz im Kontext der österreichischen Eisen- und Stahlplanung nach dem Zweiten Weltkrieg," in *Historisches Jahrbuch der Stadt Linz 1991* (Linz: Stadtarchiv, 1992), 261 - 313.

42. The revisionist literature has made a good deal about the U.S. veto of the Czech sale, but neglects to mention the Austrian role, that is of the Krauland Ministry in bringing about the U.S. veto. Einwitschläger, *Amerikanische Wirtschaftspolitik*, 45 -47. Information about the Austrian resistance to the sale in Interview Hans Blumauer-Montenave, access to which was provided by Helmut Fiereder.

43. Fiereder, "Weg zu LD und Breitband", 285 - 289.

44. Oskar Grünwald and Herbert Krämer, *Die verstaatlichte österreichische Metallindustrie* (Frankfurt: Europäische Verlagsanstalt, 1966), 35-36.

45. Hans Igler, "Die Hintergründe des Marshall-Plans in Österreich: Was täten wir, wenn wir Geld kriegen würden?," in *25 Jahre ERP-Fonds 1962 - 1987* (Vienna: 1987), 45 - 52; for planning in the Krauland Ministry see Hollerer, *Verstaatlichung und Wirtschaftsplanung*; Helmut Fiereder, "Österreichische Wirtschaftsplanung nach 1945" in *Mitteilungen des Österreichischen Staatsarchivs*, Sonderband 3 (1997): 191 - 197; Otto Lackinger, *50 Jahre Industrialisierung in Oberösterreich 1938 - 1988* (Linz: Universitätsverlag Trauner, 1997), 134-135.

46. The most telling sentence in the Iron and Steel Plan reads as follows: *"Der Umfang der zur Zeit bestehenden neuen allgemeinen Werksanlagen und einzelner erhalten gebliebener Produktionseinheiten, die jetzt ungenutzt sind oder nur teilweise ausgelastet werden können, bietet jedoch eine günstige Grundlage für die vorgesehene Eisen- und Stahlplanung. Der Wert dieser erhalten gebliebenen neuen Einrichtungen und Anlagen ist weit höher als der notwendige Investitionsaufwand zur Abrundung der Produktion und zur Erzielung wirtschaftlicher Erzeugungsmöglichkeiten."* Eisen- und Stahlplanung, I. Teil (Wien: Staatsdruckerei, 1948), 4.

47. Giblin to Gilchrist, Study of the Austrian Iron and Steel Industry, 20 January 1950, Box 11, Industry Division, RG 469, NA II.

48. Comments on the Industrial Aspects of the Austrian Long Term Program 1952/53, no date, Box 5, Economics Division, RG 260, NA II.

49. An analysis of Dr. Nemschak's comments on the Austrian Long Term Program, 27 April 1949, prepared by Industry Branch, Box 5, Economics Division, RG 260, NA II.

50. For the misgivings of the Chamber of Labor Wirlandner to Brotman, 4 Year Plan, 20 November 1948, Box 5, Economics Division, RG 260, NA II.

51. Linden to King, Austrian Criticism of the Government Four Year ECA Program, 25 February 1949, Box 7, Economics Division, RG 260, NA II.

52. Franz Nemschak, "Zur österreichischen Wirtschaftsplanung," 10 January 1949, Box 7, Economics Division, RG 260, NA II.

53. Ibid. 3, 5, 19 -20, 25 - 26, 30, 44 - 47.

54. An analysis of Dr. Nemschak's comments on Austrian Long Term Program, 27 April 1949, Box 7, Economics Division, RG 260, NA II. The principal author of the analysis was the ex-Austrian, E. G. Rothblum, a Mission expert on the finished goods industries.

55. Ibid.

**First** Austrian Long Term Program

**Second** Four Year Plan for the Rehabilitation of Austrian Industries 1948/49 - 1951/52

| | | |
|---|---|---|
| Iron and Steel Industry | 45.000 | 44.750 |
| Non-Ferrous Metals Industry | 10.000 | 4.100 |
| Metal Working Industry | 7.500 | 14.300 |
| Electrical Machinery & Equipment Industry | 6.000 | 7.000 |
| Chemical Industry | 12.000 | 13.810 |
| Textile Industry | 12.000 | 30.042 |
| Leather Producing and Leather Processing Industry | 0.000 | 2.951 |
| Building Materials Producing Industries | 0.000 | 4.853 |
| Pulp, Paper and Paper Processing Industries | 5.000 | 4.900 |
| Total | 97.500 | 126.706 |

56. Meyer to King, Conferences with Kemeth E. Brown, Steel Consultant, OSR Paris, 22 August 1949, Box 10, Industry Division, RG 469, NA II.

57. Gohn to Austrian Legation ERP Office Paris, Verbal Note, 11 August, 1949, Box 20, Administrative Division, RG 469, NA II.

58. Report on United Austrian Iron and Steel Works by William E. Brewster, Steel Consultant to the U.S. High Commissioner, Allied Commission for Austria, November 1949, Box 36, Administrative Division, RG 469, NA II. It was to be expected that Richter-Brohm, a Krauland man and opponent of Nationalization, would not survive for long the political demise of Minister Krauland. The 1949 election resulted in the ÖVP's loss of its absolute majority. The electoral change was reflected in a new distribution of ministerial responsibilities. The industrial and power utilities holdings were now administered by an SPÖ minister. In the summer of 1950, Richter-Brohm was forced to resign his position as director general, not because his National Socialist past had caught up with him, but to make room for an SPÖ man.

59. King to Chief, Industry Division OSR Paris, Letter from Dr. Nemschak, Austrian Institute for Economic Research, 14 September, 1949, Box 8, Industry Division, RG 469, NA II.

60. E.G. Rothblum, Summary of Action, Dr. Nemschak, 11 October 1949, Box 11, Industry Division, RG 469, NA II.

61. Hryntschak to Rothblum, 30 September 1949, Box 21, Administrative Division, RG 469, NA II.

62. Conversation, C.M. Cosman and Director-General Oberegger, 14 October 1949, Box 2, Industry Division, RG 469, NA II.

63. Thus the Finances Minister Margaretha strongly expressed the opinion that errors had been committed in the planning of the iron and steel sector. The planning was too "grandiose". Ladenburg to King, Conversation with Finance Minister, 19 November 1949, Box 36, Administrative Division, RG 469, NA II.

64. Rothblum to Giblin, Austrian Iron and Steel Program, 16 January, 1950, Box 11, Industry Division, RG 469, NA II.

65. Franz Nemschak, "Zur Errichtung des Breitband-Walzwerks der VÖEST," 19 January 1950, Ordner Köchl, Archiv des Geschichteclubs VÖEST. For a refutation of Nemschak's arguments VÖEST, Memorandum für die Enquete betr. den Ausbau des Blechwalzwerkes der VÖEST in Linz, 1 February 1950, Schuber 187, Koref Akten, Stadtarchiv Linz.

66. Bernhard Matuschka, Bericht über die Sitzung des Stahlkomitees OEEC vom 5. bis 6. Oktober 1949, Ordner Köchl, Archiv des Geschichteclubs VÖEST.

67. U.S. Congress, Senate, An Analysis of the ECA Program - Staff Study of the Joint Economic Committee on Foreign Economic Cooperation, presented by Mr. McCarran, 3 March 1950, 81st Cong., 2nd sess., Senate Document 142; Ruggero Ranieri, "The Marshall Plan and the Reconstruction of the Italian Steel Industry (1947 - 1954)," in *Le Plan Marshall*, 367 - 385.

68. Taucher to King, American Export License for Projects II and III (Slabbing Mill and Rolling Mill VÖEST), 12 May 1950, Box 49, Administrative Division, RG 469, NA II.

69. Secretary of Commerce to National Security Council, Export of Steel Mill Equipment to Austria, 6 June 1950, Box 5, Policy Planning Staff, State Department, RG 59, NA II.

70. Lovett to Wilson, letter 3 January 1952, Box 5, PPS, State Department, RG 59, NA II.

71. *Das österreichische Investitionsprogramm 1950/52* (Wien: Staatsdruckerei, 1950).

72. Fiereder, "Weg zu LD und Breitband", 294 - 309; Hans Jörg Köstler, "Der Weg zur Stahlerzeugung nach dem Sauerstoffaufblas-(LD)Verfahren," *Blätter für Technik-geschichte* 59 (1997): 9 - 54.

73. Grünwald and Krämer, *Verstaatlichte Österreichische Metallindustrie*, 36-38.

74. Austria seems to have given away its technology virtually free of charge. Some of this was, however, involuntary. In the U.S. the VÖEST waged a protracted legal battle with U.S. steel producers who claimed to have discovered rather than imitated the LD technology. The case was eventually decided against the Austrian company on procedural grounds. Briefs, Vereinigte Österreichische Eisen- und Stahlwerke Aktiengesellschaft versus Jones & Laughlin Steel Corporation, Civil Action No. 62 - 272, November 1958. I am indebted to Prof. Freudenberger for the legal documents.

75. OECD, The Industrial Policy of Austria (Paris, 1971), 69, as quoted in Peter J. Katzenstein, *Corporatism and Change. Austria, Switzerland, and the Politics of Industry* (Ithaca: Cornell University Press, 1984), 206; Grünwald and Krämer, *Verstaatlichte Österreichische Metallindustrie*, 38 - 39.

76. Knut Borchardt and Christoph Buchheim, "Die Wirkung der Marshall-Hilfe in Schlüsselbranchen der deutschen Wirtschaft," in *Marshallplan und westdeutscher Wiederaufstieg*, 119 - 149.

77. Christian Dirninger, ed., *Wirtschaftspolitik zwischen Konsens und Konflikt* (Vienna: Böhlau, 1995), 39 - 40.

78. Fritz Weber, "Go Heavy Metal, Austria: Bemerkungen zur Rolle der verstaatlichten Industrie im Wiederaufbau," in *Inventur 45/55. Österreich im ersten Jahrzehnt der Zweiten Republik*, ed. Wolfgang Kos and Georg Rigele (Vienna: Sonderzahl, 1996), 298 - 310.

79. Charles S. Maier, "Premises of the Recovery Program," in *Le Plan Marshall*, 15-30, here 29.

# The Marshall Plan and Austria's Hydroelectric Industry: Kaprun

*Georg Rigele*

In memorian Egon G. Rothblum (1915-1998)[1]

## Introduction[2]

In the year 1955, two important events made many Austrians proud of their country and strengthened their confidence as citizens of an independent nation: first, the regaining of full national sovereignty with the signing of the Austrian State Treaty, and second, the completion of the *Kaprun* power plant. The name of *Kaprun*, actually a village, is used to indicate a large hydroelectric power generating system consisting of three storage basins, with five giant concrete dams, and two power generating plants—the lower stage with a maximum generating capacity of 220 MW and the upper stage with 112 MW—(to mention only the most important elements). Together the two plants had a capacity to generate 615 GWh annually when they went into operation, a capacity which has been increased since then.

These sites are located in the federal provinces (*Bundesländer*) of Carinthia and Salzburg, connected by a network of water tunnels, one of them drilled through the main ridge of the Austrian Alps (*Möllüberleitungsstollen*/Moell transfer). As the official name of the site, which is "*Tauernkraftwerk Glockner-Kaprun*," indicates, one of the storage basins lies at the bottom of the Großglockner, Austria's highest mountain. In terms of the electricity business, the rationale of *Kaprun* is to accumulate water during the summer season and to generate power mainly during the peak hours in winter, when demand is highest and could not be matched otherwise.

I suppose that in the years of postwar economic reconstruction, the hydroelectric sites of *Kaprun* had an impact in Austria similar to the famous Tennessee Valley Authority project during the New Deal era in the United States.[3] One objective was to generate a high output of electric power in economically underdeveloped regions, the other one to give the crisis-shaken citizens confidence in the economic future of their nations and to build state induced landmarks, symbols of national pride.

But the successful construction of *Kaprun* was not only an Austrian achievement, it was the most important project financed by the Marshall Plan. About two thirds of the money invested between 1948 and 1955 came from ERP Counterpart Funds. I calculate that without the Marshall Plan, the completion of the *Kaprun* project would have been delayed for at least ten years.

Looking back to the 1950s, one can find many expressions of gratitude towards the US Government and the American taxpayers in the speeches and written documents of Austrian politicians and the management of the *Tauernkraftwerke AG* (the state owned company in charge of the *Kaprun* plant). In a commemorative book, published in 1955 when the upper stage dams were completed, Bruno Marek, president of the board of the *Tauernkraftwerke AG* and social democratic politician, called the plant of Kaprun a memorial, telling the story of U.S. assistance towards Austria's liberation from the conditions of war and privation.[4]

Alfred Weskamp, one of the executive managers of the *Tauernkraftwerke AG* also praised the Marshall Plan. In his contribution to the same commemorative book, he illustrated the importance of the European Recovery Program (ERP) and provided comments to the negotiations between the Austrian and U.S. Marshall Plan experts which finally led to the financing of *Kaprun*.[5]

Weskamp sketches three different periods of the Marshall Plan financing of *Kaprun*. The first period lasted from 1948 to 1950, when the Limberg dam was under construction. The U.S. side was not enthusiastic about the Austrian electric power plans because of their high costs. But the necessity to construct this main element of the project was not questioned since two sets of machines in the main stage generating plant (out of four) were already in operation when U.S. troops arrived in *Kaprun* in May 1945. (Construction of *Kaprun* had started in 1938 soon after the "Anschluß".) In order to use them efficiently it was necessary to build the 120 meter high Limberg dam to accumulate the *Wasserfallboden* storage basin.

The second period was in 1950 to 1952. After long and difficult negotiations, the representatives of the ECA finally gave their approval to an expanded electric power investment program which included the construction of the *Kaprun* upper stage dams and the upper stage generating plant.

Weskamp explained the reason for the difficulty in persuading the Americans to provide extraordinarily high sums of additional counterpart funds for the *Kaprun* project by different experiences in electric power engineering (different national approaches, cultures of engineering, or, as Thomas P. Hughes has put it, different "regional styles" of power technology[6]). The Americans, Weskamp says, were more experienced in the field of thermal power plants than in alpine hydroelectric storage plants, therefore, they had to be convinced of the Austrian preference for extensive winter storage plants in the Alps. In another commemorative book *Zehn Jahre ERP* (*Ten Years of ERP*, published in 1958) you can find a similar argument. The American experts – in the eyes of their Austrian colleagues—preferred another model of power generation with thermal plants and river power plants combined with irrigation projects (*Flußkraftwerke im Zusammenhang mit Flußregulierungen* which seems to refer to the Tennessee Valley experience).[7]

From the documents I have seen in Austrian State Archives as well as from documents of the National Archives of the United States, I learned that there were also other reasons in addition to the different approaches as to how to generate power in the best manner in a technical sense. My thesis is that the economic ties of the Austrian electric power industry of the 1920s and 1930s, some special aspects of Austria's federal traditions, and the structural change in the Austrian economy made it mandatory for Austrian economic planners and engineers to complete *Kaprun* at once. And there was something else: in the history of the Republic of Austria from 1918 to 1938, many public building programs ended unfinished, e. g. the electrification program of the Austrian federal railways. Politicians and public opinion wanted to see such a prestigious project as *Kaprun* completed because it would boost the national self-confidence of many Austrians who had suffered a "*Nichtlebensfähigkeits*" complex, namely the idea that Austria was too small and too poor to be economically viable. The completion of the great public works project of *Kaprun* in the spectacular scenery of the *Großglockner* generated a tremendous collective feeling of success.

According to Weskamp, the third period of the Marshall Plan began in 1953 when already revolving Counterpart funds (the repayments of the original Counterparts) helped to finance the expensive construction of the upper stage dams, and the first Austrian public electricity bonds (*Elektrizitätsanleihen* 1953 and 1955) marked the beginning of a sustainable capital market in Austria.

In the sections that follow, the major issues discussed will be:

1. The growth of hydroelectric power production in Austria after World War I;
2. the economic transformation during the National Socialist Regime (1938-1945), the *Alpen-Elektrowerke* (AEW) and the beginning of "Kaprun;"
3. Kaprun's move from U.S. military government to Austrian trusteeship (public administration/management) to nationalization;
4. the hydroelectric power industry as the most important beneficiary of Marshall Plan-Aid in Austria;
5. ECA decision making in the case of Kaprun or how the Austrians got everything they wanted and
6. Kaprun as a contribution to a unified Austria.

## The Growth of Austria's Hydroelectric Power Production after World War I

Within the borders of the Habsburg Empire, rich coal fields in Bohemia and Silesia and mineral oil from Galizia provided plenty of fuel for thermal power plants. The largest coal-fueled power station was the Vienna municipal power plant. In the Alpine regions, a number of medium sized hydroelectric plants contributed to the process of local system building. When the Austrian empire broke apart in 1918, the ratio between thermal and hydro power was 1:1 within the borders of today's Austria. Fuel shortages resulted in severe cuts of power supply.

In the young Austrian Republic, the electricity companies in the federal provinces started construction programs, which during the 1920s led to real growth. The electricity companies tripled their peak hydro-generating capacity from 241 MW to 725 MW between 1918 and 1933. The average annual hydro-generating capacity was more than doubled during the same fifteen years, from 1280 GWh to 2878

GWh. The actual electricity generation by hydro and thermal plants together rose from 1765 GWh in 1918 to 2550 GWh in 1929 and then fell to 2183 GWh in 1932. It rose again and reached 2890 GWh in 1937. The ratio between thermal and hydro electricity generation rose to 1:4.8 in 1937.[8]

In Austria there is still a negative attitude to these achievements, I think as an unconscious result of Nazi indoctrination, which condemned everything done before the "Anschluß". Another reason is that in the period of nationalization which took place between 1946-47 and the 1980s, when the state industries were regarded as "unsinkable ships", it was assumed that nationalization should have already taken place in 1918. We also have to take into account that after 1932, due to the Great Depression, no additional plants were built, a frustrating experience for electricity technicians and managers.

After World War I, the existing high-voltage transmission grid was improved, or rather created from scratch. Private power generation in industrial works played an important role. For example, the Styrian iron and steel corporation *Österreichisch Alpine Montan Gesellschaft* operated an independent high-voltage grid which connected their steel mills and the Styrian *Erzberg* (Iron Ore Mountain). The Austrian Federal Railways established a transmission grid reaching from Vorarlberg, the Tyrol, and Salzburg to Carinthia to supply their newly electrified lines. In the years after World War II, it was far less attractive for industrial works to generate power in their own plants since electricity provided by public utilities had become relatively cheap.

As far as the public networks of power distribution are concerned, two facts are crucial. First, the most powerful new plants, the *Achenseewerk* in the Tyrol and the *Vorarlberger Illwerke* generated electricity mainly for export to Germany. The *Vorarlberger Illwerke* were a part of the *Rheinisch Westfälische Elektrizitätswerk* (RWE) *Verbund*-system (a long-distance, high-voltage transmission grid connecting big power plants and their consumers). A 220 kV long-distance transmission line connecting the Vermunt storage plant near Bludenz in Vorarlberg with the industries of the Ruhr Territory in northwestern Germany was opened in 1931. Thomas P. Hughes has researched this history of REW in his acclaimed comparative study *Networks of Power*.[9] The main consumers of the Tyrolean electricity company *TIWAG*, which ran the *Achenseewerk* power station, were the Austrian Federal Railways, the Tyrolean public network, and the

*Bayernwerk* in Bavaria, which received the biggest export share.[10] Before 1946, no transmission lines of public networks existed between Voralberg, the Tyrol, and the eastern provinces of Austria.

The second important fact was the supply of Vienna with hydro-generated electricity. In Upper Austria, Lower Austria, and Styria, six important hydroelectric plants were opened in the 1920s and early 1930s. Two high-voltage transmission lines supplied the metropolis of Vienna with power generated by "white coal."[11]

## Economic Transformation during the National Socialist Regime (1938-1945), the *Alpen-Elektrowerke* (AEW) and the Beginning of *Kaprun*

The Anschluß had immediate consequences for electricity generation. There was an increase in electric power demand from the newly established heavy industries, for example, the later VÖEST steel mill in Linz and the Ranshofen aluminum plant. There was a high demand for electric power in the *Altreich* itself, where alpine hydro power could help to save coal.

A reorientation of industrial production took place. On the one hand, the most advanced technologies and economies of scale were established; on the other hand, the biggest new plants in the *Ostmark* delivered semi-manufactured goods like pig iron, crude steel, or aluminum ingots. In this respect, the level of production was relatively low. The hastily built aviation factories in the Vienna region were technologically advanced, but were of no use for the Austrian postwar economy (these were completely destroyed German assets in the Soviet zone).

In the National Socialist period, the traditional luxury-industry in the Vienna region continued to decline, and Vienna lost the economic activities related to her status of a capital even of a small country.[12]

Soon after the "Anschluß" construction of seven important new hydro power plants started;[13] nine others followed between 1939 and 1943.[14] In some cases, the technicians resumed existing projects. Although the *Kaprun* project existed only as a controversial planning document, construction started in May 1938. At the same time, a new company *Alpen-Elektrowerke AG* (AEW) was founded.[15] The chief engineer and executive manager of the AEW was Hermann Grengg, a very experienced Styrian engineer and a devoted pan-German. He was much acclaimed for completing the Schwabegg running water power plant (60 MW / 350 GWh) at the river Drau in Carinthia in the very short time of three and one-half years. Therefore, the AEW was allowed to continue the construction of *Kaprun* with the work force of thousands of slave-laborers from the USSR and other countries occupied by Hitler´s armies, when most of the non-weapon industry construction sites were closed due to restrictions of the war economy. As already mentioned, in 1945, two out of four sets of machines were in operation at the main stage generating plant down in the Kaprun valley. The water to power the turbines was accumulated in a makeshift way by a low earth dam. During the war, many kilometers of tunnels were dug, pipes laid, and generating equipment installed.

Another utility important for future development was the *Rodund* plant of the *Vorarlberger Illwerke* company which went into operation in 1943. Several medium sized power plants were in various stages of completion and more or less secured the supply of electricity for the postwar period. Although generating capacity in the Austrian territory had been doubled since 1938, several complete breakdowns occurred in the postwar years due to the rapidly growing demand for electricity and shortages of coal in the thermal power plants. Finally, long periods of drought reduced the actual capacity of the hydro power plants.

With the exception of Rodund, the completed utilities were running river water power plants. Such types of continuously operating plants require lower construction costs in proportion to the annual electricity output than the peak-hour alpine storage plants. Storage plants of the *Kaprun*-type are very expensive to build, because enormous quantities of concrete are required for the dams, long water tunnels must be drilled, and kilometers of heavy steel pipes must be laid. This is the reason why the American advisors in the Economic Cooperation Administration (ECA) Mission to Austria favored the running water type, when negotiations of the Austrian electricity program started.

## ***Kaprun*'s Move from U.S. Military Government to Austrian Trusteeship (public administration/management) to Nationalization**

The province of Salzburg was liberated by the U.S. Army in May 1945. During the following months, the senior technicians of the AEW were arrested by the U.S. Counter Intelligence Corps (CIC) because they were NSDAP members and had held important economic positions. The U.S. forces had a strong interest in securing power supplies in Austria after the liberation of the country, but could not prevent chaos at the construction sites of *Kaprun*.

A heavy thunderstorm caused severe damage on the construction site of the Limberg dam, where the deep excavations were filled with rocks and mud. When the forced laborers, most of them Soviet prisoners of war, left Kaprun, only a small staff of German or Austrian employees stayed with the AEW, and until 1947, only a few workers desired jobs in Kaprun, because of the poor food and clothing situation. In 1946, the special food rations for the heavy workers in Kaprun were raised from only 1800 to 2700 calories per day. That was much more than the ration for ordinary citizens, but still not enough for such heavy construction work.

The AEW company was a "German External Asset." The Austrian Government named public administrators, and when the water rights held by the AEW expired, the government took charge of the project "through nimble legal gymnastics"[16] performed by the Minister of Agriculture and Forestry. In May 1946, a "Committee of Six" named by the federal government and the provincial governments of Salzburg, Upper Austria, and Vienna was installed, but failed to manage the project efficiently.

Following an order of General Mark W. Clark and General Harry J. Collins of 30 July 1946, the *Kaprun* power plant was transferred to the Austrian government in trusteeship. Some of the U.S. officials wanted the Austrian Government to solve the problems related to *Kaprun* without U.S. aid. In a meeting on 29 August 1946, held in the office of the USACA Social Administration Division with Peter Krauland, the Austrian Minister for Economic Planning, and Vinzenz Übeleis, Minister for Transportation, it "was thoroughly clarified that the future conduct of affairs of Kaprun are strictly in the hands of the Austrians and that the complete responsibility is Austrian."[17]

In the course of the Austrian nationalization scheme of 1946-47,[18] the electricity corporation *Verbundgesellschaft*, responsible for Austrian high-voltage transmission grid and power distribution, and as its subsidy the *Tauernkraftwerke AG*, responsible for the construction and operation of *Kaprun*, were established as successors of the AEW. The question of the German assets was finally resolved in the Austrian State Treaty of 1955, but for "Kaprun" it was of no more practical importance after 1946/47. The real question was how to find workers, how to feed them, and how to finance the completion of the Limberg dam.

Nevertheless, it is of some historical interest that in November 1946 the legal division of the United States Element of the Allied Commission for Austria (USACA) decided that the *Alpen-Elektrowerke* AEW was originally financed by Austrian investments. Edward A. Mag, Head of the Counsel Branch of the Legal Division was asked for his opinion. He stated:

a. AEW is a corporation, having its principal office in Vienna, organized after the Anschluss of Austria by VIAG, a subsidiary of the Reich Finance Ministry.
b. The capital invested in AEW by VIAG was apparently obtained by the Reich Finance Ministry first by forced liquidation and transfer of the assets of *Innkredit*, an Austrian corporation to its creditor, the Austrian National Bank and then by forced transfer from the Austrian National Bank.[19]

By the end of 1947, Hal D. Huston, Deputy head of the USACA German External Assets Branch, concluded: "As a result of these manipulations it is our present point of view that AEW is not a German external asset in Austria, but that its assets were and always have been Austrian assets."[20]

Pre-Marshall Plan aid for the workers in *Kaprun* was delivered by the UNRRA and the Quakers. How seriously *Kaprun* was considered by the Austrian government is shown by the following example. In September 1946, Federal Chancellor Leopold Figl wrote a personal letter to Rudolf Leopold, Chief of the UNRRA department *Österreichhilfe der Vereinten Nationen* in the federal chancellery and asked him to find warm clothing and heavy boots for the workers at *Kaprun*. Winter was approaching, and there was urgent need for such supplies. In October, underwear, trousers, jackets, and winter overcoats for 600 men, a gift from Canada, were sent to *Kaprun*, but there were no boots available.[21]

Before the Marshall Plan went into operation in Austria, only slow progress was made at the construction sites. However, the supply of food was increased in 1947 to 3200 calories per day. Consequently, the work force grew to the required number of 2000 men. During the summer of 1947, Austrian youth organizations sent volunteers to work in *Kaprun*.[22] The project was already on the way to becoming the great symbol for Austria's reconstruction.

The U.S. authorities in Austria closely observed the *Kaprun* project.[23] In November 1946, the chief of the Economics Division, Lt. Col. James R. Rundell, recalled the situation in Kaprun since the arrival of the U.S. troops. He reported that in the spring of 1945, Josef Rehrl and others of the local government of the province of Salzburg

> took charge of Kaprun after the surrender, dismissing 3000 workers to roam the countryside looking for food and some of them engaged in pillaging. In fact this gentleman's [Rehrl's, G. R.] activities and those of his friends were so troublesome that he was ordered by Major Chittick, Military Government, to keep completely away from the job and not interfere in any way under penalty of being put in jail.[24]

It is important to recognize that the local government had few other choices but to let the forced laborers go, but there may have been a better way to do so.

Josef Rehrl was a politician of the Austrian People's Party (ÖVP), a member of the *Bundesrat* (Federal Council, the more or less powerless second chamber of the Austrian parliament), provincial governor of Salzburg from 1947 to 1949, and brother of Franz Rehrl, the provincial governor of Salzburg from 1922 to 1938. From the early planning history of *Kaprun* in the 1920s until the late 1940s, politicians of *Bundesland* Salzburg tried to gain control over the project, which caused continuous conflicts with the federal authorities.

Lt. Col. Rundell may have been informed about this matter by Eduard Hüttler, then the Austrian public administrator in Kaprun. Hüttler reported about the activities of Dr. Rehrl and his friend Dr. Hobus, a lawyer, a *Reichsdeutscher* (citizen of the German Reich) and member of the NSDAP. Hüttler reported:

> On 24 May 1946, Colonel Hyde, who was unknown to me until then, met with Dr. Hobus, the representative of Federal Counselor Rehrl, to see the construction works in Kaprun. … Rehrl, who is no expert, intends to acquire Austrian citizenship for Hobus, who … is said to have saved the power station of Kaprun of being blown up during the retreat of the Nazis. There is not a soul in Kaprun who would not laugh about this statement, because it is not true at all. Dr. Hobus was banned from Kaprun in September 1945 by the American Liaison Officer Major Trommershausen …[25]

Hüttler suggested that Hobus should be expelled from Austria, Rehrl should be released from the construction committee and the province of Salzburg should not take part in the property control of *Kaprun*. Lt. Col. Rundell concluded his report of November 1946:

> Kaprun should be completed by people who know the power business, by people who have built similar generating stations. There are two utility companies adjoining Kaprun, either one of which could handle this project; namely, the TIWAG which has lines to Kaprun, and the OKA which has hydro-generating stations in the immediate vicinity. [OKA is the electricity company of Upper Austria and TIWAG the company of the federal province of the Tyrol, G.R.]
>
> In conclusion, we would like to make the following recommendations.
>
> 1. That the Austrian Government delegate the OKA or TIWAG (preferably the former) to undertake the completion of the Kaprun project as far as Stage III.
> 2. That the Austrian Government delegate a sponsor-engineer to the project, who is a competent utility man.
> 3. That USFA [United States Forces Austria, G.R.] delegate a Consulting Engineer with whom OKA and the Austrian Government can work on special problems in connection with the project.
> 4. That USFA delegate an observer-engineer to be in touch with the work on the site.[26]

A few days later, Deputy Commanding General Ralph H. Tate wrote a letter to Peter Krauland, Minister for Economic Planning, to tell him about Lt. Col. Rundell's recommendations, but he did so in a weakened version characterizing them as "suggestions, which may be helpful," without naming the OKA or the TIWAG.[27] The RD and R Division (Reparation, Deliveries, and Restitution) had warned that objections were made by the "Committee of Six" against a contract with the Upper Austrian OKA because it "would result in political repercussions in Land Salzburg." This division also stated "that as a purely commercial project Kaprun is not economical, although cost and production figures vary widely and depend on the source consulted."[28] In fact, none of the U.S. recommendations were realized.

To understand the positions the ECA experts would take in 1950, it is important to know that as early as 1946, the United States considered “the early completion of this project vitally essential to the rehabilitation of Austria”[29] but only as far as “stage III” of the construction plan designed by the AEW went. “Stage III” meant the construction of the Limberg dam and the 12 kilometer water tunnel from a storage basin at the foot of the *Großglockner* northwards (*Möllüberleitungsstollen*/Moell transfer), but not the upper stage storage basin.

In September 1948, conditions at the construction sites were much improved. The province of Salzburg had already become Austria’s “Golden West.” Hal D. Huston, head of the German External Asset Branch, inspected the *Kaprun* project. On the first evening of his visit, he attended a large Austrian party at the *Wasserfallhaus*. The executive managers of TKW had invited 115 guests to visit the construction sites.

Houston reported that the following day:

> I had many conversations with individual workers at the dam site under conditions which permitted them to express their thoughts freely, and they are very well satisfied with the conditions as they now exist at Kaprun. They are getting a heavy ration of 3250 calories a day, the food is well prepared, their quarters are clean and comfortable, there are ample heavy work shoes and clothing and there is an atmosphere of pleasantness that did not exist when we first inspected Kaprun in 1946.[30]

This description comes near to the popular story of *Kaprun*, which was presented to the Austrian public. The workers were regarded as the “heroes of Kaprun” who provided a main share of the *Wiederaufbau*, the reconstruction of Austria.

Another difference between the 1946 and the 1948 situation is the tourists’ perception of the later report. Active participation at this time was slowly shifting from the USACA to the ECA-Mission.

## The Hydroelectric Power Industry as the Most Important Beneficiary of Marshall Plan Aid in Austria

Although the figures in the publications I have seen are contradictory in certain details, their general impact is clear.

The Austrian electricity industry received the highest amount of Counterpart loans of all industrial branches. Between 1948 and 1952, 70 percent of all investments in power plants and transmission lines were ERP funded. The *Kaprun* plant was the most expensive single project; nearly one half of all investments in new power plants were made here, and there were several other important plants under construction. In the years between 1948 and 1955, when the upper stage of the system was completed, *Kaprun* received ÖS 1,428.3 million. The entire Austrian electric power industry received ÖS 2,961.1 million.[31] Thus *Kaprun* is by far the most important single Counterpart funded project of the Marshall Plan in Austria.

To underline the massive boost of Austria's electricity industry by ERP counterpart funds, we can take a look at the situation in West Germany.[32] As in the case of Austria, the German electricity industries received the largest amount of Counterparts of all industrial branches. But even in 1950, the strongest year in Germany, investment credits from counterparts did not exceed 30 percent of annual gross capital investment in power plants. In Austria in the same year, the *Verbundkonzern*, the nationalized corporation which built nearly all major power plants including *Kaprun*, financed 91 percent of its investments by ERP Counterpart credits—91 percent compared to 30 percent in West Germany! Borchhardt and Buchheim concluded that for West Germany the Marshall Plan was essential to overcome a critical bottleneck in electricity supplies; therefore "it is certain that the ERP loans closed a financing gap and contributed decisively to the growth of West German production."[33] Considering the figures, it is easy to emphasize the same conclusion for Austria.

For the interpretation of the figures in Table I it is important to consider inflation which was a very serious problem until 1952. From 1948 to 1952, inflation exceeded the interest rates of the ERP loans. From 1949 to 1952, inflation hovered around 30 percent, while the beneficiaries of the counterpart program had to pay only 3 percent interest. Even after the stabilization and austerity program which was successfully staged by the Austrian Minister of Finance Reinhard Kamitz in 1952/53, counterpart loans remained very beneficial.

**Table 1:** ERP Counterpart Financed Loans Granted to the *Tauernkraftwerke AG*, Interest and Inflation.

| Term | Interest Rate (Percent per Annum) | Index Number of Wholesale Price / Index Number of General Consumer Price | Amount in Austrian Schillings |
|---|---|---|---|
| 1948/1983 | 3 | 8.0 | 46,600,000 |
| 1949/1977 | 3 | 28.0 | 115,000,000 |
| 1950/1977 | 3 | 32.5 | 192,500,000 |
| 1951/1978 | 3 | 34.3 / 27.5 | 325,900,000 |
| 1952/1978 | 3 | 11.2 / 13.6 | 256,500,000 |
| 1953/1980 | 3 | -5.6 / -0.8 | 266,800,000 |
| 1954/1981 | 3 | 4.5 / 2.6 | 140,000,000 |
| 1955/1982 | 5 | 3.7 / 2.5 | 84,000,000 |
| 1957/1984 | 5 | 3.8 / 4.1 | 20,000,000 |
| 1958/1985 | 5 | -2.9 / 1.1 | 60,900,000 |

**Source**: Thomas Schabel; and Österreichisches Statistisches Zentralamt.[34]

**Table 2:** ERP-Funded Investments in the Electricity Industry and Overall Investments (ERP and non-ERP) in Austrian Schillings

| Year | *Kaprun/ Tauernkraft-werke AG ERP* | *Verbund-konzern* ERP | Electricity Industry ERP | Overall Investments *Verbund-konzern* |
|---|---|---|---|---|
| 1948 | 46,600,000 | 97,986,000 | 100,000,000 | 277,130,000 |
| 1949 | 115,000,000 | 328,600,000 | 386,900,000 | 404,295,000 |
| 1950 | 192,500,000 | 426,190,000 | 443,000,000 | 470,748,000 |
| 1951 | 325,900,000 | 559,560,000 | 757,800,000 | 718,775,000 |
| 1952 | 232,000,000 | 553,519,000 | 515,400,000 | 847,019,000 |
| 1953 | 271,300,000 | 150,081,000 | 482,000,000 | 820,719,000 |
| 1954 | 160,000,000 | 452,430,000 | | 925,010,000 |
| 1955 | 84,000,000 | | | 1 461,621,000 |
| 1956 | | 284,000,000 | | 1 641,100,000 |
| 1957 | 20,000,000 | 210,000,000 | | 1 800,000,000 |

**Source**: Compiled from various data[35]

Until 1955, the construction of *Kaprun* was the primary target of the *Tauernkraftwerke AG* (*Tauernkraftwerke AG* is a subsidiary company of the *Verbundkonzern*). The figures in the first column out of Table 2 up to 1954 indicate the Kaprun project, from 1955 on other projects like the *Schwarzach* power plant are included.

In terms of actual power generation, the ERP funded construction programs resulted in double-digit growth rates. The highest growth rates ever were 29.2 percent in 1948 and 16.1 percent in 1951 when *Kaprun*'s lower stage went into full operation.

**Table 3:** Power Generation and Industrial Production

| Year | Elec. GWh | Metal GWh | Ranshofen GWh | Steel GWh | Pulp Paper GWh | Elec. Gen. Index | Alu. Prod. Index | Steel Prod. Index | Ind. Prod. Index |
|---|---|---|---|---|---|---|---|---|---|
| 1937 | 2890 | | | | | 100 | 100 | 100 | 100 |
| 1944 | 5807 | | | | | 201 | | | |
| 1945 | 3180 | | | | | 110 | | | |
| 1948 | 5326 | | 230 | | | 184 | 303 | 107 | 92 |
| 1950 | 6351 | | 300 | | | 220 | 409 | 159 | 145 |
| 1951 | 7375 | 700 | 430 | 666 | 360 | 255 | | | |
| 1952 | 8032 | | 660 | | | 278 | 834 | 195 | 147 |
| 1954 | 9847 | | 760 | | | 341 | 1300 | 264 | 194 |
| 1955 | 10751 | 1285 | 847 | 926 | 713 | 372 | 1541 | 315 | 225 |

*Columns from left to right:*

Elec. Gwh: electric power generated by public utilities (hydro and thermal)
Metal Gwh: electricity consumption of the metal industry (non iron and steel)
Ranshofen Gwh: electricity consumption of the aluminum works in Ranshofen
Steel Gwh: electricity consumption of the iron and steel industry
Pulp Paper Gwh: electricity consumption of the paper industry
Elec. Gen Index: electricity generation index (hydro and thermal)
Alu. Prod. Index: aluminum production index
Steel Prod. Index: iron and steel production index
Ind Prod. Index: overall industrial production index
**Source**: Combiled from various data[36]

Industrial consumers with high electricity needs were rapidly growing (table 3). This was due to the legacy of National Socialist economy planning, but also to the growing supply of inexpensive electricity. The state owned aluminum works in Ranshofen and chemical plants in Linz and Lenzing were among the expanding enterprises left by the Third Reich. The still very successful Austrian pulp and paper industry on the other hand, was completely run down after the war and started to modernize thanks to the Marshall Plan. The pulp and paper industry received the highest counterpart credits of all privately owned industrial branches and became a main user of inexpensive electric power from Marshall Plan funded utilities.

When we try to discuss what would have happened without the Marshall Plan or if fewer power plants had been financed by ERP Counterpart funds, prices are the crucial aspect.

Inflation rates after 1945 were much higher than the rise in electricity prices. Therefore prices did not cover the costs, and the public utilities depended on borrowed capital and state subsidies. As mentioned above, it was not attractive anymore for industrial enterprises to invest in their own power plants as they did in the 1920s, because they could buy cheaper electricity from public utilities. I owe this information to a study by the Austrian economist Wilhelm Weber printed in 1957, which was funded by the Rockefeller Foundation. According to Weber (who was assisted by Stephan Koren), an artificial demand for electricity was created; consequently, extremely high additional investments in power plants became necessary.

If there had been less Counterparts available, it seems evident that only higher prices could have compensated for capital shortages. If electricity had been subsidized to a lesser degree, the competitive position of the Austrian industry would have suffered. The Ranshofen aluminum plant might have been scaled down or closed entirely (as it finally was in 1993). A further consequence might have been falling exports, lower growth rates, or higher unemployment, all of which would have threatened Austrian economic stability.

## ECA Decision Making in the Case of *Kaprun* or How the Austrians Got Everything They Wanted

In the first period of the ERP (according to the three period model of Alfred Weskamp), most of the power plants which had been in different stages of construction in 1945 were completed or neared completion. As a result of the completion of the Limberg dam and the *Kaprun* main stage generating plant in September 1951, most restrictions for electricity consumers were lifted. Vienna especially enjoyed an improved power supply.

At the beginning of the second period, Austrian experts on electricity and politicians made plans for new power stations to meet an increasing industrial demand in Austria, and additional storage plants in the Tyrol and Vorarlberg to sell electricity abroad. To increase exports and correct the negative balance of payments, it was planned to increase the production of aluminum in Ranshofen. To provide the very large amounts of electricity required by the aluminum smelting furnaces, the Austrians wanted to proceed with the *Kaprun* project and to construct the upper stage basin. In the eyes of the ECA Special Mission to Austria, this was not a reasonable consideration at all. In 1950, Gustav Froebel, head of the Industry Division of the ECA Mission and former employee of the Baldwin Locomotive Company,[37] was strictly opposed to the upper stage project which he and his colleagues considered to be expensive and inefficient. Two years later, when construction of the upper stage dams was under way, he mentioned that the only reason it had gone ahead was that he had been in the hospital when the decision was made in 1950.[38]

How did the Austrians manage to get their pet project past the ECA officials (ÖS 719 million in Counterpart credits) against such heavy resistance?

Newly released documents in the Austrian State Archives in Vienna tell the story.[39] The documents came from the *Bundeskanzleramt: Zentralbüro für ERP-Angelegenheiten* (Federal Chancellery: Central Bureau for ERP Affairs), where most information was gathered and, foremost, where the Austrian ERP projects were prepared and presented to the ECA/MEC.[40]

Most documents of the electricity section in the "Waldbrunner Kingdom," the Ministry of Transportation and Nationalized Enterprises headed by Karl Waldbrunner (Social Democratic Party, SPÖ) have been destroyed. Waldbrunner was a powerful politician and strongly backed the electricity construction programs including *Kaprun*. Waldbrunner was an electrical engineer by profession and—facing unemployment at home—spent the years 1932 to 1937 in the USSR, where he was working on the construction of power plants.

The Central Bureau for ERP Affairs, *Zentralbüro für ERP-Angelegenheiten*—especially Wilhelm Taucher, the Austrian Government's representative, and Hans Igler, the ERP planning chief, men of the ÖVP, the People's Party mediated between Waldbrunner and the ECA.[41]

The decision whether or not to continue with the construction of the *Kaprun* upper stage plant was discussed in connection with other

"The ERP is helping Austria's Energy Industry. Light and Power for Austria: Two Years of Reconstruction in the Energy Industry"

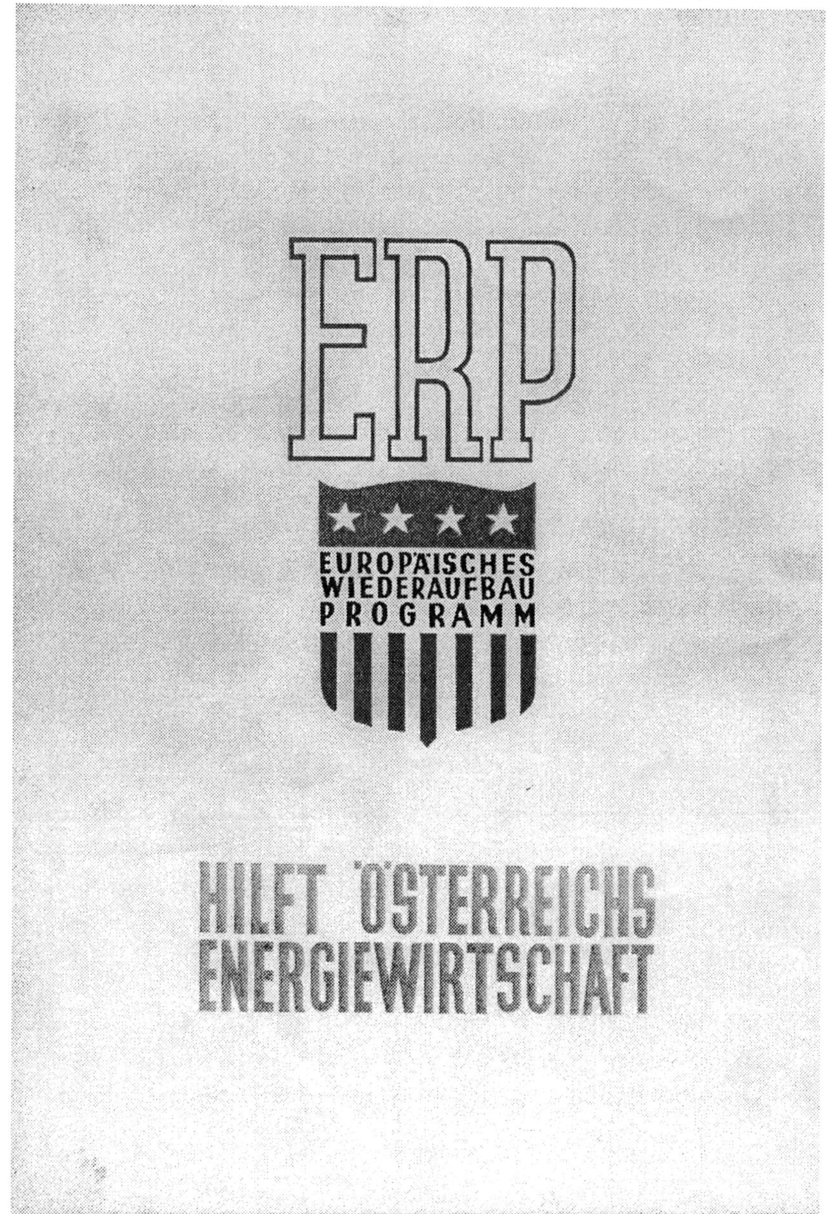


Source: *Licht und Kraft für Österreich. Zwei Jahre Neuaufbau der Energiewirtschaft*, ed. Bundesministerium fur Enegierwirtschaft und Elektrifizierung (1949)

important problems: the question of the Ranshofen aluminum plant and the question of the *Vorarlberger Illwerke* and electricity exports.

The ECA agreed with the Austrian economic planners about the importance of the *Ranshofen* plant. There was a high demand for aluminum in the western hemisphere (particularly for civil and military aviation), and Austria expected to improve her balance of payments by increasing aluminum exports. To provide the needed power it seemed logical to build additional running water power plants on the Inn river in Braunau and on the Enns river in Rosenau, both in Upper Austria. At first sight an increase in aluminum smelting meant a higher demand for basic electric load, not peak load, which was provided by *Kaprun*. The magic word used by the Austrian negotiators to convince their American partners was "winter gap" or "winter deficit," the shortage resulting from higher power demand and lower hydroelectricity supply provided by the running water plants during the winter season. During the summer season, there was a surplus of generating capacity.

Therefore the *Verbundgesellschaft* in 1950 planned an additional construction program consisting of the mentioned *Braunau* and *Rosenau* plants, increased generating capacity in the brown coal fueled *Voitsberg* thermal power plant in Styria and finally the *Kaprun* upper stage. The water accumulated in *Kaprun* during the summer should fill the winter gap. When these utilities went into operation, an additional 620 GWh annual delivery of power could be transmitted to *Ranshofen.*

In an informal note to Hans Igler, the ECA deputy chief of Mission in Austria, William Giblin, agreed that "the major problem in connection with the increased production of aluminum is the question of power. Our government would entertain a plan whereby 5 percent Counterpart funds may be used for the construction of a power plant to supply the aluminum smelter. The payment will be made in aluminum ingots."[42] This was one of several ideas as to how to finance further power plants.

While the experts of the ECA and the Austrian Central Office for ERP Affairs discussed technical details of short term (1950-52) and long term (1950-57) electric power investment programs, and searched for alternatives of financing, the shop stewards of the *Kaprun* construction workers and Minister Waldbrunner started a lobbying campaign for the upper stage project. The shop stewards passed a memorandum to Waldbunner and (via Waldbrunner and the Central Office for ERP-Affairs) to Clyde N. King, the chief of the ECA Mission to Austria. The shop stewards declared that the construction of the Kaprun upper stage was the most urgent project for the further development of Austria's hydroelectric industry and the public good. They explained the idea of the planned pump-storage-system, which is to pump water from the lower stage basin back into the upper stage basin at times of power surplus (at night) to generate electricity again during times of highest demand.[43]

For the social democratic politician Waldbrunner, it was very important to keep the workers of *Kaprun* in a good mood, because this place was a stronghold of the Communist Party and the trade union wing of the *Verband der Unabhängigen* (Association of the Independents, VdU), which attracted many former NSDAP members who worked in *Kaprun*.

In the shop steward elections in *Kaprun* of October 1949 and again in 1951, the VdU gained a relative majority. In 1951, the Communists and the right wing VdU formed a coalition. In a rare exception of postwar Austrian labor politics, the Communists had surpassed the Social Democrats (for once). This was mainly due to a corruption scandal in which a social democratic shop steward was involved.[44] This uncertain political situation might have been an important motive for Waldbrunner to table a motion in the cabinet meeting of 8 August 1950. In that meeting, he convinced his fellow Ministers and Federal Chancellor Leopold Figl that the Austrian Government must insist upon the completion of *Kaprun* as an inevitable necessity.[45] This declaration shows the considerable self-confidence of a government which insisted upon a project that it could not afford on its own means. The Austrian cabinet also knew exactly the point of view of the ECA Special Mission to Austria: no further Counterparts for *Kaprun*.[46] The experts of the ECA calculated the cost of electricity provided by the *Kaprun* upper stage project to be three times higher than by the planned *Aschach* power plant on the river Danube, which was delayed for several years (37 and 9.6 g/KWh).[47] The Aschach power plant went into operation in 1963. The maximum capacity was 287 MW and the annual generating capacity 1648 GWh (compared to 615 GWh in *Kaprun*).

A few days later, a group of experts of the ECA, the ZERP, and the Waldbrunner Ministry met in the office of Mr. Froebel to whom the position of the Austrian government was explained. But Froebel was not impressed at all by the cabinet's declaration and made a counterproposal which leads to the question of the *Vorarlberger Illwerke* and electricity exports. Fröbel argued that the best way to cover the electricity demand, including the supply of the aluminum works of Ranshofen, would be the construction of a 220 kV high-voltage transmission line from Vorarlberg to Kaprun (where the existing 220 kV line from Vienna and Upper Austria ended at this time). The electricity generated by the *Vorarlberger Illwerke* should not be exported to Germany anymore, but transmitted to Austrian power consumers. The power provided by the *Illwerke* would be of the same peak-hour quality and capacity as the energy output expected by the *Kaprun* upper stage plant. Froebel calculated that the costs of *Kaprun* were ÖS 500-600 million (which was less than the actual cost); whereas the transmission line from Vorarlberg would not cost more than ÖS 200 million.[48]

Froebel and Robert Hamilton, the public utilities specialist of ECA Mission to Austria, also criticized the *Illwerke* for selling their electricity too cheaply to West Germany. They feared that the Austrian negotiators for a new delivery treaty were negotiating from too weak a position, because they saw no other buyers than the Germans. From the U.S. point of view, a future high-voltage transmission line to the east was also seen as an opportunity to sell power generated in Vorarlberg to Italy.

On the other hand, from the official Austrian point of view, Vorarlberg as well as the Tyrol simply did not contribute to the Austrian power supply but to their regional demand and mainly to electricity export.[49] The production and consumption plans until 1953, which were calculated by the "load dispatcher" (central electricity switch control for Austria) in 1950 did not include the Tyrol and Vorarlberg.[50]

The Austrian *Verbund*system connected the seven provinces from Salzburg to Lower Austria with an extension to the *Gerlos* power plant in the Tyrol. The ECA officials regarded the use of surplus power for the manufacturing of exportable goods as the better solution than the export of power. Revenues were expected to be higher. The Austrians wanted both power exports and additional power supply for the expanding aluminum, pulp and paper, and chemical industries. Electricity exports to Germany were also seen as important for the financing of coal imports from the Ruhr Territory.

I would not rule out the threat that the government in Vienna feared: a secessionist movement in Western Austria, if the unloved east of the country and the even less liked capital, Vienna, should demand electricity generated by the waters from their mountains and glaciers.

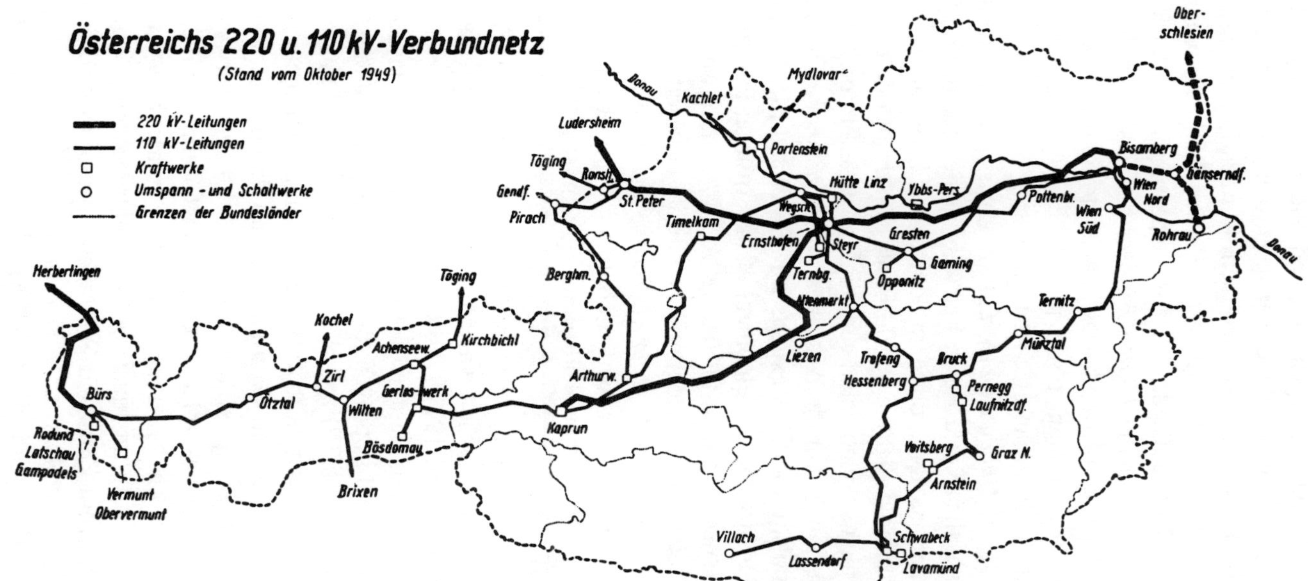


The Austrian high-voltage transmission grid in 1949 (ÖZE 1/1950)
The 110 kV transmission line in the west, which went into operation in 1946 and connected the Tyrol and Vorarlberg, did not provide enough capacity to serve as an Austrian east-west power connection. The high capacity 220 kV-link ended in Kaprun at that time. Via the Gerlospaß transmission line at least, some surplus-power generated in the Tyrol was transmitted

The importance of the *Illwerke* for the regional identity of Vorarlberg had been examined in a recent study.[51] Further, I would not rule out that in the subconscious mind and in the mentality of the Austrian energy technicians and managers, there were remains of pan-German traditions which prevented them from cutting the ties with the large *Bayernwerk*[52] and the even larger *Rheinisch Westfälisches Elektrizitätswerk* (RWE). I concede that this is speculation, but at least I can mention the fact that the *Huben I* power plant, also known as *Dorfertal*, in the East Tyrol which was planned to deliver power for Italy, was never built, although it was part of the blueprint for the future expansion of the Austrian electricity industry.

In the case of *Huben I/Dorfertal*, the Austrian government applied for loans from the World Bank, but were denied them. In September 1950, negotiations took place in Paris. The high ranking Austrian delegation was told that the World Bank would not rule out loans for such power plants which could earn high revenues in foreign exchange by exporting power, but the Austrians should present all technical and financial details to the ECA experts Mr. Cisler and Mr. Neville first.[53]

The "Plans for the Development of the Austrian Power Industry," which were negotiated with the ECA Mission, always used the expression "international program" to indicate electricity export to the German corporations RWE, *Energie-Versorgung Schwaben* (EVS), and *Bayernwerk*.[54] Negotiations with an Italian group headed by the Italian Ministry of Labor did not result in an agreement about the project in the East Tyrol.

The 220/380 kV long-distance transmission line from Vorarlberg to the east of Austria which was proposed by Gustav Froebel in 1950 went into operation in 1977.[55]

In a series of negotiations in 1950, the Austrians played out their diplomatic skills and improved their positions. The utilities-specialists Richard Polaczek (ZERP) and Robert Hamilton (ECA) agreed after a "very lively" conversation that the 220 KV high-voltage transmission line from Vorarlberg to *Kaprun* was no longer on the agenda. Hamilton finally accepted the arguments brought forward by the Austrians. When Hans Igler met William Giblin, the ECA Deputy Chief of Mission, on 18 August, they came to a common understanding about the "Kaprun"-question. A conference with high ranking ECA officials from Paris and Washington was expected to result in further progress. Walker L. Cisler (acting as consultant for ECA Washington), Mr. Southerland (Office of the Special Representative,

OSR Paris), Mr. Hamilton (ECA Wien), Rudolf Fürst (Waldbrunner Ministry) and Polaczek (BKA-ZERP) met in Innsbruck to discuss the preparation of a European energy-pool, which could bring a solution for the problems of Austrian electricity exports.[56] Walker L. Cisler, then executive vice-president, later president of Detroit-Edison Company, was one of the prominent business leaders who served in top positions in the ECA.[57] After the death of his seven- year-old son in an accident, Cisler devoted his entire life to the progress of electric power generation all around the world and also played a prominent role in the development of electric power in the USSR.[58] In a conference in Innsbruck on 21 August 1950, Cisler promised to support a fair solution in the negotiations between the *Vorarlberger Illwerke* and their Western German partners RWE and EVS, who at that time negotiated in Frankfurt a new treaty which was finally signed in 1952.[59] Due to U.S. calculations, Austria could expect additional payments in the amount of $ 4 million for electricity already delivered to Western Germany. Unfortunately, I did not find out more about the export relations of the VIW. Concerning *Kaprun* my impression is that with the involvement of ECA Washington and with Walker Cisler's assistance an improved price agreement for VIW, power exports seemed within reach.

In September 1950, a new name surfaced in the reports of the meetings of the U.S. and Austrian Marshall planners in Vienna: Wesley Cook. Cook was appointed by the CIO (Congress of Industrial Organizations) to represent organized labor at the ECA Special Mission to Austria.[60] Cook fell in love with a former member of Minister Waldbrunner's staff and married her. Waldbrunner and the ECA member to whom I owe this sentimental story witnessed the marriage.

What I definitely do not want to say is that this private relationship secured the construction of the *Kaprun* upper stage plant. But it is surprising that in the further course of negotiations in 1950, no further general objections were raised against *Kaprun*. On the contrary, most members of the ECA Special Mission to Austria now defended the Austrian power program including *Kaprun* in the Office of the Special Representative (OSR) in Paris and in the ECA Washington.

On 19 September 1950, Richard Polaczek was asked without warning to go and discuss the Austrian electricity program with Mr. Cook, Mr. Hamilton, and Mr. Froebel: This turned into a cross-examination about the program. At least at this stage in the negotiations, Froebel did not strictly oppose the *Kaprun* project which was part of the Austrian power program. Cook told Polaczek that he wished to see this program finalized in Paris and Washington.[61] He encouraged Polaczek to prepare all required information for a final meeting which took place two days later. Six members of the ECA Mission took part in this important meeting. Full agreement was achieved. Concerning the *Kaprun* upper stage plant, Wesley Cook said that he understood that this project was the most important one for Austria. He could not guarantee the program's approval by the senior ECA officials, but everybody left the meeting in an optimistic mood.[62]

By early October 1950, Wilhelm Taucher was able to tell Clyde N. King about a positive reaction of the OSR which he had received when he negotiated the power program in Paris.[63]

In September 1951, when the opening ceremony of the Limberg dam took place, new Counterpart credits had already been directed to the construction works of the upper stage.

## A Résumé: Kaprun as a Contribution to a Unified Austria

As a symbol of national pride, *Kaprun* was an important element in the process of the nation-building of Austria as a small independent democracy.

Especially during the initial period of the Marshall Plan, the *Kaprun* project was almost entirely financed by counterpart credits.

*Kaprun* helped to secure the electric power supply of Vienna. In 1949, a new 22O kV long-distance transmission line to Vienna was completed. There was an east-west division in the Austrian electric power grid, but it was a division which divided the West in two sections while *Kaprun* and the Marshall Plan kept the economic ties between the U.S. and the Soviet occupation zones alive—at least for electricity. If we consider that it took eight years after the breakdown of the Soviet satellite system to establish a parallel connection (same frequency) between the grids of Hungary, the Czech Republic, Slovakia, Poland, and the Austrian grid, one should not underestimate this factor.

In the second period after 1950/51, even more ERP credits financed the construction of the *Kaprun* upper stage. Fast growing generating capacities and low electricity prices greatly contributed to the Austrian industrial recovery. Apart from nationalization, no revolutionary change of the Austrian electricity system took place. Instead, Austria continued to follow the paths of the development of the 1920s and 1930s: expansion, integration and export. The federal provinces of Salzburg and Carinthia and, to a certain degree, the Tyrol were interconnected with the network of transmission lines which supplied the metropolis of Vienna and the Upper Austrian industries. The Tyrol and Vorarlberg continued their construction programs aimed at exporting power to Germany.

On the other hand, the fact that the political competition between the federal government and the provincial governments (as well as between the provincial governments themselves) continued, had the effect that reasonable proposals put forward by the U.S. experts were not successful. Neither the early proposal of the incorporation of the *Kaprun* power plant into the Upper Austrian electricity company OKA (or into TIWAG, the company of the Tyrol) nor the proposal of 1950 to use power generated in Vorarlberg for industrial purposes in Upper Austria became reality.[64] Instead of incorporating of *Kaprun* into one of the existing companies, in 1947, the *Tauernkraftwerke AG* (TKW) was founded. At first, its headquarters were in Zell am See near Kaprun. In 1952, the TKW planned to transfer the headquarters to the city of Salzburg, as a matter of prestige for the provincial governor of Salzburg Josef Klaus. Due to the costs, this was seen as a provocative step by the U.S. Mission for Economic Cooperation,[65] but nevertheless it was realized in the following years. Also in 1952, the treaty between the *Vorarlberger Illwerke* (VIW) and its German power purchasers was renewed. Up to the present day, electric power and political power in Austria are closely interconnected. The federal provinces especially regard their power companies as a political tool.

Thanks to the Marshall Plan, not only was inexpensive electricity provided for the Austrian industries, but traditional political structures were kept untouched. However, these structures obviously reduced the efficiency of the system of power generation.

## Conclusion

As the figures indicate, the Austrian electricity economies in the late 1940s and early 1950s depended entirely on the ERP counterpart funds. All projects for power plants and especially the *Kaprun* upper stage plant went through intensive negotiations between the Austrian Central Bureau for ERP Affairs and the ECA Special Mission to

Austria. The fact that no major changes in the Austrian projects were forced on them by the U.S. side affirmed the Austrian's self-confidence regarding their technical know-how. Because of their technical competence, they felt they had deserved the financial aid of the Marshall Plan in the first place.

## Notes

1. During 1948-54, Egon G. Rothblum played an crucial role as a senior member of the U.S. Marshallplan Administration in Austria, towards the end as head of the ECA Industry Division. I had the pleasure of getting to know him in the years before his recent death in a series of personal meetings and through an extensive personal correspondence. As one of the key witnesses to the Marshall Plan in Austria he gave me essential information about the inner workings of the ECA administration in Austria and the Austrian and American personnel involved in the ECA mission. Mr. Rothblum had been invited to the UNO Marshall Plan Conference in May 1998 but had to decline due to poor health; he died in Vienna on June 14, 1998.
   I would like to dedicate this essay to an Austrian-American gentleman, who personally suffered from Austria's fall, but then returned to help in her miraculous resurrection after World War II. His memory should be cherished as one of the legacies of the Marshall Plan in Austria.
   Egon G. Rothblum was born in Vienna on August 1, 1915. He graduated from High School and went to technical college at the "Lehr- und Versuchsanstalt der Textilindustrie"; he also studied law at the University of Vienna.
   After the "Anschluss" in 1938 he emigrated to the U.S.A. via Switzerland and Greece. In 1942 he volunteered for service in the U.S.Army. He was soon promoted from Sergeant to Lieutenant and fought in the North African and Italian campaigns and ended up in Austria, arriving with the 15th U.S.Army Group on August 21, 1945, in Salzburg. He left the Army in 1946 and became a civil servant in the War Department, USACA Economic Division. In 1950 he joined the U.S. State Department and served in the ECA Mission to Austria until 1954. he became a development specialist and worked in U.S. aid missions around the world. He retired from the State. Department in 1972 and became deputy director of the UNIDO in Vienna. After his second retirement he continued to work as a consultant. He always thought about his work in the ECA mission to Austria as one of his most important contributions to Austria's postwar economic recovery.

2. I want to thank Günter Bischof, New Orleans, Kurt Tweraser, Fayetteville, and Herbert Vopava, Vienna, for their tremendous help.

3. David E. Nye, *Electrifying America: Social Meanings of a New Technology, 1880-1940* (Cambridge, Massachusetts: The MIT Press, paperback edition 1992, fourth printing 1995), 305-326.

4. Bruno Marek, "Festgruß," in *Festschrift: Die Oberstufe des Tauernkraftwerkes Glockner-Kaprun*, ed. Tauernkraftwerke AG, and J. Götz, R. Emanovsky (Zell am See, September 1955).

5. Alfred Weskamp, "Glockner-Kaprun im kommerziellen Aspekt", in *Festschrift: Die Oberstufe des Tauernkraftwerkes Glockner-Kaprun*, ed. Tauernkraftwerke AG, J. Götz, and R. Emanovsky (Zell am See, September 1955), 27-32.

6. Thomas P. Hughes, *Networks of Power: Electrification in Western Society, 1880-1930* (Baltimore: Softshell Books edition, 1993).

7. *Zehn Jahre ERP in Österreich: Wirtschaftshilfe im Dienste der Völkerverständigung*, ed Österreichische Staatsdruckerei (Wien: Österreichische Staatsdruckerei, 1958), 67.

8. For detailed information see Oskar Vas, *Grundlagen und Entwicklungen der Energiewirtschaft Österreichs: Offizieller Bericht des österreichischen Nationalkomitees der Weltkraftkonferenz* (Wien: Verlag von Julius Springer 1930); Oskar Vas, *Die Wasserwirtschaft und ihre Bedeutung für Österreichs Wiederaufbau*, Schriftenreihe des Österreichischen Wasserwirtschaftsverbandes 5 (Wien: Springer Verlag, 1946); and Oskar Vas, *Wege und Ziele der österreichischen Elektrizitätswirtschaft* (Wien: Springer Verlag, 1952).

9. Hughes, *Networks of Power*, 404-428.

10. Manfred Pohl, *Das Bayernwerk 1919 bis 1996* (München: R. Piper, 1996), 203-206.

11. Hydroelectric power in Austria often was called *weiße Kohle*. Thomas P. Hughes uses the term "California White Coal" (Hughes, *Networks of Power*, 262-284.)

12. Dieter Stiefel, "Fünf Thesen zu den sozioökonomischen Folgen der Ostmark,"in *Politik in Österreich*, ed. Wolfgang Mantl (Wien: Böhlau Verlag, 1992), 49-61.

13. For the source of this information, see Vas, *Wasserwirtschaft*, 16. The chart shows the seven new hydro power plants started after the Anschluß.

| Name of site | River | Electricity Company | First year of operation, (which does not mean of completion) |
|---|---|---|---|
| Rodund | Ill (storage plant) | Vorarlberger Illwerke | 1943 |
| Kirchbichl | Inn | Tiroler Wasserkraftwerke TIWAG | 1941 |
| Gerloskraftwerk | Durchlaßboden (storage plant) | TIWAG | 1948 |
| Kaprun | Kapruner Ache (storage plant) | Alpen-Elektrowerke AEW | 1944 |
| Schwabegg | Drau | AEW | 1942 |
| Ering | Inn | Innwerke | 1942 |
| Ybbs-Persenbeug | Danube | Rhein-Main Donau AG | 1957 |

14. This table is from Vas, *Wege und Ziele*, Table II. For further information, see Vas, *Wasserwirtschaft*, 17.

| Name of site | River | Electricity Company (1939-1945) | First year of operation, (which does not mean of completion) |
|---|---|---|---|
| Lavamünd | Drau | AEW | 1944 |
| Unterdrauburg/ Dravograd, Slovenia | Drau | AEW | 1943 |
| Großraming | Enns | Kraftwerke Oberdonau, former OKA | 1950 |
| Staning | Enns | Kraftwerke Oberdonau, former OKA | 1946 |
| Mühlrading | Enns | Kraftwerke Oberdonau, former OKA | 1948 |
| Ternberg | Enns | Hermann Göring Werke, Linz | 1949 |
| Dionysen | Mur | STEWAG | 1944 |
| Ötz | | Westtiroler Kraftwerke | construction not resumed after the war |
| Obernberg | Inn | Innwerke | 1944 |

15. Maria Magdalena Koller, "Elektrizitätswirtschaft in Österreich 1938-1947. Von den Alpenelektrowerken zur Verbundgesellschaft" (Ph.D., Universität Graz, 1985).

16. Report of the (USACA) Special Commission on Industries under Trusteeship of Austrian Federal Government. Part V: Kaprun Project, Zell am See, 18 Octover 1946, by Ernest T. Owen (Colonel, FA, Chief, German External Assets Branch, RD&R Division) and James A. Garrison (Chief, RD&R Division), Folder Kaprun Trusteeship, Box 164, GEA, RG 260, NA.

17. Junius R Smith, Colonel QMC, Chief, Social Administration Div. to Director, Public Admin. USACA, 23 Sept. 1946, Folder Kaprun—General File, Box 164, GEA, RG 260, NA.

18. Franz Mathis, "Between Regulation and Laissez Faire: Austrian State Industries after World War II," *Contemporary Austrian Studies,* (1994): 79-90.

19. Request for an opinion by Ernest T. Owen, Col., Field Artillery, Chief, German Ext. Assets, RD&R, USACA to Legal Division USACA, 5 Nov. 1946, response of Edward A. Mag, Head, Counsel Branch, Legal Division USACA, 30. Nov. 1946, Folder Kaprun—General File, Box 164, German External Assets Branch (GEA), RG 260, National Archives (NA).

20. Hal D. Houston, Deputy head, German External Assets Branch, Memorandum to Chief, RD&R Division, 4 November 1947, Folder Kaprun—General File, Box 164, GEA, RG 260 , NA.

21. Figl to Leopold, Wien, 14. September 1946, Zl. 2718/1946 BKA-UNRRA, Archiv der Republik (AdR), Österreichisches Staatsarchiv (ÖStA), Vienna.

22. Georg Rigele, "Das Tauernkraftwerk Glockner-Kaprun—neue Forschungsergebnisse und offene Fragen," *Blätter für Technikgeschichte* 59 (Technisches Museum Wien, 1997), 55-94, 69.

23. The National Archives documents concerning *Kaprun* and the German assets of 1946-48. There some very good yet unpublished reports written by officers of the Economic Division and the Reparation, Deliveries, and Restitution Division (RD&R) and the Social Administration Division in the Headquarters of the U.S. Forces in Austria. I want to thank Professor Tweraser, who researched these files in the National Archives and sent me copies of them.
Folder Kaprun Waterrights, Folder Kaprun—General File, Folder Kaprun Trusteeship; Records of US Occupation Headquarters, WW II, USFA, USACA, German External Assets Branch (GEA), General records 1945-50, Box 164, RG 260, National Archives (NA)

24. James R. Rundell, Lt. Col. CE, Division Chief (Economic Division) to Assistent to Deputy Commissioner, 20 Nov 1946, Folder Kaprun—General File, Box 164, GEA, RG 260, NA.

25. Eduard Hüttler, 17 September 1946 (translation), Folder Kaprun Trusteeship, Box 164, GEA, RG 260, NA.

26. James R. Rundell, Lt. Col. CE, Division Chief (Economic Division) to Assistant to Deputy Commissioner, 20 Nov 1946, Folder Kaprun—General File, Box 164, GEA, RG 260, NA.

27. Ralph H. Tate, Brigadier General, to Dr. Peter Krauland, Minister for Property and Economic Planning, 10. Dec. 1946, Folder Kaprun—General File, Box 164, GEA, RG 260, NA.

28. James A. Barr, Deputy Chief, RD&R Division, USACA Section, to Dir. Public Economy, 2. Dec. 1946, Folder Kaprun—General File, Box 164, GEA, RG 260, NA.

29. Tate to Krauland, 10. Dec. 1946, Folder Kaprun—General File, Box 164, GEA, RG 260, NA.

30. Headquarters U. S. Forces in Austria, RD & D, APO 777, U. S. Army. Memorandum for the File, 27 September 1948, Subject: Kaprun by Hal D. Houston, Folder Kaprun—General File, Box 164, GEA, RG 260, NA.

31. Alfred Weskamp, "Glockner-Kaprun im kommerziellen Aspekt," in *Festschrift: Die Oberstufe des Tauernkraftwerkes Glockner-Kaprun*, ed. *Tauernkraftwerke AG*, J. Götz, and R. Emanovsky (Zell am See, September 1955), 29.

32. Knut Borchardt and Christoph Buchheim, "The Marshall Plan and Key Economic Sectors: A Microeconomic Perspective," in *The Marshall Plan and Germany*, ed. Charles S. Maier with Günter Bischof (New York: Berg, 1991), 410-451.

33. Ibid., 444.

34. Data in this chart was collected by Thomas Schabel, "Die Tauernkraftwerke AG auf dem nationalen und internationalen Kapitalmarkt," in *Vertrauen in die Kraft des Wassers: 40 Jahre Tauernkraftwerke* AG, ed. in Zusammenarbeit mit der Tauernkraftwerke AG (Wien: Verlag A. F. Koska, 1987), 125. The information regarding inflation is from Österreichisches Statistisches Zentralamt, ed., *Republik Österreich 1945-1995* (Wien: Kommissionsverlag der Österreichischen Staatsdruckerei, 1995), 97, 206.

35. Data in this chart was found in, ed., Österreichische Staatsdruckerei *Zehn Jahre ERP in Österreich: Wirtschaftshilfe im Dienste der Völkerverständigung*, (Wien: Österreichische Staatsdruckerei, 1958), 67; Alfred Weskamp, "Glockner-Kaprun im kommerziellen Aspekt," in *Festschrift: Die Oberstufe des Tauernkraftwerkes Glockner-Kaprun*, ed. *Tauernkraftwerke AG*, J. Götz, and R. Emanovsky (Zell am See, September 1955), 29; and Thomas Schabel, "Die Tauernkraftwerke AG auf dem nationalen und internationalen Kapitalmarkt," in *Vertrauen in die Kraft des Wassers: 40 Jahre Tauernkraftwerke* AG, ed. in Zusammenarbeit mit der Tauernkraftwerke AG (Wien: Verlag A. F. Koska, 1987), 126.

36. Data in this chart was found in Oskar Vas, *Wasserkraft und Elektrizitätswirtschaft in der Zweiten Republik* (Wien: Springer-Verlag, 1956), 8; ed., *Zehn Jahre ERP in Österreich: Wirtschaftshilfe im Dienste der Völkerverständigung*, ed. Österreichische Staatsdruckerei (Wien: Österreichische Staatsdruckerei, 1958), 64; and Wilhelm Weber, *Österreichs Energiewirtschaft: eine wirtschaftspolitische Untersuchung* (Wien: Springer-Verlag, 1957), 14, 19.

37. Egon G. Rothblum, letter to author, 7 January 1998.

38. Report by Sekt. Rat. Paurnfeind (BMVvB) about a meeting of 31 March 1952 with Froebel (MEC), Paurnfeind and Lang (BMVvB), Mitlacher (BKA-ZERP) and Hermann (Verbundges.), Zl. 708897-ERP/3/1952 in GrZl. 701124-ERP/3/1952.

39. Especially in the field of electricity, it is not easy to find specific documents, but thanks to the help of Herbert Vopava jun., an excellent archivist, I have seen many of them.

40. Until 1951, the U.S. ERP office in Austria was the "ECA Special Mission to Austria." After the transformation of the ECA into the MSA (Mutual Security Administration), the Mission to Austria was named "United States of America. Special Mission for Economic Cooperation," in the Austrian files quoted as "MEC."

41. Taucher to Waldbrunner, 2 February 1950, Zl. 501705-ERP/3/1950 in GrZl. 501639-ERP/3/1950, BKA-ZERP, AdR, ÖStA.

42. W. H. G. Giblin, Deputy Chief of the ECA Special Mission to Austria to Igler,10 May 1950, Zl. 511083-ERP/3/1950 bei GrZl. 501639-ERP/3/1950, BKA-ZERP, AdR, ÖStA.

43. Memo from the shop stewards to Waldbrunner, 4 August 1950, copy to BKA-ZERP/Taucher (16 August 1950), Zl. 515511-ERP/3/1950 in GrZl. 501639-ERP/3/1950, BKA-ZERP, AdR, ÖstA.
"The entire council of shop stewards of the *Tauernkraftwerke AG* and of the pool of construction companies in Kaprun, which unites the companies *Rella & Co.*, *Polensky & Zöllner*, *Hinteregger & Söhne* und *Union Baugesellschaft*, has been told by leading Austrian experts in the field of power generation that the

construction of the *Kaprun* upper stage is the most urgent task of the Austrian electricity program." (translation by the author)

44. Results of the elections for the council of shop stewards of the pool of the construction companies in Kaprun (*Arbeiterbetriebsrat der Arbeitsgemeinschaft-Kaprun*), votes/mandates:

| Election Date | SPÖ Socialists (center left social democrats) | KPÖ Communists | VdU "Independents" (dominated by former members of the NSDAP) | ÖVP Peoples Party (center right conservative party) |
|---|---|---|---|---|
| 10/12/1949 | 699/6 | 271/2 | 911/9 | 44/0 |
| 2/28/1950 | 534/8 | 150/2 | 248/4 | 34/0 |
| 10/24/1951 | 528/5 | 548/5 | 601/6 | |
| 6/18/1952 | 656/8 | 304/3 | 340/4 | 75/0 |

What the results of the election of 12 Feb 1950 tells us, is that during the winter season members of the SPÖ were less likely to be dismissed than others. Rigele, "Tauernkraftwerk," 74.

45. Bundeskanzleramt, Ministerratsdienst, Ministerratsprotokolle Figl II, Beschlußprotokoll Nr.214/1/d. This issue also was discussed at: Conference in the ECA Mission in Mr. Froebel´s office, 11 August 1950, report by Dipl.-Ing. Polaczek, Zl. 515362-ERP/3/1950 bei GrZl. 501639-ERP/3/1950, BKA-ZERP, AdR, ÖStA.

46. Conference in the ECA Mission, 12 June 1950, Zl. 510862-ERP/3/1950 bei GrZl. 501639-ERP/3/1950, BKA-ZERP, AdR, ÖStA.

47. Conference at the BKA-ZERP, Dr. Igler's office, Dr. Igler, Dr. Hauswirth, Hr. Mitlacher, and Mr. Worth, Mr. Hamilton, Mr. Fröbel, 28 June 1950, Zl. 512059-ERP/3/1950 bei GrZl. 501639-ERP/3/1950, BKA-ZERP, AdR, ÖStA.
("The three gentlemen of the ECA Mission vigorously attaked the Kaprun upper stage project ...")

48. Conference in the ECA Mission in Mr. Froebel´s office, 11 August 1950, report by Dipl.-Ing. Polaczek, Zl. 515362-ERP/3/1950 bei GrZl. 501639-ERP/3/1950, BKA-ZERP, AdR, ÖStA.

49. There were 110 KV transmission lines from Vorarlberg to the Tyrol and from the Tyrol to Salzburg, but their capacity was very limited. The Tyrol-Salzburg transmitted power from the *Gerlos* power plant eastwards and was, in a technical sense, part of the *Tauernkraftwerke*system. "Zur Inbetriebnahme der 220.000 Volt-Leitung Kaprun—Ernsthofen," in *Österreichische Zeitschrift für Elektrizitätswirtschaft*, Heft 1 (January 1950, 3. Jg.), 11.

50. Diagram of the Load Dispatcher BLV Nr. 334 "Production and Consumption in the Austrain *Verbundnetz* from 1948-1953, 15 February 1950, Zl. 505297-ERP/3/1950 bei GrZl. 501639-ERP/3/1950.

51. Diagram of the Load Dispatcher BLV Nr. 334 "Production and Consumption in the Austrain *Verbundnetz* from 1948-1953, 15 February 1950, Zl. 505297-ERP/3/1950 bei GrZl. 501639-ERP/3/1950.

52. Pohl, "Bayernwerk," 329-334.

53. Note regarding talks on 8 September 1950 in the office of Mr. Gardener, vice-president of the World Bank, Mr. Iliff, director of loans at the World Bank, Mr. Wheeler, technical expert of the World Bank, Austrian Minister of Finance Margarétha, Sekt.-Chef Dr. Hartenau, Notenbank-Präsident Rizzi, Direktor Stöger, Beilage I, MRP Nr. 218, Figl 2, 19. September 1950, BKA, AdR, ÖStA.

54. "Plans for the Development of the Austrian Power Industry," BKA-ZERP, Wien to the Austrian ERP-Office, Washington, 4 April 1950, Zl. 505944/50 bei GrZl. 500684-ERP/3/50, BKA-ZERP, AdR, ÖStA.

55. A low capacity 110 KV line went into operation in 1946, but this line was only of regional importance. Österreichische Elektrizitätswirtschafts-Aktiengesellschaft, ed., *Energie für unser Leben: 1947 bis 1997: 50 Jahre Verbund*, (Wien: Österreichische Elektrizitätswirtschafts-Aktiengesellschaft, 1997), 153-154.

56. Talks (*Aussprachen*) at ECA concerning *Kaprun* upper stage, 17 and 18 August 1950, Zl. 515362-ERP/3/1950 bei GrZl. 501639-ERP/3/1950, BKA-ZERP, AdR, ÖStA.

57. Michael J. Hogan, *The Marshall Plan: America, Britain, and the reconstruction of Western Europe*, 1947-1952 (New York: Cambridge Press), 139.

58. Egon G. Rothblum, letter to the author, 30 December 1997.

59. *Vorarlberger Illwerke AG* (Bregenz: Vorarlberger Illwerke AG 1994), 22.

60. Gene Sensenig, *Österreichisch-amerikanische Gewerkschaftsbeziehungen 1945 bis 1950* (Köln, 1987).

61. Conference at the ECA, 19 September 1950, Zl. 517751-ERP/3/1950 bei GrZl. 516613-ERP/3/1950, BKA-ZERP, AdR, ÖStA.

62. Final discussion of the Austrian program at the ECA Vienna, Mr. Giblin, Mr. Cook, Mr. Hansen, Mr. Fröbel, Mr. Arth, Mr. Hamilton for the ECA, M. Fürst, Dr. Lang for the BMVvB (Waldbrunner Ministry), Ing. Polaczek, Mr. Mitlacher for the ZERP, 21 September 1950, Zl. 517758-ERP/3/1950 bei GrZl. 516613-ERP/3/1950, BKA-ZERP, AdR, ÖStA.

63. Taucher to King, 3 October 1950, Zl. 518433/50 bei GrZl. 500684-ERP/3/50, BKA-ZERP, AdR, ÖStA.

64. Klaus Plitzner, "... zum Kaprun des Ländles! Von der repräsentativen Luxusenergie zum Spitzenstrom im europäischen Verbundnetz," in: *Technik, Politik, Identität*, ed. Klaus Plitzner (Stuttgart: GNT-Verlag, 1995), 53-93.

65. Conference at the MEC in Mr. Froebel´s office, 12 March 1952, report by Dipl.-Ing. Polaczek, Zl. 705643-ERP/3/1952 bei GrŻl. 701124-ERP/3/1952, BKA-ZERP, AdR, ÖStA.

# "Conquering the Foreigner": The Marshall Plan and the Revival of Postwar Austrian Tourism*

*Günter Bischof*

"In return for offering services and the beauties of our country, Austria will receive highly-valued foreign currency."[1]

"Austria had always had a trade deficit and that prior to World War II this deficit was largely made up by income from the tourist trade and from invisibles such as income for investments in Czechoslovakia."[2]

---

* This paper has profited from the support of many people. A one-month stay as "guest scholar" at the *Institut für die Wissenschaften vom Menschen* in Vienna allowed for excellent working conditions for immersion in Austrian tourism history and the newly opened Marshall Plan files in the Austrian State Archives. At the *Staatsarchiv* the kind advice and help of Herbert Vopava was invaluable in introducing me to the vast records of the Marshall Plan in Austria in general and the tourist section in the Ministry of Trade and Reconstruction in particular. This paper was written while I was a guest professor during the spring semester of 1998 at the History Department of the University of Salzburg, in exchange with Professor Reinhold Wagnleitner, who taught at the University of New Orleans. Our gratitude goes to our chairmen Josef Ehmer and Joe Louis Caldwell respectively who supported the idea of academic exchange against all bureaucratic odds. Without the enthusiastic help of Marianne Dirnhammer in Salzburg, this paper could not have been written. She generated my tables and graphs, fixed numerous computer problems, and was very helpful in tracking down some obscure sources. In Salzburg Robert Hoffmann and Christian Dirninger helped as well. Kurt Tweraser and Georg Rigele were extremely kind in sharing Marshall Plan documents from the National Archives (RG 469) and from the *Staatsarchiv* with me. I also profited from the advice of Dieter Stiefel, Hans Seidel, and Wilhelm Kohler. Moreover, Franz Mathis gave a sound critique of the original paper presented in New Orleans.

## Introduction

In general histories of postwar Austrian economic reconstruction, it often is assumed as an article of faith that investment funds generated through the counterpart funds of the European Recovery Program (ERP) have been crucial for the recovery of Austrian industry without presenting much empirical microeconomic evidence for the subsectors.[3] In a similar fashion, Marshall Plan funds are frequently only mentioned in passing in general histories of postwar reconstruction of Austrian tourism[4] on the national or state (*Land*) level.[5] As is the case with UFOs or the tooth fairy, people attach mythical qualities to the reconstructive powers of Marshall Plan funding without caring to know more about the exact nature of the beast. In many recent general histories[6] and in the public memory,[7] the impact of the Marshall Plan increasingly tends to be forgotten or ignored, and it is high time that the memory of the European Recovery Program be salvaged in the Austrian public mind at a time when public opinion increasingly turns anti-American.

It is the thesis of this paper that the *take-off* towards broad-based Austrian prosperity after World War II—in which tourism played a major role—would not have occurred to the same degree or with such rapid speed were it not for the Marshall Plan. Marshall funds made a decisive contribution to the postwar Austrian economic miracle, which in many ways was more impressive than the German one. While the importance of ERP counterpart investments in Austrian industry (especially the public state-owned sector) is understood by researchers, their share in the recovery of postwar tourism has not been a subject of research since the contemporaries of the Marshall Plan acknowledged it in the 1950s.[8] This is surprising, given that tourism has become Austria's most important industry and only a few tourist islands in the Caribbean and the Pacific and Indian Oceans have higher per capita incomes from tourism than Austria. Among advanced Western industrial nations, Austria may well be "the world champion of tourism" and in Europe it ranks on the top with Switzerland in tourist intensity (measured in visitor nights per inhabitant).[9] The Marshall Plan generously financed both investments in the *rebuilding* and *modernization* of hotels, spas, cable cars and ski lifts, and streets and transportation facilities between 1950 and 1955. After the revolving counterpart funds were transferred to the Austrian government in 1962, the *ERP-Fonds* in the 1960s and 1970s methodically spread the U.S. induced wealth among tourist establishments in rural areas and thus provided a major modernization incentive in some of Austria's most backward areas.[10] The overall share of ERP funds in Austrian investment funds may have become progressively less important, but they still exist and benefit the Austrian economy.[11]

ERP investments in the tourist industry had only one goal: to rebuild the existing Austrian tourist industry to attract foreign guests and *produce sufficient foreign currency* (the magical word was "*Devisenrentabilität*") to help correct the negative Austrian balance of payments.[12] Austrian officials took the year 1937 as their base year and repeated like a mantra that 6.8 million overnight stays in 1937 had produced öS 250 million in foreign currency, which then had made up the deficit in the negative balance of payments.[13]

Even before ERP officials as to directed Austrian tourist officials how to spend the ERP counterpart funds in rebuilding and modernizing existing tourist establishments, Austrian tourist officials had very similar goals. The stipulations of the American ECA officials in Vienna only strengthened the backbone of the central authorities in Vienna against the constant assault by *Länder* tourist officials to favor their respective state projects or transfer the funds directly to them for allocation. In this context, the recent opening of the tourism files of the Ministry of Trade and Reconstruction in the Vienna State Archives is a classical case study of *unresolved conflicts in Austrian federalism.* The Austrian constitution of 1920/1929, revived in 1945, provided that tourism be a preserve ("*Kompetenz*") of the *Länder*, while the central authorities in Vienna and the powerful chamber organizations were reponsible for all matters of economic reconstruction and general economic development. At a time when almost half of the hotel assets of the Austrian tourist industry had to cope with war and then occupation related damages, the built-in constitutional conflict over tourism was bound to become an explosive "states rights" issue. This dilemma in unresolved federalism as well as the fierce struggle and feeding frenzy for ERP investments funds by the state tourist organizations may well be the most important revelation characteristic of these newly opened files.

The lion's share, almost two-thirds of ERP counterpart funds invested in Austrian tourism between 1950 and 1955, went to the three Western Austrian states of Vorarlberg, Tyrol, and Salzburg (12.5 percent, 29.6 percent, and 19.5 percent respectively). These states had the most intact establishments for reviving the foreign tourist trade and thus earn foreign currency. With the French and Americans as occupiers, they also had the least oppressive occupation regimes. If we include the Upper Austria Lake District, Styria and Carinthia, 86.7 percent of ERP funds directed towards tourism went to the Western zones until the end of 1955; Soviet-occupied Vienna and Lower Austria and Burgenland got the measly rest (see Table and Graph 1 in appendix).[14] Given this concentration of ERP funds channelled into the three westernmost states of Austria, this essay focuses on the revival of tourism in Vorarlberg, Tyrol, and Salzburg, which together constitute the **locomotive** for the reconstruction of the Austrian tourist industry.

Still caught up in the martial mentality of World War II, the *Wehrmacht* veteran and economic historian Alois Brusatti summarizes the objective of Austrian tourism in the 1950s as "conquering" the foreigners, especially the Germans.[15] Indeed, postwar Austrian tourism only began to recover and take off, after the Western occupation powers dropped their visa restrictions for German tourists coming to Austria in 1951. One observer has put it this way: "At the beginning of the take-off of postwar Austrian tourism is the car—to be precise the VWbug—which carried the German guests to the back valleys and remote high mountain farms" ("*entlegenste Alm*").[16] The success story of postwar Austrian tourism was closely related to attracting German mass tourism, slowly transforming homely Austrian *Gasthäuser,* catering to local peasant populations, into big hotels attracting an international clientele. *Most often ERP funds were the financial engine driving this transformation of reconstruction from war related damages and then modernization to be internationally competitive*. The story of postwar Austrian tourism indeed must begin in the ruins left by World War II and the repercussions of the war on the postwar world. The occupation regimes seized the finest hotels surviving from the war and crowded them with its soldiers and thousands of refugees/Displaced Persons (DPs) stranded in Austria. These refugee "foreigners" were dislocated by the war and landed in Austria as unwelcome "tourists," fueling the traditional Austrian xenophobia. It becomes clear from these files that the story of postwar Austrian tourism must also address the anthropology of the Austrian "*Feindbild*" of foreigners ("*Fremde*"). At the end of the World War II, Austria was flooded with unwelcomed foreign refugees and Displaced persons (DPs). After the departure of most of them, the Austrians had to adapt to the growing presence of welcome "*Fremde*" as tourists and cash cows for the Austrian economy. Tourism officials had to constantly remind them to be *hospitable* since hospitality, they argued, was one of Austria's greatest assets as a tourist destination. An anthropologist of tourism has recently suggested that the *relationship between war and the genesis of modern mass tourism* needs to be systematically explored.[17] Indeed, Austria provides a fascinating case study for such a systematic exploration as few tourist industries in the world were more drastically impacted by World War II than Austria's.

## The War's Impact: Difficult Beginnings, 1945-46

During World War II, the *Ostmark* experienced German mass tourism on a huge scale. In Salzburg and the Salzkammergut, traditional guests such as the sophisticated Jews from Vienna and the Sudeten Germans from Czechoslovakia no longer came after the Anschluß. Jewish owned hotels were aryanized. Symptomatic of attitudes in Austria was the bad rhyme of the Viennese *Kleines Volksblatt* (22 June 1938): "*Der Alpenländler kann befreit / nach Salzburg übersiedeln, / ein Jodler grüßt die neue Zeit / als Abschied von den Jiddeln.*" Masses of German "social tourists" crowded into the Danube and Alpine *Gaue* after the Anschluß first and foremost to buy consumer products no longer available in the *Altreich*. The "*Kraft durch Freude*", "*Volkswohlfahrt*" and "*Hitler Jugend*" organized cheap tours to the picturesque alpine valleys of Austria, while the German nobility crowded the watering holes and fine hotel establishments of Salzburg. The Salzburg festival was conducted in a less eliteist manner which was associated with the "Jewish" influence of the 1920s and 1930s, and continued as a more folksy "German" event for most of the war. During the summer of 1939, before the war started, Salzburg lacked tourist beds to accomodate everyone. The *Wehrmacht* seized nine of the best hotels in the city of Salzburg to accomodate its officials. Almost 2.5 million overnight stays were registerd in Salzburg (almost 700,000 more than in 1937), and in 1940-41, more than 5 million were registered in the Tyrol (2.3 million in 1937). With the changing situation on the frontlines, during 1943 the available hotel space was increasingly set aside for soldiers recuperating from their injuries, for bomb refugees from the *Altreich*, and for forced laborers from all over Europe. Roughly 40,000 wounded soldiers alone crowded the spas of Badgastein every year. The *Reichsgau* Salzburg was not bombed until October 1944 and transmuted into the "*Lazarettgau*." By 1944 half a million foreigners spent more than 3 million overnight stays in Salzburg. Such enforced wartime tourism in the Alps only collapsed in the final months of the war, when Austria was flooded with 1.5 million refugees from all over Europe and Nazi bigwigs tried to save their skins and hide out in the Austrian lake district, where they had often vacationed during the war.[18] We can assume that many of these involuntary and "cheap" wartime tourists returned with fond memories after the war as well-to-do middle class guests, similar to American veterans of the war who returned to Normandy, Bastogne, and Remagen to relive the memory of their wartime campaigns.[19]

Mass tourism boomed in the *Ostmark* while Allied bombers and the fighting on Austrian soil wreaked havoc and destruction, especially in the cities. Thousands of houses, hotels, roads, bridges, railroad tracks, and business establishments, among other things, were levelled by Allied bombs or severely damaged, not to mention the thousands of bomb victims who died in the rubble. The bombing war hit the *Ostmark* relatively late in the fall of 1943, and hit Tyrol, Salzburg, and Vorarlberg even later in 1944. Yet bombers managed to rain such numbers of bombs on the Austrian infrastructure as to knock it out in a short time.[20] In 1946, a first assessment of the war-related destruction of the Austrian hotel industry figured that among 4,400 hotels a mere 309 had not suffered any damage. Approximately 70 percent of the hotel inventories (furniture, plates, glasses, textiles, and so on) had been destroyed. The Austrian spa industry totaled their war-related losses at almost öS 120 million.

Soon after the war was over, the still intact hotels were seized by the new occupiers. After the Nazis had seized the best hotels for their personnel during the war, the four postwar occupiers took over 50 percent of the Austrian hotels after the war to house their occupation establishments and also the Displaced Persons. It seems that hotel owners felt victimized by both occupation regimes. While such facile collation of the two occupation regimes was a typical Austrian "defense strategy," we should not forget that many of the hotel owners too had eagerly supported the Nazi cause and profitted from the wartime tourist boom.[21]

When the war ended, the putative "*Alpenfestung*," Austria, in fact, turned out to be a desperate island where millions of involuntary "*Fremde*" were stranded. In May 1945, 6 million native Austrians faced 3.7 million foreigners in their midst—the flotsam and jetsam of war. Next to 1.5 million *Wehrmacht* soldiers and their allies stranded in Austria, the country was occupied by another half million of Allied forces and some 1.7 million foreign civilian DPs. These "involuntary tourists" double- and triple-occupied every available guest bed. Yet the vast majority suffered in primitive and makeshift POW, internment and DP camps. By the end of 1945, one million DPs still remaind in Austria (see Table and Graph 2 in appendix). Many of them were the ethnic Germans expelled from Eastern Europe who were no longer repatriable. The occupation powers forced the Austrian government to take care of all DPs, including the Jewish survivors of the Holocaust who lived largely in the U.S. zone and were at times better fed than the native Austrian population. Some lived in hotels seized by the occupation powers and directly replaced the recuperating German soldiers in famous spa towns such as Badgastein where eight hotels had been seized. Such "privileges"or Jewish DPs triggered the old steretypes and scapegoating mechanisms among Austrians. Jews became the quintessential "*Fremde*" and served as symbols for all unwelcomed "foreign" DPs.[22] Seen from this perspective, the revival of postwar Austrian *Fremdenverkehr* suffered from a war-related Austrian xenophobia about an overload of foreigners ending up in the small Austrian rescue boat involuntarily and almost sinking it. The public perception of DPs was one of criminals fueling the black market and lazy and spoiled *Mitesser* favored by the occupation powers.[23] Most of the "foreigners", then, stranded by the war in Austria, were not recreational tourists and constituted a severe burden to the Austrian government with its numerous economic difficulties.

While most of the unwelcomed foreign DPs were eventually repatriated and the ethnic Germans integrated, for the benefit of tourism the foreigner had to be *reinvented as cash cow*—to be appreciated and milked. Austria had elected a government, and in the Second Control Agreement of June 1946, the Allied powers returned considerable sovereign rights back to this Figl Government—tourist affairs implicitly among them. The occupation establishment became routine during 1946/47, and even the emerging Cold War did not stop tourists from considering Austria as a possible destination since the Cold War raged in the domestic politics of most of Western Europe. First the infrastructure had to be reconstructed for a revival of tourism. Preconditions were improving border crossings for potential tourists, allowing for easier transportation, making a sufficient number of hotels available, and providing basic food rations for tourists.

In the fall of 1946, an *institutional framework* was set up to rebuild the tourism industry. The tourist section of the Ministry of Trade and Reconstruction became the focal point for coordinating all efforts in the revival of Austrian tourism. Villages and cities (local *Fremdenverkehrsvereine*) and the *Länder* had already begun to rebuild the traditional grass roots tourist organizations. Along with this reorganization came the revival of "states rights" in tourism—the provinces' traditional suspicions of losing their prerogatives to the centralizing control of Vienna. Trade and Reconstruction Minister Eduard Heinl appointed tourism expert Harald Langer-Hansel as powerful *Sektionsrat* in Division V of his Ministry to direct the efforts of rebuilding the tourism industry. In1945/46 when he had worked on tourism affairs for the American Economics Division at the Allied Council, Langer-Hansel's first goal was to secure a special aid program of $ 10 million from the American Economics Division for the reconstruction of Austrian tourism. Meeting regularly with some state tourism representatives such as the formidable Salzburg Tourism Director Hofmann-Montanus in Vienna and starting to commmunicate with state tourism organizations, Langer-Hansel established the financial needs of the industry and earmarked money for hotel repairs, renewal of interior decorations and inventory, rebuilding of the transportation infrastructure (such as comfortable railroad cars), as well as launching a marketing campaign in Western Europe and North America. He assessed the initial start-up costs for modernizing Austrian hotels to be at least öS 100 million. Lists of 300 hotels (fifty-three in Salzburg, 53 in the Tyrol, twenty-five in Vorarlberg) with a total of 30,000 beds were selected by the respective state governments to benefit from these prospective U.S. funds. In the individual states, the difficult struggle for hotel owners to get on these lists had started as well. On top of this, dicussions were held with owners from the domestic furniture, porcelain, glass, and textile industries to secure the necessary supplies for modernizing interiors, and with the Food Ministry for conceding extra allowances for foreign tourists venturing into Austria. The demand for improved transport facilities was constant. Without adequate roads and railroad services, tourists would not physically reach their destinations.[24]

The tenor among tourism officials at this early stage of reorganization was one that would ring familiar throughout the occupation decade: "the Austrian government must do everything in its might to utilize tourism for earning foreign currency for the country."

A general revival of tourism was anticipated in 1947 and Austria ought to "seize the opportunity to earn millions of dollars and foreign currency, since the Americans had saved up a lot of money during the war and many of them had encountered Europe and Austria (during the war) and were expected to return." In the end, the Finance Ministry did not support these proposals for separate U.S. aid to the tourist industry, fearing that it might compete with the much larger Austrian aid package of $ 200 million proposed to Washington. The fierce competition among the various industries for securing a maximum of U.S. aid for their specific needs had also started in the fall of 1946.[25]

Tourism did not receive the vital U.S. aid for a quick reconstruction program which it so badly needed and for which it had hoped. Yet these discussions in the fall of 1946 were not for naught. They mark the beginning of *setting the crucial agenda* for the revival of Austrian tourism needs, programs, and policy priorities.[26] They also marked the beginning of mounting pressure on the occupation powers to release the seized hotels. Austrian tourism could not be revived while the occupation personnel set aside the plushest hotels for their own comfort and often underutilized these hotels.[27] In the process of selecting the hotels for the initial *tranche* of investment credits, the Viennese authorities learned the process of consulting with the state governments and vice versa. Such a *cooperative approach* would allow for the formation of a formidable ÖVP-dominated tourist lobby by 1949, which succeeded in securing the first allocation of ERP counterpart funds. Still, the stubborn jealousies and suspicions among states that their neighbor might receive preferential treatment were never entirely overcome. It became clear early on that the western and southern states had experienced less damage and offered a more advanced tourism infrastructure. They had a better chance to attract foreign tourists and therefore had to be given highest priority for repairing and modernizing their hotel space.[28]

Moreover, the traditional top resorts such as the Arlberg region of Lech/Zürs/St. Christoph/St. Anton, Kitzbühel, and the Gastein valley held out the prospect of building up winter seasons for international skiers. Even before Marshall funds became available, the most important decision had been been made. Given the threatening Soviet occupation regime and the inability to attract tourists to Vienna and the Soviet zone, tourism would be revived first in the French and American zones and to a lesser degree in the British zone. The *westward movement of lead sectors in the Austrian economy* (especially war-related heavy industry)—already started during the war and accelerated after the war—also applied to the tourist industry and would come to characterize the postwar Austrian economy. Next to Nazi investments in Western Austria, Marshall funds were the crucial engine for this *Westverschiebung*. Fully 81 percent of ERP funds were invested in the Western zones, only 19 percent in the Soviet zone and Vienna (see Graph and Table 3 in the appendix).[29]

While establishing priorities for rebuilding Austrian tourism in the fall of 1946, a highly complex model for offering wholesale tourist packages for reviving tourism in 1947 was conceived. It would bring, for the first time after the war, larger numbers of foreigners to Austria, who would come out of their own volition for recreational purposes. The "*Ausländer-Hotelaktion*" emerged as part of Langer-Hansel's planning effort for the aborted $ 10 million U.S. aid package. He demanded that foreign tourists receive twice the calory level of the daily Austrian rations (at the time, this would have been a 2,400 calories; in fact, 4,600 calories were deemed necessary for the comfort of foreign tourists). Foreign tourists had to advance the currency by purchasing coupons in travel offices which gave the few selected Austrian hotels involved the cash to buy the food abroad.[30] The Austrian National Bank opened a special account for these tourist transactions and advanced $ 10,000 for food imports for the 1946/47 "*Winteraktion*" in Badgastein. Three hotels with 195 beds were handpicked in Badgastein. The three Western occupation powers would hand foreign tourists the necessary military permits to come to Austria.[31] The French set aside 400 of its occupied rooms for tourists from England, Belgium, and Switzerland and even advanced the food and drinks to the hotels. The French also took care of the military permits. Traffic problems did not allow hotels in the British zone to participate in this program.[32]

Such complex procedures surely did not make for a mass invasion of tourists. While no numbers are available for 1946/47, in the winter of 1947/48 foreign tourists spent 11,406 nights in Austrian hotels. In the summer of 1948, a "tourist card", to be purchased in Austrian representations abroad, made it much easier to enter the country, and 77,311 nights booked were the result. In the winter of 1948/49, there were 174,486 nightly bookings. When the Western powers returned the legal control of its borders to the Austrian government by the beginning of 1949, foreign tourists entered Austria with even fewer hassles, and 615,678 nights were booked in the summer of 1949, fifty-five times as many as only two years earlier.[33] This dramatic increase of foreign tourism in 1949 was the result of both easier border crossings into four-power occupied Austria and the easing of the desperate food situation as a result of Marshall aid. As severe import restrictions for food fell for the tourist industry, hungry Austrians no longer jealously watched foreign tourists enjoying better rations, which in 1947 had even sparked food riots. Everyone's daily lives improved; thus, foreigners were no longer viewed so suspiciously as unwanted "*Mitesser*" by the natives, particularly as their great value as foreign currency importers started to show.

## The Great Planning Debate: Origins of Marshall Aid for Austrian Tourism

In 1949, the tourist industry also began to clamor vociferously for ERP funds to rebuild and modernize its infrastructure after it had been left out in the initial U.S. aid programs and ERP allotments which secured the physical survival of the population and benefited state-owned industries. This was the result of the Austrian economic planning machinery's location in the Ministry of Property Control and Economic Planning (*Vermögenssicherung und Wirtschaftplanung*) under Minister Peter Krauland, who seems to have thrived on controversy. Upon strong Socialist pressure to start planning for the huge heavy industrial sector of former "German assets" nationalized in 1946, Krauland appointed the vigorous young economist Margarethe Ottillinger to direct and coordinate Austrian economic planning in August of 1947. This institutionalization of economic planning coincided with rather than was the result of the announcement and the initial planning phase of the Marshall Plan. Eight divisions and thirty working groups were formed in the course of 1947/48 to initiate detailed "core plans" for all subsectors of the economy. A central planning unit was supposed to coordinate the overall plan (*Konstitutionsplan*) out of the various sectoral core plans. Until the actual implementation and initiation of the European Recover Program by June 1948, these Austrian planning exercises were academic since investment funds were lacking.[34]

These prospects changed rapidly with the arrival of Marshall funds. When prospects of Marshall aid became realistic, all economic sectors handed the Ministry of Economic Planning lists of their most desirable import needs. Krauland then forwarded to the central

Austrian ERP Office in the Federal Chancellery his priority list, which in turn forwarded it to the Central European Office of the "European Cooperation Administration" (ECA) in Paris. In fact, only the iron and steel, electricity, and coal and metals industries had managed to finish their respective "core plans," which were circulated and accepted by the Krauland Ministry. This gave these largely state-owned industrial sectors a decisive advantage in securing the lion's share of ERP counterpart funds over the next four years. Some of the other economic sectors finished their plans by 1949, which came too late for initial ERP allocations.[35]

The tourist industry is a case study of belated planning. In Ottillinger's initial planning framework, tourism was lumped together with traffic, trade, and small industry in Division XII.[36] Little seems to have happened in this unit. Only the prospect of actual ERP investments funds stirred the tourist industry into motion in the first half of 1948, when a "National Working Committee for Tourism" was formed. A subcommittee (*Beschaffungsausschuß*) on securing special contingents of textiles, cutlery, glass, and porcelain for the badly depleted hotels had already been meeting in April and May. Another committee had been planning for the first conference. The crucially important *Bundesarbeitsausschuß für Fremdenverkehr* gathered for its first meeting on 1 June 1948 at the Trade Ministry in Vienna. Eugen Lanske and Harald Langer-Hansel, the Ministry's top tourism officials, chaired this important first meeting and directed and coordinated the discussions and outcomes. The 1946 lessons of *coordinated* planning effort had been learned well. The decentralization of Austrian tourism management aided by the *federal* constitution were highly visible in the composition of the delegates. Representatives from the all the federal Ministries involved in tourism affairs met with delegates from each of the nine *Länder*. The minutes of these meetings demonstrate that the Trade Ministry experts were the *Vordenker* and coordinators, but the *Länder* delegates had considerable input as well.[37] A quick summary of the detailed discussions must suffice here.

The overall goal of the *Bundesausschuß* meetings in 1948 was clear and straightforward: Austrian tourism had to coordinate its planning efforts and decide on priorities for a "core plan" to become part and parcel of the Austrian "constitution plan" and thus start benefitting from the anticipated embarrassment of riches of ERP funding. But systematic planning was needed to make the best use of scarce investment funds. During the first meeting, the representative from the Krauland Ministry, Fichtenthal explained the coordinated planning startegy and informed the delegates that tourism had be left out in the initial ERP allocations because they had not presented any detailed investement plans and priorities. Langer-Hansel explained that the priorities in the reconstruction of Austrian tourism had been identified for a while. First, the buildings still intact needed to replace and modernize the necessary inventories to resume business (*Instandsetzung*). The tourist destinations with the most likely high frequencies of foreign tourists should receive top priority. Second, only those damaged buildings which promised to attract foreigners (*Wiederaufbau*) should be rebuilt right away. But reconstruction of tourist buildings should be given the same priority as reconstruction of housing for the native population. Third, new construction (*Neubau*) should only occur in those rare cases were new foreign tourists could be attracted. All reconstruction, however, had to occur under the aegis of *modernization*, especially of baths, toilets, and kitchens. It was pointed out that spas had suffered egregiously from the heavy use and damage by the wartime and postwar occupation powers. Rebuilding of all transport facilities was given high priority. Hoffmann-Montanus stressed the importance of fostering cultural programs and festivals and of improving the training of tourist personnel, which had to be given high priority.[38]

In the end, the various methods of financing these goals were discussed. Langer-Hansel stressed that overall investment funds of öS 270 million were needed. Hotel owners had no capital for self-financing, and the government offered no tax cuts or investment credits. Austrian banks were tight with investment credits as well, and the federal government had no funds for establishing a special tourism finance fund. Moreover, in these politically uncertain times, no foreign investors were available. A special trust company for investments in hotels had already been established (*Hoteltreuhand*) for distributing U.S. relief of ERP counterpart funds. The outcome of the first meeting of the *Bundesausschuß* was that the reconstruction of Austrian tourism was entirely dependent on the allocation of ERP funds to get the initial investment program for repairs and modernization going. The catch was that the Economic Planning Ministry refused to allocate any funds to tourism without a detailed "core plan."[39]

The tourist section of the Trade Ministry thus was prompted to catch up with the much more advanced planning of the state industries. In 1948/49, a tourist core plan became the top priority. In mid-July

1948, Langer-Hansel sent all ministries involved and the planning committees on the state level his "planning directive" for a systematic tourist plan. His detailed outline envisioned investments needs of $ 75 million for the tourist industry (1948-52). Nine different planning subsections were established to fine-tune tourism's exact needs for the overall core plan (the hospitality, spa, transport, marketing, culture and sports industries being the most important ones).[40] By October 1948, Langer-Hansel sent out the agenda for the second meeting of the *Bundesarbeitsausschuß* with the "reconstruction program for Austrian tourism" and the establishment of permanent sectoral subcommittees being the top priorities.[41]

The Federal Working Committe gathered for its second meeting on 20 October 1948 in Vienna. The new Minister of Trade, Ernst Kolb of the ÖVP (a conservative administration expert from Vorarlberg), opened the gathering. In his keynote address, he urged the state representatives to *cooperate* with the Viennese ministerial and chamber authorities to overcome the constitutional "*Kompetenzkonflikt*" inherent in the organization of Austrian tourism. Kolb also addressed hidebound Austrian xenophobia and modernization fear in rural areas by telling the story of the Tyrolean innkeeper Johann Tobias Haid who opened the Ötztal valley to tourism in the nineteenth century. The "reactionary Ötztaler" spit in his face and gravely maligned him for opening up their beautiful Alpine valley to the world ("*diesen schönen Teil der Weltöffentlichkeit preisgeben wolle*"). The natives feared that decline of local morals and mores ("*die Zerrüttung der Sitten*") would accompy the advent of tourism. Such anti-modernist skepticism was typical, Kolb reminded his audience of tourism officials, but had always been premature, since tourism had turned out to be the *great engine of modernization* for the most backward alpine valleys of Austria. He stressed that "tourism was the ramrod" ("*Bahnbrecher*") in opening up hidebound villages to modernization by means of tranportation (roads, railroads, cable cars). Kolb charged the meeting to concentrate on pointing out the benefits ("*Nutzen*") of tourism for local populations and concluded about Austrian ambivalence vis-à-vis foreigners: "*Wenn uns die Fremden auch vielleicht im ersten Jahr noch wirklich Fremde sind, so sollen sie doch in der Zukunft Freunde werden.*"[42] Austrians needed to appreciate foreigners as friends and learn hospitality so they could profit from them.

Langer-Hansel pointed out that the American Marshall planners had been stressing the importance of tourism as a crucial factor in the reconstruction of the European economy. Austrian tourism needed to stay competitive with the other European countries and therefore had to participate vigorously in all the Paris Marshall Plan organizations dealing with tourism affairs. More importantly, this meeting had to make sure that the great economic importance of tourism be recognized by the other sectors of the Austrian economy to gain high priority status in allocation of investment funds. Such funds, for the time being however, were only available through Marshall funds. He demanded that tourism receive an annual allocation of öS 80 million (öS 300 million altogether) in ERP funding and stressed that many other economic sectors (such as transportation) would also profit from the revival of tourism. While Langer-Hansel demanded firm figures from the state representatives regarding their investment needs, akin to the first responses of European nations regarding their needs for Marshall funds, these parochial state representatives presented shopping lists. Burgenland demanded better bus transport to allow the Viennese to visit them; Upper and Lower Austria, Tyrol, and Vorarlberg requested money for transportation improvements and particularly ski lifts; Salzburg stressed the revival of cultural events and training opportunities for tourism personnel; and so it went. Each state single-mindedly forwarded its demands, and there was no indication that what was desperately needed was a *concerted national program* that would establish their needs as an industry vis-à-vis the other Austrian economic sectors. Eleven subcommittees were appointed to help overcome these regional priorities by arriving at a basic agreement about tourism's basic needs.[43] It seems that, in spite of the admonishments from the central Viennese authorities to cooperate in order to succeed vis-à-vis the other industries in the fierce competition for ERP funds, state officials jealously guarded their states' individual needs. These traditional "states rights" in tourism affairs ignored Minister Kolb's working motto for the conference: "*Über die Kompetenzen hinaus zur Arbeit.*"

The Tourism Section in the Trade Ministry had to enforce the cooperative spirit towards a core plan for tourism by charging the subcommittees with presenting firm plans for the subsectors, since the spa industry, for example, shared common difficulties throughout Austria. The Trade Ministry held out the hope that the industry might receive ERP funds before 1949 was over.[44] The Viennese ministerial bureaucrats and the state representatives met in the famous spa town of Bad Gastein on 1 and 2 June 1949. It might have been the venue outside of Vienna amidst the spectacular Salzburg mountain scenery, or or it might have been the serious threat from the Economic Planning Ministry in Vienna not to include tourism in the 1949 ERP investment program due to its planning lag, which marshalled the delegates towards the cooperative spirit Kolb had been demanding all along. The lion's share of the work was accomplished in the twelve subcommittees which reported to the plenary session on 2 June. In these subcommittees, the various tourism sectors at last came to realize that their common problems needed to be addressed and coordinated across Austria to get on the priority list of ERP funding.

The working group on spas was a case in point. Next to its problems with occupation related damages, the spa group gingerly raised the basic problem *of economic development versus preservation of the environment*—the perennial challenge to postwar Austrian tourism. How could the industrialization of alpine valleys such as the Gasteinertal due to the location of industrial plants and vast hydroelectric power projects be stopped? The spa officials demanded that pristine alpine valleys—tourism's greatest asset—must not become the victim of evironmental degradation by the rapidly expanding and powerful electric utility industry.[45] A few weeks later, the local priest of Dorfgastein complained to the Trade Ministry about such industrialization and its social consequences. The priest's reason against locating an industrial glass plant in his village was that it would bring industrial jobs to the village. His motives were not environmental, but both anti-modernist (in the sense Minister Kolb had mentioned in the Ötzal parable quoted above) and anti-socialist (at the time probably also anti-communist). He did not want to see factory workers settle down in his blessed valley ("*Es wäre doch ewig schade, wenn man in dieses gottgesegnete Tal Fabrikarbeiter und Fabrikarbeiterinnen ansiedeln würde.*")[46] The priest of Badgastein had already bitterly complained to his superiors how an influx of thousands of tourists and 4,000 hotel workers was destroying the social fabric and the moral values of the old family and village structure and how American "materialism and mammonism" was infecting the natives.[47] In a brilliant essay about "economic growth without industrialisation" the historian Ernst Hanisch has shown that local churches for along time had been in the vanguard of opposing tourism as a result of the hidebound clergy's anti-modernist fears about social change in the traditional and small alpine communities. The village priests usually represented the vanguard of people's anxieties about modern industrial development and technological civilization.[48]

The technocrats needed to best such attacks on the side effects of electrification/industrialization. The Transportation Ministry parried the spas resolution against hydroelectric projects in the high Alps with the perennial "*benefits of modernization*" argument. Not only were damages to nature minimal as a result of various hydroelectric energy projects, more often they even improved ("*belebt und verschönert*") the environment! Moreover, such energy projects and electrification were the basis for improving the entire economy from which tourism profitted more than anyone by way of the electrification of the railroads and the various lift projects. The technocrats in the Transport Ministry concluded: "*manche schwer zugänglichen Hochalpentäler werden durch die für die Energiebauten notwendigen Strassen Seilbahnen usw. dem Fremdenverkehr erst erschlossen.*"[49] This was the same *modernizing* argument Minister of Trade Kolb had himself used to praise the benefits of tourism for the backward alpine valleys, so tourism officials had no way of challenging it.

Both in the subcommittees on culture and tourism promotion, basic aspects of the lack of hospitality by the native population were adressed. Gasperschitz, the chairman of the tourism promotion working group and president of the Upper Austrian organization, reminded committee members in his keynote address that ERP investment funds could only go so far in promoting tourism. Reorganization of individual, local, and state tourism promotion came first. *Fremdenverkehrsförderung* had to be professionalized unter the auspices of better service—"*Dienst am Kunden, am fremden Gast.*" A modern culture and promotion of tourism had to start at the grassroots level. Local tourist organizations were the breeding ground of a broadly based organization (*Verkehrsvereine* als "*Keimzellen ... einer leistungsfähigen Organistion der Fremdenverkehrspflege*"). Moreover, solid service in hotels and pensions was the best tourism promotion ("*Ein gut geführtes Haus ist und bleibt die beste Fremdenverkehrsförderung*"). Every village needed promotion brochures. But the times had passed when promotion materials from the Nazi era could be recycled by merely covering over the Nazi symbols! Such insensitivity would surely produce serious complaints abroad. Gasperschitz concluded that modern professional tourist promotion could no longer solely rely on local "busy-bodies and old-age pensioners" ("*Die Zeit ist längst vorüber, wo man Fremdenverkehrspflege als Liebhaberei von*

*Vereinsmeiern und bastelnden Pensionisten betrieb.*")[50] Hofmann-Montanus, the outspoken tourist director of Salzburg and chair of the culture subcommittee, also noted that the natives' friendliness towards foreign guests needed to be improved by approaching the church and asking priests *to preach proper hospitality* in their edifying Sunday sermons.

The various subcommittees also raised many other important issues and passed joint resolutions on them. The transportation subcommittee moved that the Austrian railroads should offer better tariffs for tourists, especially group rates and improved mutual arrangements with Switzerland and Italy for cross-border auto tourism; time overlaps between the Bregenz and Salzburg Festivals needed to be regulated in the busy summer months, demanded Hofmann-Montanus in the culture subcommittee; the sports subcomittee asked for accelerated building of ski lifts and cable cars to be given highest priority; the education subcommittee recommended that training of tourism personnel to be accomplished through practical training rather than through a special academy or at the university level; another subcommittee pleaded for a regulation of hotel prices to prevent price-gouging, while another one agreed with the Ministry's priority list of first improving and modernizing damaged hotel space before financing new projects; the subcommittee on the hospitality industry supported the Trade Ministry's öS 300 million investment program but pleaded for a low interest rate of 3.5 percent and longer periods for paying back the ERP loans; it also recommended that the Finance Ministry plead with the occupation powers to pay higher rates for damages incurred by seized hotels which would open up additional funds for self-financing. Before the delegates departed, everyone agreed that the cooperative climate in the subcommittee and in the plenary meetings had induced unusally productive discussions.[51]

This culmination in the cooperative spirit in the tourist industry came about as a result of the threat of Krauland's Economic Planning Ministry not to include tourism in ERP counterpart allocations in 1949. Krauland had a reputation for being brainy, ambitious, independent, and condescending—in short, full of hubris and "punctilious superiority." He managed to antagonize the party leaders—Figl, Raab and Gruber—from his own conservative party.[52] When the ÖVP Minister Krauland informed the ÖVP Minister Kolb in March 1949 about his decision to exclude tourism from the next ERP funding cylce, a firestorm of protest broke loose both within the conservative

People's Party and within the tourist industry. The States' Tourist Organization (*Verkehrsverband Österreichischer Bundesländer*) sent a telegram to Chancellor Figl demanding that tourism be included in the ERP program for financial/economic (foreign currency), political, and cultural reasons: "*Ein nachhaltig geförderter Fremdenverkehr wird Österreichs Devisenschatz bereichern und seine weltpolitische und kulturpolitische Position verbreitern.*" When Figl asked Kolb to update him on this matter, the Trade Ministry's tourist section reacted angrily about the states addressing the chancellor directly out of channels. After all, no one had worked harder and been pressing for öS 300 million in Marshall funds (and öS 80 million for 1949). They drafted a letter for Kolb, who dispatched it to the chancellor informing him about their and the Chamber of Commerce's öS 300 million priority program for tourism. Once again, they put forward their central economic argument, namely tourism as a foreign currency importer for the Austrian economy, noting that "*von österreichischer Seite Dienstleistungen und die Schönheiten unseres Landes geboten werden, wofür wir die begehrten Devisen erhalten, welche in den Fällen des Exportes nur für die für unsere eigene Wirtschaft wertvollen Rohmaterialien oder Fertigwaren erhältlich sind.*" Figl was reminded that only if Austrian tourism received the necessary investment funds for its reconstruction program, could it reassume its prewar function of equalizing the Austrian balance of trade.[53] Raab also sent a letter to his friend Figl reminding him of the importance of tourism for Austria's balance of payments and the dire needs of the industry to repair war and occupation related damages. He insisted on a öS 80 million allocation in 1949 from ERP counterpart funds.[54]

Apart from the powerful economic pressure of the *tourism lobby* on the Figl government, in the election year 1949 party politics played a crucial role in reversing Krauland's unacceptable verdict of "no" to ERP aid for tourism, at a time when he was showering state-owned heavy industries close to the Socialist Party with Marshall Plan counterpart funds. On 19 March 1949 Krauland had informed representatives of the tourist industry that their demands for ERP funds were "premature." Moreover, Minister of Trade Kolb had not forwarded tourism's claims early enough. Angry at Krauland's attempt to place blame on his shoulders, Kolb unleashed an irate letter reminding Krauland that he and his tourist officials had forwarded their claims half a year ago. Kolb rightly reminded Krauland that American ERP officials had insisted all along that Austrian tourism needed to be included in ERP funding since it was a high U.S. priority in the reconstruction of the Western European economy. Kolb also reminded Krauland of the continuing occupation damages to tourist assets and bombarded him with the statistics of the success of the *Ausländer-Hotelaktion* and the dramatic increases in overnight stays and foreign currency earnings (using the Zürs success story as his example). Kolb concluded by reminding Krauland that "the tourist industry is one of the most important pillars of the ÖVP." Tourism's demands had been ignored since 1946, and the Socialists had been courting them ever since.[55] The thrust of Kolb's argument was that Krauland's obstinacy could only hurt their party in the upcoming elections.

Krauland could no longer resist the political pressure from both his own party and ECA officials, and agreed to a öS 20 million allotment for 1949 from the complimentary budget. Kolb had written letters to ÖVP ministers such as Karl Gruber, the foreign minister, asking for their support in the Cabinet. And Raab, the powerful *eminence grise* in the People's Party, whose Chamber of Commerce also lobbied for the tourist industry, had been on Kolb's side all along. The hotel association had been lobbying for Marshall funds as well. ECA headquarters in Washington had signalled to Vienna that they wanted a separate allotment for tourism rather than reallocate ERP funds from the public housing budget for tourism, as the Ministry of Trade had suggested. On 1 July 1949, Kolb proposed öS 20 million allocation for tourism from the ERP budget (öS 15 million for the reconstruction program and öS 5 million for promotion). With Krauland's support, the allocation was granted.[56] This is an excellent example how American Marshall Planners performed the very useful role of *ultimate arbiter* if partisan conflicts became self-defeating and sectoral competition became so strong that entire branches of the economy were threatened to be left out from the riches of ERP funding. Krauland's mistreatment of an ÖVP core constituency, which was particularly strong in the provinces, increased resentment within the ÖVP for the Minister of Economic Planning. His days were numbered. With Raab in the lead, the party bigwigs refused to reappoint Krautland to the new Figl Cabinet after the election in the fall of 1949. He was "retired" to the *Österreichischer Arbeiter und Angestellten Bund*, one of the ÖVP chambers.[57]

Once the the tourist industry got their small ERP allocation, the states resumed their business-as usual *Kompetenzstreit* with the federal authorities in Vienna. The cooperative spirit of the Bad Gastein conference was quickly dissipating, and the dogfight for fund distribution within the industry began in earnest. The individual states resumed their jockeying for preferential treatment even though it had been clear for a while that the ERP investments would go largely to economically more intact Western states which had a better infrastructure to offer foreign tourists. When the Chairman of the Austrian Tourist Organization, Krogner, addressed a subgroup of alpine state organizations and presented unauthorized details of the loan conditions, the tourism manager of the Vorarlberg Chamber of Commerce fired off an intemperate letter to Vienna arguing that the cities of Vienna, Salzburg, and Innsbruck supposedly were getting preferential treatment. Behind the Arlberg pass, the deep-seated Vorarlberger suspicion that the further you were from Vienna the more you were excluded from federal funding was alive and well.[58] Indeed, the Austrian Tourist Organization (*Verkehrsverband Österreichischer Bundesländer*) had passed a resolution on their 10 September 1949 meeting suggesting to cut most of the öS 5 million allotment for promotional purposes. Not only did the states suggest a key how to distribute the 20 million among the nine states, but they also insisted that the money for individual projects be allocated on the state level.[59] The hotheads in the state had to be reminded that the ECA first had to pass guidelines for the distribution of tourism funding before any funds could be allocated.

The Chamber of Commerce and the Ministry of Trade, the central authorities in charge of tourism affairs, were highly frustrated by the resumption of such extreme *Länder* parochialism. They blamed Salzburg's Hofmann-Montanus for being the wily instigator of such veritable "states rights" demands ("*Kabinettstück überspitzter Länder-politik*"). The organization of state tourist offices had no legal foundation, and Hofmann-Montanus had worked against the expertise of the central authorities ever since 1945.[60] The struggle over the distribution of funding continued throughout the fall as state organizations protested against the loan conditions established by the *Hotel Treuhand*, the special financial institution earmarked to handle and supervise fund allocation to individual projects. In late October, the Finance Ministry informed the Ministry of Trade that öS 15 million had been transferred into a special tourism account at the National Bank.[61] Withdrawals for individual hotel projects could begin but had to be confirmed in each case by the ECA authorities in Vienna.[62] Projects for repairing, modernizing, and improving hotels with funds from the first öS 20 million allotment for Austrian tourism were not dispersed before the year 1950. Three years of intense pressure and endless lobbying were finally starting to produce results, and the first loans could be applied to tourism projects.

## Conclusion

What can we learn about the inner workings of the Marshall Plan in Austria from this case study of the distribution of counterpart funds for the tourist industry? The debates had many actors and must be understood on at least two levels: 1) the *national* Austrian debates about which hardly any research has been done since the Austrian records were only opened recently (particular conflicts of interest would include intra-ministerial versus federal Chancellery/Central ERP office; states versus federal bureaucracy; provinces versus Vienna); and 2) the *international* debates between the Austrians and the various levels of the European Cooperation Administration (Vienna/Paris/Washington) including ERP funds allocation priorities about which we need to know more about as well. Based on the Austrian and U.S. ECA records, we can now begin to refine our views about "American tutelage."[63] The Americans usually set the agenda and the complex loan conditions about who qualified for ERP counterpart funds and frequently had to act as arbiters in the fierce sectoral disputes in Austria over ERP funding. One probable conclusion is that the patterns established in the tourism debates of 1946-49 tended to prevail for the rest of the era of Marshall funding and probably occurred in other economic sectors as well.

The Americans again and again had to remind the Austrian officials about their priorities for tourism funding, namely "*only those projects which seem likely to make maximum contribution to Austria's balance of payments, with a minimum of funds, and in the quickest possible way*" (emphasis added). The ECA chief in Vienna demanded in 1952—a moment in time when the U.S. started to reduce ERP/MSA funding for Austria and worried about inflationary trends and a worsening balance of payment problems—that "projects should be approved only if they promise an immediate contribution to the physical capacity of tourist centers to house more tourists, which will ordinarily imply an increase in the bed capacity." This meant favoring lead resort towns such as Salzburg, Zürs, St. Anton, Bad Gastein, and Kitzbühel.[64] Tourism officials in the Vienna ECA/MSA office came to understand the Austrian way of "doing things" and frequently had to reinforce their program guidelines, which in tourism demanded above all spreading the wealth "to many medium and smaller type modernization projects."American officials came to understand the "cartel minded finance groups" in Austria who created monopolies to undermine competition. Large Austrian nationalized banks, breweries, and insurance companies wanted to start big new hotel projects "to extend their empire by penetrating into the tourism sector." In 1952, the Austrian government wanted to start new large hotel and lift projects hoping the get such projects on the list of ERP counterpart funding with the desire of "automatically prolonguing counterpart aid to tourism for 1953, 1954, *and possibly forever*" (emphasis added). The Austrians may have succeeded with this strategy, if we consider that with the transfer of the ERP countrerpart funds to the Austrian government in 1961/62 and the establishment of the *ERP-Fonds* a *perpetu mobile* for investments was created. We also know that the Marshall planners' succeess in reforming the Austrian political economy was modest at best.[65]

This is not the place to sketch out the constant battling and competition between these various sectors for ERP tourism funds. While we do not know yet the precise details about which projects were favored and for what reasons, this essay has established some trends in ERP counterparts allocation controversies revealing the outcome of the extraordinary success story of Austrian tourism. The following points also constitute an **agenda for future research** in the subject matter of the impact of Marshall funding on the reconstruction of the Austrian tourist industry.

First, surely ERP funds were the central engine in the reconstruction and revival of Austrian tourism during the postwar occupation decade. The statistics are impressive (see Graph and Table 4 in appendix). Between 1950 and 1955, öS 525.4 Million in ERP credits were poured into tourism (the lion's share of öS 404 million for hotel reconstruction and modernization, öS 93.3 million for ski lifts and transportation, and öS 28.1 million for tourism promotion). The ECA stipulated that 40 percent of project investments had to be self-financed thus favoring viable businesses which already had a modicum of success but only needed an injection for take-off. The total ERP induced investments into tourism thus amounted to öS 828.8 million, or almost 30 percent of postwar investments into tourism (or half, if we assume that most projects might not have been started without ERP funding). Not all funds were ERP allocations, and overall, investments in tourism since the end of the war amounted to öS 1.8 billion. Fully 1,376 hotel projects were financed, adding 46,805 beds to the Austrian tourist infrastructure as well as 3,087 baths and 71 ski lifts.[66]

Second, U.S. ERP counterpart funds offered the decisive boost for the reconstruction of Austrian tourism, particularly the starting of a winter season, even though tourism only received 2-4 percent of the entire counterparts distributed until 1955 (see Graph and Table 5 in appendix).[67] In the case of tourism, even these limited funds were invested for a maximum of return. Starting a "winter season" to complement the predominant summer season was a case in point. In 1950, funding priorities began to include lift projects benefitting such a "second season." This required an accelerated building of cable cars and ski lifts. Also, ensuring that access roads such as the Arlberg Pass and the Flexen Pass road to Lech/Zürs were accessible during the winter season of heavy snowfall ("*wintersicher*") became a high priority. It appears that Marshall funds financed vital modern snow removing equipment (a *Schneefräse*) for the Arlberg region, the cradle of Austrian skiing.[68] The year 1950 was the first time when tourism received a full tranche of öS 79 million for their projected four-year, öS 300 million investment program. Of this money, öS 10 million as scheduled for improving roads in the three Western states (the Flexen, Arlberg, Bregenzerwald, Ötztal, Lechtal, Pinzgau, Pongau, and Packer roads). A quarter (öS 21.5 million) of these funds as earmarked for transportation projects such as cable cars in Lech, the Montafon, the Dachstein, and the Zillertal (on average, öS 1-2 million projects), as well as ski lifts in the Arlberg and Montafon regions (Vorarlberg), in Ischgl, Obergurgl, Lienz and Kitzbühel (Tyrol), as well as the Tauplitz, Radstadt, and Villacher Alpe.[69] The Marshall Plan hotel modernization and lift/transportation projects that were approved read like a list of "Who's Who in Austrian Tourism."[70] There is nary a prominent hotel or ski resort not funded through ERP counterparts. Ten years after the Marshall Plan, the importance of these vital funds were still gratefully remembered in Austria. Today this is hardly the case any more.

Third, the return of German tourists was crucial for the revival of postwar Austrian tourism. Just like the 1.000 Mark boycott in 1933 ruined Austrian tourism for a while, resumption of German tourists flooding across the Austrian border acclerated the recovery. The decisive takeoff of postwar Austrian tourism came with the opening of

The ERP supported tourism infrastructure by improving roads like the "*Reuttener Bundesstrasse*" in the Tyrol to make them passable in extreme winter conditions (1950).

Source: National Library, Vienna, # US 20642

the border to the Federal Republic in 1951.[71] In 1931/32, 44.7 percent of the tourists in Austria were Germans; in 1934, a mere 12.1 percent were.[72] During the time of Allied Control of the West German economy, costs and legal obstacles made crossing the border into Austria prohibitive—it took 4-6 weeks to get a visa! In 1951, the Allies relinquished the right to issue passports to the Federal Republic and the result was immediate for Austiran tourism. While the percentage of German tourists was negligible before 1950, by 1952/53 German tourists made up 54 percent of the foreign vacationers in Austria. Since the *Kleinwalsertal* was politically part of Austria, but economically part of Germany, the Vorarlberg statistics are somewhat different. The Germans already constituted 25 percent of foreign tourists in 1948 and 53 percent in 1952. Salzburg, Vorarlberg, and the Tyrol had the highest percentages of German tourists and suffered the most under the 1.000 Mark boycott before the war. In 1931/32, 85.2 percent of Tyrol's tourists had been Germans. In 1954, Germans again constituted 53 percent of Tyrol's tourists, and by the end of the 1950s, they constituted an incredible 70 percent.[73] Resumption of normal Austro-German relations was the all important accelerator for Austrian economic recovery in general and the revival of tourism in particular.

Fourth, the general statistics in overnight stays clearly illustrated how the remarkable recovery of Austrian tourism by the 1952/53 season was the result of ERP aid injection and the return of German tourists. In that season, Austria for the first time surpassed the 1936/37 figure of 20.5 million overnight stays. The 6.8 million overnight stays by foreigners in 1936/37 were already matched in 1951/52, and in 1953/54, they were surpassed by 50 percent. After 1955, more than 50 percent of tourists in Austria were foreigners.[74] Increases in foreign currency earnings were accordingly spectacular (see Graph and Table 6). Even though 50 percent more overnight stays by foreign tourists were recorded in 1954 than in 1937, the öS 2 billion earned in foreign currency lagged 8 percent behind the öS 234 millions of 1937 in buying power.[75] If the goal of foreign exchange earnings from tourism making up for the balance of payments deficit was not entirely reached, their contribution was vital. By the mid-1950s, the foreign currency earned from tourism increasingly replaced U.S. aid in making up for the deficits in the Austrian balance of payments.

Fifth, it is ironic that the Western states which complained the most about being left out by central authorities in the distribution of ERP funds, in the end received the lion's share of counterparts (see Graph and Table 7 in appendix). Maybe the lesson here was that *the louder you clamor in the West the more likely you will be heard in Vienna*. Of course, the Western states offered some of the most advanced tourist areas in Austria. By 1955, foreign tourists flooded Innsbruck and Salzburg and the famous winter resort towns of Kitzbühel, Seefeld, and the Arlberg region, as well as the spas of the

Gastein valley. While the cities of Salzburg and Bad Gastein had an almost equal number of 183,000 overnight stays, surprisingly the old spa town of Baden, next to Vienna, which was also the headquarters of the Soviet occupation forces, recorded 108,000 overnight stays.[76] Even though they attracted the majority of cash-rich foreign tourists, taken together they constituted about a third of overnight stays in Austria during this period and never reached half (see Graph and Table 8). One would need to establish their overall percentage of foreign exchange earnings to determine whether the ERP investments were economically justified. We know that, due to political reasons, they were not fair in terms of a balanced distribution of ERP counterparts throughout Austria. This is the reason why the focus of ERP counterpart distribution for the tourist industry shifted to the Soviet zone after the conlusion of the Austrian treaty and the termination of the occupation in 1955.

Sixth and last, Austrian planning and tourism officials as well as Marshall planners paid little heed to the concerns then that today still dominate the scholarly and public debates in tourism. We have noted that local worries surfaced early on that rapid economic development of the alpine valleys through mass tourism would be a mixed blessing and would lead to environmental degradation and destruction of the tradional social fabric of Austrian villages. The "urbanization," "suburbanization," and "colonization" of the Alps were not yet identified as major problems in the overdeveloped tourism economy in the Alps. "Sustainable tourism," namely that tourists not ruin what they have come to enjoy, was not yet identified as a crucial problem of modern mass tourism. Local customs and traditional folklore were still to be marshalled in the service of pleasing foreign guests. The construction boom, which led to a demise of traditional age-old architectural aesthetics ("yodel architecture") in Austrian Alpine villages, had barely set in by the end of the occupation decade. "*Überfremdung*" only surfaced in the context of the unwelcome DPs and non-German refugees whom Austrians did not want to integrate. Tourist officials only worried about how to make the xenophobic, private, and shy Alpine Austrians more hospitable. Both Austrian and American Marshall planners were technocrats fully appreciating the benefits of modernization leading to prosperity and hardly worried about long-term social or environmental consequences. Those became only clearly visible in the 1970s and brought about a reassessment of beliefs in the benefits of economic development and modernization through mass tourism.[77]

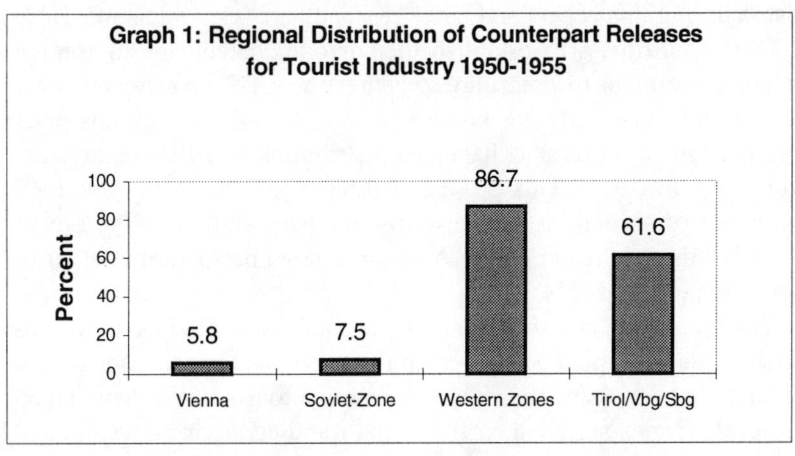


**Table 1: Regional Distribution of Counterpart Releases for Tourist Industry 1950-1955**

| | |
|---|---|
| Vienna | 5.8 |
| Soviet-Zone | 7.5 |
| Western Zones | 86.7 |
| Tirol/Vbg/Sbg | 61.6 |

Source: WIFO Monatsberichte, No. 1 (1956), 23

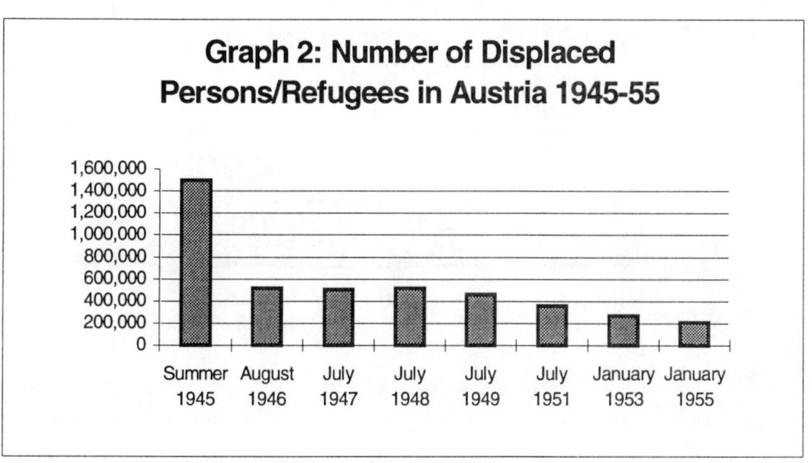


**Table 2: Number of Displaced Persons/Refugees in Austria 1945-55**

| Month/Year | Total |
|---|---|
| Summer 1945 | 1,500,000 |
| August 1946 | 519,950 |
| July 1947 | 504,454 |
| July 1948 | 520,591 |
| July 1949 | 463,617 |
| July 1951 | 360,527 |
| January 1953 | 270,816 |
| January 1955 | 209,865 |

Source: Stieber, "Lösung des Flüchtlingproblems 1945-1960", 68, 87 (Table)

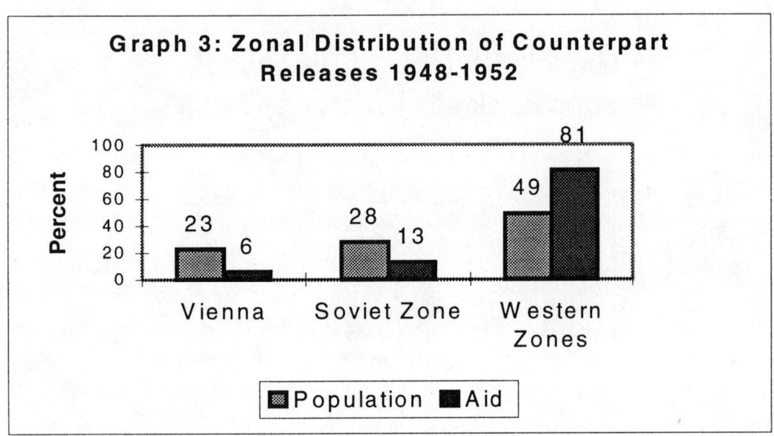


**Table 3: Zonal Distribution of Counterpart Releases 1948-1952**

| | Population | Aid |
|---|---|---|
| Vienna | 23 | 6 |
| Soviet Zone | 28 | 13 |
| Western Zones | 49 | 81 |

Source: Bischof, "Between Responsibility and Rehabilitation", 851

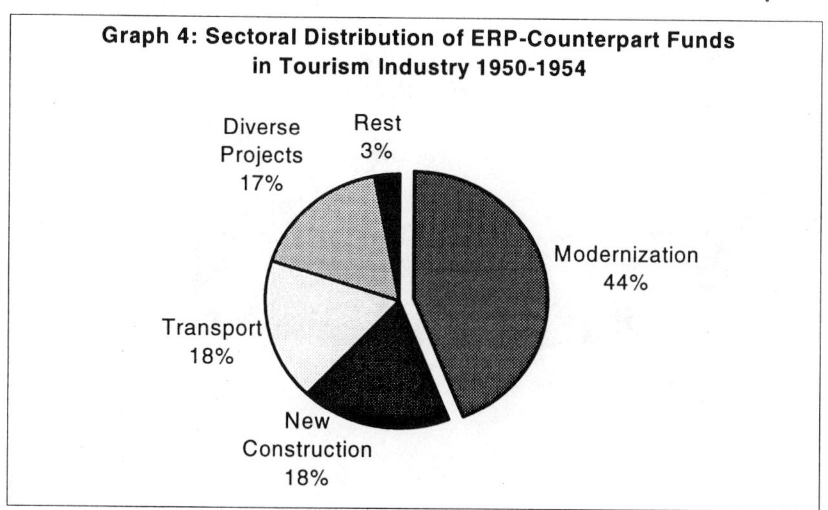


**Table 4: Sectoral Distribution of ERP-Counterpart Funds in Tourism-Industry 1950-1954**

| | % |
|---|---|
| Modernization | 44 |
| New Construction | 18 |
| Transport | 18 |
| Diverse Projects | 17 |
| Rest | 3 |

Source: "Investitionen im Fremdenverkehr", WIFO Monatsberichte, No. 3 (1955), 124

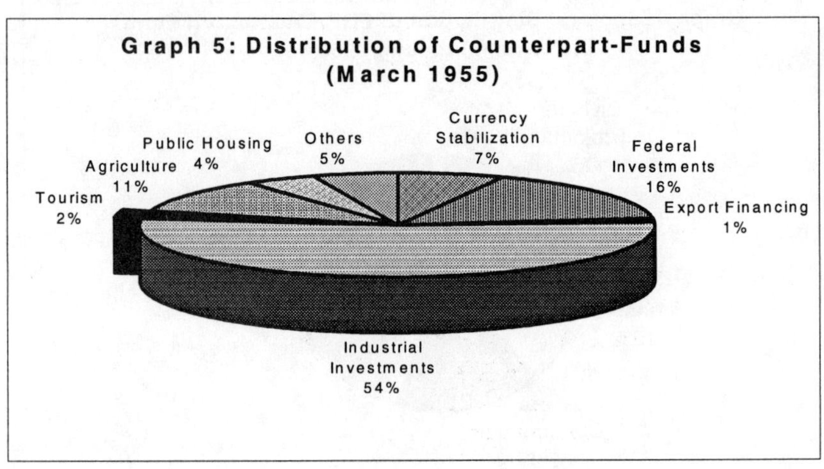


**Table 5: Distribution of Counterpart-Funds—March 1955**

| | % | ERP-Funds Mio S |
|---|---|---|
| Productivity Campaign | 2.3 | 296 |
| Currency Stabilization | 6.5 | 125 |
| Federal Investments | 15.9 | 1.529 |
| Export Financing | 1.3 | 163 |
| Industrial Investments | 51.8 | 6.137 |
| Tourism | 2.3 | 305 |
| Agriculture | 10.4 | 1.360 |
| Public Housing | 4.3 | 504 |
| Others | 5.2 | 684 |
| **Total** | 97.7 | 10.807 |

Source: Nemschak, Zehn Jahre, 24

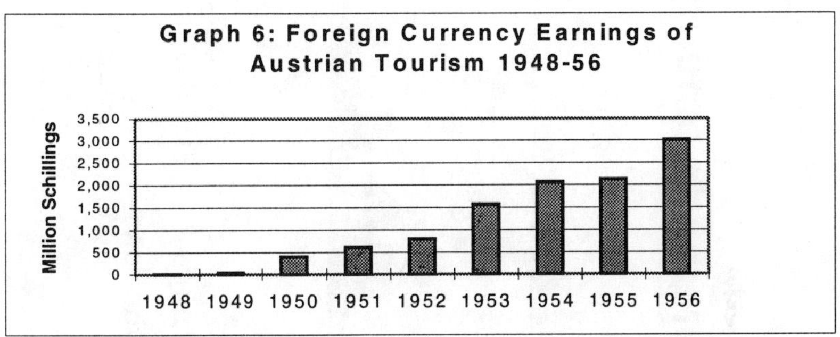


**Table 6: Foreign Currency Earnings of Austrian Tourism 1948-1956**

| | Mio S |
|---|---|
| 1948 | 10 |
| 1949 | 44 |
| 1950 | 407 |
| 1951 | 618 |
| 1952 | 806 |
| 1953 | 1.574 |
| 1954 | 2.067 |
| 1955 | 2.133 |
| 1956 | 3.020 |

Source: Schmid, "Fremdenverkehr in Salzburg, 1966, 199; Nemschak, Zehn Jahre, 57.

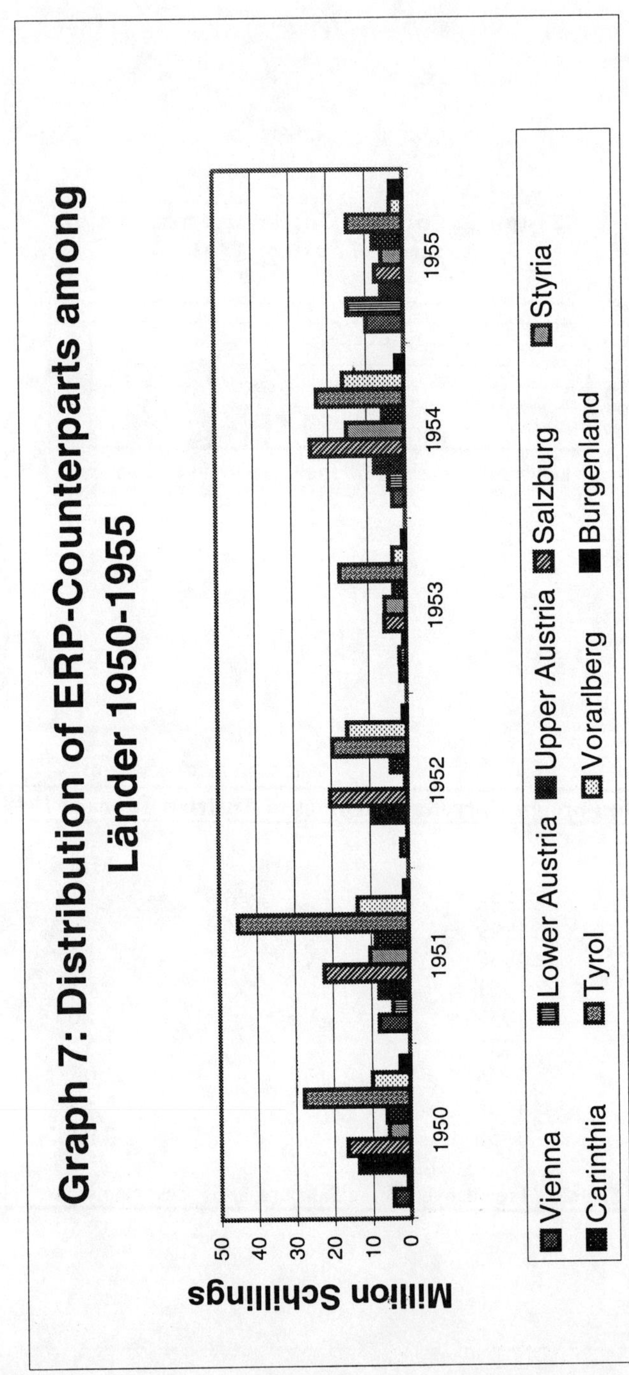
Graph 7: Distribution of ERP-Counterparts among Länder 1950-1955
Million Schillings
50
40
30
20
10
0
1950
1951
1952
1953
1954
1955
Vienna
Lower Austria
Upper Austria
Salzburg
Styria
Carinthia
Tyrol
Vorarlberg
Burgenland

**Table 7: Distribution of ERP-Counterparts among Länder 1950-1955**

| | 1950 | 1951 | 1952 | 1953 | 1954 | 1955 | 1950-55 | % |
|---|---|---|---|---|---|---|---|---|
| Vienna | 4.54 | 8.05 | 1.79 | 1.53 | 3.22 | 9.87 | 29.00 | 5.80 |
| Lower Austria | 0.81 | 4.45 | 0.10 | 1.85 | 4.31 | 14.73 | 26.25 | 5.30 |
| Upper Austria | 13.52 | 8.02 | 9.36 | 0.83 | 8.01 | 5.78 | 45.52 | 9.20 |
| Salzburg | 16.52 | 22.31 | 20.40 | 5.73 | 24.78 | 7.36 | 97.09 | 19.50 |
| Styria | 5.61 | 10.21 | 0.64 | 5.59 | 15.13 | 5.67 | 42.85 | 8.60 |
| Carinthia | 6.07 | 8.81 | 4.44 | 3.22 | 5.67 | 8.03 | 36.24 | 7.30 |
| Tyrol | 27.90 | 45.12 | 19.58 | 17.29 | 22.94 | 14.64 | 147.47 | 29.60 |
| Vorarlberg | 9.95 | 13.48 | 15.78 | 3.34 | 16.17 | 3.38 | 62.10 | 12.50 |
| Burgenland | 2.60 | 1.16 | 1.00 | 0.74 | 2.04 | 3.21 | 10.75 | 2.20 |
| **Total** | 87.52 | 121.61 | 73.09 | 40.12 | 102.27 | 72.67 | 497.27 | 100.00 |

Source: WIFO Monatsberichte, No 1 (1956), 23

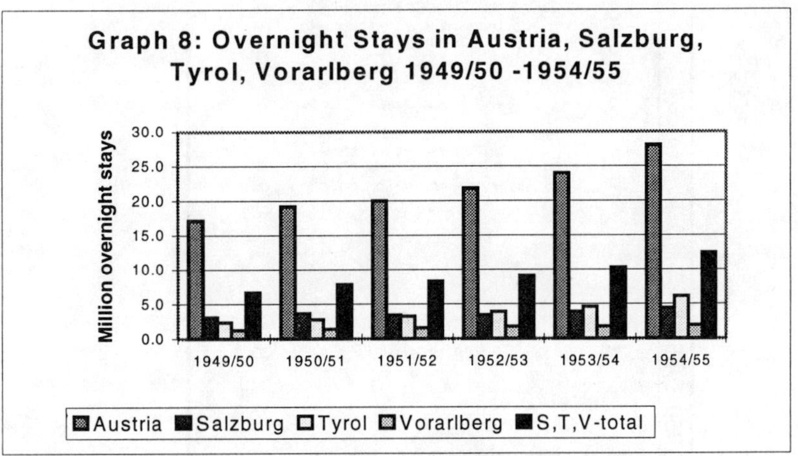


**Table 8: Overnight Stays in Austria, Salzburg, Tyrol, Vorarlberg 1949/50-1954/55**

| Year | Austria | Salzburg | Tyrol | Vorarl-berg | S,T,V-total |
|---|---|---|---|---|---|
| 1949/50 | 17.2 | 3.1 | 2.3 | 1.2 | 6.7 |
| 1950/51 | 19.2 | 3.7 | 2.8 | 1.4 | 7.9 |
| 1951/52 | 20.0 | 3.4 | 3.3 | 1.6 | 8.3 |
| 1952/53 | 21.8 | 3.4 | 3.9 | 1.8 | 9.1 |
| 1953/54 | 24.0 | 3.9 | 4.6 | 1.8 | 10.3 |
| 1954/55 | 28.1 | 4.4 | 6.1 | 2.0 | 12.4 |

Source: Anna Schmidt, "Entwicklung des Fremdenverkehrs" 195, 198 (for A, T, S); Vorarlberger Wirtschafts- u. Sozialstatistik Vol. 9 (1955), 635

## Notes

1. Letter Kolb to Figl, 27 June 1949, 98.834-V/23b/49, Bundesministerium für Handel und Wiederaufbau (BMfHuW), Archiv der Republik (AdR), Österreichisches Staatsarchiv (ÖStA), Vienna.

2. Memorandum of Conversation (Amb. Lowenthal, Byington, Allen), "Austria's Economic Position," 14 July 1952, 863.00/7-1452, Record Group 59 (RG 59) (General Records of the Department of State), National Archives (NA), Bethesda (MD).

3. See, for example, the essay by Gunther Tichy, "Wirtschaft und Wirtschaftspolitik," in *Politik in Österreich*, ed. Wolfgang Mantl (Vienna, 1992), 708; Fritz Weber, "Die wirtschaftliche Entwicklung," in *Handbuch des Politischen Systems Österreichs* ed. Herbert Dachs, et al. (Vienna, 1997), 37; and many other essays on the Austrian economy in this substantial volume which barely mentions the Marshall Plan. For a general critique of the lag in research on the Marshall Plan in Austria compared with scholarship on other recipient countries, see Günter Bischof, "Zum internationalen Stand der Marshallplan-Forschung: Die Forschungsdesiderata für Österreich," in *Zeitgeschichte im Wandel: 3. Österreichische Zeitgeschichtetage 1997*, ed. Gertraud Diendorfer, Gerhard Jagschitz, and Oliver Rathkolb (Innsbruck, 1998), 61-72; *idem*, "Der Marshall-Plan in Europa," *Aus Politik und Zeitgeschichte* B 22-23/97 (23 May 1997): 3-17.

4. I will consistently use the term tourism, used in international research for all forms of recreational and professional travel, instead of *Fremdenverkehr*, which has been the common usage in Austria up until recently. *Fremdenverkehr*—or "trafficking with foreigners"—has obvious and subtle meanings and would need to be deconstructed in the specific Austrian context.

5. Alois Brusatti, *100 Jahre Österreichischer Fremdenverkehr: Historische Entwicklung1884-1984* (Vienna, 1984); Klaus Frantz, "The Development and Regional Structure of Austrian Tourism," and Max Preglau, "Tourism Kills Tourism - Environmental, Cultural, and Economic Consequences of Tourism," in *Tourism and Culture: A Comparative Perspective*, ed. Eddystone C. Nebbel (Third Biannual University of New Orleans—University of Innsbruck Symposium) (New Orleans, 1983), 7-25, 35-63; Hanns Haas, Robert Hoffmann and Kurt Luger, eds., *Weltbühne und Naturkulisse: Zwei Jahrhunderte Salzburg-Tourismus* (Salzburg, 1994); Georg Stadler, *Von der Kavalierstour zum Sozialtourismus: Kulturgeschichte des Salzburger Fremdenverkehrs* (Salzburg, 1975); Anna Schmidt, "Die Entwicklung des Fremdenverkehrs und der Verkehrspolitik im Bundsland Salzburg," PhD., Salzburg 1990; Herbert Sohm, *Zur Geschichte des Fremdenverkehrs in Vorarlberg* (Bregenz, 1984); Adolf Lässer, *100 Jahre Fremdenverkehr in Tirol* (Innsbruck, 1989); Paul Tschurtschenthaler, "Der Tourismus im Bundesland Tirol 1918-1990", in *Handbuch zur Neueren Ge-schichte Tirols*, vol. 2/2: *Zeitgeschichte: Wirtschaft und Kultur*, ed. Anton Pelin-ka and Andreas Maislinger (Innsbruck, 1993), 113-205; the essays by Josef Fink, "Die Fremdenverkehrswirtschaft in Tirol," and Werner Karolyi, "Die Fremden-verkehrsorganisation," in *100 Jahre Tiroler Verkehrsentwicklung 1858-1958* (Innsbruck 1958); see also the splashy pictorial volume by Michael Forcher, *Zu Gast im Herzen der Alpen: Eine Bildgeschichte des Tourismus in Tirol* (Innsbruck, 1989) .

6. Most obviously in Rolf Steininger and Michael Gehler, eds., *Österreich im 20. Jahrhundert*, vol. 2: *Vom Zweiten Weltkrieg bis zur Gegenwart* (Vienna, 1997); Reinhard Sieder, Heinz Steinert, and Emmerich Talos, eds., *Österreich 1945-1955: Gesellschaft-Politik-Kultur* (Vienna, 1995); Ernst Hanisch, *Der lange Schatten des Staates: Österreichische Gesellschaftsgeschichte im 20. Jahrhundert* (Vienna, 1994).

7. Most European Marshall Plan recipient countries organized major anniversary celebrations on the fiftieth anniversary of General Marshall's Harvard speech in June 1947. President Clinton's visit to the Netherlands was the major commemorative event. Prior to that, a scholarly meeting was staged at the Clingendael Institute of the Dutch Foreign Ministry, in cooperation with the Netherlands' Atlantic Commission in The Hague, 15-16 May 1997, with representatives from all sixteen ERP participant countries. See the proceedings in *The Fiftieth Anniversary of the Marshall Plan: In Retrospect and in Prospect*. For Germany, see the symposium volume resulting from conference organized by the *Haus der Geschichte* in Bonn, which also organized a major traveling exhibit, *50 Jahre Marshall-Plan* (Berlin, 1997).
The last major commemorative volume on the achievements of the Marshall Plan in Austria was published by the Austrian government on the occasion of the ten year anniversary, see *Zehn Jahre ERP in Österreich 1948/49: Wirtschaftshilfe im Dienste der Völkerverständigung* (Vienna, 1958). Although arguably no country profited more from ERP aid than did Austria, there was no major commemorative event organized by the Austrian government or by scholars for the fiftieth anniversary of the Marshall Plan, apart from an anniversary convocation by the *ERP-Fonds* and a number of notable radio programs by Ewald Hiebl and Wolfgang Kos on the brainy channel one (Ö 1) on Austrian National Radio. Hans-Jürgen Schröder has started to reconstruct the historical memory of the Marshall Plan in Austria in his essay in this volume; for the German historical memory, see Schröder's "50 Jahre Marshall-Plan in Deutschland," *Aus Politik und Zeitgeschichte* B22-23/98 (23 May 1997): 18-29.

8. Paul Bernecker, "Die Finanzierung der österreichischen Fremdenverkehrswirtschaft aus den Mitteln des Marshallfonds," in *Der moderne Fremdenverkehr: Markt- und betriebswirtschaftliche Probleme in Einzeldarstellungen* (Vienna, 1955); *Zehn Jahre ERP in Österreich 1948/1958: Wirtschaftshilfe im Dienste der Völkerverständigung* (Vienna, 1958); Franz Nemschak, *Zehn Jahre österreichische Wirtschaft 1945-1955* (Vienna, 1955); Manfred Mautner Markhof and Franz Nemschak, *40 Jahre Österreichisches Institut für Wirtschaftsforschung 1927-1967* (Vienna, 1967), 43-9.

9. Kurt Luger and Franz Rest, "Mobile Privatisierung: Kultur und Tourismus in der Zweiten Republik," in *Österreich 1945-1995*, 655-70 (quotation 661); Frantz, "Austrian Tourism," 9ff. Today only seven Western countries (the United States, France, Italy, Spain, Great Britain, Austria, and Germany) produce almost half of the world's tourist income, see Christoph Hennig, *Reiselust: Touristen, Tourismus und Urlaubskultur* (Frankfurt, 1997), 150.

10. See the documentation *25-Jahre ERP-Fonds 1962-1987* (Vienna, 1987), now substantially updated by Kurt Löffler and Hans Fußenegger, "Die Tätigkeit des österreichischen ERP-Fonds von 1962 bis 1998," in: *80 Dollar: 50 Jahre ERP-Fonds und Marshall Plan in Österreich 1948-1998*, ed. Günter Bischof and Dieter Stiefel (Vienna, 1999), 21-61.

11. Only Austria and Germany transferred their counterpart accounts into permanent "investments funds/bank" for economic development; with these revolving funds they created investment *perpetu mobiles.* In the Federal Republic, both the *Kreditanstalt für Wiederaufbau,* and more recently the *Deutsche Ausgleichsbank,* which has been concentrating on funding the new Eastern states after unification, have been fed from the remaining counterpart funds which the initial Marshall Plan deliveries had generated. See "Geld schenken tötet unternehmerisches Denken," in *Der Marshall-Plan: Geschichte und Zukunft,* ed. Hans-Herbert Holzamer and Marc Hoch (Landsberg, 1997), and now more substantially Heinrich Harries, *Wiederafubau, Welt und Wende:Die KfW—eine Bank mit öffentlichem Auftrag* (Frankfurt, 1998).

12. "Investionen im Fremdenverkehr," *WIFO Monatsberichte,* 3/1955: 122; Informationsdienst des Bundesministeriums für Handel und Wiederaufbau (BMfHuW), 24/6/Re, 15 October 1950, "Die Etappen der ERP-Hilfe," 140.179-V/23b/50; Speech draft by the Tyrolean tourist promoter and representative (*Abgeordneter*) Josef Fink before the National Council (*Nationalrat*), 29 November 1950, 210.499-V/23b/50, BMfHuW. Unless otherwise noted, the files cited in this essay will only be from the *Fremdenverkehrssektion (*Sektion V) of the Federal Ministry of Trade and Reconstruction, which was the central authority of the Federal government coordinating Austrian tourism affairs. Some documents from the Central ERP Office in the Federal Chancellery (*Zentralbüro für ERP-Angelegenheiten, Bundeskanzleramt)* (ZERP, BKA), which coordinated all ERP matters in Austria and was the central authority corresponding with American ECA officials in Vienna, Paris, and Washington, will also be cited. All these files are in the Archives of the Republic, Austrian State Archives (AdR, ÖStA).

13. Letter Julius Raab (President, Austrian Chamber of Commerce) to Leopold Figl (Austrian Chancellor), 11 March 1949, 112.909/V-23b/2199/49. Postwar Austrian tourist development is frequently compared to the prewar base year 1937, when the prewar tourist industry was recovering from Hitler's devastating boycott of 1933 (*"Tausend Markt Sperre"*), see *WIFO Monatsberichte,* 3/1955, 121-4.

14. "Investitionen im Fremdenverkehr," *WIFO Monatsberichte,* 1/1956, 22f; for prewar developments of Austrian tourism on a national and regional level, see Georg Rigele, *Die Großglockner-Hochalpenstraße* (Vienna, 1998), 289-305.

15. Brusatti, *100 Jahre,* 155ff.

16. Gustav Zedek, "Fremdenverkehrspolitik in Österreich im letzten Vierteljahrhundert," in *Festschrift Paul Bernecker,* ed. Walter A. Ender (Vienna, 1978), 43.

17. Valene L. Smith, "War and Tourism: An American Ethnography," *Annals of Tourism Research* 25 (January 1998): 202-27.

18. For Salzburg, see Gert Kerschbaumer, "Tourismus im politischen Wandel der 30er und 40er Jahre," in *Weltbühne und Naturkulisse,* 120-8; Ernst Hanisch, *Gau der Guten Nerven: Die nationalsozialistische Herrschaft in Salzburg 1938-1945,* rev. ed., (Salzburg, 1997), 85f. For Tyrol and Vorarlberg, see Horst Schreiber, *Wirtschaft und Sozialgeschichte der Nazizeit in Tirol* (Innsbruck, 1994), 51-66.

19. V. Smith sees the "emotional tourism" (war brides) and "military tourism" (veterans's tours) as mainsprings of the postwar international tourism boom, "War and Tourism," 218f. As a student waiter for many years, I have personally met numerous such German wartime tourists coming back to Austria after the

war. To my knowledge, this important wartime link among German guests in the postwar Austrian tourism boom has not been empirically explored.

20. Erich Marx, ed., *Bomben auf Salzburg: Die "Gauhauptstadt" im "Totalen Krieg"* (Salzburg, 1995); Thomas Albrich and Arno Gisinger, *Im Bombenkrieg: Tirol und Vorarlberg 1943-1945* (Innsbruck, 1992).

21. Minutes of a meeting with American economic officials, 30 August 1946, 192.741-23/46; Letter Langer-Hansel to Economic Division/USACA, 13 September 1946, 160.210/46; Österreichische Heilbäder-, Kurorte- und Heilquellenverband, Anmeldung von Kriegsschäden, 14 December 1946.

22. Thomas Albrich, "Fremde," *Historicum*, Summer 1996, 23-8; idem, ed., *Flucht nach Eretz Israel: Die Bricha und der jüdische Exodus durch Österreich nach 1945* (Innsbruck, 1998); Gabriela Stieber, "Die Lösung des Flüchtlingsproblems 1945-1950," in *Österreich in den Fünfzigern*, ed. Thomas Albrich, et al. (Innsbruck, 1995), 67-93; idem, *Nachkriegsflüchtlinge in Kärnten und der Steiermark* (Graz, 1997); on Badgastein see Daniela Ellmauer, "Fremder/Gast: Zur Genese von Selbst- und Fremdbildern im Tourismus am Beispiel Bad Gastein," M.A. thesis, University of Salzburg 1996, 22f. A summary of the *Österreichischer Heilbäder-, Kurorte- und Heilquellenverband* of 14 December 1946 mentioned that öS 20 million worth of damage incurred during the postwar occupation, including damages through DPs, 230.012/46. Minister Heinl asked the Allied Council to vacate hotels, especially those occupied by DPs, "to modernize hotels to enable Austria to attract foreign tourists for earning foreign curreny." Heinl to Allied Council, 22 October 1946, 160.268/46.

23. The Austrian prejudices were voiced in an article in the *Arbeiter-Zeitung*, 21 August 1946, 1f, cited in Ellmauer, "Fremder/Gast," 23f. Thomas Albrich is the first scholar to have explored in depth the survival of anti-semitism in postwar Austria with his case study on Jewish DPs, see *Exodus durch Österreich: Die jüdischen Flüchtlinge 1945-1948* (Innsbruck, 1987); idem, ed., *Flucht nach Eretz Israel.*

24. "10 Millionen Dollarkredit für Fremdenverkehrszwecke-Fremdenverkehrsprogramm", Langer-Hansel an Wirtschaftsabteilung USACA, 13 September 1946, 160.210/46; "Fremdenverkehrenquete am 3. Juni 1946," 160.190/46; Hotelliste, Krogner and BM Heinl, 23 December 1946; 230.012/46; Langer-Hansel an Becker (BMfHuW), 16 December 1946, 160.351/46; Hotelliste, 160.268/46, and other documents in this file.

25. Quotation from meeting Langer-Hansel et al. with Col. Hunter and Capt. Loomis (U.S. Economic Division), 30 August 1946;. Minutes of the Meetings with representatives from the states, 4 - 6 September 1946; minutes of meeting with Major Ingham (Trade and Supply Div.), 12 September 1946; the Finance Ministry turning down this proposal for a special tourism 10 Mio. Dollar credit is recorded in the cover memo to this file, 20 January 1947, all in 192.741-23/46. On the "great debate" in Washington concerning U.S. financial aid to Austria to balance the negative trade balance, see Günter Bischof, "Between Responsiblity and Rehabiliation: Austria in International Politics, 1940-1950," PhD., Harvard University 1989, 475-96, and Hans Seidel's essay in this volume.

26. The agenda for modernizing the best existing hotels, improving interiors and inventories as well as the transport systems and initiating a marketing campaign abroad was clearly stated in Heinl to Economic Division (USACA), 18

September 1946, 192.741-23/46. The best short history of the beginnings of the revival of Austrian tourism is Langer-Hansel's "Tätigkeitsbericht" (April 1947 bis October 1949) (n.d.), 118.453-V/23b/49.

27. Letter Heinl to Allied Council, 22 October 1946, 160.268/46; Heinl to Allied Council, 13 November 1946, 160.236/46; minute of conversation with Col. Davis (GB) with attached list of hotels (about half of them occupied) available to host British tourists, 8 October 1946, 160.255/46. This pressure would only mount in the upcoming years.

28. "*Bei dem derzeitigen Stand des Fremdenbeherbergungsgewerbes und der Verkehrsmittel sowie der Besetzungsverhältnisse ist es augenscheinlich, dass hiefür in erster Linie die westlichen und südlichen Bundesländer in Frage kommen und auch da nur eine beschränkte Anzahl jener Hotelbetriebe die an sich in ihrerer früheren Ausstattung für die Unterbringung der einen gewissen Komfort verlangenden Gäste in Betracht kommen. Voraussetzung ist weiters, dass diese Häuser, falls sie von den alliierten Mächten besetzt sind, freigeben und nicht wieder beschlagnahmt werden.*" Exposé v. 25 September 1946, 160.241/46. On the revival of tourism in Carinthia in the British zone, see Brigitte Entner, "Vom Besatzer zum Urlaubsgast: Der Wiederaufbau des Devisenfremdenverkehrs in Österreich in den Jahren 1945 bis 1949 aus der Sicht der britischen Besatzungsmacht," *Zeitgeschichte* 23 (1996): 17-31.

29. Bischof, "Between Responsibility and Rehabilitation", 447-525; idem, "Foreign Aid and Austria's Economic Recovery," in *New Directions,* ed. Werner Feld (Boulder, 1986), 79-91; see also the Fraberger/Stiefel essay in this volume.

30. The first mention for the ideas that would become the "*Hotelaktion*" is by Bauernfeind from the Food Ministry: "*Die Lebensmittel würden gegen Devisen aus dem Ausland bezogen werden um Coupons, welche sich der Ausländer mit seiner Valuta, eventuell schon im Heimatland besorgt, ausgegeben zu werden.*" Minutes of meeting 4 September 1946, 192.741-23/46; the full-fledged plan is outlined in a memo by Langer-Hansel for Becker (BMfHuW), 16 December 1946, 160.351/46. For a general description of the *Hotelaktion* in 1947, however without recognizing the origins in the 1946 planning efforts briefly outlined here, see Schmidt, "Die Entwicklung des Fremdenverkehrs und der Fremdenverkehrspolitik im Bundesland Salzburg," 180-5. The complexity of the arrangements for the individual tourists is well explained by a case study in Paul Bernecker, *Der moderne Fremdenverkehr* (Vienna, 1955), 27f.

31. See minute attached to Nationalbank to Becker, 20 December 1946, 230.007/46; minutes of meeting in Economic Planning Ministry Langer-Hansel et al., 17 December 1946, 160.351/46.

32. Ibid.

33. Tätigkeitsbericht (April 1947 bis October 1949) (n.d.), Sektion V, BMfHuW, seen by Minister Kolb, 118.453-V/23b/49. This extensive report was written as a response to attacks from outside the ministry that the tourism section had failed to engage in the necessary long-term planning.

34. While outdated in its sources, still the most informative introduction to postwar economic planning is Siegfried Hollerer, *Verstaatlichung und Wirtschaftsplanung in Österreich (1946-1949)* (Vienna 1974), 132ff.

35. Ibid., 162-7; on the state sector, see also Franz Mathis, "Between Regulation and Laissez Faire: Austrian State Industries after World War II," *Contemporary Austrian Studies* 3 (1994), 79-90.

36. Hollerer, *Verstatlichung*, 134.

37. Minutes of the April and May meetings of the *Beschaffungsausschuß* and *Planungsausschuß*, as well as the invitation for the *1. Hauptsitzung des Bundesarbeitsausschußes für Fremdenverkehr* of 25 May 1948 with the agenda are in 135.787-V/23b/48; the minutes of the first meeting of 1 June 1948, dated 22 July 1948, are in 140.370-V/23b/48.

38. Ibid.

39. Ibid.

40. "Planungsrichtlinien" by Langer-Hansel with attached "Erläuterungen zum Investitionsprogramm" and "Planungschema" 14 July 1948, 135.787-V/23b/48.

41. "Information 2" of the Executive Committee of the *Bundesarbeitsauschuß*, 7 October 1948, 144.480-V/23b/48.

42. "Eröffnungsansprache des Herrn Bundesministers Ernst Kolb," in minutes of second meeting of the *Bundesarbeitsausschuß für Fremdenverkehr* of 20 October 1948, 20 November 1948, 137.397-V/23b/48.

43. Minutes of the second meeting, ibid.

44. Lanske Information sheet for the third meeting, 27 May 1949, 104.443-V/23b/49.

45. "Unterausschuss für Heilbäder- und Kurortwesen," 1 June 1949, 105.705-V-23b/49; and minutes of the second Plenarsitzung des Bundesarbeitsausschußes, 2 June 1949, 110.745-V-23b/49.

46. Letter Heinrich Ludascher (Pfarrer von Dorfgastein) to Ministry of Trade and Economic Reconstruction, 27 July 1949, 117.172-V/23b/49. The Ministry wrote back that since the 3rd meeting of the National Working Committee it was indeed well aware of these problems but that it had no legal recourse to stop such industrial plants from locating in the Gastein valley, 11 August 1949, ibid.

47. Quoted in Ellmauer, "Fremder/Gast," 15f; for a sophisticated case study of the social, environmental, and economic "modernizing" effects and repercussions of tourism on the Tyrolean village of Obergurgl, see Preglau, " Tourism Kills Tourism," 48-60.

48. Ernst Hanisch, "Wirtschaftswachstum ohne Industrialisierung: Fremdenverkehr und sozialer Wandel in Salzburg 1918-1938," in *Weltbühne und Naturkulisse*, 104-12.

49. See the various responses to the resolutions accepted by the third *Bundesarbeitsausschuss*, November 1949, 116.605-V/23b/49.

50. Gasperschitz speech in 108.650-V/23b/49; see also subommittee minutes, 105.705-V/23b/49.

51. Ibid., and minutes of plenary session, 2 June 1949, 110.745-V/23b/49.

52. See the fascinating intellectual portrait of Krauland written by the American diplomat in Vienna Cobburn Kidd, in Dowling to Department of State, 1 August 1950, 763.00/8-150, RG 59, NA. Hans Igler, who became the director of the Central Bureau of the Marshall Plan (ZERP) under Figl, had started out as an industrial planner in the ministry of Economic Planning. He characterized Krauland as coupling a highly dynamic personality with "hubris", see the oral history by Helmut Wohnout and Michael Gehler with Hans Igler, "Der Marshall-Plan war die Basis," in *Demokratie und Geschichte* 1 (1997): 94.

53. Telegram Hofmann-Montanus to Figl; letter Figl to Kolb, (n.d.); even though the telegram and Figl's letter were sent in mid-March, it is unclear from the files why Kolb addressed this important matter in June; Kolb letters to Figl and Hofmann-Montanus, 27 June 1949, all in file 98.834-V/23b/49.

54. Letter Raab to Figl, 11 March 1949, 112.909/V-23b/2199/49. The "Förderungsprogramm der Fremdenverkehrsunternehmen" of October 1948 is attached to this file. The core demand was "to be given the same priority as the export industries in all matters of reconstruction."

55. Kolb was bombarded by letters and telegrams from state tourist officials. For these, the record on Krauland's actions, and the letter from Kolb to Krauland with various official minutes, all March 1949, see the file "Finanzierungshilfe für Fremdenverkehr," 104.635-V/23b/49.

56. "Vortrag für den Ministerrat" and Kolb minute, 1 July 1949, 107.373-V/23b/49. The Cabinet (*Ministerrat*) approved funding for tourism on 4 July 1949, Kolb minute, 28 July 1949, 109.676-V/23b/49.

57. Kidd termed the ÖAAB "the tail of the People's Party dog," Dowling to Department of State, 1 August 1950, 763.00/8-150, RG 59, NA. To elucidate such ÖVP infighting, see, for background, the essays on the People's Party postwar history, party structure, and corporate tradition by Robert Kriechbaumer, Alfred Ableitinger, and Ernst Bruckmüller in *Volkspartei - Anspruch und Realität. Zur Geschichte der ÖVP seit 1945*, ed. Robert Kriechbaumer and Franz Schausberger (Vienna, 1995).

58. "*Es ist klar, dass der größte Teil der zur Verfügung stehenden Mittel für Fremdenverkehrszwecke in Wien und in den innösterreichischen Bundesländern verwendet würde, weil derjenige, welcher näher an der Krippe sitzt, eben zuerst mahlt.*" Letter Mülwerth to Kolb, 5 August 1949, 110.826-V/23b/49.

59. Letter Ilg (Governor of Vorarlberg) to Tourism Section/Ministry of Trade, 10 October 1949, 117.553-V/23b/49. Other state organizations such as the Salzburg one also lobbied the Ministry to distribute these funds quickly to the states, so they would be able to begin their reconstruction projects starving for investment funds; see Hofmann-Montanus to Ministry of Trade, 5 November 1949, 118.447-V/23b/49; see also letter Rehrl (Governor of Salzburg) to Kolb, 19 November 1949, 119.863-V/23b/49.

60. Letters Raab/Widmann (*Bundeskammer*) to Trade Ministry, 27 October 1949, and minute and draft letter Kolb to Raab, 117.856-V/23b/49.

61. ECA wanted the distribution of "short credits" (five years) at an interest rate of 3.5 percent. See Spitzmüller minutes, 27 December 1949, 112.476-V/23b/49; the *Hotel-Treuhand* had already presented a draft of its guidelines on 21 July 1949 with minute, 110.043-V/23b/49.

62. Minute, December 1949 (n.d.), 121.232-V/23b/49.

63. Wilfried Mähr, "Der Marshallplan in Österreich: Tanz nach einer ausländischen Pfeife?," in *Die bevormundete Nation: Österreich und die Alliierten 1945-1949*, ed. Günter Bischof and Josef Leidenfrost (Innsbruck, 1988), 245-72; Kurt K. Tweraser, "The Politics of Productivity and Corporatism: The Late Marshall Plan in Austria, 1950-54," *Contemporary Austrian Studies* 3 (1995): 91-115.

64. C.E. Meyer to Wilhelm Taucher (Director, of Central Bureau for ERP Affairs), 8 February 1952, Mission to Austria, Economic Program and Planning Division, Program Subject Files 1952-55, Administration-Counterpart, Box 12, Folder Tourism, RG 469 (Records of U.S. Foreign Assistance Agencies 1948-61), NA.

65. Tweraser, "Politics of Productivity"; Tweraser's and Mähr's findings of minimal U.S. success in bringing about Austrian economic reforms need to be revised in light of Hans Seidel's findings. Seidel attributes considerable success to U.S. behind-the-scenes pressure on the Figl government towards an anti-inflationary and liberalizing "stabilization program" in 1951/53, which is usually exclusively associated with Minister of Finance Reinhard Kamitz. I am grateful to Professor Seidel for showing me his chapter on the "stabilization program" in his forthcoming book on Austrian economic reconstruction; see also Seidel's essay in this volume.

66. These data are conveniently summarized in *WIFO-Monatsberichte*, No. 1 (1956), 22f; see also "Investitionen in den Fremdenverkehr," *WIFO Montsberichte*, No. 3 (1955), 121-24; Nemschak, *Zehn Jahre*, 55-57.

67. While Director of the prestigous Austrian Institute for Economic Research, Franz Nemschak noted in his authoritative study *Zehn Jahre österreichische Wirtschaft 1945-1955* (p. 24) that 2.3 percent of ERP counterparts went to tourism until March 1955, the monthly reports of his Institute, however, calculated that by the end of 1954, 3.8 percent had flowed into tourism; due to the increases in funding in 1955, as much as 4.8 percent went to tourism by the end of that year, see *WIFO Monatsberichte*, No. 1 (1956): 22.

68. See the files on the Vorarlberg government applying for funding for the "Schneefräse Lafly" in January 1948, 30.049-I/4a/1948 et al. GZ 30.049/48. Organizing the removal of snow from the streets of the high altitude alpine valleys of Western Austria was a complex affair since the Allied Council had to allot the fuel necessary for the heavy equipment, see the file "Strassenwinterdienst 1947/1948," 30.618-I/4a/1948, GZ. 30.049/48.

69. For tourism allocations, see the letter from Igler to King (ECA Mission Chief), 18 September 1950, 517.324-3/50, for fourth quarter 1950 allocations, see the letter from Taucher to King, 15 November 1950, 521.384-3/50, both GZ. 512.289-ERP/3/50, ZERP, BKA.

70. The Hotels Tyrol and Garnie in Innsbruck, Muret in St. Christoph. the spas in Goisern and Badgastein, as well as öS 2 million for the Stubnerkogel cable car in Badgastein, as well as almost öS 3 million for a cable car in St. Anton and öS 5 million for the Alpach College, on the list of tourism projects funded in 1952, see the letter from Taucher to Meyer, 10. July 1952, 713.297-3/52 and other files in GZ. 700.149-ERP/3/52, ZERP, BKA.

71. Research on the diplomatic history of postwar Austro-German economic relations is in its infancy and constitutes one of the major desiderata for postwar Austrian foreign policy in general, and economic foreign policy in the Marshall Plan era in particular. The general background and the Cold War context is adumbrated in two extensive essays by Michael Gehler in *Ungleiche Partner: Österreich und Deutschland in ihrer gegenseitigen Wahrnehmung. Historische Analysen und Vergleiche aus dem 19. Und 20. Jahrhundert*, ed. Michael Gehler, et al. (Stuttgart, 1996), 535-642; Stefan Lütgenau, "Grundstrukturen der österreichisch-deutschen Beziehungen nach 1945", in *Österreich in den Fünfzigern*, 237-58.

72. See the table in Rigele, *Großglockner-Hochalpenstraße*, 296.

73. Prewar figures, in ibid., 296-8. Austrian postwar figures in Stadler, *Kavalierstour*, 309; Vorarlberg figures, in *Vorarlberger Wirtschafts- und Sozialstatistik*, II (1955): 637f.; Tyrol figures in Tschurtschenthaler, "Tourismus im Bundesland Tirol," 156f, 203 (Table 12); for the importance of German tourists for Austria's postwar economic recovery, see also Brusatti, *10 Jahre Österreichischer Fremdenverkehr*, 157.

74. Nemschak, *Zehn Jahre*, 55f; Brusatti, *100 Jahre*, 156; for the dramatic increases after 1955 also from a regional perspective, see Frantz, " Austrian Tourism," 9-23.

75. Nemschak, *Zehn Jahre*, 56f. U.S. estimate gives different figures: the $ 6,.7 million in foreign exchange receipts of 1937 were surpassed by $ 8.36 million in 1954, see "Miscellaneous Tourism Stastistics," Jones to Ockey, 27 June 1955, Productivity and Special Assistance Division, Box 32, Folder tourism 1955, RG 469, NA.

76. Ibid.

77. For thoughtful critiques of Alpine (and Himalyan) tourism, and especially the fascinating "urbanization" analysis by Werner Bätzing and Manfred Perlik, see *Verreiste Berge: Kultur und Tourismus im Hochgebirge*, ed. Kurt Luger and Karin Inmann (Innsbruck, 1995); for "landscape devouring tourism," the "suburbanization" of the Alps and the "colonizing" effects of modern tourism, see Preglau, "Tourism Kills Tourism," 51-60, and idem, 'Kolonialisierung der Lebenswelt'?: Zum heuristischen Potential und zur empirischen Bewährung eines Theorems in der 'Bereisten'-Forschung," in *Der durchschaute Tourist: Arbeiten zur Tourismusforschung*, ed. R. Bachleitner, et al. (Munich, 1998), 49-61; for an interview with Sir Angus Stirling, former director general of the British National Trust, on "sustainable tourism," see *New Orleans Times Picayune*, 11 January 1999, B-1, B-8. For an analysis of modern tourism remarkably free of ideological bias (and therefore quite free of knee-jerk "*Tourismuskritik*"), see Hennig, *Reislust*.

# Fifty Years Later: A New Marshall Plan for Eastern Europe?

*Wilhelm Kohler*[*]

## Introduction

When several countries in Central and Eastern Europe (CEE) embarked on a path of systemic transformation in 1989/90, it soon became evident that their initial conditions were extremely bad, and catching up to Western European income levels would be a long and painful process. People felt deprived of cherished safety nets and were faced with a hitherto unknown degree and kind of uncertainty, while policy makers were confronted with the formidable task of keeping society on a sustainable track of reform which soon turned out to inflict significant income losses. There was very little help from historical experience on which to draw, or firm theoretical knowledge on which to rely. Adding to all of this the simple fact that people had meanwhile turned into a true electorate, transformation certainly was a risky endeavor.

If all of this had happened on a group of far-away islands, it would probably not have caught too much of our attention. The fact, however, that it took place at the very frontier of the Cold War made it a world event of major importance, in particular for Western Europe.

---

[*] An earlier version of this paper was presented at the conference "The Marshall Plan in Austria," University of New Orleans, May 5-7, 1998. Thanks are due to Günter Bischof for several helpful discussions on Marshall Plan issues, and to Rudi Winter-Ebmer and Herbert Matis for commenting on the first version. The simulation results reported on in the final part of the paper go back to a research project entitled "The Economic Consequences of EU's Eastern Enlargement", conducted under the auspices of the Institute for Advanced Studies, Vienna, and funded by the Kreisky Forum for International Dialogue as well as the Austrian Government.

West could not simply take a backseat and let things go their way in the East. But what should it do? On the one hand, it is true that the experiment of systemic transformation on such a grand scale was pretty much unique. On the other hand, groups of countries trying to catch up from bad initial conditions is by no means without precedence in history. After all, it is the perennial concern of development policy, and Western Europe had itself been in such a catching-up position after World War II. In all such cases, international aid had been an integral part of the strategies adopted. Hence, the issue of aid was bound to appear on the agenda for post-communist Central and Eastern Europe. For rather obvious reasons, a question often raised is whether there was—or still is—a case for a new Marshall Plan initiative for Eastern Europe. Indeed, one might even argue that the beneficiaries of the original Marshall Plan aid now have a moral obligation to step in with aid, thus facilitating a belated correction of the Yalta conference.

Obligation or not, if the Marshall Plan was successful for post-World War II Western Europe, might it now serve as a useful model for Western aid to the post-communist East? Not all observers have come up with an affirmative answer, even in the early 1990s. And now, almost ten years after the onset of transformation, the misgivings no doubt have increased. Overall, one might argue, transformation went reasonably well, and the gloomy picture starts getting brightened by success stories on business formation and growth. Big differences between individual CEE countries notwithstanding, one may therefore be tempted to forego the conclusion that at this stage a "New Marshall Plan" for these countries funded by Western Europe has no place in a well-guided strategy. This article takes a closer look at various aspects pertaining to this issue. Specifically, the Arguments for Aid section offers a critical review of principle arguments that one can put forward in favor of Western aid for Eastern Europe, placing due emphasis on the distinction between humanitarian and efficiency reasons, and drawing on recent economic research on the Marshall Plan. In the Limits to the Marshall Plan Analogy section, I shall then highlight various differences between the present position of the CEECs and the post-World War II situation and explore their potential implications in the context of Western help for CEECs along the lines of a Marshall Plan model. This will be followed a detailed discussion of the idea, sometimes coming up in policy debates, that an Eastern enlargement of the European Union (EU) involves certain key parallels to the Marshall Plan. More specifically, the section entitled Eastern Enlargement of the EU briefly characterizes EU accession from an Eastern newcomer's perspective, with special emphasis on the potential amount of transfers received, in comparison with the Marshall Plan funds that Western Europe has benefited from fifty years ago. The fifth Section then returns to a principle argument for aid expounded in general terms in the second section, arguments for Aid, namely that aid may be beneficial to the donor country if tied to trade liberalization measures. Relying on a simulation model for the Austrian economy, I shall present empirical support for this claim. The Conclusion closes the paper with a brief summary.

## Arguments For Aid: A Brief Survey

### *Helping to catch up: the simple mechanics of growth*

The most obvious argument for international aid in a catching-up situation is *humanitarian* in nature: offering help to disadvantaged people. Anecdotal evidence from individual success stories can easily lead one to forget just how big the income gap between Eastern Europe and the West still is. Table 1 gives an idea of the "distance" of some of the potential CEE EU candidates from the EU average in 1996. Even the most advanced countries exhibit a more than 40 percent income gap, and Bulgaria trails the list with a per-capita GDP which is a mere 20 percent of the EU average. Poland, which has recently been praised as a high growth performer, still lags behind by as much as 70 percent. True, these gaps are still small compared to many third world countries. But, as pointed out by Murrell, what makes this a special case is that some of these countries were in positions quite similar to EU countries no more than forty years ago. An example here is Austria and Hungary in the 1950s. These gaps will not be closed very quickly by growth differentials. For the sake of a quick numerical example, we may draw on Table 1 and assume (very optimistically) that Poland continues to grow at a rate of 6.1 percent p.a., while growth in the EU remains at 1.6 percent on average. The gap would then be narrowed from 70 percent to about 53.7 percent in ten years, and it would take as much as twenty years for the gap to be narrowed to less than 30 percent which, in turn, is the largest income gap presently observable within the EU (for Greece).

Might aid make a big difference? Not if catching-up works only through the neoclassical mechanics of growth. First of all, we should not expect countries to catch up to a common level of income, even in the very long run. They may differ in their long-run equilibrium levels of income, in which case the notion of catching-up makes sense only with respect to an individual country's long run (steady state) income level, not in the sense of an international comparison. While this is an important point in principle, it is not clear *a priori* why the CEECs should have lower long run income levels than Western European countries, let alone to pin down the difference in terms of numbers. Moreover, judging from Western countries experience, convergence to a country's own steady state is likely to be a rather slow process.[1]

In any case, the question coming up next is whether aid will have any impact on this long run income level. Here again, traditional growth theory is pessimistic: if growth takes place subject to diminishing returns of whatever is accumulated (physical capital, human capital etc.), then temporary aid will have no lasting effect. History, according to this view, does not matter where a country will ultimately end up! This, no doubt, is almost anathema to historians discussing aid. Nor does it fully capture the way that economists would want to think about it. Even from a narrow growth theory perspective, economists have pointed out several reasons why the conditions prevailing at the outset and during early phases of catching up, including transfer payments received from abroad, might have lasting effects. Modern growth theory emphasizes that path-dependence of this sort will arise whenever accumulated factors exhibit constant, rather than diminishing, marginal returns. Notice that this coin, too, has two sides. On the positive side, the effect of aid will be felt *ad infinitum*. On the negative side, however, if the marginal return to accumulated capital is constant, then a very low capital stock to start with does not carry the advantage of a high initial marginal productivity of capital. Instead, poor initial conditions will likewise leave an indefinite imprint on the development path of the economy. There is no catching-up at all![2] Typically, in such cases aid may not only affect long-run income levels, but also long run rates of income growth. However, to policy makers and people alike, short to medium run effects are no doubt of more concern than the long run steady state. Hence, even if aid were devoid of any long run effects, the truly important question seems whether it can foster growth and well-being in the short run.

But in the short run as well, the effect of aid is likely to be rather modest, if it operates only through the mechanics of investment and growth. Much depends on the details of how investment is determined, but by way of a first approximation we may draw on the famous Solow growth model.[3] In this model it can be shown that, ceteris paribus, aid in the amount of $x$ percent of GDP increases the contemporaneous growth rate of GDP per capita by $sxy\theta_k$ percentage points, where $s$ is the marginal rate of savings, $y$ is the inverse of the capital/output ratio, and $\theta_k$ is the share of capital in overall income. Invoking a Marshall Plan order of magnitude for $x = 5$, the Austrian value of $y = 0.3$ for 1992,[4] a consensus value of $\theta_k = 0.3$, and using the savings ratios from national accounts for CEECs to obtain a rough value of $s = 0.3$,[5] we obtain a temporary growth rate effect in the amount of 0.135 percentage points. Interestingly, this is pretty much what Eichengreen and Uzan have found in one of their econometric investigations of the growth effect of the Marshall Plan allotments in the Austrian case: 0.14 percent for 1948-1949, and 0.11 percent for 1949-1950. However, *a priori* expectations would rise if we were to take a more extensive view on capital, for instance by including human capital as suggested by the augmented Solow model. This would, in effect, increase the value of $\theta_k$, but even doubling its value would still not give a big stake. Also, the Solow model is, admittedly, somewhat crude in that it assumes a constant marginal savings ratio and simply equates investment with savings. Alternative models of growth, as for instance the so-called Ramsey model or much of modern growth theory, treat investment and savings in a more elaborate and satisfactory way. Within such models, one would have to be more precise as to how exactly aid is used, in order to be able to say anything about its effect. The crucial question here is how aid changes the incentives for investors.[6] Suffice it to say, without going into any detail, that in an extreme case where aid is channeled through to pure household transfers it could be devoid of any growth effect at all, but simply increase consumption. This sheds some light on why aid is seldom granted unconditionally. But still, the simple mechanics of growth strike a rather pessimistic tone on the likely effects of foreign aid on the performance of CEECs.[7]

But in their above mentioned study on the effects of the Marshall Plan, Eichengreen and Uzan carry out a counterfactual exercise which gives rise to a somewhat more optimistic view. They estimate econometric equations using—among other things—Marshall Plan allotments to explain investment, the current account, and government spending. All of these are then in turn used to explain individual countries' GDP growth. Assuming that all Marshall Plan effects have operated through either investment, the current account, or government spending gives the above mentioned minuscule effect. However, changing the econometric specification by allowing aid to explain GDP growth directly generates a wholly different picture: The Marshall Plan apparently has effected major changes through channels other than the mechanics of investment and growth. To see just what it is that gives international aid a higher leverage we have to do two things: 1. leave the realm of growth theory for a more realistic view on key problems of systemic transformation, and 2. introduce the notion of conditionality in more explicit terms. In doing so, we shall not only expand our understanding of how aid might work, but also why it might be in the interest of the donor country to grant it. More specifically, we shall encounter efficiency reasons for aid, in addition to the humanitarian reason that we have stipulated at the outset above.

*Aiming at Collective Rationality: The Efficiency Case for Aid*

In its most general form, the efficiency argument for international aid runs as follows. Suppose there is room for mutual economic improvement for two countries, but for some reason one country is either unwilling or unable to undertake whatever action is necessary for such an improvement. Then the other country might consider "bribing" its partner country into such action, hoping of course that the benefits received will over-compensate the transfers paid. To put it in less disreputable terms: this country might offer aid with appropriate conditionality attached to it.[8] This is nothing but a variant of the compensation argument which was introduced 60 years ago by Hicks and Kaldor to facilitate an evaluation of situations which cannot be Pareto-ranked.

A simple example might illustrate the point. Trade liberalization may be perceived detrimental by a large country because it fears a terms of trade deterioration. This country might then resist giving up its protectionist measures. Yet, given gains from trade and barring information problems, its partner country should be able to find some compensatory arrangement under which dismantling trade barriers is attractive for both countries. Lahiri and Raimondos-Møller have recently substantiated this point, using a theoretical model to demonstrate that tying aid to tariff reform can be used to ensure Pareto improvements. Additionally, history is replete with practical examples, including the Marshall Plan, where aid packages include a more or less explicit element of conditionality on trade liberalization. Perhaps a more realistic view would not so much emphasize that a country as a whole may lose through trade liberalization, but that its government may be unable to handle internal pressure opposing such reform. More specifically, its government may for some reason not be in a position to devise and implement suitable measures to compensate those groups among its electorate who would suffer from a loss of protection. Receiving aid from abroad may put it in a position to do so.

A somewhat subtler way that a country may gain is via trade as a channel of transmission for technological knowledge. Just as knowledge created by research and development in a given firm is to some extent transmitted to other firms and sectors within an economy through a complex input-output structure and the associated exchange relations, so it will be transmitted to other countries by trade. The crucial thing to note here is the externality: due to the public good nature of knowledge, a (potentially large) part of the benefits of research and development is external to the innovator, ready to be used without further cost by other firms whose productivity is then increased for free. Quite naturally, such an innovator cannot be expected to carry out costly research and development to a socially optimal extent. This is why most governments engage in subsidizing domestic research and development activities. If they do so in a non-cooperative way, however, they will not take into account the benefits accruing to other countries via trade. As a result, a situation might arise where they collectively under-subsidize research and development. Obviously, the first best solution would be to aim at cooperative government behavior. But if for some reason this is unachievable directly, a government may contemplate granting its neighbor-country conditional aid, particularly if that country's research and development policy is additionally plagued by fiscal constraints. Note that the argument runs in both ways, suggesting that trade liberalization may also be a very cheap and efficient way for a technologically superior country to help its neighbor to catch up. Indeed, this seems the more relevant variant of the argument in the present context. It is difficult to tell how important this aspect is in reality, but available evidence suggests it is far from trivial.[9]

The argument may be put into an even broader perspective by saying that economic prosperity as such is a public good transcending country borders.[10] We are, admittedly, entering vague and shaky ground here, but the general idea is not entirely unconvincing if applied to neighboring transition economies in the following way. To people and policy makers in the CEECs, systemic transformation may look like a trade off: current sacrifice for the sake of future prosperity. If that prosperity exerts an externality on neighboring West-European countries, transformation is likely to proceed at a sub-optimally slow speed, and maybe also to a sub-optimal extent in the long run, if optimality is defined from a global perspective. The reason again is that domestic agents are unlikely to take account of the transnational externality.[11] As before, conditional aid may be an appropriate response. In principle, this argument can be applied to all government policies aiming at domestic prosperity, but it is arguably more relevant in the present context than in others. It is worth pointing out that for this problem, and the above mentioned research and development-problem alike, international capital markets are of no help. They may be important in facilitating international borrowing for a government which temporarily faces a low tax base, but the fundamental problem here is not really one of financing. Instead, it is the cross-border external effect of prosperity which implies that the government does not do enough even if it has access to a perfect world capital market.

The efficiency arguments for aid presented so far do not shed much light on why Marshall Plan aid might have been so important to Austria and the rest of Western Europe. A further argument, however, arises in the realm of macroeconomic stabilization policy which recent research suggests was decisive for postwar Western Europe. The underlying premise here is that any country gains from a stable macroeconomic environment in its neighboring economies. Countries with big differences in inflation rates will need periodic changes in their nominal exchange rates, with the possibility of recurring exchange rate misalignments, particularly if nominal prices are sticky. As a result, trade flows between such countries will likely be disrupted from time to time. One would presumably not go as far as postulating a unified rate of inflation for neighboring countries, that is a monetary union. But it is certainly in Western European countries' interest that CEECs close the inflation gaps (see Table 1). One would actually expect that such stability gaps are easier to close in short periods of time than income gaps. Why, then, are inflation rates still so much higher in the East, and what can aid do to bring them down? Macroeconomic theory tells us that switching from an inflationary to a non-inflationary path may involve a significant temporary output loss, unless agents correctly anticipate such a switch. Similarly, if monetary authorities credibly announce such a policy shift, the output loss may, at least in theory, largely be avoided.[12] While it is plausible that policy makers in CEECs may lack credibility in this regard, it is not immediately clear why aid received from the West should be of much help in achieving lower inflation. Yet this is precisely what Eichengreen and Uzan as well as De Long and Eichengreen argue the Marshall Plan did in post-World War II Europe.

To grasp the underlying argument, one first has to recognize that inflation typically is the result of inconsistent claims on national output. Such claims are partly negotiated in nominal terms *ex ante*, for instance through wage settlements and government budgets. If they turn out *ex post* to add up to more than what is available to distribute, the resulting conflict is very often "resolved" by means of inflation, which may sufficiently reduce the claims on output in real terms. Now, if it were possible in a unified way to play this game of *ex ante* negotiation plus *ex post* inflation on a lower level of nominal claims and proportionally lower expected (and realized) inflation, the outcome would be the same in real terms for everybody. It would then be difficult to see why anybody should oppose doing so, and we would expect a quick and undelayed implementation of stabilization. However, in practice, stabilization often involves one group giving in first, or at least not all groups giving in proportionally at the same time. In this case, stabilization policy inflicts a temporary loss on certain groups (in terms of their share in real national output), to the benefit of others. In the long run, all groups will benefit from lower inflation, but only at a temporary sacrifice which is shared unequally by different groups. One can easily imagine that this gives rise to a "war of attrition" where each group hopes to avoid paying its share by delaying stabilization, and waiting until other groups have run out of either their political power or their ability to bear the cost of prolonged inflation.[13] Such a "war of attrition" analogy seems particularly relevant for periods following repressed inflation and monetary overhangs, as in post-World War II Europe or in post-communist Eastern European countries, where it is clear that the inflationary way of dealing with unresolved distributional conflicts cannot go on forever. But where in this game does foreign aid play a role? Eichengreen and Uzan and De Long and Eichengreen simply argue that by increasing the size of the pie it alleviates the conflict over how it should be distributed. More specifically, it may lower the cost of giving in first, so stabilization will succeed earlier than without aid.

**Table 1: "Distance" between CEECs and EU15-average with respect to key economic characteristics 1996**

| | GDP per capita at PPP | 1996 growth rate of real GDP | Share of agriculture in value added | Share of agriculture in employment | Unem-ployment rate | Inflation rate | Government deficit in % of GDP |
|---|---|---|---|---|---|---|---|
| **EU15** | 19499.39 | 1.60 | 2.00 | 5.00 | 11.29 | 2.66 | 0.04 |
| | | | relative to EU-average | | | | |
| **Hungary** | 0.35 | 1.00 | 3.20 | 1.67 | 0.95 | 8.86 | 0.70 |
| **Czech Rep.** | 0.57 | 4.10 | 3.25 | 1.21 | 0.31 | 3.30 | 0.16 |
| **Slovak Rep.** | 0.41 | 6.90 | 2.86 | 1.96 | 1.13 | 2.18 | 1.00 |
| **Slovenia** | 0.57 | 3.10 | 2.09 | 1.17 | 1.28 | 3.71 | -0.06 |
| **Poland** | 0.30 | 6.10 | 3.48 | 5.68 | 1.17 | 7.47 | 0.57 |
| **Romania** | 0.23 | 4.10 | 10.67 | 6.95 | 0.56 | 14.57 | 1.11 |
| **Bulgaria** | 0.20 | -10.90 | 4.39 | 4.99 | 1.11 | 46.16 | 2.51 |

EU15: average of EU15 countries, GDP in PPP US-Dollars, agricultural shares in percent
CEECs: all figures indicate the respective country figure relative to EU15-average, GDP at PPP

Source: WIIW Economic Data Base Eastern Europe
OECD National Accounts, Main Aggregates and Detailed Tables
IMF International Financial Statistics
IMF World Economic Outlook

A different scenario with a similar outcome is envisaged by Saint-Paul. Any government facing a shortage of revenue has three ways to close its budget: Finance all expenditures by means of higher contemporaneous taxation, finance a deficit through borrowing on capital markets, that is by future taxation; or—if allowed to do so—resort to money creation to finance its deficit, thereby causing an increase in the price level. The crucial point is that, given its fiscal shortage, the government's temptation to use money creation may vary with the ongoing rate of inflation. At a given rate of inflation, the incentives may just happen to be such that the government ends up choosing money creation to an extent which is consistent with this rate of inflation, in which case the rate of inflation is an equilibrium phenomenon and, therefore, stays constant. If, however, the incentives happen to be such that the government chooses a larger (or smaller) amount of money creation than is consistent with the ongoing rate of inflation, then instead of staying constant, the rate of inflation will increase (fall), thereby approaching its higher (lower) equilibrium rate. Using a simple formal model, Saint-Paul argues that the underlying incentive structure may be such that there are multiple equilibrium rates of inflation.[14] Whether an economy ends up in a high or low inflation equilibrium, then, depends on its initial combination of inflation and fiscal needs. Suppose, for instance, that the government faces a severe revenue shortage while repressed inflation is released during transformation. As a result, the economy might jump too close to the precipice of a high inflation equilibrium for it to avoid it. If, however, foreign aid provides sufficient fiscal relief, the government might find it easier and more attractive to avoid money creation, thus initiating a virtuous movement to a low inflation equilibrium instead. What aid does in this case is place the economy sufficiently close, in terms of the combination of inflation and fiscal shortage, to the desired low inflation equilibrium at a critical stage of transition. Notice that temporary aid has a permanent effect: it assists in reaching a low, instead of a high, inflation path which, once reached, remains sustainable without further aid.

### *Caveats*

Lest the reader obtain an overly optimistic impression from this discussion, let me add a few important caveats. All of the above efficiency arguments for aid fall under the category of international policy coordination to avoid collective irrationality. Economists have primarily analyzed this issue in various contexts of macroeconomic policies, but our discussion has shown that the issue really extends to other areas of economic policy. However, the relevant literature suggests that international aid is not the only, and in many instances certainly not the best, way to deal with the problem. But in some cases, it may nonetheless be more viable than in others. One can argue that the specific forms in which efficiency problems arise in the context of CEE countries in transition make aid a more promising candidate, in particular if combined with a humanitarian and/or geopolitical motive, than in the typical case considered in the economic policy coordination literature.[15]

Important additional caveats remain, nonetheless. Perhaps most importantly, it is one thing to identify an efficiency case for aid in principle, but moving from such principles to the successful implementation of a specific aid plan is a different matter. More specifically, aid has opportunity cost in the donor country, and using this aid to support a specific industry or firm likewise has an opportunity cost in the recipient country: once received, it could have been used for a different industry or firm. In other words: when it comes to implementing such a policy, the big question often is how to pick "winners" that the aid should be spent on. Obviously, the success of an aid program very much depends on the right pick. Even worse, and particularly relevant for the present case of the CEECs, an aid program may retard necessary economic reforms by relieving governments of the need to correct misguided policies. Conditionality may not be sufficiently precise to set the right incentives, or it may even set the wrong incentives. Indeed, this is precisely what some observers argue the Marshall Plan did, and it is therefore not surprising that these observers are highly skeptical as to whether the Marshall Plan could possibly act as a model for how the West should react to the challenge at the Eastern border.[16] This view which, in a sense, carries Milward's criticisms of the "folk image" of the Marshall Plan to the extreme, is by no means commonly accepted, however. We have seen above that economists have recently identified less obvious and less directly observable ways in which the Marshall Plan may have been successful or even decisive.[17] Not surprisingly, these authors are also less skeptical as to drawing on the post-War experience to suggest a Marshall Plan kind of response to the present day challenge, or at least to emphasize certain parallels. But where, exactly, do we find suggestive analogies, and perhaps more importantly, are there differences which should warrant caution?

## Limits to the Marshall Plan Analogy

*Restructuring versus reconstruction*

Perhaps most importantly, the theoretical paradigm which guides our thinking about post-World War II Europe and the Marshall Plan may be misleading for Eastern Europe, at least up to a certain point in time. While the Marshall Plan period was essentially one of reconstruction, the challenge for CEECs is restructuring, which involves a significant element of destruction. By 1945, destruction had already taken place, and the postwar era was dominated by a strong sense of reconstruction. By way of contrast, the post-communist reform process, particularly in its early phases, carried a very strong flavor of destruction (see Murrell). Figure 1 may serve to highlight and discuss this point. It juxtaposes real GDP for Marshall Plan recipient countries during and after World War II[18] with real GDP for CEECs subsequent to the start of transformation in 1989. Anchoring the comparison by placing 1989 at 1945 and by setting 1939 and 1989 equal to 100 is, admittedly, somewhat arbitrary and should be left open to debate. However, the basic message seems quite clear: while strong reconstruction-type growth in Marshall Plan countries had set in immediately after the war, particularly for the most depressed economies like those of Austria and Germany, the onset of transformation in 1989 has released strong forces of destruction. Including such countries as Russia and Ukraine, Eastern GDP growth was negative throughout until 1996. Even for the more advantageous CEECs, it took four years until very moderate GDP growth set in. Indeed, the figure suggests the metaphor of "rubber band" growth for postwar Europe,[19] while no such"rubber band" appears to have been present in 1989/90 when Eastern countries started abandoning their planning systems. The contractionary forces released thereafter may be explained in several ways. The following subsections give a brief overview.[20]

*The curse of distortions and missing institutions*

Prior to 1989/90, Eastern economies had been characterized by a heavily distorted price system dictated by central planning. Exposing them more or less overnight to world prices and competition had a devastating effect on the utilization of resources. By way of contrast, in the Marshall Plan recipient countries, price incentives had not been distorted all that much and, more importantly, were distorted for a relatively short amount of time. The price system dictates that, if prices change, those activities where the opportunity cost of resources is higher than the value of what they produce should be shut down. This part of restructuring seems to have worked quite well in the CEECs. Ideally, however, the resources freed in this way will be put to use where they generate a market value in excess of their opportunity cost. And this complementary piece of restructuring seems to have failed in the early phases of transition.

Much has been said and written on the cause of this failure, and in one way or another almost all explanations revolve around the idea of missing institutions. The legal systems and institutions necessary for the price system to deliver its success were absent to a much higher degree in the CEECs in the early 1990s than was the case in postwar Western Europe. Here, the term "institutions" should be interpreted in the broadest possible sense. The most crucial aspects are the regulatory system pertaining to business formation, property rights, the tax system, and—most important of all—a sound banking system and capital markets. Depending on the circumstances, public attitude towards these institutions may be a supportive or a retarding factor. Even though the inter-war depression had left certain misgivings, the price system was widely accepted in post-World War II Western Europe as a means to allocate scarce resources. Destruction was associated with the war, and the price system was by and large seen as supportive of reconstruction. In sharp contrast, in Eastern countries, now or at least in the early transformation periods, the price system is more or less directly associated with destruction and therefore embraced much less emphatically. Indeed, if appropriate legal systems and institutions are absent, the price system may be installed improperly, giving rise to large wind-fall gains and being open to misuse by economic crime, instead of playing the Smithian role of a beneficial invisible hand. This is certainly not conducive to a general acceptance of the price system.[21]

Getting rid of distortions is particularly difficult if macroeconomic stabilization is a simultaneous policy objective. On the one hand, adopting an undistorted price system while at the same time reducing inflation may require large reductions in nominal prices, including nominal incomes, which people are often reluctant to accept if they have money illusion. On the other hand, the above mentioned "war of attrition" is more likely to arise if macroeconomic stabilization is pur-

**Figure 1:** Real GDP and industrial production of Marshall Plan (MP) recipient countries 1939-1955 (1939=100) and CEECs and Eastern countries 1989-1996 (1989=100)

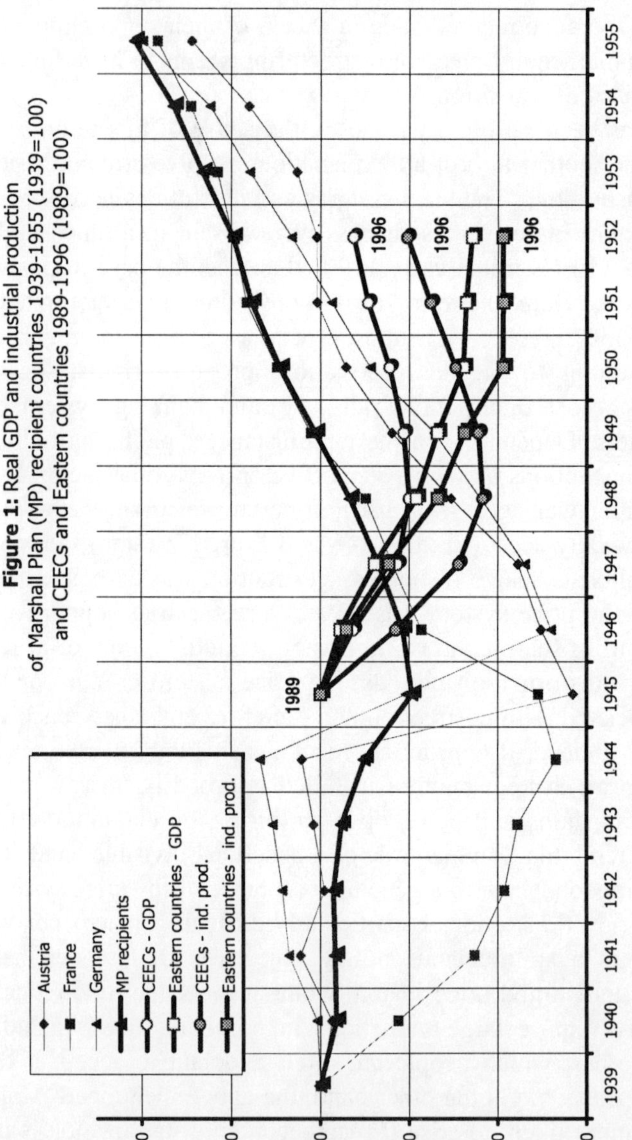


**CEECs:** Bulgaria, Czech Rep., Croatia, Hungary, Poland, Romania, Slovak Rep., Slovenia. **Eastern Countries:** CEECs plus Russia and Ukraine.
**Source:** Maddison (1995), and WIIW (1998).

**Figure 2:** GDP per-capita at PPP for Marshall Plan (MP) recipients 1939-1955 (1939=100) and CEECs and Eastern countries 1989-1996 (1989=100)

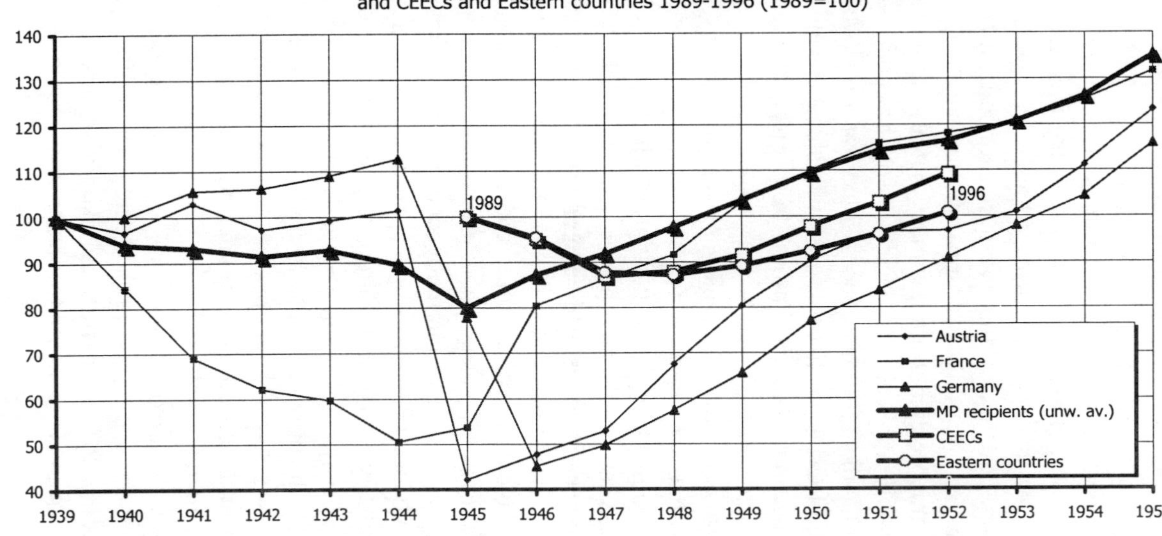


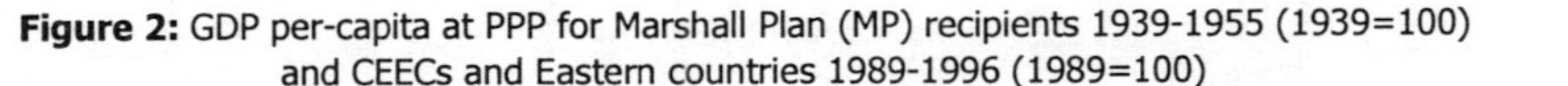

**CEECs:** Bulgaria, Czech Rep., Croatia, Hungary, Poland, Romania, Slovak Rep., Slovenia. **Eastern Countries:** CEECs plus Russia and Ukraine.
**Source:** Maddison (1995), and WIIW (1998).

sued at a time of large relative price adjustments. This gives rise to a policy dilemma: it proves difficult to achieve both an undistorted price system and lower inflation at the same time. Indeed, policy makers may feel tempted to trade in one objective for the other.[22]

### *High aspirations*

Falling incomes are particularly hard to bear, and survive politically, if they come at a time of high aspirations and expectations. Such times did not prevail in postwar Europe. In post-communist Eastern Europe, however, the Cold War rituals of mutually overselling economic success on both sides, coupled with the final defeat of the Soviet side, has left a somewhat distorted view in several parts of society regarding how much the Western economic model could deliver, and how fast. Not only is it important to realize that the price system at times imposes painful adjustment, but also to acknowledge that it is not equally applicable to all sectors of the economy. On all of these accounts, the aforementioned Cold War ritual was hardly helpful to the CEECs when it came to establishing a well-balanced view of what a decentralized system based on competition and prices can and cannot achieve.

Returning to aspirations, it is easy to get confused by different income figures that are reported on the success of economies in transition. Thus, compare Figure 1 to Figure 2 which depicts GDP *per capita*, calculated at purchasing power parities (PPP) instead of ongoing market exchange rates. Although one still observes successive periods of decline in the early 90s, the picture is no doubt somewhat brighter than was the case with Figure 1 above. Which one is right? In a sense, both are. Figure 1 gives a more or less accurate impression of how severe real contraction was in these countries, while Figure 2 tells us that we should not take this as an appropriate measure for real income losses relative to Western European countries. The difference is best understood by the following thought experiment. Imagine two regions, one of which experiences a contraction, while the other experiences a boom. Assume that prices of tradable commodities are given from world markets and remain unchanged during the period in question, assuming constant exchange rates. Under many circumstances, we would then expect prices for non-traded goods to fall in the depressed region, and to rise in the region with economic expansion. In calculating PPP, one tries to take these differential price movements into account in order to obtain comparable real income figures. Not surprisingly, applying such PPP instead of market exchange rates to obtain Eastern GDP figures gives a more favorable view of the CEECs. At the risk of oversimplification, we may say that Figure 2 takes a potential migrant's point of view, while Figure 1 is relevant to those who, for whatever reason, are determined to stay, and it is the right figure to look at if the amount of contraction is at issue.

*Trade*

Not only were distortions less prevalent in postwar Western Europe, but they were also felt with less severity than in present day Eastern Europe. The reason for this is that European postwar reconstruction took place in a much less globalized world than transformation in Eastern Europe. After the war, European economies were almost closed. Indeed, one of the key intentions of the Marshall Plan and the European Payments Union was to foster trade between European countries. Intra-European trade was deemed an essential ingredient of European postwar recovery, and these intentions were no doubt borne out. Given the limited possibility to trade with the rest of the world, and given that European countries were all in more or less equally bad shape, domestic producers felt very little competition from world markets. By way of contrast, one of the leading ideas of transformation in CEE is to quickly integrate these countries into the world economy, which has meanwhile become a global marketplace. For the countries in transition, this comes as a mixed blessing. On the one hand, being exposed to world prices almost overnight is a tremendous shock for these distorted economies, particularly since distance in almost all of its meanings has lost importance, and since some of the strongest competition comes from neighboring Western countries.[23] On the other hand, there is ample evidence from Western economies that integrated commodity markets and trade may be a powerful engine of growth.[24] Hence the long-term growth perspectives should be brighter in a globalized world. In the short run, however, the destructive forces *à la* Schumpeter may dominate and lead to a picture like the one portrayed by Figure 1.

The past seven years have already witnessed a significant increase in trade between CEECs and EU countries. Rodrik argues that this is not a pure reorientation effect. On the other hand, if judged by overall Eastern trade/GDP ratios, trade creation effects have so far been rather modest (see WIIW). Hence, we have reason to believe that there is room for further trade creation. This view is also supported by projections based on the gravity model of trade (see, for instance, Baldwin).[25] Whatever the merit of these projections, observed trade already points to an important difference between now and the Marshall Plan days: CEECs will likely turn out to be more important trading partners to Western European countries than the Marshall Plan recipients were for the United States. This is important if trade liberalization figures prominently in the conditionality element as in the case of EU enlargement. Figure 5 tries to highlight this point by depicting the relevant share of imports and exports in United States GNP for the postwar period, and in Austrian GNP for the 1980s and 1990s, respectively. Even though the CEECs covered are much smaller in their entirety than the group of Marshall Plan recipient countries, Austrian trade with these countries is more important if expressed in percent of GNP than were the Marshall Plan countries for the United States after World War II. If we believe in the projections based on the gravity model, the difference is even more pronounced. One might argue that an export share of 3.5 percent is not a lot, but this figure may substantially understate the leverage of trade liberalization. After all, trade is relatively low because there are trade barriers. As we shall see in the simulation exercise reported on below, even a 3 percent share is enough for sizable welfare gains from trade liberalization.

### *Foreign Capital*

World regions with a relatively low *per capita* level of an up-to-date capital stock should boast a high rate of return on investment and should, therefore, be able to draw foreign investment, provided only that capital markets are duly integrated so that savings can flow freely between regions. It is in this regard that we observe another difference between the Marshall Plan era and present day Europe. Presently, world capital markets are integrated to a degree which was last observed prior to World War I. In the aftermath of World War II, international capital mobility was virtually nonexistant. Quite apart from the question of convertibility, American investors were particularly shy with respect to Europe where they had sunk large amounts of money during the inter-war years. Hence, European nations found it much more difficult to gain access to world capital markets in the 1940s than after World War I (see, for instance, De Long and Eichengreen). By way of contrast, once opened to the Western world in the 1990s, Eastern European countries saw a highly receptive international capital market which had meanwhile become even more global than commodity markets. While it is true that in the early phases of transition the CEECs were facing high risk premia when drawing on foreign financing, such premia were successively reduced once investor confidence in transformation policies had been established.

Meanwhile, private capital inflows into CEECs and Eastern countries have picked up substantially, as evidenced by Figure 3 which depicts end of period stocks in percent of GDP for 1992 and 1996. Figure 4 shows that the share of private capital inflows, and in particular foreign direct investment, has increased impressively during the first half of the decade. It is tempting to draw a quick conclusion on the premise that a high responsiveness of private foreign investors to the relatively high marginal productivity of capital in Eastern Europe renders any public foreign aid program unnecessary. However, such a conclusion is valid only to the extent that the case for international aid as such relies on the lack of international capital mobility, and we have seen in the Arguments for Aid section above that there are a number of efficiency arguments for aid that in no way rest on the absence of international capital markets. Hence, while private international capital inflows no doubt are important for the CEECs' recovery and catching- up, it would be wrong to view them as a perfect substitute for aid.

### *Any Lesson?*

What are we to conclude from all of this? One might conclude from Figures 1 and 2 that by now it is simply too late. The most dire phases, so the argument might run, are over, and things look brighter. Hence aid is no longer necessary, particularly since private capital inflows have picked up quite impressively. However, in my view, the opposite conclusion is also possible, and more convincing: aid could have come too early. Given the restructuring (as opposed to the reconstruction) paradigm relevant for the early 1990s and the evidence highlighted in Figure 1, one can argue that it is only now that Eastern countries are approaching a position comparable to that of the Marshall Plan recipients in 1948, where a reasonably self-supporting growth path makes them a fertile ground for foreign aid. In other words, while such aid might have impeded necessary restructuring in times of poor institutions, it is a more promising option once institutions have started to emerge, the destructive forces of restructuring have petered out, and the reconstruction paradigm starts to prevail, as it did in the Marshall

**Figure 3:** Foreign direct investment in CEECs and Eastern countries total stock (end of period) in percent of GDP

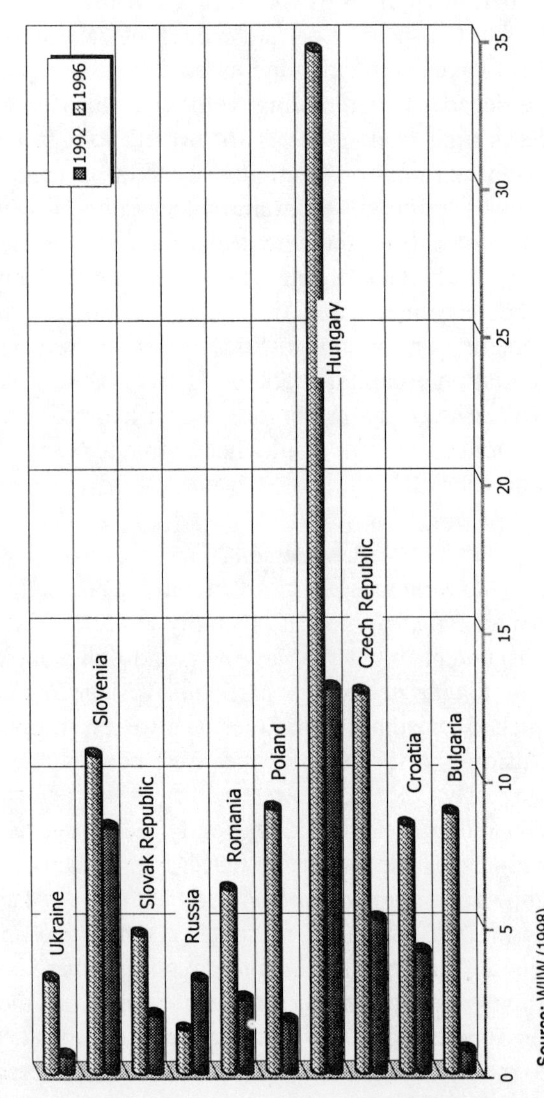


Source: WIIW (1998).

**Figure 4:** Various types of capital inflows into CEECs plus Baltics in percent of total inflows

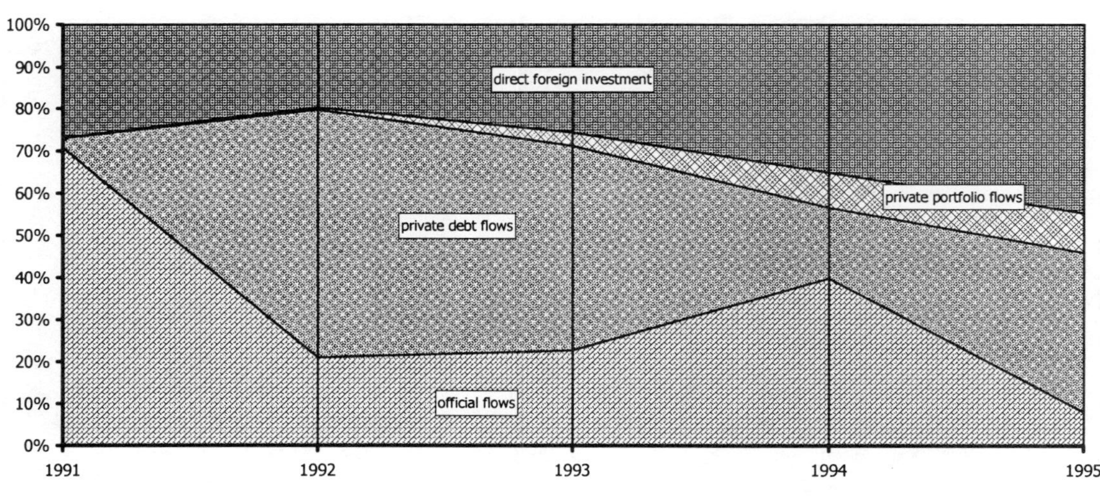


**CEECs:** as in figures 1 and 2.
**Source:** IMF World Economic Outlook, May 1997.

Plan era. This seems particularly relevant if the efficiency view of aid is adopted. It is admittedly less convincing if the humanitarian cause is in the foreground. Moreover, the above discussion supports the widely held view that aid should not be granted unconditionally. But framing such conditionality so as to make an aid package mutually advantageous for both the donor and the recipient countries is an arduous task. I shall now turn to the idea that an Eastern enlargement of the EU might constitute an appropriate design for such an aid package.

## Eastern Enlargement of the EU: Any Parallels to the Marshall Plan?

### *The policy package: a brief outline*

The European Union has reacted quite promptly to the new situation at its Eastern border by negotiating so-called Europe Agreements (EA) with several CEECs. The purpose of these agreements was to achieve a quick integration of commodity markets, which it is hoped will contribute to the catching-up process. Formal trade barriers are to be mutually abolished, except for agriculture and sensitive products like textiles and steel. The agreements, reached on a bilateral basis with ten CEECs,[26] mention full EU membership as a long-term objective. While it is true that the EAs do not contain any time schedule for negotiations on accession, it is probably fair to say that the prospect of membership was crucial for the concession that CEECs made on trade liberalization. EU enlargement and trade liberalization should thus be seen as integral parts of a single initiative. This is important in view of the simulation exercise reported on below.

However, membership would extend beyond trade liberalization in various key respects: 1. It would imply enlarging the customs union. More generally, Eastern countries would have to adopt the common EU foreign trade policy, in addition to applying the EU tariff schedule, which is lower on average than their present tariff schedule, to their trade with third countries. 2. They would be granted, and have to grant, Single Market status *vis-à-vis* all fellow EU members. This includes, but goes well beyond, commodity trade, featuring several provisions aimed at free movements of goods, services, capital, and people. Broadly speaking, the main elements are mutual acceptance of commodity standards, adoption of a common competition policy (including provisions against state aids), and a removal of all border controls.[27] 3. The CEECs would have to adopt the whole *acquis communautaire*, that is the entire stock of treaties and regulations which form the legal basis of the EU, including all provisions pertaining to future steps of integration such as monetary union and foreign policy. 4. By far the most important part of these regulations, from a CEEC's point of view, relate to the EU spending policies under the Common Agricultural Policy (CAP) and the European Structural Funds (ESF). Here, of course, the Eastern members would be net beneficiaries because all of them are a lot poorer and at the same time more agricultural than the present EU average (see Table 1).

Of course, expected aid from Brussels makes EU accession seem like a very attractive policy package to CEECs, and it is in this net transfer from Western to Eastern countries that we find an important parallel between EU enlargement and the Marshall Plan. Note that such transfers follow certain rules and guidelines, not unlike the kind of conditionality attached to ERP funds. As regards the ESF, the general aim is to reduce intra-European prosperity gaps and thus increase cohesion among European regions. More specifically, the Commission, in collaboration with national authorities, works out criteria subject to which countries and regions shall receive financial support from Brussels. We need not go into any detail here, but a point worth mentioning is that, among other things, these criteria envisage that funds from Brussels are but complementary (or even subsidiary) elements in the respective development programs. Accordingly, an important part of financing is required from domestic sources. This gives the Commission a certain leverage on the use of domestic funds, not unlike the counterpart funds of the ERP program.

*How much aid is involved?*

The EU has emphasized at the Copenhagen summit of 1993, and reiterated several times since, that its capacity to absorb new members from the East is limited, precisely because of the aforementioned net transfer. In the so-called Agenda 2000, the Commission has suggested that a first round of accession negotiations with the Czech Republic, Estonia, Hungary, Poland, and Slovenia (henceforth called CEECs-5) be started in 1998, while accession talks with the remaining five candidates (Bulgaria, Latvia, Lithuania, Romania, and the Slovak Republic) should be delayed until these countries have made further economic and political progress.[28] The Commission presents rough estimates for agricultural and structural funds that would flow into the

**Figure 5:** Share of trade with Marshall Plan (MP) countries in US GNP (left), and trade with CEECs in Austrian GNP (right), in percent

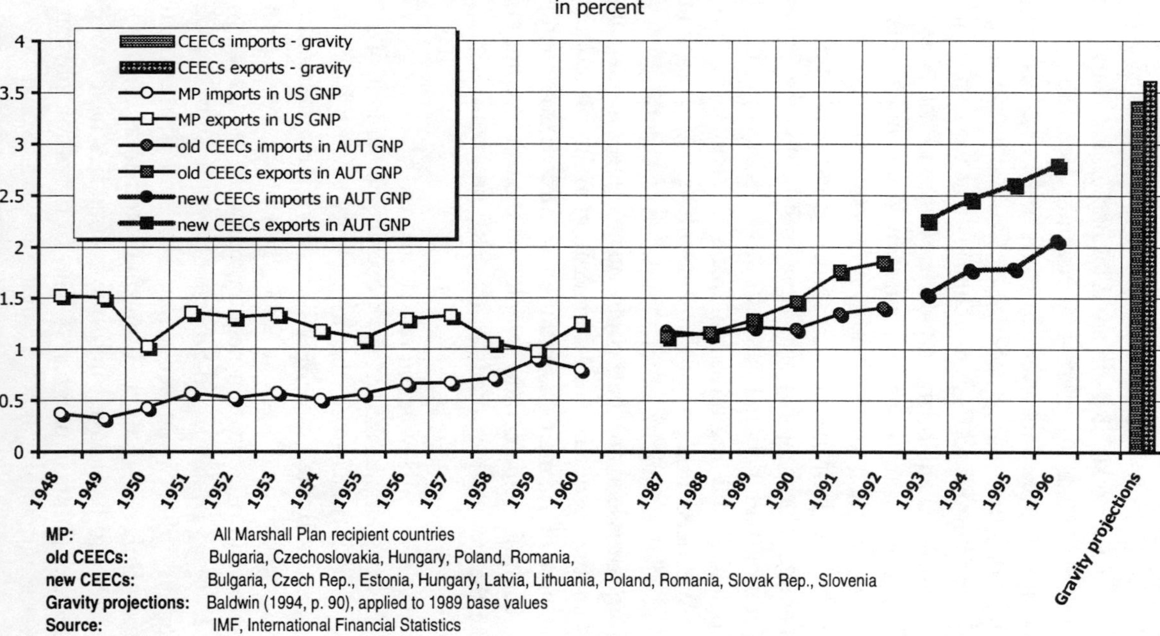


**MP:** All Marshall Plan recipient countries
**old CEECs:** Bulgaria, Czechoslovakia, Hungary, Poland, Romania,
**new CEECs:** Bulgaria, Czech Rep., Estonia, Hungary, Latvia, Lithuania, Poland, Romania, Slovak Rep., Slovenia
**Gravity projections:** Baldwin (1994, p. 90), applied to 1989 base values
**Source:** IMF, International Financial Statistics

**Figure 6:** Estimated change in incumbents' net contributions upon enlargement to CEECs-10, compared to Marshall Plan allotments 1948-1951

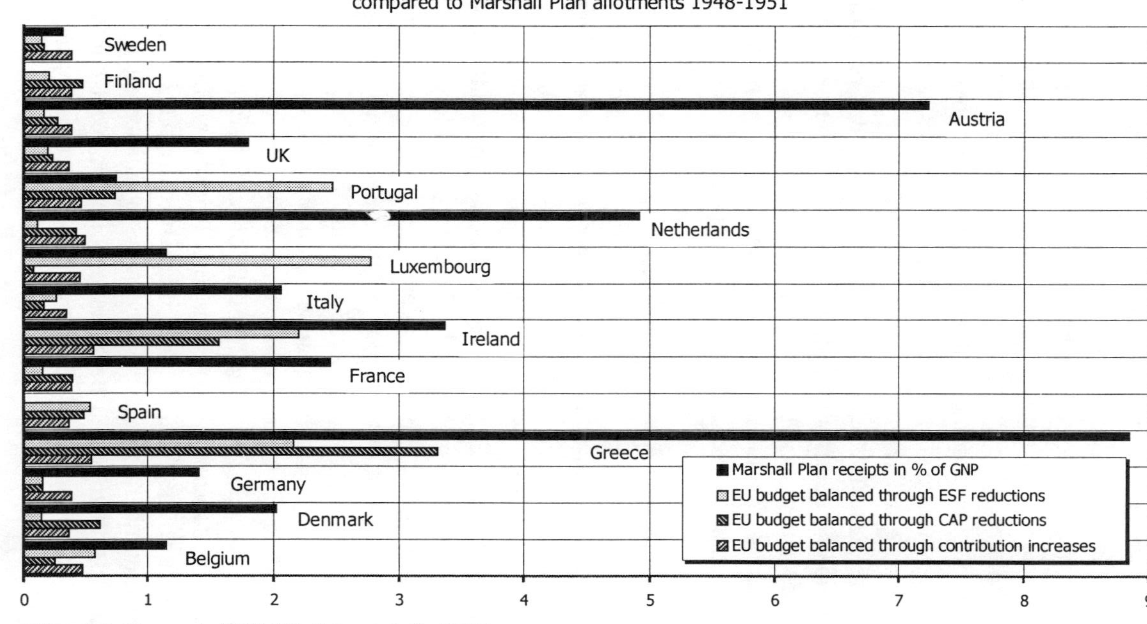


**EU contr. in % percent of GDP, MP allotments in % of GNP.**

**Source:** Own calculations for EU figures, based on Breuss and Schebeck (1996), Kostrzewa et al. (1989) for Marshall Plan figures.

above mentioned group of CEECs-5, totalling 15.5 Bn ECU for 2006. This is a gross expenditure figure. The CEECs would also have to pay contributions, of course, but there will no doubt remain a significant net cost for incumbent EU countries. For obvious reasons, the Commission report leaves entirely open how this net cost should be financed. This is a political issue that will have to be resolved in future inter-governmental negotiations.

Breuss and Schebeck present a more detailed view on how individual countries might be affected through the need to finance future net transfers to CEECs. Their estimates are based on an econometric model of EU expenditures and receipts, focusing on relevant economic characteristics of each country, and on the status quo EU expenditure policy. The overall picture is more pessimistic than the Commission estimates would suggest: the net cost of a CEECs-5 enlargement is 16.155 Bn ECU, and a CEECs-10 enlargement would impose an amount of 30.281 Bn ECU.

What are reasonable scenarios for how these costs are borne by different incumbent countries, and how important is the net inflow of funds to different new members? Figure 6 shows the effect of three different scenarios for incumbent countries: 1. Proportionally increasing contribution payments for both, incumbents and new members in such an amount that the overall EU budget is balanced,[29] 2. Proportionally reducing CAP return payments, and 3. proportionally reducing ESF funds such as would be required to balance the budget. The figure juxtaposes the increases in net contribution rates, as required according to each of these scenarios, with Marshall Plan allotments expressed in percent of GNP.[30] Figure 7 depicts net contribution payments for the CEECs-10. Several points are worth stressing. First, for all countries it matters a lot whether the enlarged EU will balance its budget through adjustments on the revenue or the expenditure side. Austria, for instance, would rather have it reduce its ESF funds than increase contribution payments. This sheds some light on the conflict that is likely to arise in future inter-governmental negotiations dealing with the precise terms of enlargement. Second, even under a balanced EU budget, net inflows of resources into the CEECs would be substantial, way above the postwar Marshall Plan allotments on average. Third, the increases in net contribution payments by incumbent members necessary to finance such aid are very modest, less than half a percentage point for most countries.[31] Thus it would take a number of years until the Western European coun-

**Figure 7:** Net contribution rates for CEECs-10 in enlarged EU, in percent of GDP

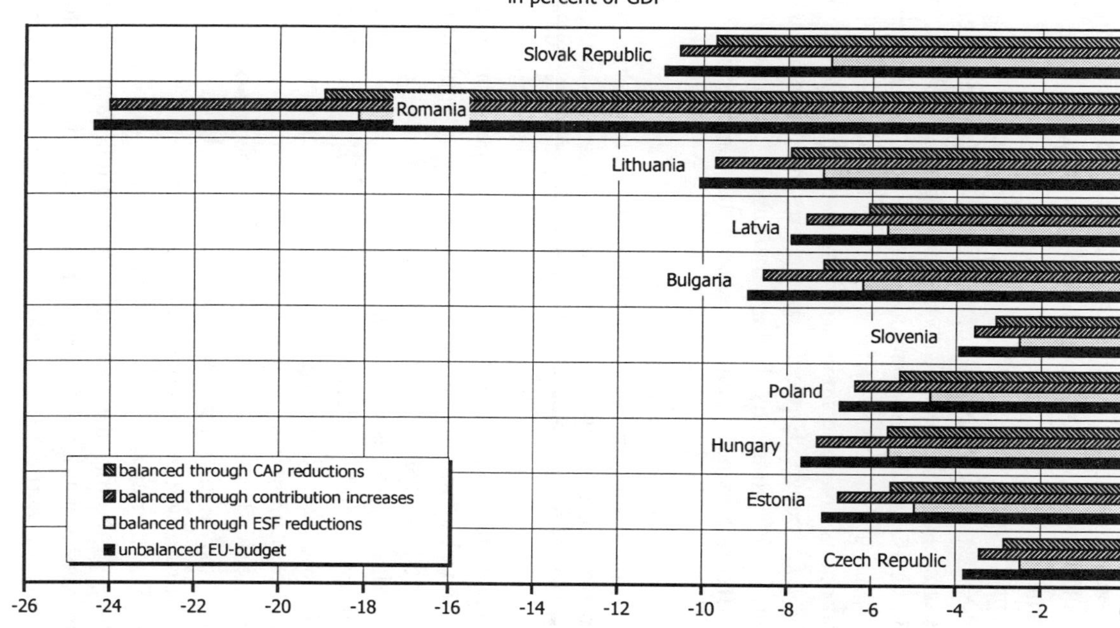


**Source:** Own calculations, based on Breuss and Schebeck (1996).

tries would have suffered an accumulated enlargement burden equal in magnitude to the funds that they had themselves received way back in the Marshall Plan years. As regards the Marshall Plan analogy, we must of course also bear in mind a further difference: then it was a one time gift; here we are talking about a more or less permanent transfer stream. It is less than perfectly permanent, however, because the CAP and ESF policies themselves will surely be subject to periodic change, depending for instance on the amount of inter-regional cohesion achieved. Hence, the above figures should likewise be interpreted as transitory, albeit with a time-span much less specific than that of Marshall Plan aid.

Before proceeding, it is worth pointing out that other authors have come to less pessimistic estimates of the financial aspects of enlargement for incumbent members. Relying on a power politics model, Baldwin, Francois, and Portes conclude that the cost of enlargement is much lower, about half of the Breuss-Schebeck estimates. Which of the two approaches is more appropriate must remain open to debate and, finally, experience. However, if we are interested in whether enlargement is advantageous for an incumbent like Austria, the pessimistic Breuss-Schebeck numbers seem a more appropriate choice.

*Is there a downside for the CEECs?*

With so much aid coming in through EU membership, is there also a downside for the new members? Some observers might point out that the CEECs would enter a Union which stands for outdated and ill-guided models of economic policy and which is, therefore, quite unattractive save for transfer reasons. In line with the "Euro-sclerosis" paradigm, such observers would argue that the EU is regulation-prone and protectionist against the outside world, and that it is plagued by over-sized welfare systems and labor market rigidities which will be felt all the more severely under Monetary Union.[32] Based on this view, one might even conclude that EU membership is not worth it despite the huge inflow of transfers. However, the view can be challenged on several grounds. First, some of these problems—labor market rigidities in particular—have very little to do with the EU, but are instead largely homemade within the countries. More generally, it is difficult to see why EU membership as such should keep the CEECs from avoiding many of the mistakes that their Western fellow members have made in the past. Second, the "Euro-sclerosis" stereotype is quite often overdone. It is not hard to find evidence that Europe today seems on the brink of a new start, and various integration efforts of the EU, starting with the Single Market initiative back in 1985, no doubt deserve a fair amount of credit. Moreover, it can be argued that broadening integration by Eastern enlargement of the EU will, in itself, further strengthen Europe's nascent liberalism, and should therefore receive priority over measures towards deepening integration.[33]

There is, admittedly, much to be said in the way of criticizing EU policies, but overall it is fair to say that they are based on a clear commitment to free trade and capital movements, restricting government subsidies, enforcing competition to have a working price mechanism, and, finally, sound macroeconomic policies. Furthermore, in its Agenda 2000, the Commission has set the stage for a fundamental overhaul of its agricultural policy, which no doubt is the weakest element of all EU structures. At any rate, given the huge transfer inflows involved (see above), the EU-CAP would hardly be a downside for new members from the East, whatever its drawbacks from a more global point of view. In all the aforementioned respects, the incremental effect of EU membership on the reform process in CEECs should, on the whole, be positive. I would not dismiss outright the concern that entering the EU may involve adopting misguided policies and reiterating errors that might seem avoidable if institutions could be designed from scratch. However, history tells that a pure "blueprint approach" towards establishing an institutional framework for a functioning market economy is very hard to implement. Instead, the evolution of such institutions normally draws on a complex web of social traditions and expectations, and EU membership offers a convenient way of importing these where ones own history does not offer much support, as in the case of CEECs. Overall, then, it seems fundamentally wrong to view EU membership for the CEECs as a simple package containing aid which has to be paid for by accepting certain disadvantages in various realms of economic policy. Instead, the appropriate paradigm is one of aid with a complex element of conditionality which, in itself, is beneficial to the CEECs. Returning to the efficiency arguments for aid expounded in the Aiming at Collective Rationality section above, one may now ask whether EU enlargement is also beneficial to incumbent EU countries. The following section tries to answer this question from an Austrian perspective.

## Enlargement from an Incumbent Country's Point of View: The Case of Austria

Public debates in EU countries on an Eastern enlargement are dominated by skepticism. In addition to the financial burden mentioned above, there is concern about import competition from the East, which causes hardships for certain sectors and individuals, potentially aggravated by labor market disruptions due to East-West migration. This does not seem to square well with the claim, indicated several times above, that the donor countries might view aid payments as a means to achieve otherwise unlikely beneficial changes. The problem with this debate is that it tends to emphasize the budgetary implications because they are highly visible and easy to understand, and to ignore the positive effects of trade liberalization because these are less obvious and more difficult to quantify. One way to get a more balanced view on the issue is to carry out a simulation study based on a theoretical model which duly captures the welfare effects from reducing trade barriers, in addition to the budgetary burden of enlargement. Such a study was carried out by Keuschnigg and Kohler.[34] The result there, indeed, is that the trade liberalization effect of enlargement should involve efficiency gains which are likely to overcompensate the Austrian budgetary burden. This section offers a few words on the kind of approach chosen, and then highlights some of the key results.

### *A simulation approach*

Our approach is to calibrate an enriched textbook model to real world Austrian data, duly emphasizing East-West trade relations, and then do "theory with numbers". More simply, we start with a numerical model which is able to reproduce a given historical data set as an equilibrium solution, we then "shock" this model by a policy scenario which captures the essential ingredients of enlargement, calculate the new equilibrium, and, finally, compare this as a sort of counterfactual equilibrium with the initial benchmark equilibrium.

We use a neoclassical model featuring optimizing agents on both the consumption and the production side of the economy. Optimization extends to savings and investment; hence, the model allows for accumulation and growth effects. We distinguish between eighteen different sectors, each producing differentiated goods using three kinds of primary inputs: physical capital, high-skilled labor, and low-skilled labor. In addition, we incorporate a full input output structure for intermediates, including imported inputs. The model envisions Austrian imports and exports of goods and services coming from and going to the EU, the potential member countries from CEE, and the rest of the world. Imports are imperfect substitutes for home produced goods. Commodity markets are characterized by monopolistic competition where free entry competes away all profits in equilibrium. In addition, we assume that Austria has unhindered access to world capital markets at a given interest rate. Given the transfer payments to the Union, a crucial aspect is government finance. We explicitly model government expenditures, including such transfer payments, as well as revenues through an elaborate tax system. Specifically, the model requires that any increase in government expenditures be either financed through increased taxation or increased government borrowing which, in turn, will either drain the savings available for investment or imply an increase in foreign debt. We thus fully account for all relevant budget constraints.

The benchmark equilibrium that we obtain by calibrating this model to real world data must be thought of as portraying the Austrian economy in an equilibrium position on its long-term growth path, equilibrium meaning fulfillment of all relevant optimality conditions as well as market clearing.[35] There are several steps in an enlargement scenario. 1. Austrian exports to the CEECs are no longer subject to tariffs (6 percent on average), nor are imports from the new Eastern members subject to the EU external tariff (3.7 percent on average). 2. There will no longer be border controls, and commodity standards shall be mutually accepted. As do other studies, we incorporate this as a fall in real trade costs from 5 percent of transaction values to zero.[36] 3. There will be additional import competition in food and agriculture where Eastern countries are known to be low cost suppliers. Using estimates consistent with Austria's own EU accession, we stipulate a fall in agricultural and food import prices from CEECs in the amount of 23 and 5 percent, respectively. 4. Finally, Austria will need to finance the increase in net transfers to the EU, whereby the relevant figures may be seen from Figure 6 above. All of these changes will displace the model economy from the initial growth path and have it run through an adjustment path approaching a new long-term equilibrium, as depicted in a schematic way by Figure 8, where it is assumed that a temporary reduction in consumption is required to facilitate investment and a subsequent shift to a higher-level growth path.

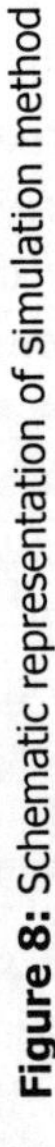

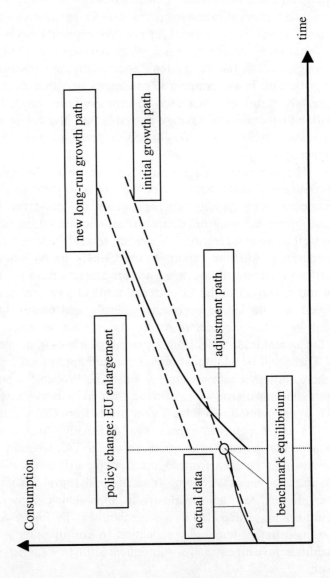


**Figure 8:** Schematic representation of simulation method

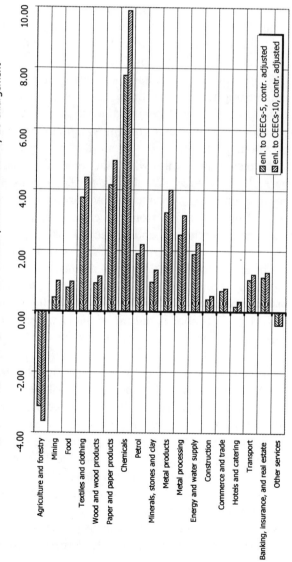

**Figure 9:** Long run changes in Austrian sectoral production caused by EU enlargement

*Simulation results*

I shall restrict myself to only a few key results. Table 2 indicates that enlargement should, in the long run, be expansionary on the capital stock by an amount of 1 to 1.3 percent, depending on the underlying scenario. The reason is that the return to investment increases, due to higher export demand and cheaper imported intermediates from CEECs. Perhaps less importantly, investors will also benefit from cheaper imported capital goods from the East. Higher capital stocks facilitate higher output; hence in the long run, GDP will be higher too. Indeed, the percentage increase is larger for GDP than for the capital stock, due to higher producer prices and a reallocation of all primary input towards sectors where such price increases are largest. It is interesting to see what the sectoral adjustment looks like in more detail. Thus, Figure 9 depicts long-term changes in sector outputs due to enlargement. Not surprisingly, agriculture experiences a severe depression, while all other sectors (except services) expand, most notably chemicals and textiles where the removal of trade barriers has the largest effect. Notice that this is perfectly consistent with textiles being on a long-term decline for other reasons. Here we are talking about a differential effect from EU enlargement.

Textiles and various other expanding sectors, like paper and paper products, are among the less skill-intensive sectors. Hence, the particular kind of expansion caused by Eastern enlargement is coupled with strong demand for unskilled labor. Looking back to Table 2, we are therefore not too surprised to find out that the wage spread between the two types of labor is only marginally widened under the CAP scenario (agricultural return payments reduced), and even narrowed under the CONTR scenario (contribution payments increased). Rather than taking it as a foregone conclusion that integrating poorer regions into richer ones will deprive low-skilled (relative to high-skilled) labor in rich regions, we should take a close look at what integration actually means on a sectoral level. In our case, both wage rates are up in the long run. Moreover, comparing these increases with the changes in the consumer price index, we identify them as real wage improvements. The explanation, of course, is that an increased capital stock affords labor a higher marginal productivity. Notice also that, far from imposing a fiscal burden on the government, enlargement swells the tax base through overall expansion, thus allowing the government to raise its lump-sum transfers to domestic households by as much as 2.2 percent under the CEECs-5-CAP scenario, for instance.

**Table 2: Macroeconomic effects of EU-enlargement**
(long run changes in percent)

| | enlargement to CEECs-5 | | | enlargement to CEECs-10 | | |
|---|---|---|---|---|---|---|
| | **CAP** | **CONTR** | **NEUTR** | **CAP** | **CONTR** | **NEUTR** |
| **Consumer price index** | 0.027 | -0.054 | -0.298 | -0.017 | -0.137 | -0.361 |
| **Wage rate - skilled labor** | 1.480 | 1.359 | 0.976 | 1.627 | 1.491 | 1.139 |
| **Wage rate - unskilled labor** | 1.468 | 1.405 | 1.109 | 1.498 | 1.569 | 1.299 |
| **Gov. budget - transfers** | 2.232 | 1.199 | -1.674 | 2.468 | 0.671 | -1.985 |
| **Disposable wage income** | 1.643 | 1.226 | 0.027 | 1.795 | 1.128 | 0.021 |
| **Overall capital stock** | 1.056 | 1.117 | 1.220 | 1.124 | 1.337 | 1.434 |
| **GDP** | 1.354 | 1.300 | 1.142 | 1.548 | 1.479 | 1.335 |
| **Welfare - equiv. Var. in % of GDP** | 0.777 | 0.576 | 0.000 | 0.864 | 0.534 | 0.000 |
| **Net contribution rate in % of GDP*** | 1.081 | 1.286 | 1.842 | 1.081 | 1.461 | 1.976 |

CAP: CAP return payments lowered to finance enlargement
CONTR: contribution payments increased to finance enlargement
NEUTR: contribution payments increased to ensure welfare neutrality
*: net of structural funds return payments

Therefore, disposable wage income increases by even more than wage income alone.

All of these are long-term changes. Figure 8 suggests that long-term growth may require a significant sacrifice in terms of forgone consumption which is required to finance investment and accumulation during the transition process. What about generations unfortunate enough to live during early periods of adjustment? The most unfortunate generations of all are those entering the economy right at the time of, or shortly after, enlargement, when adjustment lies ahead and the fruits of an enlarged capital stock cannot yet be reaped. Looking at the results in more detail would tell us that even they stand to gain, but a bottom line evaluation requires a more comprehensive summary measure which we have calculated in the following way. For each and every generation, we ask, "How much would it have to receive, or give away, by way of a compensatory transfer so as to find out that it fares just as well under enlargement than without, considering its entire life span?" To do so, one has to indulge in complex utility calculations which need not bother us here. Suppose, instead, we have succeeded, and such compensation figures are at hand for each generation. It is then tempting to add them up, applying a social discount rate to give more weight to present than to future effects. Finally, we convert the aggregate figure so obtained into a permanent income stream, and express it in percent of initial benchmark GDP. This is how one should read the welfare equivalent variation in Table 2. In other words, if Austria were to receive a yearly transfer payment equal to 0.7 percent of present GDP, granted forever throughout the entire future, then it would, of course, be possible to raise the well-being of all its present and future generations. Our simulation results imply that EU enlargement to CEECs-5 under the CAP scenario would have an effect equal to such a permanent transfer payment. Notice that this figure is substantially lower than the GDP growth figure, which is what we would expect from the above discussion pertaining to Figure 8. But it is still positive, suggesting that it is in the Austrian self-interest that the EU be enlarged. We may convey the same message from a different and slightly more provocative angle by asking, "How much could we allow the government to increase its EU net contribution rate for Austrians to find out that they are just as well-off under enlargement than without?" The NEUTR columns in Table 2 reveal that these hypothetical contribution rates substantially exceed the actual rates of slightly more than 1 percent, given in the final line of Table 1 for the two scenarios considered (CAP and CONTR).

It is important to point out that our model assumes a frictionless labor market. Thus, we rule out that Eastern enlargement causes additional unemployment. Nor do we consider migration in our simulation exercise. With regard to unemployment, it seems reasonable to assume, as a reference case at least, that workers displaced in one sector will, in the long run, be re-employed in other sectors. In the short run, however, labor reallocation tends to contribute to unemployment, adding to the plight of adjustment which, therefore, is to some extent underestimated by our results. With regard to migration, incentives no doubt are there, but it seems rather difficult to gauge likely orders of magnitude.[37] Regardless, we know from theory that an immigrant country's initial residents as a whole stand to gain, provided only that incoming labor is subject to diminishing marginal productivity and is paid its marginal product.[38] Hence, in the aggregate at least, migration is likely to improve the picture for a Western country, rather than worsen it. But this comes with a potentially troublesome distribution effect, whereby domestic workers who are substitutes for incoming labor suffer from wage pressure. Notice, however, that, absent migration, our results indicate wages would increase upon enlargement (Table 2), since an increased capital stock improves the marginal productivity of labor. Immigration would thus first moderate this wage increase, rather than directly causing a wage reduction.

## Conclusion

Let me conclude by summarizing. Comparing postwar real growth for Marshall Plan recipient countries with growth experience of CEECs in the 1990s, we have identified a crucial difference: there was immediate take-off after the war, largely dominated by reconstruction, while the economies in transition have suffered enormous contraction, essentially due to the devastating effects of initial distortions which, once removed, require enormous restructuring. It is only at the end of this decade that the CEECs come into the reconstruction phase characteristic of Marshall Plan recipients after the war. Another important difference is that restructuring and reconstruction in the 1990s takes place in a world where commodity and capital markets have become truly global, while the European countries of the Marshall Plan era were essentially closed economies. To the economies in transition, this comes as a mixed blessing: it makes restructuring all the more painful, but it also offers more opportunities for gains through international exchange of goods, ideas, and savings.

Against this background, a quick analogy to the Marshall Plan seems a doubtful justification for Western aid to the East. However, a more general discussion of aid from both a humanitarian and an efficiency point of view leaves one equally skeptical of an outright dismissal of any Marshall Plan type of aid proposal for Eastern countries in transition. We have to look into specific proposals in more detail. One such proposal holds that an enlargement of the EU towards the East would include several important Marshall Plan type elements. For most Western EU countries, the aid involved is somewhat less than the ERP funds they have received (if expressed in percent of GDP). The burden is also less to them than it was to the United States in the case of the Marshall Plan. To the Eastern countries in transition, the transfers received would be substantial, surpassing Marshall Plan magnitudes by several percentage points. Such aid would, however, come in under conditionality in the form of Eastern countries having to accept the *acquis communautaire* in all areas where the EU has adopted a common policy approach. While, admittedly, the EU may not have adopted ideal policy approaches in all these areas, the institutions and legal systems imported in this way by the CEECs are likely to be superior in many respects to what they would be able to implement on their own, given the legacy from their recent history.

Contrary to the premise underlying much of the public debate, an incumbent EU member like Austria may significantly gain by an Eastern expansion of the Union. The reason lies in gains due to trade liberalization. Such liberalization, already initiated in the so-called Europe Agreements, would have been unlikely to unravel so quickly without the prospect of EU membership for Eastern countries. Hence, it should be seen as an integral part of EU enlargement. If these gains are larger in magnitude than the budgetary burden of the transfer payments to the new members, then EU enlargement as a whole may be seen as an example of an efficiency case for aid, with transfer payments as a means to facilitate specific changes in recipient countries that are, in turn, beneficial also for the donor country. Simulation exercises carried out on the basis of a neoclassical model calibrated to real world data show that such is the case from an Austrian perspective.

## References


Alesina, A. & Drazen, A. (1991). Why are stabilizations delayed? *American Economic Review*, *81*, 1170-1188.

Baldwin R. E. (1994). *Towards an integrated Europe*. London: Centre for Economic Policy Research.

Baldwin, R. E. (1997). Concepts and speed of an eastern enlargement. In H. Siebert, (Ed.), *Quo vadis Europe?* Tübingen: J.C.B. Mohr (Paul Siebeck), 73-95.

Baldwin, R. E., Francois, J. F. & Portes, R. (1997). The costs and benefits of eastern enlargement: The impact on the EU and central Europe. *Economic Policy 24*, 127-176.

Barro R. J. & Sala-i-Martin X. (1995) *Economic growth*. New York: McGraw-Hill.

Ben-David D. & Loewy M. B. (1997). *Free trade, growth, and convergence*. Working Paper No. 6095. Cambridge, Mass.: National Bureau of Economic Research.

Blanchard, O. (1993). Panel discussion: Lessons for eastern Europe today. In R. Dornbusch, W. Nölling, R. Layard, (Eds.). *Postwar economic construction and lessons for the East today*. Cambridge, Mass.: MIT Press, 231-234.

Blanchard, O. (1997). *The economics of post-communist transition*. Oxford: Clarendon Press.

Borjas, G. J. (1995). The Economic Benefits from Immigration. *Journal of Economic Perspectives 9*, 3-22.

Breuss, F. & Schebeck, F. (1996). Ostoffnung und Osterweiterung der EU. *WIFO-Monatsberichte* 2, 139-151.

Collins, S. M. (1991). U.S. economic policy toward the Soviet Union and eastern Europe. *Journal of Economic Perspectives 5*, 219-227.

Coorey, S., Mecagni, M. & Offerdal, E. (1998). Achieving low inflation in transition economies: The role of relative price adjustment. *Finance & Development 35*, 30-33.

De Long, B. & Eichengreen, B. (1993). The Marshall Plan: History's most successful structural adjustment program. In R. Dornbusch, W. Nölling, R. Layard, (Eds.). *Postwar economic reconstruction and lessons for the East today*, Cambridge, Mass.: MIT Press, 189-230.

Eichengreen, B. (1992). A Marshall Plan for the East: Options for 1993. *Konjunkturpolitik 38*, 267-290.

Eichengreen, B. & Uzan, M. (1992). The Marshall Plan: Economic effects and implications for Eastern Europe and the former USSR. *Economic Policy* 14, 13-75.

Esposito, C. (1995). Influencing aid recipients: Marshall Plan lessons for contemporary donors. In B. Eichengreen, (Ed.). *Europe's post-war recovery*. Cambridge: Cambridge University Press, 68-90.

Europäische Kommission (1997). *AGENDA 200: Eine stärkere und erweiterte Union*. Luxemburg: Amt für amtliche Veröffentlichungen der Europäischen Gemeinschaften.

Gros, D. & Gonciarz, A. (1996). A note on the trade potential of central and Eastern Europe. *European Journal of Political Economy* 12, 709-721.

Helpman E. (1997). *R&D and productivity: The international connection*. Working Paper No. 6101. Cambridge, Mass.: National Bureau of Economic Research.

Horwitz, S. (1994). Does Eastern Europe need a new (Marshall) Plan? In P. J. Boettke, (Ed.). *The collapse of development planning*. New York: New York University Press, 210-227.

Kamm, T. (1998). The old world stands on the brink of a new epoch. *Wall Street Journal Europe*, April 9.

Keller W. (1997). *Trade and transmission of technology*. Working Paper No. 6113. Cambridge, Mass.: National Bureau of Economic Research.

Keuschnigg C. & Kohler W. (1997). *Eastern enlargement of the EU: How much is it worth for Austria*. Arbeitspapier Nr. 9723, Linz: Johannes Kepler Universität Linz, Institut für Volkswirtschaftslehre.

Keuschnigg C. & Kohler W. (1998a). *Eastern enlargement of the EU: How much is it worth for Austria*. Discussion Paper No. 1786, London: Centre for Economic Policy Research.

Kohler W. & Keuschnigg C. (1998b). Die Osterweiterung der EU: Eine österreichische Perspektive, *Wirtschaftspolitische Blätter* 45, 324-338.

Kostrzewa, W., Nunnenkamp, P. & Schmieding, H. (1998). A Marshall Plan for middle and Eastern Europe. *The World Economy 13*, 27-50.

Kristol, I. (1998). Petrified Europe. *The Wall Street Journal Europe,* Feb. 2.

Lahiri, S. & Raimondos-Møller, P. (1997). On the tying of aid to tariff reform. *Journal of Development Economics 54*, 479-491.

Maddison A. (1995). *Monitoring the world economy 1820-1992*. Paris: OECD.

Melloan, G. (1998). Communism's ghosts trouble Europe's grand plan. *Wall Street Journal Europe,* April 7.

Milward A. S. (1984). *The Reconstruction of Western Europe 1945-1951*. London: Methuen.

Mundell, R. A. (1997). The great contractions in transition economies. In M. I. Blejer, M. Škreb, (Eds.). *Macroeconomic stabilization in transition economies*. Cambridge: Cambridge University Press, 73-99.

Murrell, P. (1991). Symposium on economic transition in the Soviet Union and Eastern Europe. *Journal of Economic Perspectives 5*, 3-9.

Persson, T. & Tabellini, G. (1995). Double-edged incentives: Institutions and policy coordinations. In G. Grossman, K. Rogoff, (Eds.). *Handbook of international economics vol. III*, Amsterdam: Elsevier Science B.B., 1973-2030.

Reichlin, L. (1995). The Marshall Plan reconsidered. In B. Eichengreen, (Ed.). *Europe's post-war recovery*. Cambridge: Cambridge University Press, 39-67.

Rodrik, D. (1994). Foreign trade in eastern europe's transition: early results. In O. Blanchard, K. A. Froot, J. D. Sachs, J. D., (Eds.), *The transition in Eastern Europe, volume 2: Restructuring*. Chicago: The University of Chicago Press, 319-352.

Romer D. (1996). *Advanced macroeconomics*. New York: McGraw-Hill.

Saint-Paul, G. (1993). Economic reconstruction in France: 1945-1958. In R. Dornbusch, W. Nölling, R. Layard, R., (Eds.). *Postwar economic reconstruction and lessons for the East today*. Cambridge, Mass.: MIT Press, 83-114.

Sala-i-Martin, X. (1996). Regional cohesion: evidence and theories of regional growth and convergence. *European Economic Review* 40, 1325-1352.

WIIW Vienna Institute for Comparative Economic Studies. (1998). *Countries in transition 1997*. Vienna: Vienna Institute for Comparative Economic Studies.

## Notes

1. See Sala-i-Martin (1996) for a discussion on the empirics of this kind of convergence.

2. See Saint-Paul (1993) for more details on Marshall-Plan-type catching up in various growth models.

3. See Barro and Sala-i-Martin (1995) for a detailed account of this model.

4. This is derived from the capital stock estimates produced by the Austrian Institute for Economic Research (WIFO), and the GDP figure in the Austrian national accounts statistics.

5. See WIIW (1998).

6. See again Barro and Sala-i-Martin (1995) for accounts of these models. For a discussion of the implications in the context of the Marshall Plan, see Saint-Paul (1993).

7. This pessimistic view is further strengthened by evidence on the disappointing growth effects of aid granted to poor third world countries; see Kostrzewa, Nunnenkamp and Schmieding (1989).

8. Of course, improvement may also take the form of damage avoided. A very popular argument which is often mentioned in this vein is that transfer payments may help stabilize (or shift) the geopolitical balance of power and, thus, be advantageous for security reasons. The underlying premise here is that aid is cheaper than the military spending which would otherwise be necessary to achieve the desired outcome; see Baldwin (1997). I shall, however, not pursue this peace-dividend argument any further in this paper.

9. See, for instance, Ben-David and Loewy (1997), Helpman (1997), and Keller (1997).

10. In such general terms, the argument has been put forward in the present context by Collins (1991).

11. Notice that such a coordination problem will surely also exist between domestic agents. To the extent that it remains unresolved even domestically, it reinforces the case for foreign aid as a means to speed up transformation.

12. See Romer (1996) for a general review of the dynamics of anti-inflationary policy.

13. This idea has been formalized by Alesina and Drazen (1991).

14. A sufficient condition for such multiple equilibria to arise is that, for a given shortage of revenue, the incentive to resort to money creation increases with the rate of inflation, at least over a certain range. This obviously introduces an element of instability, with the usual consequence of multiple equilibria.

15. For a recent survey of this literature, see Persson and Tabellini (1995).

16. It is perhaps worth quoting such a critic verbatim:"... the ideas that informed the original Marshall Plan, namely that conscious, planned political intervention and design are needed to create economic institutions and guide economic growth, are the very same ideas responsible for the current economic disaster in Eastern

Europe. Given this, proposing a new Marshall Plan to solve its problems can be likened to giving free liquor to an alcoholic," see Horwitz (1994). Kostrzewa, Nunnenkamp, and Schmieding (1989) go into great detail to argue that the Marshall Plan did retard urgent economic policy reform, particularly in Germany.

17. See Eichengreen and Uzan (1992), Eichengreen (1992), De Long and Eichengreen (1993), [as well as several other authors in Dornbusch, Nölling, and Layard, eds. (1993)], Reichlin (1995), and Esposito (1995).

18. The aggregate figures exclude Greece, Ireland and Portugal. For these countries, Maddison (1995) presents figures only beginning 1947.

19. See, however, De Long and Eichengreen (1993) who emphasize that there was more to postwar European growth than such a "rubber band" effect, and that it was by no means unavoidable. On the other hand, the fact that such strong growth was experienced by countries which followed markedly different policies does indicate that there was a common factor. In addition to a "rubber band" effect, the Marshall Plan is an obvious candidate. See also the discussion by Blanchard (1993).

20. See Blanchard (1997) and Mundell (1997) for a related discussion.

21. To put it in somewhat blunter terms, systemic change does not look too attractive to the masses if the only perceivable change is that from state monopolies to private monopolies (see Melloan, 1998).

22. Coorey, Mecagni, and Offerdal (1998) argue on empirical grounds that the more frequent need of relative price adjustment makes achieving low inflation rates more difficult in transition economies than in other countries.

23. It is therefore not surprising that the contractionary element of restructuring was particularly strong in the industrial sector where traded goods loom large (see Figure 1).

24. See, again, Ben-David and Loewy (1997), Helpman (1997), and Keller (1997).

25. See, however, Gros and Gonciarz (1996) who argue that most of the trade potential has already been achieved. The simple gravity model postulates that the level of aggregate trade flows between any two countries is determined by size and distance.

26. These are (in alphabetical order): Bulgaria, the Czech Republic, Estonia, Hungary, Latvia, Lithuania, Poland, Romania, the Slovak Republic, and Slovenia.

27. See Baldwin, Francois, and Portes (1997) for more details.

28. See Europäische Kommission (1997). The CEECs-5 plus these countries will henceforth be indicated by CEECs-10.

29. EU rule does not allow the European Commission to engage in borrowing. Hence, the EU budget has to be balanced on an annual basis.

30. I have crudely "annualized" the Marshall Plan figures by dividing total allotments that have come in during the period 1948-1951 by four and then expressing this in percent of 1950 GNP figures. (Both figures were taken from Kostrzewa, Nunnenkamp, and Schmieding, 1989).

31. According to these estimates, the major exceptions are Greece and Ireland, whose net receipts would shrink considerably in an enlarged EU.

32. As an example of such a view, see Kristol (1998).

33. As an example of this more optimistic view on Europe, see Kamm (1998) and Melloan (1998).

34. Keuschnigg and Kohler (1998b) group the accession countries in accordance with the Agenda 2000 proposal, whereas the earlier papers (1997 and 1998a) are based on the initial proposal with the Slovak Republic, instead of Estonia, being part of the first round of enlargement talks.

35. To arrive at such a benchmark equilibrium, one draws on data from a large array of sources which inevitably pertain to different periods and which need to be adjusted to be mutually consistent. In our case, we use the most recent Austrian input/output table, originally dating back to 1983. We have updated it to 1992 and merged it with long-term trend values from national accounts statistics, as well as trade shares for different countries and sectors from 1994.

36. This figure may be seen as conservative consensus estimate. See Baldwin, Francois, and Portes (1997), who assume a more optimistic value of 10 percent.

37. See the above discussion pertaining to Figure 2.

38. This is the well-known "immigration surplus;" see Borjas (1995).

# NON-TOPICAL ESSAYS

## The Invasion of Austria in March 1938: *Blitzkrieg* or *Pfusch*?[1]

*Alexander N. Lassner*

The invasion of Austria on 12 March 1938 by the German *Wehrmacht* was a great victory for Hitler and his Third Reich, one that produced consternation and fear throughout the rest of Europe. For the first time since World War I, German armies crossed the sovereign boundary of a European nation to conquer additional territory.[2] The European balance of power, already shaken by the effects of German treaty revisionism, the parochial state interests of European nations, and the relationship between Berlin and Rome, was swinging decisively in favor of the Third Reich.

Even as the Anschluß occurred, a debate began over the decision taken by Kurt von Schuschnigg on 11 March 1938 not to call up the Austrian federal army and to resist the German *Wehrmacht*—which would have been, according to Schuschnigg, a "useless sacrifice"—but instead for Schuschnigg to resign the chancellorship and surrender Austria to the bosom of Nazi Germany.[3] In Austria it seems as though almost everyone has expressed himself in the so-called "resistance" controversy, and done so with august confidence. Yet the debate has not lessened with the passage of time and still inspires an abundance of books, articles, and symposiums. This body of literature has focused on a variety of issues including: Austria's internal military conditions; the international situation; and the *Wehrmacht*'s *Einmarsch* (march into) Austria on 12 March 1938.[4]

The latter category has received by far the least scholarly attention, and the three works that explore the invasion disagree as to the difficulties that the German army experienced, and among other issues as well.[5] The major dispute is "how great were the problems that the *Wehrmacht* encountered during the *Einmarsch*?" Were they insignificant and cosmetic, or serious and operationally endangering? The performance of the German army during the *Einmarsch* is the most important single factor in attempting to determine how long the Austrian *Bundesheer* could have resisted, and thus how much time might have existed to allow other factors to have come into play. An offensive operation, when undertaken with almost no prior planning and by a military force suffering heavily from its rapid expansion and material deficiencies (as was the *Einmarsch* by the *Wehrmacht*), is an extraordinarily difficult undertaking. This paper will examine the performance of the *Wehrmacht* during those days in March 1938, using archival sources from Washington D.C., England, France, Germany, Austria, and Italy. The *Einmarsch* reevaluated will then serve as a litmus test, that is, an invasion of Austria under the best of circumstances, those of no resistance and active help from Austria, as to how long the Austrian Bundesheer might have been able to resist Nazi Germany.

## Mobilization and *Aufmarsch*[6] *of the Wehrmacht*

Almost no detailed German planning existed prior to 10 March 1938 for an invasion of Austria; in fact, when instructed to prepare for the invasion, Chief of the General Staff General Ludwig Beck told General Wilhelm Keitel that "nothing [had] been done, nothing at all."[7] Beck's *protégé*, General Erich von Manstein, worked furiously that afternoon to draw up the plans for mobilization and deployment. Later that same day, Beck appointed Colonel-General Fedor von Bock as commander of the new German Eighth Army, the force that would invade Austria.

The Eighth Army was a hodgepodge of units quickly drawn from the two southern army districts (*Wehrkreise* VII and XIII) with some additional units attached. The Army comprised: the VII Army Corps made up of the 7th Infantry Division (first wave) and the 27th Infantry Division (second wave), the 1st Battalion, 25th Panzer Regiment, the only German Mountain division (first wave); the XIII Army Corps, made up of the 10th Infantry Division (first wave) and 17th Infantry Division (second wave); and the XVI Motorized Corps which consisted of the 2nd Panzer Division (first wave) and units of the SS-*Verfügungstruppe* (special readiness forces).[8] Also included in the invasion were the Herman Göring Regiment, the 97th *Landwehr* Division (territorial), and a variety of attached army troops.[9]

On 10 March at 19:00, Hitler gave the order to mobilize. Although there had been conflicting reports as to whether or not the army would meet resistance, the general consensus was that there would be none. For Hitler "battle was undesirable but resistance [would be] crushed."[10] The first *Armeetagesbefehl* of the German Eighth army issued on the afternoon of 11 March 1938 by commanding *Generaloberst* Fedor von Bock, who in the absence of Austrian mobilization, stated that "*Leisten österreichische Truppen Widerstand, so ist er mit der Waffe zu brechen.*"[11] By the morning of 12 March 1938, the German Eighth army, with just over one hundred thousand soldiers, would attempt its march into Austria.

The sudden and unexpected nature of the German mobilization was one that created enormous problems, some of which had the potential to threaten the entire invasion. Problems arose immediately and affected all units from Eighth Army command down to the company level. Given the complete surprise of the mobilization, and the fact that the *Wehrmacht* had never previously conducted a rapid or partial mobilization, such disorder is not surprising.[12]

Vital command units such as the Eighth Army's 2nd Battalion, 507th Signals Regiment were not operational until the sixth mobilization day. This understandably "*erschwert und verzögert*" the mobilization.[13] While the very late arrival of units and men to their "mobilization areas" (on or after 14 March) or their complete absence was small, it was not exceptional.[14]

Delayed mobilization can partly be explained by the unwillingness of businesses to give up their men for service.[15] In other cases, regular, reserve and "*Ergänzung*" (supplementary) personnel of the active units and many soldiers in *Landwehr* units, simply did not receive timely mobilization orders.[16] This happened for a variety of reasons including the absence of key officers from their posts when the mobilization order arrived which prevented the distribution of the order; men that were on vacation and who for several days could not be found; and the necessity of the orders being hand delivered to units. This latter circumstance was a particular problem in the 97th *Landwehr* division whose units were spread out over 240 km. east to west and 100 km. north to south.[17] In the Eighth Army itself, motorized medical units were not march-ready, partly due to the lack of personnel, until the fifth and sixth mobilization day.[18] Medical units of the XVI Motorized Corps finally arrived on the fifth mobilization day, and even then were not "*einsatzfähig*" (operational).[19] Aggravating the whole situation was the fact that many officers did not believe their orders and so created more delays while they tried to confirm the mobilization.[20]

As individual men and units began to rendezvous at mobilization points, confusion reigned as soldiers and NCOs (non-commissioned officers) arrived before the officers who knew what dispositions to make. In cases where officers were on the scene, many lacked exact and detailed orders, which disrupted the units when moving to the Austrian border. Once more, this situation was the most disruptive in the 97th *Landwehr* Division. In one of its regiments, only one officer had arrived by the end of the first day. Here too, largely because of the deferments given to skilled workers, units were short of troops. The 19th Cavalry Regiment knew as early as January 1938 that it did not have enough riders to meet its required strength, but the *Wehrkreis* (army district) VII riding school had not been able to find enough replacements.[21]

In regular army units, the late entrances by the officers and men of the 1st Artillery Battalion, 608th Artillery Regiment kept that unit from even reaching the Austrian border until 14 March. Its soldiers were rated "*zum großen Teil sehr schlecht*."[22] The accelerated pace of mobilizing the first wave divisions (2nd Panzer Division, 7th Infantry Division, 10th Infantry Division and the Mountain Division) caused them to be short approximately one sixth of their *Gefechtstärke* (battle-strength).[23]

Among those soldiers who did show up, frictions arose that quickly reduced numbers and effectiveness. In almost every German unit that took part in the invasion of Austria men were either mis-assigned or were assigned for duties for which they lacked military training or were simply unfit. *Wehrkreis* XIII (army district XIII) began by calling up men of the wrong age (60 year-olds instead of 25 to 35 year-olds), and attempted to staff an army veterinary unit with cripples from World War I and men from an insane asylum.[24] *Bäckermeister* (bakers) in the 8th Army were occasionally assigned to the artillery, while artillerists were assigned to machine gun companies. Soldiers also lied about their specialties in order to avoid unpleasant work. In the 119th *Landwehr* Infantry Regiment, men reported as communications experts who had never seen a radio.[25] More seriously, in the first wave units, men were assigned to ride horses in medical services, reconnaissance, and supply that had never ridden before, including at least one man whose qualification was only that he was a theology student. Elsewhere, men were assigned to drive vehicles who had never driven before, had no driver's license (*Führerschein*), or who had last touched a steering wheel eight years before.[26] The rate of mis-assignment varied greatly from unit to unit in both quantity and degree. The most egregious mis-assignments and lack of quality manpower affected the rear-services. Here the appointment of officers, non-commissioned officers (NCOs), and soldiers to jobs for which they had no experience was frequent and encompassed leaders and troops of gasoline re-supply columns who had "*keine Ahnung über Einsatz, Empfänge und Aufgaben seiner Kol ...* " and troops in vehicle repair companies of whom "*nicht ein Mann, der im Zivilberuf als Automechaniker tätig war.*"[27]

In all units, insufficient military training and unfitness for duty reduced operational readiness. This was common in the reserve and *Ergänzung* portions of active units of the first and second wave, and it was ubiquitous in the rear-services of all the divisions that participated in the *Einmarsch.* The XVI Motorized Corps command described all the reservists in the 3rd and 4th Panzer Regiments, 2nd Panzer Division as "*völlig wertlos*" (completely worthless); a situation that forced active soldiers to occupy reservists' positions.[28] As a consequence, fewer trained troops were available for positions that required greater expertise, and commanders had to occupy themselves with trivialities rather than command. This drastically lowered the operational capabilities of the entire Eighth Army since the 3rd and 4th Panzer Regiments comprised the total armored strength of the 2nd Panzer Division and over 4/5 of the armored strength of the entire invasion force.

Within the 7th, 10th, 17th, 27th Infantry Divisions and the Mountain Division, the reserve and *Ergänzung* troops were rated variously as "[u]*nzulänglich,*" "*untragbar,*" and "*sehr erschwert.*"[29] In the 100th Mountain Regiment, the active portion of the unit was deemed operational, but the "*große Zahl der Reservisten* [*bedeutet*] *eher ein Hindernis als eine Stärkung für die Einsatzfähigkeit ....*"[30] Four battalions in the 100th, 99th, and 79th Mountain Regiments of the Mountain Division (the 2nd and 3rd Battalion, 100th Mountain Regiment, the 1st Battalion, 99th Mountain Regiment, and the 3rd Battalion, 79th Mountain Regiment) were missing trained soldiers and equipment to such a degree that the commanders believed that it would take fourteen days for them to become *einsatzfähig*, and even then they still would not have approached the quality of the reserve units of 1914. Regimental staff estimations were that the "*kampftechnische Wert*" (battle worth) of the 2nd Battalion, 100th Mountain Regiment, and the 1st Battalion, 99th Mountain Regiment corresponded roughly on 20 March 1938 to the German volunteer corps of October 1914.[31]

The quality of the reserve and *Ergänzung* personnel in the 27th Infantry Division, the Division which would later take part in the parade in Vienna, was so bad that "*die Schlagfertigkeit einzelner Verbände in Frage gestellt* [*war*]."[32] Important units like the artillery observation detachments attached to the 7th, 10th, and 17th Infantry Divisions were heavily staffed with old, fat, untrained, and very unwilling ("*starker Unwillen*") troops that made them "*nicht einsatzfähig*".[33] The independent 1st Battalion, 25th Panzer Regiment, the spearhead of the 7th Infantry Division, lacked many *Ergänzung* troops and had a high percentage of raw recruits (50 percent) in the support services whose lack of training created problems for the unit.[34]

A dearth of motorized and horse drawn vehicles (wagons), and the poor quality of those which were available, affected the readiness and performance of all units.[35] By the afternoon of 12 March, the gasoline supply units of the 2nd Panzer Division only mustered seven of the necessary sixty-six vehicles. Only by taking the most ruthless measures could XVI Motorized Corps increase this number by the evening of 12 March.[36] Overall, the VII Army Corps alone described its *Ergänzung* motorized vehicle situation as "*nahezu katastrophal*" (almost catastrophic), with approximately 2,800 motorized vehicles which were either missing or unusable.[37] Different elements contributed to this situation. In some instances, the civilian vehicles requisitioned for wartime were still on blocks from winter storage. But it soon turned out that as civilians discovered a mobilization was taking place, many purposefully sabotaged their cars and trucks, or handed over vehicles other than those they had promised the army. Other vehicles were simply old and worn-out, or ridiculously inappropriate for the high demands to be made upon them.[38] A number of cars and trucks had partially decayed roofs, and some were so poorly balanced that they fell over when going through ditches.[39]

The heterogeneous makeup of vehicles, plus the aforementioned lack of mechanics, also created the problem of repair. The 38th Signal Battalion, 2nd Panzer Division had no less than twenty-five *different types* of vehicles, and this was not exceptional.[40] The German army simply did not possess the right equipment or the necessary personnel to fix each and every different model.[41] Of the tanks in 1st Battalion, 25th Panzer Regiment, one third were in such bad shape that they were either unusable or in repair. Many tanks and motorized transport vehicles, while able to be driven, were completely "used up."[42] The 7th Division rated 1st Battalion, 25th Panzer Regiment's tanks as "*unverwendbar für Kampf und sogar für Propagandazwecke* ..."[43] Had military operations during the Anschluß lasted more than the short time that they did, problems of repair would have drastically reduced the motorized activities of the entire Eighth Army.

Units of all types required basic and essential equipment. Ammunition and supply vehicles lacked tarpaulins, a condition that the 27th Artillery Regiment and the 608 thArtillery Regiment noted would have made, in case of rain, the "*Munition. ... größtenteils verdorben.*"[44] The 2nd Mountain Battalion, 100th Mountain Regiment, the 1st Mountain Battalion, 99th Mountain Regiment, and the 3 rdMountain Battalion, 79th Mountain Regiment of the Mountain Division were missing quantities of clothing and equipment.[45] *Landwehr* Division 97 had "*weder ein Paar Stiefel noch ein[en] Stahlhelm* ... [underscore in original]" in the entire division![46]

The German army in 1938, and throughout the war, was one that depended primarily upon the horse.[47] Even in this essential category, the mobilization pointed to serious and operation-endangering deficiencies in the *Wehrmacht*. The reserve and *Ergänzung* horses lacked shoes and were often in poor health. Whenever possible, farmers that owed the army a certain quota of horses turned over only the most shabby and decrepit animals. Reports by units in almost every Division on the *Ergänzung* situation concerning horses described the complete insufficiency of these animals and their equipment from horseshoes and saddles to reigns.[48] This situation would lead to many further problems as the march developed. The staff of the 62nd Infantry Regiment complained that it had received poor horses, with even worse equipment. Horseshoes on most horses in the regiment were in such bad shape that by the third day of operations the animals had become "*mangelhaft und kriegsunbrauchbar.*"[49]

As a result of this and the vehicle situation, many officers and NCOs, especially those in the SS-*Verfügungstruppe* and the Hermann Göring Luftwaffe Regiment, began to take whatever horses, wagons, and motor vehicles that they could lay their hands upon.[50] The 17th Infantry Division reported that because of the great difficulties of procuring replacement materials the division began to take what it could find regardless of whether that material was actually slated for its use. Once one unit undertook this sort of activity, the behavior quickly spread to all units. This method of "grabbing what one could" had to be fought *"sofort und in schärfster Weise,"* but seems to have had the worst impact on the operational capabilities of the 17th Infantry Division.[51] Within the Eighth Army as a whole, "grabbing what one could" reflected a deficiency in discipline, and represented a significant logistical problem. The result was a decidedly negative influence on operational effectiveness.

Indeed, the lack of discipline and poor conduct among some officers and troops disrupted and confused a situation that was already full of obstacles. Orders were sometimes ignored or twisted, a situation that compounded what were already serious difficulties. In the after-action report of *Wehrkreis* VII and VII Army Corps, the three main culprits were identified as: "*Geltungsbedürfnis*" (showing off), "*Besserwissertum*" (knowing everything better), and "*Rechthaberei*" (having to be right). Not to be excluded from the list were "crass and blind egoism," a "desire to be comfortable," and "incompetence."[52]

As the German units began their deployment to southern Germany, the German population exhibited a decidedly unhappy attitude toward the military action. The divisional commander for the 10th Infantry division reported that "in no place [could he] speak about enthusiasm or the happiness of the population."[53] After-action reports of the XIII Army Corps reveal that "the German population was clearly depressed."[54] Nor were these results confined to the population. In the army, especially in reserve formations made up of older soldiers, there was a marked lack of "*Wehrfreudigkeit*" (enthusiasm for military service) and willingness to serve, which sometimes had a baleful influence on the regular troops.[55] An unidentified officer of the 10th Infantry Division reported the great worries that he and his men shared regarding a possible war, between Germany and Austria, and the great relief of their friendly reception in Austria.[56] The issue of popular support, or lack thereof, in Germany and Austria often has been raised and recently has focused on Austrian unwillingness. One author has asserted that Austrian opposition to Germany would have been undermined because "the greatest portion of the population was not prepared" for armed resistance.[57] If one can speak about the fear and reluctance of the Austrian population for war one should at least take note of parallel German reluctance. What might have been the reaction of the German population if Austria had decided to mobilize and defend itself? Instead, the German population was given a morale boost two days later when they heard Hitler's "victory" speech in

Vienna. British ambassador to Germany Nevile Henderson's dispatch to British Secretary of State for Foreign Affairs Halifax on 24 March 1938 resurrected the old cliché that "nothing succeeds like success."[58]

But while the German population was dejectedly watching the mobilizing *Wehrmacht*, new obstacles materialized that disrupted its deployment to the borders of Austria. Chief among these was the operational issue of command and control. Because of the lack of motorized vehicles, especially motorcycles, and due to congested traffic on the few available roads, which were cluttered with horses, troops, wagons, and motor vehicles, divisional staffs were often unable or heavily delayed in sending and receiving orders.[59] Both 8th Army and VII, XIII, and XVI Corps commands were so overburdened with organizational aspects of the mobilization and *Aufmarsch*, "*daß sie irgendwelchen Einfluß auf den Aufmarsch nicht nehmen können.*"[60] On the tactical level, there was confusion from the start about who commanded both the SS and Herman Göring Regiments, and after they had finished commandeering vehicles and horses for their use, they joined other motorized army units which ignored orders and thrust themselves through columns of marching German troops and vehicles, producing even more chaos in a mad rush to get to the Austro-German border first. Infantry regiments frequently had to wait hours for the units to pass.[61]

The disjoining of divisions and regiments for transport by road and rail to the border not only worsened the command and control situation, but also brought about a serious and chronic new problem: the fragmenting *(zerreißen)* of units, most disastrously at the divisional and regimental levels. For its movement to the border, the 2nd Panzer Division was separated into tracked vehicles (armor) which were shipped by rail, and wheeled vehicles which undertook a road march. Unfortunately for the 2nd Panzer Division, the wheeled units had not the slightest idea where to meet the tracked components of the division. Vital support branches, such as ammunition supply and repair units of the division, were simply left behind to fend for themselves.[62]

Due to previous training exercises during winter 1937/38, the loading of trains proceeded smoothly, but at the rail heads, such as that at Passau, immense traffic jams ensued.[63] This was caused by the huge number of units attempting to navigate one rail station in route to jump-off points in and around Simbach-Schärding-Passau, and by the lack of experienced personnel.[64] German divisional transport leaders interfered with railroad officials in Passau during the loading and unloading of units. The unloaded tracked vehicles, having been previously separated from their command in order to save on wear, idled at the rail head consuming precious fuel and making the situation worse.[65] As a result, parts of the 17th Infantry Division were forced to unload outside Passau in Vilshofen and then to march to boats and other trains for movement into Austria.[66]

The complete lack of traffic regulation also confused and degraded units. More than one thousand traffic police and gendarmes only came after the start of the *Einmarsch*, instead of being in place to guide and direct it.[67] As it turned out, the low training level of these men helped little once the march had started.

By the time that the German divisions and regiments had drawn near the Austrian border, they did so as fragmented, badly inter-mixed units, frequently out of contact and control of higher commands. In short, they were barely combat formations. Each division was splintered into three or four pieces, each of which spread over tens of kilometers in several march columns, jumbled with units of other divisions.[68] For the *Einmarsch*, the spearhead 10th Infantry Division and 2nd Panzer Division lacked all essential rear services and crossed the border with only half of their allotted troops.[69] The 7th Infantry Division was completely torn asunder. In only two of many such examples, the 62nd Infantry Regiment took twenty nine and one half hours to pass through Braunau, while the 19th Infantry Regiment took thirty one and one half hours, or one and one quarter days![70] In the meantime, the 10th Engineer Battalion, 10th Infantry Division had been unable to shore up the bridge at Schärding, so what minimal wheeled strength 2nd Panzer Division possessed had to move unexpectedly to Passau.[71] Urgently required elements for sustaining combat power, notably the *Waffenmeisterwagon* (weapons maintenance vehicle) and the munitions wagons were lost in the backwash of the divisions. Some of them would be unavailable before the 7th mobilization day, a critical failing that the 10th Infantry Division believed seriously called into question "[*d*]*ie Schlagkraft und Einsatzbereitschaft der Truppe* …"[72]

## *Einmarsch*

At 08:00 on 12 March, parts of German Eighth Army invaded Austria, and circumstances continued to worsen as problem compounded problem. The much reduced spearhead of the 2nd Panzer Division, now lacking all armored, maintenance and munitions units, was three hours late in crossing the border due to the previous night's "festivities" at Schärding and Passau.[73] In general, the panzer units and all motorized units had had enough fuel to get to the Austro-German border. Once there, however, units immediately began to feel an acute gas shortage. This was due to a lack of gasoline storage at the border, lack of transport vehicles, poorly trained men (as mentioned above), the rapidity of the whole mobilization, and underestimations of fuel requirements for the rapidly mobilizing army. The Eighth Army was not able to begin solving this problem until 16 March. The 2nd Panzer Division, and the 7th and 10th Infantry Divisions were forced to make use of commercial gasoline stations in Austria, the Eighth Army noting that without these civilian stations all operations "would have come to a stop by noon on 12 March[!]"[74] For an immobilized *Wehrmacht*, Austrian resistance might well have been a disaster. Even commercial gasoline stations proved only a bad solution, as the gasoline fuel mixture in Austria was different from that upon which the Wehrmacht's vehicles normally ran. Fouled engines and breakdowns were the consequence.[75] Adding insult to injury, the huge variety of different wheeled vehicles that had been pressed into service ran on one of three types of fuel: gasoline, diesel, or a coal derivative. The problems that this caused the 2nd Panzer Division prompted the supply units to declare that such a mix of vehicles was "*untragbar*" (intolerable).[76]

The Eighth Army now entered a terrain with only a few major roads, none of which were vaguely comparable to a then German *autobahn*, and most of which were extremely narrow and poorly paved. Once in Austria, the *Wehrmacht* found only "one fully operational railroad system and a single highway suitable for motorized units."[77] The bridges were mostly wood and in shoddy condition. Furthermore, the terrain was mountainous and hilly, and in some isolated spots there was snow. "[*S*]*chlecht*[*e*] *und steil*[*e*] *Straßen*" had a profound effect upon divisions whose motor vehicles, wagons, and horses were of less than good quality.[78] The state of the transportation network would also further inhibit the already profound communications and traffic problems.

As the 10th Infantry Division "threaded" (*einfädelte*) its way down its single, tight march-street, the terrain was such that vehicles with war materials, guns, and cannons could only be dragged up roads with substantial physical help from the soldiers and the shuttling back and forth of horses.[79] Forced to "surmount" (*überwinden*) the mountains in its area, the 7th Infantry Division found its wagons too heavy and its motorized vehicles and horses inadequate for the task. The 19th and 62nd Infantry Regiments found that their *Ergänzungspferde* (supplementary horses) were simply not capable of pulling wagons loaded with munitions and equipment. The result was a high fallout of all horses in these units, since healthy ones had to pick up the slack. Part of the 19th Infantry Regiment reported that this situation had caused "*eine ganz wesentlich verringerte Gefechtsbereit*[*schaft*]....[80] In the *bergigen* land wagons were simply abandoned, and motor vehicles broke down. Heavy artillery units of the XIII Army Corps found that their horses could not pull heavy guns up Austria's mountains (deemed *unmöglich*), nor were there adequate veterinary services to help injured horses. This caused delays as officers and men searched for both vehicles and extra horses. In the meantime, artillery wagons jammed the few passable roads.[81]

By the middle of 12 March, the hindrances to the operation were substantially increased in the already overburdened and tight march-streets

> *durch eine erhebliche Zahl auf der Straße liegengebliebener Fahrzeuge der Panzerdivision, zusammengebrochener kriegsunbrauchbarer Aushebungsfahrzeuge, und durch das Tanken zahlreicher Militär=, Polizei=, und Zivilfahrzeuge an den öffentlichen Tankstellen ...*[82]

Of the 229 tanks in the 2nd Panzer Division, thirty-nine broke down during its short march to Vienna, 17 percent of its battle strength.[83] Hitler, always a man with a mind for numbers and statistics, recalled seeing "over eighty tanks immobilized by the side of the road. ..."[84] Half of these probably represented breakdowns from the disastrously equipped and trained independent 1st Battalion, 25th Panzer Regiment and/or additional out-of-gasoline tanks from the 2nd Panzer Division. The (non-motorized) 7th and 10th Infantry division and the 2nd Panzer division together suffered over 300 breakdowns of trucks and cars.[85]

The situation was made more chaotic by the above mentioned lack of discipline, and through officers and men not following orders but "arbitrarily" resting, meeting, stopping and moving where they liked.[86] Units ignored the routes to which they had been assigned, and instead frequently took what they thought to be the most direct and fastest route toward Vienna, a situation that prompted an exasperated XIII

Army Corps staff to remind all its units that the assignment of routes was the prerogative of the XIII Army corps staff alone.[87] The result was an increasingly heavy traffic situation as well as the mixing of units that produced greater obstacles for command and control and reduced operational effectiveness.

Making the traffic situation even worse, a great number of units exhibited poor marching discipline. Elements of the SS, Herman Göring Regiment, vehicles of the propaganda ministry, and regular army motorized units savagely shouldered troops and wagons off the road whenever possible. They then came to rest in critical town squares, clogging them for other units.[88] By the middle of the first day's march narrow roads, abandoned wagons, lax march discipline, and mechanical breakdowns united to produce what the 10th Infantry Division described as *Verkehrsanarchie* (traffic anarchy). Traffic was so snarled that the commander of the XIII Army Corps, General Freiherr von Weichs, believed if there had been a battle, supply columns could not have made their way forward to re-supply the troops. Supply column commanders made the same comment.[89] Nor could orders be delivered along the march-routes. In the zone of the 7th and 10th Infantry Divisions, the streets were so overloaded with a veritable wave of units going forward that vehicles bearing vital orders that tried to go against the tide could get nowhere.[90] The 7th Infantry Division described its advance as "*gelähmt*" (paralyzed), while the 10th Infantry Division reported that *"[e]s ist unmöglich zu beschreiben, was in jenen Tagen auf den Einmarschstrassen vorging.*"[91]

Nor did the traffic anarchy abate. Although it lessened during the invasion as units dropped out of the march or got clear of one another, it remained a problem throughout the operation. There were simply not enough roads for units to operate upon and those that did exist were inadequate to the demands of the invasion. When few and poor roads combined with the sheer mass of man and material that were trying to navigate them chronic traffic jams resulted. This tangle was also sustained through poor discipline, breakdowns, and the degrading of already inadequate roads.

As units attempted to pass each other on these streets, the anarchy worsened as regiments, battalions, and companies mixed with those of others. This adversely affected the ability of commanders to lead their formations, resulting in further separation. It also destroyed unit combat effectiveness. After-action reports noted that extremely serious problems would have arisen if units had been called upon to fight, because commanders would have been unable to lead effectively such fragmented units.[92]

By the time the forward elements of the 7th and 10th Infantry Divisions had made their way through the worst of the mess, during 12-14 March, they were even more torn apart than before. This was exaggerated by the differing speeds of units' vehicles within the divisions which heretofore had not been reckoned with.[93] In the 10th Infantry Division, the distance between its three infantry regiments was over 60 km.[94] Divisional artillery, anti-tank, and support units were even further behind. Only in the 10th Infantry Division were its lead three infantry regiments finally in a position on 14 March to undertake an advance relatively clear of obstruction. Yet the division's increased pace of advance led to a higher proportion of drop-outs. Troops were on the road until well into the night, traffic once more proving a hindrance, and some men were still reaching their evening lagers at 3 a.m. and 4 a.m. the next morning on roads that were now becoming rutted.[95]

Although the 10th Infantry Division achieved rapid daily advance (averaging 43 km daily), the result was that it ceased to be to a combat formation. The vital rearward services were so far behind, over 150 km, that any attempt to have them catch up with the division was abandoned. Instead, the XIII Army Corps attempted to ship these units ahead by rail and ship, but the railroads were so occupied trying to move 27th Infantry Division to Vienna for its propaganda march that the rear services of 10th Infantry Division never reached their unit.[96] Consequently, if the 10th Infantry Division had encountered anything more than token resistance, its lack of heavy weapons and logistical support would have quickly brought its advance to a halt.

The 7th Infantry Division posted considerably lower marching speeds than did 10th Infantry Division (15 km per day at its lowest). It remained torn apart, with its support units the furthest behind, and the lead elements were continually running into elements of the 10th Infantry Division maneuvering ahead of them. By 14 March, the troops of 7th Infantry Division were so exhausted from their trials that the staff asked army command for a rest day, which was granted for 16 March.[97] The condition of the 7th Infantry Division by 14 March was such that it was unfit for sustained combat and very probably incapable of advancing in the face of any organized opposition.

Matters were hardly better for the favored 2nd Panzer Division. It had lost any semblance of a combat formation. On 12 March at 11 p.m. the spearhead, consisting of the 5th and 7th Reconnaissance Battalions along with the 2nd Motorcycle Battalion, were in St. Pölten. At the same time, some mixed wheeled units were moving through Linz while others remained on the road from Passau to Linz.[98] The 3rd and 4th Panzer Regiments had not yet entered Austria. They would only filter into Vienna on 14 March between 1 a.m. and 12 noon.[99] In the face of resistance, the combat capabilities of the division, especially the 3rd and 4th Panzer Regiments with their broken-down tanks and unsatisfactory personnel, would have been highly doubtful. As the 2nd Panzer Division reported:

> *[w]enn man sich vergegenwärtigt, daß der Vormarsch der Division unter feindlicher Gegenwirkung hätte stattfinden müssen, so hätten sich sowohl bei den beschl[eunigten] ausrückenden Teilen wie auch insbesondere bei den rückwärtigen Diensten, erschütternde Folgen gezeigt, und zwar dies nicht allein im Hinblick auf Verlust, sondern es wäre möglicherweise der gesamte Einsatz der Panzer Division in Frage gestellt worden.*[100]

A similar situation affected the Mountain Division. After battling its way through the disastrous traffic and through the choked streets, during which time it came close to running out of gasoline, the 100th Mountain Regiment was faced with climbing over the Phyrn and Präbichl passes. Here it made slow and difficult progress. The demands of the advance caused 30 to 40 percent of the reserves to fall out in the first days of the march alone. In the 3rd Mountain Battalion, 100th Mountain Regiment, thirty three men fell out the first day alone. Several days into the march this number had risen to approximately two hundred and fifty men, or approximately one-third of the combat strength of the battalion.[101]

From an operational point of view, the invasion of Austria was exceptionally poor. From the first moment, frictions arose that mounted one on top of another. Officers and men arrived late to their posts and were mis-assigned or simply untrained for their duties. Wagons and motorized vehicles were frequently missing, inadequate for their tasks or unusable. Nor was the situation considerably better regarding horses, the prime mover of the *Wehrmacht*. Once inside Austria, the difficulties were aggravated through a completely inadequate road and rail network and the huge numbers of men and materiel attempting to push through. Poor discipline, lack of training, and outright incompetence worsened matters, as did mechanical breakdowns and lack of fuel. The result was that divisions, regiments, and battalions ceased to be effective combat units.

### Post Anschluß Recognition of the *Wehrmacht's* Performance

The failure of the German military during the invasion of Austria only became known slowly and incompletely during the months following the event, and was never fully recognized as the mitigated disaster that it was. The French military *attachés* in Berlin and Vienna did not venture out of their respective areas and saw little more than what the Germans wanted them to see. The French military *attaché* in Berlin lamented the fact that the French had nobody in the area of the mobilization and *Einmarsch,* a situation which forced them to rely on information supplied entirely by the Germans.[102] The result would be a drastic mis-assessment of German performance that heavily contributed to French despair of resisting Nazi Germany.[103]

The Italians did somewhat better. Their military *attaché* in Vienna drove through the immediate suburbs of the city before midnight on 12 March, as far as Klosterneuburg, and saw just a little of the huge mess that characterized the *Einmarsch.* He reported seeing vehicles and motorcyclists at 23:30 and not seeing anything else until another group arrived at 3:00am on 13 March. The condition of their arrival prompted him to write that "every connection among single elements had been lost. ... a sign of lack of marching discipline."[104] In the parade itself, to which only Italian, Polish, and Yugoslav representatives were invited, the best tanks of the 2nd Panzer Division were used along with the best equipped and trained portions of the 27th Infantry Division.[105]

The British military *attaché* in Berlin requisitioned a car on 13 March and drove from Berlin through Dresden and Prague to Vienna. From Vienna he traveled the road Vienna-Linz-Salzburg-Munich. During the drive, he reported that most of the German mechanized units had only finally passed Wels on 14 March and that as late as 15 March the public gas stations were either completely dry or still reserved for the *Wehrmacht*. The troop trains "gave every evidence of having been very hastily put together and loaded."[106] Although it eventually took a bit more time for British intelligence to digest the fact that the German army was not what the Germans pretended it was, this information was one of the first pieces of evidence that led Britain to revise drastically its net assessment of the German army.[107]

After World War II, General Heinz Guderian, one of Hitler's trusted Generals, characterized the Anschluß as an operation that was performed "satisfactorily." He minimized the failure of the *Wehrmacht* in Austria in his pursuit of self-aggrandizement.[108] Guderian had the audacity to deny that gas shortages almost ended the invasion, that the road to Vienna was continuously blocked, and that units were poorly trained and performed dismally. Winston Churchill, in his memoirs, was close to the mark precisely because he must have based his judgments on the reports that were coming in from the perspicacious British military *attaché*. Churchill wrote:

> [a] triumphal entry into Vienna was [Hitler's] dream. ... [T]he Nazi party in [Vienna] had planned a torchlight procession to welcome the conquering hero [on 12 March]. But nobody arrived. The cause of this hitch leaked out slowly. The German war machine had lumbered falteringly over the frontier and come to a standstill near Linz.[109]

Although Churchill may have erred in the details, he was correct in the tenor of his commentary. Like some great malfunctioning clockwork, the Wehrmacht lurched and shuddered forward. Throwing springs and spitting cogs, it grated to a halt in the suburbs of Vienna. Hitler himself later took note of the poor performance of the *Wehrmacht* in Austria in March 1938 and the substantially better performance it gave in Czechoslovakia in March 1939.[110]

## The Question of Austrian Resistance

The Austrian *Bundesheer*, consisting of seven infantry divisions, one independent brigade and one armored division, was a developing army in March 1938.[111] As such, it faced shortages that would have compromised a sustained Austrian resistance of more than several weeks. The most egregious of these was the lack of artillery ammunition both in the infantry divisions and in the independent artillery regiment, which amounted to approximately a ten to twelve days supply.[112] This might have been extended through the careful conservation of sheils as practiced by all armies when short of ammunition; nevertheless, after the ammunition was depleted it would have had a highly negative effect upon the defensive capabilities of the

*Bundesheer*. The Austrian army was also not as well trained as the *Wehrmacht*.[113]

Although the *Bundesheer*'s artillery regiments were still equipped with large numbers of World War I vintage artillery, these had been modernized through the use of new ammunition and technical refinements that together had extended both lethality and range.[114] The equipment had also been lightened for use in the mountainous terrain of Austria. Here, for example, the 80 mm field cannon (World War I vintage) proved very effective.[115] Since the *Wehrmacht* was experiencing problems moving its artillery into Austria exactly because it had not considered the problems that mountainous terrain might pose, it is possible that the first days of the invasion would have actually given Austria an important, if temporary, advantage in artillery.

Most important for defense against German armor was the Austrian-made 47 mm anti-tank cannon which could easily penetrate the armor of any German tank at that time at over 1000 m.[116] By March 1938, the *Bundesheer* deployed 270 of these guns with more than enough ammunition to decimate the armor of the Eighth Army.[117] Against the 229 tanks of the German 2nd Panzer Division, the *Bundesheer* mustered 72 Italian Fiat-Ansaldo M 35 tanks. In comparison to the 184 Panzer Is in the German 2nd Panzer Division, the Fiat-Ansaldos were equal; only against the forty-five panzer IIs of the 2nd Panzer Division were they moderately inferior.[118] The *Bundesheer* possessed light infantry weapons (rifles, mortars, machine-guns) that compared favorably with those of the German *Wehrmacht*.[119]

Austrian defense plans, as set down in the "Jansa Plan," anticipated a German assault and had been begun in the fall of 1935 by Austrian Chief of the General Staff Alfred Jansa together with his divisional commanders. They provided not only for the mobilization and deployment of the entire *Bundesheer* and auxiliary formations against the *Wehrmacht*, but also for the creation of street blockades and the destruction of bridges and roads in order to hamper the advance of the German army.[120] The mobilization required a minimum of four days for the active army. If necessary, a hastily mobilized 4th Infantry Division (Linz), the Motorized division and the *frontmiliz* (a paramilitary organization) would fight a withdrawal from the Austro-German border to the assembly area of the main body of the *Bundesheer* between the Traun and Enns rivers west of Steyr.[121] The four day mobilization time was, on the surface, the greatest shortcoming in Jansa's defense plans. But the problems of the German *Wehrmacht* were large enough to have provided the needed time, even considering that the *Bundesheer* would have experienced problems during its mobilization. The Austrian *Bundesheer* in March 1938 was an army with still unsolved and operationally inhibiting problems, but it possessed sufficient equipment and manpower, a modern armored doctrine, and a well thought out defensive plan.[122] Though it could not hope ultimately to prevail against the resources of Germany, Austria very probably had enough military strength for a one to two week defensive battle in Austria's rugged terrain; if the enemy were not too acute.

The monumental shortcomings of the *Wehrmacht* illustrate what might have happened if Austria had resisted by mobilizing early on 11 March after first detecting the then mobilizing *Wehrmacht*. The Eighth Army reported that if the Austrian *Bundesheer* had mobilized, the *Wehrmacht* could not have been ready before 13 March to cross the frontier.[123] Considering the difficulties that were occurring for the *Wehrmacht* during its mobilization and march to the Austrian border, a delay until 15 or 16 March is eminently believable. Here was the time Austria needed for its mobilization. Against the huge problems that the *Wehrmacht* experienced in mobilizing, Jansa's estimation of four days for the mobilization of the active Austrian army does not seem so much operationally slow as it does realistic.[124] The evidence examined suggests that once the *Wehrmacht entered* Austria, a war between the two countries probably would have lasted one and one half to two weeks, and perhaps as long as three weeks. The first wave 7th and 10th Infantry Divisions needed one week to march to Vienna under the best possible circumstances, active and essential aid from the Austrians and no fighting, and arrived in dismal shape. Even in this undertaking command units were pushed to their limits. Without the aid of Austrian gasoline stations, the 2nd Panzer Division and the motorized portions of all Infantry and Mountain Divisions could have gone nowhere before 15-16 March; if they had attempted to do so, they would have found themselves out of fuel in an active combat zone.

When Hitler gave the order for mobilization plans to be drawn up on 10 March, he did so for a *Wehrmacht* that faced grave deficiencies. In this vein, it is essential to realize that the German army in March 1938 was a "phase shift" less qualitatively and quantitatively, than the German army that invaded Poland in 1939.[125] Beginning in October

1934, the *Wehrmacht* began systematically tearing apart established divisions in order to raise new ones. Selected established divisions lost no less than 40 percent of their established strength in this process, along with their equipment, weapons, and horses. In 1936 and 1937 alone the army created two corps headquarters, twelve regular divisions, four reserve divisions and twenty-one *Landwehr* divisions. It also motorized four infantry divisions. The stresses that this put upon military readiness were substantial. Further, at the end of 1937, the *Wehrmacht* released its draftees with two years experience and took in large quantities of raw recruits which, along with the reserve and *Ergänzung* portions, significantly reduced the operational capabilities of all divisions. German army after-action reports indicated as much.[126]

The *Wehrmacht* still faced many and critical shortcomings in doctrine, training, and discipline. For example, the concepts of full command by radio and of Panzer Corps were still one and two years away, respectively. No less were the shortages in vehicles, equipment, and ammunition in March 1938, a situation to which Chief of the German General Staff Ludwig Beck had drawn attention shortly after the meeting recorded and known to posterity as the "Hossbach Memorandum" in November 1937.[127] In March 1938, the *Wehrmacht*, for example, had only ten days of light mortar ammunition. One scholar has characterized the situation as late as April 1939 (slightly more than one year after the Anschluß) as one in which the field army

> had no supply of arms and equipment. . . [and of] the infantry divisions thirty four had only some of the required weapons and equipment, the reserve forces possessed only 10% of the weapons that they required and that the overall munitions supply was down to 15 days.[128]

In March 1938 the main battle tank of the German army was still the *Panzerkampfwagen* I, which mounted only two machine-guns and had between 13mm and 7mm of armor plating, hardly enough protection to stop fire from machine guns, and no better than the tanks of the Austrian *Bundesheer*. The *Panzerkampfwagen* II was little better.

Doctrinally, there would be no possibility of German combined air-ground operations and little possibility of significant landings/air assaults behind Austrian lines. As late as the campaign in Poland in September 1939, Beck's view of combined air-ground operations was that it was still "a completely new land."[129] Although the German *Luftwaffe* had hastily thrown together two companies of paratroopers in order to take the airport in Vienna in case of Austrian resistance, they would have fallen right on top of the Austrian 2nd Battalion, 5 th Infantry Regiment stationed near the airport and with numerous reinforcements near at hand in Vienna.[130] It is difficult to imagine how these could have been reinforced and supplied to obtain significant results. They were primarily intended for propaganda. The German army did not yet have paratroopers of the quantity and quality to conduct anything bordering on the operation that would be *Eben Emael* during the French Campaign in 1940. These troops would only be the result of two further years of intensive training (not to mention a substantial portion of luck). The improvised nature of the German invasion left no time for the extensive planning that German airborne operations in Austria would have needed in order to be undertaken.

The *Luftwaffe* too was experiencing crippling problems. At the beginning of 1938, the German army was still flying its first generation aircraft. To take but one important example, the German army was still operating Ar-68 biplanes as its primary fighter. Only by autumn 1938 would the *Luftwaffe* have any significant number of Me-109s, the Ar-68s replacement.[131] The "in commission" rates and air crew readiness of the *Luftwaffe* were also low. On 1 August 1938, only 453 fighters and 742 bombers, dive bombers and ground attack planes were "in commission."[132] In terms of air crews only 1084 were fully operational, while 909 were partially operational.[133] Against this, the weak Austrian *Luftwaffe* mustered somewhere between 150-250 machines, only a small percentage of which were "in commission" and of a modern enough type to have been effective.[134]

The German *Luftwaffe* could have attempted to bomb Vienna and other towns and interdict supply. But what probable effect would this "strategic bombing" have had? First of all, only a small portion of the German *Luftwaffe* (about three hundred planes) was on hand for the *Einmarsch.* The *Luftwaffe* would have had to re-deploy its serviceable fighters and bombers along with fuel and logistical support to southern Germany. Further, it would have to plan a campaign and to select targets in Austria. Only then could any sort of systematic destruction begin. The two German bombers which were being produced in March 1938, the Do-17 and the He-111, have been characterized as "twin-engined aircraft, which possessed neither the speed nor the bomb-carrying capacity [500 kilograms at this time] to act as strategic bombers."[135] As discussed above, poor air crew readiness rates and in commission rates would have further reduced the effect that bombing could have had on Austria. On the basis of this evidence, we may presume that an air war against Austria would have had little immediate effect beyond the destruction of the fledgling Austrian *Luftstreitskräfte* (air force). Only after one to two weeks might the German *Luftwaffe* have begun to have had a significant effect on Austrian armaments and munitions industries, and the interdiction of supply.

War is without question one of the most entropic activities humankind undertakes. When bullets fly and men die, everything becomes more disordered, difficult, and unpredictable. Units not only fight with less than perfect information but are subject to information overload.[136] The German 7th Infantry Division itself noted that if it had come into battle, it would substantially reduced its already slow march (at its lowest 15 km per day) in order to be effective and that battle would have made everything more arduous.

The problems of the *Wehrmacht* were great enough that combat opportunities would have presented themselves to the weak *Bundesheer* to bleed, disrupt, and slow the German spearheads with small hit and run attacks as it fell back toward Vienna. Fedor von Bock, the commander of the Eighth Army noted:

> [e]s *steht außer Zweifel, daß bei feindlicher Gegenwehr von der Erde und namentlich aus der Luft die Ereignisse auf der Straße Passau-Linz-Wien zu einer Katastrophe hätten führen können.*
>
> *Aehnliche Dinge können sich nach kriegerischen Erfolgen wiederholen. Die Schwierigkeiten werden dann durch zurückströmende Verwundete und Gefangene, zurückfahrende Leerkolonnen und an der Straße liegendes zusammengeschossenes Gerät usw. noch größer sein.*[137]

Nevertheless, Austrian resistance had its limits and could not have been successful if the war had remained local. The question remains whether diplomatic or military pressure from other European nations might have saved the small Danubian state.

## Conclusion

Recently, Gerhard Weinberg addressed officers and cadets at the U.S. Military Academy at West Point, New York. During his lecture, he came to the subject of one of the greatest distortions to which people have given credence since the end of World War II, that of the "good" German generals who were not Nazi and had no idea about the Final Solution.[138] Less pernicious but no less distorting is the enduring myth of the "invincible" *Wehrmacht* which sprang, ready formed, from the rib of Guderian, which went on to conquer most of Europe and Western Russia, and which only really lost because of Hitler's half-witted and irrational commands. Much recent scholarship has finally made clear the enormous difficulties which affected the creation and development of the *Wehrmacht*. The German army reached and maintained the levels of effectiveness that it did only as the result of slow laborious work, brutally honest self-criticism, and much practice, not from some "inherent" German ability.[139] German commanders complained that they lacked essential motorized vehicles, maps, and trained soldiers because they could not get orders to units and command effectively without them, not, as it has been suggested, because they would have liked some extras.[140]

It is important to understand that the image of the "swift and efficient" Anschluß was largely the result of a few lead armored cars and motorcycles that rushed down winding Austrian roads at breakneck speeds; obsolete aircraft that landed at the Vienna airport; and part of the 27th Infantry Division (*...Schlagfertigkeit einzelner Verbände in Frage gestellt haben...)* which was shipped to Vienna by train, since no other infantry units could reach Vienna to participate in the scheduled victory parade.[141] In this last maneuver, the German army was only successful because of the substantial help and cooperation afforded by the Austrian *Bundesbahn*.[142] At times, the military operation bordered on the comic and in strict terms was a mitigated operational disaster. Nevertheless, like the North Vietnamese Tet Offensive thirty years later, operational disaster does not equal military disaster. The Nazi propaganda machine, parts of which were busy running down German soldiers in their rush to get to Vienna on 12 and 13 March, would prove as successful as it had ever been.

In Germany, however, the beginning of a transformation was taking place as a result of the lessons learned from the Anschluß.[143] Clausewitz wrote, "[there] are only two sources of ... [military] spirit. ... [t]he first is a series of victorious wars; the second, frequent exertions of the army to the utmost limits of its strength."[144] Despite the gross problems that the *Wehrmacht* had encountered, the Anschluß fulfilled the first of these requirements in spirit and the second of these in practice. In the wake of a miserable performance, the *Wehrmacht* drew critical and realistic conclusions that would help to make it the instrument of French and British defeat in 1940.

## Notes

1. "Lightning War or Bungling War."

2. It is not my intention to become involved in the debate as to whether or not the Anschluß "really" constituted a legal or an illegal act, an adequate summary of which is provided in Robert H. Keyserlingk, *Austria in World War II: An Anglo-American Dilemma* (Montreal: McGill-Queen's University Press, 1988), 27-29. It should be enough to note that *without* some form of armed force it had been impossible (from the time of Hitler's *Machtergreifung* in 1933 until 12 March 1938), and probably would have continued to be extremely difficult, for Nazi Germany to have brought about an Anschluß. In the event, which was nothing short of a coercive act, I do not believe that one can speak of "legality" in any meaningful sense of the word. At best we can say that force was used and then recognized as the law since not enough people's interests or fears reached that critical point at which they were willing to go to war.

3. Kurt von Schuschnigg, *The Brutal Takeover*, trans. Richard Barry (New York: Atheneum, 1971), 277.

4. With regard to Austria's internal military situation, such issues as the matériel of the Austrian *Bundesheer*, its defense plans, the reliability of the officer corps and troops, and the morale of the Austrian people have all received attention. Here the essential point has been if and how well the *Bundesheer* could have fought. To take some examples Emil Liebitzky, the Austrian military *attaché* in Italy between 1933-38 in his *Nachlass* has stated that the reliability of the *Bundesheer* was without question, a statement that corresponds to what Chief of the General Staff from 1935-38 Field-Marshal Alfred Jansa, Schuschnigg, and 2[nd] Infantry Division commander Major General Karl Borneman wrote after the war. Other authors such as postwar Field-Marshal Kubena, Ludwig Jedlicka, and Erwin Steinböck have illuminated the problems of *matériel* which the *Bundesheer* faced, especially that of equipment and ammunition. Emil Liebitzky, *Nachlässe und Sammlungen*, B/1030, Österreichische Staadtsarchiv: Kriegsarchiv, Wien. (hereafter referred to as ÖSK); Alfred Jansa, *Nachlässe und Sammlungen*, 07R143/1, ÖSK; Karl Borneman, *Nachlässe und Sammlungen*, C/1119, ÖSK; Field-Marshal Kubena "Die Presse" 16 April 1947; Ludwig Jedlicka, *Ein Herr im Schatten der Parteien: Die militär-politische Lage Österreichs 1918-1938* (Graz: Böhlau, 1955); Ludwig Jedlicka "Warum hat das Bundesheer nicht geschossen? Die militärpolitische Vorgeschichte des 13. März 1938" in *Wien Aktuell*, Heft 3 (March 1978); Erwin Steinböck, *Österreichs militärliches Potentziell im Märtz 1938* (Vienna: Verlag für Geschichte und Politik, 1988).
   Externally, authors have focused on the international situation as the source of dispute. Those who argue that Schuschnigg made the right decision point to Austria's abandonment by France, England, Italy, and the rest of Europe. This

school of thought, the "useless sacrifice" school, I consider to be best represented by the two apologia of Kurt von Schuschnigg. Works that fall into this school include, for example, those by Ludwig Jedlicka, Hubertus Trauttenberg, and Erwin A. Schmidl. Schmidl's argument is more refined and nuanced than previous ones. The great weakness in this school of thought is twofold. First, it holds the following as a syllogism: Schuschnigg did not offer resistance because all of Europe had abandoned Austria thus, if Schuschnigg had offered resistance none of Europe would have aided Austria. This is assuredly an incorrect deduction, and there is evidence to support the contention that a resistance by Austria might have provoked reactions ranging from resistance to the Nazi regime from within Germany, to a European wide conflict. Second, it either ignores or drastically overvalues the abilities of the German *Wehrmacht* in 1938. Kurt von Schuschnigg *Im Kampf gegen Hitler: Die Überwindung der Anschlußidee* (Vienna: Fritz Molden, 1969); Kurt von Schuschnigg, *The Brutal Takeover*; Ludwig Jedlicka "Warum hat das Bundesheer nicht geschossen?"; Hubertus Trauttenberg, "Die Abwehrvorbereitungen gegen einen deutschen Angriff im Bereich der 4. Division in den Jahren 1936-1938," Militärwissenschaftliche Hausarbeit, Linz, 1972; Erwin Schmidl *Der "Anschluß" Österreichs: Der Deutsche Einmarsch im März 1938* (Bonn: Bernard and Graefe Verlag, 1994).

One hears the argument that even if the Austrian Bundesheer could not have resisted for long (the estimates usually being several days) thus achieving a "symbolic resistance," it should have been undertaken. Even if a "symbolic resistance" would not have saved the country, the argument continues, at least it would have provided some measure of moral balm in the aftermath of the German *Angriff*. That this argument is one largely based on the *ex post facto* results of non-resistance has not stopped its propagation.

5. The first of these works, written by Friedrich Fritz and originally published in 1968, covered the days immediately preceding the invasion, and the *Einmarsch* itself in chronological order. For the most part, this publication is a superficial, descriptive work with little in the way of critical analysis. The author, in his last chapter, "*War Verteidigung möglich*?", avoids taking a stand as to the results of a possible military confrontation. After mentioning the military problems of both Germany and Austria, he categorically asserts that no country would have helped Austria if she had chosen to fight and therefore that resistance by the small Danubian state would have been useless. Friedrich Fritz *Der Deutsche Einmarsch in Österreich 1938* (Vienna: Österreichischer Bundesverlag Gesellschaft, 1985). Williamson Murray dealt with the *Einmarch* more completely than it had been dealt with up until that time. Yet his focus was much wider than the Anschluß, and beyond his obvious thesis of the changing European balance of power, one of his chief focal points was on Munich and a possible war in the fall of 1938 as the result of a German attack against Czechoslovakia. Nevertheless, Murray's research on the Austrian invasion clearly revealed a *Wehrmacht* in disarray, and in light of his research on the subject, the author is of the opinion that any attack by Germany in early 1938 was bound to encounter enormous difficulties as a result of the great problems that the *Wehrmacht* faced at that time. Discussion with Williamson Murray, September 1996; Williamson Murray, *The Change in the European Ballance of Power, 1938-1939* (Princeton: Princeton University Press, 1984).

Most recently, Erwin A. Schmidl has examined the *Einmarsch* in 1938, and his work has refined the research done both by Fritz and Murray. A major portion of the book is concerned with describing the march into Austria by the

*Wehrmacht*, and the reception of the Germans by the Austrians during that event. In doing so, Schmidl has examined aspects of both the Austrian *Bundesheer* and the German *Wehrmacht* and made a variety of assessments. Unfortunately, Schmidl does not address Murray's evidence and comes to a very different conclusion: that the invasion by Germany was, despite "*zahlreiche*[r] *Pannen*" [numerous breakdowns], indicative of a German army that had its weaknesses "*vielfach überbewertet*" [greatly exaggerated] by the likes of Winston Churchill in his memoirs. Schmidl clearly implies that the German army which invaded Austria on 12 March 1938 had problems, but that they were not extremely serious and operationally inhibiting. Thus, the German army (in combination with the mobilization problems of the Austrian army) would likely have quickly subdued the small Danubian state. Schmidl *Der "Anschluß" Österreichs*, 254, 208.

Schmidl and Fritz principally utilized archives in Germany and Austria, while Murray's research was primarily based upon archives in the United States and England.

6. "March-out [to the border of Austria and Germany]"

7. Telford Taylor, *Sword and Swastika: Generals and Nazis in the Third Reich* (New York: Simon and Schuster, 1952), 182. As is well known, the sketchy plans that did exist were drawn-up in case of a Habsburg restoration in Austria.

8. First wave divisions were supposed to be the most combat ready, with the highest percentage of active manpower and most complete equipment. Because of the rapid and uneven expansion of the *Wehrmacht* in the mid to late 1930s, however, this was not always the case.

9. My thanks to Edward Macdonald for his help in the National Archives. Bericht über den Einsatz der 8. Armee im März 1938, Dresden 18. Juli 1938, Der Oberbefehlshaber der Heeresgruppenkommando 3, T-79/14/000447 [Group/Roll/ Frame No.], National Archives Records Service, Washington, D.C. [hereafter referred to as NARS]. See either the appendices of Fritz, or that of Schmidl for a complete listing (and unit breakdown) of the German and Austrian forces during the *Einmarsch*. Although both authors based their identification of the XVI as a "Panzer Corps" on actual source material, the original document itself is misleading. *No Panzer Corps were created prior to 1940*. The XVI was a Motorized Corps. The amount of units on both sides is large enough, reasons of space preclude its publication here. Fritz, *Der deutsche Einmarsch*; Schmidl, *Der "Anschluß" Österreichs*.

10. Bericht über den Einsatz der 8. Armee im März 1938, Dresden 18. Juli 1938, Der Oberbefehlshaber der Heeresgruppenkommando 3, T-79/14/000447, NARS.

11. "Austrian troops that resist are to be broken with force of arms." Armeetagesbefehl Nr. 1, Mühldorf, 11.3.38, A.O.K. 8, RH 20-8/274, p. 5-6, Bundesarchiv/Militärarchiv, Freiburg [hereafter referred to as BA/MA].

12. Erfahrungsbericht über den "Einsatz Österreich," Nürnberg 6.5.1938, Generalkommando XIII. Armeekorps (Wehrkeiskommando XIII), RH 26-17/173, p.5, BA/MA.

13. "Aggravated and delayed." Berichte des Armeeoberkommandos, RH 20-8/274, p.24, BA/MA. Army command also found that some of its officers were not up to their duty, and that there was the need for more officers. Erfahrungsbericht

über den "Einsatz Österreich," Nürnberg 6.5.1938, Generalkommando XIII. Armeekorps (Wehrkeiskommando XIII), RH 26-17/173, p 12, BA/MA.

14. "Mobilization areas" were the locations to which troops had to report inside of Germany and before their march to the Austrian border. See, for example, the situation of the gasoline supply column of the 7th Infantry Division, which by 13 March could only muster half of its required twenty-six motorized vehicles and two-thirds of its troops. Erfahrungsbericht z. großen Übung "Einsatz Österreich" im März 1938, Passing 28.3.1938, Gr.Kw.Kol.f.Betriebsstoffe C 22 [7th Infantry Division], RH 26-7/170b, p. 1,3, BA/MA. See also Erfahrungsbericht Österreich, Berlin 13.4.38, Korpskommando XVI Armeekorps, RH 53-13/63, p.13, BA/MA.

15. Erfahrungsbericht über den "Einsatz Österreich," Nürnberg 6.5.1938, Generalkommando XIII. Armeekorps (Wehrkeiskommando XIII), RH 26-17/173, p. 25, BA/MA.

16. The *ergänzung* portions of active divisions made up from 10 to 20 percent of the personnel in combat units and as much as 95 percent of personnel in the rear services. Georg Tessin, *Deutsche Verbände und Truppen 1918-1939* (Osnabrück: Biblio Verlag, 1974), 218-219.

17. Erfahrungen beim "Einsatz Österreich," 26.April 1938, Wehrsatzinspektion Nürnberg, T-79/275/000001-000010, NARS; Erfahrungsbericht der Landwehr-Division 97 über "Einsatz Österreich," 22.4.1938, Landwehr-Kommandeur München, RH 26-7/170b, p. 3, BA/MA. See also the reports by units in the 7th Division, for example, Erfahrungsbericht über den "Einsatz Österreich," K.W.W. Komp. (mot) 27, RH 26-7/170b, p.1, BA/MA.

18. "Mobilization day" is counted with 11 March as being the first such day. Thus the fifth mobilization day would be the 15 March. Erfahrungsbericht über den "Einsatz Österreich," Nürnberg 6.5.1938, Generalkommando XIII. Armeekorps (Wehrkeiskommando XIII), RH 26-17/173, p. 18, 23, 43, BA/MA.

19. They lacked, for example, medicine, equipment, and over one-third of their officers. Erfahrungsbericht Österreich, Berlin 13.4.38, Korpskommando XVI Armeekorps, RH 53-13/63, p. 37, BA/MA.

20. Erfahrungsbericht über Mobilmachung und Demobilmachung anläßlich des "Einsatz Österreich," 21.4.1938, 27. Division Nr. 200/38 g. Kdos., T-79/14/000575, NARS; Erfahrungsbericht über den "Einsatz Österreich," 6.5.1938, Generalkommando XIII. Armeekorps (Wehrkreiskommando XIII), T-79/274/000910, NARS.

21. Mob. Erfahrungen, 27. April 38, Wehrersatz-Inspektion Nürnberg Nr. 1987 geh./ Gru.Ia., T-79/223/000509-512, NARS.

22. "for the most part very bad;" Erfahrungsbericht über Mobilmachung und Demobilmachung anläßlich des "Einsatz Österreich," Landesberg 11.IV.38, I./A.R. 608 i. Abw., RH 53-7/433, p. 6-10, BA/MA.

23. Bericht über den Einsatz der 8 Armee im März 1938, Dresden 18 Juli 1938, Der Oberbefehlshaber der Heeresgruppenkommando 3, T-79/14/000453, NARS. See also, for example, "Erfahrungsbericht," 20.3.38, Panzer Regiment 3, Gr. 1a op., RH 53-13/63, p. 76, BA/MA; Erfahrungsbericht, 38, 23.3.38, Nachrichten Abteilung, RH 53-13/63, p. 116-8, BA/MA.

24. Erfahrungsbericht über den "Einsatz Österreich," 6.5.1938, Generalkommando XIII. Armeekorps (Wehrkreiskommando XIII), T-314/525/000347, NARS. This situation might almost be amusing were it not for the fate the mentally disturbed and retarded were meeting at the hands of the Nazis. See Michael Burleigh, *Death and Deliverance: "Euthanasia" in Germany 1900-1945* (Cambridge: Cambridge University Press, 1994).

25. Erfahrungsbericht über Mobilmachung und Demobilmachung anläßlich des "Einsatz Österreich," 21.4.1938, 27. Division Nr. 200/38 g. Kdos., T-79/14/000580, NARS; Mob. Erfahrungen, 27. April 38, Wehrersatz-Inspektion Nürnberg Nr. 1987 geh./Gru.Ia., T-79/223/000510-513, NARS.

26. Fernspruch, 15.3.38, übermittelte der Ia des Gen. Kdos. XIII dem Ia der 10. Division, RH 26-10/118, p. 3/34, BA/MA; Erfahrungen bei der Probe-Mobilmachung, Obergrafendorf 23.3.38, Infantrie Regiment 19, RH 26-7/645, p. 1-2, BA/MA; [No title. Probably an after-action report from 7. Infantry Division] RH 26-7/170b, p. 3, 5, BA/MA.

27. "no idea about the mission, and duty of his column;" "not a man that was active in his civil job as an auto-mechanic." [No title. Probably an after-action report from 7$^{th}$ Infantry Division] RH 26-7/170b, p. 3 BA/MA; Erfahrungen bei der Probemobilmachung, Bad Reichenhall 8.April 1938, Stab Geb. Jäg. Reg. 100, RH 37/6717, p. 3-5, BA/MA; Erfahrungsbericht über den "Einsatz Österreich," Schrobenhausen 23.3.1938, K.W.W. Komp. (mot) 27, RH 26-7/170b, p. 1, BA/MA; Erfahrungsbericht zur Probe-Mobilmachung, München 28. März 1938, Kw. Werkstattzug C 23 der Korps Nachschub Abtl. 407, RH 26-7/170b, p. 1, BA/MA. See especially the *Erfahrungs-berichte* of the 2$^{nd}$ Panzer Division and the 27$^{th}$ Infantry Division, for example, Erfahrungsbericht über die Mobilmachung der Nachschubeinheiten der 2. Pz.Div., Floridsdorf 22.3.38, Nachub-Führer an 2. Pz. Div., RH 53-13/63, p. 130, BA/MA; Erfahrungsbericht über Mobilmachung und Demobilmachung anläßlich des "Einsatz Österreich," Augsburg 21.4.38, 27. Division, RH 53-7/508, p. 6/7-8/9, BA/MA.

28. The situation was so bad that fully one-third of the tanks still had to be driven by raw recruits without the necessary training. Erfahrungsbericht Österreich,13.4.38, Korpskommando XVI Armeekorps, RH 53-13/63, p. 13, BA/MA; "Vorläufiger Erfahrungsbericht über Ablauf der Mobilmachung und Vormarsch bis Wien," 27 März 1938, 2. Panzer Division, RH 53-13/63, p. 54, BA/MA; Erfahrungsbericht, 24.3.38, 2. Panzer Brigade, RH 53-13/63, p. 71, BA/MA.

29. "inadequate," "intolerable," and "badly aggravated;" Fernspruch, 15.3.38, übermittelte der Ia des Gen. Kdos. XIII dem Ia der 10. Division, RH 26-10/118, p. 2/33, BA/MA; [No title. Probably an after-action report from the 7$^{th}$ Infantry Division] RH 26-7/170b, p. 4, BA/MA; Erfahrungsbericht über Mobilmachung und Demobilmachung anläßlich des "Einsatz Österreich," Augsburg 21.4.38, 27. Division, RH 53-7/508, p.3/4, BA/MA; Erfahrungsbericht beim "Einsatz Österreich," Nürnberg 16.5.38, 17. Division, RH 37-850, p. 1-2, BA/MA. See also, for example, the after-action reports of Infantry Regiment 61, II/Infantry Regiment 19, I/Infantry Regiment 62, RH 26-7/645 BA/MA; Erfahrungsbericht, Generalkommande VII Armeekorps RH 53-7/128, p. 9/13, BA/MA; Erfahrungsbericht der Infantrie-Regiment 14 anläßlich des "Einsatz Österreich," Konstanz 14. April 1938, Infantry Regiment 14, RH 37/5031, p. 4-5, BA/MA; Erfahrungsbericht, Bad Mergentheim 1. April 1938, III/Infantry Regiment 55, RH 37/6664, p. 3, BA/MA.

30. "largest number of the reservists amounted to more of a hindrance than a strengthening of the operational capabilities [of the unit]." Erfahrungen bei der Probe-Mobilmachung und beim Einmarsch Österreich, Bad Reichenhall 13.4.38, Geb. Jäg. Reg. 100, RH 37/6711, p. 7, BA/MA. Regarding the term *einsatzfähig* (operational) it is essential to note that this term was *not* used synonymously to mean fully combat ready. See for example, the report by the Staff of the 100th Mountain Regiment which noted that although 3rd Mountain Battalion, 100th Infantry Regiment was *einsatzfähig*, it was "*nicht voll auf der von einer aktiven Feldtruppe zu fordernden Höhe* ..." (not completely up to the demands of an active field unit ...). Erfahrungen bei der Probemobilmachung, Bad Reichenhall 8. April 1938, Stab Geb. Jäg. Reg. 100, RH 37/6717, p. 1, BA/MA. Units were denoted *einsatzfähig* that were at the same time identified as either questionable or not suitable for combat. *Einsatzfähig* was used to denote a unit that had been able to be mobilized in a more or less complete fashion, and then able to join the march into Austria but which may have had significant combat inhibiting problems. A unit deemed not *einsatzfähig* was one that was unable even to mobilize properly and march out to the border. The German army high command (*Oberkommando des Heeres*) officially instituted a rating system which reflected these nuances in September 1939. This was a four level rating for units that were *einsatzfähig* and included the following ratings: 1) "[e]*insatzfähig für alle Aufgaben*" (operational for all assignments); 2) "operational, though only partly for the attack"; 3) "fully operational for defensive assignments"; and 4) "partly operational for defensive assignments." Units that were below a IV rating were "*nicht einsatzfähig*." Beurteilung des Kampfwertes der Divisionen Mitte Dezember 1939, 13.12.1939, Generalstab des Heeres, RH 2/1520, p. 68, BA/MA.

31. Erfahrungen bei der Probemobilmachung, Bad Reichenhall 8. April 1938, Stab Geb. Jäg. Reg. 100, RH 37/6717, p. 2-3, BA/MA; Erfahrungen bei der Probemobilmachung zum Einsatz Österreich, Bad Reichenhall 7.4.1938, III./Geb. Jäg.Reg. 100, RH 37/6717, p. 1-3, BA/MA.

32. "the battle-worthiness of particular units was called into question." Erfahrungsbericht über Mobilmachung und Demobilmachung anläßlich des "Einsatz Österreich," Augsburg 21.4.38, 27. Division, RH 53-7/508, p.3/4, BA/MA.

33. Fernspruch, 15.3.38, übermittelte der Ia des Gen. Kdos. XIII dem Ia der 10. Division, RH 26-10/118, p. 10, BA/MA; aus Erfahrungsberichten über der Einsatz Österreich, Nürnberg 21. April 1938, 17. Division, RH 26-17/174a, p. 1-4, BA/MA; Erfahrungsbericht, 7 April 1938, 7. Division, RH 26-7/645, p. 9, BA/MA. See also, for example, Erfhrungsbericht über die Mobilmachung der Nachschubeinheiten der 2. Panzer Division, 22.3.38, Nachub-Führer, RH 53-13/63, p. 138, BA/MA.

34. Erfahrungsbericht über den "Einsatz Österreich," Nürnberg 6.5.1938, Generalkommando XIII. Armeekorps (Wehrkeiskommando XIII), RH 26-17/173, p. 22-23, BA/MA; Erfahrungen bei der Probemobilmachung, 30.3.38, I./Panzer-Regiment 25, RH 26-7/645, p.1, BA/MA. It should at least be mentioned that morale in all units was lowered by the lack of clothing and the poor shape of clothing. In the 97th *Landwehr* Division, clothing "*spottet*[*e*] *jeder Beschreibung*" (defied description). Socks were full of holes, and uniforms were dirty and "*zerfetzt*" (torn into rags). Geheime Kommandosache: Erfahrungen beim "Einsatz Österreich," 26. April 1938, Wehrsatzinspektion Nürnberg Nr. 1300/38 g. k., T-79/275/000019, 000030, NARS; Erfahrungsbericht der Landwehr-Division 97 über "Einsatz Österreich,"22.4.1938, Landwehr-Kommandeur München II/Nr.

800 geh., T-79/253/000071-000079, NARS.

35. Showing a contempt even for their "fellow Germans," SS troops stole the vehicles they needed from civilians and from other army units, especially in the realm of the 17th Infantry Division. Erfahrungsbericht über den "Einsatz Österreich, 23. März 1938, K.W.W.Komp.(mot.) 27 O 142, T-79/14/000710, NARS.

36. Erfahrungsbericht über die Mobilmachung der Nachscchubeinheiten der 2. Panzer Division, 22.3.38, Nachub-Führer, RH 53-13/63, p. 130-133, BA/MA.

37. Erfahrungen beim Einmarsch Österreich, München 5.1939, Generalkommando VII Armeekorps, RH 53-7/128, p.6, BA/MA; Erfahrungsbericht über den "Einsatz Österreich," 6.5.1938, Generalkommando XIII. Armeekorps (Wehrkreiskommando XIII), T-314/525/000360, NARS; Erfahrungsbericht über den "Einsatz Österreich," 6.5.1938, Generalkommando XIII. Armeekorps (Wehrkreiskommando XIII), T-79/274/000933, NARS. The 10th Infantry Division had similar comments. See Fernspruch, 15.3.38, übermittelte der Ia des Gen. Kdos. XIII dem Ia der 10. Division, RH 26-10/118, p. 7/38, BA/MA.

38. Erfahrungsbericht über den "Einsatz Österreich," 6.5.1938, Generalkommando XIII. Armeekorps (Wehrkreiskommando XIII), T-314/525/000360-000366, NARS.

39. Mob. Erfahrungen, 27. April 38, Wehrersatz-Inspektion Nürnberg Nr. 1987 geh./Gru.Ia., T-79/223/000516, NARS; Erfahrungsbericht über den "Einsatz Österreich," 6.5.1938, Generalkommando XIII. Armeekorps (Wehrkreiskommando XIII), T-79/274/000970, NARS.

40. Troops of this unit were hard pressed to keep their vehicles running during the short period of the invasion. They were only partly successful because they took the most extreme measures, and because of the short duration of the invasion. Erfahrungsbericht, Wien 23.3.38, Nachrichten Abteilung 38, RH 53-13/63, p. 120, BA/MA.

41. Mob. Erfahrungen, 27. April 38, Wehrersatz-Inspektion Nürnberg Nr. 1987 geh./Gru.Ia., T-79/223/000516, NARS; Erfahrungsbericht über den "Einsatz Österreich," 6.5.1938, Generalkommando XIII. Armeekorps (Wehrkreiskommando XIII), T-79/274/000970, NARS.

42. Mobilmachung, Erlangen 30.3.1939, I./Panzer Regiment 25, RH 26-7/645, p. 1-2, BA/MA; Erfahrungen der I./Panzer-Regiment 25, Erlangen 7.4.38, I./Panzer Regiment 25, RH 26-7/645, p. 1-2, BA/MA.

43. "unusable for battle as well as propaganda purposes;" Kurze Darstellung der Ereignisse, München 29.4.1938, 7. Division, RH 26-7/170b, p. 14, BA/MA.

44. "the munitions. ... in large part spoiled;" Erfahrungsbericht über Mobilmachung und Demobilmachung anläßlich des "Einsatz Österreich," Augsburg 21.4.1938, 27 Division, RH 53-7/508, p. 28, BA/MA; Erfahrungsbericht über Mobilmachung und Demobilmachung anläßlich des "Einsatz Österreich," Landsberg 11.IV.38, I/A.R. 608, RH 53-7/433, p. 22/24, BA/MA.

45. Erfahrungen bei der Probemobilmachung, Bad Reichenhall 8. April 1938, Stab Geb. Jäg, Regt., RH 37/6717, BA/MA; Erfahrungen bei der Probemobilmachung, Bad Reichenhall 2. April 1938, 10. Kompanie, RH 37/6717, p. 1, BA/MA.

46. "neither *one* pair of boots nor *one* steel helmet ..." Erfahrungsbericht der Landwehr-Division 97 über "Einsatz Österreich," München 22.4.38, Landwehr-Kommandeur München, RH 26-7/170b, p. 3, BA/MA.

47. See Martin Van Creveld, *Supplying War: Logistics from Wallenstein to Patton* (Cambridge New York: Cambridge University Press, 1977); see also, Richard DiNardo, *Mechanized Juggernaut or Military Anachronism? Horses and the German Army in World War II* (Westport, CT: Greenwood Press, 1991).

48. Erfahrungsbericht über den "Einsatz Österreich, 23. März 1938, K.W.W. Komp.(mot.) 27 O 142, T-79/14/000711, NARS.

49. Erfahrungen bei der Probemobilmachung, Strannersdorf 27.3.1938, Stab [Infantry].R[egiment]. 62, RH 26-7/645, p. 1-2, BA/MA.

50. Erfahrungen beim "Einsatz Österreich," München 5. 1938, Generalkommando VII Armeekorps, RH 53-7/128, p. 15/19, BA/MA; Erfahrungsbericht der Landwehr-Division 97 über [den] "Einsatz Österreich," München 22.4.38, Landwehr-Kommandeur München, RH 26-7/170b, p. 18, BA/MA.

51. "immediately and in the sharpest manner." Erfahrungsbericht beim "Einsatz Österreich," Nürnberg 16.5.1938, 17. Division, RH 37/850, p. 2, BA/MA. See also, for example, Erfahrungsbericht über die Mobilmachung, München 21. März 1938, D.9 L.Inf.Kol.J.R.19 [7th Division] , RH 26-7/170b, p. 2, BA/MA.

52. This lack of discipline would continue to be a problem for the Eighth Army throughout the operation. Erfahrungen aus "Einsatz Österreich"; Ausführung von Befehlen, 19.4.1938, Der Kommandierende General des VII. Armeekorps und Befehlshaber im Wehrkreis VII Nr. 2918/38 geh., T-79/15/000225, NARS.

53. Erfahrungsbericht über den "Einsatz Österreich," 6.5.1938, Generalkommando XIII. Armeekorps (Wehrkreiskommando XIII), T-314/525/000435, NARS.

54. Erfahrungsbericht über den "Einsatz Österreich," 6.5.1938, Generalkommando XIII. Armeekorps (Wehrkreiskommando XIII), T-79/274/000913, NARS.

55. Erfahrungsbericht über Mobilmachung und Demobilmachung anläßlich des "Einsatz Österreich," 21.4.1938, 27. Division Nr. 200/38 g. Kdos., T-79/14/000576 NARS; Erfahrungsbericht hinsichtlich Änderung der K.St.N., K.A.N. usw., 13.4.38, 7. Division Ib Az. Mob.A/VIII Nr. 1717/38 g.Kdos., T-79/14/000693, NARS. See also the intelligent and introspective article by Wilhelm Deist, "Überlegungen zur 'widerwilligen Loyalität' der Deutschen bei Kriegsbeginn" in *Der Zweite Weltkrieg: Analysen, Grundzüge, Forschungsbilanz*, ed. Wolfgang Michalka (Weyarn: Seehamer Verlag, 1997), 235.

56. [report by unnamed officer of the 10th Infantry Division] Box 7n2719, p. 5-6, Archives Militaires du Château de Vincennes, Paris.

57. Schmidl, *Der "Anschluß" Österreichs*, 57.

58. Henderson to Halifax 24 March 1938. DBRP, Series 3, Vol. 1, No. 115.

59. Erfahrungsbericht, München 25.4.1938, Artillerie Regiment 7 [7th Inf.Div.], RH 26-7/645, p. 2, BA/MA; Kurze Darstellung der Ereignisse, München 29.4.1938, 7. Division, RH 26-7/170b, p. 15, BA/MA; Erfahrungsbericht Österreich, Berlin 13.4.1938, Korpskommando XVI Armeekorps, RH 53-13/63, p. 21, BA/MA; Berichte der Armeeoberkommandos, RH 20-8/274, p. 25, BA/MA. The XVI

Motorized Corps exclaimed that by 13 March the 2nd Panzer Division was almost uncontrollable and had "*keinerlei Möglichkeit zur Verbindungsaufnahme, Erkundung, Befehlsübermittlung und Versorgung.*" (no possibilities for contact [with headquarters], reconnaissance, the transmission of orders [or] supply). Erfahrungsbericht Österreich, Berlin 13.4.38, Korpskommando XVI Armeekorps, RH 53-13/63, p. 21, BA/MA. It is *vital* to understand that the command of motorized units by radio was not perfected at this time. The greatest strides in commanding motorized and non-motorized units by radio were made during the spring maneuvers of 1939. As late as the Polish Campaign, the German army still was unsure if such command would work in practice. "Die operativen Nachrichtenverbindungen des deutschen Heeres im Polenfeldzug 1939," Berlin 1.7.1942, Kriegswissenschaftliche Abteilung des Generalstabes des Heeres, RH 60/v. 1, p. 1-2, BA/MA,

60. "that they could not exert some kind of influence on the march [to the border]." Berichte des Armeeoberkommandos, BA/MA, RH 20-8/274, p. 25.

61. [report by unnamed officer of the 10th Infantry Division] Box 7n2719, p. 5-6, Archives Militaires du Château de Vincennes, Paris; Kurze Darstellung der Ereignisse, München 29.4.1938, 7.Division, RH 26-7/170b, p. 6, BA/MA

62. Erfahrungsbericht über den "Einsatz Österreich," 6.5.1938, Generalkommando XIII. Armeekorps (Wehrkreiskommando XIII), T-79/274/000948, NARS; Berichte des Armeeoberkommandos, RH 20-8/274, p. 26, BA/MA

63. Erfahrungen bei der Mrobilmachung, Strannersdorf 27.3.1938, Stab J.R. 62, RH 26-7/645, p. 5-6, BA/MA; Erfahrungsbericht über den "Einsatz Österreich" März/April 1938, Nürnberg 6.5.1938, Generalkommando XIII. Armeekorps, RH 26-17/173, p. 49/52, BA/MA.

64. At Passau, for example, the 10th and 17th Infantry Divisions and the 2nd Panzer Division all piled up on top of one another. This situation worsened due to the difficulties units had restarting the engines of vehicles made frigid by the blast of wind accompanying movement by train. The 7th Infantry Division also reported heavy delays and problems. Kurze Darstellung der Ereignisse, München 29.4.1938, 7.Division, RH 26-7/170b, p. 2, BA/MA; "Vorläufiger Erfahrungsbericht über Ablauf der Mobilmachung und Vormarsch bis Wien," Wien 27. März 1938, 2. Panzer Division, RH 53-13/63, p. 53, BA/MA.

65. Erfahrungsbericht über den "Einsatz Österreich" März/April 1938, Nürnberg 6.5.1938, Generalkommando XIII. Armeekorps, T-79/274/000948, 000958, NARS; "Vorläufiger Erfahrungsbericht über Ablauf der Mobilmachung und Vormarsch bis Wien," Wien 27. März 1938, 2. Panzer Division, RH 53-13/63, p. 53, BA/MA.

66. Kurze Darstellung des Einsatz des Korpskommandos XIII zum Erfahrungsbericht "Einsatz Österreich," RH 26-17/173, p. 4, BA/MA.

67. Berichte des Armeeoberkommandos, RH 20-8/274, p. 25, BA/MA.

68. Erfahrungsbericht über den "Einsatz Österreich" März/April 1938, Nürnberg 6.5.1938, Generalkommando XIII. Armeekorps, RH 26-17, p. 19/22, 56/59, BA/MA.

69. Berichte des Armeeoberkommandos, RH 20-8/274, p. 26, BA/MA.

70. Kurze Darstellung der Ereignisse, München 29.4.1938, 7.Division, RH 26-7/170b, p. 4, BA/MA.

71. Erfahrungsbericht über den "Einsatz Österreich" März/April 1938, Nürnberg 6.5.1938, Generalkommando XIII. Armeekorps, T-79/274/000959, NARS.

72. "the battle-strength and assignment readiness of the troops;" Fernspruch, 15.3.38, übermittelte der Ia des Gen. Kdos. XIII dem Ia der 10. Division, RH 26-10/118, p. 6/37, BA/MA; Erfahrungsbericht über den "Einsatz Österreich" März/April 1938, Nürnberg 6.5.1938, Generalkommando XIII. Armeekorps, RH 26-17, p. 17/20, 27/30, BA/MA.

73. "Mobilmachung," Grumpoldskirchen 24.3.38, Panzer Regiment 4. Gr. Ia Op., RH 53-13/63, p. 96-97, BA/MA; Erfahrungsbericht, 24.3.38, Panzer Brigade 2., RH 53-13/63, p. 71, 74, BA/MA; Erfahrungsbericht Österreich, Berlin 13.4.38, Korpskommando XVI Armeekorps, RH 53-13/63, p. 8-10, BA/MA.

74. Erfahrungsbericht Österreich, Berlin 13.4.38, Korpskommando XVI Armeekorps, RH 53-13/63, p. 17-18, BA/MA; Erfahrungsbericht über den "Einsatz Österreich" März/April 1938, Nürnberg 6.5.1938, Generalkommando XIII. Armeekorps, T-79/14/000462, NARS. The 10th Infantry Division reported that it had to make use of public gasoline stations and even this was not adequate: "*Es darf nicht vorkommen, daß Fahrzeuge wegen Betr[iebs]toffmangel liegen bleiben*! [underscored in original]" ("It may not come to pass that *motorized vehicles break-down because of lack of gasoline*"). Besondere Anordnungen für die Versorgung der Div. am 13.3.38, 10 Division Ib, Div. Stbs Qu., RH 26-10/547, BA/MA. See also Schmidl's discussion which, despite a conclusion that is inconsistent with the data, covers the evidence in this matter exhaustively. Schmidl, *Der "Anschluß" Österreichs*, 152-155.

75. Schmidl, *Der "Anschluß" Österreichs*, p. 153.

76. Erfahrungsbericht über die Mobilmachung der Nachschubeinheiten der 2. Panzer Division, Floridsdorf 22.3.38, Nachschub-Führer an 2. Panzer Division, RH 53-13/63, p. 131, BA/MA.

77. Quoted in Murray, *The Change in the European Balance of Power*, 143.

78. "bad and steep streets;" Kurze Darstellung des Einsatz des Korpskommandos XIII zum Erfahrungsbericht "Einsatz Österreich," RH 26-17/173, p. 4, BA/MA; Fernspruch, 15.3.38, übermittelte der Ia des Gen. Kdos. XIII dem Ia der 10. Division, RH 26-10/118, p. 8/11, BA/MA.

79. Fernspruch, 15.3.38, übermittelte der Ia des Gen. Kdos. XIII dem Ia der 10. Division, RH 26-10/118, p. 6/9, 9/12, BA/MA; Erfahrungsbericht Einsatz Österreich [10th Inf.Div.] , box 7n264, p. 6, Archives Militaires du Château de Vincennes, Paris. Reports of the 7th Infantry Division were similar. See, for example, Kriegstagebuch des Korps Kommandos VII, Führungsgruppe Ia, RH 53-7/1442, p. 11, BA/MA.

80. "essential lessening of combat readiness ..." Kurze Darstellung der Ereignisse, München 29.4.1939, 7.Division, RH 26-7/170b, p. 6-7, BA/MA; Erfahrungsbericht über die Mobilmachung, Markersdorf 23.3.1938, 13.(J.G.)/Jnf. Reg. 19, RH 26-7, 645, p. 1-2, BA/MA; Erfahrungen bei der Probemobilmachung, Ruprechtshofen 22.3.1938, I./Jnf. Reg. 62, RH 26-7/645p. 2,4-5, BA/MA.

81. Erfahrungen bei der Probemobilmachung, Bad Reichenhall 8.April 1938, Stab Geb. Jäg. Reg. 100, T-79/14/000672, NARS; Fernspruch, 15.3.38, übermittelte der Ia des Gen. Kdos. XIII dem Ia der 10. Division, RH 26-10/118, p. 23/54, 24/55, BA/MA.

82. "mountainous;" "impossible;" "through an increasing number of motor vehicles of the Panzer-division that were abandoned in the street, as well as broken-down and battle-unusable drafted vehicles, and finally through the refueling of numerous military-, police-, and civil motor vehicles in public gasstations." Berichte des Armeeoberkommandos, RH 20-8/274, p. 26, BA/MA. See also, Erfahrungsbericht über den "Einsatz Österreich" März/April 1938, Nürnberg 6.5.1938, Generalkommando XIII. Armeekorps, RH 26-17, p. 62/65, BA/MA.

83. Erfahrungsbericht Österreich, Berlin 13.4.38, Korpskommando XVI Armeekorps, RH 53-13/63, p. 37, BA/MA.

84. This number may also have reflected tanks that ran out of gas and then were later refueled. Quoted in Murray, *The Change in the European Balance of Power*, 148.

85. Ibid.; Erfahrungsbericht Österreich, Berlin 13.4.38, Korpskommando XVI Armeekorps, RH 53-13/63, p. 37, BA/MA.

86. Kurze Darstellung der Ereignisse, München, 29.4.1938, 7.Division, RH 26-7/170b, p. 6, BA/MA.

87. Berichte des Armeeoberkommandos, RH 20-8/274, p. 26, BA/MA; Fernspruch, 15.3.38, übermittelte der Ia des Gen. Kdos. XIII dem Ia der 10. Division, RH 26-10/118, p. 21/52, BA/MA.

88. Erfahrungsbericht über den "Einsatz Österreich," 6.5.1938, Generalkommando XIII. Armeekorps (Wehrkreiskommando XIII), T-79/274/000963, NARS.

89. Erfahrungsbericht über den "Einsatz Österreich," 6.5.1938, Generalkommando XIII. Armeekorps (Wehrkreiskommando XIII), T-314/525/000402, 000383, NARS.

90. Erfahrungsbericht, München 25.4.1938, Artillerie Regiment 7, RH 26-7/645, p. 2, BA/MA. In this particular example, the artillery regiment reported that because its orders were being routed to it through the infantry regiment headquarters, and since the artillery regiment was out of contact with this headquarters, they received no orders at all. The divisional staff for 10th Infantry Division also reported its inability to get orders through and the problem of command and control within its regiments. See Fernspruch, 15.3.38, übermittelte der Ia des Gen. Kdos. XIII dem Ia der 10. Division, RH 26-10/118, p.24/55, BA/MA.

91. "it is impossible to describe, what occurred on the march streets in those days." Kurze Darstellung der Ereignisse, München 29.4.1938, 7.Division, RH 26-7/170b, p. 6, BA/MA; [report by unnamed officer of the 10th Infantry Division] Box 7n2719, p. 6, Archives Militaires du Château de Vincennes, Paris.

92. Erfahrungsbericht hinsichtlich Änderung der K.St.N. usw., 13.4.38, 7. Division Ib Az. Mob.A/VIII Nr. 1717/38 g. Kdos, T-79/14/000697, 000670, 000671, NARS. See also, Erfahrungsbericht über Mobilmachung und Demobilmachung anläßlich des "Einsatz Österreich," Augsburg 21.4.1939, 27.Division, RH 53-

7/508, p. 36/37, BA/MA; Erfahrungsbericht über den "Einsatz Österreich," Nürnberg 6.5.1938, Generalkommando XIII. Armeekorps, RH 26-17/173, p. 75/78, BA/MA.

93. Erfahrungsbericht, München 26.4.1938, Panzer Abwehr Abteilung 7 [7th Inf.Div.], RH 26-7/645, p. 7, BA/MA.

94. [Map], Kriegstagebuch 10th Div., Einsatz Österreich, RH 26-10/574, BA/MA.

95. Fernspruch, 15.3.38, übermittelte der Ia des Gen. Kdos. XIII dem Ia der 10. Division, BA/MA, RH 26-10/118, p. 23/54;

96. Kurze Darstellung des Einsatzes des Korpskommandos XIII, zum Erfahrungsbericht "Einsatz Österreich,"RH 26-17/173, p. 4/178, 5/179, BA/MA.

97. Kriegstagebuch des Korps Kommandos VII, Einsatz Österreich, RH 53-7/1442, p. 12, 14, 17, BA/MA.

98. "Erfahrungsbericht," Mödling, 20.3.38, Panzer Regiment 3. Gr. Ia Op, RH 53-13/63, BA/MA; "Mobilmachung," Grumpoldskirchen, 24.3.38, Panzer Regiment 4. Gr. Ia Op, RH 53-13/63, BA/MA; Erfahrungsbericht, 24.3.38, 2. Panzer Brigade, RH 53-13/63, p. 73-75, BA/MA.

99. Erfahrungsbericht Österreich, Berlin 13.4.38, Korpskommando XVI Armeekorps, RH 53-13/63, p. 12-13, 22, 25, BA/MA.

100. "If one visualizes that the advance of the division would have had to have taken place under enemy fire, the results would have been shocking in those parts of the division that had moved out quickly, and especially the rear services. The consequences would not just have been in losses, but it would [have been] possible to place the entire mission of the Panzer Division into question." "Vorläufiger Erfahrungsbericht über Ablauf der Mobilmachung und Vormarsch bis Wien," Wien, 27. März 1938, 2. Panzer Division, RH 53-13/63, p. 66, BA/MA.

101. Erfahrungen bei der Probe-Mobilmachung und beim Einmarsch Österreich, Bad Reichenhall 13.4.1938, Geb.Jäg.Reg.100, RH 37/6711, p. 7, 9, BA/MA; Erfahrungen bei Probemobilmachung zum Einsatz Österreich, Bad Reichenhall 7.4.1938, III./Geb.JägReg.100, RH 37/6717, p. 1, 7, 9, BA/MA. German battalions had an established strength of approximately 1000 men of which no more than 750 were part of the *Gefechtsstärke* (combat strength).

102. "Mobilisation, Cencentration et Mouvements de la 8 ème Armée allemande" 28 Mars 1938, from the French military attaché in Berlin Renondeau to Monsieur le Ministre de la Guerre é Etat-Major de l'Armée, box 7n2601, #265, p. 25-26, Archives Militaires du Château de Vincennes, Paris.

103. "Opérations militaires en Autriche" 16 Mars 1938 from the French military attaché in Berlin Renondeau to Monsieur le Ministre de la Guerre é Etat-Major de l'Armée, box 7n2601, #220, Archives Militaires du Château de Vincennes, Paris; "L'Occupation de L'Autriche par L'Armée Allemande" Juillet-Août 1938, État-Major de l'Armée, box 7n2719, D74, Archives Militaires du Château de Vincennes, Paris.

104. "Truppe tedesche in Austria. Parata" 16 March 1938, From the Italian military attaché in Vienna Mondini to Al Comando del Corpo di Stato Magiore, Gabinetto 322, Vienna, #105, p. 2-3, Ministeri Afferi Esteri, Rome.

105. Regiments were paired down to approximately 750 men per regiment from their normal 3000 man compliment. "Truppe tedesche in Austria. Parata" 16 March 1938, From the Italian military attaché in Vienna Mondini to Al Comando del Corpo di Stato Magiore, Gabinetto 322, Vienna, #105, p. 4, Ministeri Afferi Esteri, Rome.

106. Memorandum by the British military attaché to Berlin, 16 March 1938, Foreign Office, 371/22318, R2933, No. 256, Public Record Office, London.

107. Unfortunately, the British then began to overestimate the abilities of the *Wehrmacht.* See Paul Kennedy, "British Net Assessment," in *Calculations: Net Assessment and the Comming of World War II* , ed. Allan R. Millett and Williamson Murray (New York: Maxwell Macmillan International, 1992), chapter 2.

108. Guderian and Liddell-Hart both undertook, after the war, a campaign of distortion to give themselves all the credit for developing modern armored warfare. For an accurate picture of armored war development in Germany during the 1920s and 1930s, see James S. Corum, *The Roots of Blitzkrieg: Hans von Seekt and German Military Reform* (Lawrence, KS: Kansas University Press, 1992). Guderian is an untrustworthy author and his works should be read with great caution.

109. Quoted in Heinz Guderian, *Panzer Leader* (abridged), trans. Constantine Fitzgibbon (New York: Ballantine Books, 1957), 36. Perhaps a triumphal march into Vienna was Guderian's dream as well.

110. Murray, *The Change in the European Balance of Power*, 148.

111. The standing strength of these units was approximately 60,000 men, and they were expandable upon mobilization to 120,000 men. See Erwin Steinböck, *Österreichs militärliches Potentziell im Märtz 1938* (Vienna: Verlag für Geschichte und Politik, 1988).

112. Erwin Steinböck, "Die bewaffnete Macht Österreichs 1938" in *Anschluß 1938: Protokoll des Symposiums in Wien am 14. Und 15. März 1978* (Vienna: Verlag für Geschichte und Politik, 1981), 130. The exact supply depended upon the particular unit and equipment in question. Erwin Schmidl has argued against Steinböck's calculated number of ten to eleven days of artillery ammunition. Schmidl's assessment is that the Austrian artillery had only enough ammunition for two to three days. His argument is based on four points: 1) some ammunition that Steinböck counted was actually "not available" for use (for example rounds that were getting dusty in the courtyards of barracks); 2) that young soldiers were apt, in their nervousness, to fire off more rounds than necessary; 3) that as the defending army the *Bundesheer* would use more ammunition. The author's fourth point is more involved. The *Bundesheer* had neither dive bombers nor attack planes, as the Germans had. These planes, Schmidl argues, assumed some of the weight that had been performed traditionally by the German artillery. Thus the German artillery statistics from the Polish and French campaigns that Steinböck used when estimating an accurate daily rate of ammunition consumption were lower than what the Austrians would have used. Because the *Bundesheer* did not possess such aircraft, its artillery's rate of ammunition consumption would have been higher. See Schmidl, *Der "Anschluß" Österreichs*, 46, 96f.

Schmidl's argument is unconvincing. In the first place, he offers no statistics on how many rounds were "getting dusty." One imagines these were most likely for decoration and probably did not represent a significant number. Second, although it may be true that young soldiers are often nervous and fire more than necessary, this is not a problem in artillery fire which is a systematized group effort (in relatively calm surroundings) and subject to very exact control. One might picture infantry soldiers shooting off excess rifle rounds, but it is difficult to imagine them ignoring their officers and NCOs and as a group firing artillery pieces *ad infinitum*. Even if it were possible for "raw" artillerists to fire excessively, artillery units were (and are) supplied on a *by day* basis limiting the amount of shells they could use at any one time. Third, it is just as often the attacker who uses more ammunition for such activities as pre-attack bombardment and counter-battery fire and not the defender. There is no conclusive evidence to support the assertion that defensive activities inherently and consistently used more ammunition. Although Schmidl points to German use of more artillery rounds in the defensive battles later in World War II as evidence, one might equally point to the U.S. Army artillery in Korea (using the same weaponry as in World War II) where no such difference existed. There are many other possible explanations for higher German artillery usage later in the war, for example, an increase in the number of guns per unit. Fourth, Schmidl's calculation that dive bombers and attack planes relieved the German artillery of certain roles does not mean that German artillery fired less as a result. Dive bombers and attack planes were force multipliers, that is, they provided the German army with firepower *in addition* to the artillery. German artillery fired as frequently as before, but was able to concentrate more on targets that were susceptible to its fire and/or to provide more support missions.

The key to the discussion of rate of ammunition usage actually lies in the resistance of the artillery cannons themselves. Artillery has always been limited by the enormous stresses that firing shells puts on the barrels of the cannons. Steinböck's figure of each Austrian artillery gun using approximately fifty rounds per day is actually a bit high. A daily usage rate of between twenty-five to thirty rounds is much more likely if the guns were not to wear out in a short time. Fifty rounds per day would have been the upper safe limit. In order to use ammunition at the rate Schmidl identifies, Austrian cannons would have had to fire over 150 to 200 rounds per day destroying their own guns in the process. I would like to thank two of my Ohio State University colleagues for their valuable insight: Conversation with Major Kelly Jordan, United States Army, 30 December 1998, Conversation with Captain Ronald Kyle, United States Army (ret.), 2 January 1998.

Finally, artillery ammunition was made in Austria at the *Enzesfelder Metallwerke* and might have been able to be moved onto an emergency (day and night) production footing if war had broken out, the newly manufactured shells going directly from the factory to the front lines. This might have extended the ammunition supply beyond ten to twelve days. Russian factories would undertake similar measures in dire circumstances, as when T-34 tanks in Stalingrad rolled off of the production line and almost immediately into combat.

113. General Ritter von Leeb remarked in autumn 1938 that there was still a great variance between the quality of Austrian and German units. Murray, *The Change in the European Balance of Power*, 152.

114. Erwin Steinböck, "Die bewaffnete Macht Österreichs 1938" in *Anschluß 1938: Protokoll des Symposiums in Wien am 14. Und 15. März 1978* (Vienna: Verlag für Geschichte und Politik, 1981), 115. Then Artillery Inspector of the *Bundesheer* Robert Martinek had an important impact on the Austrian artillery

branch through the making lighter of artillery pieces, the refinement of training, the development of new range-finding and firing procedures, and in artillery reconnaissance. Most of these refinements would be carried over into the *Wehrmacht.* Though he did not survive the war, Martinek claimed in 1937 that these refinements had made the Austrian artillery arm so flexible and useful that no other army in the world could match it. Dolf Berdach and Erich Dethlefsen, *General der Artillerie Robert Martinek: Lebensbild eines Soldaten* (Neckargemünd: Kurt Vowinckel Verlag, 1975) 14-17, 110-111; Robert Martinek, "Die Waffentechnische Entwicklung der Artillery," *Wehr und Waffen: Monatsschrift für den Soldaten von gestern, heute, und morgan,* 2. Jg. (July 1937): 4-5. It is worth noting that the French army still deployed the World War I vintage 75mm artillery cannon during the invasion of France in 1940, and it proved one of the more potent weapons in either the French or German arsenals.

115. N. Oe. Lichtes Artreg. Nr. 3 an Bundesministerium für Landesverteidigung, 20 April 1937, Bundesministerium für Landesverteidigung, 35 3/5 Sektion III 1937, 35 3/5 1654 [box, document], Österreichisches Staatsarchiv: Neues Politisches Archiv, Wien; N. Oe. Lichtes Artreg. Nr. 4 an der Generaltruppeninspectorat, 19 February 1937, Bundesministerium für Landesverteidigung, 35 3/5 Sektion III 1937, 35 3/5, 1654, Österreichisches Staatsarchiv: Neues Politisches Archiv, Wien.

116. The Austrian 47mm M35/36 anti-tank cannon could penetrate 40 mm of armor at 90° at 1000 m and 40 mm of armor at 60° at 600 m. German panzers provided the following protection: Panzer I (models A and B), 13 mm front and 7mm side armor at 90°; Panzer II (model D) 20mm front and 14mm side at 90°. *No Panzerkampfwagon IIIs took part in the invasion of Austria.* Dunkin Crow, *Armored Fighting Vehicles of Germany: World War II* (New York: Arco Publications Inc., 1978), 14-15, 32; Peter Gschaider: "Das österreichische Bundesheer 1938 und seine Überführung in die deutsche Wehrmacht," Ph.D. diss., Universität Wien, 1967, 33.

117. Erwin Steinböck, "Die bewaffnete Macht Österreichs 1938," 130.

118. Both the Fiat-Ansaldo M 35 and *Panzerkampfwagon* I were characterized by thin armor (less than 13 mm), machine-guns as main armament, and two man crews. The *Panzerkampfwagon* II's great advantage was entirely in its 20 mm cannon as main armament, but with hardly enough penetration to knock out the M 35 at any distance. Erfahrungsbericht Österreich, Berlin 13.4.38, Korpskommando XVI Armeekorps, RH 53-13/63, p. 37, BA/MA; Erwin Steinböck, "Die bewaffnete Macht Österreichs 1938," 111, 113.

119. Peter Gschaider, "Das österreichische Bundesheer 1938," 30-35.

120. [Alfred] Jansa an Kommando 4. Division, 11 November 1935, Bundesministerium für Landesverteidigung, 1- 1935, 1 5/1 10040, Österreichisches Staatsarchiv: Neues Politisches Archiv, Wien

121. Alfred Jansa, *Nachlässe und Sammlungen*, 07R143/1, ÖSK; Hubertus Trauttenberg, "Die Abwehrvorbereitungen gegen einen deutschen Angriff," passim.

122. On the development of Austrian doctrine, see Manfried Rauchensteiner, "Zum operativen Denken in Österreich 1918-1938," *Österreichische Militärische Zeitschrift*, 16. Jg. (März 1978).

123. Berichte des Armeeoberkommandos, RH 20-8/274, p. 26, BA/MA.

124. The Austrian army had taken note of the problems associated with mixing raw recruits, reserve troops, and soldiers who had not served since World War I during its 1937 maneuvers. [unnamed author], "Die Schlußübungen unserer bewaffneten Macht," *Wehr und Waffen: Monatsschrift für den Soldaten von gestern, heute, und morgan,* 2. Jg. (Oktober 1937).

125. I use the term "phase shift" to denote two different armies as behaviorally different as, for example, water from ice. The German army that invaded Poland was similarly inferior to that which invaded France, which in turn was substantially less than that which marched into Russia in June 1941.

126. Reports indicated that new recruits had not yet completed basic training and had no small or large unit training. Murray, *The Change in the European Balance of Power,* 21; Georg Tessin, *Deutsche Verbände und Truppen*, 218-219, 230-231; Burkhard Mueller-Hillebrand, "*Das Heer 1933-1935*," vol. 1, (Darmstadt: Mittler, 1954), 59-60.

127. Wilhelm Deist, *The Wehrmacht and German Rearmament* (Toronto: University of Toronto Press, 1981), 90-98.

128. Ibid., 88.

129. Quoted in Manfred Messerschmidt, "German Military Effectiveness between 1919 and 1939," in *Military Effectiveness*, ed. Allan R. Millett and Williamson Murray, vol. 2 (Boston: Unwin Hyman, 1988), 240.

130. A small band of three companies of paratroopers also was dropped in the vicinity of Graz on 13 March. Schmidl, *Der "Anschluß" Österreichs*, 167-170.

131. Williamson Murray, "German Air Power and the Munich Crisis" in *War and Society*, 2 (1977), 111.

132. Of this number, only *one* dive bomber was operative. These statistics come from the Public Record Office London, and are exact copies of those that exist in the BA/MA Freiburg. Unfortunately, no statistics in either archive exist prior to August 1938. Statistics for March 1938 would probably have been similar, though with a higher number of "in commission" fighters since a greater number of accidents occurred during the summer months of 1938 as the *Luftwaffe* changed from the Ar-68 to the Me-109. Williamson Murray, "German Air Power and the Munich Crisis," 112; Luftwaffe Strength and Serviceability Tables, 1 August 1938, Compiled from records of VI Abteilung Quartermaster General's Department of German Air Ministry, AIR 20/7706, Public Record Office, London; Rüstungsstand der Fliegertruppe, 1 August 1938, VI Abteilung, RL 2 III 700, BA/MA.

133. Williamson Murray, "German Air Power and the Munich Crisis," 112-113.

134. The amount of usable aircraft for the Austrian *Luftwaffe* may have been as low as fifty machines. There is disagreement between authors as to the exact numbers of planes in the Austrian Luftwaffe in 1938. Fred Haubner puts the figure at approximately 150 machines, while Othmar Tuider's number is 250. Fred Haubner, *Die Flugzeuge der österreichischen Luftstreitkräfte vor 1938*, Bd. 2, (Graz: H. Weishaupt, 1982); Othmar Tuider, *Die Luftwaffe in Österreich 1938-1945* (Vienna: Bundesverlag, 1985), 12-13.

135. The German *Luftwaffe* had increased these payloads by 1940. Murray, "German Air Power and the Munich Crisis," 110-111.

136. The great philosopher of war Karl von Clausewitz codified this phenomenon in his term "friction."

137. "[i]t remains without a doubt, that because of enemy resistance on the ground and especially from the air, the events on the street Passau-Linz-Wien could have lead to a catastrophe. Similar things could have repeated themselves after [our] battlefield successes. In that case the difficulties would still be greater because of wounded and prisoners streaming to the rear; empty columns [of trucks?] driving back; shot-up equipment lying in the street; etc." Berichte des Armeeoberkommandos, RH 20-8/274, p. 27, BA/MA.

138. Lecture by Gerhard Weinberg, U.S. Military Academy, West Point, NY, February 1997.

139. Manfred Messerschmidt, "German Military Effectiveness between 1919 and 1939," in *Military Effectiveness*, ed. Allan R. Millett and Williamson Murray, vol. 2 (Boston: Unwin Hyman, 1988); Williamson Murray, *German Military Effectiveness* (Baltimore: Nautical and Aviation Publishing Co. of America, 1992); Russell A. Hart, "Learning Lessons: Military Adaptation and Innovation in the American, British, Canadian and German Armies during the 1944 Normandy Campaign," Ph.D. diss., The Ohio State University, 1997; Richard R. Muller, "The German Air Force and the Campaign against the Soviet Union, 1941-1945," Ph.D. diss., The Ohio State University, 1990; Williamson Murray and Allan R. Millet, ed., *Military Innovation in the Interwar Period* (Cambridge, New York : Cambridge University Press, 1996).

140. Schmidl, *Der "Anschluß" Österreichs*, 208.

141. Gen. St. d. H. (I. Abt.), 12.3.38, T-79/14/000460, NARS.

142. Berichte des Armeeoberkommandos, RH 20-8/274, p. 29, BA/MA.

143. The German invasion of Czechoslovakia in March 1939 continued to point out serious shortcomings in the *Wehrmacht*. See Erfahrungsbericht "Einsatz Sudetendeutschland," 15.11.1938, Generalkommando XIII. Armeekorps (Wehrkreiskommando XIII) Nr. 5800/38 g. Kdos. Ib., T-314/525/000536.

144. Karl von Clausewitz, *On War*, ed. and trans. Michael Howard and Peter Paret (Princeton, NJ: Princeton University Press, 1984), 179.

# "Neutral," Host, and "Mediator": Austria and the Vienna Summit of 1961*

*Martin Kofler*

## Introduction

The Vienna Summit on 3 and 4 June 1961 heated up the Cold War and led to the construction of the Berlin Wall ten weeks later. The first and only meeting of U.S. President John F. Kennedy and the Soviet Chairman Nikita Khrushchev changed their mutual perceptions decisively and influenced their attitudes during the Cuban Missile Crisis of October 1962.[1] Cold War studies have analyzed the K-K-talks in the light of summit politics[2] or within the JFK years,[3] but nobody ever looked at the host's perspective in a detailed way. Austrian historians just focused on press reports and used few sources[4] or only dedicated a few useful paragraphs to the Vienna Summit in broad overviews.[5]

The event requires fresh analysis. Why did the Soviets and the Americans decide to get together in the city of Vienna? How did the

---

* This case study is part of my forthcoming dissertation on "'Neutral'? Austria between Kennedy and Khrushchev 1960-1963" with Prof. Rolf Steininger of the Institute of Contemporary History at the University of Innsbruck/Austria. The article is based on an extensively revised research seminar paper with Dr. Günter Bischof at the History Department of the University of New Orleans (U.N.O.). I want to thank Dr. Bischof, Dr. Michael Gehler, Roman Urbaner, and Dr. Gerald Steinacher for their critical remarks. I am very thankful for a research grant from the Eisenhower Center, back then under the leadership of Dr. Stephen Ambrose which allowed me to spend two weeks at the John F. Kennedy Library in Boston. Chairperson Dr. Joe Caldwell at U.N.O.'s History Department kindly agreed to a "Boebel fellowship" to finance a visit to the National Archives in College Park, Maryland.

Austrian government and the Austrian people react? What was the summit's benefit for the central European country's active foreign policy of neutrality? Answers to these questions give insight in the role of a neutral "player" in the East-West power game—one of the so-called "third actors" according to Günter Bischof that was not weak at all.

## The K-K-Summit: The Top-Level

To discuss Austria's part in the Vienna Summit, a short review of the event's history is indispensable. The presidential election of John F. Kennedy in November 1960 seemed to promise a period of détente in the Cold War. The previous two years at the end of Dwight Eisenhower's second term resulted in inconsistent policies regarding the special case of Germany. Khrushchev had finally withdrawn his 1958 Berlin ultimatum during his visit to the United States in September 1959, but he decided to break up the Four-Power Summit in Paris in mid-May 1960 after the Soviets had downed a U.S. U-2 spy plane over their territory. The leader in the Kremlin sought to defend himself in the light of severe criticism within the Communist world over his doctrine of "peaceful coexistence" and negotiations with the West—and decided for a harsher line in the Cold War. Whereas he especially turned to the Third World openly supporting Lumumba in the Congo and Castro in Cuba, he did not heat up the Berlin crisis.[6] On the contrary, Khrushchev proclaimed in a speech in East Berlin on 20 May to wait six to eight months to reschedule the summit conference with the new U.S. President; though there was no intention "of letting the grass grow under its feet forever"[7] about his aim of a German peace treaty.

The Chairman sent out feelers to Kennedy in late 1960 even before the President-Elect's inauguration.[8] Based on former Soviet and East German documents, new studies stress Khrushchev's willingness to a compromise with the West, but only from a position of strength and using West Berlin as a lever. Fear of a nuclear and revanchist Federal Republic of Germany (FRG) as well as support of the economically weak German Democratic Republic (GDR) with its refugee problem lay at the basis of the Kremlin's top priority pre-occupation with Germany.[9]

But Khrushchev waited more than two months after U.S. Ambassador to Moscow Llewellyn Thompson handed him a letter from Kennedy on 9 March 1961 that expressed hopes for a meeting. This was no coincidence. During this time span, important developments delayed a Soviet answer. In April 1961, Yuri Gagarin succeeded in the first space flight, and Kennedy stumbled into the Bay of Pigs disaster on Cuba. Khrushchev felt strengthened and perceived JFK as a weak, young fellow. He also knew that something had to be done about the increasing flow of refugees that left East Germany through the loophole of West Berlin.[10]

The Chairman seized his chance with a letter to Kennedy in mid-May; the President agreed to talks that should take place in Vienna.[11] The official U.S. note announced the meeting on 19 May as a first personal contact and a general exchange of opinions without negotiations that would take place on 3 and 4 June in between Kennedy's visits to Charles De Gaulle in France and Harold Macmillan in London.[12]

As the authors of the State Department's briefing papers for the President had assumed and several U.S. ambassadors and officials had stressed, Khrushchev would focus on his number one issue, Berlin, and Kennedy should not waver.[13] New Soviet evidence supports the interpretation of the Chairman's pushy attitude. He exclaimed in a special session of the *Politburo* right before the summit that the "favorable situation [after the Bay of Pigs] must be exploited." Khrushchev believed that, under pressure, Kennedy would make concessions, especially on Berlin.[14]

The two statesmen's priorities clashed, and the Vienna Summit heated up the Cold War. Kennedy was in favor of disarmament as well as a test ban treaty. He wanted to both preserve the status quo and warn of miscalculations about U.S. indecisiveness. Khrushchev wanted at least an interim agreement on Berlin: "to remove this thorn, this ulcer." Therefore, he pressured the President, who stood absolutely firm as advised. Then the Chairman confronted JFK with another Berlin ultimatum, a repetition of November 1958, handing over a memorandum. If the United States did not want to sign a German peace treaty that would fix the present situation of two German states, the Soviet Union would go for a separate one with the GDR at the end of the year. In that case, the state of war would end, the access rights to West Berlin would be turned over to the East Germans, and a "free city" of West Berlin would be created.[15]

About two months later, in mid-August 1961, the East German regime built the Berlin Wall that helped to reduce tensions in the long run. Whereas Kennedy was shocked after Vienna[16] and initiated crisis management in the U.S. decision-making process, Khrushchev returned to Moscow with the impression of a young and indecisive leader in the White House. But the Chairman miscalculated, because nuclear rhetoric and bluff did not intimidate JFK in changing his opinion on the Berlin question.[17] After long internal discussions in the administration between "hawks" and "doves," Kennedy agreed to a not only cautious and flexible, but also firm stand.[18] In a serious radio and TV report on 25 July, he announced an increase in the defense budget—the third one after March and May[19]—to convince the Kremlin of utmost U.S. determination. Deterred by the growing nuclear danger, Khrushchev decided to achieve an immediate goal, the Wall. In doing so, he hoped to cut the flow of refugees, strengthening East Germany, to control its impatient leader Walter Ulbricht and not to provoke the West. He did not sign a separate peace treaty. The status quo remained.[20] Kennedy accepted this step, saying internally: "It's not a very nice solution, but a wall is a hell of a lot better than a war."[21] Khrushchev stepped back from his ultimatum of Vienna in October 1961,[22] but the Berlin Crisis lingered into 1962/63.[23]

## Why Vienna?

It was not clear-cut from the beginning that Khrushchev and Kennedy would get together in Vienna/Austria in June 1961. Ironically, the old Habsburg capital had almost become the meeting place of Khrushchev and Eisenhower in 1955, but Foreign Minister Vyacheslav Molotov did not succeed in this Soviet proposal, because John Foster Dulles feared a bad effect on Germany. It was impossible for the U.S. Secretary of State to reward Austria with a summit for becoming neutral right after the State Treaty. So Geneva was the chosen spot. Dulles did not want Austria to play any role as a mediator between East and West. He might have been quite angry, when the Austrian Chancellor Julius Raab mentioned his country's interest in a summit in Vienna in mid-1958 for which the Soviets had opted.[24]

When Thompson presented Kennedy's proposal for an "informal exchange of views" to Khrushchev in March 1961, the Ambassador mentioned his President's suggestions of Vienna or Stockholm as possible locations. The time could be around early May. The Soviet ruler called it a "good beginning" and "seemed inclined [to] prefer Vienna but did not rule out Stockholm." He expressed how useful it would be to become acquainted with Kennedy and even hoped to be able to invite him to the USSR.[25]

The event's date was set quickly in mid-May. Deputy Assistant Secretary for European Affairs Richard Davis contacted the Austrian Ambassador in Washington, Wilfried Platzer, informally on 15 May. He stressed that both the United States and the Soviet Union would regard Vienna as the most suitable city for a soon-to-be-definite meeting. The U.S. government especially emphazised Vienna and asked for an answer in the affirmative.[26] The next day JFK received a letter from Khrushchev via the Soviet Ambassador Mikhail Menshikov that called for a summit. Kennedy stated that "Vienna is a place which appeared to be mutually agreed upon," but first he wished to talk to Secretary of State Dean Rusk and "with the Austrians."[27] The same day, 16 May, Rusk gave his go-ahead,[28] and the *Ministerrat* (Council of Ministers) in Vienna gave its approval.[29] Everything was settled.

Two sources give more insight in the choice of the Austrian capital. Khrushchev points out in his memoirs that the meeting had to be held on neutral territory: "Helsinki, Geneva, and Vienna were all considered, as far as I remember. Kennedy was in favor of Vienna, while we wanted to meet in Helsinki." In the end, the Soviets agreed on Austria with its "policy of neutrality."[30] Whatever places were discussed, the aspect of neutrality lay on Khrushchev's mind. There was no problem at all to accept Kennedy's proposal, and the Chairman himself had leaned toward Vienna in his meeting with Thompson.

The U.S. Ambassador to Moscow gave his Austrian colleague Heinrich Haymerle some information on the decision-making process one month after the summit in early July. First, Vienna and Stockholm arose as possible locations in a special session with Kennedy in February. Thompson suggested the two cities to Khrushchev who did not (!) show any preference. Later "Vienna was the only option discussed" ("*sei eigentlich nur mehr von Wien die Rede gewesen*"); he did not know when Stockholm had been dropped. The Soviets had never proposed a different place, although Thompson had heard in the meantime that Moscow had contacted Oslo. But Norway had turned down the offer, because it was unable to host a summit.[31]

# The Vienna Summit the Cartoonist's Perspective

Three cartoonists' views of the Kennedy-Chrushchev "Vienna Summit" of 1961

Süddeutsche Zeitung
Das große Bockspringen des John F. Kennedy

"FACE TO FACE"

From: *U.S. News & World Report*, Jun 19, 1961, p. 38; *Der Spiegel*, June 7, 1961, p. 15; *U.S, News & World Report*, Jun 5, 1961.

## Austrian Views from the Inside, Views of Austria from the Outside

After the Austrian help for refugees during the Hungarian Crisis in 1956 and the Austrian protest against U.S. overflights during the Lebanon Crisis in 1958, the Vienna Summit proved to be the next step in the country's successful step-by-step emancipation process from both the Soviet Union and the United States. Following the State Treaty and the Neutrality Law of 1955, Austria had to find its way in the international arena with its more dynamic neutrality.[32] Despite the conservative People's Party Chancellor Julius Raab's steps toward a more independent foreign policy, Austrian diplomats quietly assured U.S. officials of their country's western orientation but strict "military" neutrality in late 1958.[33] But in an early 1959 article in *Foreign Affairs*, the Austrian State Secretary and soon-to-be Foreign Minister, the Socialist Bruno Kreisky, put the country's "military" neutrality not only as "exclusively a matter of its own determination," but also as "somewhere between the [practical] Swedish and the [constitutional] Swiss" models.[34] Within his newly established Ministry for Foreign Affairs, the pro-Western Kreisky also tried to build up connections with Austria's Eastern European Communist neighbors. On the other hand, Raab was focusing on the Soviet Union.[35]

During Khrushchev's visit in Austria in July 1960 right after the U-2 affair and the aborted Paris Summit, the Austrian government took a new stand when it stressed its sole and only right to interpret its neutrality's violation and rejected a Soviet guarantee. The Chairman had not only used the country as a stage for tirades against Eisenhower and Adenauer, but also hailed its neutrality as a model of the Soviet doctrine of "peaceful coexistence"—a neutrality that he was willing to defend. Finally, after heavy criticism by the United States, the Federal Republic of Germany, the Austrian press, public, parliament, and some cabinet members, Chancellor Raab disassociated Austria and himself from Khrushchev's verbal attacks against the West. Foreign Minister Kreisky had remained in the background throughout Khrushchev's visit and even agreed with the very harsh, patronizing attitude of U.S. Ambassador to Vienna, H. Freeman Matthews, by criticizing Raab.[36]

Circumstances were quite different in mid-1961: Alfons Gorbach of the People's Party had succeeded Raab as Chancellor. Austria had been a member of the European Free Trade Association (EFTA) for more than a year. Kennedy quite appreciated the neutral status of Austria compared to Dulles' uncompromising line.[37] There were no bilateral problems between the *Ballhausplatz* and the White House. As the State Department's briefing paper on Austria for the Vienna Summit stated: Besides "European economic integration" and the "South Tyrol dispute," the United States' "failure to return all Austrian assets" might represent the only question raised by the Austrians informally with the President or members of the U.S. delegation.[38] Matthews added the policy toward Communist China to these three aspects in his letter of advice to Rusk on 26 May.[39]

The Austrian Grand Coalition government took the opportunity to host the top-level meeting between the Eastern and Western superpowers to gain prestige in the world and to present its successful policy of active neutrality. While the Austrian press reacted rather pessimistically to the announcement of the summit (with the exception of the Communists), Kreisky and Gorbach concentrated on its importance for Austria in special interviews for the newspaper *Die Presse* on 3 June. The Socialist Foreign Minister welcomed the talks and said that Austria's acknowledged neutrality was the reason Vienna was chosen as the meeting's location. The Austrian capital was no bridge, but rather a meeting spot ("... *keine Brücke, wohl aber ein Begegnungsort* ..."). The conservative Chancellor expressed his satisfaction with the summit and the choice of Vienna. He stressed the significance for Austria even more, because the U.S. administration had proposed a neutral Laos following the Austrian model.[40]

The Chancellor became enthusiastic in interviews right after the meeting which, in his opinion, had upgraded Austria's neutrality. The country would be delighted to offer its facilities for similar events in the future and would gain a Swiss-like international reputation. Gorbach also declared Austria would be pleased if the United Nations moved its headquarters to Vienna (the Soviets had already suggested this step several times, though not during the summit). In a commentary, Kreisky doubted such a move because of its material, technical, and political implications.[41] The Austrian embassies in Bonn and Moscow sent reports about press and radio coverage to Vienna that emphasized the city's perfect performance during the summit as well as the country's well-maintained neutrality.[42]

Kreisky clearly sided with Kennedy. The important 9 June circular to all Austrian embassies and missions already showed the Foreign Minister's pro-western attitude. It called the summit a "success for Kennedy" ("*Erfolg für Kennedy*") who had impressed Khrushchev mightily. Contrary to press reports, the U.S. president was not [sic!]

disappointed after the talks. The Austrian government welcomed this first contact that had allowed Kennedy to demonstrate the West's resolve to hold its position, thereby preventing the other side from entertaining ideas to the contrary.[43]

Thanking Kennedy for a letter with a photograph on 5 July, Kreisky expressed his happiness about the summit's taking place in Vienna. The Soviet Chairman had had to realize that he faced a man who would not only fight for the ideas of democracy with full power but who would also endorse a policy with prospect of success: "I am convinced that Mr. Khrushchov [sic!] respects that fact, and it has given us all great confidence" ("*Das hat - davon bin ich überzeugt -, Herrn Chruschtschow Respekt und uns allen viel Vertrauen gegeben.*").[44]

The meeting was no stage for talks related to Austria. Nevertheless, the Austrians tried. Whereas Kreisky took the chance for a twenty minute talk with Secretary of State Rusk on European Integration and neutrality on late 3 June, Gorbach raised the topic of "Sixes and Sevens" the same evening, but Khrushchev declined to discuss it. However, several other Soviet officials, including Foreign Minister Andrei Gromyko, expressed Moscow's view on the Common Market to the Austrians.[45]

The Austrian Government tried to provide "exact equality of treatment" to both delegations, but the people of Vienna "allowed their country's neutrality to impose no impediment":[46] they opted for the Kennedys and ignored the Kremlin leader. In letters to the U.S. President before the summit, Austrians had asked for his help in effecting peace and aiding South Tyrol. These letters also stressed the country's status of neutrality.[47] When Khrushchev arrived by train on 2 June, the Viennese gave him a cold and reserved reception. They remembered not only the ten years of Soviet occupation in Eastern Austria after WWII but also the Chairman's blustering visit of the previous year. On the contrary, thousands cheered for Kennedy and his wife Jackie at the *Schwechat* airport the next day despite the rain.[48]

What about Khrushchev's and Kennedy's perceptions of neutral Austria? Both were fond of its neutrality, but both had quite different recollections. The Raab government had helped the Soviet leader to gain prestige inside and outside the USSR with his first "great international victory,"[49] the Austrian State Treaty of 1955. In this matter Khrushchev had overruled Foreign Minister Molotov. The bold

Raab Cabinet took the opportunity and declared Austria's "perpetual neutrality." The Four Power occupation came to an end.[50]

After the Chairman had hailed the country's neutrality as a model and even claimed to be willing to defend it during his visit in 1960,[51] he mentioned his move against Molotov in his conversations with Kennedy in Vienna a year later. The reversal of previous leaders' decisions and the situation in Laos were the general background.[52] Back in Moscow, Khrushchev thanked the Austrian Government for its efforts to ensure "most favourable conditions" for both sides and the citizens of Vienna "for their kind and cordial attitude toward us."[53] Erroneously, both in his radio/TV-report on 15 June and in his memoirs, Khrushchev stressed some Austrian positive feeling toward the Soviet Union in 1961 because of the State Treaty and the Chairman's role to it.[54] Rauchensteiner even calls this aspect as well as Khrushchev's stay in Austria in 1960 quite a "*Heimvorteil*" for the Soviets during the summit.[55] This interpretation neglects the Viennese people's negative feelings about the Soviets which reached back to WWII and the occupation period up to the Chairman's unpleasant visit the previous year. The Austrians supported JFK and the United States.

Kennedy not only praised Austria's neutrality from his Western view of freedom and democracy, but also referred to the historical context. Besides the fact of his holiday on the Carinthian *Wörther See* in the late 1930s, the President told Ambassador Platzer at a reception in early February 1961 how much he liked Austria: above all, he appreciated the country's behavior in the Hungarian Crisis.[56] During their lunch on 4 June, JFK expressed his hope to Khrushchev not to return from this meeting in Vienna, "a city that is symbolic of the possibility of finding equitable solutions," with a problem involving U.S. national security and reputation.[57] He was proven wrong—the new Berlin Crisis erupted.

But even in his disillusionment at the end of the meeting, Kennedy thanked the Austrian government in his farewell speech at the airport, saying that he departed from a country where problems had been solved under protection of the people's interests.[58] In his 6 June radio/TV-report to the U.S. people about the "very sober" and "somber" meeting, the President also mentioned the hearty welcome of the Viennese who knew "what it is to live under occupation, and ... what it is to live in freedom."[59] In NSC 6020, the basic U.S. National Security document on Austria dated 9 December 1960 and still valid in June 1961, Washington expressed the will to maintain a continued pro-Western (as well as independent and stable) Austria, to make "all feasible attempts to influence Austria to interpret its military neutrality" for such Western orientation, and to resist Communist influence.[60]

## The Secret "Kreisky" Channel

Right after the end of the 1961 summit, Khrushchev revived the secret Austrian channel to the Western powers in his talks to Foreign Minister Bruno Kreisky. The Soviet Chairman had already tried to get in touch with the Mayor of West Berlin, Willy Brandt, via Kreisky in March 1959 and during his visit to Austria the following year. At that time, in early July 1960, the Soviets asked the Austrian Foreign Minister to bring a Berlin memorandum to Brandt's attention because he might be "thinking of the future" and might be "looking for a way out of the blind alley which has come about."[61] The United States took a firm line, and Brandt rejected Khrushchev's feelers—the Mayor's Socialist friend in Vienna had to suffer the consequences.[62]

Whereas Kennedy had already left for London, Khrushchev stayed in Vienna one day longer. His memoirs explain why. In a conversation with the Austrian Foreign Minister on 4 June 1961 Khrushchev did not just hear of a "gloomy" JFK before the departure: "To tell the truth, I recounted for Kreisky everything I'd told Kennedy. I knew that what I said would get back to Kennedy—and it would also be passed on to Willy Brandt."[63]

Khrushchev was right, at least there is evidence regarding his statements' transmission to the United States. Kreisky already briefed U.S. Ambassador Matthews on 5 June (!) about his talk with the Kremlin leader. According to the Austrian politician who called the summit a huge success for Kennedy, Khrushchev had been impressed by the President's sense of responsibility and his knowledge. Then Kreisky repeated exactly the Soviet attitude on the German/Berlin question that the Chairman had expressed to JFK. There had to be a peace treaty with both German states, because reunification was impossible. In case of Western refusal, Khrushchev would be determined to sign a separate peace treaty with the GDR around the end of the year. There might be a crisis, but no war. Khrushchev had also stressed that he was still interested in a contractual solution with the West on Berlin "for instance following the model of the Austrian State Treaty" ("*etwa nach dem Muster des österreichischen Staatsvertra-*

*ges*").[64] West German and U.S. diplomats had informed their Austrian colleagues about the K-K-dispute right after the meeting, but had never mentioned Khrushchev's Berlin ultimatum.[65]

Kreisky's function as an important player in the East-West powergame continued when the Executive Committee discussed his proposal of a rocket trade during the dangerous Cuban Missile Crisis of October 1962.[66] During Kreisky's visit to the United States about one month before Kennedy's assassination in late 1963, the President invited the Foreign Minister to the White House for consultation.[67]

## Austria—A Perfect Host

To complete the picture, one has to add that the Austrian government assembled a security force of 7,000 during the Vienna Summit,[68] but especially wanted to make their special guests' stay very comfortable. Therefore, the country presented itself as a richly cultural nation—and succeeded masterfully. The peak was the first day's gala evening in the imperial Habsburg castle of *Schönbrunn* based on the invitation of the Austrian President Adolf Schärf. The world-famous Vienna Philharmonic Orchestra played and the ballet of the *Wiener Staatsoper* performed to the tunes of the *Donauwalzer* to entertain the two Ks as well as their wives, Jackie and Nina Petrovna.[69] On Sunday morning, 4 June, the Kennedys attended the Holy Mass at St. Stephen's Cathedral, officiated by Cardinal Franz König, and listened to the Vienna Boys' Choir. Khrushchev visited the Soviet war memorial on the *Schwarzenbergplatz*.[70] JFK thanked President Schärf in a letter on 12 June for the Austrian kindness and concluded: "Your generous hospitality made an indispensable contribution to our meeting."[71]

## Conclusion

The Kennedy-Khrushchev summit in Vienna in June 1961 had four major results for Austria. First, the country became a meeting point between East and West, thereby gaining much prestige in the international arena. Second, Gorbach and Kreisky could show Austria's successful policy of active neutrality, though with a differing attitude between the more impetuous Chancellor from the People's Party and his more cautious Foreign Minister from the Socialist Party. Austria's process of emancipation from the USA and USSR since the State

Treaty of 1955 moved to another level. The Kremlin especially hailed Austria's "positive" neutrality as a model for its doctrine of peaceful coexistence and even suggested moving the UNO-headquarters to the city on the Danube. John F. Kennedy above all praised the country's behavior during the Hungarian Uprising in 1956. There were no real problems between Washington and Vienna—as long as the country remained pro-Western.

Third, Khrushchev used the Austrian Foreign Minister as a "secret channel" to the Americans. After unsuccessful feelers to Brandt via Kreisky in 1959/60, the Soviet Chairman tried once more right after the summit had ended. As Khrushchev had intended, Kreisky indeed briefed U.S. Ambassador Matthews the next day about the Soviet leader's statements and talked about the new Berlin ultimatum. In fact, the Foreign Minister acted secretly as a mediator—but also clearly stressed his pro-Western attitude in his communication with the Americans. Fourth, the Austrian government was a perfect host. It provided the necessary security means and it could present itself as a great cultural nation.

The Austrian Coalition government tried hard to treat the two delegations equally. But only the anti-Communist people of Vienna could do "officially" what the Austrian politicians could just express "inofficially:" they took sides when they openly cheered for the young Kennedy and ignored Khrushchev.

## Notes

1. For the long-lasting consequences of the Vienna Summit, see for instance Michael R. Beschloss, *The Crisis Years: Kennedy and Khrushchev 1960-1963* (New York: HarperCollins, 1991), 382-84; Michael Jochum, *Eisenhower und Chruschtschow: Gipfeldiplomatie im Kalten Krieg 1955-1960* (Paderborn: Schöningh, 1996), 205-10.

2. Elmer Plischke, *Diplomat in Chief: The President at the Summit* (New York: Praeger Publishers, 1986), 326-34; Gordon R. Weihmiller, *U.S.-Soviet Summits: An Account of East-West Diplomacy at the Top, 1955-1985* (Lanham: University Press of America, 1986), 43-48; Barbara Kellerman, "Leaders and Leaders - Ten Soviet-American Summits," in *Essays in Honor of James MacGregor Burns*, ed. Michael R. Beschloss and Thomas E. Cronin (Englewood Cliffs: Prentice Hall, 1989), 206-24, here 208f.

3. The best accounts are: Beschloss, *Crisis Years*, 191-225; James N. Giglio, *The Presidency of John F. Kennedy* (Lawrence: University Press of Kansas, 1991), 74-78; Richard Reeves, *President Kennedy: Profile of Power* (New York: Touchstone, 1993), 156-73; and Harald Biermann, *John F. Kennedy und der Kalte Krieg: Die Außenpolitik der USA und die Grenzen der Glaubwürdigkeit*

(Paderborn: Schöningh, 1997), 114-21. An insufficient account is provided by Andreas Wenger, "Der lange Weg zur Stabilität: Kennedy, Chruschtschow und das gemeinsame Interesse der Supermächte am Status quo in Europa," *Vierteljahrshefte für Zeitgeschichte* 46 (January 1998): 69-99, here 80f. Still useful texts include: Arthur M. Schlesinger, Jr., *A Thousand Days: John F. Kennedy in the White House* (Boston: Houghton Mifflin, 1965; repr., New York: Fawcett Premier, 1971), 333-48; Theodore C. Sorensen, *Kennedy* (New York: Harper, 1965), 543-50; and Honoré M. Catudal, *Kennedy and the Berlin Crisis: A Case Study in U.S. Decision Making* (Berlin: Berlin Verlag, 1980), 99-118.

4. Erika Weinzierl, "Das 'Wiener Gipfeltreffen' Chruschtschow-Kennedy 1961," in *Politik und christliche Verantwortung: Festschrift für Franz-Martin Schmölz*, ed. Gertraud Putz et al. (Innsbruck: Tyrolia-Verlag, 1992), 135-60.

5. Manfried Rauchensteiner, *Die Zwei: Die Große Koalition in Österreich 1945-1966* (Vienna: Österreichischer Bundesverlag, 1987), 431f; Oliver Rathkolb, *Washington ruft Wien: US-Großmachtpolitik und Österreich 1953-1963* (Vienna: Böhlau, 1997), 49-51, 94, 268, 270f, 275; but incorrect: Hugo Portisch, *Österreich II: Jahre des Aufbruchs - Jahre des Umbruchs* (Vienna: Kremayr & Scheriau, 1996), 134-40.

6. Regarding Khrushchev's motivation on the U-2 and the Paris Summit, see above all Vladislav Zubok and Constantine Pleshakov, *Inside the Kremlin's Cold War: From Stalin to Khrushchev* (Cambridge: Harvard University Press, 1996), 202-7; *Khrushchev Remembers: The Last Testament*, ed. Strobe Talbott (Boston: Little, Brown and Company, 1974), 443-61. More generally, see John Lewis Gaddis, *We Now Know: Rethinking Cold War History (Oxford:* Clarendon Press, 1997), 138-43.

7. *The Current Digest of the Soviet Press* 12 (22 June 1960) 3-7, here 6.

8. Beschloss, *Crisis Years*, 40-45.

9. See Zubok/Pleshakov, *Kremlin's Cold War*, 195 99, Hope M. Harrison, "Ulbricht and the Concrete 'Rose': New Archival Evidence on the Dynamics of Soviet-East German Relations and the Berlin Crisis, 1958-1961," *Cold War International History Project* Working Paper No. 5 (May 1993), 4-7, 12, 16, 19, 54f; Vladislav M. Zubok, "Khrushchev and the Berlin Crisis (1958-1962)," *Cold War International History Project* Working Paper No. 6 (May 1993), 3-11; and Michael Lemke, *Die Berlinkrise 1958 bis 1963: Interessen und Handlungsspielräume der SED im Ost-West-Konflikt* (Berlin: Akademie-Verlag, 1995), 102-7; compare these to the critical appraisal Gerhard Wettig, "Die sowjetische Politik während der Berlinkrise 1958 bis 1962: Der Stand der Forschungen," *Deutschland Archiv* 30 (1997): 383-98.

10. See especially Harrison, "Ulbricht," 36; Beschloss, *Crisis Years*, 77-83, 87f, 150-60.

11. Ibid., 162f.

12. *Archiv der Gegenwart*, 1961, 9099.

13. The most important briefing papers of 23, 25, and 26 May 1961 are in the (G-1), (G-2), and (G-3) folders "USSR-Vienna Meeting Background Documents 1953-1961, Briefing Material," Countries Files, President's Office Files (POF), box 126, John F. Kennedy Library/Boston (JFKL); Beschloss, *Crisis Years*, 175-78;

Martin Kofler, "'To Eliminate This Thorn, This Ulcer': Chruschtschow, Kennedy und die Berlin-Frage beim Wiener Gipfeltreffen 1961" (unpublished manuscript).

14. Anatoly Dobrynin, *In Confidence: Moscow's Ambassador to Americas Six Cold War Presidents (1962-1986)* (New York: Random House, 1995), 45; see also Aleksandr Fursenko and Timothy Naftali, *"One Hell of a Gamble": Khrushchev, Castro, and Kennedy, 1958-1964* (New York: W. W. Norton & Company, 1997), 124-26, 129-31.

15. The transcripts of the meeting's conversations are in "USSR Khrushchev Talks (President)" folder, Countries Files, National Security Files (NSF), box 187, JFKL; quote in conversation Khrushchev-JFK, 4 June 1961 (10:15 A.M.). Ibid.; also in: *Foreign Relations of the United States (FRUS), 1961-1963, Vol. XIV, Berlin Crisis 1961-1962* (Washington D.C.: United States Government Printing Office, 1993), 87-96, here 90.

16. Biermann, *Kennedy*, 120.

17. Zubok/Pleshakov, *Kremlin's Cold War*, 248; see also Gerald S. and Deborah H. Strober, *"Let us begin anew": An Oral History of the Kennedy Presidency* (New York: HarperCollins, 1993), 356f; Hans Kroll, *Lebenserinnerungen eines Botschafters* (Cologne: Kiepenheuer & Witsch, 1967), 494; and Andrei Sakharov, *Memoirs* (New York: Chekhov, 1990), 217.

18. Adrian W. Schertz, *Die Deutschlandpolitik Kennedys und Johnsons: Unterschiedliche Ansätze innerhalb der amerikanischen Regierung* (Cologne: Böhlau, 1992), 100-19.

19. *Public Papers of the Presidents of the United States: John F. Kennedy (JFKP)*, 1961 (Washington D.C.: United States Government Printing Office, 1962), 533-40.

20. Harrison, "Ulbricht," 47-51, 55; Zubok, "Khrushchev," 26.

21. Quoted in Kenneth O'Donnell and David F. Powers with Joe McCarthy, *"Johnny, we hardly knew ye:" Memories of John Fitzgerald Kennedy* (Boston and Toronto: Little, Brown, 1970), 303.

22. Schlesinger, *Thousand Days*, 372.

23. Lemke, *Berlinkrise*, 173-227; Wettig, "Politik," 396-98.

24. Rathkolb, *Washington*, 80, 85, 88.

25. Thompson to Rusk, 10 March 1961, folder "USSR Security 1/61-5/61," Countries Files, POF, box 125a, JFKL; also: Beschloss, *Crisis Years*, 77f, 80f.

26. Platzer to Außenministerium, 15 May 1961, Zl. 23676/61, GZ. 23618-6/61, II-Pol/USA-1, Bundesministerium für Auswärtige Angelegenheiten, Österreichisches Staatsarchiv/Archiv der Republik (BMfAA, ÖStA/AdR); memorandum of conversation Davis-Platzer, 16 May 1961, 611.61/5-1661, Central Decimal File, 1960-63, General Records of the Department of State, RG 59, National Archives (NA).

27. Memorandum JFK-Menshikov, 16 May 1961, folder "USSR General 9/5/61-17/5/61," Countries Files, NSF, box 177, JFKL.

28. Beschloss, *Crisis Years*, 163.

29. Copy of Ministerrat's decision, 16 May 1961 (*Verschluß!!!*), Zl. 23818, GZ. 23618-6/61, II-Pol/USA-1, BMfAA, ÖStA/AdR, also: Weinzierl, "'Wiener Gipfeltreffen'," 135.

30. Talbott, *Last Testament*, 492.

31. Haymerle to Kreisky, 3 July 1961 (*Vertraulich!*), Zl. 27388/61, GZ. 23618-6/61, II-Pol/USA-1, BMfAA, ÖStA/AdR; Thompson to Secretary of State, 18 May 1961, 611.61/5-1861, Central Decimal File, 1960-63, RG 59, NA.

32. As an introduction see Helmut Kramer, "Strukturentwicklung der Außenpolitik (1945-1990)," in *Handbuch des Politischen Systems Österreichs*, ed. Herbert Dachs et al., 2nd expanded edition (Vienna: Manzsche Verlags- und Universitätsbuchhandlung, 1992), 637-57, here 641-43; for the term "*Emanzipation*," see Rauchensteiner, *Die Zwei*, 332f.

33. *FRUS, 1958-1960, Vol. IX: Berlin Crisis 1959-1960: Germany; Austria* (Washington D.C.: United States Government Printing Office, 1993), 789f, 794-96.

34. Bruno Kreisky, "Austria draws the balance," *Foreign Affairs* 37 (January 1959): 269-81, quotes 275f.

35. Oliver Rathkolb, "Austria's 'Ostpolitik' in the 1950s and 1960s: Honest Broker or Double Agent?" *Austrian History Yearbook* XXVI (1995): 129-45, here 140f.

36. Martin Kofler, "Berlin, Neutrality, and Cold War Propaganda: Nikita Khrushchev's Visit in Austria in 1960" (M.A. thesis, University of New Orleans, 1998) posted as a "working paper" on the CenterAustria homepage **Centeraustria.uno.edu**.

37. See the overviews of Michael Gehler and Wolfram Kaiser, "A Study in Ambivalence: Austria and European Integration 1945-95," *Contemporary European History* 6 (1997): 75-99; Michael Gehler and Rolf Steininger, ed., *Österreich und die Europäische Integration 1945-1993: Aspekte einer wechselvollen Entwicklung* (Vienna: Böhlau Verlag, 1993); for the shift within the new administration, see Oliver Rathkolb, "The Foreign Relations between the U.S.A. and Austria in the late 1950s," *Contemporary Austrian Studies* 3 (1995): 24-38, here 33.

38. Background paper "Austria: General," 24 May 1961, folder "USSR-Vienna Meeting Background Documents 1953-1961 (G-3) Briefing Material, Background Papers," Countries Files, POF, box 126, JFKL.

39. Matthews to Secretary of State, 26 May 1961, 611.61/5-2661, Central Decimal File, 1960-63, RG 59, NA.

40. See: *Die Presse*, 3 June 1961; Weinzierl, "'Wiener Gipfeltreffen'," 135-42.

41. *Archiv der Gegenwart*, 1961, 9134, 9140; the newly founded International Atomic Energy Agency already had its seat in Vienna since 1957. Hans G. Knitel, "Wien als Sitz internationaler Organisationen und als internationale Konferenzstadt," *Österreichisches Jahrbuch für Politik* (1985): 471-94, here 489.

42. Press report Schöner, 9 June 1961, Zl. 25533/61, GZ. 25533-6/61, II-pol/Deutschland West-6, BMfAA, ÖStA/AdR; comments "Radio Moskau" in: "Pressemappe 1 Jänner-Juli 1961", II-pol/UdSSR-6, BMfAA, ÖStA/AdR.

43. Circular Außenministerium, 9 June 1961, Zl. 25889-6/61, GZ. 23618-6/61, II-pol/USA-1, BMfAA, ÖStA/AdR.

44. Kreisky to Kennedy, 5 July 1961, folder "Austria 1961," Countries Files, POF, box 111, JFKL [Department of State's translation].

45. Matthews to Secretary of State, 7 June 1961, box 13, and 6 June 1961, 12 June 1961, box 16, Classified General Records, 1959-1961, Vienna Embassy, Austria, RG 84, NA.

46. John Fisher, First Secretary of the U.S. Embassy Vienna to Department of State, 8 June 1961, ibid.

47. See the numerous letters of Austrians to the U.S. embassy in Vienna in late May and early June 1961: Folder "Vienna Meeting-Advice-Austria-Part A," General Correspondence Files, POF, box 25, JFKL.

48. *Die Presse*, 3, 4 June 1961; Beschloss, *Crisis Years*, 191f; Weinzierl, "'Wiener Gipfeltreffen'," 143; Charles E. Bohlen, *Witness to History* (New York: Norton, 1973), 480; Dean Rusk, *As I Saw It (as told to Richard Rusk)* (New York: W.W. Norton & Company, 1990), 220; compare these to Talbott, *Last Testament*, 493.

49. Jerrold L. Schecter and Vyacheslav V. Luchkov, ed., *Khrushchev Remembers: The Glasnost Tapes* (Boston: Little, Brown and Company, 1990), 79f.

50. See Günter Bischof, "Eisenhower, the Summit, and the Austrian Treaty, 1953-1955," in *Eisenhower: A Centenary Assessment*, ed. Günter Bischof and Stephen E. Ambrose (Baton Rouge: Louisiana University Press, 1995), 136-61, here 155-61; see also Gerald Stourzh, *Um Einheit und Freiheit: Staatsvertrag, Neutralität und das Ende der Ost-West-Besetzung Österreichs 1945-1955*, 4th completely revised and expanded ed. (Vienna: Böhlau Verlag, 1998), 335-485.

51. Kofler, "Berlin," 9-12.

52. Conversation Khrushchev-JFK, 4 June 1961 (10:15 A.M.), folder "USSR Khrushchev Talks (President)," Countries Files, NSF, box 187, JFKL; also in: *FRUS, 1961-1963, Vol. XXIV, Laos Crisis* (Washington D.C.: United States Government Printing Office, 1994), 234.

53. D. C. Watt, ed., *Documents on International Affairs 1961* (London: Oxford University Press, 1965), 286-302, here 288.

54. Talbott, *Last Testament*, 493.

55. Rauchensteiner, *Die Zwei*, 431.

56. Platzer to Außenministerium, 9 February 1961, Zl. 18272/61, GZ. 18272-4/61, II-pol/USA-1, BMfAA, ÖStA/AdR; *JFKP*, 1961, 438.

57. Conversation Khrushchev-JFK, 4 June 1961 (Lunch), folder "USSR Khrushchev Talks (President)," Countries Files, NSF, box 187, JFKL.

58. *JFKP*, 1961, 438f.

59. Ibid., 441-46, here 442.

60. NSC 6020, 9 December 1960, Lot 63 D 351, Records Relating to State Dept. Participation in the Operations Coordinating Board and the National Security Council, 1947-1963, RG 59, NA.

61. Full translation of original Russian text in Bennett to Department of State, 22 July 1960, 762.00/7-2260, RG 59, NA.

62. Hanns Jürgen Küsters, "Konrad Adenauer und Willy Brandt in der Berlin-Krise 1958-1963," *Vierteljahrshefte für Zeitgeschichte* 40 (October 1992): 483-542, here 493-97, 517-19; Kofler, "Berlin," 23-25; see also the memoirs of Willy Brandt, *People and Politics: The Years 1960-1975* (Boston and Toronto: Little, Brown and Company, 1978), 99-102; Bruno Kreisky, *Im Strom der Politik: Erfahrungen eines Europäers* (Berlin: Siedler, 1988), 10-24; Hans J. Thalberg, *Von der Kunst, Österreicher zu sein: Erinnerungen und Tagebuchnotizen* (Vienna: Hermann Böhlaus Nachf, 1984), 252-57; and Egon Bahr, *Zu meiner Zeit* (Munich: Karl Blessing Verlag, 1996), 127-29, which give the wrong date with early 1961; Kroll, *Lebenserinnerungen*, 463f; *Der Spiegel,* 7 July 1960, headline "Wrong Address" ("*Falsche Adresse*").

63. Talbott, *Last Testament*, 500f.

64. Note Generalsekretär Martin Fuchs, 6 June 1961, Zl. 25916/61, GZ. 23618/61, II-pol/USA-1, BMfAA, ÖStA/AdR; Weinzierl, "'Wiener Gipfeltreffen'," 152-54.

65. Notes of the leading diplomats in the Außenministerium's section II Walter Wodak, June 5 1961, Zl. 24788-6/61, GZ. 23618-6/61 and Kurt Waldheim, June 5 1961, Zl. 24799-4/61, June 6 1961, Zl. 25028-4/61, GZ. 23618-4/61, II-pol/USA-1, BMfAA, ÖStA/AdR.

66. Ernest May and Philip D. Zelikow, ed., *The Kennedy Tapes: Inside the White House during the Cuban Missile Crisis* (Cambridge, MA: The Belknap Press of Harvard University Press, 1997), 513, 534, 593, 600.

67. Rathkolb, *Washington*, 55f.

68. *The New York Times,* 3 June 1961.

69. See: Beschloss, *Crisis Years*, 207-209; Rose Fitzgerald Kennedy, *Times to Remember* (New York: Doubleday, 1974), 374.

70. Beschloss, *Crisis Years*, 209f; for the full U.S. program see: Folder "Trips-Vienna, Austria 3/6/61-4/6/61," Subjects Files, POF, box 107, JFKL; *Die Presse*, 3 June 1961.

71. Kennedy to Schärf, 12 June 1961, folder "Austria 1961", Countries Files, POF, box 111, JFKL.

# Postindustrial Cleavages and Electoral Change in an Advanced Capitalist Democracy: The Austrian Case

*Markus M. L. Crepaz and Hans-Georg Betz*

For much of the post-1945 period, West European party systems were widely regarded as relatively stable structures reflecting the well-entrenched sociostructural cleavage patterns of the past.[1] Starting in the late 1960s, most West European democracies experienced growing electoral volatility, the defection of some portion of the electorate to newly emerging parties, an increase in unconventional political behavior, and an upsurge of new social movements. Although these developments generally had more than a negligible impact on the mainstream parties, they failed to bring about a fundamental change of the structure of the established party systems. Despite a significant increase in partisan dealignment, social tracers such as religion, language, ethnicity, and class continued "to play a crucial role in determining partisan preferences."[2]

Given the profound socioeconomic and sociocultural transformation of West European societies since the late 1960s, the resilience of party systems might come as a surprise. In the early 1980s, there were widespread expectations that the "postindustrial revolution" would entail a substantial restructuring of traditional cleavages along a new axis, separating the "proponents of the established industrial order" from the "supporters of New Politics goals." In the wake of dramatically rising education levels and the diffusion of postmaterialist values among Western European youth, generational turnover was expected to expedite the erosion of traditional cleavage patterns while bolstering a "secular realignment in voting patterns."[3]

as far as they occurred, could still largely be accommodated by the established parties. Support for "new politics" parties remained rather circumscribed.[4] Green, alternative, and other left-libertarian parties, while managing to establish themselves as viable political competitors in a number of West European countries, failed to fundamentally alter the direction of political competition.

Since the beginning of the 1990s, this picture has dramatically changed. The almost complete collapse of the established party system in Italy; the considerable increase in volatility of the Swiss party system; the extensive fragmentation of the party systems in France or Belgium; and the growing elasticity of the German party system in recent years indicate that Western European party systems have entered a period of extensive turmoil, turbulence, and instability.

These developments have occurred at a time of momentous geopolitical, socioeconomic, and sociostructural change associated with the collapse of the Cold War system and the acceleration of global economic integration. It seems therefore appropriate to revisit the question of the effect of socioeconomic and sociostructural change engendered by postindustrialism on West European party systems. Focusing on the case of Austria is one way to explore this question.

For much of the postwar period, the Austrian party system had a reputation of being highly stable. During the past decade, however, Austria has gone through an electoral revolution which has led to a profound transformation of the country's party landscape. This political transformation was a direct result of socioeconomic change that began in the 1980s and accelerated in the early 1990s as a result of the opening of Austria's eastern borders and the preparations for Austria's membership in the European Union. This process is discussed in the second section of this article. In the first section, a theoretical framework linking socioeconomic and sociocultural change to political change is advanced. These theoretical propositions to an empirical test using data from a recent national survey.

## Postindustrialism and Sociopolitical Change

Theories on postindustrialism generally agree that postindustrial societies are characterized first, a shift from the production of manufactured goods to the production of services, and second by a "new centrality" of theoretical knowledge and technical information.[5] In recent years, these two developments have been intensified both by the information revolution and the competitive pressures of a rapidly integrating global market.

The information revolution has brought together science and technology as "a continuing interaction," making research and development "an essential component of production activity." As a result, human resources have increasingly replaced physical resources as the central component of the production process.[6] Globalization, in turn, has put pressure on advanced industrial societies to shift from routinized mass production to flexible, high value-added production and from production-supporting services to sophisticated human-oriented services using a smaller, highly trained, but less specialized labor force.[7] The result has been a decrease in manufacturing employment, a widening "wage premium for skill," and, more generally, a "significant increase in labor-market instability and insecurity," including rising unemployment, which affects particularly low-skilled workers.[8]

Postindustrialization results in a fundamental transformation of the social structure of traditional industrial societies. Most directly, it implies the rapid expansion of professional, managerial, and technical jobs at the expense of traditional routine manufacturing operations increasingly being replaced by flexible machines. At the same time, the expansion of postindustrialism occasions a dramatic increase in demand for "abstract conceptual, technical, and alphanumeric skills."[9]

At the same time, postindustrialization entails profound sociocultural change. Postindustrial societies are characterized by a dramatic increase in individual choices and life chances furthered by the growing importance of education, which emphasizes the individual pursuit of credentials and generally promotes an ethos of individual effort and merit. This leads to the dissipation and dissolution of traditional identities, forcing individuals to design their own "social biography."[10] At the same time, postindustrialization also entails the individualization of risks, giving rise to new forms and dimensions of social inequality.

Postindustrial sociostructural and sociocultural change has a significant impact on political orientation. Politics in industrial societies has largely been shaped by a basic conflict between the middle and working class over the just distribution of material gains. As a result, there has generally been a strong relationship between social class and party preference. Once industrial societies have turned into postindustrial societies, traditional class differences have eroded, and with them class voting. The result has been a shift from class-based to a value-based pattern of political polarization that pits materialist against postmaterialist value orientations.[11]

Those who subscribe to this interpretation generally attribute the rise of postmaterialist values during the past several decades to the postwar generations' formative experience of steadily increasing material security that characterized much of the period between the late 1940s and the early 1970s. This interpretation offers a plausible explanation for the sociocultural impact of the postwar experience of robust economic growth and rapidly rising mass affluence. However, it is based on a premise which the experience of postindustrialism has rendered largely obsolete.

The dramatic rise in affluence in the postwar period was largely the result of a system of industrial mass production which, combined with an expanding welfare state, allowed even low-skilled manual labor to lead a middle-class life. This logic no longer holds in postindustrial societies. Whereas the postwar period was characterized by rising mass affluence and growing material and physical security, postindustrial societies are characterized by growing insecurity and rising inequality. Postindustrial value formation is bound to reflect these new realities. The driving mechanism behind the postwar shift in values was the experience of mass affluence as the central new feature of the postwar period. The core feature of postindustrialism is the centrality of knowledge and human capital. This makes education the central determinant of postindustrial value formation. In postindustrial societies, education not only crucially determines professional opportunities and life chances, but also attitudes toward central socioeconomic and sociocultural issues. These attitudes, in turn, are informed by a person's position on risk, insecurity, and inequality, the central features underlying postindustrialism. This gives rise to a number of distinct value cleavages.

Postindustrial societies are meritocratic societies, where differences in income and status increasingly reflect theoretical knowledge and technical skills.[12] Postindustrialization, in turn, tends to stimulate skepticism about the desirability of social intervention and planning while engendering support for a substantial deregulation of markets. The result is a value cleavage that pits market liberals against the defenders of a socially and community-regulated distribution of resources.

Postindustrial societies are knowledge societies. Most of the new and highly demanding jobs in the service and information sector provide room for considerable individual creativity and autonomy. It has been submitted that persons with advanced degrees are generally more attracted to interesting and challenging, rather than merely well-remunerated, work. This results in a new and increasingly important value cleavage pitting social libertarians who put a high price on individual autonomy and self-realization, equality, and the free choice of lifestyle, against authoritarians who value traditional morals, respect for authority, and sociocultural conformity.[13]

Postindustrial societies generate growing demands for individual autonomy and challenging and interesting work. This suggests that postindustrialism is conducive to the continued promotion of non-materialist values, including support for environmental protection and aesthetic values, even if—as in the case of environmentalism—they might be at odds with neoliberal values. This means that the cleavage pitting postmaterialists against those who prefer job security, high wages, and economic growth to challenging work and protecting the natural environment remains important.

What are the implications of postindustrial sociostructural and sociocultural change on politics? We start from two competing views. In the first view, the transition to postindustrialism leads to the disintegration of traditional social groups, subcultures, and milieus while setting in motion processes of social fragmentation and individualization.[14] Individualization, in turn, diminishes the salience of those factors that traditionally influenced individual political orientations, such as religion or social class. The result is a "postmodern" reconstruction of politics characterized by a "process of particularization of voting choice" accompanied by a fundamental decline of cleavage politics, which means that voters respond to new developments "in ways that are impossible to anticipate."[15]

The second perspective maintains that postindustrial sociostructural change, while promoting processes of individualization and social fragmentation, gives rise to a limited number of distinct new social groups with shared identities. The resulting recomposition of the social structure of postindustrial societies occasions new lines of political conflict that follow a new postindustrial logic.[16] In this view, the growing importance of theoretical knowledge and the growing demands for cognitive ability and analytical skills divides society into winners and losers.[17] The logic of postindustrialism suggests that whichever category people find themselves in is largely determined by sociostructural factors, such as education, and increasingly also age and gender.[18] Together with new value orientations, these sociostructural factors form the basis of new postindustrial cleavages which, in turn, have a strong influence on political behavior. The following section tests these propositions using Austrian data.

## Postindustrialization and the Bifurcation of the Electorate Market in Austria

During the past two decades, Austria has experienced broad socioeconomic and sociostructural change, transforming it from a predominantly industrial to an increasingly postindustrial society. Until the early 1980s, Austria (together with Germany) distinguished itself by its large manufacturing sector. In 1981, some 43.2 percent of the labor force were employed in industry and construction, and 55.4 percent were employed in service industries. By 1989, the share of the secondary sector had declined to 36.1 percent, and the service sector had grown to 60 percent.[19] A comparison of the trends in the core segments of the secondary and tertiary sectors illustrates these developments even more clearly (see Table 1). Between 1981 and 1991, the percentage of persons employed in manufacturing declined from 30.5 percent to 26.1 percent of the labor force; at the same time, employment in typically postindustrial services (financial and business services, insurance, personal, social, and public services) increased from 25.7 to 31.4 percent.

The shift from industrial to postindustrial employment structures was accompanied by a significant transformation of the educational composition of the labor force (see Table 2). Between 1981 and 1991, the percentage of workers with only compulsory education fell from 40.6 to 29.4 percent; the percentage of those with secondary education or more increased from 8.5 to 11.4 percent. These developments occurred in both the manufacturing and service sector, but it was most pronounced in the postindustrial service sector, where by 1991, more than a quarter of the labor force had received at least a secondary education.

**Table 1:** Changes in the Core Sectors of the Austrian Labor Force, 1971-1991

| | 1971 | 1981 | 1991 |
|---|---|---|---|
| | | *Manufacturing* | |
| in 1,000 persons | 972.3 | 1,038.7 | 960.5 |
| percent of total labor force | 31.4 | 30.5 | 26.1 |
| | | *Postindustrial Services* | |
| in 1,000 persons | 630.5 | 875.8 | 1,156.3 |
| percent of total labor force | 20.4 | 25.7 | 31.4 |

**Source**: Lorenz Lassnigg and Peter Prenner, *Wandel der österreichischen Wirtschafts- und Berufsstrukturen* (Vienna: Institute for Advanced Studies, 1997).

The third important socioeconomic feature of the 1980s was a significant rise in unemployment. Until the early 1980s, Austria enjoyed one of the lowest unemployment rates in the Organization of Economic Cooperation and Development (OECD).[20] Between 1981 and 1989, however, unemployment more than doubled, from 2.4 percent to 5 percent. For the Austrians, having become accustomed to being shielded against the vicissitudes of the labor market, this was a new experience which gave rise to considerable concern.[21]

Socioeconomic and sociostructural change in Austria accelerated in the early 1990s as a result of the opening of the eastern borders (*Ostöffnung*) and Austria's decision to join the European Union (EU). *Ostöffnung* exposed Austrian industry to increasing competitive pressures from low-wage producers in central Europe "whose areas of comparative advantage closely coincide with Austria's own traditional areas of export specialisation," that is, resource and labor-intensive goods. In response, Austria had to adjust "towards those areas within which it had hitherto been weak and where capacity is underdeveloped: i.e. toward higher-technology manufactures, and value-added services."[22] Structural readjustment was reinforced by the preparations for Austria's entrance into the European Union. Starting in the late 1980s, Austria embarked on a comprehensive privatization program. By the early 1990s, the state had divested itself of the majority of state-owned industries.

**Table 2:** Changes in the Educational Composition of the Labor Force, 1971-1991, percent of labor force

| | 1971 | 1981 | 1991 |
|---|---|---|---|
| Education | | | |
| compulsory | 51.2 | 40.6 | 29.4 |
| higher | 3.4 | 8.5 | 11.4 |
| | | *Manufacturing* | |
| compulsory | 51.4 | 43.2 | 33.6 |
| higher | 2.8 | 3.4 | 4.4 |
| | | *Postindustrial Services* | |
| compulsory | 36.0 | 29.1 | 21.0 |
| higher | 19.4 | 22.9 | 26.4 |

**Source**: Lorenz Lassnigg and Peter Prenner, *Wandel der österreichischen Wirtschafts- und Berufsstrukturen* (Vienna: Institute for Advanced Studies, 1997).

As a result of the structural adjustment measures, between 1991 and 1994, more than 70,000 jobs were lost in the production sector, and official unemployment rose to 6.5 percent.[23] However, what kept unemployment relatively low was a dramatic increase in early retirement and disability pensions, which significantly eased the pressure on the labor market, while burdening the pension system.[24] A series of takeovers of Austrian privatized firms by foreign (especially German) companies soon after Austria's entrance into the EU led to new job losses when foreign companies relocated part of the production of their newly acquired subsidiaries to central Europe.[25] In 1996 and 1997, unemployment reached a series of new record highs, reported by the major Austrian newspapers in an increasingly alarmist tone which reflected the public's growing anxieties.[26] Between 1991 and 1997, the percentage of Austrians who said they were afraid of losing their job increased from 36 to 71 percent.[27]

Postindustrial structural change and growing exposure to globalization pressures in Austria during the past two decades have been accompanied by a profound transformation of the Austrian party system. Until the early 1980s, the Austrian party system distinguished itself by its high degree of stability and concentration. For most of the postwar period, political power rested with two major parties, the Austrian People's Party (ÖVP) and the Social Democrats (SPÖ), which governed the country in a grand coalition from 1945 to 1966 and again from 1986 until today. In the 1970s, the ÖVP and SPÖ accounted for roughly 93 percent of the valid vote. The only other electorally significant party was the small Freedom Party (FPÖ) which averaged between 5 and 6 percent of the vote in the 1960s and 1970s. With an average Pedersen index of 3.2, Austria was the least volatile of all West European polities in the twelve elections between 1945 and 1983.[28]

The Austrian party system owed its stability to the persistence of strong linkages between political parties and traditional, mutually exclusive subcultures (*Lager*) that emerged in the nineteenth century, dividing society along religious, class, and ideological lines. After the war, the major parties, in order to alleviate the profound historical animosities between the *Lager*, created a bipartisan patronage system (*Proporz*) that allowed them to extend their reach over much of the Austrian population, making the allocation of jobs, contracts, and even housing dependent on party affiliation. The *Proporz* system strengthened subculture cohesion and assured continued party loyalty even after the subcultures started to erode. The party state was further strengthened by a highly hierarchical, elitist, and often secretive system of economic concertation which, with its mandatory membership in workers, farmers, and employers (chamber of commerce) chambers and its high union density, made Austria the paradigm case of societal corporatism.[29]

The hyperstability of the Austrian party system ended in the mid-1980s. Within little more than a decade, support for the two major parties declined from 90 percent in 1983 to roughly two thirds of the valid votes in 1995, with the rest going to three minor political parties. A recalculation of the voter distribution, this time with reference to the eligible voters, reveals the full extent of change. The data show three developments: first, a significant increase in the number of non-voters and invalid votes, which by 1994 represent the third largest "party" in Austria; second, a dramatic increase in support for the three minor parties, which in 1994 surpassed that of the ÖVP; and third, an even more dramatic decline of support for the two major parties, which between 1970 and 1995 lost more than a third of their voters.

**Table 3:** Election Results in Austria, 1945-1995, in percent of valid votes

| | ÖVP | SPÖ | FPÖ | KPÖ | Greens | LF | ÖVP+SPÖ |
|---|---|---|---|---|---|---|---|
| 1945 | 49.8 | 44.6 | 5.4 | 94.4 | | | |
| 1949 | 44.0 | 38.7 | 11.7 | 5.1 | | | 82.7 |
| 1953 | 41.3 | 42.1 | 10.9 | 5.3 | | | 83.4 |
| 1956 | 46.0 | 43.0 | 6.5 | 4.4 | | | 83.4 |
| 1959 | 44.2 | 44.8 | 7.7 | 3.3 | | | 89.0 |
| 1962 | 45.4 | 44.0 | 7.1 | 3.0 | | | 89.4 |
| 1966 | 48.3 | 42.6 | 5.4 | 0.4 | | | 90.9 |
| 1970 | 44.7 | 48.4 | 5.5 | 0.9 | | | 93.1 |
| 1971 | 43.1 | 50.0 | 5.5 | 1.4 | | | 93.1 |
| 1975 | 43.0 | 50.4 | 5.4 | 1.2 | | | 93.4 |
| 1979 | 41.9 | 51.0 | 6.1 | 1.0 | | | 92.9 |
| 1983 | 43.2 | 47.7 | 5.0 | 0.7 | 3.3 | | 90.9 |
| 1986 | 41.3 | 43.1 | 9.7 | 0.7 | 4.9 | | 84.4 |
| 1990 | 32.1 | 42.7 | 16.6 | 0.6 | 6.8 | | 74.8 |
| 1994 | 27.7 | 34.9 | 22.5 | 0.3 | 7.4 | 6.0 | 62.6 |
| 1995 | 28.3 | 38.1 | 21.9 | 0.3 | 4.8 | 5.5 | 66.4 |

**Source:** Wolfgang C. Müller, Fritz Plasser and Peter A. Ulram (eds.) *Wählerverhalten und Parteienwettbewerb* (Vienna: Signum-Verlag: 1995), 526-527.

The result was a significant increase in the effective number of parties from a mean of 2.2 in the 1945 to 1983 period to 3.4 in 1995, as well as a dramatic increase in electoral volatility, with the Pedersen index reaching 10.5 in 1995. Symptomatic of the new instability was the collapse of the grand coalition in 1995, only one year after its formation, followed by equally inconclusive elections that led to a rehash of the grand-coalition government. Those benefiting from the decline of the major parties were three new parties: the Greens, the Freedom Party (FP), and the Liberal Forum (LIF).

The Greens emerged in the early 1980s in opposition to the government's nuclear energy policy. Initially an electoral alliance of rival environmental groups, a united party was founded in 1987. Despite internal conflicts and confrontations, the party managed to establish itself in the Austrian party system, gaining between 5 and 7 percent of the vote. The Greens promote environmentalism, the protection of civil liberties and minority rights, and a thorough democratization of all areas of society, including politics and the economy. Like their counterparts in Germany, Switzerland, and Belgium, the Greens are a left-libertarian party, rejecting both "centralized-bureaucratic governance" and "instrumental market exchange" in favor of "more communitarian, but voluntary, modes of social and political self-organization."[30]

**Table 4:** Voter Distribution, 1970-1995, in percent of valid votes

| | Eligible voters in 1,000 | no-voters/ invalid | SPÖ | ÖVP | FPÖ | Greens | LiF |
|---|---|---|---|---|---|---|---|
| 1970 | 5,045.8 | 9.05 | 44.03 | 40.65 | 5.01 | | |
| 1971 | 4,984.4 | 8.58 | 45.75 | 39.42 | 4.98 | | |
| 1975 | 5,019.3 | 8.09 | 46.34 | 9.47 | 4.96 | | |
| 1979 | 5,186.7 | 8.82 | 46.52 | 8.21 | 5.53 | | |
| 1983 | 5,316.4 | 8.71 | 43.50 | 39.46 | 4.55 | 3.0 | |
| 1986 | 5,461.4 | 11.16 | 38.31 | 36.69 | 8.65 | 4.39 | |
| 1990 | 5,628.9 | 16.41 | 35.76 | 26.80 | 13.90 | 5.64 | |
| 1994 | 5,774.0 | 19.76 | 28.02 | 22.20 | 18.05 | 5.86 | 4.79 |
| 1995 | 5,768.3 | 19.16 | 31.96 | 23.76 | 18.38 | 4.04 | 4.65 |

**Source:** Wolfgang C. Müller, Fritz Plasser and Peter A. Ulram (eds.) *Wählerverhalten und Parteienwettbewerb* (Vienna: Signum-Verlag: 1995) 526-527.

The Freedom Party traces its roots to the nineteenth century. In the immediate postwar period, it represented the "third" (German-national) *Lager* which rejected the notion of an independent Austrian identity. The party gradually distanced itself from its historical legacy, moving closer to West European liberalism. The development came to an end in 1986, when the FPÖ underwent a fundamental strategic and programmatic reorientation, which transformed the FPÖ into a completely new party. Under its new chairman, Jörg Haider, the party became the by far most successful radical right-wing populist party in Western Europe, garnering a record 27.6 percent of the vote in the 1996 European election. It achieved this success with a program that called for a fundamental transformation of Austria's institutional and political structure, the introduction of a radical market liberalism, a revival of traditional values, and the enforcement of harsh anti-immigration measures.[31]

The third new party, the Liberal Forum (LiF), was founded in the spring of 1993 by Heide Schmidt and fellow FPÖ dissidents who objected to Haider's aggressive anti-immigration campaign. Against strong opposition from the major parties and the FPÖ, the LiF managed to overcome Austria's 4 percent hurdle in both 1994 and 1995, gaining a little more than 5 percent of the vote. The LiF's leadership made a conscious effort to create a niche in the electoral market. Thus Heide Schmidt adopted the question of equal legal status for non-conventional partnerships as one of the party's first major issues, leading critics to charge the LiF with being an ultra left-wing "gays' party." The question of homosexual rights is part of a broad range of civil rights demands including equal rights for women, minorities, and immigrants, and the "decriminalization" of drug use. At the same time, the party promotes a delicately balanced program that combines calls for individual entrepreneurship, achievement, private initiative, and an unrestricted market with a pronounced concern for social solidarity and the environment.[32]

Evidence suggests that the transformation of the Austrian party system has, to a significant degree, been a product of electoral realignment, which occurred in several waves and from which the FPÖ benefited most. Post-election studies suggest that, in 1986 and 1990, the FPÖ gained a roughly equal number of former SPÖ and ÖVP voters (130,000 from each in 1986; 180,000 from the ÖVP and 155,000 from the SPÖ voters in 1990) while in 1994, it gained more than twice as many former SPÖ as ÖVP voters (246,000 versus 111,000). Against that, the Greens and the LiF mobilized a significant number of first-time voters. Thus in 1994, roughly a third of the LiF's support (some 83,000 votes) came from new voters, the rest from the other parties (SPÖ: 38,000; ÖVP: 37,000), including the FPÖ (40,000) and the Greens (55,000).[33]

As a result of their dramatic losses in the late 1980s and early 1990s, the two major catch-all parties have increasingly been reduced to their core traditional constituencies. In 1994, the percentage of union members among SPÖ voters (42 percent) and persons with strong religious attachments among ÖVP voters (50 percent) was considerably higher than, for instance, among their German counterparts (SPD: 28 percent; CDU/CSU: 18 percent). At the same time, support for the two major parties was increasingly concentrated among more voters. In

1994, roughly 58 percent of SPÖ and ÖVP voters were older than forty-four years old.[34] By contrast, the new parties have consciously marketed themselves as representatives of a new politics in an attempt to appeal to floating and new voters. This suggests that the electoral realignment of the past ten years has led to a bifurcation of the Austrian party system. The question is whether and to what extent the increasing postindustrialization of the Austrian employment structure in the 1980s and the growing exposure of the Austrian economy to new competitive pressures in the 1990s have created new value dispositions reflected in the dramatic gains of new parties since the mid-1980s.

## Values versus Resentment: The Logic of Postindustrial Politics in Austria

This empirical investigation is based on an Austria-wide representative survey consisting of 1,538 individual interviews. The survey was conducted in the summer of 1993, primarily to gauge the Austrian public's attitudes toward EU membership, but also to monitor the development of public opinion on a wide variety of economic, social, and political issues and choices.[35] For this analysis, a limited number of questions which provide measures of values pertinent to this investigation have been selected.

For this study, those respondents who indicated they could imagine voting for one of the three new parties were selected. By not limiting the sample of respondents to strong partisans, this analysis has been consciously biased in favor of the hypothesis that *postindustrialization leads to a particularization of voting choice*. Our competing hypothesis is that *support for the new parties stems from a combination of sociostructural factors (including education, age, and perhaps also gender) and value patterns*. Ideally, it would be expected that potential supporters of the Greens would be better educated and hold a combination of postmaterialist and left-libertarian values; potential supporters of the Liberal Forum be better educated and hold a combination of neoliberal and left-libertarian values; and potential supporters of the Freedom Party would have significantly lower levels of education and hold a combination of authoritarian and materialist values.[36]

Since our dependent variables are of a binary nature, we have decided to employ logistic regression analysis. The advantage of this method over other maximum likelihood methods such as logit or probit is that the coefficients, standard errors, and significance levels can be more intuitively interpreted. In addition, logistic regression offers superior goodness of fit measures. Most of the value items represent forced questions asking the respondent to choose between two diametrically opposed items, for example, between economic growth at the price of environmental degradation, or environmental protection at the price of potential unemployment.

Our choice of variables is largely derived from the literature on value change, postindustrialization, and globalization. With regard to the latter, we have included a statement on the European Union and on immigration. EU membership, particularly after the Maastricht decision, entails significant competitive pressures for market liberalization which are generally associated with globalization. It thus forms an intricate part of the neoliberal wave.[37] Immigration has become a major challenge to affluent societies, where labor migrants are increasingly seen as unwelcome competitors for scarce jobs; political refugees, as a growing drain on the dwindling resources of the welfare state; and foreigners, in general, as a threat to sociocultural cohesion.[38] Much of the ensuing debate has been couched in terms of sociocultural exclusion versus multicultural integration. Immigration has thus become a major aspect of the libertarian/authoritarian value cleavage. In addition to attitudinal variables, traditional sociostructural variables as well as variables measuring economic voting and political alienation as control variables have also been included (see Appendix).

The results of our model disprove the hypothesis that postindustrialization leads to electoral particularization. On the contrary, at least in the Austrian case, *support for new parties follows rather distinct sociostructural and sociocultural patterns*. These patterns hold particularly strong for the two libertarian parties, the Greens and the Liberal Forum. Against that, support for the radical populist right is considerably less grounded in a coherent pattern than the recent literature on the radical right might lead one to expect.

Potential supporters of both libertarian parties distinguish themselves by their age and high level of education. Our results indicate that the younger the voters, the more they sympathize with the Greens and the Liberal Forum, while age is not a statistically significant predictor for the Freedom Party. This is somewhat surprising, given Jörg Haider's attempt to present himself as a youthful and dynamic alternative to the established political class. Similarly, education is sig-

**Table 5:** Logistic Regression Estimates of Party Sympathizers

Note: The vote for "Freedom Party Sympathizers," "Green Party Sympathizers," and the "Liberal Forum Sympathizers" are the binary dependent variables (For operationalization, exact wording of questions and coding scheme, see Appendix).

| Socio-structural variables: | Freedom Party Sympathizers | Green Party Sympathizers | Liberal Forum Sympathizers |
|---|---|---|---|
| Age | -.01 (1.35) | -.04 (46.93)*** | -.02 (18.32)*** |
| Education | .11 (1.34) | .22 (5.35)** | .28 (11.16)*** |
| Gender | -.41 (9.06)*** | .14 (.08) | .16 (1.40) |
| Household net-income | -.004 (.06) | .002 (.001) | .02 (2.93)* |
| Working Class | .34 (5.66)** | -.29 (2.56)* | .02 (.016) |
| Libertarianism/ Authoritarianism: | | | |
| More Participatory Democracy | -.02 (.06) | .14 (3.44)* | -.02 (.16) |
| Law and order | -.02 (.20) | -.09 (2.73)* | -.003 (.025) |
| Xenophobia | .37 (39.42)*** | -.33 (23.68)*** | -.24 (18.16)*** |
| Neo-Liberalism: | | | |
| Too much state interventionism | .14 (7.93)*** | .01 (.025) | .16 (11.37)*** |
| Pro-European Union | -.09 (1.82) | -.37 (.18) | .18 (7.96)*** |

| | | | |
|---|---|---|---|
| Materialism/ Postmaterialism: | | | |
| People are more important than money | -.11 (7.17)*** | .05 (.92) | -.10 (6.50)** |
| Environmenta-lism | -.06 (.99) | .33 (18.76)*** | .09 (2.33) |
| Alternative Hypotheses: | | | |
| Personal economic situation | -.02 (.034) | .11 (1.09) | .02 (.066) |
| Economic situation of Austria | -.16 (1.66) | .072 (.25) | .13 (1.22) |
| Disenchantment with politics | .37 (14.26)*** | .11 (.84) | -.01 (.005) |
| Intercept | -3.15 (17.83)*** | -.36 (.18) | -1.96 (7.51)*** |
| Degrees of Freedom | 1262 | 1259 | 1251 |
| Percent correctly predicted | 2.41 | 81.25 | 70.0 |
| Goodness of fit measure (Significance) | .40 | .71 | .42 |

The values in parentheses refer to the Wald statistic. The stars refer to the significance level of the Wald statistics which follows a chi-square distribution. *=significant at the .1 level. **=significant at the .05 level. ***=significant at the .01 level. The large observed significance level of the goodness of fit statistic indicates that this model does not differ significantly from the "perfect" model.

nificantly and positively connected to sympathizers of the two libertarian parties, that is the better educated a person, the more likely he or she is to sympathize with them. Against expectations, education is not significantly correlated with potential support for the FP. Instead, what distinguishes its sympathizers from those of the two libertarian parties is class and gender, which are both highly significant. This data show that potential support for the radical right in Austria is strongest among working-class males. This means that education is overshadowed by the importance of the variable class. This result contrasts sharply with earlier findings which saw FP support as "evenly spread over the entire occupational structure." While this might have been the case in the late 1980s, by the early 1990s, the radical right was on its way to becoming a working class party.[39]

To summarize, this analysis of the sociostructural data confirms that support for new parties in Austria closely follows a postindustrial logic. Support for the two libertarian parties is most likely to come from those groups whose sociostructural profile allows them to adapt most easily to postindustrialization or who are most likely to benefit from it. Support for the radical right is most likely to come from those groups whose sociostructural profile makes them particularly vulnerable to the pressures of postindustrial socioeconomic change. In what follows the link between sociostructural and sociocultural patterns is investigated.

The findings generally confirm expectations with respect to value cleavages. However, the results are far from clear cut. With respect to the battery of variables that measure libertarianism versus authoritarianism, only Green sympathizers are significantly in favor of more participatory democracy, whereas no clear pattern emerges for potential supporters of either the LiF or the FP. This is somewhat surprising. Surveys have found that a substantial majority of FP supporters are highly skeptical toward parliamentary democracy, preferring instead decisions to be "carried through swiftly by a strong man."[40] In a similar vein, it is only among Green sympathizers that the question of law and order evokes a statistically significant (negative) response. Given the fact that this item is a core measure of authoritarianism and that the fear of crime has been found to be a strong motive among supporters of right-wing parties such as the French Front National or the German Republikaner, the lack of significant concern among FP sympathizers is particularly notable.[41]

The one item which registers highly significantly for all three groups is xenophobia. The more opposed a person is to immigration, the more likely he or she is to sympathize with the FP, while the opposite is true for the two libertarian parties. The significance of these results leaves no doubt that attitudes toward the influx and presence of foreigners have a major influence on potential support for new parties in Austria. However, these findings do not support one of the major assumptions in the literature on the radical right, namely that "the themes of racism and cultural intolerance are embedded in broader right-wing political dispositions that are prominent among identifiable social groups."[42]

The two variables "too much state intervention" and "support for the European Union" were designed to measure the degree of neo-liberalism. Consistent with our expectations, both items register significantly with LiF sympathizers, while neither item seems particularly important for potential Green supporters. This is somewhat surprising given the party's strong opposition to Austrian membership in the EU. The same holds true for the FP, which in the early 1990s gradually abandoned its traditional support for EU membership to become its most vocal opponent. Surveys have shown, however, that FP supporters have been split on the question. This is also reflected in our unconclusive results. Finally, like potential LiF supporters, FP sympathizers are strongly and significantly opposed to state intervention. In view of the FP's radical, liberal economic program, this result might not be surprising. It is somewhat surprising, however, given the sociostructural base of potential FP support. Thus one might expect working class members to favor state intervention in order to protect jobs. This issue will be discussed later when the question of political alienation is entertained.

The two items "people are more important the money" and "environmentalism" measure attitudes relating to the materialism/post-materialism dimension. We find that persons who hold that money is more important than people (which we consider a strong materialist position), significantly favor the LiF or the FP. Surprisingly, however, potential support for the Green Party is not significantly correlated with the opposite (nonmaterialist) position. Not surprisingly, potential Green support is highly correlated with protection of the environment, even at the cost of job losses. Neither FP nor LiF sympathizers show a significant preference on this question.

Potential electoral support could be explained by factors other than the ones explored so far. Three of the most prominent alternative hypotheses that have been advanced to explain citizens' political preferences have been included herein. The literature on economic voting suggests that people's voting behavior is dependent on how individual voters are affected by economic conditions, that is, whether they are personally affected – the so-called "pocketbook voter" – or whether they take into consideration the economic conditions of the country as such – the so-called "socio-tropic voter." The survey provides two questions that relate to these concepts. However, neither economic variable is statistically significant. The third alternative hypothesis states that electoral behavior increasingly reflects voter protest. Voter protest is a result of growing alienation with respect to the established political parties and the political class in general.[43] The findings suggest that neither the potential supporters of the LiF nor those of the Greens are motivated by political alienation. Disenchantment, however, is clearly a major factor for those who sympathize with the Freedom Party, on a par with xenophobia.

The strong feelings of alienation and disenchantment with respect to the political class among FP sympathizers might also explain their pronounced opposition to state intervention. The German philosopher Max Scheler has argued that resentment arises when there is a "discrepancy" between the political or traditional status of a group and its "factual" power, particularly when it is confronted with "lasting situations which are felt to be injurious but beyond one's control—in other words, the more the injury is experienced as a destiny."[44] Thus, behind resentment is always a pronounced experienced of powerlessness. We would contend that FP sympathizers' opposition to state intervention is largely motivated by political resentment in response to the growing inability and unwillingness on the part of the government and political establishment to protect the individual against the effects of global economic change. This links political resentment to the second major factor motivating FP sympathizers—xenophobia. Immigrants serve as an almost perfect target for resentment. Not only are they the most visible symbols of a fundamentally changing world, but they very often also represent a low-skilled, blue-collar workforce doing jobs that the indigenous population no longer is prepared to perform. The devaluation of blue-collar work closes the gap between foreign and indigenous workers, providing, as it were, a dramatic illustration of the latter's status loss.

## Conclusion

Much of the recent literature on political change in advanced capitalist societies assumes that postindustrialization has a significant impact on both electoral choice and party politics. In this essay, we have attempted to develop a theoretical model that links sociostructural change with political change via sociocultural change and have tested it empirically. The results of this empirical study provide little support for the thesis that individualization and social fragmentation characteristic of postindustrial societies result in a progressive particularization of voting behavior. On the contrary, the case of Austria suggests that support for new parties is grounded in a combination of sociostructural and sociocultural factors that largely follow from the logic of postindustrial change.

However, the resulting patterns are far less pronounced than the theoretical framework would have led one to expect. Although electoral support does appear to be broadly grounded in value cleavages, these cleavages are far less consistent and coherent than the theoretical model used in this analysis would have suggested. Thus, while potential support with the LiF is significantly correlated with neo-liberal value positions, there is no significant link to social libertarian positions, despite the party's conscious programmatic appeal to these positions. Although education appears to become an increasingly important determinant of political choice, class still retains some of its predictive power. Additionally, while support for the two libertarian parties is largely grounded in left-libertarian and neo-liberal value patterns, support for the radical right is more an expression of protest than of consistent authoritarian dispositions. The growing political importance of working class resentment as a foundation for right-wing electoral success is among the most important findings of this case study.

If there is one central issue to postindustrial politics, it is immigration. This case study shows that the question of immigration is the only issue that is significant for the potential supporters of all three new parties. The reason is that immigration, perhaps more than any other issue, appeals to a wide range of different aspects of a new, value-based politics. For the libertarian left, it is part of a larger question of minority rights and multiculturalism; for neoliberals, immigration is inseparably connected to larger concerns about the free flow of goods and labor and about open markets while also resonating with more traditional concerns for individual and citizen rights; finally, for the radical right, immigration represents both a threat to traditional identities as well as a burden on an already overloaded welfare state.

It is hardly surprising that radical right-wing parties have used appeals to nationalism and latent racism as a way of manipulating the resulting need for psychological compensation. Recent studies on the evolution of the French Front National from a lower middle-class party into a predominantly working-class party and on the sociostructural and sociocultural profile of the Belgian *Vlaams Blok* come to similar conclusion. They suggest that working-class political alienation represents an important new political challenge to advanced capitalist democracies confronting the transition to postindustrialism.

The challenge is how to respond constructively to worker anxiety and disenchantment. In several West European democracies where radical right-wing populist parties have made significant gains during the past few years, the political class' official response has been to warn of the dangers of a revival of fascism. Not only has this response been largely ineffective, it has also failed to confront the fundamental reasons behind successful radical right-wing mobilization, which are largely related to the profound structural transformation engendered by postindustrialization and, increasingly, globalization. Those voicing their grievances and anxieties at the ballot box do so for rational reasons. As long as the established politicians are not prepared to address them effectively, postindustrial politics will remain far from benign.

## Appendix: Explanation of Data Interpretation

The survey was conducted in German. Here are our translations of the questions and the coding scheme of the variables.

The political preference variables were based on the following questions: "Could you imagine voting for the Liberal Party of Austria under the leadership of Jörg Haider in the next general election?" ("Freedom Party Vote"). Respondents could indicate either "yes" (1) or "no" (0). The leadership of Heide Schmidt ("Liberal Forum Vote") and the "Grün-Alternativen" under the leadership of Madeleine Petrovic ("Green Party Vote").

### *Structural Variables*

Males were coded 0, females were coded 1. "Age" is a continuous variable. The variable "income" represents net household income and is divided into eighteen groups from low to high income categories (1-18). The variable "education" consists of four categories: compulsory school (1), apprenticeship (2), junior college ("Matura") (3), and advanced university degree (4). The variable "working class" was derived from a question that asked respondents about their professional status. "Working class" is a composite index of respondents who indicated "worker" and "skilled worker and apprentice". This group was coded (1), while everybody else was coded (0). Of the 1525 responses, 505 put themselves into the categories "worker" and "skilled worker and apprentice."

*Authoritarian/Libertarian*

The variable "participatory democracy" consists of two statements. The first reads: "In the future it will be crucial that as many people as possible will participate in all areas of the public and economic sphere" (5). The second reads: "It's best if one person knows what's going on, who gives unmistakable commands, to which everybody subordinates him/herself" (1). Respondents were asked to place themselves on a five point scale (1 representing "complete agreement" with the first statement and 5 representing "complete agreement" with the second statement).

The "law and order" variable consists of a sixfold ranking to the following statement: "I would like to live in a society in which law and order are appreciated." Respondents were shown six cards which they had to rank in order. The card on top was considered to be the most important issue (1) while the card on the bottom the least important (6). Here are the other cards which were shown to the respondents (besides the "law and order" card): "I would like to live in a society in which traditional values are appreciated and respected", "I would like to live in a society in which all citizens participate in all decisions"; "I would like to live in a society in which effort will be rewarded"; "I would like to live in a society which is open for new ideas and change"; and lastly, "I would like to live in a society in which man is more important than money."

The variable "xenophobia" consists of two statements. The first reads: "Foreigners are not only necessary for our economy, they also enrich our daily life as a result of their different lifestyle." The second reads: "The many foreigners in Austria create not only disadvantages for Austrian workers, but also endanger our lifestyle." Respondents were asked to place themselves on a five point scale (1 representing "complete agreement" with the first statement and 5 representing "complete agreement" with the second statement).

*Neo-liberalism*

The variable "state interventionism" consists of two statements. The respondents were asked to place themselves on a five point scale where both ends meant "complete agreement." The first reads: "It is the state's obligation to intervene anywhere where there are problems and where people are hurting" (1). The second reads: "We already have too much state. Individuals should help themaselves through their own efforts" (5).

The variable "Pro-European Union" is based on the following question: "If there were a referendum in Austria next Sunday regarding whether Austria should join the European Union, how would you vote?" The respondents had four choices: "I would definitely vote for Austria to join the EU" (4); "I would rather vote for Austria to join the EU" (3); "I would rather not vote for Austria to join the EU" (3); or "I would definitely vote for Austria to not join the EU" (1).

*Materialism/Postmaterialism*

The variable "People are more important than money" is derived from a question which states: "I want to live in a society in which people count more than money." Respondents were asked to rank their preference on a scale from "most important" (1) to "least important" (6).

The variable "Environmentalism" consists of two statements. Respondents had to place themselves on a five point scale whereby 1 indicated "complete agreement" with the first statement and 5 indicated also "complete agreement" with the second statement which was the polar opposite of the first statement. The first statement reads: "In order to protect jobs we have to continue to bet on economic growth even if that will sometimes come at the cost of negatively affecting nature and the environment." The second reads: "In order to protect our nature and environment we have to distance ourselves from further economic growth, even if that means that might sometimes lead to problems of joblessness."

*Alternative Hypotheses*

The variable "personal economic situation" was derived from the following question: "Think about your future: What will your financial economic situation be in one year from today?" The answer key listed the following options: "very secure" (4), "rather secure" (3), "rather insecure" (2), and "very insecure" (1). The variable "economic situation of Austria" represents the respondents' attitudes to the following question: "Think for a moment about the Austrian economy: How do you feel about the Austrian economic situation?" The respondents had four choices: "very good" (4), "rather good" (3), "rather bad" (2), and "very bad" (1).

The variable "disenchantment with politics" was based on the following question: "How often do you feel that politics fails when dealing with decisive questions?" Respondents could choose between these answers: "all the time" (5), "sometimes" (3), "rarely" (2), "never" (1). The numbers in parentheses indicate the coding scheme.

## Notes

1. Seymour M. Lipset and Stein Rokkan, "Cleavage Structures, Party Systems, and Voter Alignments: An Introduction," in *Party Systems and Voter Alignments: Cross-National Perspectives* ed. Seymour M. Lipset and Stein Rokkan (New York: Free Press, 1967); Richard Rose and Derek W. Urwin, "Persistence and Change in Western Party Systems since 1945," *Political Studies* 18 (1970): 287-319.

2. Peter Mair, "Continuity, Change and the Vulnerability of Party," *West European Politics*, 12 (1989): 172.

3. Russell J. Dalton, Scott C. Flanagan and Paul Allen Beck, "Political Forces and Partisan Change," in *Electoral Change in Advanced Industrial Democracies: Realignment or Dealignment?* ed. Russell J. Dalton, Scott C. Flanagan and Paul Allen Beck (Princeton: Princeton University Press, 1984), 456; Scott C. Flanagan and Russell J. Dalton, "Parties under Stress: Realignment and Dealignment in Advanced Industrial Societies," *West European Politics* (1984): 11.

4. Jeff Manza, Michael Hout, and Clem Brooks, "Class Voting in Capitalist Democracies since World War II: Dealignment, Realignment, or Trendless Fluctuation?" *Annual Review of Sociology* 21 (1995): 137-162.

5. Manuel Castells, *The Rise of the Network Society* (New York: Blackwell, 1996).

6. C. T. Kurien, *Global Capitalism and the Indian Economy* (New Delhi: Orient Longman, 1995): 60.

7. Philip Cerny, "Globalization and the Changing Logic of Collective Action," *International Organization* 49 (1995): 613-616.

8. Dani Rodrik, *Has Globalization Gone To Far?* (Washington: Institute for International Economics, 1997), 11.

9. Daniel Bell, "The Third Technological Revolution," *Dissent* (Spring 1989): 168.

10. Ulrich Beck, "Jenseits von Stand und Klasse," *Merkur* 38 (1984): 485-497.

11. Ronald Inglehart, *Culture Shift in Advanced Industrial Society* (Princeton: Princeton University Press, 1990), 258-264; Oddbjørn Knutsen, "The Impact of Old Politics and New Politics Value Orientations on Party Choice—A Comparative Study," *Journal of Public Policy* 15 (1995): 1-63.

12. Peter Drucker, "Knowledge Work and Knowledge Society: The Social Transformations of This Century," Edwin L. Godkin Lecture, Harvard University, May 1995.

13. See Scott Flanagan, "Value Change in Industrial Society," *American Political Science Review* 81 (1987): 1303-1319; Herbert Kitschelt, *The Transformation of European Social Democracy* (Cambridge: Cambridge University Press, 1994), chapter one; Etienne Schweisguth, "Status Tension," in *The Impact of Values*, ed. Jan W. Van Deth and Elinor Scarbrough (London: Oxford University Press, 1995): 332-354.

14. Jan Pakulsi and Malcolm Waters, "The Reshaping and Dissolution of Social Class in Advanced Society," *Theory and Society* 25 (1996): 667-691.

15. Cees van der Eijk, Mark Franklin, Tom Mackie, and Henry Valen, "Cleavages, Conflict Resolution and Democracy," in *Electoral Change*, Mark Franklin, Tom Mackie, Henry Valen et al. (Cambridge: Cambridge University Press, 1992): 427, 430.

16. See Herbert Kitschelt, "Class Structure and Social Democratic Party Strategy," *British Journal of Political Science* 23 (1993): 299-337.

17. Flanagan and Dalton, "Parties under Stress," 12-13.

18. See Gøsta Esping-Andersen, "Postindustrial Class Structures: An Analytical Framework," in Gøsta Esping-Andersen, ed., *Changing Classes* (London: Sage, 1993), 17.

19. *Quarterly Economic Review 1982*, Annual Supplement, 5; *EIU Country Profile Austria 1990-1991*, 18.

20. See Fritz Scharpf, "Economic and Institutional Constraints of Full-Employment Strategies: Sweden, Austria, and Western Germany, 1973-1982," in *Order and Conflict in Contemporary Capitalism*, ed. John H. Goldthorpe (Oxford: Clarendon Press, 1984): 258.

21. Emmerich Tálos, "Gesellschaftsspaltung in Österreich?" in *Zweidrittelgesellschaft*, ed. Ehrenfried Natter and Alois Riedlsperger (Vienna: Europverlag, 1988): 71-103.

22. *OECD Economic Surveys: Austria* (Paris: OECD, 1995), 65.; see also Karl Aiginger, Rudolf Winter-Ebmer, and Josef Zweimüller, "Eastern European Trade and the Austrian Labor Market," *Weltwirtschaftliches Archiv* 132 (1996): 477-483.

23. See "Industrie erlebt radikalen Umbruch," *Der Standard*, 28 November 1996; "Österreich bleibt auf der Kriechspur," *Der Standard*, 1/2 February 1997.

24. See OECD, *OECD Economic Surveys:Austria* (Paris: OECD, 1997), 25, 113; by 1997, one sixth of the overall costs of pensions were spent on a record of more than 200,000 early retirees. See "Ein Sechstel aller Kosten entfällt auf Frührentner," *Der Standard*, 21/22 June 1997, 6.

25. "Das große Fressen," *Der Spiegel*, September 1997.

26. See, for example, "Drei Milliarden für arbeitslose Kellner," *Der Standard*, 15 November 1996, 25; "Keine Horrorquote von acht Prozent," *Der Standard*, 23 November 1996; "Hochsaison für Arbeitslosigkeit," *Der Standard*, 6 August 1997, 15.

27. "Die Ängste und Sorgen der Österreicher," "market" Institut für Meinungs- und Mediaforschung, Linz, March 1997.

28. The Pedersen index is the sum of the absolute differences in the percentages of votes for all parties between two consecutive elections divided by two. For Austria, see Christian Haerpfer, "Austria," in *Electoral Change in Western Democracies*, ed. Ivor Crewe and David Denver (New York: St. Martin's Press, 1985), 264-286; Frederick C. Engelmann, "The Austrian Party System: Continuity and Change," in *Parties and Party Systems in Liberal Democracies*, ed. Steve Wolinetz (London: Routledge, 1988): 84-104.

29. See Christian Haerpfer and Ernst Gehmacher, "Social Structure and Voting in the Austrian Party System," *Electoral Studies* 3 (1984): 25-46; Marcus Crepaz, "An Institutional Dinosaur: Austrian Corporatism in the Postindustrial Age," *West European Politics* 18 (1995): 64-88, see also *Austrocorporatism*, CAS III (1995).

30. Herbert Kitschelt, "Austrian and Swedish Social Democrats in Crisis," *Comparative Political Studies* 27 (1994): 6; for the party program see *Leitlinien grüner Politik* (Vienna: Impuls, 1990).

31. Hans-Georg Betz, *Radical Right-Wing Populism in Western Europe* (New York: St. Martin's Press, 1994), chapter four; for the party's program, see Jörg Haider, *Österreicherklärung zur Nationalratswahl 1994* (Vienna, 1994); also by Haider, *Vom Parteienstaat zur Bürgerdemokratie: Der Weg zur dritten Republik* (Vienna, no date).

32. Liberales Forum, *Das Programm*, Vienna, 1994; *Die offensive Mitte*, Vienna, 1996.

33. Fritz Plasser, "Die Nationalratswahl 1986: Analyse und politische Konsequenzen," *Österreichische Monatshefte* 42 (August 1986): 19; Fritz Plasser and Peter A. Ulram, "Abstieg oder letzte Chance der ÖVP" *Österreichische Monatshefte* 46 (July 1990): 8-9; Erich Neuwirth, "Statistische Wählerstromanalyse der Nationalratswahl 1994," in *Wählerverhalten und Parteienwettbewerb*, ed. Wolfgang C. Müller, Fritz Plasser, and Peter A. Ulram (Vienna: Signum, 1995), 461-462.

34. Fritz Plasser and Peter A. Ulram, "Konstanz und Wandel im österreichischen Wählerverhalten," in *Wählerverhalten und Parteienwettbewerb*, 18.

35. The survey is entitled "*Gesellschaftlicher Monitor*" (societal monitor). It was conducted by the polling institute of Dr. Fessel+GfK under the guidance of Professor Peter Ulram using a stratified, multi-stage, clustered random sampling method with a margin of error of +/- 2 percent. Included in the survey were men and women ages fourteen and above. We would like to thank Professor Ulram for providing us with the data set and allowing us to use it.

36. The last hypothesis is derived from a proposition advanced by Inglehart, *Culture Shift*, 277.

37. Dan D. Marshall, "Understanding Late-Twentieth-Century Capitalism: Reassessing the Globalization Theme," *Government and Opposition* 31 (1996): 206.

38. One the link between immigration and global socioeconomic change, see Hélène Pellerin, "Global Restructuring in the World Economy and Migration: The Globalization of Migration Dynamics," *International Journal* 48 (1993): 240-254; Jean-Pierre Garson and Agnès Puymoyen, "New Patterns of Migration," *The OECD Observer* 192 (1995): 8-12; Rodrik, *Has Globalization*, Chapter One.

39. Herbert Kitschelt, *The Radical Right in Western Europe* (Ann Arbor: University of Michigan Press, 1995): 190.

40. Election polls confirm this trend. Between 1986 and 1995, the percentage of blue- collar workers among the FPÖ electorate rose from 10 to 34 percent. In the 1996 European election, 50 percent of the working-class vote went to the radical right. See Plasser, Ulram, Neuwirth, and Sommer, 1995, p. 45; and Fritz Plasser, Peter A. Ulram, and Franz Sommer, *Analyse der Europawahl '96: Muster und Motive* (Vienna: Fessel+GfK, 1996): 30.

41. In 1993, 59 percent of FP supporters, but only 19 percent of the Austrian population agreed with this statement fully or in part. *SWS-Rundschau* 33 (1993): 483-484.

42. A recent survey found that, unlike Front National supporters, FP supporters were somewhat less concerned about falling victim to violent crime than was the average population. "Die Ängste und Sorgen der Österreicher," 4.

43. Kitschelt, *Radical Right*, 257.

44. Max Scheler, *Ressentiment* (New York: Schocken, 1961), 50.

# Book Reviews

## Brigitte Hamann: *Hitler's Wien: Lehrjahre eines Diktators* (Munich: R. Piper, 1996).

*Steven Beller*

Brigitte Hamann's book about the Vienna of Hitler's youth has been a great success since its publication, and deservedly so. It is now available in English, published by Oxford University Press, and it is, as Ian Kershaw's magisterial first volume of his Hitler biography attests, widely accepted as by far the best book on these formative years of "young Adolf" that has yet appeared. It is pointless to quibble with this assessment, because *Hitler's Wien* is an immense contribution to our understanding Hitler's early development, or, even more importantly, to our not misunderstanding what it was about Vienna that shaped Hitler so. It is also, apart from its central preoccupation with Hitler, a brilliant corrective to some of the rosier perspectives that have appeared over the last decades about *fin-de-siècle* Vienna and the joyously decaying Habsburg Monarchy.

That said, it has at its center an immense paradox about Hitler's relation to Vienna, which I am not sure Hamann can explain, even if she wanted to, namely that Hitler, living in a strongly anti-Semitic society and supporting rabidly anti-Semitic political leaders, was not, according to Hamann, himself anti-Semitic while in Vienna, and only became so after he had left the city. Vienna may have been an even more anti-Semitic environment than was previously thought, but Hitler's anti-Semitism was not Vienna-induced, and only came afterward, as a result of the war and the post-war turmoil, as Hitler was looking for something to mesh his diffuse views into a winning political platform (p. 502). Vienna was deeply anti-Semitic, but Hitler's (and by implication Nazism's) anti-Semitism was not Viennese in cause, even if it was in form. This paradox means that the book, no matter how many smaller questions of false rumor and supposition, legend and myth it is able to clear up, leaves us with another, even larger and more critical question left unanswered about the sources of Nazism and the Holocaust: if Hitler's anti-Semitism did not come from his youth and his experience in Vienna, where did it come from?

Hamann's suggested answer, that Hitler, emulating Karl Lueger, essentially adopted anti-Semitism after the war for practical, political purposes, is deeply unsatisfactory spiritually, but also intellectually, knowing what we do about Hitler's subsequent "career." Explaining Hitler is an arduous and gut-wrenching enough exercise without having to address the idea that the Holocaust, the intentional genocide of a whole people, has its origins in the pragmatic decision by a young politician that racial anti-Semitism was the most effective way of rallying a crowd. Hamann's explanation as to why Hitler chose falsely to project his anti-Semitism back to his time in Vienna, because this way his development would appear more 'organic' and hence more acceptable to biologistic and racist German nationalists also is not very convincing. Even if Hitler had come to his anti-Semitic views during the war, in the trenches, or as a result of his injuries and temporary blindness, I cannot understand why he would not have claimed this really rather heroic setting for his "revelation" about the role Jews played in world affairs. Surely this would have made his *Fronterlebnis* even more compelling.

Instead Hitler chose to stress in *Mein Kampf* the role Vienna played in prompting this "conversion", even though, as Hamann emphasizes and illustrates with impressively marshalled evidence, Hitler had Jewish business partners, Jewish discussion partners, and Jewish patrons. He even attended the musical salon of a Jewish family, the Jahodas, and was never reported by a credible witness as having uttered any anti-Semitic remarks, indeed, is reported as having said many positive things about the Jews (p. 498). If we do not accept Hamann's explanations of her paradoxical claims (a very anti-Semitic Vienna and a non-anti-Semitic Viennese Hitler), we are really left at a loss as to how to explain them. As posed by Hamann's book, these paradoxes probably cannot be satisfactorily resolved, but they can if we are not quite so absolute in our interpretation as the author herself is after reviewing the ample evidence which she has amassed so painstakingly and admirably. The solution to the paradox at the heart of this book is that there really is not as much of a paradox as Hamann thinks. This different, less rigid view of the evidence eventually makes more sense of Hamann's book than Hamann herself does, even if it is not quite so controversial, not so dramatic a conundrum, and indeed leads to rather a banal conclusion.

The one part of the conundrum, the quite horrifying context of the Vienna in which Hitler lived and "studied," with its dire poverty, political paralysis, racism and anti-Semitism, has rarely been depicted as well or as convincingly as here. The reader is very elegantly led through this dismal world by following Hitler's footsteps. First the provincial background and family background is related; then young Adolf's move to Vienna provides the occasion for an introduction to the world of Viennese modernism, and the fact that Hitler had barely anything to do with that world (except admiring Mahler's productions of Wagner at the opera). There follows a chapter on Vienna as the center of imperial power, and Hitler's frequent visits to the spectators' gallery of the parliament (*Reichsrat*) are the setting for Hamann's detailed and entertaining description of the complete paralysis of that body, caused by the nationalities' question, which she rightly sees as a formative experience for Hitler's estimate of parliamentary democracy. The failed art student's plunge into destitution is the occasion for a description of the dire social conditions in the Habsburg capital, and his eventual refuge in the *Männerheim* in Brigittenau, a bastion of social democracy, is used by Hamann to explore Hitler's attitudes towards the workers' movement and the "threat"of socialism. The best part of the book is Hamann's description of the thought, if we can call it that, of Hitler's ideological idols, those people whose books he was reading so assiduously while at the *Männerheim*. The life and work of Guido von List, Lanz von Liebenfels, Hanns Hörbiger, and others, is clearly, and mercilessly, summarized, producing a fine picture of just how crazy the "thinkers" of the Far Right in Vienna were. The one point where Hamann hits a false note is in her description of Otto Weininger. She recognizes that Weininger's thought is far more sophisticated than Hitler's interpretation of it, or indeed of most people's interpretation, but she still gets Weininger quite wrong. She does not quite grasp the distinction which Weininger was trying to make between sexual types (Man and Woman) and actual men and women; she completely misinterprets Weininger's attitude to emancipation; and she is too hasty to attribute his suicide to his supposed Jewish self-hatred. That aside, though, the chapter on racial thinkers and "world explainers" is excellent, and, strange to say, very funny, if one enjoys black comedy. The story related by Hamann of Lanz von Liebenfels desperately trying to make Julius Ofner, a Jewish politician whom he admired, of the "blond race" is only one of many surreal moments described in these pages.

Her chapter on Hitler's political role models is also of a very high standard. She provides accounts of Georg von Schönerer, Franz Stein, Karl Hermann Wolf, and Karl Lueger, which, taken together, produce a vivid and very depressing picture of what the political climate must have been like in Vienna during Hitler's time. Her handling of Lueger is especially good, making the point that, even if his anti-Semitism was indeed instrumental rather than meant, the opportunism involved makes Lueger's behavior even more reprehensible. She is also quite frank about the extreme violence of much of Lueger's rhetoric, as well as, described later in the book, the way in which it was Lueger and the Christian Socials, who in 1905-6, long before 1917, were equating Russian socialism with some sort of Jewish conspiracy. The book then proceeds to discuss the Czech presence in Vienna and the often violent response of both German Nationalists and Christian Socials to it, with a fascinating description of the crisis caused by a set of Viennese Czechs taking a tour of the "teutonic" Wachau in 1909. This is followed by chapters on the Jews and on Hitler's attitude toward women, before the book concludes with the narration of Hitler's last period in Vienna and his departure for Munich.

The chapter on Jews has its interesting moments, and is good on discussing anti-Semitic ideology in Vienna, but it is one of the less successful of the book, particularly when it comes to the position of Jews in Austrian and Viennese society, because it is clearly working without much knowledge of recent research. The roots of Theodor Herzl's Zionism are completely misunderstood, and the presence of "Russian" Jews in Austria and Vienna greatly exaggerated, as is the number of "assimilated and baptized" Jews (an interesting categorization in itself) who Hamann believes would have been added to the number of Jews in Vienna recorded by the census, which only counted "religious Jews" (*Glaubensjuden*). There actually were far fewer baptized Jews than one might think, and the extent of intermarriage was also rather low in absolute numbers, making the numbers of those of Jewish descent also not as high as some have assumed. Hamann does speak admiringly of the Viennese-Jewish "symbiosis" which she sees as so important to Vienna's becoming such an important center of modernist culture, but at times she lapses into a phraseology which in current academic debates might cause eyebrows to be raised. She writes of assimilation having almost produced a "solution" for the Jewish Problem in Vienna; freely writes of *Ostjuden* and *Westjuden*; describes the liberal politician, Eduard Suess, as a *Halbjude*, and Albert Gessmann, Lueger's right-hand man, as a *getaufter Jude*. Gessmann may well have been partially of Jewish descent, but he was not a Jew who had been baptized, even if we allow for the phrase "baptized Jew" to make any sense at all. She exhibits, in other words, something of a tin ear when it comes to modern sensibilities about anti-Semitism and the Jewish Question.

The problems with the chapter on Jews are exceptional, however, in a book which overall is a major contribution to the historical understanding of pre-war Vienna and the roots of Nazi ideology there, which is compelling to read, and which is generally an excellent work of history. This is despite (some might say because of) the fact that Hamann's endnotes and bibliography show a breathtaking disregard for most of the recent historiography of "Vienna 1900." This might be because, in a work such as this, the emphasis is either on primary and contemporary sources, or on keeping the distractions of scholarship to a minimum. Nevertheless, it is rather odd to see a chapter about pre-war Austrian politics which does not cite one modern Austrian scholar, or not to see in a book about the seamier side of Vienna any citations from the collection *Glücklich ist, wer vergisst?* That book has its flaws, but it was one of the first to pioneer the theme of which Hamann's book also makes much: the sheer nastiness of life for so many of turn-of-the-century Vienna's inhabitants.

The relative absence of Austrian historiography might be explained by Hamann's at times strained relationship with academic historians in her adopted country, where she is known mainly as a writer of books about the Habsburgs rather than as a "historical scientist." The easiest way to explain the scarcity of references to recent scholarship on "Vienna 1900" in the English-speaking world is the fact that this is a book written in German for a German-reading audience, but it is nevertheless striking how little Hamann has taken advantage of the rather extensive body of anglophone research now available on subjects relevant to her topic. Lueger, for instance, is discussed with a passing reference to Richard Geehr, but none at all to John Boyer's work. Carl Schorske is cited once, on Herzl, but there are no references to the various works on Viennese Jewry, such as those by Robert Wistrich, nor are there many to the various articles and books published in English which have dealt directly with the issues Hamann addresses. The excellent essay by Ivar Oxaal, "The Jews of Young Hitler's Vienna: Historical and Sociological Aspects" is absent, even though it is available in German; even more unfortunately, while J. Sydney Jones's *Hitler in Vienna* is cited, the far superior study by William Jenks, *Vienna and the Young Hitler*, is not, even though it takes an approach which anticipates Hamann in very many ways.

At times, this lack of sufficient grounding in the current state of academic research does affect the quality of Hamann's work. The examples given above of her misunderstanding of Weininger, and her rather clumsy and inaccurate handling of the chapter on Jews, subjects on which I have more specialized knowledge than on other subjects in the book, suggest to me that specialists in those other areas might make similar criticisms of Hamann's treatment of those topics. On the other hand, the overall effect of the book remains a most powerful one, which leads to a conclusion, uncomfortable for an academic historian, that perhaps detailed knowledge of current historiography and methodological theory is not as important as a diligent ferreting in the sources and the ability to tell a story well. What Hamann has indubitably achieved is showing once and for all that everything that the later Führer had to say about the German *Volk*, the Aryan race, and the threat from world Jewry, could have been obtained from his studies of the Viennese anti-Semitic press, and that Vienna did indeed, with its examples of Schönerer, Wolf, Lueger and company, provide an excellent apprenticeship for a future racist demagogue.

Yet, Hamann states, Hitler was not an anti-Semite when he was in Vienna. He was a German nationalist, a racist, an anti-clerical, a hater of the socialists and of the, for him, supranational racial mixing of the Habsburg Monarchy; but he said nice things about Jews, was not reliably reported to have said anything anti-Semitic, had Jewish friends, and dealt with Jewish customers and business partners. How does one square the context of a very nasty anti-Semitic context with this apparent lack of any impact of all this anti-Semitic rhetoric and ideology on Hitler's own views, before about 1918?

The explanation lies in the fact that, closely seen, the second part of the conundrum is not nearly as well proven as the first, and is, in any case, not as absolutely at odds with the idea of a strongly anti-Semitic Viennese context, or even with Hitler's own account of his becoming anti-Semitic. Hamann really never proves that Hitler was not anti-Semitic, she simply shows that there is no direct evidence that he was. Her main evidence for saying so is, as already related, that he sold his pictures with the help of Jews and to Jewish dealers in frames, and was also reported by the few sources which she deems reliable as having said some complimentary things about Jews, the Jewish religion, the Jewish race, and the Jewish ability to survive (p. 239-42, 496-503). The bulk of this evidence comes from the account of Reinhold Hanisch, who was Hitler's first business partner, but whom Hitler denounced to the police in the spring of 1910 after deciding that Hanisch was ripping him off. Hamann rejects the evidence of August Kubizek, Hitler's closest friend in Linz and in his first year in Vienna, that Hitler was already anti-Semitic when he came to Vienna, because she supposes that Kubizek was trying, after the war, to blame his own anti-Semitism on his erstwhile friend. She is probably correct in this supposition; obversely, though, she accepts Hanisch's testimony at face value, despite recognizing that Hanisch's interest was in discrediting the, by that time (1939), fiercely anti-Semitic Hitler, his old enemy. She may be correct here too, although it is also likely that Hanisch at least colored his account to put Hitler in the worst (most non-anti-Semitic) light he could. If we assume that Hanisch is reliable, then two points need to be made: Hanisch's account of Hitler only goes up to the spring of 1910, when Hanisch and Hitler fell out, and many of the remarks which Hitler is reported by Hanisch as making can very easily be given an anti-Semitic interpretation. The idea that Jews had a different smell; that the scions of Jews are often radical, with terroristic tendencies; and that according to the Talmud, Jews could unfairly exploit Gentiles without punishment, are not exactly philo-Semitic, and are indeed classic weapons in the anti-Semite's ideological armory. It is true that another witness, the "Brünner anonymous" confirms that in 1912 Hitler still consorted with many Jews in the *Männerheim* and reports him as saying that "the Jews were a clever people [*Volk*], who held together better than the Germans," but again, this last statement is deeply ambivalent, confirming at least two deeply held anti-Semitic beliefs about Jewish "cleverness" and Jewish racial solidarity. Hamann's own evidence about Hitler's views on Jews is thus not as clear as she thinks concerning Hitler's not having said anything anti-Semitic.

Hamann's evidence is also, odd though this may seem, largely compatible with what Hitler had to say about his own conversion to an anti-Semitic worldview. Hitler did not claim to have always been an anti-Semite; instead, he stated that he became one when confronted with the evidence provided by the Jewish role in Viennese culture, society, and socialist politics. One can actually doubt whether, as a German Nationalist from his youth in Linz, he was quite as free of anti-Semitic prejudice as he claimed in *Mein Kampf*, but it is quite possible that he had not straightened out in his mind the various superstitious and bigoted beliefs about Jews which a boy of his background, from Austrian Catholic, peasant stock, would have almost inevitably possessed. As an admirer of Gustav Mahler, he, like the first wave of German Nationalists, might have thought assimilated, acculturated Jews as having somehow overcome their Jewishness. He might have thought himself as, therefore, not anti-Semitic when he arrived in Vienna, as he indeed claimed. According to his own timetable in *Mein Kampf*, it took Hitler roughly two years for his liberal "heart" to be overcome by the rational arguments of his "head" and for him to adopt an anti-Semitic worldview. His attendance at the musical salon of an assimilated Jew, Rudolf Jahoda, in 1908 is not therefore at all surprising, because Hitler, on his own admission, was not yet "anti-Semitic." It was only, Hitler claimed, after a confrontation with a kaftanned, traditionalist Jew, that he realized for the first time that Jews were not Germans at all, but rather of a completely different race. It was this fact which then made him look at Viennese society anew, and, after many spiritual struggles, find the Jewish involvement in that society ubiquitous and pernicious. The story of the kaftanned Jew might be completely apocryphal, but much of the rest of Hitler's story is actually confirmed by Hamann's account. She does see him as preoccupying himself with the Jewish Question in his reading at the *Männerheim*, and Hitler's own account of an internal struggle would also be reflected in his having read not only anti-Semitic but also philo-Semitic literature. Moreover what Hamann sees as inconsistencies in Hanisch's reporting of Hitler's views on Jews could also be evidence of Hitler's own inconsistencies, of his own inner struggle. What is clear, though, is that by this time Hitler did, as he claimed in *Mein Kampf*, think of Jews as being a separate race, a crucial step by his own account on the way to his anti-Semitism. Hitler might have been inaccurate about the time it took for his anti-Semitism to congeal, but Hanisch's evidence does not in itself mean much except that it delays the completion of Hitler's slow conversion until past April 1910, that is, by a few months.

There remain Hitler's business contacts with Jews after this date, the evidence that he was "getting on well with Jews" in 1912, and that his later friend, Rudolf Häusler, did not notice any pronounced anti-

Semitism in Hitler in the period just before their joint move to Munich. These points should certainly give us pause in completely accepting Hitler's version of events, but even they do not contradict it all that much. That Hitler had become dependent on Jews for selling and buying his paintings is deeply ironic, but this would not have been the first time that an anti-Semite had been forced to deal with Jews in the business world, and, if I am right about Hitler having basic prejudices against Jews from his Austrian provincial background, then the psychology of dependence on members of what should be an alien and inferior group is itself a possible explanation for the exacerbation of such resentments into a more visceral hatred, all the more potent for having been repressed. After all, given that the people on whom he depended at the time for keeping his head above water, his business partners and customers, were Jews, it would be rather surprising if he had not repressed any anti-Semitic feelings and kept such thoughts to himself when trying to sell his work and when taking part in the discussions in the hostel, where his Jewish business associates were present and listening.

This is speculation, and it may well be that Hitler had indeed not reached the radical conclusions about a Jewish world conspiracy that later marked his apocalyptic thinking. Häusler's claim that Hitler was not noticeably anti-Semitic tends to lead to this conclusion. The question I have here, though, is when does anti-Semitism become so extreme as to be noticeable? Hamann herself quotes Franz Joseph as saying: "*Ja, ja, man tut natürlich alles, um die Juden zu schützen, aber wer ist eigentlich kein Antisemit?*" Her point is to cast doubt on the emperor being actually philo-Semitic, but it is in any case, as her book amply shows, a very good question. Who indeed was not anti-Semitic in Vienna, especially in the sort of circles that Hitler moved? What would truly have been remarkable was if Hitler had *not* had any anti-Semitic prejudices, as he claims. That he was not pronouncedly anti-Semitic might well be explained by the fact that anti-Semitism of a basic kind was virtually omnipresent, except among Jews (and even then not always).

It would have been quite possible, moreover, for Hitler to have had anti-Semitic ideas and to have had "friendly" discussions with Jews about them, especially if the Jews involved, rejecting the assimilatory assumptions of the liberal Jewish establishment, had believed in the distinct nature of the Jews as a group, whether from religious or more "national" grounds. After all, Hitler's belief in the

Jews as a separate race, and his fears, derived from the thought of Guido von List, of racial miscegenation, would have allowed him to argue sympathetically with Jews who held Zionist beliefs about the need for Jews to separate from German society and found their own state. Hamann recounts a debate Hitler had with Neumann at the hostel in which Neumann, perhaps to tease Hitler but perhaps as part of a serious discussion of Zionism, claimed that if the Jews really left Austria this would be bad for the Austrian economy because they would take all their capital with them. Hitler responded by saying that this would not happen, because the money, being Austrian and not Jewish, would be confiscated before the Jews left. Neumann made a joke then about the coffeehouses in the Leopoldstadt, at least, suffering loss of custom, and perhaps this was a "jovial" discussion, but I think it does say something about Hitler's state of mind, and the sort of discussions he was having with his Jewish "friends," that he was discussing the exodus of the Jews from Austria and contemplating the confiscation of property of those Jews leaving. In this context, it is worth noting that Hitler in *Mein Kampf* claims to have had confirmation of the "national character of the Jews" from none other than the Zionists.

The evidence thus does not really point to Hitler not having any anti-Semitic views in Vienna, as Hamann supposes. Rather, Hitler appears as someone who has quite accepted the German nationalist, anti-Semitic claim that Jews are indeed a separate race, and that, therefore, they have no place in a truly pure, German society, which must have been Hitler's ideal. In the dismal reality of the polyglot, multi-racial, melting pot Vienna, Hitler might have reckoned that it was acceptable to deal with Jews, who, as individuals, seemed decent enough. He would not have been the only Viennese anti-Semite to use this somewhat casuistic logic at the time; Lueger, an idol, was a good role model here. He would not have been so stupid as to jeopardize his livelihood by antagonizing his Jewish acquaintances unnecessarily, so he phrased his basically anti-Semitic and racist views in ambivalently complimentary ways, stressing for instance his admiration for the ability of the Jews (Jewish race) to survive over the millennia, or comparing Jewish racial discipline favorably with that of the Germans, or, again, stressing Jewish intellectuality as an admirable strategy for giving Jews superiority over the less educated, naive Germans. He could also dismiss ritual murder allegations as superstitious nonsense (because it was), and it did not take too much to defend Heinrich

Heine's right to be respected, or to claim to regard Jacques Offenbach and (the baptized) Felix Mendelssohn-Bartholdy as examples proving that Jews could be artists, especially if this was during the time when he was still "struggling" with his anti-Semitic conclusions. It might be the case that Hitler, though clearly a racist, clearly a staunch German Nationalist and hater of socialist internationalism, did not care as much about the anti-Semitism that all his favorite ideologues and politicians, without exception, shared. Why then, as Hamann stresses, did he spend so much time studying the Jewish Question, even if he consulted pro-Jewish works as well?

It is possible that Hitler was misleading his readers in *Mein Kampf* by claiming that his anti-Semitic worldview was fixed by the time he left Vienna. It might be that he shortened his chronology somewhat (although I still do not see why he needed to do so), but the evidence presented by Hamann actually confirms his account in *Mein Kampf* more than it disproves it, and it certainly shows Hitler to have been well on the way to seeing the Jews as a group which should not exist within German society (and this was after all, the position, expulsion, which the National Socialists held until the beginning of the Second World War). When Hitler left Vienna in 1913, much of his later anti-Semitic ideology was already in place. His experience in the war and its catastrophic aftermath might well have radicalized his views, as it did those of so many others. It would have been strange if it had not. Only when he embarked, by "inspiration" or accident, on his career as politician was he forced to articulate his views in a more or less coherent way. It was then that he used a radical form of racial anti-Semitism as the cement of his views, but there is no convincing reason to think that he had not already started on the path to this conclusion during his time in Vienna.

Much as Hamann in effect maintains that Hitler, despite the Viennese context she describes so well, remains a German and not an Austrian problem, the signposts pointing to the roots of Hitler's racial anti-Semitism point very much at Vienna, not Germany. It was not only the rhetoric of Viennese anti-Semitism which Hitler employed to make his mark as a politician. One of the reasons he was able to use it so well is the simple fact that he actually believed in it, and had done so for quite some years, from his time as a destitute painter of postcards in Vienna. The ideology he shaped and helped to power with such evil consequences, Nazism, remains as much an Austrian problem as it does a German one.

# Peter Katzenstein, ed., *Mitteleuropa: Between Europe and Germany* (New York: Berghahn Books, 1997).

*Lonnie Johnson*

Eric Hobsbawn, with his customary wit, recently has observed that "the tradition which regards Europe not as a continent but as a club, whose membership is open only to candidates certified as suitable by the club committee, is almost as old as the name 'Europe:'"[1] Analogously, the members of the most influential European club today, the European Union (EU), determine the rules of membership for their Europe: who gets in, who is on the waiting list, and who stays out. At the beginning of 1989, who would have imagined that the old western European club would be making territorial gains in the East—with German unification or the accession of Austria, Sweden, and Finland to this club in 1995—or seriously draw up criteria for accepting new members, such as the ten states of "Central and Eastern Europe" or Cyprus, Malta, and Turkey? Furthermore, did anyone seriously consider the enlargement of NATO even as a policy development scenario before the revolutions of 1989?

Peter Katzenstein had edited an interesting book, *Mitteleuropa: Between Europe and Germany*,[2] which addresses the problems of the position of Germany in Europe and central Europe since 1989, on the one hand, and informs readers about the problems of transition in four Central European states (Poland, the Czech Republic, Slovakia, and Hungary), on the other. The historical presence and interest of Germany in "the East" and issues of bilateral political and economic relationships provide a common core for these four country studies, which also are thematically interrelated insofar as they address the role of German models of privatization, social welfare and corporatism in their discussions of post-1989 developments. A fine article on the rise and fall of the central European cooperation of the Visegrad group concludes this collection of articles.

Katzenstein is fully aware of the problematic nature and nebulous status of the concept of central Europe (or *Mitteleuropa*) and points out in his Introduction to this volume that "... there is no agreement about where it starts precisely, and where it ends."[3] The absence of an independent article on Austria in this *Mitteleuropa* volume may be a source of concern to some Austrianists or Austrians, who could argue that the Austrian concept of *Mitteleuropa* was and is substantially different than the German one. Furthermore, there are concepts of Central Europe that may exclude Germans, Austrians, or both, from being bona fide Central Europeans, too.[4]

Valerie Bunce, in his article "The Visegrad Group: Regional Cooperation and European Integration in Post Communist Europe," is a bit more terminologically exacting, when he distinguishes between central European states for the sake of his presentation (Poland, Hungary, and Czechoslovakia, or the Czech and Slovak republics after 1993), central Europe in "geographical terms" (add Germany, Austria, Rumania, Bulgaria, the five successor states of the former Yugoslavia, Albania, and Greece); "eastern Europe" as an "expansive term" (include the Baltic states, Belarus, Ukraine, Moldova, and Russia); and "Eastern Europe" in terms of the Communist period (subtract all of the successor states of the USSR and leave Poland, Czechoslovakia, Hungary, Rumania, Bulgaria, plus add Yugoslavia and Albania).[5] It is perhaps worth noting—and this is an issue we shall return to—that none of the above definitions correspond to the states of "Central and Eastern Europe" as defined by the European Union. This "policy region" initially consisted of three states (Poland, Czechoslovakia, and Hungary) that sought association with the EU in 1991; it subsequently was increased to six states (to include applications by the Czech Republic, Slovakia, Rumania, and Bulgaria in 1993) and then to ten (by the addition of Slovenia, Estonia, Latvia, and Lithuania in 1995). In 1994-96, all ten of the these "associated" states formally applied to join the EU, and in 1998 the EU concluded "Accession Partnerships" with them. The EU frequently uses the acronym CEEC: "Central and Eastern European countries."[6]

Katzenstein is especially sensitive to the German connotations of *Mitteleuropa* and knows that the ghosts of Friedrich Naumann and

Adolf Hitler associatively lurk behind the German term of *Mitteleuropa* for many central Europeans. However, he also recognizes that the Federal Republic of Germany has the capacity to play a leading role in promoting the enlargement of the European Union, and that it—in virtue of its size, political and economic potential, and regional interests—more than any other EU member state will determine the pace of the integration of central European states into the European Union.[7] Katzenstein is undoubtedly correct when he notes that "[m]ultilateral regimes are inhibiting unilateral German initiatives along the lines of traditional power politics."[8] The "Europeanization of Germany," the anchoring of the Federal Republic of Germany in the processes of European integration, undoubtedly will go down in history as on of Helmut Kohl's great political achievements; the "Germanization" of Europe or central Europe are fears that the success of European integration has dispelled to a great extent. As long as the countries of central Europe are not in the EU, they are going to look to Germany, Katzenstein maintains, and Germany is going to be the driving force in enlargement, which will make them look to Germany once again.

As the easternmost representatives of the European Union in central Europe and the maintainers of the integrity of the EU's "external frontier" (of "*Schengenland*"[9]), Germany and Austria have a number of common interests. (There is an excellent analysis of the consequences of restrictive German and EU asylum immigration policy for the "Europeanization" of Polish migration policy in this volume, which illustrates to what extent the states of central Europe have been compelled to "import" western policies and have begun to serve as a buffer zone for asylum seekers and (illegal) immigrants for the EU.)[10] In political terms, the enlargement of the European Union is an issue of equally high priority on German and Austrian policy agendas because it effects their immediate frontiers and neighbors. On a *per capita* basis, Austria has been just as important as Germany as an economic player in central Europe. However, the fact that Austria is approximately one-tenth the size of Germany puts its relative economic clout into perspective.

In light of Austria's accession to the European Union on 1 January 1995 along with Finland and Sweden, Austria has participated fully in the processes of European integration, but it has waffled on the issue of NATO membership. Austria's declaration of permanent neutrality in 1955 was a product of the Cold War, and neutral Austria played an indisputably important role in a divided Europe up until 1989. Since then, however, Austrian neutrality has become meaningless for all practical purposes—there really is no one left to be "neutral against" —and those Austrian politicians, predominantly Social Democrats, who are determined to hold on to Austrian neutrality as long as possible, have prevented Austria from participating fully in the process of NATO enlargement. In this respect, Austrian integration into western European security arrangements, despite its membership in NATO's Partnership for Peace program, is incomplete.

Are Germany's neighbors to the east and southeast worried about burgeoning German influence; should they be? Indeed, the historical relationships of the states of central Europe to Germany vary considerably. The "weight of the memories of past German policies," Katzenstein notes, are "less powerful in Poland than in the Czech Republic, and virtually absent in Hungary and the Slovak Republic."[11] Reconciliation is a classic bilateral issue, and German-Polish reconciliation has been an ongoing, if somewhat intermittent, process since the initiation of West German *Ostpolitik* in the 1970s. Although the claims of German expellees and the status of indigenous German minorities in Poland are sensitive issues, they have been managed judiciously.

The issue of historical memory is more problematic with the Czech Republic, because neither Czechs nor Germans had an opportunity to address openly the problems of their more recent common history and crimes (1918-1948) before 1989. In early 1990, the newly appointed Czechoslovak ambassador to the United States, Rita Klímová, also expressed her concerns that a "Germanization of Central and Eastern Europe" could be executed using "the peaceful and laudable methods of market economics" and that "the German-speaking parts of Europe, including Austria, may succeed, where the Habsburgs, Bismarck, and Hitler failed."[12] Perhaps this is a particularly Czech historical reflex. Czech prosperity ultimately will depend—as the prosperity of Austria and other smaller neighboring states of Germany do—on the extent to which Germany becomes its most important export market and trading partner in terms of imports. In their contribution to Katzenstien's *Mitteleuropa* volume, two Czech scholars, Hynek Jerabek and Frantisek Zich, address the structural as well as psychological and historical problems of the renewed German presence as investors in the Czech Republic (with case studies of the Volkswagen-Skoda deal and German participation in the privatization and internationalization of media), and the outline the problem of the German presence, expulsion, and subsequent claims in the Czech borderlands (before the joint Czech-German reconciliation statement of 1997).

German banks of the present do not have the same ominous imperial presence as German tanks of the past, and in light of the introduction of the Euro on January 1, 1999, one may legitimately ask how "national" any one European national economy, banking community, or currency really is. The German deutsche mark virtually has ceased to exist, along with the currencies of the ten other EU member states participating in the Euro, and all of these currencies will factually disappear with the introduction of new notes and coins in 2002. The dynamics of old German national economic imperialism were relatively clear; the dynamics of the type of asymmetrical relationships and dependencies which the European Union (or "Euroland") has created or will create with the states of Central and Eastern Europe are not as transparent.

## Mitteleuropa's Treatment of Individual Countries

Although all professional anti-Communists in the West before 1989 believed in the superiority of the political and economic formula of "democracy plus capitalism" and ultimately were convinced that this combination would prevail over communism, no one in the West expected the victory of capitalist democracy to be as sudden and as complete as it was. Consequently, no one in the West really bothered to seriously think about possible models for the transition from socialism "back" to capitalism, and much of the theoretical work that has been done since 1989 is *post facto*: attempting to find models for what is actually happening under the broad concept of "transition" which has been displaced by the concept of "transformation."[13] The contribution about Poland in this volume does a fine job of describing the reorganization of the political landscape of Poland since 1989, especially with reference to the role of the Roman Catholic Church, and it elaborates on how "transformative corporatism" has arisen to cope with the problems of simultaneous democratization, liberalization, and marketization. The Polish experiment with neo-liberalism was short-lived, and corporatism appears to have become the model for negotiating transition. Although the corporatist players in central Europe may have the same names—representatives of organized labor and agriculture, industry and management, and the state—the game rules of post-socialist societies and assets of post-socialist economies are substantially different from those of western Europe. Transformative corporatism "... takes into account both conflictual societal interests and the need for a modicum of social peace, ... [in a] fundamental process of bargaining between states and interest groups and strives to integrate states with markets."[14] The authors of this contribution are of the opinion that Poland is in the process of developing a "distinctive form of political economy that resembles some of the main features of European polities without duplicating them."[15]

In his article on post-socialist transition in Hungary, Péter Gedeon distinguishes between the domestic needs and interests driving the transition toward capitalism and the relative influence of German, European, and international organizations as constraining and enabling agents on domestic political and economic actors in the realms of privatization, social policy, and monetary policy. Gedeon emphasizes the difference between the principle desirability of emulating the institutional models of Western economic and social policies and the prospects of realistically being able to do so under post-socialist circumstances characterized by scare resources, austerity, and uncertainty. He also predicts that there will be a substantial disparity between intentions and outcomes in terms of the evolution of institutional structures and policies and assumes that "the process of post-socialist transformation aiming to emulate the existing model of Western modernity will take an idiosyncratic form."[16]

The economies and the institutions central European states will get undoubtedly will be different than the ones that they want, or, as Gedeon observes: "Policies in the post-socialist transition are shaped by the presence or absence of institutional reform." Although "during the first years of the transition the existing circumstances did not require ... a direct adaptation to EU policy standards,"[17] this situation also has changed dramatically in the interim. The EU is has assumed a substantial role in the process of institutional reform in the states of "Central and Eastern Europe." The prerequisites of accession to the European Union include more than "the stability of institutions guaranteeing democracy, the rule of law, human rights, and respect for and protection of minorities; the existing of a functioning market economy; [and] the capacity to cope with competitive pressure and market forces within the Union ..."[18] They also require accession seekers to bring domestic institutions, policies, laws, and regulations into line with the so-called *acquis communautaire*: roughly 80,000 pages of EU law and code. Institutional reform something the "five new *Länder*" of the Federal Republic of Germany were spared for the most part, because west German institutions, laws, and code were introduced more or less *en bloc* in the former GDR in the course of unification—is in many respects the biggest task of transformation, not only because it is so far reaching, but also because it ultimately determines the prospects of democratization and marketization. According to the EU, the satisfactory adoption of the *acquis* is a prerequisite of accession, and this clearly places the burden of externally dictated institutional reform on the shoulders of the countries seeking accession.

Valerie Bunce's article on the rise (1990-1993) and decline (1993-1996) of Visegrad cooperation is a particularly informative piece. Visegrad cooperation had its initial roots in a "strong interest in regional cooperation expressed by the new leaders of the region, high uncertainty and shared fears [of the USSR before and Russia after 1991], a clear agenda for regional action and strong support for such regional initiatives expressed by the European Community" as well as shared experiences of protest before 1989 and expectations and agendas for transformation shortly thereafter.[19] Bunce identifies a number of different variables, all of which fed into the demise of regional cooperation, including the break up of Czechoslovakia; Slovak-Hungarian tensions on economic and minority issues; the fact that cooperation and being lumped together with other "Eastern European" states such as the Baltic states and Rumania and Bulgaria would not contribute to their objectives of full membership in the EU or NATO; and actions and statements by Western governments and institutions that have encouraged individualistic approaches. Post-socialist solidarity among the states of "Eastern Europe" has been replaced by processes of political and economic differentiation, and the EU, in turn, has made it perfectly clear that each accession candidate will be judged upon the basis of its individual accomplishments, merits, and credibility.

Furthermore, the list of top contenders among the ten states of "Central and Eastern Europe" has changed in recent years. Poland, the Czech Republic, Slovakia, and Hungary indisputably were the four original leaders, until Vladimir Meciar led the Slovak Republic on a peculiar *Sonderweg* that led away from "Europe," but otherwise nowhere. (The contribution on Slovakia in *Mitteleuropa* does a fine job of providing the reader with insights into the problems and peculiarities of the Slovak situation and argues that the processes of transformation there have been much more successful than generally recognized.) In July 1997, the EU published individual "opinions" on the progress the ten accession candidates had made toward fulfilling the political, economic, and institutional criteria for accession, and these opinions were updated by "reports" in November 1998. In the course of 1998, the EU also divided the ten contenders of "Central and Eastern Europe" into two different groups: five "pre-accession" states that have been invited to begin negotiations on accession (the Czech Republic, Estonia, Hungary, Poland, and Slovenia) and the rest (Bulgaria, Estonia, Lithuania, Romania and Slovakia), who have been promised that they may qualify to be brought into the ranks of the "first wave" applicants. In global terms, Hungary appears to lead the first wave states, along with the Czech Republic and Poland, followed by Slovenia and Estonia. Slovakia is obviously gaining ground and improving its position as the lead second wave state—and its prospects have improved since Meciar's departure from power in 1998. It is followed by Latvia and, finally Bulgaria and Romania.[20]

Furthermore, the enlargement of the European Union is not an issue upon which the current fifteen member states currently agree. Benefactors of the current EU subsidies scheme (in the south) are not especially interested in competing for EU subsidies with the states of "Central and Eastern Europe," and the taxpayers of EU member states (in the north), who are paying directly more into EU coffers than they are getting back in the form of EU programs or subsidies, are becoming increasingly restive with their net losses.[21] In other words, Mediterranean Europe has no pressing interest in the enlargement of the EU, and the rest of Europe is reticent about paying for it. As a result the earliest possible date for the beginning of enlargement is pushed back farther. The major problem is that the European Union must reform itself—especially in terms of its agricultural policy and subsidies practicesbefore it has the capacity to absorb new members, and this is contingent upon the timely realization of the so-called "Agenda 2000"—the EU's structural, political, and fiscal plan for 2001-2006. Enlargement may well have to wait.

## Difficulties with Definitions

Where was or where is central Europe or Central Europe? In his recent magisterial history of Europe, Norman Davies has pointed out that "Central Europe," like the "Heart of Europe" is truly an elusive concept, of which he ultimately disapproves.[22] In terms of cultural and historical regions, central Europe undoubtedly belongs to that part of Europe which was drawn into the sphere of the Roman Catholic form of Christianity in the early Middle Ages, as opposed to the Byzantine-Orthodox sphere of the Christian world in southeastern, and later, in eastern Europe. Although this cultural fault line between the Roman West (western Christendom) and the Orthodox East was exceptionally fluid—and additionally further blurred by Uniate churches as an East-West or "hybrid" from of Christianity—it roughly corresponded to the fluctuating eastern frontiers of Poland-Lithuania and the eastern and southern frontiers of the Kingdom of Hungary. If one is prepared to use ethnic, linguistic, confessional, and denominational diversity as primary categories of defining European culture, the crescent along this frontier from L'viv in the western Ukraine to Dubrovnik on the Adriatic *was* perhaps the most European part of Europe.

This frontier of Catholic Central Europe corresponds, in turn, more or less to the historical patterns of a "German presence" in the region (up until their expulsion at the end of World War II), ranging from the activities of the Teutonic Knights and the Hanseatic League in the Baltic, to German burghers in Polish towns and cities or German-speaking Jews, and including the "Saxons" of Transylvania, the "Schwabians" in the Danube Valley between Budapest and Belgrade, or the (former) German linguistic islands in Slovenia and Croatia. If one is prepared to assume a longer historical perspective, the demonization of the German presence in central Europe is historically unfounded to a great extent because the German-speaking world was the filter through which western European ideas were transmitted to central Europe; Germany and Austria were sources and models of modernization for their central European neighbors. The frontier of this *Mitteleuropa* may correspond to the more benign Habsburg or, after 1867, the Austro-Hungarian version of *Mitteleuropa* as well as the more aggressive imperial German versions of Naumann's German "economic space" or Hitler's *Lebensraum*.

Furthermore, "Western Europe," in its varying manifestations, was and has remained the primary point of cultural orientation and self-definition for the peoples of central Europe from their initial conversions to Christianity up until the present. Those nations living between the eastern frontiers of the German-speaking world and the western frontiers of the Orthodox East undoubtedly consider themselves "Central European." This is an elective category as well as a mode of self-perception.

Confronted with the choice of being "Eastern" Europeans (read Russian and Soviet here) or "Southeastern" Europeans (read Ottoman and Balkan here), Central Europeans not only always have preferred to define themselves as "Central European" but also have identified with what perhaps best can be called the grand Central European narrative of Western European cultural orientation. The peculiar asymmetry that exists is that central Europeans always have been aware of being or have aspired to be western European; however, as a chronically "backward" region, central Europe never has managed to reach western European levels of development.[23] Furthermore, western Europeans rarely have demonstrated a substantial amount of interest in their "eastern" neighbors, nor are they frequently aware of the fact that central Europeans consider themselves not only good, but also in some cases, the best (western) Europeans. The tradition of Polish national exceptionalism, for example, is based on the chronic European neglect of Poland as a western European polity.[24]

If the western European club corresponds to the European Union, there is a Central European club, too. In his Introduction, Katzenstein asks if the Baltic states are in central Europe.[25] Using the "Catholic-German" criteria stated above, one would have to include them and take a more serious look at the role of the Baltic Sea in European history, because this body of water, admittedly less appealing to the European imagination than the Mediterranean, has played a vital role in the histories of all of the peoples who have inhabited its shores and their hinterlands. During the thirteenth and fourteenth centuries, the Hanseatic League built up a trading network that reached from Novograd in Moscovy in the east to Bruges and London in the west.[26] In other words, it was not only the crusading of the Teutonic Knights but also the commerce of the Hanseatic League that drew the Baltic states into to the sphere of western European civilization. If given a choice of points of historical orientation today, the inhabitants of Tallinn or Riga undoubtedly will prefer Copenhagen, Stockholm, Hamburg, Amsterdam, or London over St. Petersburg or Moscow, and if a "Europe of regions" is to counterbalance the centralizing potential of European integration, the Baltic may well come into its own.

Katzenstein also asks if Serbia, Croatia, Slovenia, Rumania, and Bulgaria are in central Europe.[27] Indeed, if Central Europe itself is a sub-club of countries that consider themselves more western in terms of their historical cultural orientation and more eligible for western Europe than the countries of eastern and southeastern Europe, Slovenia (historically as a part of Habsburg Austria and economically as the wealthiest republic of former Yugoslavia) is included.[28] Croatia (as part of the historical kingdom of Hungary) certainly is in the historical club of central Europe, and its chauvinistic national ideology relies heavily on the terminological repertoire of Central Europe. However, after 1991 Croatia and Serbia both politically disqualified themselves from belonging to the Central European club. (The status of Bosnia-Herzegovina as a potentially central European state is negotiable.) Finally, self-proclaimed Central Europeans rarely include Rumania and Bulgaria their club, and Macedonia and Albania are definitely out.

"Balkan" is usually a pejorative term, as Maria Todorova has shown in her fascinating book *Imagining the Balkans*. Todorova is especially harsh in her critique of the evolution of the "Central Europe" from "an idea" in the 1980s to a "political program" in the 1990s. The "ideal of intellectual solidarity in the region [of the former Soviet bloc] all but disappeared ..." after 1989, according to Todorova, and it was replaced by "Central European" divisiveness to a great extent, as "the Balkans were evoked as the constituting other to Central Europe along side Russia."[29] After the collapse of the old Communist East, Todorova interprets the attempts to redefine the region in terms of central, eastern, and southeastern Europe as misleading, discriminatory, and exclusionary, not only in terms of the ideological agendas behind scholarly precedents for regional differentiation (for example, the Polish-America Oskar Halecki in the 1950s and 1960s and the Hungarian Jenö Szücs some twenty years later[30]), but also in terms of the political intent of the central European (Polish, Hungarian, Czech, and Slovak) proponents of the Central European idea as it became, however briefly, a regional political program that relied on the same distinctions.[31]

Todorova's book is well worth reading, although one may argue that the "exclusion" of southeastern Europe from central Europe that she describes so eloquently sometimes seems to question the indisputable merits of methodologically differentiating between central, eastern, and southeastern Europe in terms of their patterns of development. Gale Stokes recently has reaffirmed defining the subregions of "Eastern Europe"—the thirteen countries between Russia and the German-speaking world from Finland in the north to Greece in the south—in terms of central, southeastern, and eastern Europe which, in turn, may be distinguished using three "defining fault lines": the Catholic-Orthodox divide; the frontiers between Christian (Habsburg and Russian) and Ottoman empires; and a "third fault line of economic differentiation [that] runs approximately along the Elbe river south and west to Trieste." Stokes traces the different historical trajectories in these regions and comes to the conclusion that for the generation after World War II it appeared that these "ancient fault lines had been erased by the homogenizing internationalism of Stalinism and Communism, not to mention by industrialization and modernization, but after 1989 it became clear that they had not."[32]

In *Imagining the Balkans*, Todorova was reticent about what it was like being an academic and intellectual in pre-1989 Bulgaria. If "Central Europe" was an idea or a debate that turned into a political program, it would have been interesting if she had taken this opportunity to inform us about her personal experience with the presence or absence of the Central European idea and the Central European debate in Bulgaria in the 1980s. Be that as it may, the point I wish to make here is that as exclusionary as traditional European discourse about the Balkans may be, the *discourse* has not been the source of the exclusion of the states of southeastern Europe from Central Europe as much as their less auspicious structural and political points of departure in terms of their pre-1989 heritages and their subsequent lag in reform since them.

In her critique of Central European intellectuals and dissidents turned politicians, Todorova seems to underestimate the fact that a head of state, such as Vaclav Havel, did not have much in common, personally or politically, with the newly elected post-Communist representatives of Rumania and Bulgaria, such as Ion Iliescu or Andrei Lukanov. Rumania and Bulgaria also have suffered from a comparative lack of expatriate-émigré-exile advocacy in the West because, unlike Hungary, Czechoslovakia, or Poland, their respective levels of emigration to the West since the nineteenth century—and the consequent establishment of emigrant communities abroad that provide the basis for "ethnic lobbying"have been comparatively low. Nor did Romania or Bulgaria have upheavals, such as 1956, 1968, or 1981, that led to the establishment expatriated political and intellectual lobbies in the West.

In his analysis of the Visegrad group, Valerie Bunce points out, for example, that "the history of these three countries [Poland, Czechoslovakia, and Hungary] under state socialism, the victory of the opposition in the first competitive elections after socialism, and the similarities of their geographical location, as well as their agendas for transformation, all worked to homogenize in effect the structure, the experiences, the interests, and the goals of the new regimes ..."[33] In contrast, one may ask if the revolutions in Rumania and Bulgaria were as successful in dislodging the old political elites to the same extent as they were in Poland, the Czech Republic, Slovakia, and Hungary. They were not, and both countries had to wait until the end of 1996 or the beginning of 1997, respectively, to make definitive transitions to genuinely post-Communist governments. The fact that the Rumanian and Bulgarian revolutions took so long to come to fruition also is indicative of the fact that neither of these countries seemed to have developed the same kind of (central European) momentum in the 1980s that carried the Visegrad states into the 1990s.

So where is Central Europe? Perhaps a consensus never will be reached on the term, but there are a number of attributes that various "definitions" seem to share. Central Europe corresponds geographically to that part of Europe that was drawn into the sphere of the Roman Catholic Europe in the early Middle Ages. This, in turn, underlines the importance of the western Christian-Eastern Orthodox divide as a primary category for the methodological tripartition of this part of Europe into central, eastern, and southeastern Europe.

The concept of Central Europe relies on two grand narratives: the religious narrative of western or Roman Catholic Christianity ("Western Christendom") and the secular narrative of the Enlightenment (the "democratic West" or modernization). Roman Catholicism drew Central Europe into the west and established the primary patterns of Central European cultural orientation. As historically important as the western Christian orientation of central Europe is, it is—perhaps with the exception of Polish Catholicism—rarely politically operative today, although it may serve as an important historical or ideological argument for the proponents of post-Cold War theories of "cultural" or "civilizational" conflict. In light of the high level of secularization in all parts of Europe, it would be difficult to argue that western Christianity is a primary motive for the exclusion of the Orthodox and Orthodox/Islamic "constituting others" in Europe: Russia and the Balkans.[34]

The secular tradition of the Enlightenment ultimately appears to be more important in Central *and* Western Europe. Starting with the Enlightenment, this was "the West" to which progressive Central Europeans aspired to belong, and this is "the West" the European Union professes to represent. If western Europe is based upon a community of enlightened, secular, and liberal values that produce freedom and prosperity to the extent that proponents of the European Union maintain it is, then these are the values which the EU uses to ascertain potential membership in the European club: democracy, market economics, and institutions which guarantee the functioning of both. One also should not forget that economic interests are the major driving force in the processes of European integration. One market and one currency are in the process of redefining "one Europe" and the "other Europe," too.

In terms of its economic and political development, central Europe historically has lagged behind western Europe, but it also has stayed ahead of eastern and southeastern Europe in quantifiable terms. The economic development and the political experience of central European states in "Eastern Europe" between 1945 and 1989 was substantially different than in eastern and southeastern Europe and contributed to giving the states of central Europe a head start on the road "back to Europe."

Finally, Germany and Austria are in Central Europe in historical terms, but they are in western Europe in political and economic ones, unless German and Austrian politicians, as representatives of prospering EU democracies, wish to emphasize their special commitments to their eastern neighbors, who, in turn, do not want to be central European, but aspire to full membership in the western European club. Central Europe can perhaps best be defined as that part of "old" Eastern Europe that eventually will make it into the political and economic haven of the West, and this makes it a negotiable term. It will be interesting to see whether the frontiers of the European Union ultimately will end up corresponding to the limitations inherent in the concept of Central Europe at some point in the not so distant future.

## Notes

1. Eric Hobsbawn, "The Curious History of Europe" in *On History*, ed. Eric Hobsbaum (New York: New Press, 1997), 222.

2. Peter J. Katzenstein, ed., *Mitteleuropa: Between Europe and Germany* (Oxford: Berghann Books, 1997), 292 pp.

3. Ibid., p. 4. Specialists, editors, and librarians also seem to disagree on the issue of capitalizing central Europe. See the December 1997 Listserve discussion on HABSBURG archived under the query "Eastern/Central Europe, eastern/central Europe": <http://h-net2.msu.edu/logs/logs.cgi> [path: H-NET E-mail Discussion Groups/HABSBURG/Discussion logs/December 1997]. In the following, I will capitalize Central Europe when it refers to a concept of ideological import; analogous to the practice of "West" and "East."

4. In *Central Europe: Enemies, Neighbors, Friends*, (New York: Oxford University Press, 1996), I have identified at least seven different "definitions" of "Central Europe": *Mitteleuropa* (in the German imperial sense); German-Jewish Central Europe; the Central Europe of small (non-Germanic) nations (the Palacky-Masaryk tradition); the notalgic, *k.u.k* or Austro-Hungarian version of *Mitteleuropa* (without imperial Germans) which is related to the Austro-Hungarian version of *Mitteleuropa* in the 1970s and 1980s (Kreisky-Kadar-Busek); the *Mitteleuropa* of the West German left and peace movement in the 1980s; the "Central Europe" of Eastern European dissidents and intellectuals (for example, Milosz, Kundera, Konrad); and finally the "Central and Eastern Europe" of the European Union. See pp. 6-12. For recent Austrocentric reflections on Central Europe see Erhard Busek, *Mitteleuropa: Eine Spurensicherung* (Vienna: Kremayr and Scheriau, 1997); or Milo Dor, *Mitteleuropa, Mythos oder Wirklichkeit: auf der Suche nach der größeren Heimat* (Salzburg: Müller, 1996).

5. Katzenstein, *Mitteleuropa*, footnote 4, 240-41.

6. Readers interested in an overview of EU enlargement policy, relevant documents, and reports should consult the EU website: <http://europa.eu.int/comm/dg1a/enlarge/>

7. Katzenstein, *Mitteleuropa*, 9-11.

8. Katzenstein, *Mitteleuropa*, 37-38.

9. With the exception of the United Kingdom and Ireland, all EU members have signed the Schengen Agreement and Convention which provides for free movement of persons between the respective member states, regardless of their citizenship, once the have entered one of the participating member states. The consequences of Schengen for asylum and immigration policy as well as the control of the EU ports of entry and external frontiers are obvious.

10. Katzenstein, *Mitteleuropa*, 67-81. Readers interested in the evolution of Austrian policy should consult Heinz Fassmann and Rainer Münz, *Einwanderungsland Österreich? Historische Migrationsmuster, aktuelle Trends und politische Maßnahmen* (Vienna: Jugend and Volk, 1995) or, for a longer historical perspective, Gernot Heiss and Oliver Rathkolb, eds., *Asylland Wider Willen: Flüchtlinge in Österreich im europäischen Kontext seit 1914* (Vienna: Jugend and Volk, 1995).

11. Katzenstein, *Mitteleuropa*, 38.

12. Cited in "USA helfen Prag. 'Germanisierung' soll verhindert werden," *Die Presse*, 22 February 1990, 1.

13. The "transition" from socialism and planned economies to democracy and markets in principle occurred quickly. "Transformation" is a bit more cautious and reflects the experimental and tentative nature of the processes at work after the introduction of new political and economic regimes.

14. Katzenstein, *Mitteleuropa*, 56.

15. Ibid.

16. Ibid. 106.

17. Ibid., 148.

18. Commission of the European Communities, "The Europe Agreements and Beyond: A Strategy to Prepare the Countries of Central and Eastern Europe for Accession," COM (94), 320 final, Brussels, 7 July 1994, 1. EU authorities agreed upon the accession criteria a the Copenhagen European Council Meeting in June 1993.

19. Katzenstein, *Mitteleuropa*, 251, 258.

20. Full texts of the "opinions" and "reports" are available on the EU website: "Commission Opinions concerning the Applications for Membership to the European Union presented by the candidate Countries" <http://europa.eu.int/comm/dg1a/enlarge/a genda2000_en/opinions/opinions.htm>; "Reports on progress towards accession by each of the candidate countries"; <http://europa.eu.int/comm/dg1a/enlarge/ report_11_98_en/index.htm>.

21. See Katzenstein, *Mitteleuropa*, 28-29.

22. Norman Davies, *Europe: A History* (Oxford and New York: Oxford University Press, 1996), 14-15.

23. See, for example, Daniel Chirot, *Origins of Backwardness in Eastern Europe: Economics and Politics from the Middle Ages Until the Early Twentieth Century* (Berkley: University of California Press, 1989); and Ivan T. Berend, *Central and Eastern Europe, 1944-1993: Detour from the Periphery to the Periphery* (Cambridge: Cambridge University Press, 1996).

24. See the contribution on the Polish Catholic church in *Mitteleuropa: Between Europe and Germany*, 57-67. If European culture is synonymous with Roman Catholicism, Poland may be the most "European" country in Europe.

25. Katzenstein, *Mitteleuropa*, 4.

26. See David Kirby, *Northern Europe in the Early Modern Period: The Baltic World, 1492-1772*, (London: Longman, 1990).

27. Katzenstein, *Mitteleuropa*, 4.

28. In *Bloodlines: A Journey into Eastern Europe* (Vancouver and Toronto: Douglas and McIntyre, 1993), 73, Myrna Kostash, a Canadian-Ukrainian author and essayist, described the way she felt—as an advocate of some kind of Slavic solidarity—in Slovenia in the following manner: "We are so far 'West' that I feel marooned, cast among Slavs, who are not Slavs."

29. Maria Todorova, *Imagining the Balkans* (New York: Oxford University Press, 1997), 155, 156.

30. In the Introduction to *The Price of Freedom: A History of East Central Europe from the Middle Ages to the Present*, (London: Routledge, 1992), 1-4, Piotr Wandycz underlines the importance of Halecki and Szücs in establishing the terminology of (East) Central Europe. Perhaps the most important point Szücs

makes in his seminal article "The Three Historic Regions of Europe," *Acta Historica Scientiarum Hungaricae* 29 (1982), 131-194, is that western Christian forms of feudal contractual subordination provided a more fertile ground for the development of civil society than the Orthodox (in particular Russian) forms of fealty. For Szücs, the potential for the development of constitutional and democratic habits was greater in the Roman West than in the Orthodox East.

31. Todorova, *Imagining the Balkans*, Chapter 6 "Between Classification and Politics: The Balkans and the Myth of Central Europe," 140-160.

32. See Gale Stokes, "Eastern Europe's Defining Fault Lines" in his *Three Eras of Political Change in Eastern Europe* (New York: Oxford University Press, 1997), 7-23.

33. Katzenstein, *Mitteleuropa*, 258.

34. Although one might disagree with some of the premises or terminology Samuel P. Huntington uses in his controversial *The Clash of Civilizations and the Remaking of the World Order* (New York: Touchstone, 1996), such as "civilizational paradigm" and "logic of civilizations," his premise that there must be limits to the enlargement of the European Union and NATO is sound. Huntington's assumption that the limits of enlargement ultimately will correspond to the "great historical line that has existed for centuries separating Western Christian peoples from Muslim and Orthodox peoples" (158) appears to be realistic, and his assertion that the (Orthodox) Greeks and the (Moslem) Turks are in many regards the most problematic members of the EU and NATO, respectively, is correct.

# Günther Nenning: *'Forum.' Die berühmtesten Beiträge zur Zukunft von einst von Arrabal bis Zuckmayer* (Vienna: Amalthea, 1998).

*V.R. Berghahn*

Günther Nenning begins his commemorative volume with fanfare, calling *Forum* not only "the most significant cultural journal of Austria," but also the country's only intellectual periodical which has had "a significant long-term impact in the entire German-speaking lands" (p. 7). More than that, "until today and probably also tomorrow and the day after tomorrow *Forum* remains unsurpassed in the variety of its topics, intellectual weight of its authors, and elegance as well as originality of its offerings."

There is a good deal of truth in these claims. Starting in 1954 under the editorship of Friedrich Torberg (until 1965), thereafter of Nenning (until 1985) and of Gerhard Oberschlick (until 1995, when it finally folded), *Forum* certainly left its mark if we look at the complete list of contributors and the index of their articles assembled at the end of the volume. Indeed, it is almost more interesting to ask who among the cultural elites in Europe and the rest of the world did not, at one time or another, publish in the journal than to find out who did.[1] Many of these contributions, to be sure, were translations of essays that appeared elsewhere. But it is probably no exaggeration to say that the topics covered offer a kaleidoscope of the major issues that occupied the West from the height of the Cold War in the early 1950s until its end in the 1990s. Of these hundreds of contributions, Nenning has selected 108 for this volume.

These selections are organized in seven sections which may be said to reflect the great themes of this dramatic period and, in line with the traditions of the journal, start off with fundamental ideological conflicts. For, as Nenning, stresses in his Introduction, "anti-communism was the hardcore of the good old *Forum.* Founder Friedrich Torberg was a European figure of resistance to all things totalitarian, whether it was defeated Hitlerism or continuing Stalinism. Among all anti-communists he was the most rabid and the most gifted" (p. 7). After Torberg's retirement there were inevitable changes in editorial policy, but Nenning is no doubt correct when he writes that the anti-totalitarian stance remained the thread that also runs through the journal's later volumes.

The first ideological theme presented in this volume revolves around the question of whether Bertold Brecht should be performed in the West, and Nenning proudly records as proof of *Forum's* pluralism, that most authors were in favor of putting Brecht on stage. But it pays off to look for the date of publication at the end of each contribution. Just as the patterns of the East-West conflict itself changed, so did the arguments about the merits and demerits of Brecht's work. Significantly, the section ends with Ernst Bloch's 1967 examination of *Mahagonny.* Here Bloch takes the view that Brecht always tried to generate *Nachdenklichkeit* in his audiences—a "pensiveness" that resisted seduction by cheap slogans, that got to the essence of things, "in the West as well as in the East" (p. 63).

The essences of the divided world that defined our postwar existence are at the center of the next section which covers the dialogues between Christians and non-Christians between 1954 and 1978. Accordingly, we find Friedrich Heer, Karl Barth, and Hans Küng next to Georg Lukács, Hannah Arendt, Leszek Kolakowski, Ernst Bloch, Max Horkheimer, Herbert Marcuse, and, last but not least, Rudi Dutschke. Reminding us that the Cold War era was not just about political and philosophical exchange and conflict, but also produced several cultural revolutions, the next section contains, apart from disquisitions about revolutionary politics, Alice Schwarzer's interview with Simone de Beauvoir about feminism, a discussion between Bernard Wolfe and Henry Miller about literature and pornography, as well as pieces by Norman Mailer and Nenning about sexual and gender relations. Since this third section deals with "revolutions of all kinds," an intriguing essay by Claude Lévi-Strauss on the rights of humans, animals, and plants and the perils of survival on our small planet is thrown in for good measure.

Two further sections focus on high and low culture. The final section on Austrian politics, old and new, offers ruminations by prominent Austrians on the state of mind of their fellow-citizens and their country's future.

Yet, however fascinating it may be to leaf through the volume in order to sample the essays of some of the most eminent authors of the time to get a sense of an era that is now history, it is a pity that Nenning has not written a longer introduction that provides a fuller exploration of the context for all those readers who are not of the editor's generation or are not European cultural historians. After all, the volume was published to coincide with what would have been the ninetieth birthday of *Forum's* first editor. But it is only on pages 206/7 that we learn a bit more about this flamboyant figure of Austria's postwar political and cultural life. Here Nenning reprints the obituary he wrote in January 1980, a few months after Torberg's death. No less important, here we learn that Torberg had for years prevented the performance of Brecht's plays in Vienna. We are also informed that Torberg, the militant anti-communist, who was born in Vienna and was a Jewish refugee from Nazism in the United States, had sub-titled his journal "Austrian Monthly for Cultural Freedom" and received funding for it from the Congress for Cultural Freedom (CCF). Through this link, *Forum* was part of a "family" of international periodicals that included *Der Monat* in West Germany, *Preuves* in France, *Encounter* in Britain, and *Tempo Presente* in Italy.

*Der Monat* was the oldest among these, established in 1948 by Melvin Lasky, an American in postwar Berlin with connections to the U.S. intelligence community. Funding came until 1953 from the U.S. High Commission in West Germany. But when budget cuts by Congress in Washington forced the High Commission to withdraw its subsidies, Lasky created his own publishing company. Unable to turn *Der Monat* into a commercially viable enterprise, he sought refuge under the larger roof of the CCF, an international association based in Paris, that also organized prestigious anti-communist cultural congresses, art exhibitions, and exchange programs.[2] At this point, Nenning's obituary become a bit cloudy. He speaks of "rumors" that the CIA funded the CCF, adding, rather meekly, that "that is probably true" (p. 206). Nenning knew better, even when he wrote his piece: the CIA did indeed finance the CCF, although he claims that *Forum* became independent of this source as early as 1962, when he found alternative support "in the deep Austrian well of red-black subsidies and advertisements."

Rather than being distracted by the funding and the upheaval that the CCF went through when all this was discovered in 1966/67, it is important to contextualize Nenning's timid revelations. In other words, there is a much larger story to be told here, of which postwar Austria was an integral part. It is the story of European liberals and social democrats, who, while fiercely anti-communist, were at the same time committed to combating widespread criticism of the United States as a cultural power. The Austrian members of this Atlantic network were opposed to the restorative tendencies in society and politics. This is why Nenning reports that Torberg, the anti-Stalinist, allowed him, as a young co-editor from 1958, to "write as *rosarot* as I wanted, also Austro-Marxist, and even pro-Brecht" (p. 206). Clearly, *Forum* was a periodical that was open to non-conformist views as long as they were not totalitarian, right or left. It was pointedly cosmopolitan.

Accordingly, it was also working hard to counteract the criticisms that the so-called "Cocacolonization" of Austria was producing among intellectuals and the bourgeoisie.[3] Torberg, the returnee from his American exile, wanted to reinforce the Westernization of Austria. This seemed all the more important in a country that suffered not only from Habsburg nostalgia but that had also positioned itself between East and West in political and economic terms. For Torberg and his American friends in the CCF this did not include ideological neutralism, but involved a clear option in favor of the West and its hegemonic power, the United States.

Perhaps Nenning will tell this story in his memoirs. Better still would be a few historians who will research not only the Salzburg Seminar[4], but also, for example, the Ford Foundation's backing for an institute of advanced study in Vienna. This will lead them to Paul Lazarsfeld's visits to Vienna, who, prevented from writing his *Habilitation* in Vienna in the early 1930s and after gaining a Rockefeller Foundation fellowship in 1933 to go to the United States, now returned as an American citizen and esteemed Columbia University sociologist to advise Ford about its effort to strengthen links with Austrian intellectual life. Unfortunately, the letter Lazarsfeld wrote to the Foundation in June 1959 was not too optimistic:[5]

> As to the Austrian situation at large, I find it as depressing as before. No brains, no initiative, no collaboration. Someone should make a study to find out how a country can be

intellectually so dead, and at the same time have such wonderful musical festivals. There is also on the conservative side and in large parts of the University a real anti-Americanism. I should add, however, that a paranoic element of mutual distrust is characteristic of today's personal relations among Austrians themselves.

If we look at this larger milieu in which *Forum* operated, it becomes more comprehensible why Torberg and Nenning printed so many articles from intellectuals from all over the world and fought not only communism, but also the reservations many fellow countrymen felt about modern culture and the West. In fact they both fought to Cold Culture Wars at the same time. Seen in this light, this volume serves as no more than a welcome appetizer, suggesting plenty of fascinating work about Austrian culture and the Austrian-American relationship after 1945 that is still to be done.

## Notes

1. Here is a very random selection of contributors: F. Abendroth, T.W. Adorno, I. Aichinger, F.R. Allemann, S. Allende, G. Anders, L. Aragon, H. Arendt, W.H. Auden, I. Bachmann, L. Barzini, S. de Beauvoir, K. Bednarik, J. Berger, I. Birnbaum, E. Bloch, H. Böll, F. Bondy, F. Borkenau, W. Brandt, M. Brod, M. Buber, W. Burian, A. Camus, E. Canetti, N. Chomsky, W. Daim, M. Djilas, H. Von Doderer, T. Draper, W. Duwe, I. Fetscher, E. Fischer, E. Fromm, C. Gatterer, F. Geyrhofer, G. Girardi, H. Gollwitzer, G. Grass, P. Gutjahr, W. Haas, P. Hamm, K. Harpprecht, V. Havel, F. Heer, W. Hofmann, I. Illich, K. Jelenski, R.A. Kann, B. Kautsky, E. Kmölniger, L. Kolakowski, B. Kreisky, A. Krims, J. Langenbach, N. Leser, G. Lukács, E. Mandel, H. Marcuse, H. Menningen, , G. Mikes, L. Mnacko, R. Nitsche, A. Noll, H. Pataki, A. Pelinka, H. Politzer, J.-P. Sartre, A. Schnitzler, O.F. Schuh, I. Silone, S. Spender, M. Sperber, M. Springer, G. Steiner, E. Stengel, P. Turini, R. Urbach, K. Vorhofer, H. Weigel, F. Willnauer, H. Winter, P. Zahl, and C. Zuckmayer.

2. For histories of the CCF, see Pierre Grémion, *Intelligence de l'Anticommunisme* (Paris: Fayard, 1995); and Peter Coleman, *The Liberal Conspiracy* (New York: Free Press, 1989).

3. See Reinhold Wagnleitner, *Coca-Colonization und Kalter Krieg* (Vienna: Verlag für Gesellschaftskritik, 1991).

4. A history of the Salzburg Seminar is being written by Oliver Schmidt, Harvard University.

5. Quoted in Christian Fleck, "Autochthone Provinzialisierung. Universität und Wissenschaftspolitik nach dem Ende der nationalsozialistischen Herrschaft in Österreich," *Österreichische Zeitschrift für Geschichtswissenschaften* 7 (1996): 92.

# Rigele Georg: *Die Großglockner-Hochalpenstraße: Zur Geschichte eines österreichischen Monuments* (Vienna: WUV-Universitätsverlag, 1998).

*Peter Thaler*

There was a time when large-scale construction projects were important symbols of national pride. In a manner that might seem alien to a younger generation raised under the influence of environmentalism, massive infrastructural undertakings were seen as a measure of a country's progressiveness and societal advancement. Next to hydroelectric plants such as the famous storage power station at Kaprun, Alpine road constructions such as the Brenner autobahn with its towering *Europabrücke* and the panoramic road along the slopes of the *Großglockner* mountain were among the foremost symbols of technological prowess in inter- and early postwar Austria.

The young Austrian historian Georg Rigele specializes in examining the relationship between landscape and culture. In his 1993 dissertation, he contrasted the Alpine *Großglockner-Hochalpenstraße*, or Glockner road, the Vienna *Höhenstraße* that crosses the scenic hills surrounding the Austrian capital. In the richly illustrated study he now presents, Rigele expands his examination of the Glockner road into a comprehensive look at the origin, completion, and societal background of this challenging construction project.

Rigele adopts a broad interdisciplinary approach that integrates diverse sources ranging from technical drawings and financial accounts to literary adaptations of the Glockner road theme. He first introduces the reader to the pre-history of the project, which begins with the modest dirt road constructed by the non-governmental Alpine Club around the turn of the century. Then, he analyzes the plans for an expansion of this traffic route into a full-scale Alpine crossing, which circulated in the primarily affected provinces of Carinthia, Salzburg, and Tyrol in the 1920s. In the central portion of the book, the author details the progress of the construction project from its inception in 1930 to its ultimate completion in 1935. In this context, he illuminates the pivotal contributions of the leading engineer, Franz Wallack, and the Salzburg governor Franz Rehrl to the realization of the project. Finally, Rigele places the road construction into the context of employment as well as tourism policy and examines the ecological debate that pitted government and technocracy against the private, but influential, Alpine Club and its supporters.

Particularly interesting is the author's examination of the contemporary political atmosphere. Although construction was started by a democratically elected government in 1930, the decisive second phase of the project occurred under the auspices of the authoritarian conservative government of Engelbert Dollfuss and Kurt Schuschnigg. The conservatives saw the Glockner road as a symbol that could both bolster their own stature as modern can-do politicians and reinforce a sense of patriotism rooted in the natural beauty of the Austrian landscape. This patriotic appeal leads Rigele to view the Glockner road as a central contribution to the developing Austrianism of the authoritarian government and a precursor of the distinctly Austrian national imagery of the postwar era.

*Die Großglockner-Hochalpenstraße* presents a rich picture of a construction project that is interesting from both an economic and a symbolic point of view. The panoramic Alpine crossing in the vicinity of Austria's highest mountain peak appealed to the public; it seems one of the most noteworthy facts presented that statistically, every single privately registered Austrian car used the Glockner road 1.42 times during the short period between 1935 and 1937. Rigele has integrated a wide selection of sources, which allows the reader to get a comprehensive impression of the geographical, technical, economic, and human parameters of so massive an undertaking.

Although the author is also interested in the relationship between the construction project and its broader political and economic environment, its influence appears to be predominately unidirectional—from the macro to the micro-level. Since it depended on public financing, the progress of the Glockner road construction was determined by contemporary Austrian politics. The impact of the road on national politics, by contrast, was more limited. The extensive statistical data presented lead to the conclusion that the Glockner road did not significantly alter the overall tourist flow. While annual employment peaks of around 2000 people were hardly insignificant, they did not make a serious dent in Austria's contemporary unemployment figures, which reached into the hundreds of thousands. Even the patriotic significance of the project is relativized by the author's acknowledgment that the symbolism of Glockner road proved just as compatible with the imagery of German nationhood between 1938 and 1945 as with prior and subsequent adaptations to a purely Austrian framework.

The story of a massive Austrian road-building project of the interwar era reminds us of changing perceptions of progress, modernity, and quality of life. While Rigele's book introduces us to the national and political symbolism of public construction projects, it also shows us that they reflect more than shape their political environment. Thus, the main relevance of this well-researched study remains within a framework of technological history and the development of auto tourism.

# Anton Pelinka: *Austria. Out of the Shadow of the Past* (Boulder: Westview, 1998).

*Kurt Tweraser*

For the last twenty years, the Austrian political, economic, and social landscape has been undergoing profound changes with seemingly no end in sight. The political business has become more unpredictable, prediction and interpretation more hazardous. The classic political milieus no longer hold; political decisions deal with the short-run. The results of electoral contests do not convey clear meanings. What motivates the Austrian voter? Is it a shift to the right, a chance of teaching the establishment a lesson, a reaction inspired by anxiety, a return to normalcy? Does the trend go towards depoliticization, or do we witness the repoliticization of society, or are we in the presence of a total transformation of politics?

Fortunately for American readers, Anton Pelinka, professor of Political Science at the University of Innsbruck who is well known on both sides of the Atlantic, provides us with an analysis and explanation of modern Austrian history and politics in a mercifully short, but profound, and well written book. In a felicitous blend of political science and *Zeitgeschichte*, he applies the tools of comparative systems analysis to Austria, comparing the country with other European political systems that are at approximately the same stage of development (Denmark, Belgium) as well as comparing contemporary Austria with an Austria that existed in the past. In the course of these comparisons, Pelinka explains how Austria got from there to here. It is almost impossible, and for a reviewer slightly annoying, not to describe this work in superlatives. Each chapter of the book, a *tour de force* in its own right, brings into sharp focus different aspects of Austrian politics and society.

The book starts with a brief analysis of Austria's complex image at home and abroad and her changing identities. Another chapter delivers a superb analysis of the Austrian political culture, describing consociational democracy as it developed after the failure of the centrifugal democracy of the First Republic and the catalytic years of authoritarian and totalitarian rule. Based on their painful memories of past conflicts and the unifying experience of occupation by foreign powers, Austria's deeply opposed "black" and "red" elites came together in an elaborate power sharing and grand coalition cartel after 1945. Originally a "cartel of anxiety," consociational democracy developed into a stable duopoly in which the Austrian People's Party (Österreichische Volkspartei, ÖVP) and the Socialist Party of Austria (Sozialistische Partei Österreichs, SPÖ) and their respective corporatist complements (Chamber of Commerce, Agricultural Chambers, Federation of Austrian Trade Unions, ÖGB, and Chamber of Labor) succeeded in establishing and maintaining the pillarization and concentration of the politico-economic system as a valid means of representation since these groups encompassed the overwhelming majority of the Austrian population.

However, by taming and institutionalizing elite competition, the grand compromise of 1945 eventually unleashed a dynamic that dispersed cartels and fostered the emergence of forces more in tune with pluralist democracy. Pelinka identifies the generation gap, education, and gender as the forces of change and transformation of consociational democracy, replacing to a considerable extent the old cleavages of class and religion. He concludes that the history of consociational democracy in Austria is the history of self-elimination by success. The cleavages responsible for the old *Lager* mentality disappeared-and so did the old camps.

In a chapter on the constitutional structure of Austria, Pelinka rightly stresses the fact that the "real" constitution was provided by the dominance of political parties and interest organizations at the expense of Parliament, the Federal President, and the Judiciary. However, the decline of the party state and the increase of the individualistic perceptions of politics permitted the formal constitutional agencies to gain a new independence. The formal constitution increasingly matters politically.

Another important chapter reviews political parties, elections and interest groups, the churches, and the media. In it, Pelinka highlights the main features of Austrian corporatism (social partnership) such as the complex interpenetration of parties and interest groups illustrated by the existence of party factions within major interest groups, and, by the large number of interest group officials who, in the past, served as members of Parliament. Further, he refers to the Austrian *Proporz* system, whereby the *Lager* have been represented in public administration and the management of nationalized industries and banks. In a chapter titled "A Farewell to Corporatism," Pelinka discusses the challenges to the Austrian corporatist arrangements, particularly to the mandatory membership in the chamber system. The conditions that made Austro-corporatism possible, such as the reduction of bargaining partners to two, centralized leadership, internal discipline, informality of decision-making, and reasonableness of demands, have been undermined in the 1980s and 1990s. Factors that disrupted stability and political harmony were new social movements challenging the philosophy of economic growth and male superiority. The social partnership has been unable to integrate the ecological and feminist movements and their political representatives. The globalization of the economy and the single European market has eroded the ability of Austro-corporatism and Austro-Keynesianism to steer the economy. At any rate, the simple dichotomy of representing the interest of capital and labor no longer worked. The chambers apparently lost touch with society resulting in a legitimacy crisis of the corporatist organizations.

Along with the corporatist legitimacy crisis went the disintegration of the traditional two-and-a half party system. Voters were becoming increasingly fickle. The percentage of late deciders, floating voters, and non-voters increased. In successive elections, beginning in 1983, the party system underwent a process of deconcentration. The old cleavages were fading (also see the Crepaz/Betz essay in this volume). Since social partnership was built around the power symmetry in the party system, the advent of new parties (a revitalized Freedom Party, Freiheitliche Partei Österreichs, FPÖ; the Green Party; and the Liberal Forum, LIF) was bound to weaken, if not destroy the corporatist system. Austria, in line with other Western democracies, experienced a gradual opening of the structures of consociationalism, thus increasing uncertainty in party competition. Furthermore, the corporatist organization seemed to be rather slow in adapting to the changing political environment, and seemed politically detached and technocratic in their solution to problems. Their political party complements, displaying greater adaptive capabilities to increased competition in the electoral arena, began to emancipate themselves from their corporatist organizations in order to survive. Pelinka is careful, however, not to pronounce the death knell of Austro-corporatism. A slim network of corporatist intermediation which has surrendered much of its power to the logic of the market may surwive.

The chapter titled "A Farewell to Neutrality" highlights the importance of taking the international dimension into account when analyzing democratic consolidation and transition. Politics at the domestic and international levels are fundamentally interdependent. While domestically Pelinka still discerns a strong positive attitude towards neutrality, Austrian neutrality lost its *raison d'etre* with the end of the Cold War. Pelinka draws our attention to a similar interdependence on the economic realm, where a hitherto successful system slowly disintegrated. Linking the Schilling to the Deutsche Mark and Austria's economic fortune to Germany, and then to Europe, gradually has diminished state intervention and subsidies. The globalization of national economies, in conjunction with poor management and scandals relating to patronage, misappropriation of funds, and illegal arms deals with foreign countries meant that the Austrian government could no longer ignore the challenge of market efficiency and saw no alternative to large-scale privatization. Calming the fears of a second Anschluß as a consequence of the high dependence of Austria's economy on Germany's economy, Pelinka points out that economic dependence no longer correlates with political dependence. Pan-Germanism as a political program in Austria is dead. Austria's economic dependence is no longer specifically Austrian. The country is now a player among others in a single market with a single currency.

In, perhaps, the most brilliant chapter, Pelinka sheds light on Austria's darker side, sketching the social and political history of a nation which was deeply involved in the criminal activities of National Socialism and had a hard time liberating itself from the thicket of NS lies and myths. Rather than overcoming national socialist and authoritarian mentalities such as anti-Semitism, the political and social elites stumbled from one embarrassment to another. In the 1980s anti-Semitism in Austria acquired not a new importance but a new candor, reaching a highpoint triggered by the Waldheim affair. Much more important than Waldheim himself was the public reaction to the affair which, like a flash of lightning, illuminated Austrian anti-Semitism and Austria's Nazi past. Pelinka does not neglect to mention some positive consequences arising from the Waldheim affair, such as the official recognition of Austria's co-responsibility for the Holocaust and the crackdown on rightwing extremism by the police and the criminal courts.

In the same chapter, Pelinka also addresses the question of whether or not the FPÖ under the leadership of Jörg Haider represents neo-Nazism or right populism. Pelinka regards the FPÖ as a populist anti-statist party, defined by its hostility to mainstream parties and the establishment; at times, the party has shown signs of a hidden authoritarian agenda. Rather than demonize Haider, Pelinka explains the rise of the FPÖ with the move towards a post-industrial society which has produced an authoritarian response from a section of the electorate, especially blue collar males. Of the three reasons for voting FPÖ, solving the "foreigner problem," fighting corruption and mismanagement, eliminating waste in public spending, only the first reason is clearly racist, whereas the other two are traditional protest motives and legitimate in a liberal democracy. Thus, Pelinka correctly sees the rise of the FPÖ under Haider primarily as a backlash to the impact of societal and economic modernization (individualization, decline of the welfare state, immigration) on the part of the losers in this process. He argues convincingly that there is no danger of a revival of National Socialism in its Hitler-era form.

Finally, in the last chapter, Pelinka brings the reader up to date on Austria's future. His message is straightforward: Austria is westernizing. The characteristics used to describe Austria since 1945 are fading: its stability through corporatist arrangements, its ability to be Western and neutral simultaneously, its strong social democratic outlook, its Catholic character, and its stubborn insistence on having been the victim of Nazi aggression. Westernization is a general process of emancipation: the constitution is gaining autonomy from the party state as well as from the corporate state; Parliament is becoming more autonomous from the administration; political parties and economic interest groups are beginning to dissociate; and the economy has reached a degree of autonomy from political interference previously unknown in the Second Republic. However, the emancipation process has its darker side, too. The gap between the haves and the have-nots is widening. The decline of the welfare state ushers in a two-thirds society, excluding a significant portion of the population from prosperity. Thus, Austria's farewell to Catholicism, to socialism, to corporatism, and to neutrality is decreasing security for an increasing number of Austrians.

Ultimately, Pelinka's book is the finest example of a concise work on modern Austrian politics in English that has been released in recent years and should take its place beside Kurt Steiner's *Politics in Austria* from 1972. It is a brilliant synthesis of the scholarly literature on the Second Republic, reflecting the outstanding work of Austrian scholars, and Pelinka's own substantial production.

# Ingrid Bauer: "Welcome Ami Go Home" Die Amerikanische Besatzung in Salzburg 1945-1955.

## Erinnerungslandschaften aus einem Oral History Projekt

# (Salzburg: Verlag Anton Pustet, 1998)

*Petra Goedde*

The last decade has seen a remarkable outpouring of new scholarship on the impact of the U.S. occupation on Germany and Austria. While earlier studies extensively covered military, economic, and political aspects of the occupation, the new wave of scholarship concentrates on social and cultural aspects. Ingrid Bauer's "Welcome Ami Go Home," a collection of critically edited oral interviews, provides a useful documentary supplement to this new group of monographs. The book reveals the ambivalent and, as the title suggests, often contradictory attitudes of Austrians toward the U.S. occupation forces between 1945 and 1955.

The book's objective, in Bauer's words, is to document how individuals experienced reality and the world of the occupation (p. 9). Together with a team of researchers, she interviewed sixty Salzburg citizens about their memories of the U.S. presence in Austria in the first postwar decade. To that group Bauer added another twenty interviews she had conducted for an earlier project. Through the creation of a website, Bauer also reached some occupation participants and witnesses who had left the Salzburg area, among them occupation soldiers and Austrian war brides who emigrated to the United States. The eighty interviews as well as the web-site contributions form the documentary basis of the book. The interviews are embedded in descriptive and analytical chapters which place the testimonies in historical context or critically interpret the merits of the sources.

As the introduction of the book shows, Bauer appears to be well aware of the possibilities and limits of her source base. Memories, Bauer notes, are never simple reflections of past lives and thoughts. They are necessarily colored by the individuals' social, cultural, and political environment, their gender, as well as by the events and transformations in their life stories (p. 9-10). Oral histories can add depth to our understanding of the past, yet they can also produce a distorted image of it. The critical recorder of those testimonies has to be aware of the peculiarities of an individual's historical place. The purpose of the book, according to the author, thus goes beyond the recording of personal experiences during the occupation. It also tries to link these testimonies to existing scholarship and thus create a fuller picture of the period (p. 15). The result is an impressive collection of multiple voices from the past and the present that both describe and reflect on a wide variety of issues concerning the U.S. impact on this area during the first postwar decade.

Separate chapters explore the question of whether Austrians saw Americans as conquerors or liberators; how they dealt with the Nazi legacy; the personal interactions between occupiers and occupied; and Austrians' shifting images of the Americans. The testimonies reveal the ambivalence with which Austrians viewed the invaders. While few of the interviewees questioned the victors' right to take control of Austrian affairs, many laced their comments with an air of cultural superiority, perhaps as a way to compensate for the sense of military and economic inferiority. As one witness summarized: "I learned already as a child [she was born in 1943] that the people here accepted the Americans as the ones who had the money, who could afford more, had cars and the like. But the culture [Bildung] was with us" (p. 212). Another admitted that he and his compatriots looked down on the Americans because "we realized they were not quite on our level [niveau]" (p. 214). Testimonies like these reveal the persistence of stereotypes that dated back to the prewar period. Especially during the 1920s when Europe for the first time confronted U.S. consumerism, traditionalists lamented the Americanization of European culture. In the eyes of these critics, "Americanism" became a synonym for materialism, mass consumption, and superficial mass entertainment.

Yet the interviews also reveal the transmutability of these images. In particular, young Austrians found the openness and youthfulness of American GIs appealing. Furthermore, they were drawn to the icons of U.S. popular culture. The music of Bill Haley and Elvis Presley became as much part of Austrian youth culture as Coca Cola, chewing gum, and blue jeans. Young Austrians used these U.S. cultural symbols to break out of the narrow confines of their parents' tradition of folk music and provincialism (p. 223). The U.S. presence in Austria allowed youth to transcend the boundaries of Austria's troubled historical legacy and embrace a new identity of internationalism and modernism that in the postwar period became identified with the United States.

The Austrian battle between cultural nationalism and internationalism was indicative of a global postwar trend. As U.S. troops occupied bases all over the world, U.S. culture interacted and sometimes clashed with indigenous cultures. In Germany, where U.S. troops were stationed in large numbers and where, as in Austria, the military government pursued a policy of denazification and cultural re-education, the same conflicted attitudes toward the Americans prevailed. Germans, as Austrian, vacillated between regarding Americans as liberators or conquerors. They, like Austrians, frowned upon their female compatriots' relationships with American GIs, and some retaliated violently against women who dated Americans and against GIs themselves.

Race relations exhibited similarly ambiguous, sometimes contradictory tendencies in both countries. In the interviews Austrians, often emphasized the black soldiers' friendliness toward children. Similar testimonies can be found among Germans. Yet they did not necessarily reveal a new acceptance of racial diversity that stood in marked contrast to Nazi ideology. Rather, they indicated the transformation of a threatening stereotype—that of the crude animalistic barbarian—into a non-threatening one—that of the childlike, naive, and essentially good-natured simpleton. Another indicator for the continued prevalence of racism in Austria and Germany was the strong opposition in both countries to mixed relationships (p. 170). In addition, Germans, at least, were far more likely to complain about misconduct of African-Americans than that of white soldiers. By the same token, white officers were much more likely to give credence to complaints about black soldiers' misconduct and were far more likely to discipline those soldiers for their transgressions. Crime statistics in Germany showed a far higher rate among black Gis than among white ones. The U.S. perspective on Austrians and the military mission in Salzburg surfaces only occasionally in Bauer's study. When it does, it provides rare insight into the reciprocity of the relationship and the mutuality of influence. Particularly fascinating is the realization of the incompatibility of some of the recollections. Americans, for instance, generally had a far better impression of Austrian hospitality than Austrians had. The author recorded several Austrian admissions of acts of aggression against the occupation forces (p. 14, 36-40). Yet testimonies of Americans' experience in Austria remain largely anecdotal in this study and serve primarily as useful illustrations of the subjective nature of the experience on both sides.

Scholars of postwar Austria will find this to be an indispensable resource. It adds to the growing pool of oral histories in Germany and Austria that document World War II and the early phase of the Cold War. The accounts illustrate the importance of the presence of U.S. troops in the consciousness of Austrians during the first decade after the war. They also demonstrate that the encounter with a foreign culture in day-to-day interactions prompted Austrians to reassess their own cultural idiosyncrasies. As a result, some embraced Austrian culture with renewed fervor leading to a more nationalist stand, while others questioned the continued relevance of Austrian traditions in the face of new influences from abroad. Most Austrians found themselves somewhere between these two poles. A few rejected some and embraced other aspects of U.S. culture.

Those who are looking for a comprehensive interpretation of the postwar Austrian-American relationship, however, will be disappointed. Bauer cites an abundance of secondary literature in conjunction with the oral testimonies, but in many instances she shies away from advancing her own critical reading of the evidence. For instance, Bauer contrasts a witness's testimony of an uprising in a prisoner of war camp in 1947 with a historian's very different interpretation of the same events (p. 97). But she lets these two contradictory statements stand side by side without offering her own critical commentary. The book also could have greatly benefited from conclusions to each chapter, and most importantly from an interpretative concluding chapter to the book. It appears that Bauer places too much confidence in the testimonies of the eyewitnesses and the interpretations of those who have studied the period in the past, and too little confidence in her own ability to make sense of these disparate views. Bauer might have intentionally kept to a minimum her own interpretations of these documents, so as to not obscure the authenticity of the voices she records. Or she might have concluded that the diverse and sometimes contradictory testimonies revealed no overarching pattern that would have pointed toward a comprehensive interpretation of the era. In any case, this volume constitutes a great resource for students of the Austrian experience with U.S. troops.

## ANNUAL REVIEW

# Survey of Austrian Politics 1998

*Reinhold Gärtner*

Elections to the State Diet in Lower Austria;
Presidential Elections 1998;
Rosenstingl and the FPOE;
The European Union-Presidency;
Catholic Church;
Walter Kohn wins Nobel;
Economic Data.

### Elections to the State Diet in Lower Austria

On 22 March, the State Diet of Lower Austria was re-elected. In the 1993 elections, the ÖVP had 44.3 percent, the SPÖ 33.9 percent, and the FPÖ 12 percent. Additionally the LiF (Liberals) had 5.1 per-ent and the Greens 3.2 percent. In 1998, however, the ÖVP increased its percentage to 44.9 percent, the FPÖ to 16.1 percent and Greens to 4.65 percent. The SPÖ (down to 30.4 percent) and the LiF (down 2.1 percent) were the losers; the LiF couldn't even surmount the 4 percent hurdle necessary for seats in the Diet.

**Table 1:** Results of the State Diet Elections 1998, Votes and Seats Gained

| | Votes/Percentage | Change in Votes +/- (in percent) | Seats | Change in Number of Seats +/- |
|---|---|---|---|---|
| ÖVP | 405,900/44.9 | + 0.6 | 27 | + 1 |
| SPÖ | 274,980/30.4 | - 3.5 | 18 | - 2 |
| FPÖ | 145,514/16.1 | + 4.0 | 9 | + 2 |
| Grüne | 40,639/4.6 | + 1.3 | 2 | + 2 |
| LiF | 19,279/2.1 | - 3.0 | 0 | - 3 |
| Others | 18,386/1.9 | + 0.5 | 0 | +/- 0 |

**Source**: *Willkommen in Nideröserreich*
<http://www.noel.gv.at/politik/wahlen/98_ltg/index.htm>

Only 71.9 percent of the persons entitled to vote went to the ballots (in comparison to 75.5 percent in 1993 and to 89.1 percent in the 1995 national elections). The new (and old) governor is Ludwig Pröll (ÖVP).

## Presidential Elections 1998

On 19 April, the new Austrian President was elected, and former President Thomas Klestil succesfully ran for re-election. For the first time since 1945, neither the SPÖ, ÖVP, or FPÖ nominated a candidate. Thomas Klestil, the ÖVP-candidate in 1992 again and again pointed out that he was an independent candidate in 1998. Gertrud Knoll was independent, too, as was Richard Lugner. The LiF was the only political party represented in parliament which had its own candidate (Heide Schmidt). The fifth candidate was Karl Walter Nowak, a right-wing outsider. The poll was at a remarkably low of 73.8 percent (in comparison to 81 percent in 1992).

An interesting candidate was Gertraud Knoll. Knoll was head (*Superintendentin*) of the protestant church in Burgenland and thus we had—or the first time in the Second Republic—high-ranked representative of a religions community running for presidency.

**Table 2:** Results of Austrian Presidential Elections 1998

| Candidate | Votes | Percentage |
|---|---|---|
| Dr. Thomas Klestil | 2,626,860 | 63.49 |
| Mag. Gertraud Knoll | 559,943 | 13.54 |
| Dr. Heide Schmidt | 458,491 | 11.08 |
| Ing. Richard Lugner | 411,378 | 9.94 |
| Karl Walter Nowak | 801,741 | 1.95 |

**Source**: *Der Standard*, 20 April 1998.

Thomas Klestil is the seventh president since 1945, four of them running successfully for re-election (Adolf Schärf, Franz Jonas, Rudolf Kirchschläger, and Klestil). Klestil is the first president who was not nominated by a political party. Renner, Körner, Schärf, and Jonas were SPÖ candidates, Kirchschläger was nominated by the SPÖ (at though he was not a party member), Waldheim was nominated by the ÖVP (at though he was not a party member), and Klestil at though a member of the ÖVP and ÖVP candidate in 1992—ran as independent candidate in 1998. Until 1980, the poll was more than 90 percent; since then it decreased to 87.3 percent in 1986 and 80.1 percent in 1992.

**Table 3:** Austrian Presidents and their Length of Tenure, 1945 to the Present

| President | Tenure |
|---|---|
| Dr. Karl Renner | 20 Dec. 1945 - 31 Dec. 1950 |
| Dr. Theodor Körner | 21 June 1951 - 4 Jan. 1957 |
| Dr. Adolf Schärf | 22 May 1957 - 28 Feb. 1965 (reelected 28 April 1963) |
| Franz Jonas | 9 June 1965 - 24 April 1974 (reelected 25 April 1971) |
| Dr. Rudolf Kirchschläger | 8 July 1974 - 8 July 1986 (reelected 18 May 1980) |
| Dr. Kurt Waldheim | 8 July 1986 - 24 May 1992 |
| Dr. Thomas Klestil | since 24 May 1992 (reelected 19 April 1998) |

**Source**: *Der Standard*, 20 April 1998.

## Rosenstingl and the FPÖ

In the Spring of 1998 the FPÖ was confronted with a political (and financial) scandal. Peter Rosenstingl, an FPÖ member of parliament, fled to Brazil in May 1998. Rosenstingl left a financial disaster for the FPÖ in Lower Austria; he is alleged to have left the FPÖ of Lower Austria with debts of some öS 500 Million (some 36 Million EURO). In autumn, another FPÖ member of parliament, Walter Meischberger, was found guilty of bribery.

The Rosenstingl scandal led to the resignation of Bernhard Grazter, head of the FPÖ in Lower Austria. As a result of the possible convictions, FPÖ might of Rosenstingl, Meischberger, and Gratzer soon lack of experience a herefore unheard of credibility. According to polls, the FPÖ is seen by most the Austrians as the party which successfully uncovers scandals. This image of a "clean and tidy" party might be seriously damaged by Rosenstingl and the like.

According to opinion polls, the FPÖ has lost ground. At the end of 1998, the SPÖ led opinion polls with some 40 percent; the ÖVP was supported by some 26 percent, the FPÖ was below 20 percent, the Greens were at 6 percent, and the Liberals were at 5 percent. Whether or not the FPÖ can gain ground again will be seen in 1999 when elections in the Tyrol, Carinthia, and Salzburg, and national elections and European Union elections are held.

Throughout 1998, Jörg Haider threatened his party with resignation from politics; regardless at the end of 1998 Haider was still chairman of the FPÖ. If 1998 was the "*Jahr der Bewährung*" (year of proving oneself), the elections in 1999 will be decisive for the future role of the FPÖ in Austrian politics.

## EU-Presidency

From 1 July until 31 December, Austria—for the first time—presided over the European Union (the presidency changes from one country to another every six months). During these six months of European Union Presidency, the most outstanding events were the Vienna Summit in December and the preparation for the introduction of the EURO on 1 January 1999). On 31 December, the exchange rates of national currencies to EURO were fixed: one EURO equals 13.7603 Austrian schillings. EURO cash will be introduced on 1 January 2002. The layout of the EURO banknotes was created by Robert Kalina, an Austrian, and Minister of Finance Rudolf Edlinger signed the banknotes as president on 31 December 1998.

On 1 January 1999, Germany assumed the presidency after Austria.

## Catholic Church

The troubles within Austria's Catholic Church continued in 1998. In March, the monastery of Gottweig was visited by a benedictine commission led by the American abbot primate Marcel Rooney. Though Rooney pointed out that the Groer affair was not the main point of investigation, the case had effects on the visit. Cardinal Hans

Groer retired in September amid allegations of having sexually abused male students at a catholic school over twenty years ago. Nevertheless, the visitors reported to the pope in Rome.

In June, Pope John-Paul II visited Austria for the third time, and this visit, too, was over shadowed by the Groer-case and by serious troubles within the Austrian Catholic Church. Bishop Kurt Krenn, a stout conservative hardliner, clashed with the rest of the Austrian bishops, including Cardinal Schönborn from Vienna, on the other. Bishop Weber initiated a "*Dialog für Österreich*" (dialogue for Austria) which should be a platform for discussions. In November, Austria's bishops made an "ad limina visitation" in Rome and presented their problems to Pope John Paul II. The (not very surprising) result was a more or less vague answer from the Pope.

The crisis within the church will continue during the next years. According to a survey published in the catholic weekly *Die Furche* 83 percent of Austrians think that this situation might have negative consequences for the church. In 1997, some 33,000 catholics left the church; during the last fifteen years, the percentage of Austrian catholics decreased from 92 percent to 75 percent.

## Walter Kohn wins Nobel Prize

The 1998 Nobel Prize for Chemistry was awarded to Walter Kohn together with the britih mathematician John Pople. Although Kohn is officially an American, he was born in Vienna in 1923. In 1938, after the Anschluß, Kohn was expelled from school (*Akademisches Gymnasium* in Vienna) for being Jewish, and in 1939 Kohn emigrated to the United States. Kohn's parents were murdered in Auschwitz.

In January 1999, Kohn visited his former school in Vienna.

## Economic data

In 1998, the rate of inflation was 0.8 percent, 0.4 percent lower than in the European Union. Austrian businesses employed 3,075,900 people, 0.7 percent increase in comparison to 1997, and 298,600 of them non-Austrians, 0.1 percent decrease in comparison to 1997. Approximately 237,800 people were unemployed, 1.9 percent increased compared to 1997. GNP was at öS 2.628 billion, or some 191 billion EURO.

The number of bancruptcies decreased; however liabilities, increased to öS 35 billion (sone 2.5 billion EURO from öS 34 billion in 1997. One of the reasons for this increase were the bankruptcies of Rieger Bank and Diskont-Bank.

## Outlook

1999 will be an interesting election year. On 7 March, the State Diet in Tyrol, Salzbzurg and Carinthia will be newly elected. In June, there are elections for the European Parliament, and in autumn, the State Diet elections in Vorarlberg and the National Council Elections will be held. The present situation is depicted in Table 4 below.

**Table 4:** Party Representation per Election in percent

| Party | National elections 1995 | Carinthia 1994 | Salzburg 1994 | Tyrol 1994 | Vorarlberg 1994 | EU 1996 |
|---|---|---|---|---|---|---|
| SPÖ | 38.1 | 37.4 | 27.0 | 19.8 | 16.3 | 29.2 |
| ÖVP | 28.3 | 23.8 | 38.6 | 47.3 | 49.9 | 29.6 |
| FPÖ | 21.9 | 33.3 | 19.5 | 16.1 | 18.4 | 27.6 |
| Greens | 4.8 | 1.6 | 7.3 | 10.7 | 7.7*<br>1.6** | 6.8 |
| LiF | 5.5 | 2.6 | 5.8 | 3.4 | 3.5 | 4.2 |

* GAV: Die Grünen - Grüne Alternative
** GBL: Grüne Bürgerliste - Die Grünen Vorarlbergs

FURTHER LITERATURE

*Der Standard*
*Die Presse*
*News*
*Profil*
*Willkommen in Niederösterreich* <http://www.noel.gv.at>

# List of Authors

*Siegfried Beer*, Associate Professor of Modern History, University of Graz

*Stephen Beller*, Historian, Washington D.C.

*Matthew Paul Berg*, Assistant Professor of European History, John Carroll University, Cleveland, Ohio

*Volker Berghahn*, Seth Low Professor of History, Columbia University

*Hans-Georg Betz*, Professor of Political Science, John Hopkins School of Advanced International Studies, Washington, D.C.

*Markus M. L. Crepaz*, Professor of Political Science, University of Georgia, Athens, GA

*Günter Bischof*, Professor of History and Associate Director, CenterAustria, University of New Orleans

*Ingrid Fraberger*, Historian, Vienna

*Hans Fußenegger*, Deputy Director of the *ERP-Fonds*, Vienna

*Reinhold Gärtner*, Associate Professor, University of Innsbruck, and secretary of "*Gesellschaft für politische Aufklärung*"

*Petra Goedde*, Lecturer in History, Princeton University

*Lonnie Johnson*, Executive Secretary, Austrian Fulbright Commission

*Martin Kofler*, PhD candidate, University of Innsbruck, and Contemporary History Editor, *Studienverlag*, Innsbruck

*Wilhelm Kohler*, Professor of Economics, University of Linz

*Andrea Komlosy*, Assistant Professor, University of Vienna

*Ferdinand Lacina*, Former Minister of Finance, Vienna; Senior Advisor, Erste Bank, Vienna

*Alexander Lassner*, PhD candidate, The Ohio State University, Columbus, Ohio

*Jill Lewis*, Lecturer in Modern History, University of Wales Swansea

*Kurt Löffler*, Director of the *ERP-Fonds*, Vienna

*Anton Pelinka*, Professor of Political Science, University of Innsbruck, and Director, *Institut für Konfliktforschung*, Vienna

*Georg Rigele*, Historian, Vienna

*Hans Seidel*, Former State Secretary of Finance and Senior Associate, *Institut für Österreichische Wirtschaftsforschung*, Vienna

*Hans-Jürgen Schröder*, Professor of Modern History, University of Giessen

*Dieter Stiefel*, Professor of Economic and Social History, University of Vienna, Executive Secretary of the Schumpeter Society, Vienna

*Peter Thaler*, Historian, University of Minnesota, Minneapolis. Minnesota

*Kurt Tweraser*, Professor of Political Science Emeritus, University of Arkansas, Fayetteville, Arkansas